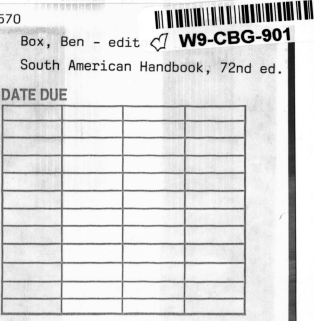
GUAYAQUIL: (5934) 200277 - 205115 • QUITO: (5932) 254510 - 564969
• USA/CANADA TOLL FREE 1-800-82 SAETA.

If you're looking for the best Latin American coverage read this.

If you want to make sure you take in the spectacular contrasts of Latin America, you want to make sure you fly out with Iberia or Viasa.

Together, Iberia (the international airline of Spain) and Viasa (the international airline of Venezuela) link Europe to a range of destinations that's not only proved impossible to beat – it's never been matched.

The Iberia Group brings you closer to the sun-drenched beaches of the Caribbean, the glacial beauty of Tierra del Fuego and the distinctive colonial architecture of cities like Lima, by serving an incredible 26 locations.

In fact, Iberia has continued to expand and strengthen its links since establishing the first air connection between Europe and Latin America over 50 years ago.

ARUBA
ASUNCION
BOGOTA
BUENOS AIRES
CANCUN
CARACAS
CARTAGENA
GUATEMALA
HAVANA
LIMA
MANAGUA
MEXICO
MIAMI
MONTEVIDEO
PANAMA
PORLAMAR
PUNTA CANA
QUITO
RIO DE JANEIRO
SAN JOSE
SAN JUAN
SAN PEDRO SULA
SANTO DOMINGO
SAN SALVADOR
SANTIAGO DE CHILE
SÃO PAULO

In addition Viasa now offers the greatest choice of flights from Caracas to the whole of Latin America. So with Iberia and Viasa all your needs are covered.

What's more, by flying with Iberia or Viasa, you are guaranteed comfort and style. Whether you choose the exceptional value of the established 'Latin American Saver' fares in Economy Class or decide to treat yourself to the

luxury of First or Business Class, the Iberia Group gives you the best choice and the best value fares.

So if you're looking for the best Latin American coverage, you don't have to read between the lines, simply contact your local travel agent and ask about the Iberia Group, or call Iberia today on

0171-830 0011

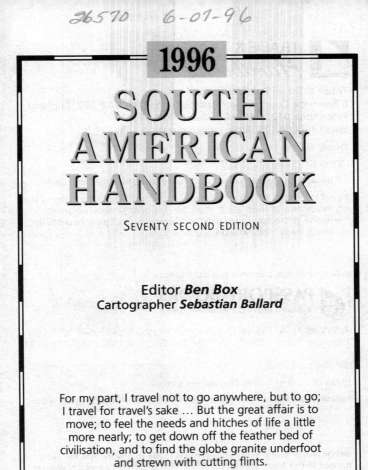

1996

SOUTH AMERICAN HANDBOOK

SEVENTY SECOND EDITION

Editor *Ben Box*
Cartographer *Sebastian Ballard*

For my part, I travel not to go anywhere, but to go;
I travel for travel's sake … But the great affair is to
move; to feel the needs and hitches of life a little
more nearly; to get down off the feather bed of
civilisation, and to find the globe granite underfoot
and strewn with cutting flints.
Robert Louis Stevenson

2

TRADE & TRAVEL
Handbooks

Trade & Travel Publications Ltd
6 Riverside Court, Lower Bristol Road, Bath BA2 3DZ, England
Telephone 01225 469141   Fax 01225 469461
Email 100660.1250@compuserve.com

©Trade & Travel Publications Ltd., September 1995

ISBN 0 900751 60 6   ISSN 0309-4529

CIP DATA: A catalogue record for this book is available from the British Library

In North America, published and distributed by

PASSPORT BOOKS
a division of *NTC Publishing Group*

4255 West Touhy Avenue, Lincolnwood (Chicago), Illinois 60646-1975, USA
Telephone 708-679-5500   Fax 708-679-2494   Email NTCPUB2@AOL.COM

ISBN 0-8442-8881-0

Library of Congress Catalog Card Number 95-69407

Passport Books and colophon are registered trademarks of NTC Publishing Group

**IMPORTANT: While every endeavour is made to ensure that the facts
printed in this book are correct at the time of going to press, travellers
are cautioned to obtain authoritative advice from consulates, airlines,
etc, concerning current travel and visa requirements and conditions
before embarking. The publishers cannot accept legal responsibility for
errors, however caused, that are printed in this book.**

**MAPS – Publisher's note: a number of frontiers in the area covered by this
Handbook are disputed and the subject of territorial claims by various
countries in the region. Neither the coloured nor the black and white
maps in this book are intended to have any political significance or
purport to show authenticated international boundaries.**

Cover illustration by Suzanne Evans

Printed and bound in Great Britain by Clays Ltd., Bungay, Suffolk

CONTENTS

4

PREFACE

In *The Creature in the Map*, his book on Sir Walter Ralegh and other seekers of gold in what is now Venezuela, Charles Nicholl writes, "Where was El Dorado?

"The first and sensible answer is, nowhere...There have been remarkable discoveries in Latin America this century...There are probably others waiting to be found, but El Dorado will not be among them...In another sense, of course, El Dorado certainly did exist...as an idea in people's minds, as a destination for their journeys...". Ralegh's chart marked El Dorado as a city on the shores of a Lake Manoa. Even though modern day maps show no such lake or city, the place names and historical allusions provoke a sense of mystery. Anyone travelling in Latin America today will know of Kevin Healey's incomparable maps. It was therefore with great sadness at the news of his death that work began on this edition. Although so very different in approach from 16th-century charts, Kevin's dedication to accuracy provides his greatest legacy in that his maps also have the power to inspire adventure.

A failure to map areas where riches are thought to lie led partly to the recurrence of war between Ecuador and Peru over their disputed border in the Cordillera del Cóndor. The historical reasons behind the dispute are well-documented; the motives for the latest outbreak of fighting are less clear-cut than the international desire for its conclusion and the economic aftermath (especially in Ecuador). The effect on tourism was shortlived. The number of visitors to Ecuador remains high and in Peru tourism continues to rally after the doldrums of recent years.

The editor visited Ecuador and the Galápagos Islands in September/October 1994 (thanks are given at the end of the Ecuador chapter). He formed his own ideas about places visited for the first time, or revisited, but these impressions may well differ from those of our correspondents and of the tourists who so generously write to us. A consequence of Ecuador being so popular is that many travellers generate many opinions. More than ever over the past year it has been remarkable how many opposing views of the same places have been received. It is worth bearing in mind that besides "one man's meat" being "another man's poison", the quality of service may change between high and low season.

Readers familiar with the *Handbook* will notice that the **Information for Visitors** sections are now in two columns. This is the start of a process to make the book conform to the style of the other *Handbooks* in the Trade and Travel series. Hotel price categories have been narrowed at the upper end of the range to account for price rises in some countries and for the opening of more luxury hotels. The lower price categories remain unchanged. Some readers suggest that we omit the higher-priced establishments because "no one uses that part of the hotel list". This is not the case, even though the most visible part of the readership is probably that which stays in the cheaper places. The *Handbook's* comprehensiveness aims now, as it has done for many years, to "cater particularly for the requirements of the budget traveller, while at the same time paying due regard to the interests of the better-off" (1978 Preface).

Special thanks for their work on this edition go to our regular subeditors Cherry Austin, Sarah Cameron, John Hale, Charlie Nurse, Peter Pollard and the new members of the team, Alan Murphy (widely-travelled in South America, who subedited Argentina and helped with the final stages of editing) and Amanda Purves (who has lived in Venezuela and updated that chapter). Peter Pollard travelled to Colombia in 1995. Richard Robinson did a lot of research for the Venezuela chapter in late 1994. We are most grateful to our correspondents in the region, who are thanked at the end of the relevant chapters, and also to John Lewis for his annual reports from the business centres of the region. Finally we should like to thank Jo Morgan, Ann Griffiths and Claudia Golding for their tireless work in transferring all the material to disk.

The Editor

THE EDITOR

Ben Box

A doctorate in medieval Spanish and Portugese studies provided very few job prospects for Ben Box, but a fascination for all things Latin. While studying for his degree, Ben travelled extensively in Spain and Portugal. He turned his attention to contemporary Iberian and Latin American affairs in 1980, beginning a career as a freelance writer at that time. He contributed regularly to national newspapers and learned tomes, and after increasing involvement with the *South American Handbook*, became its editor in 1989. Although he has travelled from the US/Mexico border to southern Chile (not all in one go) and in the Caribbean, Ben recognises that there are always more places to explore. He also edits the *Mexico and Central American Handbook* and jointly edits the *Caribbean Islands Handbook* with Sarah Cameron. To seek diversion from a household immersed in Latin America, he plays village cricket in summer and cycles the lanes of Suffolk.

HOW TO USE THIS HANDBOOK

The South American Handbook is the most complete and up-to-date package of information for independent travellers on the sub-continent of South America (from the Darién Gap to Tierra del Fuego) currently in print. Its text is updated every year for the new edition which is published on 1 September. The text is based on the Editors' travels, contributions from national tourist authorities, notes from correspondents living in the countries we cover, detailed material and maps which Handbook users send us, and the extensive sources of information on Latin America available in London and elsewhere.

Editorial Logic Users of the Handbook will find that we employ a logical system of arrangement, which we believe is the most useful for travellers. The capital city is (with one exception, dictated by geography—Chile) the first place covered in detail. The territory is then divided into subsections which are numbered on the country contents and map as well as in the text. In the subsections, towns appear in sequence along a route, which falls within the natural geography of the region. The routes cover the most interesting places to visit and do not necessarily constitute the shortest possible distance from A to B. Details are also given of any interesting excursions or other sights that are off the route. Travellers can therefore plan their own itineraries according to the time available, and their own special interests.

Cross Referencing and Indexing There is a complete index at the end of the book. Personalities as well as place names and sites of interest are now included. The key used is as follows: Archaeological site ▲; Beach or Marine Resort ♠; Colonial City ♣; Festival, religious or otherwise ☆; Historical site ✳; Inland Resort ✱; Market, or traditional shopping ✿; National Park, Natural Feature, recommended Zoological or Botanical Garden ◆; People ❑.

To make it easier for Readers to find their way around the text, we have a comprehensive system of cross-references. For ease of use, the "see page" entry has been highlighted in heavier type. On the page referred to, you will find the entry again emphasised in some form of heavier type.

Maps The South American Handbook maps within the text are undergoing a programme of updating, improvement and expansion. Three types are used:

A Country Maps These appear at the start of each country chapter and show main access routes (not necessarily major roads in all cases), main towns, and divisions of the country as described in the text. These divisions are numbered on the map, in the country's contents list and at the text divisions in the chapter. The numbers are not recommendations as to which parts of the country are most interesting to visit, they are only for easy identification.

B Regional Maps The subsections of the country listed in the country contents has, where appropriate, its own regional map. These give extra information on a more detailed scale and show the main physical features, towns, means of communication and points of interest.

C City and Town Maps Generally these are detailed maps of town centres, showing means of access to bus and railway stations and airports. The main points of interest are indicated by means of a numbered key.

MAP SYMBOLS

International Border	——·—·—	Capital Cities	▫
State / Province Border	———·———	Cities / Towns	○
Main Roads (National Highways)	15	Bus Stations	🅱
Other Roads	———	Hospitals	🅷
Jeepable Roads, Tracks, Trails, Paths, Ferries	- - - · · · - - -	Post Office	PO
Railways, Station	┼─■─┼	Tourist Office	🄸
Contours (approx)	〜〜	Key Numbers	27
Mountains	⩕	Airport	✈
Rivers	*Rio Torola*	Church	✝
Waterfall	⌇	Camp site	⛺
Bridges	≍	Refuge	⌂
Built Up Areas	▨	Lodge with facilities	⌂
Lakes, Dams, Reservoirs	〜	Wild Life Parks, Biological Reserves, Bird Sanctuaries	◆
Sand Banks, Beaches	⣿	Archaeological Sites	▲
National Parks, Gardens, Stadiums	▨	Text Subdivisions	•·•·•·
Fortified Walls	▲▲▲		SAH 0

Introduction and Hints This first section in the book gives information and hints that apply generally to all the countries we cover on:

- ❏ travel to and in Latin America ❏ photography
- ❏ money ❏ surface transport
- ❏ law enforcement ❏ hitchhiking
- ❏ security ❏ motoring and motorcycling
- ❏ responsible tourism ❏ hiking and trekking
- ❏ travelling with children ❏ river boats
- ❏ camping ❏ cycling
- ❏ language

Health Information This major section by Dr David Snashall of St Thomas's Hospital Medical School, London, gives details of the health risks common in South America, and the sensible precautions travellers should take to combat them.

Country Sections Information is set out country by country in a constant sequence as follows:

- ❏ List of contents
- ❏ Description of physical geography

history	people
economy	present form of government
music and dance	

- ❏ Survey of Cities, Towns and places of interest

things to do	things worth seeing
where to stay	eating out
services for visitors	

❏ Information for visitors
　　　documentation
　　　food
　　　the best time for visiting
　　　currency regulations

how to get there
health precautions
clothing
other essential information

All those readers who have written with valuable updating material are listed with thanks at the end of each chapter.

Note The aim of the **Music and Dance** sections (specially written for us by Nigel Gallop) has been to give an overview of the traditional and popular music and dances of each country. Considerations of space and the desire to avoid a tedious inventory has meant that by no means every song style, dance or instrument has been noted. As to the performers mentioned, the choice has also been selective, giving preference to those who have achieved local fame over those who, for commercial or political reasons, have based themselves in Europe or North America and are probably already familiar to the overseas visitor. Readers may also notice that space has not been devoted to the forest indians, who are nevertheless present in most of the countries covered and whose music and dancing tends to exist only in its isolated cosmos, rarely relating to, or connecting with, national or regional musical cultures. Also not discussed, at present, is the classical music of the region.

Hotels and Restaurants In large cities, lists of hotels and restaurants include only those establishments for which positive recommendations have been received. In smaller towns, these lists contain both the favourable recommendations and others. In general, restaurants are grouped by neighbourhood and by type of cuisine.

Prices Our hotel price ranges, for double rooms with taxes and service charges but without meals unless stated, are as follows:

L1	Over US$200	**L2**	US$151-200	**L3**	US$101-150
A1	US$81-100	**A2**	US$61-80	**A3**	US$46-60
B	US$31-45	**C**	US$21-30	**D**	US$12-20
E	US$7-11	**F**	US$4-6	**G**	Up to US$3

Other abbreviations used in the book (apart from pp = per person; a/c = air conditioned; rm = room(s) in a hotel; flr = floor; rec = recommended; T = telephone; TCs = travellers' cheques; s/n = "sin número", no street number) should be self-explanatory.

We are grateful to those travellers, listed below, who have sent us important information for the "Introduction and Hints" section which follows: Mrs Carol Baillie (Grand Cayman, Cayman Islands), Dave Blackburn (Luton, UK) and Emily Smith (North Carolina, USA), Tim Burford (Linton, UK), Mark Davies and Tiffany Story (Amersham, UK and Santa Barbara, USA), Dr J Rudolf Dietrich (Basle, Switzerland), Gerd Dörner (Darmstadt, Germany), Patrick Ganahl (Wolfhausen, Switzerland), Michael Gonin (Canberra, Australia), Marten H Jacobsen and Brit R Lauritsen (Denmark), Sonja Jovanovic and Andrew Thompson (London, UK) a helpful letter, Kay Leissner (Gottingen, Germany), Gilles Lalonde (Quebec, Canada) a detailed account, M Leufgens and M Jollands (Alsdorf, Germany), Richard Leuwin (Antigua, Guatemala), Peter Koenen (Bocholt, Germany) and Scott Mattoon (San Francisco, USA), Marie-Helene Boone and Ulrich Nanz (Stuttgart, Germany), Jonathan Paisner (London, UK), Jerry Peek (Sepastopol, USA), Paul Schneider (Venice, USA), The Schweers (somewhere in Colombia), Ludwig Seitz (Dossenheim, Germany), Ron and Dorothy Thyer (Blackburn, Australia), and Ollo Wiemann (Trier, Germany).

WILL YOU HELP US?

We do all we can to get our facts right in the **SOUTH AMERICAN HANDBOOK**. Each section is thoroughly revised each year, but the territory is vast and our eyes cannot be everywhere. If you have enjoyed a tour, trek, train trip, beach, museum or any other activity and would like to share it, please write with all the details. We are always pleased to hear about any restaurants, bars or hotels you have enjoyed. When writing, please give the year on the cover of your *Handbook* and the page number referred to. In return we will send you details of our special guidebook offer.

Thank you very much indeed for your help.

TRADE & TRAVEL
Handbooks

Write to The Editor, *South American Handbook*, Trade & Travel,
6 Riverside Court, Lower Bristol Road, Bath BA2 3DZ. England
Fax 01225 469461   Email 100660.1250@compuserve.com

INTRODUCTION AND HINTS

AIR TRAVEL TO AND WITHIN LATIN AMERICA

Travel to and in South America All the main airlines plying to each country are given in the "Information for Visitors" sections. Airlines will only allow a certain weight of luggage without a surcharge; this is normally 30 kg for first class and 20 kg for business and economy classes, but these limits are often not strictly enforced when it is known that the plane is not going to be full. If you have special baggage requirements, check with an agency for the anomalies which exist on different weight allowances one way, for example. Passengers seeking a larger baggage allowance can route via USA, but with certain exceptions, the fares are slightly higher using this route. On the other hand, weight limits for internal flights are often lower; best to enquire beforehand.

Paul Davies, of Journey Latin America, has told us:

1 It is no longer generally cheaper to fly from London rather than a point in Europe to Latin American destinations; fares vary from airline to airline, destination to destination and according to time of year. Check with an agency for the best deal for when you wish to travel.

2 Most airlines offer discounted fares of one sort or another on scheduled flights. These are not offered by the airlines direct to the public, but through agencies who specialize in this type of fare*. The very busy seasons are 7 Dec–15 Jan and 10 July–10 Sept. If you intend travelling during those times, book as far ahead as possible.

3 Other fares fall into three groups, and are all on scheduled services:
   A Excursion (return) fares with restricted validity eg 5-90 days. Carriers are introducing flexibility into these tickets, permitting a change of dates on payment of a fee.
   B Yearly fares: these may be bought on a one-way or return basis. Some airlines require a specified return date, changeable upon payment of a fee. To leave the return completely open is possible for an extra fee. You must, fix the route (some of the cheapest flexible fares now have 6 months validity).

---

*In London, these include Journey Latin America, 16 Devonshire Road, Chiswick, London W4 2HD (T 0181-747 3108); Trailfinders, 48 Earl's Court Road, London W8 6EJ (T 0171-938 3366); South American Experience, 47 Causton Street, Pimlico, London SW1P 4AT (T 0171-976 5511); Last Frontiers, Swan House, High Street, Long Crendon, Buckinghamshire, HP18 9AF (T 01844 208405); Passage to South America, 41 North End Road, West Kensington, London W14 8SZ (T 0171-602 9889); STA Travel, Priory House, 6 Wrights Lane, London W8 6TA (T 0171-938 4711), Cox & Kings Travel, St James Court, 45 Buckingham Gate, London (T 0171-873 5001). (Ed.)

C Student (or Under 26) fares. (Do not assume that student tickets are the cheapest; though they are often very flexible, they are usually more expensive than A or B above). Some airlines are flexible on the age limit, others strict. One way and returns available, or "Open Jaws" (see below). NB There is less availability in the busy seasons (see above).

4 For people intending to travel a linear route and return from a different point from that which they entered, there are "Open Jaws" fares, which are available on student, yearly, or excursion fares.

5 Many of these fares require a change of plane at an intermediate point, and a stopover may be permitted, or even obligatory, depending on schedules. Simply because a flight stops at a given airport does not mean you can break your journey there—the airline must have traffic rights to pick up or set down passengers between points A and B before it will be permitted. This is where dealing with a specialized agency (like Journey Latin America!) will really pay dividends. There are dozens of agencies that offer the simple returns to Rio or Lima at roughly the same (discounted) fare. On multi-stop itineraries, the specialized agencies can often save clients hundreds of pounds.

6 Although it's a little more complicated, it's possible to sell tickets in London for travel originating in Latin America at substantially cheaper fares than those available locally. This is useful for the traveller who doesn't know where he will end up, or who plans to travel for more than a year. Because of high local taxes (see paragraph 7) a one-way ticket from Latin America is more expensive than a one-way in the other direction, so it's always best to buy a return. Taxes are calculated as a percentage of the full IATA fare; on a discounted fare the tax can therefore make up as much as 30-50% of the price.

7 Certain Latin American countries impose local tax on flights originating there. Among these are Ecuador, Peru, Bolivia, Uruguay, Colombia and Mexico. This often applies if you happen to have bought a ticket, say, London—Rio—Santiago—Lima—Los Angeles and then on to Australia.

8 There are several cheap French charters to Colombia, Ecuador, Peru, Bolivia and the southern countries, but no-one in the UK sells them.

Travellers starting their journey in continental Europe may try: Uniclam-Voyages, 63 rue Monsieur-le Prince, 75006 Paris for charters. The Swiss company, Balair (owned by Swissair) has regular charter flights to South America (every second week to Recife and Rio). For cheap flights in Switzerland, Globetrotter Travel Service, Renweg, 8001 Zürich, has been recommended. Also try Nouvelles Frontières, Paris, T (1) 41-41-58-58; Hajo Siewer Jet Tours, Martinstr 39, 57462 Olpe, Germany, T (02761) 924120. The German magazine *Reisefieber* is useful.

9 If you buy discounted air tickets *always* check the reservation with the airline concerned to make sure the flight still exists. Also remember the IATA airlines' schedules change in March and October each year, so if you're going to be away a long time it's best to leave return flight coupons open.

In addition, check whether you are entitled to any refund or re-issued ticket if you lose, or have stolen, a discounted air ticket. Some airlines require the repurchase of a ticket before you can apply for a refund, which will not be given until after the validity of the original ticket has expired. The Iberia group, for example, operates this costly system.

10 Note that some South American carriers change departure times of short-haul or domestic flights at short notice and, in some instances, schedules shown in the computers of transatlantic carriers differ from those actually flown by smaller, local carriers. If you book, and reconfirm, both your transatlantic and onward sectors through your transatlantic carrier you may find that your travel plans have been based on out of date information. The surest solution is to reconfirm your outward flight in an office of the onward carrier itself.

AeroPerú operates Sudameripass, a 45-day return ticket which is one of the cheapest ways of flying around the continent. If starting a journey in Miami, Mexico City or Cancún, it costs US$1,099 for up to 6 coupons on AeroPerú's network; if starting in Buenos Aires or Los Angeles it costs US$1,299. Extra coupons can be bought for US$100 each. There are seasonal permutations. Check with JLA for up-to-date details. Also worth noting here are Varig's Stopover Programme, which offers special rates for accommodation and transfers for Varig passengers throughout Latin America, and the Mercosur Airpass. The latter applies to Brazil, Argentina, Uruguay and Paraguay, using 9 local carriers, available to any passenger with a return ticket to a Mercosur country. It must be bought in conjunction with an international flight; minimum stay is 10 days, maximum 30, at least 2 countries must be visited. Maximum number of coupons is eight. Fares are calculated on a mileage basis and range from US$225 to US$870.

Miami is a good place for connections between South and Central America and Europe. Non-US citizens should note that it is very difficult to check air tickets purchased outside the USA through an agent in Miami and that it is unlikely that you will be allowed by US Immigration to enter the USA without an onward ticket already in your possession. Continental Airlines' hub, Houston, is another good place for connections.

Beware buying tickets from the general sales agents in Europe of minor Latin American airlines. They are sometimes incorrectly made out and therefore impossible to transfer or cash in. If you buy internal airline tickets in Latin American countries you may find cash refunds difficult to get if you change your plans: better to change your ticket for a different one. On the other hand you can save money by buying tickets in a country with a black exchange market, for local currency, for flights on its national airline. Overbooking by Latin American airlines is very common (largely due to repeated block bookings by travel agents, which everyone knows will not be used), so always reconfirm the next stage of your flight within 72 hrs of your intended departure. And it does no harm to reconfirm yet again in the last 24 hrs, just to show them you mean it, and turn up for the flight in good time (at least 2 hrs before departure).

We advise people who travel the cheap way in Latin America to pay for all transport as they go along, and not in advance. This advice does not apply to people on a tight schedule: paying as you go along may save money, but it is likely to waste your time somewhat. The one exception to this general principle is in transatlantic flights; here money is saved by booking as far as possible in one operation. International air tickets are very expensive if purchased in Latin America. If buying airline tickets routed through the USA, check that US taxes are included in the price.

The national airlines of Argentina, Bolivia, Brazil, Chile, Colombia, Peru and Venezuela operate airpass schemes within those countries at a set price. See the respective country sections.

The Amerbuspass covers the whole of Latin America, from Mexico City to Ushuaia, and entitles the holder to 15-20% discounts on tickets with participating operators; bookable in all Latin American capitals, Europe, Asia, Africa, Oceania, it is valid for 9,999 miles, up to 180 days. Unlimited stopovers, travel with either a confirmed or open itinerary. Contact TISA Internacional, B Irigoyen 1370, Oficina 25/26, 1138 Buenos Aires, Argentina, T 27-6591/631-1108, F 953-5508, or Av Larrazabal 493, Buenos Aires, PO Box 40 Suc 1 (B), 1401 Buenos Aires.

Travel to the USA Until July 1988 all foreigners (except Canadians) needed visas to enter the USA. Despite subsequent relaxations of visa requirements for British air travellers with round-trip tickets to the USA, it is advisable to have a visa to allow entry by land, or on airlines from South and Central America which are not "participating carriers" on the Visa Waiver scheme. If you are thinking of travelling via the USA, or of visiting the USA after Latin America, you are strongly advised to get your visa from a US Consulate in your own country, not while travelling.

The US Department of Agriculture places restrictions on agricultural items brought to the United States from foreign countires as well as those brought to the mainland from Hawaii, Puerto Rico, and the US Virgin Islands. Prohibited items can harbour foreign animal and plant pests and diseases that could seriously damage America's crops, livestock, pets and the environment.

Because of this threat, travellers are required to list on the Customs' declaration form any meats, fruits, vegetables, plants, animals, and plant and animal products they are bringing into the country. The declaration must list all agricultural items carried in baggage, hand luggage and in vehicles coming across the border.

USDA inspectors will confiscate illegal items for destruction. Travellers who fail to declare items can be fined up to US$100 on the spot, and their exit from the airport will be delayed. Some items are permitted. Call 301-436-5908 for a copy of the helpful pamphlet, "Travelers Tips". The best advice is to check before purchasing an agricultural item and trying to bring it back into the United States.

Shipping Voyages on passenger-carrying cargo vessels between South America and Europe, the USA, or elsewhere, are listed here: the Blue Star line sails from Tilbury to Hamburg, Bremen, Antwerp, thence to Montevideo via the Brazilian ports of Salvador, Santos and Rio de Janeiro, returning via Rio Grande, Santos, Salvador and Recife, and Rotterdam. 12 passengers are carried; fare to Montevideo, £1,610, round trip £3,010 pp. The Grimaldi Line sails from Tilbury to Brazil (Vitória, Rio, Santos, Paranaguá), via Hamburg, Amsterdam and Antwerp, round trip about 42 days, £2,400-3,900, also from Genoa to Paranaguá, Santos and Rio for £840-1,105 (T Genoa 010-55091, London 0171-930 5683, Rio 021-253 6599). The Dobson Line has services from the UK to Caribbean, Central and South American ports; itineraries change frequently and usually calls in port are quite long, fare is about £50 pp per day, incl meals.

Various German companies sail to the E coast of South America: either Tilbury, Hamburg, Bremen, Antwerp to Salvador, Santos and Recife, returning to Rotterdam and Tilbury (£3,000-3,300 round trip); or Felixstowe, Bremen, Hamburg, Rotterdam, Antwerp, Le Havre, Rio de Janeiro (21 days, £1,800-1,950), Santos, Buenos Aires (25 days, £2,200-2,350), Rio Grande, Santos, Felixstowe. Flensburger Befrachtungskontor UC Hansen of Germany has a 50-day round trip Antwerp, Manaus, Itacoatiara, Belém, Rouen/Honfleur, Bremen, costing £3,000. Fyffes has regular sailings Portsmouth-Suriname, 6 passengers on a banana boat, 35-38 day round trip, £1,980 pp.

From the USA, Ivaran Lines serve East Coast USA, Brazilian ports, Montevideo and Buenos Aires; the *Americana* container ship carries 80 passengers in luxury accommodation (New Orleans, Houston, Puerto Cabello, La Guaira, Rio, Santos, Buenos Aires, Montevideo, Rio Grande do Sul, Itajaí, Paranaguá, Santos, Salvador, Fortaleza, Bridgetown, San Juan, Veracruz, Tampico, New Orleans, £6,645-11,340 pp round trip, fares depend on season, one-way N or S possible). Ivaran also have the *San Antonio*, carrying 12 passengers on the route Port Elizabeth (New Jersey), Baltimore, Norfolk, Savannah, Miami, Puerto Cabello, La Guaira, Rio, Santos, Buenos Aires, Montevideo, Rio Grande do Sul, Itajaí, Santos, Rio (possibly Salvador and Fortaleza), Port Elizabeth; 44-day round trip £4,085-4,825 pp, one-way subject to availability. Lykes Line sail from Miami/New Orleans to Cartagena, then through the Panama Canal to Guayaquil, Callao and Valparaíso (a round trip costs US$3,300-3,500 pp). Egon Oldendorff carries passengers on its USA or Canada/South America routes.

From Europe and USA to the west coast of South America: the Mediterranean Shipping Company has vessels from Felixstowe, Antwerp, Hamburg, Bremerhaven and Le Havre to the US ports of New York, Charleston, Miami and Houston (among others). From these four ports, the same company sails to Guayaquil, Callao, Arica and Valparaíso. Transatlantic fares range from £850 (Felixstowe or Le Havre-New York) to £1,370 (Antwerp-Houston); US-South America fares range from £590 (Guayaquil-New York) to £2,020 (New York-Arica). A round trip from the USA to South America, embarking and disembarking at the same port costs £2,930 (Europe-USA round trip £2,080). Passengers buying round trips are given preference; one-way tickets are practically impossible to come by in the autumn and winter months, but can be bought in summer.

Our thanks are due to John Alton of Strand Cruise and Travel Centre, Charing Cross Shopping Concourse, The Strand, London WC2N 4HZ, T 0171-836 6363, F 0171-497 0078, for the above information. Enquiries regarding passages should be made through agencies in your own country, or through Strand Cruise and Travel Centre. In the USA, contact Freighter World Cruises, 180 South Lake Ave, Pasadena, CA 91101, T (818) 449-3106, or Travltips Cruise and Freighter Travel Association, 163-07 Depot Road, PO Box 188, Flushing, NY 11358, T (800) 872-8584. Do not try to get a passage on a non-passenger carrying cargo ship to South America from a European port; it is not possible.

Details on shipping cars are given in **Motoring**, below, and in the relevant country sections.

Note Some countries in Latin America officially require travellers who enter their territory to have an onward or return ticket. (Look under "Information for Visitors" sections for the countries you intend to visit.) In 1994-95 this regulation was rarely enforced by any country. (It does not apply to travellers with their own vehicles.) In lieu of an onward ticket out of the country you are entering, any ticket out of another Latin American country (or a ticket home) may suffice, or proof that you have sufficient funds to buy a ticket (a credit card will do).

DOCUMENTATION AND SECURITY

Passports   Remember that Latin Americans, especially officials, are very document-minded. You should always carry your passport in a safe place about your person, or if not going far, leave it in the hotel safe. If staying in a country for several weeks, it is worth while registering at your Embassy or Consulate. Then, if your passport is stolen, the process of replacing it is simplified and speeded up. Keeping photocopies of essential documents, including your flight ticket, and some additional passport-sized photographs, is recommended

Remember that it is your responsibility to ensure that your passport is stamped in and out when you cross frontiers. The absence of entry and exit stamps can cause serious difficulties: seek out the proper migration offices if the stamping process is not carried out as you cross. Also, do not lose your entry card; replacing one causes a lot of trouble, and possibly expense. Citizens of countries which oblige visitors to have a visa (eg France) can expect more delays and problems at border crossings.

If planning to study in Latin America for a long period, make every effort to get a student visa in advance.

Identity and Membership Cards   Membership cards of British, European and US motoring organizations have been found useful for discounts off hotel charges, car rentals, maps, towing charges, etc. Student cards must carry a photograph if they are to be of any use in Latin America for discounts. (If you describe yourself as a student on your tourist card you may be able to get discounts, even if you haven't a student card). Business people should carry a good supply of visiting cards, which are essential for good business relations in Latin America. Identity, membership or business cards in Spanish or Portuguese (or a translation) and an official letter of introduction in Spanish or Portuguese are also useful.

If you are in full-time education you will be entitled to an International Student Identity Card, which is distributed by student travel offices and travel agencies in 77 countries. The ISIC gives you special prices on all forms of transport (air, sea, rail etc), and access to a variety of other concessions and services. If you need to find the location of your nearest ISIC office contact: The ISIC Association, Box 9048, 1000 Copenhagen, Denmark T (+45) 33 93 93 03.

Money   is best carried in US dollar travellers' cheques (denominations of US$50 and US$100 are preferable, though one does need a few of US$20) or cash. Sterling and other currencies are not recommended. Travellers' cheques are convenient but they attract thieves (though refunds can of course be arranged) and you will find that they are more difficult than dollar bills to change in small towns. Though the risk of loss is greater, many travellers take part of their funds in US dollar notes; better rates and lower commissions can usually be obtained for them. In many countries, US dollar notes are only accepted if they are in excellent condition (ie no writing, stamps, rips or other blemish; take brand new notes if you can). Low-value US dollar bills should be carried for changing into local currency if arriving in a country when banks or *casas de cambio* are closed (US$5 or US$10 bills). They are very useful for shopping: exchange shops (*casas de cambio*) tend to give better exchange rates than hotels or banks. The better hotels will normally change travellers' cheques for their guests (often at a rather poor rate), but if you're travelling on the cheap it is essential to keep in funds; watch weekends and public holidays carefully and never run out of local currency. Take plenty of local currency, in small denominations, when making trips into the interior. Spread your money around your person: less chance of thieves finding it all. Don't leave cash in your shoe, it may become too damaged to exchange or use.

We recommend in general the use of American Express, Visa or Thomas Cook US$ travellers' cheques, but should point out that less commission is often charged on Citibank or Bank of America cheques, if they are cashed at Latin American branches of those banks. These cheques are always accepted by banks, even though they may not be as well known outside banks as those of American Express, Visa or Thomas Cook. It is a good idea to take two kinds of cheque: if large numbers of one kind have recently been forged or stolen, making people suspicious, it is unlikely to have happened simultaneously with the other kind. Several banks charge a high fixed commission for changing travellers' cheques—sometimes as much as US$5-10 a cheque—because they don't really want to be bothered. Exchange houses (*casas de cambio*) are usually much better for this service. Some establishments may ask to see the customer's record of purchase before accepting travellers' cheques.

Most of the countries described in this book have freedom of exchange between US dollars and the local currency. A few have a parallel rate of exchange which is not always better than the official rate. Local conditions are described in the relevant chapters. Changing money on the street: if possible, do not do so alone. If unsure of the currency of the country you are about to enter, check rates with more than one changer at the border, or ask locals or departing travellers.

An increasingly popular and easy way of obtaining funds while travelling is with a credit card via an automatic telling machine (ATM). The Visa and Mastercard/

Plus/Cirrus networks are widespread. We give outlets' names in the text, but check before leaving home, as variations occur. Frequently, the rates of exchange on ATM withdrawals are the best available. It is also straightforward to obtain a cash advance against a credit card and, in the text, we give the names of banks that do this.

For purchases, credit cards of the Visa and Mastercard (Eurocard, Access) groups are useful, and American Express (Amex), Carte Blanche and Diners Club can be used. Conceal them very carefully (*not* under the insole of a shoe, however: that may render them unusable!), and make sure you know the correct procedure if they are lost or stolen. Credit card transactions are normally at an officially recognized rate of exchange (sometimes, if there are several, the least favourable one); you may find it much cheaper to pay cash and get the parallel rate. Many establishments in Latin America charge a fee of about 5% on credit card transactions (irrespective of any taxes); although forbidden by credit card company rules there is not a lot you can do about this, except get the charge itemized on the receipt and complain to the card company. For credit card security, insist that imprints are made in your presence and that any imprints incorrectly completed should be torn into tiny pieces. Also destroy the carbon papers after the form is completed (signatures can be copied from them).

NB In many countries, one can get at least US$500 in Amex travellers' cheques on the American Express card (US$1,000 on the gold card). One can also obtain cash at American Express via personal cheques, eg Eurocheque. If you are having additional sums of money sent out during a tour of Latin America, try to have it sent to one of the countries where you can easily exchange dollar travellers' cheques for dollars cash; see under the individual countries below for the current situation. Remember that a transfer of funds, even by telex, can take several days, and charges can be high; a recommended method is, before leaving, to find out which local bank is correspondent to your bank at home, then when you need funds, telex your own bank and ask them to telex the money to the local bank (confirming by air mail). It is possible to obtain money within hours by this method.

Whenever you leave a country, sell any local currency before leaving, because the further away you get, the less the value of a country's money. **Note** If departing by air, do not leave yourself too little money to pay the airport departure tax, which is never waived.

Americans should know that if they run out of funds they can usually expect no help from the US Embassy or Consul other than a referral to some welfare organization. Find out before you go precisely what services and assistance your embassy or consulate can provide if you find yourself in difficulties.

Law Enforcement Whereas in Europe and North America we are accustomed to law enforcement on a systematic basis, in general, enforcement in Latin America is achieved by periodic campaigns. The most typical is a round-up of criminals in the cities just before Christmas. In December, therefore, you may well be asked for identification at any time, and if you cannot produce it, you will be jailed. At first sight, on arrival, it may seem that you can flout the law with impunity, because everybody else is obviously doing so. If a visitor is jailed his friends should take him food every day. This is especially important for people on a diet, such as diabetics. It must also be borne in mind that in the event of a vehicle accident in which anyone is injured, all drivers involved are automatically detained until blame has been established, and this does not usually take less than 2 weeks.

Never offer a bribe unless you are fully conversant with the customs of the country. (In Chile, for instance, it would land you in serious trouble if you tried to bribe a *carabinero*.) Wait until the official makes the suggestion, or offer money in some form which is apparently not bribery, eg "In our country we have a system of on-the-spot fines (*multas de inmediato*). Is there a similar system here?" Do not assume that an official who accepts a bribe is prepared to do anything else that is illegal. You bribe him to persuade him to do his job, or to persuade him not to do it, or to do it more quickly, or more slowly. You do not bribe him to do something which is against the law. The mere suggestion would make him very upset. If an official suggests that a bribe must be paid before you can proceed on your way, be patient (assuming you have the time) and he may relent.

Security Generally speaking, most places in Latin America are no more dangerous than any major city in Europe or North America. In provincial towns, main places of interest, on day time buses and in ordinary restaurants the visitor should be quite safe. Nevertheless, in large cities particularly, crime exists, most of which is opportunistic. If you are aware of the dangers, act confidently and use your common sense you will lessen many of the risks. The following tips, all endorsed by travellers, are meant to forewarn, but not alarm, you. Keep all documents secure; hide your main cash supply in different places or under your clothes: extra pockets sewn inside shirts and trousers, pockets closed with a zip or safety pin, moneybelts (best worn below the waist rather than outside or at it or around the neck), neck or leg pouches, a thin chain for attaching a purse to your bag or under your clothes and elasticated support bandages for keeping money and cheques above the elbow or below the knee have been repeatedly recommended (the last by John Hatt in *The Tropical Traveller*). Keep cameras in bags (preferably with a chain or wire in the strap to defeat the slasher) or briefcases; take spare spectacles (eyeglasses); don't wear wrist-watches or jewellery. If you wear a shoulder-bag in a market, carry it in front of you. Backpacks are vulnerable to slashers: a good idea is to cover the pack with a sack (a plastic one will also keep out rain and dust) with maybe a layer of wire netting between, or make an inner frame of chicken wire. Use a pack which is lockable at its base.

Ignore mustard smearers and paint or shampoo sprayers, and strangers' remarks like "what's that on your shoulder?" or "have you seen that dirt on your shoe?" Furthermore, don't bend over to pick up money or other items in the street. These are all ruses intended to distract your attention and make you easy for an accomplice to steal from. If someone follows you when you're in the street, let him catch up with you and "give him the eye". While you should take local advice about being out at night, do not assume that daytime is safer than nighttime. If walking after dark, walk in the road, not on the pavement/sidewalk.

Be wary of "plainclothes policemen"; insist on seeing identification and on going to the police station by main roads. Do not hand over your identification (or money—which he should not need to see anyway) until you are at the station. On no account take them directly back to your lodgings. Be even more suspicious if he seeks confirmation of his status from a passer-by. If someone tries to bribe you, insist on a receipt. If attacked, remember your assailants may well be armed, and try not to resist.

It is best, if you can trust your hotel, to leave any valuables you don't need in safe-deposit there, when sightseeing locally. Always keep an inventory of what you have deposited. If you don't trust the hotel, lock everything in your pack and secure that in your room (some people take eyelet-screws for padlocking cupboards or drawers). If you lose valuables, always report to the police and note details of the report—for insurance purposes.

When you have all your luggage with you at a bus or railway station, be especially careful: don't get into arguments with any locals if you can help it, and lock all the items together with a chain or cable if you are waiting for some time. Take a taxi between airport/bus station/railway station and hotel, if you can possibly afford it. Keep your bags with you in the taxi and pay only when you and your luggage are safely out of the vehicle. Make sure the taxi has inner door handles, in case a quick exit is needed. Avoid night buses; never arrive at night; and watch your belongings whether they are stowed inside or outside the cabin (roof top luggage racks create extra problems, which are sometimes unavoidable—make sure your bag is waterproof). Major bus lines often issue a luggage ticket when bags are stored in the bus' hold, generally a safe system. When getting on a bus, keep your ticket handy; someone sitting in your seat may be a distraction for an accomplice to rob you while you are sorting out the problem. Finally, never accept food, drink, sweets or cigarettes from unknown fellow-travellers on buses or trains. They may be drugged, and you would wake up hours later without your belongings. In this connection, never accept a bar drink from an opened bottle (unless you can see that that bottle is in general use): always have it uncapped in front of you.

For specific local problems, see under the individual countries in the text.

Drugs Users of drugs, even of soft ones, without medical prescription should be particularly careful, as some countries impose heavy penalties— up to 10 years' imprisonment—for even the simple possession of such substances. In this connection, the planting of drugs on travellers, by traffickers or the police, is not unknown. If offered drugs on the street, make no response at all and keep walking. Note that people who roll their own cigarettes are often suspected of carrying drugs and subjected to intensive searches. Advisable to stick to commercial brands of cigarettes—but better still not to smoke at all.

ACCOMMODATION

Hotels For about US$10, a cheap but not bad hotel room can be found in most countries, although in some of the Andean countries you may not have to pay that much. For the indigent, it is a good idea to ask for a boarding house—*casa de huéspedes, hospedaje, pensión, casa familial* or *residencial*, according to country; they are normally to be found in abundance near bus and railway stations and markets. Good value hotels can also be found near truckers' stops/service stations; they are usually secure. There are often great seasonal variations in hotel prices in resorts. Note that in the text "with bath" usually means "with shower and toilet", not "with bath tub". Remember, cheaper hotels don't always supply soap, towels and toilet paper; in colder (higher) regions they may not supply enough blankets, so take your own or a sleeping bag. Useful tips: book even cheap hotels in advance by registered mail, if you receive no reply don't worry; ask the car rental agency employees at the airport for advice when you arrive, as long as they are not busy they may have better value recommendations than airport tourist offices; always ask for the best room. To avoid price hikes for gringos, ask if there is a cheaper room.

Experiment in International Living Ltd, "Otesaga", West Malvern Road, Malvern, Worcestershire, WR14 4EN, T 01684-562577, F 562212, or Ubierstrasse 30, 5300 Bonn 2, T 0228-95-7220, F 0228-35-8282, can arrange stays with families from 1 to 4 weeks in Chile, Ecuador and Brazil; EIL has offices in 38 countries. This has been recommended as an excellent way to meet people and learn the language.

Note The electric showers used in innumerable hotels should be checked for obvious flaws in the wiring; try not to touch the rose while it is producing hot water.

Youth Hostels Organizations affiliated to the Youth Hostels movement exist in Argentina, Brazil, Colombia, Chile, Peru and Uruguay. There is an associate organization in Ecuador. Further information in the country sections and from the IYHA.

Meals In all countries except Brazil and Chile (where cold meats, cheese, eggs, fruit etc generally figure) breakfast usually means coffee or tea with rolls and butter, and anything more is charged extra. In Colombia and Ecuador breakfast usually means eggs, a roll, fruit juice and a mug of milk with coffee; say "breakfast without eggs" if you do not want that much. There is a paragraph on each nation's food under "Information for Visitors". Vegetarians should be able to list all the foods they cannot eat; saying "Soy vegetariano/a" (I'm a vegetarian) or "no como carne" (I don't eat meat) is often not enough. Most restaurants serve a daily special meal, usually at lunchtime, which is cheap and good. Other than that you can expect to pay between US$10-15 on breakfast and dinner per day.

Camping There is a growing network of organized campsites, to which reference is made in the text immediately below hotel lists, under each town. If there is no organized site in town, a football pitch or gravel pit might serve. Obey the following rules for "wild" camping: (1) arrive in daylight and pitch your tent as it gets dark; (2) ask permission to camp from the parish priest, or the fire chief, or the police, or a farmer regarding his own property; (3) never ask a group of people— especially young people; (4) never camp on a beach (because of sandflies and thieves). If you can't get information from anyone, camp in a spot where you can't be seen from the nearest inhabited place, or road, and make sure no one saw you go there. In Argentina and Brazil, it is common to camp at gas/petrol stations. As Béatrice Völkle of Gampelen, Switzerland, adds, camping wild may be preferable to those organized sites which are treated as discotheques, with only the afternoon reserved for sleeping.

If taking a cooker, the most frequent recommendation is a multifuel stove (eg MSR International, Coleman Peak 1), which will burn unleaded petrol or, if that is not available, kerosene, *benzina blanca*, etc. Alcohol-burning stoves are simple, reliable, but slow and you have to carry a lot of fuel: for a methylated spirit-burning stove, the following fuels apply, *alcohol desnaturalizado, alcohol metílico, alcohol puro (de caña)* or *alcohol para quemar*. Ask for 95%, but 70% will suffice. In all countries fuel can usually be found in chemists/pharmacies. Gas cylinders and bottles are usually exchangeable, but if not can be recharged; specify whether you use butane or propane. Gas canisters are not always available. The Camping Clube do Brasil gives 50% discounts to holders of international campers' cards.

Toilets Many hotels, restaurants and bars have inadequate water supplies. **Almost without exception used toilet paper should not be flushed down the pan, but placed in the receptacle provided.** This applies even in quite expensive hotels. Failing to observe this custom will block the pan or drain, a considerable health risk. It is quite common for people to stand on the toilet seat (facing the wall—easier to balance), as they do in Asia. If you are concerned about the hygiene of the facility, put paper on the seat.

Cockroaches These are ubiquitous and unpleasant, but not dangerous. Take some insecticide powder if staying in cheap hotels; Baygon (Bayer) has been recommended. Stuff toilet paper in any holes in walls that you may suspect of being parts of cockroach runs.

ETIQUETTE AND LANGUAGE

Travellers' Appearance There is a natural prejudice in all countries against travellers who ignore personal hygiene and have a generally dirty and unkempt appearance. Most Latin Americans, if they can afford it, devote great care to their clothes and appearance; it is appreciated if visitors do likewise. How you dress is mostly how people will judge you. Buying clothing locally can help you to look less like a tourist. The general prejudice previously reported against backpacks has virtually disappeared, unless carried by those whom officials identify as "hippies". One tip we have received; young people of informal dress and life-style may find it advantageous to procure a letter from someone in an official position testifying to their good character, on official-looking notepaper.

Some countries have laws or prejudices against the wearing by civilians of army-surplus clothing. Men wearing earrings are liable to be ridiculed in more "macho" communities (eg parts of Argentina). A medium weight shawl with some wool content is recommended for women: it can double as pillow, light blanket, bathrobe or sunscreen as required. For men, a smart jacket can be very useful.

Courtesy Remember that politeness—even a little ceremoniousness—is much appreciated. In this connection professional or business cards are useful. Men should always remove any headgear and say "con permiso" ("com licença" in Brazil) when entering offices, and be prepared to shake hands (this is much commoner in Latin America than in Europe or North America); always say "Buenos días" (until midday) or "Buenas tardes" ("Bom dia" or "Boa tarde" in Brazil) and wait for a reply before proceeding further; in a word, don't rush them! Always remember that the traveller from abroad has enjoyed greater advantages in life than most Latin American minor officials, and should be friendly and courteous in consequence. Never be impatient; do not criticize situations in public: the officials may know more English than you think and they can certainly interpret gestures and facial expressions. Be judicious about discussing politics with strangers. Politeness can be a liability, however, in some situations; most Latin Americans are disorderly queuers. In commercial transactions (buying a meal, goods in a shop, etc) politeness should be accompanied by firmness, and always ask the price first.

Politeness should also be extended to street traders; saying "No, gracias" with a smile is better than an arrogant dismissal. Whether you give money to beggars is a personal matter, but your decision should be influenced by whether a person is begging out of need or trying to cash in on the tourist trail. In the former case, local people giving may provide an indication. Giving money to children is a separate issue, upon which most agree: don't do it. There are occasions where giving food in a restaurant may be appropriate, but first inform yourself of local practice.

Moira Chubb, from New Zealand, suggests that if you are a guest and are offered food that arouses your suspicions, the only courteous way out is to feign an allergy or a stomach ailment. If worried about the purity of ice for drinks, ask for a beer.

Language Without some knowledge of Spanish you can become very frustrated and feel helpless in many situations. English, or any other language, is absolutely useless off the beaten track. Some initial study, to get you up to a basic Spanish vocabulary of 500 words or so, and a pocket dictionary and phrase-book, are most strongly recommended: your pleasure will be doubled if you can talk to the locals. Not all the locals speak Spanish, of course; apart from Brazil's Portuguese, you will find that some Indians in the more remote highland parts of Bolivia and Peru, and lowland Indians in Amazonia, speak only their indigenous languages, though there will usually be at least one person in each village who can speak Spanish (or Portuguese).

The basic Spanish of Hispanic America is that of south-western Spain, with soft "c's" and "z's" pronounced as "s", and not as "th" as in the other parts of Spain. Castilian Spanish is readily understood, but is not appreciated when spoken by non-Spaniards; try and learn the basic Latin American pronunciation. There are several regional variations in pronunciation, particularly in the River Plate countries, which are noted in the Argentine section "Information for Visitors". Differences in vocabulary also exist, both between peninsular Spanish and Latin American Spanish, and between the usages of the different countries.

If you are going to Brazil, you should learn some Portuguese. Spanish is not adequate: you may be understood but you will probably not be able to understand the answers. Language classes are available at low cost in a number of centres in South America, for instance Quito. See the text for details, under **Language Courses**.

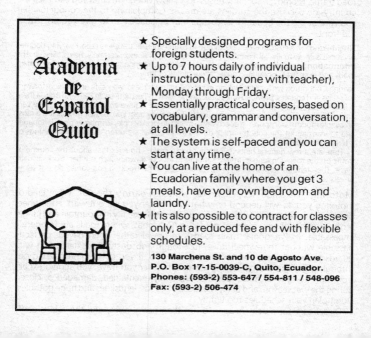

INTERNAL SURFACE TRANSPORT

Before you start, remember that distances are great and journeys by land are long: plan accordingly and do not try to do too much in the time available.

Surface Transport The continent has a growing road system for motor traffic, with frequent bus services. The buses are often comfortable; Brazil, Chile and Venezuela are the best; Colombia is quite good, Ecuador not far behind; Bolivia has good and bad; Peruvian buses are generally poor because of economic problems and the difficulties of Andean terrain. In mountainous country, however, do not expect buses to get to their destination, after long journeys, anywhere near on time. Do not turn up for a bus at the last minute; if it is full it may depart early. Tall travellers are advised to take aisle rather than window seats on long journeys as this allows more leg room. When the journey takes more than 3 or 4 hrs, meal stops at country inns or bars, good and bad, are the rule. Usually, no announcement is made on the duration of a stop: follow the driver, if he eats, eat. See what the locals are eating—and buy likewise, or make sure you're stocked up well on food and drink at the start. For drinks, stick to bottled water or soft drinks or coffee (black). The food sold by vendors at bus stops may be all right: watch if locals are buying, though unpeeled fruit is of course reliable. (See above on **Security** in buses.)

In most countries trains are slower than buses. They do tend, however, to provide finer scenery, and you can normally see much more wildlife than from the road—it is less disturbed by one or two trains a day than by the more frequent road traffic. Moreover, so many buses now show video films that you can't see the countryside because the curtains are drawn. Complaining to the conductor that you cannot see the beautiful landscape may persuade him to give you his seat at the front.

Hitchhiking This custom is quite common in Latin America; travellers report varying degrees of success in virtually all countries. Neatness of appearance certainly helps. See in the **Information for Visitors** sections for local conditions. If trying to hitchhike away from main roads and in sparsely-populated areas, allow plenty of time.

Joanna Codrington writes: Hitchhiking in Latin America is reasonably safe and straightforward for males and couples, provided one speaks some Spanish/Portuguese. In Peru and Bolivia there is little private transport and trucks charge about $2/3$ the equivalent fare. But elsewhere cars and trucks will carry you free of charge, and will generally treat you as their guests. It is a most enjoyable mode of transport—a good way to meet the local people, to improve one's languages and to learn about the country. Truck drivers in particular are often well versed in things of interest one is passing, eg crops and industries.

Here are a few general hints: in remoter parts, make enquiries first about the volume of traffic on the road. On long journeys, set out at crack of dawn, which is when trucks usually leave. They tend to go longer distances than cars. Some trucking companies do not allow drivers to take hitchhikers.

Motoring Binka and Robin le Breton write: *Preparing the Car* What kind of motoring you do will depend on what kind of car you set out with. Four-wheel drive is not necessary, but it does give you greater flexibility in mountain and jungle territory, although you may not get far in Amazonas, where roads are frequently impassable. In Patagonia, main roads are gravel rather than paved: perfectly passable without four-wheel drive, just rough and dusty. Consider fitting wire guards for headlamps, and for windscreens too, if you don't mind peering out through a grill like a caged chimpanzee. Wherever you travel you should expect from time to time to find roads that are badly maintained, damaged or closed during the wet season, and delays because of floods, landslides and huge potholes. Don't plan your schedules too tightly.

Diesel cars are much cheaper to run than petrol ones, and the fuel is easily available; in Venezuela you may have to look hard for it outside Caracas. Most towns can supply a mechanic of sorts, and probably parts for Bosch fuel injection equipment. Watch the mechanics like a hawk, since there's always a brisk market in spares, and some of yours may be highly desirable. That apart, they enjoy a challenge, and can fix most things, eventually.

For prolonged motoring over 3000 metres, you may need to fit high altitude jets on your carburettors. Some fuel injection engines need adjusting too, and ignition settings may have to be changed: check the manufacturer's recommendations. The electronic ignition and fuel metering systems on modern emission controlled cars are allergic to humidity, heat and dust, and cannot be repaired by bush mechanics. Standard European and Japanese cars run on fuel with a higher octane rating than is commonly available in North, South or Central America, and in Brazil petrol (gasolina) is in fact gasohol, with a 12% admixture of alcohol. A high compression fuel injection engine will not like this. Unleaded fuel is available in Chile, Colombia and Ecuador, and to a small extent in Argentina. The most easily maintained petrol engined cars, then, are the types manufactured in Latin American countries, ie pre-emission control models such as the VW Kombi with carburettors and conventional (non-electronic) ignition, or the old type Toyota Landcruisers common in Central America. Older model American cars, especially Ford or GM pickups, are easily maintained, but high fuel consumption offsets this advantage. (Note that Colombia does not have a network for spares and repairs of VW, while Ecuador, Venezuela and Brazil do. Argentina is very expensive for maintenance of any make of car.)

Preparing the car for the journey is largely a matter of common sense: obviously any part that is not in first class condition should be replaced. It's well worth installing extra heavy-duty shock-absorbers (such as Spax or Koni) before starting out, because a long trip on rough roads in a heavily laden car will give heavy wear. Fit tubes on "tubeless" tyres, since air plugs for tubeless tyres are hard to find, and if you bend the rim on a pothole, the tyre will not hold air. Take spare tubes, and an extra spare tyre. Also take spare plugs, fan-belts, radiator hoses and headlamp bulbs; even though local equivalents can easily be found in cities, it is wise to take spares for those occasions late at night or in remote areas when you might need them. You can also change the fanbelt after a stretch of long, hot driving to prevent wear (eg after 15,000 km/10,000 miles). If your vehicle has more than one fanbelt, always replace them all at the same time (make sure you have the necessary tools if doing it yourself). If your car has sophisticated electrics, spare "black boxes" for the ignition and fuel injection are advisable, plus a spare voltage regulator or the appropriate diodes for the alternator, and elements for the fuel, air and oil filters if these are not a common type. (Some drivers take a spare alternator of the correct amperage, especially if the regulator is incorporated into the alternator.) Dirty fuel is a frequent problem, so be prepared to change filters more often than you would at home: in a diesel car you will need to check the sediment bowl often, too. An extra in-line fuel filter is a good idea if feasible (metal canister type preferable to plastic), and for travel on dusty roads an oil bath air filter is best for a diesel car. It is wise to carry a spade, jumper cables, tow rope and an air pump. Fit tow hooks to both sides of the vehicle frame. A 12 volt neon light for camping and repairs will be invaluable. Spare fuel containers should be steel and not plastic, and a siphon pipe is essential for those places where fuel is sold out of the drum. Take a 10 litre water container for self and vehicle. Note that in some areas gas stations are few and far between. Fill up when you see one: the next one may be out of fuel. Some countries have periodic fuel conservation strategies which means you can't get any after a certain hour in the evening, and often not at weekends either.

Apart from the mechanical aspects, spare no ingenuity in making your car secure. Your model should be the Brink's armoured van: anything less secure can be broken into by the determined and skilled thief. Use heavy chain and padlocks to chain doors shut, fit security catches on windows, remove interior window winders (so that a hand reaching in from a forced vent cannot open the window). All these will help, but none is foolproof. Anything on the outside—wing mirrors, spot lamps, motifs etc—is likely to be stolen too. So are wheels if not secured by locking nuts. Try never to leave the car unattended except in a locked garage or guarded parking space. Remove all belongings and leave the empty glove compartment open when the car is unattended. Also lock the clutch or accelerator to the steering wheel with a heavy, obvious chain or lock. Street children will generally protect your car fiercely in exchange for a tip. Be sure to note down key numbers and carry spares of the most important ones (but don't keep all spares inside the vehicle).

Documents   A *carnet de passage* is no longer necessary in any country (but please see **Additional notes** below). Land entry procedures for all countries—with the exception of Colombia—are simple, though time-consuming, as the car has to be checked by customs, police and agriculture officials. All you need is the registration document in the name of the driver, or, in the case of a car registered in someone else's name, a notarized letter of authorization. Most countries give a limited period of stay, but allow an extension if requested in advance. Of course, do be very careful to keep **all** the papers you are given when you enter, to produce when you leave. Bringing a car in by sea or air is much more complicated and expensive: generally you will have to hire an agent to clear it through customs, expensive and slow. Insurance for the vehicle against accident, damage or theft is best arranged in the country of origin, but it is getting increasingly difficult to find agencies who offer this service. In Latin American countries it is very expensive to insure against accident and theft, especially as you should take into account the value of the car increased by duties calculated in real (ie non devaluing) terms. If the car is stolen or written off you will be required to pay very high import duty on its value. A few countries insist on compulsory third party insurance, to be bought at the border: in other countries it's technically required, but not checked up on (Venezuela seems to be the only country where it is easy to obtain—Ed). Get the legally required minimum cover, not expensive, as soon as you can, because if you should be involved in an accident and are uninsured, your car could be confiscated. If anyone is hurt, do not pick them up (you may become liable). Seek assistance from the nearest police station or hospital if you are able to do so. You may find yourself facing a hostile crowd, even if you are not to blame.

Journey's End   When you finally reach your destination, what happens to the car? Shipping it back is one alternative. From Brazil, Grimaldi line to Genoa is the cheapest: there are also frequent sailings from Montevideo and Buenos Aires to most other destinations. The other alternative is to sell the car. Until now, this has been virtually impossible except in Paraguay, but the economic liberalization in Argentina, Chile and Brazil makes it legal—if not simple—to import cars into those countries. Probably safer not to count on it though, unless you have the sort of car in great demand, like a Mercedes saloon. You can sell anything in Paraguay if you have the time. Legalizing the permanent import of a temporarily imported car costs about 30% of its street value. If you leave it to the buyer to "take care of" obtaining the correct documentation, you should not expect to receive a very favourable price. Dealers are adept at taking advantage of the fact that they can wait, and you cannot, so be prepared for "on—off—on again" dealing.

Car Hire The main international car hire companies operate in all countries, but they do tend to be very expensive, reflecting the high costs and accident rates. Hotels and tourist agencies will tell you where to find cheaper rates, but you will need to check that you have such basics as spare wheel, toolkit and functioning lights etc. You'll probably have more fun if you drive yourself, although it's always possible to hire a car with driver. If you plan to do a lot of driving and will have time at the end to dispose of it, investigate the possibility of buying a second hand car locally: since hiring is so expensive it may well work out cheaper and will probably do you just as well.

Car Hire Insurance Check exactly what the hirer's insurance policy covers. In many cases it will only protect you against minor bumps and scrapes, not major accidents, nor "natural" damage (eg flooding). Ask if extra cover is available. Also find out, if using a credit card, whether the card automatically includes insurance. Beware of being billed for scratches which were on the vehicle before you hired it.

Additional notes on motoring A great deal of conflicting information surrounds what documents are required in addition to the vehicle's registration. According to the RAC in the UK there are three recognized documents for taking a vehicle into South America: a *carnet de passages* issued by the Fedération Internationale de l'Automobile (FIA – Paris), a *carnet de passages* issued by the Alliance Internationale de Tourisme (AIT-Geneva), and the *Libreta de Pasos por Aduana* issued by the Federación Interamericana de Touring y Automóvil Clubs (FITAC). The following list gives official requirements, with comments about actual practice: **Argentina** requires a written undertaking that the car will be exported after a given period, either of the *carnets*, or the *libreta* (in practice, nothing is asked for beyond the title document, except at remote border crossings which may demand a *libreta*); **Bolivia**, *libreta* only; **Brazil**, a written undertaking only (nothing asked for); **Chile**, either *carnet*, or the *libreta* (in practice nothing asked for), insurance is obligatory; **Colombia**, either *carnet* or, according to a law of 31.12.1992, you have to purchase a bond on entry to the value of 10% of your vehicle (in practice, early 1995, nothing asked for), insurance is necessary; **Ecuador**, until 1995 either *carnet*, or the *libreta* was essential, but latest reports indicate that neither is now required (ask at an embassy in advance); **Paraguay**, either *carnet*, or the *libreta*; **Peru**, either *carnet*, the *libreta* and, for caravans and trailers, an inventory (the consulate in London says that a *libreta* is necessary, but if you cannot obtain one a written declaration that the car will leave Peru, authorized at a Peruvian consulate before leaving your home country, will do instead, in addition a traveller reports that *Formulario 015*, which can be requested at the border, entitles visitors to bring a vehicle into Peru duty free for 3 months, it is not extendable, it is free, but our correspondent was charged US$35 anyway); **Uruguay**, the *libreta* or the FIA *carnet* only (in practice nothing asked for); **Venezuela**, either *carnet* or the *libreta* (the consulate in London says a *Certificado de uso por turismo* must be completed at a Venezuelan embassy before arrival, no other documents required; in the USA the vehicle's title document must be legalized by a Venezuelan consul, US$100, this, plus title and a letter of intent from your shipper's agent must be taken to US customs at least 2 days before sailing, no *libreta* or *carnet* needed). In view of this confusion, contact the automobile clubs of the countries you intend to drive in and get their advice. In general, in 1994, motorists in South America seemed to fare better with a *carnet de passages* than without it.

The *libreta*, a 10-page book of three-part passes for customs, should be available from any South American automobile club member of FITAC; cost seems to be US$200, half refundable. The *carnet de passages* is issued only in the country where the vehicle is registered (in the UK it costs £65 for 25 pages, £55 for 10 pages, valid 12 months, either bank indemnity or insurance indemnity, half of the premium refundable value of the vehicle and countries to be visited required), available from the RAC or the AA. In the USA the AAA seems not to issue the *carnet*, although the HQ in Washington DC may give advice. It is available from the Canadian Automobile Association (1775 Courtwood Crescent, Ottawa, K2C 3JZ, T 613-226-7631, F 613-225-7383) for Canadian and US citizens, cost in late 1994 C$450; full details obtainable from the CAA. For this information thanks go to Paul Gowen, RAC Touring Information

Manager, Binka Le Breton, Mark Simril (who wrote to us and whose experiences were reported in *South American Explorer* No 30, November 1991), and other motorists.

While a normal car will reach most places of interest, high ground clearance is useful for badly surfaced or unsurfaced roads and for fording rivers: 4-wheel drive is recommended for mountain terrain and unmade roads off the beaten track.

If you want to buy a second-hand car, check for corrosion if making the deal in a coastal city and always check, if not change, the full set of tyres.

Shipping a vehicle From Europe or the USA you can either go to Panama and take the new *Crucero Express* ferry from Colón to Cartagena (Colombia), or shop around for the best value sailing to whichever port best suits your travelling plans. Try Boyd Steamship Corporation (T Balboa 636311), Buenaventura or Guayaquil; Sudamericana de Vapores (T Cristóbal 293844), Buenaventura; Central American Lines (T Colón 412880, Panama City 361036), Cartagena; Vencaribe (T Cristóbal 450461, Panama City 521258) or Cía Transatlántica España (T 696300) for Venezuela. Alternatively you can ship a vehicle from Europe to Brazil, Uruguay or Argentina. Vehicles can also be shipped from the USA. You have to get a special exemption in order to be allowed to be carried to Colombia in a non Colombian vessel, which takes time to obtain. Anything left using the car while it is being shipped will be stolen. As long as your vehicle is not over 2.28m high, it can go in a container, but permission must be obtained for any belongings to remain in the car, and separate insurance for effects purchased. If the car is going ro-ro (drive on), it should be empty of all belongings, unless they are thoroughly secured.

A book containing much practical information on South American motoring conditions and requirements, as well as being a travelogue, is *Driving to Heaven*, by Derek Stansfield (available from the author, Ropley, Broad Oak, Sturminster Newton, Dorset DT10 2HG, T/F 01258-472534, £8.85 plus postage, if outside the UK).

Motorcycling The following advice was received from Ashley Rawlings of Bath (England): People are generally very amicable to motorcyclists and you can make many friends by returning friendship to those who show an interest in you.

The Machine should be off road capable: my choice would be the BMW R80/100/GS for its rugged and simple design and reliable shaft drive, but a Kawasaki KLR 650s, Honda Transalp/Dominator, or the ubiquitous Yamaha XT600 Tenere would also be suitable. Buying a bike in the States and driving down works out cheaper than buying one in the UK. A road bike can go most places an off road bike can go at the cost of greater effort.

Preparations: Many roads in Latin America are rough. Fit heavy duty front fork springs and the best quality rebuildable shock absorber you can afford (Ohlins, White Power). Fit lockable luggage such as Krausers (reinforce luggage frames) or make some detachable aluminium panniers. Fit a tank bag and tank panniers for better weight distribution. A large capacity fuel tank (Acerbis), +300 mile/480 km range is essential if going off the beaten track. A washable air filter is a good idea (K&N), also fuel filters, fueltap rubber seals and smaller jets for high altitude Andean motoring. A good set of trails-type tyres as well as a high mudguard are useful. Get to know the bike before you go, ask the dealers in your country what goes wrong with it and arrange a link whereby you can get parts flown out to you. If riding a chain driven bike, a fully enclosed chaincase is useful. A hefty bash plate/sump guard is invaluable.

Spares: Reduce service intervals by half if driving in severe conditions. A spare rear tyre is useful but you can buy modern tyres in most capital cities. Take oil filters, fork and shock seals, tubes, a good manual, spare cables (taped into position), a plug cap and spare plug lead. A spare electronic ignition is a good idea, try and buy a second hand one and make arrangements to have parts sent out to you. A first class tool kit is a must and if riding a bike with a chain then a spare set of sprockets and an 'o' ring chain should be carried. Spare brake and clutch levers should also be taken as these break easily in a fall. Parts are few and far between, but mechanics are skilled at making do and can usually repair things. Castrol oil can be bought everywhere and relied upon.

Take a puncture repair kit and tyre levers. Find out about any weak spots on the bike and improve them. Get the book for international dealer coverage from your manufacturer, but don't rely on it. They frequently have few or no parts for modern, large machinery.

Clothes and Equipment: A tough waterproof jacket, comfortable strong boots, gloves and a helmet with which you can use glass goggles (Halycon) which will not scratch and wear out like a plastic visor. The best quality tent and camping gear that you can afford and a petrol stove which runs on bike fuel is helpful.

Security: Not a problem in most countries. Try not to leave a fully laden bike on its own. An Abus D or chain will keep the bike secure. A cheap alarm gives you peace of mind if you leave the bike outside a hotel at night. Most hotels will allow you to bring the bike inside. Look for hotels that have a courtyard or more secure parking and never leave luggage on the bike overnight or whilst unattended.

Documents: Passport, International Driving Licence, bike registration document are necessary. The *carnet de passages* seems only to be absolutely necessary for Ecuador (Customs may allow you through in transit for a limited period), but in 1994 riders fared much better with a *carnet de passages* than without it. Get your licence endorsed by police in Bolivia.

Shipping: Bikes may be sent from Panama to Colombia by cargo flight (eg CAC). This costs approx US$150 for a 200kg bike (1994 price). You must drain the fuel, oil and battery acid, or remove the battery, but it is easier to disconnect and seal the overflow tube. Tape cardboard over fragile bits and insist on loading the bike yourself. The Darién Gap is impossible unless you carry the bike. See the Colombia chapter for the *Crucero Express* which carries motorbikes between Panama and Colombia.

Border Crossings Do not try to cross borders on a Sunday or a holiday anywhere as you are charged double the rate in Central America and a charge is levied on the usually free borders in South America. I found South American customs and immigration inspectors mostly as friendly, polite and efficient. Central America, however, was a different story and it was sometimes very difficult to find out exactly what was being paid for. If in doubt ask to see the boss and/or the rule book.

Cycling Hallam Murray writes: Since the early 1980s, bicycle technology has improved in leaps and bounds. With the advent of Kevlar tyres and puncture-resistant inner tubes it is now theoretically possible to cycle from Alaska to Tierra del Fuego without so much as a single puncture. For the traveller with a zest for adventure and a limited budget there is unlikely to be a finer way to explore. At first glance a bicycle may not appear to be the most obvious vehicle for a major journey, but given ample time and reasonable energy it most certainly is the best. It can be ridden, carried by almost every form of transport from an aeroplane to a canoe, and can even be lifted across one's shoulders over short distances. On my most recent journey from Lake Titicaca to Tierra del Fuego—largely on unpaved roads, many of which would have defeated even the most robust car or truck—I was often envied by travellers using more orthodox transport, for I was able to travel at my own pace, to explore more remote regions and to meet people who are not normally in contact with tourists.

Choosing a Bicycle: The choice of bicycle depends on the type and length of expedition being undertaken and on the terrain and road surfaces likely to be encountered. Unless you are planning a journey almost exclusively on paved roads—when a high quality touring bike such as a Dawes Super Galaxy would probably suffice—I would strongly recommend a mountain bike. The good quality ones (and the cast iron rule is **never** to skimp on quality) are incredibly tough and rugged, with low gear ratios for difficult terrain, wide tyres with plenty of tread for good road-holding, cantilever brakes, and a low centre of gravity for improved stability. Expect to pay upwards of US$800 for such a machine. Although touring bikes, and to a lesser extent mountain bikes, and spares are available in the larger Latin American cities, remember that in the developing world many indigenous manufactured goods are shoddy and rarely last. In some countries, such as Mexico, Chile and Uruguay, imported components can be found but they tend to be extremely expensive. (Shimano parts are generally the easiest to find.) Buy everything you possibly can before you leave home.

Bicycle Equipment: A small but comprehensive tool kit (to include chain rivet and crank removers, a spoke key and possibly a block remover), a spare tyre and inner tubes, a puncture repair kit with plenty of extra patches and glue, a set of brake blocks, brake and gear cables and all types of nuts and bolts, at least 12 spokes (best taped to the chain stay), a light oil for the chain, tube of waterproof grease, a pump secured by a pump lock, a Blackburn parking block (my choice for the most invaluable accessory and they are cheap and virtually weightless), a cyclometer, a loud bell, and a secure lock and chain. *Richard's Bicycle Book* makes useful reading for even the most mechanically minded.

Luggage and equipment: Strong and waterproof front and back panniers are a must. When packed these are likely to be heavy and should be carried on the strongest racks available. Poor quality racks have ruined many a journey for they take incredible strain on unpaved roads. A top bag cum rucksack (eg Carradice) makes a good addition for use on and off the bike. I used a Cannondale front bag for my maps, camera, compass, altimeter, notebook and small tape-recorder. My total luggage weighed 27 kg—on the high side, but I never felt seriously overweight. (Other panniers rec are Ortlieb – front and back – which is waterproof and almost "sandproof", and Karimoor.) "Gaffa" tape is excellent for protecting vulnerable parts of panniers and for carrying out all manner of repairs. My most vital equipment included a light and waterproof tent, a 3 season sleeping bag, an Optimus petrol stove (the best I have ever used for it is light and efficient and petrol can be found almost everywhere; also rec is the MSR XGK II multi-fuel stove – Andrew Dobbie, Swansea), a plastic survival bag for storing luggage at night when camping, 4 elastic straps, 4 one-litre water bottles, Swiss Army knife, torch, candle, comprehensive medical kit, money belts, a hat and sunglasses to protect against hours of ferocious tropical sun and small presents such as postcards of home, balloons and plastic badges. A rubber mouse can do wonders for making contact with children in isolated villages.

All equipment and clothes should be packed in plastic bags to give extra protection against dust and rain. (Also protect all documents, etc carried close to the body from sweat.) Always take the minimum clothing. It's better to buy extra items en route when you find you need them. Naturally the choice will depend on whether you are planning a journey through tropical lowlands, deserts, high mountains or a combination, and whether rain is to be expected. Generally it is best to carry several layers of thin light clothes than fewer heavy, bulky ones. Always keep one set of dry clothes, including long trousers, to put on at the end of the day. I would not have parted with my incredibly light, strong, waterproof and wind resistant goretex jacket and overtrousers. I could have sold them 100 times over and in Bolivia was even offered a young mule in exchange! I took two pairs of training shoes and found these to be ideal for both cycling and walking.

Useful Tips: Wind, not hills is the enemy of the cyclist. Try to make the best use of the times of day when there is little; mornings tend to be best but there is no steadfast rule. In parts of Patagonia there can be gusting winds of 80 kph around the clock at some times of year, whereas in other areas there can be none. Take care to avoid dehydration, by drinking regularly. In hot, dry areas with limited supplies of water, be sure to carry an ample supply. For food I carried the staples (sugar, salt, dried milk, tea, coffee, porridge oats, raisins, dried soups, etc) and supplemented these with whatever local foods I could find in the markets. Give your bicycle a thorough daily check for loose nuts or bolts or bearings. See that all parts run smoothly. A good chain should last 2,000 miles, 3,200 km or more but be sure to keep it as clean as possible—an old toothbrush is good for this—and to oil it lightly from time to time. Always camp out of sight of a road. Remember that thieves are attracted to towns and cities, so when sight-seeing, try to leave your bicycle with someone such as a café owner or a priest. Country people tend to be more honest and are usually friendly and very inquisitive. However, don't take unnecessary risks; always see that your bicycle is secure (most hotels will allow bikes to be kept in rooms). In more remote regions dogs can be vicious; carry a stick or some small stones to frighten them off. Traffic on main roads can be a nightmare; it is usually far more rewarding to keep to the smaller roads or to paths if they exist. Most towns have a bicycle shop of some description, but it is best to do your own repairs and adjustments whenever possible. In an emergency it is amazing how one can improvise with wire, string, dental floss, nuts and bolts, odd pieces of tin or "Gaffa" tape!

The Expedition Advisory Centre, administered by the Royal Geographical Society, 1, Kensington Gore, London SW7 2AR has published a useful monograph entitled *Bicycle Expeditions*, by Paul Vickers. Published in March 1990, it is available direct from the Centre, price £6.50 (postage extra if outside the UK). (In the UK there is also the Cyclist's Touring Club, CTC, Cotterell House, 69 Meadrow, Godalming, Surrey, GU7 3HS, T 0483-417217, for touring, and technical information.)

Most cyclists agree that the main danger comes from other traffic. A rearview mirror has been frequently recommended to forewarn you of vehicles which are too close behind. You also need to watch out for oncoming, overtaking vehicles, unstable loads on trucks, protruding loads etc. Make yourself conspicuous by wearing bright clothing and a helmet.

Ryan Flegal of Los Angeles, California, says that, instead of taking your own expensive bicycle from home with the attendant need for specialized tools and high risks of loss, one can buy a bike in Latin America. "Affix a sturdy rear rack, improvise securing luggage to the bicycle, and go. Carry only a patch kit and wrench to remove the wheel, and rely on the many bike mechanics in the area to do the rest". A steel frame is more durable when heavily laden and can be welded if damaged, unlike aluminium. If undertaking your own maintenance, make sure you know how to do it, and research what tyres you will need, before you go.

River Transport Geoffrey Dempsey has sent us the following note, with particular reference to Amazonia:

Because expanding air services have captured the lucrative end of the passenger market, passenger services on the rivers are in decline. Worst hit have been the upper reaches; rivers like the Ucayali in Peru, but the trend is apparent throughout the region. The situation has been aggravated for the casual traveller by a new generation of purpose-built tugs (all engine-room and bridge) that can handle up to a dozen freight barges but have no passenger accommodation. In Peru passenger boats must now supplement incomes by carrying cargo, and this lengthens their journey cycle. In the face of long delays, travellers might consider shorter "legs" involving more frequent changes of boat; though the more local the service, the slower and more uncomfortable it will be.

Hammocks, mosquito nets (not always good quality), plastic containers for water storage, kettles and cooking utensils can be purchased in any sizeable riverside town, as well as tinned food such as sardines, meat loaf, frankfurters, ham and fruit. Fresh bread, cake, eggs, fruit—papayas, bananas, pineapples, oranges etc—are available in most villages. Cabin bunks are provided with thin mattresses but these are often foul. Replacements can be bought locally but rolls of plastic foam that can be cut to size are also available and much cheaper. Eye-screws for securing washing lines and mosquito nets are useful, and tall passengers who are not taking a hammock and who may find insufficient headroom on some boats should consider a camp-chair. The writer yearned for a cushion.

HM Wams (Amsterdam) endorses the recommendation of taking hammock, mosquito net and food, adding that in Venezuelan Amazonas hitching rides on boats is possible if you camp at the harbour or police post where all boats must register. Take any boat going in your direction as long as it reaches the next police post. See the special section on the Brazilian Amazon, p 539.

Travelling with Children   We are grateful to Tim and Arlene Frost, of New Zealand, for the following notes and to Linda and Lawrence Foster, of Wembley, Hallam and Carole Murray, of London, SW11, and Tim Butler and Valerie Fraser, of Lima, for additional suggestions:

People contemplating overland travel in South America with children should remember that a lot of time can be spent waiting for buses, trains, and especially for aeroplanes. On bus journeys, if the children are good at amusing themselves, or can readily sleep while travelling, the problems can be considerably lessened. If your child is of an early reading age, take reading material with you as it is difficult, and expensive to find. A bag of, say 30 pieces, of Duplo or Lego can keep young children occupied for hours. Travel on trains, while not as fast or at times as comfortable as buses, allows more scope for moving about. Some trains provide tables between seats, so that games can be played. Beware of doors left open for ventilation especially if air-conditioning is not working.

Food can be a problem if the children are not adaptable. It is easier to take biscuits, drinks, bread etc with you on longer trips than to rely on meal stops where the food may not be to taste. Avocados are safe, easy to eat and nutritious; they can be fed to babies as young as 6 months and most older children like them. A small immersion heater and jug for making hot drinks is invaluable, but remember that electric current varies. Try and get a dual-voltage one (110v and 220v).

Fares: On all long-distance buses you pay for each seat, and there are no half-fares if the children occupy a seat each. For shorter trips it is cheaper, if less comfortable, to seat small children on your knee. Often there are spare seats which children can occupy after tickets have been collected. In city and local excursion buses, small children generally do not pay a fare, but are not entitled to a seat when paying customers are standing. On sightseeing tours you should *always* bargain for a family rate—often children can go free. (In trains, reductions for children are general, but not universal.)

All civil airlines charge half for children under 12, but some military services don't have half-fares, or have younger age limits. Children's fares on Lloyd Aéreo Boliviano are considerably more than half, and there is only a 7kg baggage allowance. (LAB also checks children's ages on passports.) Note that a child travelling free on a long excursion is not always covered by the operator's travel insurance; it is adviseable to pay a small premium to arrange cover.

Hotels: In all hotels, try to negotiate family rates. If charges are per person, always insist that two children will occupy one bed only, therefore counting as one tariff. If rates are per bed, the same applies. In either case you can almost always get a reduced rate at cheaper hotels. Occasionally when travelling with a child you will be refused a room in a hotel that is "unsuitable". On river boat trips, unless you have very large hammocks, it may be more comfortable and cost effective to hire a 2-berth cabin for 2 adults and a child. (In restaurants, you can normally buy children's helpings, or divide one full-size helping between two children.)

Travel with children can bring you into closer contact with Latin American families and, generally, presents no special problems—in fact the path is often smoother for family groups. Officials tend to be more amenable where children are concerned and they are pleased if your child knows a little Spanish or Portuguese. Moreover, even thieves and pickpockets seem to have some of the traditional respect for families, and may leave you alone because of it!

Hiking and Trekking   Hilary Bradt, the well-known trekker, author and publisher, writes: A network of paths and tracks covers much of South America and is in constant use by the local people. In countries with a large Indian population—Ecuador, Peru and Bolivia, for instance—you can walk just about anywhere, but in the more European countries, such as Venezuela, Chile, and Argentina, you must usually limit yourself to the many excellent national parks with hiking trails. Most South American countries have an Instituto Geográfico Militar which sells topographical maps, scale 1:100,000 or 1:50,000. The physical features shown on these are usually accurate; the trails and place names less so. National Parks offices also sell maps.

Hiking and backpacking should not be approached casually. Even if you only plan to be out a couple of hours you should have comfortable, safe footwear (which can cope with the wet—Ed) and a daypack to carry your sweater and waterproof (which must be more than showerproof). At high altitudes the difference in temperature between sun and shade is remarkable. The longer trips mentioned in this book require basic backpacking equipment. Essential items are: backpack with frame, sleeping bag, closed cell foam mat for insulation, stove, tent or tarpaulin, dried food (not tins), water bottle, compass. Some but not all of these things are available locally.

When planning treks in the Andes you should be aware of the effects and dangers of acute mountain sickness, and cerebral and pulmonary oedema (see Health Information, **p 36**). These can be avoided by spending a few days acclimatizing to the altitude before starting your walk, and by climbing slowly. Otherwise there are fewer dangers than in most cities. Hikers have little to fear from the animal kingdom apart from insects (although it's best to avoid actually stepping on a snake), and robbery and assault are very rare. You are much more of a threat to the environment than vice versa. Leave no evidence of your passing; don't litter and don't give gratuitous presents of sweets or money to rural villagers. Respect their system of reciprocity; if they give you hospitality or food, then is the time to reciprocate with presents.

For trekking in mountain areas, where the weather can deteriorate rapidly (eg in Torres del Paine), trekkers should consider taking the following equipment (list supplied by Andrew Dobbie of Swansea, who adds that it "is in no way finite"): **Clothing**: warm hat (wool or man-made fibre), thermal underwear, T-shirts/shirts, trousers (quick-drying and preferably windproof, never jeans), warm (wool or fleece) jumper/jacket (preferably two), gloves, waterproof jacket and over trousers (preferably Gore-Tex), shorts, walking boots and socks, change of footwear or flip-flops. **Camping Gear**: tent (capable of withstanding high winds), sleeping mat (closed cell - Karrimat - or inflatable - Thermarest), sleeping bag (3-season minimum rating), sleeping bag liner, stove and spare parts, fuel, matches and lighter, cooking and eating utensils, pan scrubber, survival bag. **Food**: very much personal preference but at least two days more supplies than you plan to use; tea, coffee, sugar, dried milk; porridge, dried fruit, honey; soup, pasta, rice, soya (TVP); fresh fruit and vegetables; bread, cheese, crackers; biscuits, chocolate; salt, pepper, other herbs and spices, cooking oil. **Miscellaneous**: map and compass, torch and spare batteries, pen and notebook, Swiss army knife, sunglasses, sun cream, lip salve and insect repellent, first aid kit, water bottle, toiletries and towel.

Maps and Guide Books Those from the Institutos Geográficos Militares in the capitals (see above) are often the only good maps available in Latin America. It is therefore wise to get as many as possible in your home country before leaving, especially if travelling by land. A recommended series of general maps is that published by International Travel Map Productions (ITM), World Wide Books and Maps, 736A Granville Street, Vancouver BC, V6Z 1G3, Canada, compiled with historical notes, by the late Kevin Healey. Available are South America South, North East and North West (1:4,000,000), Amazon Basin (1:4,000,000), Ecuador (1:1,000,000), The Galapagos Islands (1:500,000), Easter Island (1:30,000), Argentina (1:4,000,000), Central America (1:1,800,000), Panama (1:800,000), Guatemala and El Salvador (1: 500,000), Costa Rica (1:500,000), Belize (1:350,000), Mexico (1:3,300,000), Mexico City (1:10,000), Mexico South (1:1,000,000), the Yucatán (1:1,000,000) and Baja California (1:1,000,000). Details of Bradt Publications' Backpacking Guide Series, other titles and imported maps and guides are mentioned in our country "Information for Visitors" sections.

A very useful book, highly recommended, aimed specifically at the budget traveller is *The Tropical Traveller*, by John Hatt (Penguin Books, 3rd edition, 1993).

The South American Explorers' Club is at Avenida Portugal 146 (Casilla 3714), Lima, Peru (T 425-0142), 1254 Toledo, Apartado 21-431, Eloy Alfaro, Quito, Ecuador (T 566-076), and 126 Indian Creek Road, Ithaca, NY 14850, USA T (607) 277-0488. (For further details see under Lima and Quito.) The South American Explorers Club is represented in the UK by Bradt Publications.

The Latin American Travel Advisor is a quarterly news bulletin with up-to-date detailed and reliable information on countries throughout South and Central America. The publication focuses on public safety, health, weather and natural phenomena, travel costs, the economy and politics. It includes maps, tables, and charts comparing different countries and analyzing trends. Every issue has a feature article, a detailed column about each country and a 2-page summary called *The Continent at a Glance*. Available by mail or fax. For a free sample copy contact PO Box 17-17-908, Quito, Ecuador, F 593-2-562-566, E-Mail rku@pi.pro.ec.on Internet.

Literature This Handbook does not at present have space to contain sections on Latin American literature. Interested readers are recommended to see Jason Wilson, *Traveller's Literary Companion, South and Central America* (Brighton, UK: In Print, 1993), which has extracts from works by Latin American writers and by non-Latin Americans about the various countries and has very useful bibliographies.

GENERAL ADVICE

Responsible Tourism Mark Eckstein of David Bellamy Associates writes:
Much has been written about the adverse impacts of tourism on the environment and local communities. It is usually assumed that this only applies to the more excessive end of the travel industry such as the Spanish Costas and Bali. However it now seems that travellers can have an impact at almost any density and this is especially true in areas "off the beaten track" where local people may not be used to western conventions and lifestyles, and natural environments may be very sensitive.

Of course, tourism can have a beneficial impact and this is something to which every traveller can contribute. Many National Parks are part funded by receipts from people who travel to see exotic plants and animals, the Galápagos (Ecuador) and Manu (Peru) National Parks are good examples of such sites. Similarly, travellers can promote patronage and protection of valuable archaeological sites and heritages through their interest and entrance fees.

However, where visitor pressure is high and/or poorly regulated, damage can occur. It is also unfortunately true that many of the most popular destinations are in ecologically sensitive areas easily disturbed by extra human pressures. This is particularly significant because the desire to visit sites and communities that are off the beaten track is a driving force for many travellers. Eventually the very features that tourists travel so far to see may become degraded and so we seek out new sites, discarding the old, and leaving someone else to deal with the plight of local communities and the damaged environment.

Fortunately, there are signs of a new awareness of the responsibilities that the travel industry and its clients need to endorse. For example, some tour operators fund local conservation projects and travellers are now more aware of the impact they may have on host cultures and environments. We can all contribute to the success of what is variously described as responsible, green or alternative tourism. All that is required is a little forethought and consideration.

It would be impossible to identify all the possible impacts that might need to be addressed by travellers, but it is worthwhile noting the major areas in which we can all take a more responsible attitude in the countries we visit. These include, changes to natural ecosystems (air, water, land, ecology and wildlife), cultural values (beliefs and behaviour) and the built environment (sites of antiquity and archaeological significance). At an individual level, travellers can reduce their impact if greater consideration is given to their activities. Canoe trips up the headwaters of obscure rivers make for great stories, but how do local communities cope with the sudden invasive interest in their lives? Will the availability of easy tourist money and gauche behaviour affect them for the worse, possibly diluting and trivialising the significance of culture and customs? Similarly, have the environmental implications of increased visitor pressure been considered? Where does the fresh fish that feeds the trip come from? Hand caught by line is fine, but is dynamite fishing really necessary, given the scale of damage and waste that results?

Some of these impacts are caused by factors beyond the direct control of travellers, such as the management and operation of a hotel chain. However, even here it is possible to voice concern about damaging activities and an increasing number of hotels and travel operators are taking "green concerns" seriously, even if it is only to protect their share of the market.

Environmental Legislation Legislation is increasingly being enacted to control damage to the environment, and in some cases this can have a bearing on travellers. The establishment of National Parks may involve rules and guidelines for visitors and these should always be followed. In addition there may be local or national laws controlling behaviour and use of natural resources (especially wildlife) that are being increasingly enforced. If in doubt, ask. Finally, international legislation, principally the Convention on International Trade in Endangered Species of Wild Fauna and Flora (CITES), may affect travellers.

CITES aims to control the trade in live specimens of endangered plants and animals and also "recognizable parts or derivatives" of protected species. Sale of Black Coral, Turtle shells, protected Orchids and other wildlife is strictly controlled by signatories of the convention. The full list of protected wildlife varies, so if you feel the need to purchase souvenirs and trinkets derived from wildlife, it would be prudent to check whether they are protected. Every country included in this Handbook is a signatory of CITES. In addition, most European countries, the USA and Canada are all signatories. Importation of CITES protected species into these countries can lead to heavy fines, confiscation of goods and even imprisonment. Information on the status of legislation and protective measures can be obtained from Traffic International, UK office T (01223) 277427.

Green Travel Companies and Information The increasing awareness of the environmental impact of travel and tourism has led to a range of advice and information services as well as spawning specialist travel companies who claim to provide "responsible travel" for clients. This is an expanding field and the veracity of claims needs to be substantiated in some cases. The following organizations and publications can provide useful information for those with an interest in pursuing responsible travel opportunities.

Organizations Green Flag International Aims to work with travel industry and conservation bodies to improve environments at travel destinations and also to promote conservation programmes at resort destinations. Provides a travellers' guide for "green" tourism as well as advice on destinations, T (UK—01223) 890250. **Tourism Concern** Aims to promote a greater understanding of the impact of tourism on host communities and environments; Southlands College, Wimbledon Parkside, London SW19 5NN, T (UK—0181) 944-0464). **Centre for Responsible Tourism** CRT coordinates a North American network and advises on N American sources of information on responsible tourism. CRT, 2 Kensington Rd, San Anselmo, California USA. **Centre for the Advancement of Responsive Travel** CART has a range of publications available as well as information on alternative holiday destinations. T (UK—01732) 352757.

Publications *The Good Tourist* by Katie Wood and Syd House (1991) published by Mandarin Paperbacks; addresses issues surrounding environmental impacts of tourism, suggests ways in which damage can be minimised, suggests a range of environmentally sensitive holidays and projects.

Souvenirs Remember that these can almost invariably be bought more cheaply away from the capital, though the choice may be less wide. Bargaining seems to be the general rule in most countries' street markets, but don't make a fool of yourself by bargaining over what, to you, is a small amount of money.

If British travellers have no space in their luggage, they might like to remember Tumi, the Latin American Craft Centre, who specialize in Mexican and Andean products and who produce cultural and educational videos for schools: at 23/2A Chalk Farm Road, London NW1 8AG (F 0171-485 4152), 8/9 New Bond Street Place, Bath BA1 1BH (T 01225 462367, F 01225 444870), 1/2 Little Clarendon St, Oxford OX1 2HJ (T/F 01865-512307), 82 Park St, Bristol BS1 5LA (T/F 0117 929 0391). Tumi (Music) Ltd specializes in different rhythms of Latin America. See *Arts and Crafts of South America*, by Lucy Davies and Mo Fini, published by Tumi (1994), for a fine introduction to the subject. In Edinburgh there is a Mexican shop called Azteca. There are similar shops in the USA; one good one is on the ground floor of Citicorp Center, Lexington Avenue and 53rd Street, New York.

Mail Postal services in most countries are not very efficient, and pilfering is frequent. All mail, especially packages, should be registered. Some travellers recommend that mail should be sent to one's Embassy (or, if a cardholder, American Express agent) rather than to the Poste Restante/General Delivery (*Lista de Correos*) department of a country's Post Office. Some Embassies and post offices, however, do not keep mail for more than a month. If there seems to be no mail at the Lista under the initial letter of your surname, ask them to look under the initial of your forename or your middle name. Remember that there is no W in Spanish; look under V, or ask. For the smallest risk of misunderstanding, use title, initial and surname only. (If you're a British male, and all else fails, ask them to look under "E" for "Esquire"!—Geoffrey van Dulken.) If having items sent to you by courier (eg DHL), do not use poste restante, but an address such as a hotel: a signature is required on receipt.

Phones US travellers should know about AT&T's "USA Direct", by which you can connect with an AT & T operator without going through a local one. It is much cheaper than operator-assisted calls and is widely available. Sprint and MCI are also available; details given under individual countries. Other countries have similar systems, eg UK, Canada; obtain details before leaving home.

Communicating by fax is a convenient way of sending messages home. Many places with public fax machines (post offices, telephone companies or shops) will receive messages as well as send. Fax machines are often switched off; you may have to phone to confirm receipt.

World Band Radio Richard Robinson writes: South America has more local and community radio stations than practically anywhere else in the world; a shortwave (world band) radio offers a practical means to brush up on the language, sample popular culture and absorb some of the richly varied regional music. International broadcasters such as the BBC World Service, the Voice of America and the Quito-based Evangelical station, HCJB, keep the traveller abreast of news and events, in both English and Spanish.

Compact or miniature portables are recommended, with digital tuning and a full range of shortwave bands, as well as FM, long and medium wave. Detailed advice on radio models (£150 for a decent one) and wavelengths can be found in the annual publication, *Passport to World Bank Radio* (Box 300, Penn's Park, PA 18943, USA). Details of local stations is listed in *World TV and Radio Handbook* (WRTH), PO Box 9027, 1006 AA Amsterdam, The Netherlands, US$19.95. Both of these, free wavelength guides and selected radio sets are available from the BBC World Service Bookshop, Bush House Arcade, Bush House, Strand, London WC2B 4PH, UK, T 071-2557 2576.

Photography Always ask permission before photographing people. The price of film varies from country to country, being cheapest in Chile (in the Iquique and Punta Arenas Tax Free Zones) and Paraguay (always check the expiry date). Cheap film can also be bought in the USA. Pre-paid Kodak slide film cannot be developed in South America; it is also very hard to find. Kodachrome is almost impossible to buy. Fuji film is usually harder to find than Kodak. Some travellers (but not all) have advised against mailing exposed films home; either take them with you, or have them developed, but not printed, once you have checked the laboratory's quality. Note that postal authorities may use less sensitive equipment for X-ray screening than the airports do. Modern controlled X-ray machines are supposed to be safe even when a slow film passes through it dozens of times, but it is worth trying to avoid X-ray as the doses are cumulative. Many airport officials will allow film to be passed outside X-ray arches; they may also hand-check a suitcase with a large quantity of film if asked politely.

Dan Buck and Anne Meadows write: A note on developing film in South America. Black and white is a problem. Often it is shoddily machine-processed and the negatives are ruined. Ask the store if you can see an example of their laboratory's work and if they hand-develop.

Jeremy Till and Sarah Wigglesworth suggest that exposed film can be protected in humid areas by putting it in a balloon and tying a knot. Similarly keeping your camera in a plastic bag may reduce the effects of humidity.

Travelling Alone   Many points of security, dress and language have been covered already. These additional hints have been supplied by women, but most apply to any single traveller. When you set out, err on the side of caution until your instincts have adjusted to the customs of a new culture. If, as a single woman, you can befriend a local woman, you will learn much more about the country you are visiting. Unless actively avoiding foreigners like yourself, don't go too far from the beaten track; there is a very definite "gringo trail" which you can join, or follow, if seeking company. This can be helpful when looking for safe accommodation, especially if arriving after dark (which is best avoided). Remember that for a single woman a taxi at night can be as dangerous as wandering around on her own. At borders dress as smartly as possible. Travelling by train is a good way to meet locals, but buses are much easier for a person alone; on major routes your seat is often reserved and your luggage can usually be locked in the hold. It is easier for men to take the friendliness of locals at face value; women may be subject to much unwanted attention. To help minimize this, do not wear suggestive clothing and, advises Alex Rossi of Jawa Timur, Indonesia, do not flirt. By wearing a wedding ring, carrying a photograph of your "husband" and "children", and saying that your "husband" is close at hand, you may dissuade an aspiring suitor. If politeness fails, do not feel bad about showing offence and departing. When accepting a social invitation, make sure that someone knows the address and the time you left. Ask if you can bring a friend (even if you do not intend to do so). A good rule is always to act with confidence, as though you know where you are going, even if you do not. Someone who looks lost is more likely to attract unwanted attention. Do not disclose to strangers where you are staying. (Much of this information was supplied by Alex Rossi, and by Deirdre Mortell of Carrigaline, Co Cork).

Final Hints   Everybody has his/her own list. In addition to items already suggested above, those most often mentioned include air cushions for slatted seats, inflatable travel pillow for neck support, strong shoes (and remember that footwear over 9½ English size, or 42 European size, is difficult to obtain in Latin America except Argentina and Brazil); a small first-aid kit and handbook, fully waterproof top clothing, waterproof treatment for leather footwear, wax earplugs (which are almost impossible to find outside large cities) and airline-type eye mask to help you sleep in noisy and poorly curtained hotel rooms, sandals (rubber-thong Japanese-type or other), a polyethylene sheet 2 x 1 metres to cover possibly infested beds and shelter your luggage, polyethylene bags of varying sizes (up to heavy duty rubbish bag size) with ties, a toilet bag you can tie round your waist, if you use an electric shaver, take a rechargeable type, a sheet sleeping-bag and pillow-case or separate pillow-case—in some countries they are not changed often in cheap hotels, a 1½-2m piece of 100% cotton can be used as a towel, a bedsheet, beach towel, makeshift curtain and wrap; a mosquito net (or a hammock with a fitted net), a straw hat which can be rolled or flattened and reconstituted after 15 mins soaking in water, a clothes line, a nailbrush (useful for scrubbing dirt off clothes as well as off oneself), a vacuum flask, a water bottle, a small dual-voltage immersion heater, a small dual-voltage (or battery-driven) electric fan,

tea bags, a light nylon waterproof shopping bag, a universal bath- and basin-plug of the flanged type that will fit any waste-pipe (or improvise one from a sheet of thick rubber), string, velcro, electrical insulating tape, large penknife preferably with tin and bottle openers, scissors and corkscrew—the famous Swiss Army range has been repeatedly recommended (for knife sharpening, go to a butcher's shop), collapsible drinking beaker, electric motor-cycle alarm for luggage protection, a flour sack and roll of wire mesh for ditto, alarm clock or watch, candle, torch (flashlight)—especially one that will clip on to a pocket or belt, pocket mirror, small transistor radio earphones, pocket dictionary, pocket calculator, an adaptor and flex to enable you to take power from an electric-light socket (the Edison screw type is the most commonly used), a padlock (combination lock is best) for the doors of the cheapest and most casual hotels (or for tent zip if camping), spare chain-lengths and padlock for securing luggage to bed or bus/train seat. Remember not to throw away spent batteries containing mercury or cadmium; take them home to be disposed of, or recycled properly.

Useful medicaments are given at the end of the "Health Information" section (**p 47**); to these might be added some lip salve with sun protection, and pre-moistened wipes (such as "Wet Ones"). Always carry toilet paper. Natural fabric sticking plasters, as well as being long-lasting, are much appreciated as gifts. Dental floss can be used for backpack repairs, in addition to its original purpose. **Never** carry firearms. Their possession could land you in serious trouble.

A note for **contact lens wearers**: most countries have a wide selection of products for the care of lenses, so you don't need to take kilos of lotions. Lens solution can be difficult to find in Peru and Bolivia and outside major cities. Ask for it in a chemist/pharmacy, rather than an optician's.

Be careful when asking directions. Women probably know more about the neighbourhood; men about more distant locations. Policemen are often helpful. However, many Latin Americans will give you the wrong answer rather than admit they do not know; this may be partly because they fear losing face, but is also because they like to please. You are more likely to get reliable information if you carefully refrain from asking leading questions.

Lastly, a good principle is to take half the clothes (trousers with plenty of pockets are very useful), and twice the money, that you think you will need.

HEALTH INFORMATION

The following information has been compiled for us by Dr David Snashall, who is presently Senior Lecturer in Occupational Health at the United Medical Schools of Guys and St Thomas' Hospitals in London and Chief Medical Advisor of the British Foreign and Commonwealth Office. He has travelled extensively in Central and South America, worked in Peru and in East Africa and keeps in close touch with developments in preventative and tropical medicine. We incorporate also some welcome observations on the text by Dr C J Schofield, editor of Parasitology Today.

THE TRAVELLER to Latin America is inevitably exposed to health risks not encountered in Britain or the USA, especially if he/she spends time in the tropical regions. Epidemic diseases have been largely brought under control by vaccination programmes and public sanitation but, in rural areas, the latter is rudimentary and the chances of contracting infections of various sorts are much higher than at home.

There are English-speaking doctors in most major cities. If you fall ill the best plan may be to attend the out-patient department of a local hospital or contact your Embassy representative for the name of a reputable doctor. (We give the names of hospitals and some recommended doctors in the main city sections.— Ed.) Medical practices vary from those at home but remember they have particular experience in dealing with locally-occurring diseases.

Self-medication is undesirable except for minor complaints but may be forced on you by circumstances. Whatever the circumstances, be wary of medicines prescribed for you by pharmacists; many are poorly trained and unscrupulous enough to sell you potentially dangerous drugs or old stock they want to get rid of. The large number of pharmacies throughout Latin America is a considerable surprise to most people, as is the range of medicines you can purchase over the counter. There is a tendency towards over-prescription of drug mixtures and in general this should be resisted. Many drugs are manufactured under licence from American or European companies so the trade names may be familiar to you. This means that you do not need to carry a whole chest of medicines, but remember that the shelf-life of some items, especially vaccines and antibiotics, is markedly reduced in tropical conditions. Buy your supplies at the better outlets where they have refrigerators, even though it is more expensive. Check the expiry date of all preparations you buy.

Immigration officials sometimes confiscate scheduled drugs (Lomotil is an example) if they are not accompanied by a doctor's prescription.

With the following precautions and advice, you should keep as healthy as usual. Make local enquiries about health risks if you are apprehensive and take the general advice of European or North American families who have lived or are living in the country.

Before you go take out medical insurance. You should have a dental check-up, obtain a spare glasses prescription, a spare oral contraceptive prescription and, if you suffer from a chronic illness (such as diabetes, high blood pressure, ear or sinus troubles, cardiopulmonary disease or a nervous disorder) arrange for a check-up with your doctor, who can at the same time provide you with a letter explaining the details of your disability, if possible in English and Spanish (or Portuguese for Brazil). Check current practice in malaria prophylaxis (prevention).

Inoculations Smallpox vaccination is no longer required anywhere in the world. A major outbreak of cholera occurred, unusually, in Peru in 1990-91 and most other Latin American countries were affected subsequently. The epidemic continues, spread by travellers and fuelled by insanitary living conditions, untreated sewage and polluted water supplies. A vaccine against cholera is available but is not very effective and is not recognized as necessary for international travel by the World Health Organization. Nevertheless some immigration officials are demanding it in Latin America, so this should be borne in mind. Cholera is largely a water borne disease, either in drinking water, or via food which has been washed in contaminated water, or seafood which has been living in such water. The usual food hygiene precautions should protect the traveller from cholera; if they don't, the treatment is rapid rehydration with water and salts and sometimes the use of antibiotics.

The following vaccinations are recommended:

Yellow fever: this is a live vaccine not to be given to children under 9 months of age or persons allergic to eggs. Immunity lasts 10 years. An international certificate of yellow fever vaccination will be given and should be kept because it is sometimes asked for.

Typhoid (monovalent): one dose followed by a booster in a month's time. Immunity from this course lasts 2 to 3 years. An oral preparation is now available and a newer, more expensive vaccination against typhoid, Typhim Vi, less likely to cause post-injection symptoms.

Poliomyelitis: this is a live vaccine generally given orally and a full course consists of three doses with a booster in tropical regions every 3 to 5 years.

Tetanus: one dose should be given with a booster (vital) at 6 weeks and another at 6 months, and 10-yearly boosters thereafter are recommended.

Children should, in addition, be properly protected against diphtheria, and against pertussis (whooping cough), measles and HIB, which tend to be more

serious infections than at home. Measles, mumps and rubella vaccine is now widely available but those teenage girls who have not had rubella (German measles) should be tested and vaccinated. Consult your doctor for advice on tuberculosis inoculation: the disease is still widespread.

Infectious Hepatitis (jaundice) is endemic throughout Latin America and seems to be frequently caught by travellers. The main symptoms are pains in the stomach, lack of appetite, lassitude, and the typical yellow colour of the skin. Medically speaking there are two different types, the less serious but more common is hepatitis A, for which the best protection is the careful preparation of food, the avoidance of contaminated drinking water and scrupulous attention to toilet hygiene. Human normal immunoglobulin (gamma globulin) confers considerable protection against the disease and is particularly useful in epidemics; it should be obtained from a reputable source and is certainly useful for travellers who intend to live rough: they should have a shot before leaving and have it repeated every 6 months. The dose of gamma globulin depends on the concentration of the particular preparation used, so the manufacturer's advice should be taken. A smaller dose than usual can be given if exposure is for one or 2 months only. At last a vaccine is now in production and generally available against hepatitis A. Trials have shown it to be safe and effective. It is more expensive than gamma globulin, but the protection is better and lasts longer. Three doses over 6 months would appear to give immunity lasting up to 10 years; then boosters would be required. Havrix monodose is now available, and Junior Havrix.

The other, more serious, version is hepatitis B which is acquired usually by injections with unclean needles, blood transfusions, as a sexually transmitted disease and possibly by insect bites. This disease can be effectively prevented by a specific vaccination requiring three shots over 6 months before travelling but this is quite expensive. If you have had jaundice in the past it would be worthwhile having a blood test to see if you are immune to either of the two types because this might avoid the necessity for vaccination or gamma globulin.

Other vaccinations might be considered in the case of epidemics, eg meningitis. There is an effective vaccination against **rabies** which should be considered by all travellers, especially those going to remote areas and if there is a particular occupational risk, ie zoologists or veterinarians.

AIDS in South America is increasing in its prevalence, as in most countries, but is not wholly confined to the well known high risk sections of the population, ie homosexual men, intravenous drug abusers, prostitutes and children of infected mothers. Heterosexual transmission is now the dominant mode and so the main risk to travellers is from casual sex. The same precautions should be taken as when encountering any sexually transmitted disease. The AIDS virus (HIV) can be passed via unsterilized needles which have been previously used to inject an HIV positive patient, but the risk of this is very small indeed. It would however be sensible to check that needles have been properly sterilised or disposable needles used. If you wish to take your own disposable needles, be prepared to explain what they are for. The risk of receiving a blood transfusion with blood infected with the HIV virus is greater than from dirty needles because of the amount of fluid exchanged. Supplies of blood for transfusion should now be screened for HIV in all reputable hospitals so again the risk must be very small indeed. Catching the AIDS virus does not usually produce an illness in itself; the only way to be sure if you feel you have been put at risk is to have a blood test for HIV antibodies on your return to a place where there are reliable laboratory facilities. The test does not become positive for many weeks. Presently the higher risks are probably in Brazil and the West Indies.

Common Problems, some of which will almost certainly be encountered, are:

Heat and Cold Full acclimatization to high temperatures takes about 2 weeks and during this period it is normal to feel relatively apathetic, especially if the relative humidity is high. Drink plenty of water (up to 15 litres a day are required when working physically hard in the tropics), use salt on your food and avoid extreme exertion. Tepid showers are more cooling than hot or cold ones. Large hats do not cool you down, but do prevent sunburn. Remember that, especially in the highlands, there can be a large and sudden drop in temperature between sun and shade and between night and day, so dress accordingly. Warm jackets and woollens are essential after dark at high altitude.

Altitude Acute mountain sickness or *soroche* can strike from about 3,000 metres upwards. It is more likely to affect those who ascend rapidly (eg by plane) and those who over-exert themselves. Teenagers are particularly prone. Past experience is not always a good guide: the author, having spent years in Peru travelling constantly between sea level and very high altitude, never suffered the slightest symptoms, then was severely affected climbing Kilimanjaro in Tanzania.

On reaching heights above 3,000 metres, heart pounding and shortness of breath, especially on exertion, are almost universal and a normal response to the lack of oxygen in the air. *Soroche* takes a few hours or days to come on and presents with headache, lassitude, dizziness, loss of appetite, nausea and vomiting. Insomnia is common and often associated with a suffocating feeling when lying in bed. Keen observers may note their breathing tends to wax and wane at night and their face tends to be puffy in the mornings—this is all part of the syndrome. The treatment is rest, pain killers (preferably not aspirin-based) for the headache and anti-sickness pills for vomiting. Oxygen may help at very high altitudes. Various local panaceas ("Coramina glucosada", "Effortil", "Micoren") have their advocates and *mate* (or *te*) *de coca* (an infusion of coca leaves, widely available) certainly alleviates some of the symptoms.

On arrival at places over 3,000 metres, a few hours' rest in a chair and avoidance of alcohol, cigarettes and heavy food will go a long way towards preventing *soroche*. Should the symptoms be severe and prolonged it is best to descend to lower altitude and re-ascend slowly or in stages. If this is impossible because of shortage of time or if the likelihood of acute mountain sickness is high then the drug Acetazolamide (Diamox) can be used as a preventative and continued during the ascent. There is good evidence of the value of this drug in the prevention of *soroche* but some people do experience funny side effects. The usual dose is 500 mg of the slow-release preparation each night, starting the night before ascending above 3,000 metres. (Detailed information is available from the Mountain Medicine Centre, c/o Dr Charles Clarke, Dept of Neurological Sciences, St Bartholomew's Hospital, 38 Little Britain, London EC1A 7BE—Ed.)

Other problems experienced at high altitude are sunburn, excessively dry air causing skin cracking, sore eyes (it may be wise to leave your contact lenses out) and stuffy noses. It is unwise to ascend to high altitude if you are pregnant, especially in the first 3 months, or if you have any history of heart, lung or blood disease, including sickle-cell.

There is a further, albeit rare, hazard due to rapid ascent to high altitude called acute pulmonary oedema. The condition can affect mountaineers; but also occurs in Andean natives returning from a period at the coast. The condition comes on quite rapidly with breathlessness, noisy breathing, cough, blueness of the lips and frothing at the mouth. Anybody developing this must be brought down as soon as possible, given oxygen and taken to hospital.

Rapid descent from high places will aggravate sinus and middle ear infections, and make bad teeth ache painfully. The same problems are sometimes experienced during descent at the end of a flight.

Despite these various hazards (mostly preventable) of high-altitude travel, many people find the environment healthier and more invigorating than at sea-level.

Intestinal Upsets Practically nobody escapes this one, so be prepared for it. Most of the time it is due to the insanitary preparation of food. Don't eat uncooked fish or vegetables, fruit with the skin on (always peel your fruit yourself), food that is exposed to flies, or salads. Tap water is rarely safe outside the major cities, especially in the rainy season, and stream water is often contaminated by communities living surprisingly high in the mountains. Filtered or bottled (make sure it is opened in your presence—Ed) water is usually available and safe. If your hotel has a central hot-water supply, this is safe to drink after cooling. Ice for drinks should be made from boiled water but rarely is, so stand your glass on the ice cubes rather than putting them in the drink. Dirty water should first be strained through a filter bag (available from camping shops) and then boiled or treated. Water in general can be rendered safe in the following ways: boil for 5 mins at sea level, longer at higher altitudes; or add 3 drops of household bleach (but not modern treated bleaches) to 1 pint of water and leave for 15 mins; or add 1 drop of tincture of iodine to 1 pint of water and leave for 3 mins. Commercial water-sterilizing tablets are available, for instance Sterotabs from Boots, England. (Also recommended are compact water filters, for instance Travel Well, Pre Mac (Kent) Ltd, Tunbridge Wells, or the Swiss-made Katadyn.)

Fresh, unpasteurized milk is a source of food poisoning germs, tuberculosis and brucellosis. This applies equally to ice-cream, yoghurt and cheese made from unpasteurized milk. Fresh milk can be rendered safe by heating it to 62°C for 30 mins followed by rapid cooling, or by boiling it. Matured or processed cheeses are safer than fresh varieties. Heat-treated (UHT), pasteurized or sterilized milk is becoming more available. Fruit juice should be pure, not diluted with water.

Diarrhoea – Diagnosis and treatment Diarrhoea is usually caused by eating food which is contaminated by food poisoning germs. Drinking water is rarely the culprit. Seawater or river water is more likely to be contaminated by sewage and so swimming in such dilute effluent can also be a cause. Infection with various organisms can give rise to diarrhoea, eg viruses, bacteria (eg Escherichia coli, probably the most common cause), protozoa (amoeba), salmonella and cholera. The diarrhoea may come on suddenly or rather slowly. It may or may nor be accompanied by vomiting or by severe abdominal pain and the passage of blood or mucus when it is called dysentery. How do you know which type you have and how to treat it?

If you can time the onset of the diarrhoea to the minute (acute) then it is probably due to a virus or a bacterium and/or the onset of dysentery. The treatment, in addition to rehydration is Ciprofloxacin 500 mgs every 12 hrs. The drug is now widely available as are various similar ones.

If the diarrhoea comes on slowly or intermittently (sub-acute) then it is more likely to be protozoal, ie caused by an amoeba or giardia and antibiotics will have little effect. These cases are best treated by a doctor, as is any outbreak of diarrhoea continuing for more than 3 days. Sometimes blood is passed in sub-acute amoebic dysentery and for this you should certainly seek medical help. If this is not available then the best treatment is probably Tinidazole (Fasigyn) 1 tablet 4 times a day for 3 days. If there are severe stomach cramps, the following drugs may help but are not very useful in the management of acute diarrhoea: Loperamide (Imodium, Arret) and Diphenoxylate with Atropine (Lomotil). They should not be given to children.

Any kind of diarrhoea whether or not accompanied by vomiting responds well to the replacement of water and salts taken as frequent small sips of some kind of rehydration solution. There are preparatory preparations consisting of sachets of powder which you dissolve in boiled water, or you can make you own by adding half a teaspoonful of salt (3.5 grams) and 4 tablespoonfuls of sugar (40 grams) to a litre of boiled water.

Thus the lynchpins of treatment for diarrhoea are rest, fluid and salt replacement, antibiotics such as Ciprofloxacin for the bacterial types and special diagnostic tests and medical treatment for the amoeba and giardia infections. Salmonella infections and cholera can be devastating diseases and it would be wise to get to a hospital as soon as possible if these were suspected. Fasting, peculiar diets and the consumption of large quantities of yoghurt have not been found useful in calming travellers diarrhoea or in rehabilitating inflamed bowels. Oral rehydration has on the other hand, especially in children, been a lifesaving technique and it should always be practised whatever other treatment you use. As there is some evidence that alcohol and milk might prolong diarrhoea they should probably be avoided during and immediately after an attack. Diarrhoea occurring day after day for long periods of time (chronic diarrhoea) is notoriously resistant to amateur attempts at treatment and again warrants proper diagnostic tests (most towns with reasonable-sized hospitals have laboratories for stool samples). There are ways of preventing travellers diarrhoea for short periods of time by taking antibiotics, but this is not a foolproof technique and should not be used other than in exceptional circumstances. Doxycycline is possibly the best drug. Some preventatives such as Enterovioform can have serious side effects if taken for long periods.

Paradoxically, constipation is also common, probably induced by dietary change, inadequate fluid intake in hot places and long bus journeys. Simple laxatives are useful in the short term (the Editor recommends Senokot) and bulky foods such as maize, beans and plenty of fruit are also useful.

Insects These can be a great nuisance, especially in the tropics, and some, of course, are carriers of serious diseases. The best way of keeping them away at night is to sleep off the ground with a mosquito net and to burn mosquito coils containing pyrethrum. The best way to use insecticide aerosol sprays is to spray the room thoroughly in all areas and then shut the door for a while, re-entering when the smell has dispersed. Tablets of insecticide are also available which, when placed on a heated mat plugged into a wall socket, fill the room with insecticide fumes in the same way. The best repellents contain di-ethyl-meta-toluamide (DET) or di-methyl phthalate—sold as "Deet", "Six-Twelve Plus", "Off", "Boots' Liquid Insect Repellent", "Autan", "Flypel". Liquid is best for arms and face (care around eyes) and aerosol spray for clothes and ankles to deter chiggers, mites and ticks. Liquid DEET suspended in water can be used to impregnate cotton clothes and mosquito nets.

If you are bitten, itching may be relieved by baking-soda baths, anti-histamine tablets (care with alcohol and driving), corticosteroid creams (great care—never use if any hint of sepsis) or by judicious scratching. Calamine lotion and cream have limited effectiveness and antihistamine creams (eg Antihisan, May & Baker) have a tendency to cause skin allergies and are, therefore, not generally recommended.

Bites which become infected (commonly in the tropics) should be treated with a local antiseptic or antibiotic cream, such as Cetrimide BP (Savlon) as should infected scratches.

Skin infestations with body lice (crabs) and scabies are, unfortunately, easy to pick up. Use gamma benzene hexachloride for lice and benzene benzoate solution for scabies. Crotamiton cream (Eurax, Geigy) alleviates itching and also kills a number of skin parasites. Malathion lotion 5% (Prioderm) kills lice effectively, but do not use the toxic agricultural insecticide Malathion.

Ticks attach themselves usually to the lower part of the body often after walking in areas where cattle have grazed. They take a while to attach themselves strongly but do swell up as they suck your blood. The important thing is to remove them gently so that they do not inject any disease into your body and if the head part of the tick is left inside the skin it may cause a nasty allergic reaction some days later, and become infected. Don't use petrol, vaseline, lighted cigarettes etc, to remove the tick but, with a pair of tweezers, remove the beast gently by gripping it at the attached (head) end and rock it out very much the way that a tooth is extracted.

Certain tropical flies which lay their eggs under the skin of sheep and cattle also occasionally do the same thing to humans with the unpleasant result that a maggot grows under the skin and this presents as a boil or pimple. The best way of removing these is to cover the boil with oil, vaseline or nail varnish so as to stop the maggot breathing, then to squeeze it out gently the next day.

Malaria in South America is theoretically confined to coastal and jungle zones but is now on the increase again. Mosquitoes do not thrive above 2,500 metres so you are safe at altitude. There are different varieties of malaria, some resistant to the normal drugs. Make local enquiries if you intend to visit possibly infected zones and use one of the following prophylactic regimes. Start taking the tablets a few days before exposure and continue to take them for 6 weeks after leaving the malarial zone. Remember to give the drugs to babies and children also. Opinion varies on the precise drugs and dosage to be used for protection; all the drugs may have some side effects, and it is important to balance the risk of catching the disease against the albeit rare side effects. The increasing complexity of the subject as the malarial parasite becomes immune to the new generation of drugs has made concentration on the physical prevention of being bitten by mosquitoes more important, ie the use of long-sleeved shirts/blouses and long trousers, repellents and nets. Clothes are now available impregnated with the insecticide Permethrin or Deltamethrin, or it is possible to impregnate the clothes yourself. Wide meshed nets impregnated with Permethrin are also becoming available, are lighter to carry and less claustrophobic to sleep in.

Prophylactic regimes:
Proguanil (Paludrine Zeneca 100 mg, 2 tablets daily) or Chloroquine (Avloclor; Zeneca, Malarivon; Wallace MFG, Nivaquine, May & Baker; Resochin, Bayer; Aralen 300 mg base (2 tablets) weekly).
   Where there is a high risk of Chloroquine-resistant falciparum malaria, take Chloroquine plus Proguanil in the above-mentioned doses.
   Some authorities are recommending alternative drugs for prophylaxis, eg Mefloquine, Doxycycline. Before going to a malarial area, seek expert advice since changes worldwide in the subject are so rapid.

You can catch malaria even when sticking to the above rules, although it is unlikely. If you do develop symptoms (high fever, shivering, headache, sometimes diarrhoea) seek medical advice immediately. If this is not possible, and there is a great likelihood of malaria, the *treatment* is:

Normal types: Chloroquine, a single dose of 4 tablets (600 mg) followed by 2 tablets (300 mg) in 6 hrs and 300 mg each day following.
Falciparum type or type in doubt: take local advice: a combination of quinine and Fansidar or Halofantrine.

If Falciparum type malaria is definitely diagnosed, it is wise to get to a good hospital as the treatment can be complex and the illness very serious.
   Pregnant women are particularly prone to malaria and should stick to Proguanil as a prophylactic. Chloroquine may cause eye damage if taken over a very long period. The safety of Fansidar has been questioned and, at the time of writing, it is not recommended for prophylaxis.

Chagas' Disease (South American Trypanosomiasis) is a chronic disease, very rarely caught by travellers, but very difficult to treat. It is transmitted by the simultaneous biting and excreting of the Reduvid bug (Triatoma or Rhodnius), also known as the *vinchuca*, or *barbeiro*. Somewhat resembling a small cockroach (coloured black and red, or black and yellow), this nocturnal "kissing bug" lives in poor adobe houses with dirt floors often frequented by oppossums. If you cannot avoid such accommodation, sleep off the floor with a candle lit, use a mosquito net, keep as much of your skin covered as possible and wash any bites thoroughly with soap and water, or a disinfectant.

Sunburn　The burning power of the tropical sun, especially at high altitude, is phenomenal. Always wear a wide-brimmed hat and use some form of suncream lotion on untanned skin. Normal temperate-zone suntan lotions (protection factor up to 7) are not much good; you need to use the types designed specifically for the tropics, or for mountaineers or skiers, with protection factors up to 15. These are often not available in South America; a reasonable substitute is zinc oxide ointment. Glare from the sun can cause conjunctivitis, so wear sunglasses, especially on tropical beaches, where high protection-factor sunscreen cream should also be used.

Snakebite　If you are unlucky enough to be bitten by a venomous snake, spider, scorpion or sea creature, try (within limits) to catch the animal for identification. The reactions to be expected are: fright, swelling, pain and bruising around the bite, soreness of the regional lymph glands, nausea, vomiting and fever. If any of the following symptoms supervene, get the victim to a doctor without delay: numbness and tingling of the face, muscular spasms, convulsion, shortness of breath and haemorrhage. The tiny coral snake, with red, black and white bands, is the most dangerous, but is very timid.

　　Commercial snakebite and scorpion kits are available, but only useful for the specific type of snake or scorpion for which they are designed. The serum has to be given intravenously so is not much good unless you have had some practice at making injections into veins. If the bite is on a limb, immobilize the limb and apply a tight bandage between the bite and the body, releasing it for 90 seconds every 15 mins. Reassurance of the bitten person is very important because death from snakebite is very rare. Do not slash the bite area and try to suck out the poison because this sort of heroism does more harm than good. Hospitals usually hold stocks of snake bite serum. Best precaution: don't walk in snake territory with bare feet or sandals—wear proper shoes or boots.

Spiders and Scorpions　These may be found in the more basic hotels in the Andean countries. If bitten by *Latrodectus* or *Loxosceles* spiders, or stung by scorpions, rest and take plenty of fluids, and call a doctor. Precaution: keep beds away from the walls, and look inside shoes in morning.

Other Afflictions　Remember that **rabies** is endemic throughout Latin America so avoid dogs that are behaving strangely, and cover your toes at night to foil the vampire bats, which also carry the disease. If you are bitten by a domestic or wild animal, don't leave things to chance. Scrub the wound with soap and water and/or disinfectant, try to have the animal captured (within limits) or at least determine its ownership where possible and seek medical assistance at once. The course of treatment depends on whether you have already been satisfactorily vaccinated against rabies. If you have (and this is worthwhile if you are spending lengths of time in developing countries) then some further doses of vaccine are all that is required. Human diploid cell vaccine is the best, but expensive: other, older kinds of vaccine such as that derived from duck embryos may be the only types available. These are effective, much cheaper and interchangeable generally with the human derived types. If not already vaccinated then anti-rabies serum (immunoglobulin) may be required in addition. It is wise to finish the course of treatment whether the animal survives or not.

Dengue fever has made its appearance in southern Mexico and the lower-lying parts of Central America; also in Brazil. No treatment: you must just avoid mosquito bites.

Typhus can still occur, carried by ticks. There is usually a reaction at the site of the bite and a fever: seek medical advice.

Intestinal worms are common, and the more serious ones such as **hookworm** can be contracted from walking barefoot on infested earth or beaches. Various other tropical diseases can be caught in jungle areas, usually transmitted by biting insects; they are often related to African diseases and were probably introduced by the slave trade from Africa. **Onchocerciasis** (river-blindness), carried by blackflies, is found in parts of Mexico and Venezuela. Cutaneous **leishmaniasis** (Espundia) is carried by sandflies and causes a sore that won't heal; wearing long trousers and long-sleeved shirts in infectious areas helps to avoid the fly. Epidemics of meningitis occur from time to time. Be careful about swimming in piranha- (or caribe-) infested rivers. It is a good idea not to swim naked: the candiru fish can follow urine currents and become lodged in body orifices; swimwear offers some protection.

Dangerous animals Apart from mosquitoes, the most dangerous animals are men, be they bandits or behind steering wheels. Think carefully about violent confrontations and wear a seatbelt, if you are lucky enough to have one available to you.

Prickly heat, a very common, intensely itchy rash, is avoided by frequent washing and by wearing loose clothing. Cured by allowing skin to dry off through use of powder, and spending 2 nights in an air-conditioned hotel! **Athlete's foot** and other fungal skin infections are best treated with Tinaderm or Canestan.

Psychological disorders First time exposure to countries where sections of the population live in extreme poverty or squalor and may even be starving can cause odd psychological reactions in visitors. So can the exceptional curiosity extended to visitors, especially women. Simply be prepared for this and try not to over-react.

When you return home Remember to take your anti-malarial tablets for 6 weeks. If you have had attacks of diarrhoea, it is worth having a stool specimen tested in case you have picked up amoebic dysentery. If you have been living rough, a blood test may be worthwhile to detect worms and other parasites. If you have been exposed to bilharzia by swimming in lakes, etc, check by means of a blood test when you get home, but leave it for 6 weeks because the test is slow to become positive. Report any untoward symptoms to your doctor and tell the doctor exactly where you have been and, if you know, what is the likelihood of diseases to which you were exposed.

Basic supplies The following items you may find useful to take with you from home: sunglasses (if you use clip-on sunglasses, take a spare pair – Ed), ear plugs, suntan cream, insect repellent, flea powder, mosquito net, coils or tablets, tampons, condoms, contraceptives, water sterilizing tablets, anti-malaria tablets, anti-infective ointment, dusting powder for feet, travel sickness pills, antacid tablets, anti-diarrhoea tablets, sachets of rehydration salts and a first aid kit.

Health packs containing sterile syringes, needles, gloves, etc, are available for travellers from various sources (eg Schiphol airport, Amsterdam); one such is made by Safa of Liverpool, UK. Emergency dental kits are available at leading retail outlets and dentists, made by Dental Save, 144 High St, Nailsea, Avon, BS19 1AP, UK, T 01275-810291, F 01275-858112, also available from Fiona Mahon Associates, PO Box 204, Hayes, Middx, UB4 9HN, UK, T 0181-842 3141, F 0181-845 7370.

Further information on health risks abroad, vaccinations, etc, may be available from a local travel clinic. If you wish to take specific drugs with you such as antibiotics, these are best prescribed by your own doctor. Beware, however, that not all doctors can be experts on the health problems of tropical countries. More detailed or more up-to-date information than local doctors can provide are available from various sources.

In the UK there are hospital departments specializing in tropical diseases in London, Liverpool, Birmingham and Glasgow and the Malaria Reference Laboratory at the London School of Hygiene and Tropical Medicine provides free advice about malaria, T 0891-600-350. In the USA the local public health services can give such information and information is available centrally from the Centres for Disease Control in Atlanta, T (404) 332 4559.

There are in addition computerized databases which can be accessed for a specific destination, up to the minute information. In the UK there is MASTA (Medical Advisory Service to Travellers Abroad), T 0171-631 4408, Tx 895 3474, F 0171-436 5389 and Travax (Glasgow, T 0141-946 7120, extension 247).

Further information on medical problems overseas can be obtained from the book by Richard Dawood (Editor) – *Travellers Health, How to Stay Healthy Abroad*, Oxford University Press, 1992, £7.99. We strongly recommend this revised and updated edition, especially to the intrepid traveller heading for the more out of the way places. General advice is also available in the UK in "Health Advice for Travellers" published jointly by the Department of Health and the Central Office of Information available free from your UK Travel Agent.

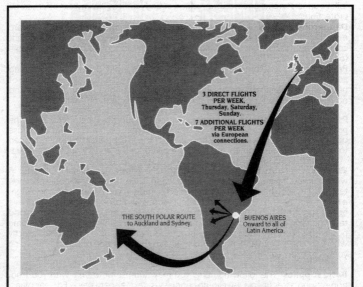

3 DIRECT FLIGHTS PER WEEK,
Thursday, Saturday, Sunday.

7 ADDITIONAL FLIGHTS PER WEEK
via European connections.

THE SOUTH POLAR ROUTE
to Auckland and Sydney.

BUENOS AIRES
Onward to all of Latin America.

NEW, FROM JULY 1995, 3 DIRECT FLIGHTS PER WEEK, LONDON/BUENOS AIRES.

From 1st July 1995, Aerolineas Argentinas increases its direct London to Buenos Aires flights from <u>two to three weekly.</u> These, together with seven additional European services, offer your clients a comprehensive choice to meet their travel needs - every day to Argentina.

● Arrive Buenos Aires for breakfast ● Onward Services to Santiago, Montevideo, La Paz, Rio, Sao Paulo, and all of Latin America ● Two weekly flights to Auckland and Sydney ● Advantageous 'Round the World' fare structures ● Competitive rates for Latin America and Australasia ● 747 comfort with inflight service to match.

RESERVATIONS 0171 494 1001
SALES DEPT 0171 494 1074 • FAX 0171 494 1002

FOR BUSINESS OR PLEASURE

AEROLINEAS ARGENTINAS

Aerolineas Argentinas, 54 Conduit Street, London WIR 9FD.

ARGENTINA

Maps: Country map, 50; Buenos Aires and surroundings, 60; Buenos Aires centre, 63; Buenos Aires & the Pampas, 85; Córdoba, 95; Córdoba environs, 101; North-West Argentina, 103; Tucumán, 105; Salta, 111; Mendoza, 131; North and East of Mendoza, 136; San Juan 138; San Juan centre, 139; North-East Argentina, 150; Iguazú Falls, 165; Puerto Iguazú and Misiones Province, 168; Bariloche, 177; Patagonia, 189; Puerto Madryn region, 193; Trelew, 197; Río Gallegos, 204; El Calafate 207; Southern Santa Cruz and P.N. Los Glaciares, 210; Ushuaia, 217.

INTRODUCTION

ARGENTINA is the second largest country in area in South America, equivalent to 29% of that of Europe. It stretches 3,460 km from N to S and 1,580 km from E to W. Apart from the estuary of the Río de la Plata its coast line is 2,575 km long. Its W frontier runs along the crest of the high Andes, a formidable barrier between it and Chile. Its neighbours to the N are Bolivia and Paraguay and (in the NE) Brazil. To the E is Uruguay. Its far S limit is the Beagle Channel. The area figures exclude the sector of Antarctica claimed by Argentina.

Argentina is enormously varied both in its types of land and its climates. Geographers usually recognize four main physical areas: the Andes, the North and Mesopotamia, the Pampas, and Patagonia.

The first division, the Andes, includes the whole length of the Cordilleras, low and deeply glaciated in the Patagonian S, high and dry in the prolongation into NW Argentina of the Bolivian Altiplano, the high plateau. S of this is the very

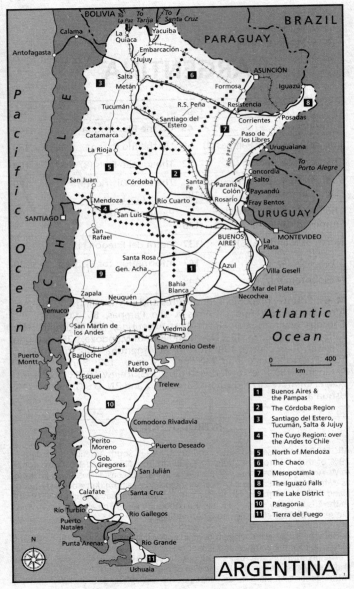

ARGENTINA

1	Buenos Aires & the Pampas
2	The Córdoba Region
3	Santiago del Estero, Tucumán, Salta & Jujuy
4	The Cuyo Region: over the Andes to Chile
5	North of Mendoza
6	The Chaco
7	Mesopotamia
8	The Iguazú Falls
9	The Lake District
10	Patagonia
11	Tierra del Fuego

parched desert and mountain region S of Tucumán and W of Córdoba. The oases strung along the eastern foot of the Andes—Jujuy, Salta, Tucumán, Catamarca, La Rioja, San Juan, Mendoza and the small town of San Rafael—were the first places to be colonized by the Spaniards.

The second division, the North and Mesopotamia, contains the vast forested plains of the Chaco, and the floodplain and gently rolling land known as the Argentine Mesopotamia lying between the rivers Paraná and Uruguay. The Province of Misiones in the NE is actually on the great Paraná plateau. These plains cover 582,750 sq km.

The third division, the pampa, takes up the heart of the land. These vast, rich plains lie S of the Chaco, E of the Andes, W of the Atlantic and the Río Paraná and N of the Río Colorado. The eastern part, which receives more rain, is usually called the Humid Pampa, and the western part the Dry Pampa. The Pampas stretch for hundreds of km in almost unrelieved flatness, covering some 650,000 sq km.

The final division is Patagonia, the area S of the Río Colorado—a land of arid, wind-swept plateaux cut across by ravines. In the deep S the wind is wilder and more continuous. There is no real summer, but to compensate for this the winters are rarely severe. Patagonia has about 780,000 sq km.

Three-quarters of Argentina's territory cannot be cultivated without irrigation but only 400,000 ha are artificially watered.

Climate ranges from sub-tropical in the N to cold temperate in Tierra del Fuego, but is temperate and quite healthy in the densely populated central zone. From mid-Dec to the end of Feb Buenos Aires can be oppressively hot and humid, with temperatures ranging from 27°C (80°F) to 35°C (95°F) and an average humidity of 70%. Beware of the high pollen count in the pollinating season if you have allergy problems. The winter months of Jun, Jul and Aug are best for a business visit, though spring weather in Buenos Aires is often very pleasant indeed. The skiing season in Bariloche ends by Aug 30. Corrientes and Misiones provinces are wet in Aug and especially Sep.

History When, in the early 16th century, the first Europeans came to Argentina, the native Indians had already halted the Inca drive S from Peru through Bolivia into N Argentina. The Spaniard Juan de Solís landed on the shores of the Plata estuary in 1516, but he was killed and the expedition failed. Magellan touched at the estuary four years later, but turned S to make his way into the Pacific. In 1527 both Sebastian Cabot and his rival Diego García sailed into the estuary and up the Paraná and the Paraguay. They formed a small settlement, Sancti Spiritus, at the junction of the Caraña and Coronda rivers near their confluence with the Paraná, but it was wiped out by the Indians about two years later and Cabot and García returned to Spain. Eight years later, in 1535, Pedro de Mendoza, with a large force well supplied with equipment and horses, founded a settlement at Buenos Aires. The natives soon made it too difficult for him; the settlement was abandoned and Mendoza returned home, but not before sending Juan de Ayolas with a small force up the Paraná. Ayolas set off for Peru, already conquered by Pizarro, leaving Irala in charge. It is not known for certain what happened to Ayolas, but in 1537 Irala and his men settled at Asunción, in Paraguay, where the natives were friendly. There were no further expeditions from Spain to colonize what is now called Argentina, and it was not until 1573 that the settlement at Asunción sent forces S to establish Santa Fe and not until 11 June 1580 that Juan de Garay refounded the settlement at Buenos Aires. It was only under his successor, Hernando Arias de Saavedra (1592-1614), that the new colony became secure.

In the meantime there had been successful expeditions into Argentina both from Peru and Chile—the first, from Peru, as early as 1543. These expeditions led, in the latter half of the 16th century, to the foundation at the eastern foot of the Andes of the oldest towns in Argentina: Santiago del Estero, Tucumán, Córdoba,

Salta, La Rioja and Jujuy by Spaniards from Peru following the old Inca road, and San Juan, Mendoza, and San Luis by those from Chile, across the Andes. Peru was given the viceroyalty over all the Spanish possessions in South America in 1543.

For 270 years after its foundation Buenos Aires was of little importance. Spanish stress was upon Lima, and Lima did not send its treasures home by way of Buenos Aires but through Panama and the Caribbean. Buenos Aires was not allowed by Spain to take part in any overseas trade until 1778; its population then was only 24,203. It was merely a military outpost for Spain to confront the Portuguese outpost at Colonia, across the estuary, and lived, in the main, by smuggling. Even when in 1776 the Viceroyalty of Río de la Plata was formed, it made little difference to Buenos Aires as a capital, for its control of the *cabildos* (town councils) in distant towns was very tenuous. When the British, following Spain's alliance with Napoleon, attacked Buenos Aires in 1806 and again in 1807 before being repulsed by local levies, there was no inkling of its future potential. But the defeat of these attacks, known as the Reconquista, had one important result: a great increase in the confidence of the *porteños* (the name given to those born in Buenos Aires) to deal with all comers, including the mother-country, whose restrictions were increasingly unpopular. On 25 May 1810, the *cabildo* of Buenos Aires deposed the viceroy and announced that it was governing henceforth on behalf of King Ferdinand VII, then a captive of Napoleon. Six years later, when Buenos Aires was threatened by invasion from Peru and blockaded by a Spanish fleet in the River Plate, a national congress held at Tucumán declared independence on 9 July 1816. The declaration was given reality by the genius and devotion of José de San Martín, who boldly marched an Argentine army across the Andes to free Chile, and (with the help of Lord Cochrane, commander of the Chilean Navy), embarked his forces for Peru, where he captured Lima, the first step in the liberation of Peru.

When San Martín returned home, it was to find the country rent by conflict between the central government and the provinces. Disillusioned, he retired to France. The internal conflict was to last a long time. On the one hand stood the Unitarist party, bent on central control; on the other the Federalist party, insisting on local autonomy. The latter had for members the great *caudillos*, the large landowners backed by the *gauchos*, suspicious of the cities. One of their leaders, Juan Manuel de Rosas, took control of the country in 1829. During his second term as Governor of Buenos Aires he asked for and was given extraordinary powers. The result was a 17-year reign of terror. His rule was an international scandal, and when he began a blockade of Asunción in 1845, Britain and France promptly countered with a three-year blockade of Buenos Aires. But in 1851 Justo José de Urquiza, Governor of Entre Ríos, one of his old henchmen, organized a triple *entente* of Brazil, Uruguay, and the Argentine opposition to overthrow him. He was defeated in 1852 at Caseros, a few km from Buenos Aires, and fled to England, where he farmed quietly for 25 years, dying at Southampton.

Rosas had started his career as a Federalist; once in power he was a Unitarist. His downfall meant the triumph of federalism. In 1853 a federal system was finally incorporated in the constitution, but the old quarrel had not been solved. In 1859, when the constitution was ratified, the capital was moved to Paraná, the province of Buenos Aires seceded, and Buenos Aires, under Bartolomé Mitre, was defeated by the federal forces under Urquiza. Two years later Buenos Aires again fought the country, and this time it won. Once again it became the seat of the federal government, with Bartolomé Mitre as its first constitutional president. (It was during his term that the Triple Alliance of Argentina, Brazil, and Uruguay defeated Francisco Solano López of Paraguay.) There was another political flare-up of the old quarrel in 1880, ending in the humiliation of Buenos Aires, which then ceased to be the capital of its province; a new provincial capital was founded at La Plata, 56 km to the SE. At that time a young colonel, Julio A Roca, was finally subduing all the Indian tribes of the pampas and the South. This was an event which was to make possible the final supremacy of Buenos Aires over all rivals.

Politically Argentina was a constitutional republic with a very restricted suffrage up to the passage in 1912 of the Sáenz Peña law, which established universal manhood suffrage. From 1916 to 1930 the Unión Cívica Radical (founded in 1890) held power, under the leadership of Hipólito Yrigoyen and Marcelo T de Alvear, but lost it to the military uprising of 1930. Though seriously affected by the world depression of the 1930s, Argentina's rich soil and educated population had made it one of the ten wealthiest countries in the world, but this wealth was most unevenly distributed, and the political methods followed by the conservatives and their military associates in the 1930s denied the middle and working classes any effective share in their own country's wealth and government. In 1943 came another military coup, which had a distinctly fascist tinge; in 1946 emerged, as President, Gen Juan Domingo Perón, who based his power on an alliance between the army and labour; his contacts with labour were greatly assisted by his charismatic wife Eva (since commemorated in the rock-opera "Evita") and the living conditions of the workers were greatly improved—but at the expense of the economic state of the country. By the time a military coup unseated Perón in 1955 serious harm had been done; ever since, Argentina has been a politically divided society and has been struggling to recover its lost economic health.

An uneasy alternation of three military and two constitutional regimes followed between 1955 and 1973. Perón lived in exile in Madrid and his supporters were excluded from power by the armed forces. The military seized power in 1966 but were discredited by a deteriorating economy and the emergence of several guerrilla groups in a climate of tension and violence. Gen Perón again became President in Oct 1973, but died on 1 July 1974, leaving the Presidency to his widow, Vice-President María Estela Martínez de Perón. A chaotic political situation, of which a high level of violence (including guerrilla warfare) was a regrettable feature, followed his death; by Mar 1976 conditions in the country, both of violence and of economic crisis, had deteriorated to the point when the military felt again obliged to intervene. Sra de Perón was deposed from the Presidency by a military junta, led by Gen Jorge Videla, and guerrilla warfare and the other features of dissidence were repressed with great brutality: about 9,000 people (according to official statistics; human rights organizations believe the total at least doubles this) disappeared without trace during the so-called 'dirty war'. General Videla was appointed President in 1978 by the military leaders, for a three-year term. His nominated successor, Gen Roberto Viola took over as President for three years in Mar, 1981 but was replaced by Gen Leopoldo Galtieri in Dec 1981. The latter was in turn replaced in Jun 1982 by Gen (ret) Reynaldo Bignone.

Confidence in the military ebbed when their economic policies began to go sour in 1980. In 1982-83 pressure for a democratic restoration grew apace particularly after the South Atlantic conflict with Great Britain in 1982. General elections on 30 October 1983 were won by the Unión Cívica Radical (UCR), with Dr Raúl Alfonsín, its candidate, elected as president. During 1985 Generals Videla, Viola and Galtieri were sentenced to long terms of imprisonment for their parts in the 'dirty war', which caused friction between the Government and the armed forces. President Alfonsín's popularity gradually waned as his Government failed to solve economic problems. When Alfonsín was defeated by Dr Carlos Saúl Menem of the Partido Justicialista (Peronists) in May 1989, Alfonsín stepped down early because of economic instability. Strained relations between the Peronist Government and the military led to several rebellions, which Pres Menem attempted to appease by pardoning the imprisoned generals. His popularity among civilians declined, but in 1991-92 the Economy Minister, Domingo Cavallo, succeeded in restoring confidence in the economy and the Government as a whole. After triumphing in Oct 1993 congressional elections at the expense of the UCR, the Peronists themselves lost some ground in April 1994 elections to a constituent assembly. The party to gain most was Frente Grande, a broad coalition of left wing groups and disaffected Peronists, who captured the votes, especially in Buenos Aires, of those dissatisfied with conventional politics. Among the causes of the lost confidence were unrestrained corruption and a pact in Dec 1993 between Menem and Alfonsín pledging UCR support for constitutional changes which included re-election of the president for a second term of 4 years.

By the 1995 elections, the majority of the electorate favoured stability over constitutional concerns and returned Pres Menem, without recourse to a second ballot. The Peronists also increased their majority in congress. Menem's chief priority was to reduce unemployment, although this would be difficult given the government's insistence that the provinces restructure their finances and reduce inefficiencies. Despite the country's overall economic improvement, most provinces have not enjoyed prosperity. In early 1995, a series of revelations by army personnel concerning the disappearance of thousands of Argentines in the 1970s and 1980s reopened the wounds of the "dirty war", despite official attempts to suppress discussion of the subject.

The Transformation of the Pampas   The pampas, the economic heart of the country, extend fanwise from Buenos Aires for a distance of between 550 and 650 km. Apart from three groups of *sierras* or low hills near Córdoba, Tandil and Bahía Blanca, the surface seems an endless flat monotony, relieved occasionally, in the SW, by sand dunes. There are few rivers. Drinking water is pumped to the surface from a depth of from 30 to 150m by the windpumps which are such a prominent feature of the landscape. There are no trees other than those that have been planted, except in the *monte* of the W. But there is, in most years, ample rainfall. It is greatest at Rosario, where it is about 1,020 mm, and evenly distributed throughout the year. The further S from Rosario, the less the rain. At Buenos Aires it is about 940 mm; it drops to 535 at Bahía Blanca, and is only 400 along the boundary of the Humid Pampa. The further from Rosario, too, the more the rainfall is concentrated during the summer. Over the whole of the pampa the summers are hot, the winters mild, but there is a large climatic difference between various regions: at Rosario the growing season between frosts is about 300 days; at Bahía Blanca it falls to 145 days.

When the Spanish arrived in Argentina the pampas were an area of tall coarse grasses. The cattle and horses they brought with them were soon to roam wild and in time transformed the Indian's way of life. The only part of the pampa occupied by the settlers was the so-called Rim, between the Río Salado, S of the capital, and the Paraná-Plata rivers. Here, in large *estancias*, cattle, horses and mules in great herds roamed the open range. There was a line of forts along the Río Salado: a not very effective protection against marauding Indians. The Spaniards had also brought European grasses with them; these soon supplanted the coarse native grasses, and formed a green carpet surface which stopped abruptly at the Río Salado.

The *estancia* owners and their dependent *gauchos* were in no sense an agricultural people, but towards the end of the 18th century, tenants—to the great contempt of both *estanciero* and *gaucho*—began to plant wheat in the valleys along the Paraná-Plata shore. The fall of Rosas in 1852, and the constitution of 1853, made it possible for Argentina to take a leap forward, but it must be remembered that its civilized population at that time was only 1,200,000.

The rapidly rising population of Europe during the latter half of the 19th century and the consequent demand for cheap food was the spur that impelled Argentina (as it did the United States and Canada) to occupy its grasslands and take to agriculture. This was made possible by the new techniques already developed: agricultural machinery, barbed wire, well-drilling machines and windpumps, roads and railways, and ocean-going steamships. Roads were, and are, a difficulty in the pampa; the soil lacks gravel or stones to surface the roads, and dirt roads become a quagmire in wet weather and a fume of dust in the dry. Railways, on the other hand, were simple and cheap to build. The system grew as need arose and capital (mostly from Britain) became available. The lines in the pampa radiate out fanwise (with intricate inter-communication) from the ports of Buenos Aires, Rosario, Santa Fe and Bahía Blanca. Argentina, unlike most other countries, had extensive railways before a road system was built.

The occupation of the pampa was finally achieved by a war against the Indians in 1878-83 which virtually exterminated them. Many of the officers were given gifts of land of more than 40,000 ha each. The pampa had passed into private hands on the old traditional pattern of large estates.

Cattle products—hides, tallow, and salt beef—had been the mainstay of Argentine overseas trade during the whole of the colonial period. In the early 19th century wool challenged the supremacy of cattle. The occupation of the grasslands did not, at first, alter the complexion of the foreign trade; it merely increased its volume. In 1877, however, the first ship with refrigeration chambers made it possible to send frozen beef to England, but the meat of the scrub cattle was too strong for English taste. As a result, pedigree bulls were imported from England and the upgrading of the herds began. The same process was applied to sheep. But the improved herds could only flourish where there were no ticks—prevalent in the N—and throve best where forage crops were available. Argentina adopted as its main forage crop alfalfa (lucerne), a plant like clover which proved extremely suitable on the pampa. It has since been supplemented with barley, oats, rye, maize, sorghum and oilseeds.

A striking thing about the Pampas is the bird life. Flamingoes rise in a pink and white cloud, heron egrets gleam white against the blue sky, pink spoonbills dig in the mud and rheas stalk in the distance. Most fascinating are the oven birds, the *horneros*, which build oven-shaped nests six times as big as themselves on the top of telegraph and fence posts.

The transformation of the pampa has had two profound effects. Because its newly-created riches flowed out and its needs flowed in mainly through Buenos Aires, that port grew from comparative insignificance into one of the great cities in the world. Also, the transformation of the Humid Pampa led, through immigration, to a vast predominance of the European strain. The first immigrants settled NW of Santa Fe in 1856. Between 1857 and 1930 total immigration was over six million, almost all from Europe. The process has continued; Italians have been by far the most numerous, followed by Spaniards, and then, far behind, groups of other Europeans and Latin Americans. British and North Americans normally came as stockbreeders, technicians and business executives.

The Argentine People In the Federal Capital and Province of Buenos Aires, where almost 40% of the population lives, the people are almost exclusively of European origin. In the far northern provinces, colonized from neighbouring countries, at least half the people are *mestizos* though they form about 15% of the population of the whole country. It is estimated that 12.8% are foreign born and generally of European origin, though there are also important communities of Syrians, Lebanese, Armenians, Japanese and, most recently, Koreans.

Not surprisingly, the traditional image of the Argentine is that of the *gaucho*; *gauchismo* has been a powerful influence in literature, sociology and folklore, and is celebrated each year in the week before the 'Day of Tradition', 10 Nov.

In the highlands of the NW, in the Chaco, Misiones and in the SW, there are still some indigenous groups. The exact total of the Indian population is unknown; estimates vary from 100,000 to 300,000. As was noted above, the pampas Indians were virtually exterminated in the 19th century; the Indians of Tierra del Fuego are extinct. Surviving peoples include the Wichi and others in Salta and Jujuy provinces (see p 108), various Chaco Indians (see p 147) and tribes related to the Mapuche and Tehuelche nations in the SW. A number of organizations represent indigenous interests, but any legislation, under federal law, has to be enacted separately by each province.

The Economy   Argentina is one of the more highly developed countries of the region and is potentially one of the richest farming countries in the world. The importance of agriculture and livestock production is shown by the fact that this sector still provides over 50% of export earnings with sales of cereals, oilseeds, meat and processed foodstuffs. Although Argentina has lost its dominant position as an exporter of cereals and beef, it has great resources in relation to its population. Per capita income is therefore relatively high. Agriculture accounts for 6% of gdp. There has been a shift from livestock to crop production since the 1960s in line with changes in relative prices and the introduction of new technology which has sharply increased crop yields. Cereals account for a substantial proportion of crop production although the area sown to oilseeds has risen steeply, now exceeding that of wheat, and producing about 15 million tonnes of soyabeans and sunflower seed a year. Livestock, faced with stiff competition abroad from other exporting countries, has declined in importance. The cattle stock fell from around 57 million head in the late 1970s to 50m in 1993.

The manufacturing sector has developed behind high import protection barriers; it accounts for 22% of gdp and benefits from increased agricultural activity, so that natural resource-based and labour-intensive industries such as food processing, textiles and clothing are reasonably dynamic. Food processing and beverages account for a quarter of manufacturing output and a fifth of industrial employment. Investment in manufacturing remained low in the 1980s and early 1990s, first because of hyperinflation depressing domestic demand, then during the recession that followed the introduction of Menem's market reforms. In 1994, many companies restructured in readiness for the full implementation of the Mercosur common market in 1995 and to cope with the elimination of government support. The financial crisis that hit Argentina as a result of Mexico's late-1994 economic crisis led to reduced expectations for manufacturers through 1995. A shortage of credit, lower domestic demand and the knock-on effect of Brazil's economic problems all heralded weaker performance.

Energy development has been a priority with emphasis on hydro and nuclear power sources to reduce dependence upon thermal power. Argentina is virtually self-sufficient in oil; production in 1993 was 210 million barrels. There is an exportable surplus of natural gas and petroleum derivatives. The country's hydroelectric potential lies on the rivers Paraná and Uruguay in the N and on the network of rivers in Río Negro and Neuquén provinces. In 1992 hydroelectricity accounted for 34.8% of power generation, fossil fuels 52.6%, with nuclear power plants supplying the balance. Hydroelectricity's share was set to grow substantially after 1993 with Yacyretá, on the Paraná, and Piedra del Aguila, in the Andes, coming on stream. This would also reduce the incidence of power cuts.

Extremely high rates of inflation were recorded in the 1980s through a combination of large fiscal deficits, monetary expansion and a high velocity of circulation. These were difficult to contain because of structural imbalances in the economy caused by inadequate levels of investment and inefficiencies and corruption in both the public and private sectors. The Government introduced several stabilization programmes, the first of which was the Austral Plan, named after the new currency, but none was successful. The economic crisis deepened as management of public finances deteriorated, leading to hyperinflation and a sharp contraction in output and investment as confidence was eroded and the economy became increasingly dollarized. The Government which took office in July 1989, attempted to curb hyperinflation through a wide range of measures. Structural economic reform initially brought further recession, unemployment and declining living standards. After 1993, however, investment began to recover. Inflation fell from 171.7% in 1991 to 10.6% in 1993 and 3.9% in 1994, while gdp growth in excess of 6% was recorded in both 1993 and 1994 (8.9% in 1991, 8.7% in 1992). Much of the increase in economic growth and confidence was attributed to a currency convertibility law, which required the domestic currency to be fully backed by US dollars, so that monetary expansion was limited by the growth in international reserves. The government insisted that the convertibility law would not be modified in the wake of the Mexican financial crisis of Dec 1994. Despite capital flight of about US$8.5bn which caused severe problems in the banking system, high levels of domestic debt, rising unemployment to 12% of the workforce and the threat of recession, devaluation of the peso was ruled out. Instead, austerity measures were introduced and substantial aid was sought from multilateral institutions to help restructure the financial sector.

The external debt rose sharply in the 1980s to US$65bn in 1991, making Argentina the third largest debtor in the region. Debt rescheduling agreements negotiated with commercial bank creditors, new loans and IMF financing facilities, and World Bank loans all collapsed as the Government failed to implement fully its policy commitments. By the early 1990s, Argentina was seriously in arrears to commercial banks although arrears to multilateral agencies had been cleared. The Government sought to reduce its commercial bank commitments by cancelling debt through privatization. Despite an early failure of the sale of Aerolíneas Argentinas in 1992, the government pressed ahead with the sale of state companies. The largest, Yacimientos Petrolíferos Fiscales (YPF, the state oil company), was privatized in 1993. In 1992 the Government started negotiations to restructure its commercial bank debt by securitizing it into bonds, following the Mexican model of debt or debt service reduction. A successful conclusion was

Argentina : fact file

Geographic

Land area	2,780,400 sq km
forested	21.6%
pastures	51.9%
cultivated	9.9%

Demographic

Population (1994)	33,880,000
annual growth rate (1989-94)	1.3%
urban	86.9%
rural	13.1%
density	12.2 per sq km
Religious affiliation	
Roman Catholic	91.6%
Birth rate per 1,000 (1994)	19.6
	(world av 26.0)

Education and Health

Life expectancy at birth,	
male	68 years
female	74 years
Infant mortality rate	
per 1,000 live births (1992)	34.0
Physicians (1988)	1 per 326 persons
Hospital beds	1 per 205 persons
Calorie intake as %	
of FAO requirement	131%
Population age 25 and over	
with no formal schooling	5.7%
Literate males (over 15)	95.5%
Literate females (over 15)	95.1%

Economic

GNP (1993)	US$244,091mn
GNP per capita	US$7,290
Public external debt (1992)	
	US$46,835mn
Tourism receipts (1992)	US$3,090mn
Inflation (annual av 1990-93)	30.3%
Radio	1 per 1.6 persons
Television	1 per 4.7 persons
Telephone	1 per 7.0 persons

Employment

Population economically active (1990)	
	12,305,346
Unemployment rate (1989)	7.3%
% of labour force in	
agriculture	12.0
mining	0.5
manufacturing	19.9
construction	10.1
Military forces	69,800

Source Encyclopaedia Britannica

reached in April 1993, signalling Argentina's reentry into the international financial community.

Government   The country's official name is República Argentina (RA), the Argentine Republic. The form of government has traditionally been a representative, republican federal system. Of the two legislative houses, the Senate has 46 seats, and the Chamber of Deputies 254. By the 1853 Constitution (amended in 1880) the country is divided into a Federal Capital (the city of Buenos Aires) and 23 Provinces. Each Province has its own Governor, Senate and Chamber of Deputies. The municipal government of the Federal Capital is exercised by a Mayor who is directly elected. The Constitution grants the city autonomous rule.

Communications   Argentina has only four good seaports: Buenos Aires, La Plata, Rosario and Bahía Blanca. Necochea/Quequén is also a good port, but the swell can sometimes prevent ships entering or sailing for days. The two great rivers flowing southward into the Plata, the Paraná and the Uruguay, are not very reliable shipping routes. The Colorado and the Negro rivers in northern Patagonia are navigable by small vessels only. Internal air services are highly developed.

Most of Argentina is served by about 214,613 km of road, but only 28% are paved and a further 17% improved. The 34,183 km (1987) of railway line, owned mostly by British companies until they were taken over by the State in 1948, used to carry less than 10% of passengers and freight, until privatization in the early 1990s caused an even greater reduction in rail's share of national transportation.

Music and Dance   Buenos Aires contains a third of the country's population and its music is the Tango. Indeed to the outside world there is no other Argentine music. Although also sung and played, the Tango was born as a dance just before the turn of the 20th century. The exact moment of the birth was not recorded by any contemporary observer and continues to be a matter of debate, though the roots can be traced. The name "Tango" predates the dance and was given to the carnivals (and dances) of the black inhabitants of the Río de la Plata in the early l9th century. Elements of the black tradition were taken over by whites, as the black population declined into insignificance. However, the name "Tango Americano" was also given to the Habanera (a Cuban descendent of the English Country Dance) which became the rage in Spain and bounced back into the Río de la Plata in the middle of the 19th centry, not only as a fashionable dance, together with the polka, mazurka, waltz and cuadrille, but also as a song form in the very popular "Zarzuelas", or Spanish operettas. However the Habanera led not a double, but a triple life, by also infiltrating the lowest levels of society directly from Cuba via sailors who arrived in the ports of Montevideo and Buenos Aires. Here it encountered the Milonga, originally a Gaucho song style, but by 1880 a dance, especially popular with the so-called "Compadritos" and "Orilleros", who frequented the port area and its brothels, whence the Argentine Tango emerged around the turn of the century to dazzle the populace with its brilliant, personalized footwork, which could not be accomplished without the partners staying glued together. As a dance it became the rage and, as the infant recording industry grew by leaps and bounds, it also became popular as a song and an instrumental genre, with the original violins and flutes being eclipsed by the *bandoneón* button accordion, then being imported from Germany. In 1911 the new dance took Paris by storm and returned triumphant to Buenos Aires. It achieved both respectability and notoriety, becoming a global phenomenon after the First World War. The golden voice of the renowned Carlos Gardel soon gave a wholly new dimension to the music of the Tango until his death in 1935. After losing some popularity in Argentina, it came to the forefront again in the 1940s (1920-50 is considered the real golden age). Its resurgence was assisted by Perón's decree that 50% of all music played on the radio must be Argentine, only to suffer a second, much more serious decline in the face of rock music over the past two decades. To see the Tango and Milonga danced in Buenos Aires today, you need to visit one of the clubs or *confiterías* where it is specially featured, see Buenos Aires **Nightclubs and Folklore.** Apart from Carlos Gardel, other great names connected with the Tango are Francisco Canaro (Uruguayan), Osvaldo Pugliese and Astor Piazzolla, who has modernized it by fusion with jazz styles (*nuevo tango*). Whilst the majority of Argentine young people will agree that the Tango represents the soul of Buenos Aires, don't expect them to dance it or listen to it. They are more likely to be interested in the country's indigenous rock music.

If the Tango represents the soul of Buenos Aires, this is not the case in the rest of the country. The provinces have a very rich and attractive heritage of folk dances, mainly for couples, with arms held out and fingers clicked or handkerchiefs waved, with the "Paso Valseado" as the basic step. Descended from the Zamacueca, and therefore a cousin of the Chilean Cueca and Peruvian Marinera, is the slow and stately Zamba, where the handkerchief is used to greatest effect. Equally popular throughout most of the country are the faster Gato, Chacarera and Escondido. These were the dances of the Gaucho and their rhythm evokes that of a cantering horse. Guitar and the *bombo* drum provide the accompaniment. Particularly spectacular is the Malambo, where the Gaucho shows off his dextrous footwork, the spurs of his boots adding a steely note to the rhythm.

Different regions of the country have their own specialities. The music of Cuyo in the W is sentimental and very similar to that of neighbouring Chile, with its Cuecas for dance and Tonadas for song. The NW on the other hand is Andean, with its musical culture closer to that of Bolivia, particularly on the Puna, where the Indians play the *quena* and *charango* and sound mournful notes on the great long *erke*. Here the dances are Bailecitos and Carnavalitos, while the songs are Vidalitas and the extraordinary high pitched Bagualas, the very essence of primeval pain. In the NE provinces of Corrientes and Misiones, the music shares cultural similarities with Paraguay. The Polca and Galopa are danced and the local Chamamé is sung, to the accordion or the harp, the style being sentimental. Santiago del Estero is the heartland of the Chacarera and the lyrics are often part Spanish and part Quichua, a local dialect of the Andean Quechua language. Down in the Province of Buenos Aires you are more likely to hear the Gauchos singing their Milongas, Estilos and Cifras and challenging each other to a Payada or rhymed duel. Argentina experienced a great folk revival in the 50's and 60's and some of the most celebrated groups are still drawing enthusiastic audiences today. These groups include Los Chalchaleros and Los Fronterizos, the perennial virtuoso singer and guitarist, Eduardo Falú and, more recently, León Gieco from Santa Fe.

BUENOS AIRES AND THE PAMPAS (1)

Apart from the capital itself, with its museums, theatres, public buildings, parks and shopping, this region contains the Tigre Delta (waterways, lunch spots) and Atlantic coastal resorts. Of these the most famous is Mar del Plata.

The Río de la Plata, or River Plate, on which Buenos Aires lies, is not a river but an estuary or great basin, 160 km long and from 37 to 90 km wide, into which flow the Ríos Paraná and Uruguay and their tributaries. It is muddy and shallow and the passage of ocean vessels is only made possible by continuous dredging. The tides are of little importance, for there is only a 1.2m rise and fall at spring tides. The depth of water is determined by the direction of the wind and the flow of the Paraná and Uruguay rivers.

Buenos Aires, the capital, spreads over some 200 sq km (together with Gran

BUENOS AIRES 2b

Railway Stations:
T1. Retiro
T2. Lacroze
T3. Once
T4. Constitución
T5. Buenos Aires

Buenos Aires, the area is 4,326 sq km). The population of the Federal Capital itself is about 2.92 million, but the population of greater Buenos Aires (including the suburbs in the province of Buenos Aires) is 10.87 million.

NB Extreme humidity and unusual pollen conditions may affect asthma sufferers.

Buenos Aires has been virtually rebuilt since the beginning of this century and very few of the old buildings are left. In the centre, which has maintained the original lay-out since its foundation, the streets are often very narrow and are mostly one-way. Its original name, "Santa María del Buen Ayre" was a recognition of the good winds which brought sailors across the ocean.

The heart of the city, now as in colonial days, is the Plaza de Mayo, with the historic Cabildo, the Town Hall, where the movement for independence from Spain was first planned; the pink Casa Rosada (Presidential Palace); the Municipalidad (City Hall); and the Cathedral, where San Martín, the father of Argentine independence, is buried. (For a note on the Mothers of the Plaza de Mayo, **see p 66**). Within a few blocks are the fashionable church of Nuestra Señora de la Merced and the main banks and business houses.

Running W from the Plaza, the Avenida de Mayo leads 1½ km to the Congress building in the Plaza del Congreso. Halfway it crosses the wide Avenida Nueve de Julio. A tall obelisk commemorating the 400th anniversary of the city's founding stands in the Plaza de la República. The Av Nueve de Julio itself, one of the widest in the world, consists of three carriageways separated by wide grass borders. In the N the Av Nueve de Julio meets the Avenida del Libertador, the principal way out of the city to the N and W.

North of the Plaza de Mayo is the shopping, theatre and commercial area. The city's traditional shopping centre, Calle Florida (with excellent newsstands), is in this district. This is the popular down-town meeting place, particularly in the late afternoon; it is reserved for pedestrians only and the buskers in the 500 block are worth visiting. Another shopping street is Avenida Santa Fe, which crosses Florida at the Plaza San Martín; it has become as touristy and as expensive as Florida. Avenida Corrientes is the entertainment centre, a street of theatres, restaurants, cafés and night life. Close by, in Calle Lavalle (part reserved to pedestrians) and in nearby streets, there are numerous cinemas and many good and reasonable restaurants.

East of the Plaza de Mayo, behind the Casa Rosada, a broad avenue, Paseo Colón, runs S towards San Telmo and the picturesque old port district known as the Boca, where the Riachuelo flows into the Plata. The Boca is reached by bus 152 from Av LN Alem, or bus 29 from Plaza de Mayo, in the centre, US$0.50. For a tour of the Boca, start at Plaza Vuelta de Rocha, near Av Pedro de Mendoza and Dr Del Valle Iberlucea, then walk up Caminito, the little pedestrian street used as a theatre and an art market. Visit the Museo de Bellas Artes de la Boca (**see p 64**). The Boca, mostly Italian, has its own distinctive life and parts of it are becoming touristy, but the area, with the adjacent industrial and meat-packing suburb of Avellaneda across the high Avellaneda bridge, is generally dirty and run down, and assaults occasionally take place.

One of the few places which still have late colonial and Rosista buildings is the *barrio* of San Telmo, S of Plaza de Mayo, centred on Plaza Dorrego along the slope which marks the old beach of the Río de la Plata. It is a recognized artistic centre, with plenty of cafés and a pleasant atmosphere; and there is a regular Sat and Sun morning antiques market at the Plaza Dorrego (**see p 75**). The 29 bus connects the Boca with San Telmo, and passes the end of Calle Florida, the shopping street. East of San Telmo on the far side of the docks, the spacious Av Costanera runs along the Plata estuary. A stretch of marshland (claimed from the river by a system similar to the one used in the construction of the Dutch polders) forms the interesting **Costanera Sur Wildlife Reserve**, which has many *coypu* (large rodents) and many types of birds, including the rare black-headed duck and the curve-billed reed hunter. The entrance is at Av Tristán Achabal Rodríguez 1550 (reached by buses 4 and 2); it opens daily from 0700-2000 (free, guided tours available), but much can be seen from the road before then (binoculars useful). There are three trails ranging from 2 km to 6 km long. In summer it is very hot with little shade. For details, contact Fundación Vida Silvestre, Defensa 245, 6 piso, 1075 Buenos Aires, T 331-4864/343-3778.

The theatre retains its hold on the people of Buenos Aires. About 20 commercial theatres play the year round. Recommended is the Teatro Liceo. There are many amateur theatres. You are advised to book as early as possible for a seat at a concert, ballet, or opera.

NB Street numeration: numbers start from the dock side rising from E to W, but N/S streets are numbered from Av Rivadavia, 1 block N of Av de Mayo rising in both directions. Calle Juan D Perón used to be called Cangallo and MT de Alvear is still referred to by its old name, Charcas.

Principal Public Buildings

Casa de Gobierno on the E side of the Plaza de Mayo, and called the Casa Rosada because it is pink, contains the offices of the President of the Republic. (The Foreign Minister's offices are at the Palacio de San Martín, Plaza San Martín). The Casa Rosada is notable for its statuary, the rich furnishing of its halls and for its libraries, but it is not at present possible to visit the interior. The Museo de los Presidentes is on the lower floors (see under **Museums**). A tunnel connects the Casa Rosada with the port (Perón used this to escape in 1955).

The **Cabildo** on the W side of the same Plaza, the old town hall, was put up in 1711 but has been rebuilt several times. Its original structure, fittings and furniture were replaced in 1940 and it was declared a national monument. See under **Museums**.

Old Congress Hall on the S of the Square, built 1863, is a National Monument. It has been encircled and built over by a palatial bank building. Open Thur, 1500-1700, free.

Palacio del Congreso (Congress Hall) to the SW at the far end of Avenida de Mayo, of great size and in Greco-Roman architecture, is the seat of the legislature. It contains the Senate and the Chamber of Deputies. There is limited accommodation for the public at the sittings. It is open from 1700 onwards. Queue in front of desk assigned for minor parties, there they take your passport and give you a ticket for your seat and a pink slip to reclaim your passport. You may stay as long as you wish, but must remain seated. A guided tour (in English) can be taken on Mon, Tues and Fri at 1100 and 1700 when Congress is not sitting. Behind the building is a large white statue of Columbus. This is a quiet area, beware of robbery.

Teatro Colón, one of the world's great opera houses, overlooks Avenida 9 de Julio, with its main entrance on Libertad, between Tucumán and Viamonte. The Colón's interior is resplendent with red plush and gilt; the stage is huge, and salons, dressing rooms and banquet halls are equally sumptuous. Open daily to visitors (not Sun), opening hours vary according to time of year, guided tours Mon-Fri 0900-1600, Sat 0900-1200, in Spanish, French and English, US$5 (children US$2), from entrance at Viamonte 1180, rec. Closed Jan-Feb, check times in advance, T 382-0554. Tickets, sold several days before performance, on the Calle Tucumán side of the theatre. The season runs from Apr to early Dec, and there are concert performances most days. The cheapest seat is US$6 (available even on the same day), and there are free performances most days (Tues-Fri) at 1730 in the Salón Dorado—check programme in the visitors' entrance.

The **Bolsa de Comercio**, built in 1916, a handsome building, contains a stock exchange (entrance 25 de Mayo y Sarmiento), and a grain exchange (entrance at the corner of Av Corrientes and Bouchard, opposite Luna Park).

Churches

All historic churches are open 1630-1900; some at 0900-1100 also.

The **Cathedral**, Rivadavia 437, on the N of Plaza de Mayo is flanked by the former residence of the Archbishop. On this site was built the first church in Buenos Aires, which after reconstruction in 1677 collapsed in 1753 and the rebuilding was not completed until 1823. The eighteenth century towers were never rebuilt, so that the architectural proportions have suffered. A frieze upon the Greek façade represents Joseph and his brethren. The tomb (1878) of the Liberator, General José de San Martín, is imposing.

The **Church of San Ignacio de Loyola**, at Calles Alsina and Bolívar 225, founded in 1710, is the oldest Colonial building in Buenos Aires. It has two lofty towers. The **San Francisco**, Calles Alsina and Defensa, controlled by the Franciscan Order, was inaugurated in 1754 and given a new façade in 1808.

La Merced, Calles Juan D Perón and Reconquista 207, was founded 1604 and rebuilt 1732. One of the altars has a wooden figure of Nuestro Señor, carved during the 18th century by an Indian in Misiones. It has one of the best organs in the country, and one of the few fine carillons of bells in Buenos Aires.

Santo Domingo, on Defensa and Av Belgrano, was founded in 1756. During the British attack on Buenos Aires in 1806 some of Whitelocke's soldiers took refuge in the church. The local forces bombarded it (some of the hits can still be seen on one of the towers); the British capitulated and their regimental colours were preserved in the church. Adjoining is the Salón Belgraniano (with relics of General Belgrano and much colonial furniture). There are summer evening concerts in the church; check times.

El Pilar, Junín 1904, is a jewel of colonial architecture dating from 1732, in a delightful setting of public gardens. A fine wooden image of San Pedro de Alcántara, attributed to the famous 17th century Spanish sculptor Alonso Cano, is preserved in a side chapel on the left. The clock in the steeple is the oldest in the city, made by the Englishman Thomas Windmills, c 1740.

Next to it is the **Cemetery of the Recoleta**, entrance at Junín 1822 near Museo de Bellas Artes (see below). It is one of the sights of Buenos Aires (open 0700-1800). Evita Perón is buried there; her tomb is now marked besides the inscription, Familia Duarte—wardens will point out the grave. "A Doric portico gives on to the main, paved, cypress-lined avenue of a little city of the dead. At the end of the avenue there is a great bronze statue of the resurrected Saviour; on either side, hard up against each other, like houses in a street, there are the family vaults of the Argentine patricians. Every possible style of architecture is represented." G S Fraser, in *News from Latin America*. Bus 110 along Esmeralda, to Recoleta, then 10 mins walk or 8 blocks from Pueyrredón Subte station. On Sun there is a good craft market near the entrance. A cultural centre alongside the Recoleta cemetery specializes in contemporary local art with many free exhibitions by young artists. Another well known cemetery is that of La Chacarita, reached

To
La Recoleta

Parera

oping

Perezuzuno

Arroyo

Juncal

Av. Callao

Montevideo

Arenales

Av. Santa Fe

M.T. de Alvear

Paraguay

Av. Córdoba

Cerrito

Libertad

Talcahuano

Uruguay

Paraná

Montevideo

Av. Corrientes

Sarmiento

Juan D. Perón

Bartolomé Mitre

Rodriguez Peña

Av. Callao

Rivadavia

Av. de Mayo

H. Yrigoyen

Alsina

Moreno

Virrey Cevallos

L. Sáenz Peña

Av. Entre Ríos

Solís

To
Palermo Parks,
Aeroparque

Av. del Libertador

Basavilbaso

Malpú

San Martín

Dr. R. Rojas

Dársena
Norte

Av. Antártida Argentina

Sulpacha

Esmeralda

Malpú

C. Pellegrini

Av. Córdoba

Viamonte

Tucumán

Lavalle

Florida

San Martín

Reconquista

25 de Mayo

Av. Leandro N. Alem

Av. Eduardo Madero

Av. Corrientes

Diagonal Norte

Carabelas

Av. de Mayo

Diagonal Sur

Av. Belgrano

Venezuela

México

Chile

Av. Independencia

Estados Unidos

Carlos Calvo

Humberto 1°

Bernado de Irigoyen

Lima

Salta

Av. 9 de Julio

Av. Rosales

Av. La Rabida

Av. Huergo

Dr. Guiffra

To
Castanera
Sur Wildlife
Reserve

N

23. "Presidente Sarmiento",
    museum ship
24. Museo Nacional Ferroviario
    at Retiro Station
25. Central Post Office
26. National Tourist Office x3
26. Buenos Aires Municipal
    Tourist Office

To
Ezeiza
Airport

25 de Mayo

Autopista 25 de Mayo

Av. San Juan

Cochabamba

Chacabuco

Perú

Bolívar

Defensa

To
Dársena
Sur

Av. Juan de Garay

Brasil

Av. Caseros

Tacuari

Piedras

Lima

Salta

To
La Boca

Al. Brown

Not to Scale

1. Plaza de Mayo
2. Plaza del Congreso
3. Plaza de la República,
   & Obelisk
4. Plaza San Martín
5. Plaza de la Fuerza Aérea
6. Parque Lezama
7. Plaza Constitución
8. Plaza Lavalle
9. Plaza Libertad
10. Parque Colón
11. Plaza Dorrego
12. Cathedral
13. San Ignacio de Loyola
14. San Francisco
15. Cabildo & Museum
16. Casa Rosada & Museo
    de los Presidentes
17. Municipalidad
18. Palacio del Congreso
19. Teatro Colón
20. Museo Histórico Nacional
21. Museo de la Ciudad
22. Teatro Municipal General
    San Martín & Museo
    Municipal de Arte Moderno

BUENOS AIRES
Centre

by Subte to the Federico Lacroze station, which has the much-visited, lovingly-tended tombs of Juan Perón and Carlos Gardel, the tango singer.

Museums, Libraries, Art Exhibitions Note: State museums and parks are free on Wed. Check opening hours with Tourist Office.

Museo de Gobierno (basement of Casa Rosada), Hipólito Yrigoyen 218 (open Wed-Thur 0900-1400, Fri, Sun 1400-1800). Historical memorabilia, particularly of former Presidents, 19th century tunnels.

Museo de Bellas Artes (National Gallery), Avenida del Libertador 1473, T 803-0802. In addition to a fine collection of European works, particularly strong in the 19th century French school, there are paintings representing the conquest of Mexico, executed 300 or 400 years ago, many good Argentine works incl new 19th and 20th century exhibits, and wooden carvings from the Argentine hinterland. Open Tues-Sun 1330-1930, Sat 0930-1930 (closes Jan-Feb). Entrance US$1 (Thur free), ISIC holders free. Warmly rec.

The Museo Nacional de Arte Decorativo is at Av Libertador 1902, collecions of painting, furniture, porcelain, crystal, sculpture; classical music concerts Wed and Thur, closed Tues, otherwise 1500-1900, T 802-6606, US$1, half-price to ISIC holders, closed Jan. The building is shared with the **Museo Nacional de Arte Oriental**, permanent exhibition of Chinese, Japanese, Hindu and Islamic art; open Wed-Mon, 1500-1900 (closed Jan), T 801-5988.

Biblioteca Nacional (The National Library), founded in 1810. About 500,000 volumes and 10,000 manuscripts, now housed in futuristic new building at Av del Libertador 1600 y Agüero 2502, T 806-6155, where only a fraction of the stock is available. Cultural events and festivals held here.

Museo Histórico Nacional, Defensa 1600, in San Telmo. Trophies and mementoes of historical events, divided into halls depicting stages of Argentine history. Here are San Martín's uniforms, a replica of his sabre, and the original furniture and door of the house in which he died at Boulogne. Open Thur-Sun 1400-1800. Entrance US$1; discount for ISIC and Youth card holders. For guided tours in English, French or Portuguese, T 27-4767/26-4588. Closed Jan-Feb.

Museo de la Ciudad, Alsina 412, open Mon-Fri, 1100-1900, Sun, 1500-1900, open all year, US$0.50 (Wed free), T 331-9855. Permanent exhibition covering social history and popular culture, special exhibitions on daily life in Buenos Aires changed every two months, and a reference library open to the public.

Museo y Biblioteca Mitre, San Martín 336, preserves intact the household of President Bartolomé Mitre; has coin and map collection and historical archives. Open Tues-Fri 1300-1800, US$1, T 394-8670.

Museo de Ciencias Naturales at Avenida Angel Gallardo 478, facing Parque Centenario. It houses palaeontological, zoological, mineralogical, botanical, archaeological and marine sections. Meteorites from Campo del Cielo on display. Open all year, daily, 1400-1900, US$0.20. Library, Mon-Fri, 1100-1700; T 982-5243.

Museo de la Dirección Nacional del Antártico, Angel Gallardo 470, in the Museo de Ciencias Naturales, Tues, Thur and Sun, 1400-1800. Specimens of flora, fauna and fossils and a library of taped birdsong, T 44-7327.

Museo Municipal de Arte Moderno, San Juan 350, with a salon at Avenida Corrientes 1530, 9th floor: international exhibitions and a permanent collection of 20th century art; open Mon-Fri 1000-2000, Sat and Sun 1200-2000, US$1.50 (US$1 at the salon, Wed free), T 374-9426.

Museo Municipal de Artes Plásticas Eduardo Sivori, Junín 1930 (in Cultural Centre, La Recoleta) and Corrientes 1530 8th floor, emphasis on 19th and 20th century Argentine art, entry US$1, open daily 1600-2000.

Museo de Bellas Artes de la Boca, Pedro de Mendoza 1835, Boca, has many works on local life, contemporary Argentine painting, also sculptures and figureheads rescued from ships. Tues-Fri 0900-1700, Sat-Sun 0900-1200, 1400-1800, T 21-1080, entrance free.

Museo de la Asociación Evaristo Carriego, Honduras 3784, tango museum of the writer, open Mon-Fri 1300-2000.

Museo de Motivos Populares Argentinos José Hernández, Av Libertador 2373, widest collection of Argentine flokloric art, with rooms dedicated to Indian, colonial and Gaucho artefacts; handicraft sale and library. Open Tues-Fri 1300-1700, Sat and Sun 1500-1900. T 802-7294 for guided visits in English or French. Entrance US$0.50 (closed in Feb).

Museo del Instituto Nacional Sanmartiniano, Gral Ramón Castilla and Av A M de Aguado; Mon-Fri 0900-1200 and 1400-1700; Sat, Sun 1400-1700. Replica of San Martín's house in exile in Boulogne-sur-Mer.

Museo de Arte Español Enrique Larreta, Juramento 2291, in Belgrano (entrance on Av Rafael Obligado). Sat-Sun 1500-1945; Mon-Fri 0900-1300, 1500-1945. Closed Thur and Jan. The home of the writer Larreta, with paintings and religious art; T 783-2640 for guided tour in language other than Spanish. Also **Biblioteca Alfonso El Sabio**, Mon-Fri, 1300-1930.

Museo del Cabildo y la Revolución de Mayo, Bolívar 65, is the old Cabildo building, converted into a museum in 1940. It contains paintings, documents, furniture, arms, medals, maps, recording the May 1810 revolution, and memorabilia of the 1806 British attack; also Jesuit art. Entry US$1 (retired persons free). Open Tues-Fri 1230-1900, Sun 1500-1900. T 334-1782 for English tours. Library, Mon-Fri, 1100-1900.

Museo de Arte Hispanoamericano Isaac Fernández Blanco, Suipacha 1422. Contains a most interesting and valuable collection of colonial art, especially silver, plus watercolours by Carlos Pellegrini, in a beautiful colonial mansion. Open Tues-Sun, 1500-1800, admission US$1. Thur free; closed Jan. For guided visits in English or French T 393-6318; guided tours in Spanish Sat, Sun 1530 and 1730.

Museo y Biblioteca Ricardo Rojas, Charcas 2837 (Tues-Fri 1400-1800). The famous writer Rojas lived in this beautiful colonial house for several decades. It contains his library, souvenirs of his travels, and many intriguing literary and historical curios.

Museo Numismático del Banco Central, San Martín 275, 2nd floor, fascinating, well kept, Mon-Fri 1000-1600, free, overlooks central foyer, ask guard for directions. Not to be confused with **Museo Numismático e Histórico del Banco Nacional**, B Mitre 326, 1st floor, coins and notes, furniture and historical documents, Mon-Fri 1000-1600, T 342-4041, ext 607.

"Presidente Sarmiento", Costanera Norte y Viamonte, next to Yacht Club, a sailing ship used as a naval training ship until 1961; now a museum. Open Sat-Sun 1400-1830, open all year, US$2.

Bank of London and South America (now Lloyds Bank, BLSA), Bartolomé Mitre and Reconquista, has a miniature museum on its fifth floor. Open during banking hours; the building, designed by SEPRA (Santiago Sánchez Elia, Federico Peralta Ramos, and Alfredo Agostini) and completed in 1963 is worth seeing. Next door is the **Banco de Córdoba**, designed by the brilliant Córdoba architect Miguel Angel Roca, completed in the early 1970s.

Museo Nacional de Aeronáutica, Av Costanera Rafael Obligado 4550, next to Jorge Newbery airport. Many civil and military aircraft, plus displays of navigational material, documents, equipment. Thur, Sat, Sun, holidays 1400-1900 (summer hours vary), T 773-0665.

Museo Nacional Ferroviario, Av Libertador 405, behind Retiro station. Mon-Fri, 0900-1800, Sat 0900-1200, free, T 325-5353. Archives 1100-1800. For railway fans, locomotives, machinery, documents of the Argentine system's history. Building in very poor condition.

Museo del Teatro Colón, Tucumán 1161. Mon-Fri 1000-1800. Documents and objects related to the theatre since 1908. T 35-5414/5/6, closed in summer.

Museo Histórico Saavedra (also known as the Museo Histórico de la Ciudad de Buenos Aires, not to be confused with Museo de la Ciudad), Crisólogo Larralde (Republiquetas) 6309. Tues-Sun, 1400-1800. City history from the eighteenth century, furniture, arms, documents, jewellery, coins and religious art; daily guided tours. T 572-0746. Free on Wed; closed Feb.

Museo de la Policía Federal San Martín 353, 7th and 8th floors, worth visiting. Interesting but extremely gruesome forensic section (for strong stomachs only, no one under 15 admitted),T 394-6857, Tues-Fri 1400-1800, US$1.

Museo Penitenciario Argentino Antonio Ballue, Humberto I 378, entrance US$1. Museum of the penal system, T 361-5803; Tues-Fri 1000-1200, 1400-1700, Sun 1000-1200, 1300-1700.

Museo del Teatro Nacional Cervantes, Córdoba 1199.

Museo Internacional de Caricatura y Humorismo, Lima 1037, open Mon, Tues, Thur, Fri, 1700-2000, Sat 1200-1700, originals of cartoons and caricatures of 20th century, but small international section, admission US$0.05.

Museo de Armas, Santa Fe 750. All kinds of weaponry related to Argentine history, incl the Malvinas conflict, plus Oriental weapons, T 312-9774, Wed-Fri 1500-1900, closed 15 Dec-14 Mar, US$1.

Museo de Telecomunicaciones in a magnificent building on the Costanera Sur, Av de los Italianos 851, T 312-5405 (used to belong to Cervecería Munich), Fri, Sat, Sun 1400-1800.

Jewish Museum, Libertad 773, religious objects relating to Jewish presence in Argentina, Tues-Thur 1600-1900.

Museo Histórico Sarmiento Cuba 2079, Belgrano, the National Congress and presidential offices in 1880; documents and personal effects of Sarmiento; library of his work, Wed-Fri 1430-1900, Sat, Sun, holidays 1500-1900, T 783-7555.

Museo Etnográfico J B Ambrosetti, Moreno 350, anthropological and ethnographic collections from around the world, incl Bolivian and Mapuche silverwork, US$1, Tues-Fri 1400-1600, Sat-Sun 1400-1900, T 342-4970.

Parks and Squares

Parque Lezama, Calles Defensa and Brasil, originally one of the most beautiful in the city, has been somewhat vandalized. There is a hippy fair at weekends and the park is very lively on Sun. It has an imposing statue of Pedro de Mendoza, the founder of the original city in 1535. The tradition is that the first founding took place on this spot. The Museo Histórico Nacional (**see above p 64**) is in the park.

The **Palermo Parks**, officially known as the Parque Tres de Febrero, with their magnificent avenues and the city's Bois de Boulogne. They are famous for their rose garden, Andalusian Patio, Japanese garden (admission US$2) with fish to feed and the Hipódromo Argentino, the Palermo race course, with seats for 45,000 (Sun, 1500, entry: US$3, senior citizens free). Opposite the parks are the Botanical and Zoological Gardens (the Zoo and Japanese Garden are closed on Mon). Nearby are the Municipal Golf Club, Buenos Aires Lawn Tennis Club, riding clubs and polo field, and the popular Club de Gimnasia y Esgrima (Athletic and Fencing Club). The **Planetarium** (just off Belisario Roldán, in the Park), is open Fri, Sat and Sun only (1930), entry US$2.50. At the entrance are several large meteorites from Campo del Cielo (**see p 148**). Reached by Subte line D. The **Show Grounds** of the Argentine Rural Society, next to Palermo Park, entrance on Plaza Italia, stage the Annual Livestock Exhibition in July, known as Exposición Rural.

The **Municipal Botanical Gardens**, Santa Fe 3951, entrance from Plaza Italia (take Subte, line D), contain characteristic specimens of the world's vegetation. The trees proper to the several provinces of Argentina are brought together in one section. The Gardens, closed at night, contain the Museo del Jardín Botánico, whose collection of Argentine flora is open daily 1000-1800, T 71-2951. The Gardens are full of stray cats, fed regularly by local residents. The **Zoo**, opp the Botanical Gardens, has been privatized and is open Tues-Fri 0930-1830, Sat-Sun 0930-1900, guided visits available, US$4 entry for adults, children under 13 free.

Plazas The most interesting is the Plaza de Mayo, containing so many public buildings, where the **Mothers of the Plaza de Mayo** march in remembrance of their children who disappeared during the crisis of the 1970s (their address is H Yrigoyen 1442). The Mothers still march anti-clockwise round the central monument every Thur at 1530, with photos of their "disappeared" loved-ones pinned to their chests. Others are the Plaza San Martín, with a monument to San Martín in the centre and, at the N end, a monument to those who fell in the South Atlantic conflict of 1982; the former Plaza Británica, now known as the Plaza de la Fuerza Aérea, with the clock tower presented by British and Anglo-Argentine residents, "a florid Victorian sentinel, royal crest upon its bosom" (frequently vandalized); in Plaza Canadá (in front of the Retiro Station) is a Pacific Northwest Indian totem pole, donated by the Canadian government; the Plaza Lavalle, which has secondhand bookstalls at the Calle Lavalle end; the Plaza del Congreso, the largest in the city, with a waterfall, floodlit at 2145; Plaza Francia, between Centro Cultural Recoleta and Museo de Bellas Artes, "hippy" fair on Sat and Sun, pleasant trees. There is also the great Plaza de la República, with a 67-metre obelisk at the junction between the Diagonal Norte, Av 9 de Julio and Avenida Corrientes.

Warning Buenos Aires is mostly a safe city, but street crime has risen since 1988, especially in the tourist season. Be particularly careful when boarding buses and near the Retiro train station. Beware of bagsnatching gangs in parks, markets and in the Subte, especially on Sun: they are not violent, but particularly skilful. See also **Security**, p 223, on mustard-spraying. If your passport is stolen, remember to get a new "entrada" stamp at the Dirección Nacional de Migraciones. Also changing money on the street is fraught with difficulties and can be dangerous: stick to the *cambios*.

Hotels All hotels, guest houses, inns and camping sites are graded by the number of beds available, and the services supplied. The Dirección de Turismo fixes maximum and minimum rates for 1, 2 and 3-star hotels, guest houses and inns, but there have been complaints that at 3 stars and below the ratings do not provide very useful guidance. Four and five-star hotels are free to apply any rate they wish. Hotels in the upper ranges can often be booked more cheaply through Buenos Aires Travel Agencies.

5-star hotels in our **L1-2** range are: *Caesar Park*, Posadas 1232, T 814 5146, covered pool, solarium; *Park Hyatt*, Cerrito 1433, T 326-1234, F 326-3032, new; *Libertador*, Av Córdoba y Maipú, T 322-2095, *Plaza*, Florida 1005, T 318-3000, good restaurant; *Alvear Palace*, Av Alvear 1891, T 804-4031/4041, an older-style hotel, near Recoleta, with roof garden, shopping gallery, elegant, good; *Sheraton*, San Martín 1225, T 311 6330, good buffet breakfast; *Claridge*, Tucumán 535, T 322-7700, highly rec, but not its restaurant; *Panamericano/Holiday Inn Crowne Plaza*, Carlos Pellegrini 525, T 393 6017; **L2** *Bauen*, Callao 360, T 476 1600.

4-star are *Etoile*, Presidente Roberto Ortiz 1835 in Recoleta, T 804 8603, outstanding location, rooftop pool, rooms with kitchenette, rec. **L3** *Bisonte Palace*, MT de Alvear y Suipacha, T 328-6621, very good, welcoming and **L3** *Gran King*, Lavalle 560, T 393

4012/4052, helpful, English spoken; **A2** *Torre*, Olleros 4186, T 552 6126; **L3** *Cambremon*, Suipacha 30, T 345-0118, F 345-4552, interior rooms very good, but front rooms noisy; **L2** *Regente Palace*, Suipacha 964, T 328 6628, very good, central, helpful, English spoken, buffet breakfast, sports facilities, will store luggage; **L2** *Crillón*, Santa Fe 796, T 312 8181; **A1** *Carsson*, Viamonte 650, T 322-3601, F 392 3551, good location, comfortable, friendly, quiet except rooms on street (ending in 17); **A1** *Los Dos Chinos*, Brasil 780, T 300 2021; **A1** *Bristol*, Cerrito 286, T 382-3228, F 382-3384, good breakfast; **L3** *Camino Real*, Maipú 572, T 322-3162, pleasant, clean, central; *Liberty*, Corrientes 632, T 325 0261, with breakfast, English spoken, luggage stored, clean, various sized rooms; **A2** *City*, Bolívar 160, T 342 6481, clean, rec; *Italia Romanelli*, Reconquista 647, T 312-6361, comfortable, rec; **L3** *Gran Hotel Buenos Aires*, MT de Alvear 767, T 312-3001, rundown but clean.

Other hotels: **A3** *Waldorf*, Paraguay 450, T 312-2079, clean, comfortable and plush, rooms of varying standards, garage, a/c, rec; **A2** *Gran Orly*, Paraguay 474, T/F 312-5344, good location, old fashioned, helpful, good lunches, English spoken, has some rooms for 4, will hold mail for guests, arranges tours and taxis; **L3** *Principado*, Paraguay 481, central, helpful, friendly; **L3** *Bisonte*, Paraguay 1207, T 394 8041, a/c, TV, bar, modern, central, good value; **A1** *Savoy*, Av Callao 181, T 372-5972, friendly and helpful; **A2** *Victory*, Maipú 880, T 314-0655, clean, a/c, modern, heating, TV, comfortable, front rooms noisy, luggage storage unreliable; **A3** *Plaza Roma*, Lavalle 110, breakfast incl, rec; **B** *Central Argentino*, Av del Libertador 174, T 312-6742, secure, clean, near Retiro stations, rec; **A1** *Embajador*, Pellegrini 1181, T 393 9485, good; **A3** *Goya*, Suipacha 748, T 322 9269, with bath, a/c, quiet, clean, nr Buquebus; **A2** *Eibar*, Florida 328, T 325 0969, breakfast incl, quiet, friendly, helpful, dingy, rundown.

A3 *San Antonio*, Paraguay 372, T 312 5381, with bath, nice atmosphere, garden, clean, rec; **A3** *Regidor*, Tucumán 451, T 393 9615, a/c, clean, breakfast incl, rec; **L3** *Lafayette*, Reconquista 546, T 393 9081; **B** *Central Córdoba*, San Martín 1021, T 312-8524, very central, clean, helpful, quiet, good value, will arrange transport to Ezeiza airport, US$35; **A3** *Promenade*, MT de Alvear 444, T 312-5681, 3-star, no charge for credit cards, breakfast extra, helpful, stores luggage, rec; **A2** *Regis*, Lavalle 813, T 327-2613, good value, nice atmosphere, quiet at back; **A2** *Sarmiento Palace*, Sarmiento 1953, T 953 3404, clean, comfortable, English spoken, rec; **B** *Orleans*, Callao 680, clean, small rooms, safe and friendly; **A3** *Gran Hotel de la Paix*, Rivadavia 1187, T 383 7140, old but good, clean, large rooms; *Majestic*, Libertad 121, T 351-949, Subte Lima, colonial, very clean, good value, breakfast incl, street facing rooms noisy; **A3** *Gran Hotel Hispano*, Av de Mayo 861, T 342-3472, spacious, clean, pleasant patio, stores luggage; **A3** *Astoria*, Av de Mayo 916, friendly, very clean; **C** *Marbella*, Av Corrientes 3193, T 887118, modernized, clean, friendly, quiet, breakfast pricey, fans, English spoken, highly rec, no credit cards; **A3** *Mundial*, Av de Mayo 1298, T 383 0011, with bath, clean, comfortable; **A2** *Orense*, Mitre 1359, good service, cooking facilities, basic, rec; **A2** *Deauville*, Talcahuano 1253, T 811 5732, a/c, restaurant and bar, garage, rec; **A3** *Super*, Gallo 1637, nr Av Santa Fe (Subte D, Agüero), T 824 1021, out of centre, a/c, pleasant.

B *Tres Sargentos*, Tres Sargentos 345, T 312 6081, clean, secure, modernized in 1994-95, new bathrooms, good value; **D** *Micki*, Talcahuano 362, T 371-2376, clean, no a/c, basic, good value; *Sportsman*, Rivadavia 1426, near Plaza Congreso, T 381-8021/2, clean, old fashioned, cheaper without bath, rec (10% discount for ISIC and youth card holders); **B** *Chile*, Av de Mayo 1297, T 383-7877, clean, friendly, noisy; **C** *La Argentina*, Av de Mayo 860, with bath, clean, friendly, central, very noisy; *Maipú*, Maipú 735, popular, hot water, clean, friendly, basic, stores

luggage, laundry facilities, T 322-5142, rec; **B Uruguay**, Tacuarí 83, T 334 2788, central, clean, friendly, good value, rec; **A3 Ayacucho Palace**, Ayacucho 1408, T 806 0611, 10 mins from centre bus 10, T 806 0611, 2 star, better value than central hotels, rec; **C Hispano Argentino**, Catamarca 167, T 975 543, some rooms with bath, clean, quiet, convenient; **A2 Ecuador**, Adolfo Alsina 2820, nr Plaza Once, T 956-0533, rec; **C Gran Vía**, Sarmiento 1450, T 371-5763, with bath, clean, friendly; **B Aguirre**, Aguirre 1041, T 773-5027, clean, safe. **B Versalles**, Arenales 1394, T 811-5214, W of Av 9 de Julio, friendly, basic, clean, shower, no breakfast, fine staircase and mirrors; **C Central**, Alsina 1693, with bath.

C range: **Frossard**, Tucumán 686, T 322-1811, inexpensive, hot showers, but not quiet (10% discount to ISIC members); **O'Rei**, Lavalle 733, T 393-7186, basic, central, gloomy, unfriendly, popular; **Bahía**, H Yrigoyen 3062, hot showers, pleasant, clean, safe, central but noisy (10% discount to ISIC members), rec; **Sarmiento**, Sarmiento 1162, T 350305, clean, central, popular, back rooms quieter, good value; **Vila Seca**, Av de Mayo 776, T 340-952, basic, friendly; **Petit Mitre**, B Mitre 4315, T 981-7768, offers 10% discount to ISIC and youth card holders; **Ceballos Palace**, Virrey Ceballos 261, 2 blocks from Congreso, T 372 7636, with bath, safe (next to police HQ). **Bolívar**, in Bolívar (San Telmo), with bath, clean; **Mediterráneo**, Rodríguez Peña 149, T 476 2852, with bath, basic, central, helpful, safe, stores luggage, limited cooking facilities, fridge, some rooms are dark, rec; **Plaza**, Rivadavia 1691, friendly, T 40-9747, many cheap hotels on Calle 25 de Mayo, none under US$15, all dirty.

Youth Hostel, Brasil 675 near Constitución station (Subte C from bus terminal, last stop), T 362-9133, E pp with YHA card (ISIC card accepted), incl breakfast, sheets provided, hot water 24 hrs, clean, basic, rec, no cooking facilities, cheap meals, doors closed 1200-1800 and from 0200, single women not admitted. Women should be aware that they could attract unwelcome attention near Constitución station as prostitutes operate there. New **Youth Hostel Del Aguila**, Espinosa 1628, E pp, hot water, cooking and laundry facilities, T 581-6663 (buses 24, 105, 106, 109, 146), rec.

Apartments   Contracts are usually for at least one year and owners will demand a guarantor or a deposit covering at least 6 months rent (security or cash). One agent is Sr Aguilar, Florida 520, 3°-314, T 322-4074. An agency which arranges sharing apartments (often with senior citizens), is Martha Baleiron, Esmeralda 1066, 5°"F", T 311 9944. US$50 fee if an apartment is found, US$10 if not. All agencies should provide contracts which should be read carefully. To rent flats on a daily basis try **Edificios Esmeralda**, Marcelo T de Alvear 842, T 311-3929, cleaning incl. Facilities for up to 6 persons; also **Edificio Suipacha**, Suipacha 1235, T/F 322-6685, US$120 per day. Also **Aspen Apartment Hotel**, Esmeralda 933, T 313-9011, US$136 per day; **Edificio Lemonde**, San Martín 839, T 313-2032, rec, though apartments overlooking road are noisy; **Residencial Trianon**, Callao 1869, T 812-3335, US$75-85 per day.

NB   All the rates quoted are subject to alteration. It should be noted that for the most part they are the basic or minimum rates. Room tax is 15% and is not always incl in the price. Check when booking into a hotel whether breakfast is incl or not. Air conditioning is a must in high summer, but be prepared for frequent power cuts. Many of the cheaper hotels in the central area give large reductions on the daily rate for long stays. Hotels with red-green lights or marked **Albergue Transitorio** are hotels for homeless lovers (for stays of 1½-2 hrs).

Camping   About 15 km out at Lomas de Zamora, US$3 pp per night, incl swimming pool, take bus 141 from Plaza Italia to Puente La Noria then No 540 to Villa Albertini which passes the entrance; information on all sites is available from the Automóvil Club Argentino and from the national tourist information office, which has a free booklet, *1ra Guía Argentina de*

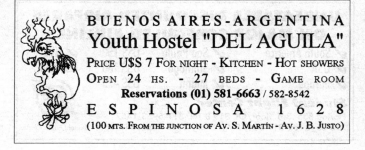

Campamentos.

Good camping equipment and fuel from Fugate (no sign), Gascón 238 (off Rivadavia 4100 block), T 982-0203, also repairs equipment. Outside Mountain Equipment, Donado 4660, T 541-2084, and Acampar, H Yrigoyen 2835, T 783-0209. Munor, H Yrigoyen 283, Martínez, and Panamericana y Paraná, Martínez (Shopping Unicenter, 3rd level). Good camping stores also at Guatemala 5908 and 5451. Camping gas available at Mitre 111, Todo Gas, Paraná 550, and El Pescador, Paraguay y Libertad. Every kind of battery (incl for Petzl climbing lamps) at Callao 373. Cacique Camping manufacture camping equipment and clothing; their two shops: Arenales 1435, Barrio Norte, and San Lorenzo 4220, Munro, Provincia Buenos Aires, T 762 0261, F 756 1392 also sell the *South American Handbook*.

Restaurants "The Buenos Aires Herald" publishes a handy *Guide to Good Eating in Buenos Aires* (with a guide to local wines) by Dereck Foster. There is also *El Libro de los Restaurantes de Buenos Aires*, published annually, describing the city's major restaurants. Eating out in Buenos Aires is very good but is getting more expensive, especially in the posher places which charge in dollars. In 1995 good restaurants were charging US$30 and up pp; more modest places were charging US$20-25 pp. **NB** In many mid to upper range restaurants, lunch is far cheaper than dinner. Lunch or dinner in a normal restaurant cost US$7-12 (cutlet, salad, ¼ of table wine, dessert); a portion at a *comidas para llevar* (take away) place cost US$2.50-3.50. Many cheaper restaurants are *tenedor libre*, eat as much as you like for a fixed price.

The following list, for reasons of space, not quality, gives only those restaurants easily accessible for people staying in the city centre. In the banking district, between Av Corrientes and Plaza de Mayo: *Clark's*, Sarmiento 645, in old English outfitter's shop (also at Junín 1777), well cooked food, very expensive, busy, fish and lamb specialities (set lunch very good value); *Bolsa de Comercio*, 25 de Mayo 359, downstairs at the Stock Exchange, good but expensive; *London Grill*, Reconquista 455, British, busy, famous for roast beef and turkey curries; *El Pulpo*, Tucumán 400, seafood, great variety, big portions; *Sabot*, 25 de Mayo 756, good business lunches; *Brizzi*, Lavalle 445, business lunches, good and worth the price; *Blab*, Florida 325, sole, veal, pork specialities; *La Pipeta*, San Martín 498, serving for 30 years, closed Sun; *La Estancia*, Lavalle 941, popular with business people, excellent grills and service, expensive (US$30-40); *La Casona del Nonno*, Lavalle 827, popular, *parrilla* and pasta; *ABC*, Lavalle 545, traditional, good value if a bit dull; *El Palacio de la Papa Frita*, Lavalle 735 and 954, Corrientes 1612, 10% discount for ISIC and youth card holders; *Emporio de las Papas Fritas*, Maipú 431, good *parrillas*, good value; *La Rural*, Suipacha 453, rec for *parrillada* and *bife de lomo* but expensive, English-speaking head waiter is excellent; *Pizzería Roma*, Lavalle 800, cheap and good quality, delicious spicy *empanadas* and *ñoquis*, good breakfasts; *Los Inmortales*, Lavalle 746, specializes in pizza, also good. There are other locations; some serve *à la carte* dishes which are plentiful, and are open from 1500-2000 when most other restaurants are closed. *El Figón de Bonilla*, rustic style, L N Alem 673, good, another branch at Junín 1721; *Los Troncos*, Suipacha 732, good grills, expensive; *Catalinas*, Reconquista 875, seafood (very expensive though). A few blocks from this district: *El Aljibe*, at *Sheraton*, smoked salmon, tournedos Rossini, baby beef; *Dolli*, Av del Libertador 312, nr Retiro, very good food, fairly expensive; *La Chacra*, Córdoba 941 between Suipacha and 9 de Julio, expensive but good; *Bice*, Av Dávila 192, mostly Italian, good, about US$50 pp.

Walking up Avenida Quintana, you reach La Recoleta cemetery; on the corner is *La Biela* (see **Tea Rooms**, etc, below) and, opp, *Café de la Paix*. Turning left, towards Av Las Heras: *Gato Dumas*, Junín 1745, expensive but has good fixed price menus; *La Bianca*, Junín 1769, very good value for BsAs, lunch US$16 pp; *Harper's*, Junín 1773; *Hippopotamus*, Junín 1787, dinner expensive, good value executive lunch; *Munich Recoleta*, Junín 1871, good steaks, pleasant atmosphere, US$20 pp, no credit cards. On Roberto M Ortiz: *Lola*, No 1805, good pasta, lamb and fish but expensive; *Don Juan*, No 1827; *La Tasca de Germán*, No 1863, highly rec, European. Nearby, 2 blocks from Recoleta towards Av Callao, *Au Bec Fin*, Vicente López 1827, reservations needed, open 2000-0200 daily. In the San Telmo area: *El Sabor Escondido*, Cochabamba 435, good and reasonably priced; *Calle de Angeles*, Chile 318, nice setting in an old, covered street, high standards; *El Comité*, Carlos Calvo 375, good, but very dear; *El Repecho de San Telmo*, Carlos Calvo 242, excellent, expensive, reserve in advance (T 362-5473). For ice cream, *Sumo*, Independencia y Piedras. The Costanera along the river front is lined with little eating places: *El Rancho Inn* is best, try also *Happening* and *Los Años Locos*, good beef, *parrilla*, cold buffet. *Bulls and Bears*, Av R Obligado (Costanera Norte) s/n y J Salguero, very good grill, take colectivo 33 from Retiro or on LN Alem, or take taxi; in same area, but more elegant and more expensive is *Clo Clo*, La Pampa y Costanera, reservation required. Typical *parrilla* at *Rodizio*, Costanera Norte, opp Coconor, far end of Aeroparque, self-service and waiter service, other branches, eg Av Callao y Juncal, good value, popular.

Near the Teatro Colón: *Tomo Uno*, Carlos Pellegrini 521 (*Hotel Panamericano*), expensive, trout, mignon, shrimp, home-made pasta, closed Sun; *Posta del Gaucho*, Pellegrini 625, accepts Visa; *Edelweiss*, Libertad 432, tuna steaks, pasta, grill, expensive and famous; *La Emiliana*, Av Corrientes 1443, excellent, rec. By Congreso: *La Cabaña*, Entre Ríos 436, old tavern style, excellent food, pricey (US$40); *Quorum*, Combate de los Pozos 61, behind Congress, popular with politicians.

Typical Boca restaurants on Necochea, but check the hygiene. There are several others in the same street. They all serve antipasto, pasta and chicken; no point in looking for beef here. All bands are loud. The seafood restaurant *La Barca*, on river bank near Avellaneda bridge, rec; also rec for seafood and good value, *Viejo Puente*, Almirante Brown 1499. *El Pescadito*, P de Mendoza 1483, rec for pasta and seafood.

Other recommendations: *Pippo*, Montevideo 341, large pasta house, good simple food, very popular, also at Paraná 356; *Chiquilín*, Montevideo 321, pasta and meat, good value; *Nazarenas*, Reconquista 1132, good for beef, expensive, rec; *El Ceibal*, Av Las Heras 2379, inexpensive, very good *empanadas*; *Ostramar*, Santa Fe 3495 y Julián Alvarez (Subte station Ortiz, then walk back towards town), good quality fish; *El Salmón II*, Reconquista 1014, large portions of good food, not cheap.

Other Italian: *Broccolino*, Esmeralda 776, excellent, very popular, try *pechuguitas*; *Mama Liberata*, Maipú 642, excellent. 3 famous *pizzerías* in the centre are on Corrientes: *Banchero*, No 1298; *Las Cuartetas*, No 838, and *Los Inmortales*, No 1369, same chain as above. *Il Gatto*, Corrientes 959, popular and reasonably priced; *El Cuartito*, Talcahuano, excellent pizzas.

Swedish food at *Swedish Club*, Tacuarí 147, open to non-members. Hungarian: *Budapest*, 25 de Mayo 690, cheap. British: *The Alexandria*, San Martín 774, curries, fish and seafood, nice bar.

Vegetarian: *Granix*, Florida 126 and 467 *tenedor libre* US$8, bland but filling, lunchtime Mon-Fri. *Ever Green* is a chain of *tenedor libre* vegetarian restaurants, branches: Paraná 746, Tucumán 666, Sarmiento 1728 and Cabildo 2979; *Yin Yang*, Paraguay 858, excellent (health-food shop too, lunch only, closed Sun); *La Esquina de las Flores*, Córdoba 1599, excellent value, also good health-food shop; *Los Angeles*, Uruguay 707, US$5 for salad bar, main meal and dessert, rec; *La Huerta*, Paraguay 445, T 311-0470, macrobiotic, rec; *La Huerta II*, Lavalle 895, 2nd floor, *tenedor libre*, US$7, reasonable.

Oriental: *Chung Kiu*, Paraguay 725, Chinese, *tenedor libre*, US$6 with one drink; *La Cantina China*, Maipú 976, one of the oldest; *Nuevo Oriental*, Maipú near Lavalle, Chinese *tenedor libre*, US$6, good choice; another *tenedor libre* Chinese place on Av San Martín 1 block from Av 1B Justo, wide variety, US$6, good value; *Tsuru*, ground floor of *Sheraton*, authentic Japanese, small, rec.

Pumper-nic is a chain of rather pricey fast food restaurants. 2 *McDonalds* in the centre, one on Florida, one on Lavalle. *The Embers*, Callao 1111, fast food, 10% discount for ISIC and youth card holders. Try also restaurants in Supercoop stores at Sarmiento 1431, Lavalle 2530, Piedras y Rivadavia and Rivadavia 5708.

Cheap meals at *Los Teatros*, Talcahuano 354, good (live music 2300-0100, open 24 hrs). *Pizzalandia*, on Brasil (near Youth Hostel) serves cheap *empanadas*, *salteñas* and pizzas. Good snacks all day and night at Retiro and Constitución railway termini. For quick cheap snacks the markets are rec, eg El Retiro market on the 900 block of Av Libertador. *Tío Ivan*, Florida 142 Boston Gallery, cheap sandwich bar, 10% discount for ISIC and youth card holders; good sandwich bar at Lavalle 1610. Stalls of the Cooperadora de Acción Social offer cheap snacks, and can be found in several public areas, eg near the Recoleta. The snack bars in underground stations are also cheap. *DeliCity* bakeries, several branches, very fresh pastries, sweets, breads, authentic American donuts.

For restaurants with shows, see **Night Clubs and Folklore** below.

Tea Rooms, Cafés and Bars *Richmond*, Florida 458 between Lavalle and Corrientes, genteel (chess played between 1200-2400); well-known are the *Confitería Suiza*, Tucumán 753, and the *Florida Garden* at Florida and Paraguay. *Confitería Ideal*, Suipacha 334, old, faded, good service, cakes and snacks, rec. Many on Av Libertador in the Palermo area. *Café Querandí*, Venezuela y Chacabuco, popular with intellectuals and students, good atmosphere, well known for its Gin Fizz. *Café Piazza*, Rivadavia 1400 block, excellent coffee, pretty setting. The more bohemian side of the city's intellectual life is centred on Avenida Corrientes, between Cerrito and Callao, where there are many bars and coffee shops, such as *La Paz* (open very late, Corrientes 1599, T 46-5542, 10% discount for ISIC and youth card members). *Pub Bar Bar O*, Tres Sargentos 415, good music and prices, gives similar discount. *El Molino*, Rivadavia and Callao, popular with politicians, Belle Epoque décor, frequent art sales, good value. *Café 1234*, Santa Fe 1234, good and reasonable. *Clásica y Moderna*, Callao y Paraguay, bookshop at back, expensive but very popular, open 24 hrs. Excellent ice-cream at *Freddo*, Av Santa Fe y Callao, or Ayacucho y Quintana. Next door (Quintana y Recoleta) is café *La Biela*, restaurant and *whiskería*, one of the places to be, elegant. Similarly popular, *Café Victoria*,

Roberto M Ortiz 1865, whiskería/sandwichería, typical of the Recoleta area. On Lavalle there are *whiskerías* and *cervecerías* where one can have either coffee or exotic drinks. *Barila*, Santa Fe 2375, has excellent confectionery. *Café Tortoni*, Av de Mayo 825-9, delicious cakes, coffee, a haunt of artists, very elegant, over 100 years old, interesting *peña* evenings of poetry and music. On Sat at 2315, it becomes a 'Catedral del Jazz', with Fenix Jazz Band, US$1 entrance. *Café El Verdi*, Paraguay 406, also has live music. *Babilonia*, Guardia Vieja 3360, popular, shows, bar, music, young, rocker crowd and intellectuals; *Parakultural New Border*, Chacabuco 1072, mostly avant-garde theatre, popular; *Die Schule*, Alsina 1760, hard rock bar with avant-garde theatre. A "bohemian, bizarre" bar is *El Dorado*, H Yrigoyen 971; gay bar, *Café de Abril*, Aráoz 2300 block. Good bars in San Telmo around Plaza Dorrego, eg *El Balcón de la Plaza*, and on Humberto I. Watch whisky prices in bars: much higher than in restaurants. Most cafés serve tea or coffee plus *facturas*, or pastries, for breakfast, US$2.50-3. Bakery shops sell 10 *facturas* for US$2.

Airline Offices Aerolíneas Argentinas (AR), Calle Perú 2; reservations and enquiries, T 393-5122, reservations 362-5008/6008. **Austral Líneas Aéreas**, Corrientes 485, T 49-9011/325-0505. Líneas Aéreas del Estado (LADE), Calle Perú 714, T 361-0278/0853, erratic schedules, uniformed office. Líneas Aéreas Privadas Argentinas (LAPA), Av Santa Fe 1970, T 812-3322 (reservations), or Aeroparque Puente Aéreo section, T 772-9920, cheapest fare to main tourist centres. AeroPerú, Santa Fe 840, T 311-6079. **Varig**, Florida 630, T 329-9201. **Lan Chile**, Paraguay 609 Piso 1, T 311-5334, 312-8161 for reconfirmations. See **Introduction and Hints**, or Brazil chapter for Mercosur Airpass.

Banks and Exchange Most banks charge very high commission especially on cheques (as much as US$10). Banks open Mon-Fri 1000-1500, be prepared for long delays. US dollar bills are often scanned electronically for forgeries, while cheques are sometimes very difficult to change and you may be asked for proof of purchase. American Express cheques are less of a problem than Thomas Cook. Practices are constantly changing. Lloyds Bank (BLSA) Ltd, corner of Reconquista and Bartolomé Mitre, Visa cash advances provided in both US dollars and pesos. It has 10 other branches in the city, and others in Greater Buenos Aires. **Royal Bank of Canada**, corner of Florida and JD Perón; branch at Av Callao 291. **Citibank**, B Mitre 502, changes only Citicorps TCs, no commission; branch at Florida 746. **First National Bank of Boston**, Florida 99. **Bank of America**, JD Perón y San Martín changes Bank of America TCs am only, into US$ at very high commission; branch at Paraguay 901 doesn't take American Express or Thomas Cook cheques. Banco Tornquist, Mitre 531, Crédit Lyonnais agents, advance cash on visa card. **Banco Holandés**, Florida 361. **Deutsche Bank**, B Mitre 401, changes Thomas Cook cheques, both give cash advances. Banco Roberts, 25 de Mayo 258, changes Thomas Cook without commission. Thomas Cook rep, **Fullers**, Esmeralda 1000 y MT de Alvear. American Express offices are at the corner of Arenales 707 y Maipú, by Plaza San Martín, T 312-0900, where you can apply for a card, get financial services and change Amex TCs (1000-1500 only, no commission into US$ or local cash). **Client Mail** in same building, Mon-Fri 0900-1800, Sat 0900-1300. **Mastercard**, Hipólito Yrigoyen 878 (US$500 limit for cash advance), or **Deutsche Bank**, Mitre 401; Mastercard ATMs (look for Link-Mastercard/Cirrus) at several locations, mostly Banco Nacional del Lavoro.

There are many *casas de cambio*, some of which deal in TCs; most are concentrated around San Martín and Corrientes (*Cambio Topaz*, No 1394-1400, recently rec, also *Casa Piano*, San Martín 345-347, changes TCs into pesos or US$ cash for 2-3% commission, *Cambios Trade Travel*, San Martín 967, 3% commission on TCs, and *Exprinter*, Suipacha 1107); open from Mon-Fri 1000-1600, Sat closed. Many *cambios* will exchange US$ TCs for US$ cash at commissions varying from 1.25 to 3%. If all *cambios* closed, try Mercadería de Remate de Aduana, Florida 8, or Eves, Tucumán 702, open until 1800 (but count your change). On Sat, Sun and holidays, cash may be exchanged in the *cambio* in some of the large supermarkets (eg *Carrefour*, Paseo Alcorta Shopping Center, open daily 1000-2200). There is no service charge on notes, only on cheques. Major credit cards usually accepted but surcharges were common in 1993/4. General Master Card office at Hipólito Yrigoyen 878, open 0930-1800, T 331-1022/2502/2549; another branch at Florida 274 (open 1000-1730). Visa, Corrientes 1437, 2nd floor, T 954-3333/2000, for stolen cards. Other South American currencies can only be exchanged in *casas de cambio*.

Cultural and Trade Associations Argentine Association of English Culture, Suipacha 1333 (library for members only); **British Chamber of Commerce**, Av Corrientes 457; British Council, MT de Alvear 590, Piso 4, T 311-9814/7519, F 311-7747 (open 1000-1200, 1430-1630). Goethe Institut, Av Corrientes 311, German library (open 1300-1900 exc Wed, and 1000-1400 first Sat of month) and newspapers, free German films shown, cultural programmes, German language courses; in the same building, upstairs, is the German Club, Corrientes 327. Alliance Française, Córdoba 946. USA Chamber of Commerce, Diagonal

Norte 567; **US Information Library** (Biblioteca Lincoln), Florida 935, reference and lending library, free, no identification needed, but take passport to become a member, on first five days of each month only, fixed address needed (closed Sat, Sun). **St Andrew's Society**, Perú 352.

Clubs **American Club**, Viamonte 1133, facing Teatro Colón, temporary membership available; **American Women's Club**, Av Córdoba 632, 11 piso. **English Club**, 25 de Mayo 586, T 311-9121, open for lunch only; temporary membership available to British business visitors. The American and English Clubs have reciprocal arrangements with many clubs in USA and UK. **Swedish Club**, Tacuari 147. **Organización Hebrea Argentina Macabi**, Tucumán 3135, T 962-0947, social and sporting club for conservative Jews.

Embassies and Consulates All open Mon-Fri unless stated otherwise. **Bolivian Consulate**, Belgrano 1670, 2nd floor, T 381-0539, open 0900-1400, visa while you wait. **Brazilian Consulate**, Carlos Pellegrini 1363, 5th floor, open Mon-Fri, 0930-1400, visa takes 1 day, T 394-5260/5264. **Paraguayan Consulate**, Las Heras 2545, 0900-1400, T 322-6536. **Peruvian Consulate**, San Martín 691, 6th floor, T 311-7582, 0900-1400, visa US$5, takes 1 day. **Uruguayan Consulate**, Ayacucho 1616, open 1000-1800, T 821-6031, visa takes up to 1 week. **Chilean Embassy**, Tagle 2762, T 394-6582, Mon-Thur 0930-1330, 1530-1830, Fri 0915-1430. **Ecuadorean Embassy**, Quintana 585, 9th and 19th floors, T 804-6408.

US **Embassy and Consulate General**, Cerviño 4320, T 777-4533/7007, 0900-1730, consulate, visas 0800-1100, calls between 1500 and 1700 (US Embassy Residence, Av Libertador 3502). **Australian Embassy**, Av Santa Fe 846 (Swissair Building), T 312-6841, Mon-Thur 0830-1230, 1330-1730, Fri 0830-1315. **Canadian Embassy**, Tagle 2828, T 312-9081. **South African Embassy**, Marcelo T de Alvear 590, 7 piso, T 311-8991/7, Mon-Thur 0900-1300, 1400-1630, Fri 0900-1330. **Israeli Embassy**, Av de Mayo 701, piso 9, T 342-6653. **Japanese Embassy**, Paseo Colón 275, 9 y 11 piso, T 343-2561, 0900-1300, 1430-1800.

Austrian Embassy, French 3671, T 802-1400, 0900-1200. **Belgian Embassy**, Defensa 113-8, T 331-0066/69, 0800-1300. **British Embassy**, Luis Agote 2412/52 (near corner Pueyrredón & Guido), T 803-7070, open 0915-1215, 1415-1615. **Danish Embassy**, L N Alem 1074, 9 piso, T 312-6901/6935, 0900-1230, 1500-1730. **Finnish Embassy**, Av Santa Fe 846, 5 piso, T 312-0600/70, Mon-Thur 0830-1700, Fri 0830-1200. **French Embassy**, Av Santa Fe 846, 3 piso, T 312-2425, 0900-1200. **German Embassy**, Villanueva 1055, Belgrano, T 771-5054/9, 0900-1200. **Greek Embassy**, R S Peña 547, 4 piso, T 342-4958, 1000-1300. **Irish Embassy**, Suipacha 1380, 2 piso, T 325-8588, 1000-1230. **Italian Embassy**, Billinghurst 2577, consulate at MT de Alvear 1149, T 325-6132, 0900-1300. **Netherlands Embassy**, Edificio Buenos Aires, Av de Mayo 701, 19° piso, T 334-4000, 0900-1200, 1300-1530. **Norwegian Embassy**, Esmeralda 909, 3 piso B, T 312-2204, 0900-1430. **Spanish Embassy**, Mariscal Ramón Castilla 2720, esq Av del Libertador 2075, T 811-0078, 0900-1330, 1500-1730. **Swedish Embassy**, Corrientes 330, 3 piso, T 311-3088/9, T 1000-1200. **Swiss Embassy**, Av Santa Fe 846, 12 piso, T 311-6491, open 0900-1200.

Night Clubs and Folklore Tango: *El Caminito de San Telmo*, Balcarce, good show costing US$25 incl two drinks, best atmosphere at weekends; nearby are *Casablanca*, Balcarce 668, T 331-4621, excellent show, costing US$40 pp incl drinks, and *La Ventana*, Balcarce 425, Mon-Sat shows at 2230, T 331-3648/334-1314, very touristy but very good show, US$50 for show, dinner and unlimited wine, through an agency, 20% discount for ISIC and youth card holders, from Asatej office (see **Useful Addresses** below). Tango shows also at *Bar Sur*, Estados Unidos 299, and *Antigua Tasca de Cuchilleros*, Carlos Calvo 319, T 362-3811/28, pleasant surroundings, show US$20, show and dinner, US$32, both in San Telmo. Good show also at *La Veda*, Florida 1, reasonable meal with wine and other drinks. *Viejo Buzón*, Corrientes y Rodríguez Peña, good tango, no dinner but plenty of dancing, locals and tourists; *Café Mozart*, Esmeralda 754, tango, jazz, theatre, no dinner; *La Casa de Aníbal Troilo*, Carlos Calvo 2540, good singers and bands, for tourists; *Tango Danza*, José María Moreno 351, Fri, Sat, Sun, from 2200; *Salón La Argentina*, Rodríguez Peña 361, Thur-Sun, 2200, more modern-style tango. *Michelangelo*, Balcarce 433, T 334-4321, impressive setting, concert café in an old converted monastery, various types of music incl tango and folklore, Tues-Sun. The best affordable tango bars are in the Boca, but it is increasingly difficult to find authentic tango for locals; most are tourist-oriented. Four rec places are *Café Homero*, J A Cabrera 4946, Palermo, *Tarquino*, Brasil y Perú, *Italia Unita*, JD Perón 2535 and *Tortoni* (see below). Authentic tango at Cochabamba 444, pay US$5 when leaving, young crowd, rec; lessons also available. *La Cumparsita*, Chile 302, T 361-6880, authentic tango, US$50 for 2 incl wine; *Mesón Español*, Rodríguez Peña 369, T 35-0516, good folk music show and good food; *Galería Tango Argentino*, Boedo 722 y Independencia, T 93-1829/7527, Wed-Sat, less touristy than others, dinner (usually), show and dancing, has dancers and tango lessons (Mon-Fri, 1800-2100), well-known bands. *Paladium*, San Martín 954, tango/bolero dance hall; *Volver*, Corrientes 837, Mon-Fri, 1800-2100. Andean music at *Ollantaytambo*, Estados Unidos 541. Tango lessons at *Champagne Tango*, Rio de Janeiro 387, Tues, Fri, Sun.

Recommended night club/discos incl *Hippopotamus*, Junín 1787, Recoleta, French restaurant (lunch and dinner), fashionable night club; *Le Club*, small and exclusive, Quintana 111; *Cemento*, Estados Unidos 700 block, disco with live shows, usually hard rock and heavy metal, popular with younger crowd, as are *La City*, Alvarez Thomas y El Cano, and *Halley*, Corrientes 2020, heavy metal and hard rock. Also rec: *Mama Baker*, Santa Fe 2800; *Cinema*, Av Córdoba 4633, inside a former cinema; *El Dorado*, Hipólito Yrigoyen y 9 de Julio, interesting, different; *El Nacional*, Reconquista 915, in tunnels formerly used for smuggling; *El Angel*, Corrientes 1768 y Callao; *Club Coco Bahiano*, Carlos Calvo y Balcarce, live Brazilian music, crowded and friendly, open Fri and Sat till 0700, entry incl one drink US$9, rec. *Cachaça Tropical*, on Brasil (1 block from Plaza Constitución), big disco with Latin American music, good meeting place. *Roxy*, Rivadavia 1900 block, rock and roll, reggae, rec; *New York City*, Alvarez Thomas 1391, T 552-4141, young and middle-aged clientele, popular, chic, well-established. On the Costanera: *El Cielo*, on riverside, techno music popular with politicians, models, actors, etc; *Caix*, mega-disco with panoramic view of the river, young, trendy. *Age of Communication*, M T de Alvear 400 block, for the beautiful, young and rich. Gay discos: *Bunker*, Anchorena 1170, Thur-Sun; *Experiment*, C Pellegrini 1085, open nightly; *Enigma*, Esmeralda y Paraguay, also for heterosexuals. Some discos serve breakfast for additional charge at entry. Generally it is not worth going to discos before 0230 at weekends. Dress is usually smart.

Bars and restaurants in San Telmo district, with live music (usually beginning 2330-2400): *Players*, Humberto I 528 (piano bar); *Samovar de Rasputin*, Almte Brown, edge of Parque Lezama, good blues, dinner and/or show. Cover charges between US$5 and US$20, or more.

Jazz: *El Subsuelo*, JD Perón 1372, good bands featured; *Oliverio*, Paraná 328, excellent live jazz features the great Fats Fernández, Fri-Sat 2330 and 0100; *Café Tortoni*, Av de Mayo 829, T 342-4328, traditional jazz downstairs, Fri-Sun 2315, Fri tango concert 2130, rec, entry US$6; *Clásica y Moderna* Callao 893, expensive but classy, jazz usually on Wed night, no shows weekends.

Bailantas are music and dance halls where they play popular styles which for years have been despised as "low class". They are now fashionable among the upper classes. A popular place is *Fantástico*, Rivadavia 3400 block; also *Terremoto Bailable*, Paraguay y Thames; *Metropolis*, Santa Fe at Plaza Italia. For salsa: *El Club*, Yerbal 1572, friendly, for all ages, not trendy, all welcome; *La Salsera*, Yatay 961, highly regarded salsa place.

Cultural Events The Luna Park stadium holds pop/jazz concerts, ballet and musicals, at Bouchard 465, nr Correo Central, T 311-5100, free parking at Corrientes 161. Check "Musimundo" record shop on Santa Fe or Florida for latest information on rock concerts. Tickets to see big names can be very reasonable. Teatro Alvear, Corrientes 1659, T 46-9470, has free concerts Fri at 1300, usually Orquesta de Tango de BsAs. Tango Week, leading up to National Tango Day (11 Dec), has free events all over the city; details posted around the city and at tourist offices. Teatro Municipal General San Martín, Av Corrientes 1530, organizes many cultural activities of which quite a few are free of charge, incl concerts Sat and Sun evenings; the theatre's Sala Leopoldo Lugones shows international classic films, Sat-Sun, US$2. Free concerts at ProMusica music shop, Florida 638; schedule in window. Centro Cultural General San Martín, Sarmiento 1551, and the Centro Cultural de Recoleta, Junín 1930, next to the Recoleta cemetery have many free activities. Free lunchtime seasonal concerts on the lower ground floor of the Galería Pacífico on Florida. Also worth a visit for the architecture and murals. Theatre ticket agency, La Cartelera, Lavalle 828. Look for details in main newspapers and weekly paper *La Maga*, US$3 from news stands. **NB** From mid-Dec to end-Feb most theatres and concert halls are closed.

Cinemas The selection of films is as good as anywhere else in the world and details are listed daily in all main newspapers. Films are shown uncensored. Tickets best booked early afternoon to ensure good seats (average price US$7 in 1995). Tickets obtainable, sometimes cheaper, from ticket agencies (*carteleras*), such as *Vea Más*, Paseo La Plaza, Corrientes 1600, local 19 (the cheapest), *Cartelera*, Lavalle 742, T 322 9263, *Teatro Lorange*, Corrientes 1372, T 372-7386, and *Cartelera Baires*, Corrientes 1372, local 25. Some cinemas offer 50% discounts on Wed. Almost all foreign films are shown with subtitles. Many cinemas on Lavalle, around Av Santa Fe and Callao and in Belgrano (Av Cabildo and environs). Film club at *Faro Gandhi*, Montevideo 453 on Fri and Sat evenings, showing old, foreign and "art" films, US$1.50, open to non-members. Free films at Asociación Bancaria, Sarmiento 337/341, T 313-9306/ 312-5011/17, once a month (Wed); old films at Cine en la Cinemateca Argentina, Sarmiento 2255, T 952-2170 (half price of other cinemas, plus 20% discount for ISIC holders), and at Sarmiento 2150, T 48-2170. ISIC holders also entitled to discounts at Cine IFT Sala 1, Boulogne Sur Mer 549

(50%). On Sat nights many central cinemas have *trasnoches*, late shows starting at 0100.

Urgent Medical Service (day and night) (Casualty ward: *Sala de guardia*) T 34-4001/4. *British Hospital*, Perdriel 74, T 23-1081, US$14 a visit; cheap dental treatment at Av Caseros y Perdriel 76. *German Hospital*, Pueyrredón 1658, between C Berutti and C Juncal, T 821-7661. Both maintain first-aid centres (*centros asistenciales*) as do the other main hospitals. *Children's Hospital* (Ricardo Gutiérrez), Bustamante 1399, T 86-5500. *Centro Gallego*, Belgrano 2199, T 47-3061. *Hospital Juan A Fernández*, Cerviño y Bulnes, good, medical attention. If affected by pollen, asthma sufferers can receive excellent treatment at the *University Hospital de Clínicas José de San Martín*, Córdoba 2351, T 821-6041, US$6 per treatment.

Innoculations *Centro Médico Rivadavia*, S de Bustamante 2531, Mon-Fri, 0730-1900 (bus 38, 59, 60 or 102 from Plaza Constitución), or *Guardia de Sanidad del Puerto*, Mon and Thur, 0800-1200, at Av Ing Huergo 690, T 334-1875, free, bus 20 or 22 from Retiro, no appointment required (typhus, cholera, Mon-Fri 0800-1200; yellow fever, Tues-Thur 1400-1600, but no hepatitis; take syringe and needle, particularly for insulin and TB). Buy the vaccines in *Laboratorio Biol*, Uriburu 159, or in larger chemists. *Hospital Rivadavia*, Calles Las Heras y Tagle, for polio inoculation. Free. Any hospital with an infectology department will do hepatitis A.

Language Schools *Verbum Language School*, Lavalle 357, 3°C2, T/F 393-8228, frequently rec, accommodation and social events offered. *Instituto de Lengua Española para Extranjeros*, Lavalle 1619, 7th C and 3rd E, T 375-0730, F 864-4942, US$15 per hour, rec by individuals and organizations alike. *Bromley Institute*, Paraná 641, 1A, T 40-4113, courses in Spanish, Portuguese, French, English, high standards, well-regarded, rec. Free Spanish classes at *Escuela Presidente Roca*, Libertad 581, T 35-2488, Mon-Fri, 1945-2145 (basic level only). Spanish classes also at *Instituto del Sur*, Av Callao 433, 9 S, T/F 49-8421, individual lessons, cheap; *Estudio Buenos Aires*, San Martín 881, 4° piso, T 312-8936, owner also lets out rooms; *Link Educational Services*, Arenales 2565, piso 5° B, T 825-3017. *Universidad de Buenos Aires*, 25 de Mayo, offers cheap, coherent courses. *AmeriSpan Unlimited* has an affiliated school; contact PO Box 40513, Philadelphia, PA 19106, USA, T 800-879-6640 or, outside N America 215-985-4522, F 215-985-4524, E-mail info@amerispan.com. For other schools teaching Spanish, and for private tutors look in *Buenos Aires Herald* in the classified ads. Enquire also at Asatej (see **Useful Addresses**).

Schools which teach English to Argentines include: International House, Pacheco de Melo 2555, British-owned and -run; Berlitz, Av de Mayo 847 (low rates of pay); Santiago del Estero 324; American Teachers, Viamonte y Florida, T 393-3331. There are many others; vacancies are advertised in the *Buenos Aires Herald*. Before being allowed to teach, you must offically have a work permit (difficult to obtain) but schools may offer casual employment without one (particularly to people searching for longer-term employment); if unsure of your papers, ask at Migraciones (address below). There are many "coordinadoras", usually women, who do not have an institute but run English "schools" out of their homes by hiring native English-speakers and sending them out on jobs. Pay varies between 10 and 25 pesos, depending on where you teach and on negotiation; the pay is usually better than in a fixed institute. Adverts occasionally appear in the *Herald*, but most contacts are by word of mouth.

Laundries *Tintorería Constitución*, Av Santiago del Estero 1572 (suits only). Many dry cleaners and many launderettes, eg Marcelo T de Alvear 861, in centre; Junín 15 y Rivadavia, Mon-Sat 0800-2100; Junín 529 y Lavalle; Rivadavia 1340; *Laverap*, Paraguay 888 y Suipacha, Córdoba 466, Local 6, T 312-5460, US$6.50 per load (10% discount to ISIC and youth card holders, also at Brasil y Bolívar and Rodríguez Peña 100-200), Arenales 894, Solís nr A Alsina (cheaper). The laundry at Brasil 554 costs US$2.50 per load, more for valet service. *Marva*, Juan D Perón 2000 y Ayacucho.

Libraries Harrods (2nd floor) on Florida. See also Biblioteca Nacional, under **Museums**, and **Cultural and Trade Associations**.

General Post Office (Correo Central – now privatized, Correos Argentinos, improved service), corner of Sarmiento and LN Alem, Mon-Fri, 0800-2000. *Poste Restante* on 1st floor (US$2.25 per letter); poor reports; very limited service on Sat (closes 1400). Fax service US$5 per minute. Philatelic section open Mon-Fri 1000-1800. Centro Postal Internacional, for all parcels over 1 kg for mailing abroad, at Av Antártida Argentina, near Retiro station, open 1100 to 1700. Check both Correo Central and Centro Postal Internacional for *poste restante* (US$1.15 to collect letters).

Telecommunications The State company Entel has now been privatized and the city is split into two telephone zones, owned by Telecom and Telefónica Argentina. Av Corrientes 705 (open 24 hrs) for international phone calls, fax, public telex in basement; alternatively in Central Post Office (more expensive), also telex. Other offices at San Martín 322, on Santa Fe 1841, on Agüero/Las Heras, and at Lavalle 613. *Fichas* or *cospeles* (tokens) for calls in the city from public telephone boxes cost US$0.25, obtained at newspaper stalls, cigarette *kioskos* and Telecom or Telefónica Argentina offices. Many phones now use phone cards costing 5 and 10 pesos (break off the corner tab before using); the cards of the two companies are interchangeable. (Payphones in Telecom and Telefónica Argentina offices reportedly use 5 cent coins.) International telephone calls from hotels may incur a 40%-50% commission in addition to government tax of about the same amount. For more details see **Postage and Telephone Rates** in Information for Visitors.

NB Since privatization, many phone prefixes in the city have been changed: 34 became 342, 30 - 343, 37 - 383, 38 - 381, 59 - 581, 45 - 476 or 372 depending on location, and 47 - 951. Further changes are likely and will be indicated on the first pages of the phone directory, or dial 110 to ask the operator.

Places of Worship The **Holy Cross**, Calle Estados Unidos 3150, established by the Passionists. **St John's Cathedral** (Anglican), 25 de Mayo 282 (services, Sun 0900 in English, 1030 in Spanish), was built half at the expense of the British Government and dedicated in 1831. **St Paul's, St Peter's, St Michael and All Angels** and **St Saviour's** are Anglican places of worship in the suburbs. **St Andrew's**, Calle Belgrano 579, is one of the 8 Scottish Presbyterian churches. The **American Church**, Corrientes 718, is Methodist, built in 1863; service at 1100. **First Methodist** (American) Church, Av Santa Fe 839, Acassuso. **German Evangelical Church**, Esmeralda 162. **Swedish Church**, Azopardo 1422. The **Armenian Cathedral** of St Gregory the Illuminator at the Armenian Centre, and the **Russian Orthodox Cathedral** of The Holy Trinity (Parque Lezama) are interesting.

Synagogues The most important in Buenos Aires are the Congregación Israelita en la República Argentina, Libertad 705 (also has a small museum), and, the oldest, the Templo Israelita at Paso 423 (called the Paso Temple), traditional and conservative. An important orthodox temple is the Comunidad Israelita Ortodoxa, the seat of the rabbis of Argentina, Ecuador 530, T 862-2701. The Comunidad Betel, Av Elcano 3424, and the B'nai Tikvah, Vidal 2049, are for reformed worshippers. Congregación Emanu-El (reformed sect), Tronador 1455, take bus 140 from Av Córdoba to Alvarez Thomas block 1600, then turn right into Tronador.

Shopping Most shops close lunchtime on Sat. Visit the branches of *H Stern*, for fine jewellery at the Sheraton and Plaza Hotels, and at the International Airport. *Kelly's*, Paraguay 431, has a very large selection of reasonably-priced Argentine handicrafts in wool, leather, wood, etc. Excellent leatherwork at *LYK*, Paraguay y Maipú. *Artesanías Argentinas* (*ARAR*), at Montevideo 1386, T 812-2650, a non-profitmaking organization selling handicrafts (clothing, weaving, basketware, wooden goods etc) all with certificate of origin, expensive. *Campanera Dalla Fontana*, Reconquista 735, leather factory which is fast, efficient and reasonably priced for made-to-measure clothes. Good quality leather clothes factory at Boyacá 2030, T 582 6909 to arrange time with English speaking owner. *Aída*, Florida 670, can make a leather jacket to measure in 48 hours. *Creaciones Vartán*, Calle 97, No 2622, San Andrés (Colectivo 363), T 753-6660, good quality leather goods. *El Guasquero*, Av Santa Fe 3117, traditionally made leather goods. *Galería del Caminante*, Florida 844, has a variety of good shops with leather goods, arts and crafts, souvenirs, etc. Apart from shops on Florida and Santa Fe (especially between 1000 and 2000 blocks), Av Corrientes has many shops for men's clothes between 600 and 1000 blocks, and the shops on Arenales N of Av Santa Fe, and on Av Alvear on the way to Recoleta, have been rec. Av Cabildo in Belgrano district can be reached by 152 bus from Retiro for good shopping between 1600 and 2800 blocks. Many boutiques and places for casual clothes in Martínez suburb. *Pasaje de Defensa* is a beautifully restored colonial house containing small shops, on Defensa 791 in the San Telmo area. Calle Defensa is good for antique shops. There is a shopping mall, *Patio Bullrich*, between Av del Libertador y Posadas, at Montevideo, entrances on Posadas and Av del Libertador (No 750); boutiques are very expensive, but leather goods are of high quality. A new mall, very smart and expensive, is **Alto Palermo**, at Coronel Díaz y Santa Fe. **La Plaza Shopping Centre**, at Corrientes 1600, has a few restaurants and an open-air theatre. **Paseo Alcorta**, Av Alcorta y Salguero, 4 levels, cinemas, supermarket, stores, many cheap restaurants (take colectivo 130 from Correo Central); **Galerías Pacífico**, on Florida, between Córdoba and Viamonte, where the Bellas Artes museum used to be, is now a beautiful shopping mall with many exclusive shops and fast food restaurants in basement. Also good set-price restaurant on 2nd floor and concerts on lower-ground floor (**see Cultural Events, p 73**). **Galerías Broadway**, Florida 575, for cheap electronic goods, CDs, tapes. In the **Munro district** on Av Mitre either side of Calle Ugarte (buses, 130, 314, 41 from Av del Libertador, 50 mins) are cheap and varied fashion clothes incl jeans, fake designer labels, some secondhand. For cheap clothes and electrical goods try Mercadería de Remate de Aduana, Florida 8 (downtown).

Markets Sunday markets for souvenirs, antiques, etc: **Plaza Dorrego (San Telmo)** with food, dancers, buskers, Sun 0900-1700, on Humberto I and Defensa (entertaining, not cheap, an interesting array of "antiques"). **Feria Hippie**, in Recoleta, near cemetery, big craft and jewellery market, Sat and Sun, good street atmosphere, expensive. Also **Feria de Las Artes** (Fri, 1400-1700) on Defensa y Alsina. Sat craft, jewellery, etc market, at **Plaza Belgrano**, nr Belgrano station on Juramento, between Cuba y Obligado, 1000-2000. Handicraft markets at weekends at Parque Lezama and Plaza Italia, which also has a used book market Fri and Sat, a few stalls have English books, some stay open throughout the week. Another secondhand book market is at Plaza Lavalle in front of Tribunales, a few English titles (ask around), weekdays only. At **Parque Rivadavia**, Rivadavia 4900, around the ombú tree, records, books, magazines, stamps and coins, Sun 0900-1300, **Plazoleta Primera Junta**, Rivadavia and Centenera, books and magazines, Sat 1200-2000, Sun 1000-2000. **Parque Patricios**, Av Caseros entre Monteagudo y Pepiri, 1000-2000, antiques, books, art and stamps. **Plazoleta Santa Fe**, Santa Fe and Uriarte (Palermo) old books and magazines, same times as Primera Junta, and again, plastic arts in the **Caminito**, Vuelta de Rocha (Boca), 1000-1800. Sat market in **Plaza Centenario**, Díaz Vélez and L Marechal, 1000-2100 local crafts, good, cheap hand-made clothes. **Auction sales**: some bargains at weekday pm auctions, Edificio de Ventas, Banco de la Ciudad de Buenos Aires, Esmeralda 660. Souvenirs can be found in area around San Martín and Paraguay (not markets). Interesting market of gaucho items at Mataderos (unsafe area), bus 126 from Plaza de Mayo, 50 mins (Sun); closed in the summer.

Bookshops Many along Av Corrientes, W of Av 9 de Julio, though most have no foreign language sections. Try **Yenny** (No 571) for new English classics and **Fausto** (No 1316 and 1243) for second-hand selection. **ABC**, Av Córdoba 685 (limited selection of second-hand and best selection of new English books, good selection of German books) and Av del Libertador 13777 in Martínez suburb. **Joyce, Proust y Cía**, Tucumán 1545, 1st floor, T 40-3977, paperbacks in English, Portuguese, French, Italian, classics, language texts, etc, good prices. **Librería Rodríguez**, Sarmiento 835, good selection of English books and magazines, has another branch on Florida, 300 block; French bookshop at Calle Rivadavia 743; **Librería Goethe**, Lavalle 528, good selection of English and German books. Italian books at **Librería Leonardo**, Av Córdoba 335, also (with newspapers and magazines) **La Viscontea**, Libertad 1067. **Liberarte** has a good selection of alternative books and magazines in Spanish, international videos to rent, CDs, especially jazz and blues, concerts and shows in hall downstairs. Secondhand/exchange inside shopping arcade under Av 9 de Julio at the Obelisco, but poor stock. Also in the plaza behind the main post office (Corrientes 50). **Asatej Bookshop**, Florida 835, 1° of 104, T 312-8476, sells this Handbook "at the best price". Good bookshop at Florida 340, **El Ateneo** (basement, good selection of English books), **Kel Ediciones**, Talcahuano 1063, and Laprida 2488 in Florida suburb, also maintain a good stock of English books and sells South American Handbook. Prices at **Harrods** on Florida are lower than most. **LOLA**, Viamonte 976, 20D, T 476 0518, specializes in Latin American Natural History books. For used and rare books: **Fernández Blanco**, Tucumán 712; **Casa Figueroa**, Esmeralda 970; and **L'Amateur**, Esmeralda 882. Second-hand English language books from **British and American Benevolent Society**, Catamarca 45 (take train to Acassuso), and from **Entrelibros**, Av Cabildo 2280 and Santa Fe 2450, local 7.

Foreign newspapers at news stands on Florida, and at kiosk at Av Corrientes y Maipú.

Every Apr the Feria del Libro is held at the Centro De Exposiciones, F Alcorta y Pueyrredón, Recoleta; exhibitions, shows and books for sale in all languages.

Camera Repairs and Film Developing Film developing to international standards. There are many Kodak labs around Talcahuano. Fotospeed, Av Santa Fe 4838 (20% discount to SAHB owners!) for quality 2-hour service. For developing slides Esmeralda 444, fast service, and Kinefot, Talcahuano 244. 1-hr developing service is hard to find outside Buenos Aires. Camera repairs: several good shops on Talcahuano 100-400 blocks. Try also Casa Schwarz, Perú 989, international brands; Golden Lab, Lavalle 630, good prices for film; Horacio Calvo, Riobamba 183, all brands and variety of rare accessories, rec; fast service at Tacuarí 75; for Olympus cameras, Rodolfo Jablanca, Corrientes 2589. German spoken at Gerardo Föhse, Florida 890, fast, friendly.

Sports Association and rugby football are both played to a very high standard. Soccer fans should not miss a visit to see Boca Juniors : matches Sun 1500-1800 (depending on time of year), Wed evenings, entry US$10 (stadium open weekdays for visits). Soccer season Sep-May/Jun, with a break at Christmas; rugby season Apr-Oct/Nov. Ice-hockey is becoming popular. Cricket is played at 4 clubs in Greater Buenos Aires between Nov and Mar. Polo: the high handicap season is Oct to Dec, but it is played all year round (low season Apr-Jun). Argentina has the top polo teams; a visit to the national finals at Palermo in Nov or Dec is rec. Horse racing at Palermo and San Isidro, a large, modern race course 25 mins from the city centre by train or road, is popular throughout the year. Riding school at Palermo, US$5 an hour.

The Tigre Boat Club, founded in 1888, is open to British or American visitors for a small fee and a limited period. The leading golf clubs are the Hurlingham, Ranelagh, Ituzaingó, Lomas, San Andrés, San Isidro, Sáenz Peña, Olivos, Jockey, Campos Argentinos and Hindú Country Club; visitors wishing to play should bring handicap certificate and make telephone booking. Weekend play possible only with a member. Good hotels may be able to make special arrangements. Municipal golf course in Palermo, open to anyone at any time. Tennis, squash and paddle tennis are popular: there are 5 squash clubs. The Argentine Tennis Open is in Nov; ATP tour. There are many private clubs. For aerobics try the San Martín Club, San Martín 645, T 311-9191, or the Gimnasio Olímpico Cancillería, Esmeralda 1042, no membership required.

Motor racing: Formula 1 championship is no longer held in Argentina, but efforts are being made to restore it. There are lots of rallies, stock racing and Formula 3 competitions, mostly from Mar to mid-Dec.

Gambling Weekly lotteries. Football pools, known as *Prode*.

Chess Club Argentino de Ajedrez, Paraguay 1858, open daily, arrive after 2000; special tournament every Sat, 1800. High standards.

Tours A good way of seeing Buenos Aires and its surroundings is by BAT, Buenos Aires Tur, Lavalle 1444, T 40-2304, almost hourly departures, or Autobuses Sudamericanos (TISA), information and booking office at Bernardo de Irigoyen 1370, 1st floor, Offices 25 and 26, T 27-6591, F 26-7933, or Av Larrazábal 493, T 642 7028 (Liniers). Prices range from US$13 to US$65. Also run buses to all major South American cities. At same address is Transporte Aero Costa Atlántica (TACA), passenger charter services to Mar del Plata, Villa Gesell, Pinamar and Santa Teresita, T 26-7795. For reservations in advance for sightseeing or other tours, with a 20% courtesy discount to *South American Handbook* readers, write to Casilla de Correo No 40, Sucursal 1(B), 1401 Buenos Aires. A 3-hour city tour of Buenos Aires in English and Spanish is run by City Tours, US$12, rec, as is Eurotur (T 312-6170), in English. Some tours incl dinner and a tango show, or a gaucho *fiesta* at a ranch, eg at *Santa Susana Estancia* (excellent food and dancing, although the gaucho part is somewhat showy). Bookable through most travel agents, US$50-65.

Travel Agents Among those rec are *Exprinter*, Suipacha 1107, T 312-2519, and San Martín 170, T 331-3050, Galería Güemes (especially their 5-day, 3-night tour to Iguazú and San Ignacio Miní); *American Express*, Arenales y Maipú; *Furlong*, Perón 338, T 318-3200, Thomas Cook representatives; *ATI*, Esmeralda 561, very efficient and helpful, with branches in Brazil; *Turismo Feeling* ("don't be put off by the name") L Alem 762, T 311-9422, excellent and reliable horseback and skiing trips; *Astra Travel*, Tucumán 358, 5th floor, English spoken by director, efficient; *Versailles*, Callao 257, 13th floor N, helpful, friendly; *Turismo Flyer*, Reconquista 621, 8° piso, T 313-8224, F 312-1330, English, Dutch and German spoken, accepts credit cards, rec. *Germania*, Lavalle 414, T 393-1265/0035, excellent service (English not spoken), especially for tours to the N, branch in Salta. *Lihue Expeditions*, Maipú 926, T 311-9610, helpful with all arrangements, especially wildlife tours and *estancia* visits. *Círculos Mágicos*, Uruguay 864, 3rd floor, T 815-2803, books visits to *estancias* at competitive rates. *Eves Turismo*, Tucumán 702, T 393-6151, helpful and efficient, rec for flights; *City Service*, Florida 890, T 312-8416/9; *Travel Up*, Maipú 474, 4° piso, T 326-4648; *Folgar*, Esmeralda 961, 3° piso E, T 311-6937. *Ruta 40*, P O Box 5210, 1000 Buenos Aires, T 782-7427, F 783-5557, jointly run by Federico Kirbus, the traveller and author (see **Tourist Information** in **Information for Visitors**). English is widely spoken.

Tourist Information National office at Santa Fe 883 with maps and literature covering the whole country. Open 1000-1700, Mon-Fri; T 312-2232, 312-5550. Has a guide to campsites throughout Argentina. Other offices at Aeroparque, T 773-9891/05 and at Ezeiza, T 480-0224/0011.

There are also helpful *Casas de Turismo* for most provinces (open Mon-Fri usually, 1000-1800, depending on office, check): **Buenos Aires**, Av Callao 237, T 40-7045; others on Callao are **Córdoba** (332, T 49-4277, F 476-2725), **Chaco** (322, T 476-0961, F 49-3777), **La Rioja** (745, T 326-1140, F 812-1339), **Mendoza** (445, T 40-7301, F 49-8296). Others: **Río Negro**, Tucumán 1920, T 40-7066, F 476-2126; **Chubut**, Paraguay 876, T 311-0428, F 313-7757; **Entre Ríos**, Suipacha 844, T 313-9327, F 312-5985; **Formosa**, H Irigoyen 1429, T 381-7048, F 381-2037; **Mar del Plata**, Santa Fe 1175; **Jujuy**, Santa Fe 967, 6th floor, T 393-6096; **Misiones**, Santa Fe 989, T 322-0677, F 393-1615; **Neuquén**, JD Perón 687, T/F 326-6812; **Salta**, Diagonal Norte (Roque Sáenz Peña) 933, T 326-1314; **Santa Cruz**, 25 de Mayo 377, 1st floor, T 343-3653, F 342-1667; **Catamarca**, Córdoba 2080, T 46-6893, F 46-6892; **Corrientes**, San Martín 333, 4th floor, T 394-7432, F 394-2808; **La Pampa**, Suipacha 346, T/F 326-0511; **San Juan**, Sarmiento 1251, T 382-5580, F 382-4729; **San Luis**, Azcuénaga 1083, T/F 822-0426; **Santa Fe**, Montevideo 373, 2nd floor, T 40-1825, F 40-4610; **Santiago**

del Estero, Florida 274, T 326-2720, F 326-5915; **Tucumán**, Mitre 836, 1st floor, T 345-2495, F 345-4924; **Tierra del Fuego**, Av Santa Fe 919, T/F 322-8855; **Patagonia**, Av de Mayo 801, T 342-0101; **Villa Gesell**, B Mitre 1702, T 46-5098, F 46-5199; **Bariloche** hotel, flat and bungalow service in Galería at Florida 520, room 116 (cheapest places not listed). Calafate bookings for *Refugio and Autocamping Lago Viedma*, excursions with Transporte Ruta 3 and lake excursions with Empresa Paraíso de Navegación booked from Turismo Argos, Maipú 812, 13th floor C, T 392-5460. (For bookings for *Hotel La Loma*, Calafate and further information on the area contact Paula Escabo, Av Callao 433, piso 8° P, T 371-9123.) For tourist information on Patagonia and bookings for cheap accommodation and youth hostels, contact Asatej, see **Useful Addresses** below.

Municipalidad de Buenos Aires, Sarmiento 1551, 5th floor open Mon-Fri 0930-1730, has an excellent free booklet about the city centre and maps. Further offices at Aeroparque (Aerolíneas Argentinas), Mon-Fri, 0830-2000 and Sat 0900-1900, and Ezeiza/Pistarini Airport, Mon-Fri 0830-2200; kiosks at Florida y Diagonal Norte and Florida y Córdoba, open at 0830-2030 Mon-Fri and 0900-1900 Sat, also small information stand on 2nd floor of Galerías Pacífico.

On Fri, the youth section of *Clarín* (*Sí*) lists free entertainments; *Página 12* has a youth supplement on Thur called *NO*, the paper lists current events in *Pasen y Vean* section on Fri; also the weekly *La Maga* and Sun tourism section of *La Nación*. *Where in Buenos Aires*, a tourist guide in English, published monthly, is available free in hotels, travel agencies, tourist kiosks on Florida, and in some news stands. The *Buenos Aires Times* is a bilingual monthly newspaper covering tourist topics, available in some hotels. A good guide to bus and subway routes is *Guía Peuser*; there is one for the city and one covering Greater Buenos Aires. A similar guide and map is "Lumi": both are available at news stands. Also handy is Auto Mapa's pocket-size "Plano guía" of the Federal Capital, available at news stands, US$8, or from sales office at Santa Fe 3117; Auto Mapa also publishes an increasing number of regional maps, Michelin-style, high quality. Country-wide maps at Instituto Geográfico Militar, Cabildo 301 (see **Maps** in Information for Visitors).

Useful Addresses Youth Hostel Association—information for all South America, Talcahuano 214, piso 3, T 45-1001 (post code: 1013 Buenos Aires). Buenos Aires hostels at Brasil 675, Nicasio Oroño 1593 and Espinosa 1628. **NB** A YHA card in Argentina costs US$20, ISIC cards also sold. Secretariat open Mon-Fri 1300-2000. (There are very few hostels near Route 3, the main road S from Buenos Aires.) **Asatej**, Argentine Youth and Student Travel Association, information for all South America, noticeboard useful for single travellers, booking for hotels and travel, the *Sleep Cheap Guide* lists economical accommodation in Argentina, Bolivia, Chile, Brazil, Uruguay and Peru (though limited), ISIC cards sold, English and French spoken, very helpful but limited travel information, Florida 835, piso 3, oficina 315, T 311-6953, F 311-6840, also Student Flight Centre at oficina 319 B, be prepared for a long wait and take US$ cash. **YMCA** (Central), Reconquista 439. **YWCA**, Tucumán 844. **Salvation Army**, Rivadavia 3255. **Municipalidad**, Av de Mayo 525, facing Plaza de Mayo. **Central Police Station**, Moreno 1550, T 38-8041 (emergency, T 101 from any phone, free). **Migraciones** (Immigration), Antártida Argentina 1365 (visas extended mornings only), T 312-3288/7985/8661, from 1230-1700. **Comisión Nacional de Museos y Monumentos y Lugares Históricos**, Av de Mayo 556; professional archaeology institute.

Local Bus services (*colectivos*) cover a very wide radius, are clean, frequent, efficient and very fast (hang on tight). The basic fare is US$0.50; US$0.90 to the suburbs. Have coins ready for ticket machine as drivers no longer sell tickets. **NB** The number of the bus is not sufficient indication of destination, as each number has a variety of routes, but bus stops display routes of buses stopping there and little plaques are displayed in the driver's window. "Lumi" guide to all routes is available at news stands, US$7.50.

Tram A green and white old-fashioned street car operates on Sat and holidays 1600-1930 and Sun 1000-1300, 1600-1930 (not Easter Sun), free, along the streets of Caballito district. Operated by Asociación de los Amigos del Tranvía, T 476-0476.

Underground Railways ("Subte") Five lines link the outer parts of the City to the centre. "A" line runs under Calle Rivadavia, from Plaza de Mayo up to Primera Junta. "B" line from central Post Office, Avenida L N Alem, under Av Corrientes to Federico Lacroze railway station. "C" line links Plaza Constitución with the Retiro railway station, and provides connections with all the other lines. "D" line runs from Catedral, under the Diagonal Norte, Córdoba, Santa Fe and Palermo to Ministro Carranza (5300 block of Av Santa Fe; from Palermo to the end of the line is single track, running a shuttle service). Note that on Line "D" Canning station has become Scalabrini Ortiz; 9 de Julio station interconnects with Diagonal Norte ("D" and "C") and Carlos Pellegrini ("B"). "E" line runs from Bolívar (nr Plaza de Mayo) through San Juan to Avs Directorio and José María Moreno. The fare is US$0.45, the same for any direct trip or combination between lines; tokens (*fichas*) must be bought at booking offices (*boleterías*); buy a few in advance to save time. System operates 0530-2215, but some lines close before 2200. Line A, the oldest was built in 1913, the oldest underground in South America. Some trains date from the early part of the century too. The oldest and nicest station is Station Perú. Some stations on lines C and D have some very fine tile-work. Backpacks and luggage allowed. Beware bag-and jewellery-snatchers and pickpockets, particularly when doors are about to close. The tourist office gives out a map, which can also be bought on station platforms together with a booklet giving bus schedules.

Taxis are painted yellow and black, and carry *Taxi* flags. Fares are shown in pesos. The meter starts at 0.96 when the flag goes down; make sure it isn't running when you get in. A charge is sometimes made for each piece of hand baggage (ask first). Tips not usual. Beware of overcharging especially with remise (private clubs) and late at night. Remise service leaves from Constitución station, T 27-8111. Four common taxi driver tricks are 1) to take you on a longer than necessary ride; 2) to switch low-denomination notes for higher ones proffered by the passenger (don't back down, demand to go to the police station); 3) to grab the passenger's baggage and prevent him/her from leaving the taxi (scream for help); 4) to quote "old" prices for new, eg "quince" (15) for 1.50 pesos, "veinte y seis" (26) for 2.60 pesos, etc. If possible, keep your luggage with you. Worst places are the 2 airports and Retiro; make sure you know roughly what the fare should be before the journey. (As examples, from Aeroparque to: Ezeiza 32 pesos, Congreso 7 pesos, Plaza de Mayo 6 pesos, Retiro 5 pesos, La Boca 9 pesos.) Fares double for journeys outside city limits (General Paz circular highway). Alberto Pommerenck, T 654 5988, offers reasonable $1/2$ day hire, knows suburban leather factories well, good driver.

Car Hire Cars for hire, expensive, can be got through hotel reception clerks. There is a 20% tax on car hire. It is difficult to hire cars during holiday periods, best to book from abroad. Use of Avis Car Credit card with central billing in one's home country is possible. See also **Information for Visitors**. Driving in Buenos Aires is no problem, provided you have eyes in the back of your head and good nerves. **Avis**, Cerrito 1527, T 326-5542; **A1 International**, San Luis 3138, T 963-3489/961-6666; **Hertz**, Ricardo Rojas 451, T 312-1317. There are several national rental agencies, eg **ALV**, Av Alvear 1883, T 805-4403; **Ricciard Libertador**, Av Libertador 2337/45, T 799-8514; **Localiza**, Paraguay 1122, T 375-1611.

Motoring Associations See p 227 for details of service. Parking, safely, at El Balneario within the old port, but ask the military post for permission first.

Airports Most international flights use Ezeiza airport (officially referred to as Ministro Pistarini), 35 km from the centre by a good divided lane highway, which links with the General Paz circular highway round the city. The airport has a duty free shop (expensive, for arrivals and departures), exchange facilities (US$5 fixed commission, but no commission for US$ cash), post office (open 0800-2000) and its hotel, the *Internacional*, is closed for renovation (no other hotels nearby). There is a *Devolucion IVA* desk (return of VAT) for purchases such as leather goods. Airport information, T 480-0217. Reports of pilfering from luggage; to discourage this have your bags sealed after inspection at special counter by Your Packet International SA, US$5-10 per piece. Free hotel booking service at Tourist Information desk – helpful, with list of competitively-priced hotels.

Manuel Tienda León runs a comfortable bus service between Ezeiza and the company offices at Santa Fe 790, next to *Hotel Crillon* (T/F 315-0489, F 311-3722, or airport T/F 480-0597/0374—24 hrs), every 20 mins until 1700, every 30 mins 1700-2200, US$14, return US$25, allow 50 mins for journey; at Ezeiza their stand is in Arrivals, if you have a hotel reservation, a minibus will drop you off at any hotel in the centre. Alternatively, if in a group of 2 or more, call Mary Maxwell, T 801 0546 (Spanish only) – competitive and efficient service to and from the airport. Best to call her in advance. Both airport ("rojos") and city ("amarillos") **taxis** are allowed to operate from Ezeiza; they have separate departure points: "rojos" in front of the central hall, "amarillos" 50 m to the left of the "Espigón Internacional". Fixed-price **remise taxis** can be booked from the Manuel Tienda León counter at Ezeiza, US$49 (incl US$2 toll) payable in advance. The taxi fare of US$30, however long the journey, is fixed by government, in reality drivers charge US$45 or more, or illegally use the meter (bargaining possible, essential when going from city to airport). Avoid unmarked cars at Ezeiza no matter how attractive the fare may sound; drivers are adept at separating you from far more money than you can possibly owe them. Always ask to see the taxi driver's licence; if you think you have been cheated, T 343-5001 to complain. If you take an "amarillo", the Policía Aeronáutica on duty notes down the car's licence and time of departure. Local electric trains go to Ezeiza suburb from the Constitución station. The train, marked "Ezeiza" costs US$0.80, and takes 40 mins. 1 block from the Ezeiza station, colectivo No 502 goes to the airport, US$0.60, and takes 20 mins.

No 86 **buses** (white and blue, marked "Fournier") also run to the centre from outside the airport terminal to the right, (*servicio diferencial* takes 1½ hrs, US$5, *servicio común* 2¼ hrs, US$1) between 0500 and 2400, US$3.50. To travel to Ezeiza, catch the bus in Plaza de Mayo or, preferably, at Av de Mayo y Perú—make sure it has "Aeropuerto" sign in the window as many 86s stop short of Ezeiza. Only one bag is normally allowed and passengers with backpacks may be charged double fare. A display in immigration in the terminal shows choices and prices of all ways into the city.

All internal flights, services to Punta del Este and Montevideo and flights from Latin American countries with an intermediate stop in Argentina are handled by Jorge Newbery Airport, usually known as Aeroparque, 4 km N of the centre near the New Port, T 771-2071. Duty free facilities as at Ezeiza. Tourist information, and luggage deposit, US$5 per piece. Exchange, Banco de la Nación (open until 2100, rates as in town). Manuel Tienda León bus also serves Aeroparque (see above for downtown address). Remise taxis for the centre cost US$10-15 depending on destination, reliable. Avoid unofficial taxis which can demand up to US$40. AR and Austral offer minibus services to Aeroparque every 20 mins, US$5. Local bus 45 runs from outside the airport to the Retiro metro and railway station, then follows Av L N Alem and Paseo Colón to La Boca (if going to airport take a 33 signed to Aeroparque, not all go there); *colectivos* 56 and 160 also go to Aeroparque; US$0.50. None is advisable with bulky luggage.

Manuel Tienda León operates buses between Ezeiza and Jorge Newbery airports, stopping in city centre, US$15. AR offer free transfers between Ezeiza and Aeroparque to passengers whose incoming and connecting flights are both on AR: ask at AR desk for a voucher.

Aerolíneas Argentinas and Austral offer daily flights to the main cities, for details see text under intended destination; **see also p 226** for the Visit Argentina fare. If travelling in the S, book ahead if possible with LADE, whose flights are cheaper than buses in most cases.

Passenger Boats The *Buenos Aires Herald* (English-language daily) notes all shipping movements. Flota Fluvial del Estado (Corrientes 489, T 311-0728) organizes cruises from Buenos Aires, Dársena Sur (dock T 361-4161/0346); up the Paraná river. South Coast, down to Punta Arenas and intermediate Patagonian ports, served by the Imp & Exp de la Patagonia and Elma (state shipping line). Very irregular sailings. For connections with Uruguay, **see p 81.**

Railways On 10 March 1994, the government withdrew its funding for Ferrocarriles Argentinos, handing responsibility for all services to the provinces through which the lines run. Few provinces accepted the responsibility, because of lack of resources. Most trains have therefore been suspended. Those that were operating in May 1995 are given below, but note that this can change at any moment.

There are 4 main terminals: **Retiro**: Services in operation: Mitre line to Córdoba, suspended Mar 1994; Tucumán, Mon and Fri, returning Thur and Sun, 14 hrs, US$50 pullman, US$40 1st, US$35 tourist (service being run by Tucumán provincial government). The terminal has a left-luggage facility, US$1.50 per bag per day.

Constitución: Ferrocarril Nacional Roca (Southern)—T 304-0021. Bariloche (via Bahía Blanca), Wed and Sun 0740 (but very unreliable service and future uncertain in early 1995), US$65 pullman, US$60 1st, US$44 tourist; San Antonio Oeste, US$30, 22 hrs; Mar del Plata 7 times daily from 0100-1830, US$30 pullman, US$19 1st, US$14 tourist; continues to Miramar. Necochea, Mon, Wed, Fri 2100 (daily in summer), returns Tues, Thur, Sun, US$20.50 pullman, US$16 1st class, US$14 2nd. The Automóvil Club Argentino provides car transporters for its members (see **ACA** in **Information for Visitors**).

Federico Lacroze: Ferrocarril Nacional Urquiza (North-Eastern)—T 55-5214. No services except the Tren Histórico. Every Sun a Scottish 1888 Neilson steam engine pulls old wooden carriages, either to Capilla del Señor with lunch or a folkloric show at an *estancia* (dep 1000, return 1900), or to Zárate across the Zárate-Brazo Largo bridges over the Paraná river (dep 0900). Prices from US$25-65, T 799-4263/856-5917/46-4186.

Once: Ferrocarril Nacional Sarmiento (Western)—T 87-0041/2/3, for services in the province of Buenos Aires.

NB The railways maintain an information centre and booking office at Maipú 88, but it is largely inactive. For Ferrocarriles Argentinos T 331-3280. There is a money-back scheme if the ticket is changed, ranging from 90% of the fare if within 96 hrs of purchase to 40% within 24 hrs of your trip.

Buses The long-distance bus station, Estación Terminal de Omnibus, is behind Retiro, on Av Ramos Mejía and Antártida Argentina (Subte C); T for information 311-6073/6088. All long distance buses leave from here. All offices are on the E side on the ground floor. There are too many bus companies to list them all, but at the information desk on the 2nd floor you can get information and prices of all the companies. The passage between the bus station and Retiro is packed with market stalls and is narrow (beware pickpockets), as are the turnstile exits from the platforms, all designed to inconvenience those with luggage (although, as one correspondent points out, this also slows down anyone trying to make a speedy escape with someone else's belongings). There are two left-luggage offices (US$5 per piece), open 0600-2300. Some bus companies charge extra for luggage (illegally). Fares may vary according to time of year and advance booking is advisable Dec-Mar. Some companies may give discounts, such as 20% to YHA or student-card holders and foreign, as well as Argentine teachers and university lecturers. Travellers have reported getting discounts without showing evidence of status, so it's always worth asking. For further details of bus services and fares, look under proposed destinations. There is a bank at the bus station. There are cinemas, cafés, shops, toilets and news stands, all overpriced. (Further modifications to improve comfort, including a special section for international travellers, were due to be completed by May 1995.) TISA is the agent for Amerbuspass, see above under **Tours** and in **Introduction and Hints**, **Travel To and In South America**.

Hitchhiking For Pinamar, Mar del Plata and nearby resorts, take bus for La Plata to Alpargatas *rotonda* roundabout. For points further S, take bus 96 to Ruta 3—the Patagonia road. Best to hitch from a service station where trucks stop. The police control point at Km 43 (S) is reported to be friendly and will help to find a lift for you. For Mendoza try truck drivers at the wine warehouses near Palermo station (take Subte to Puerto Pacífico, at Buenos Aires al Pacífico train station, at viaduct crossing Av Santa Fe/Av Cabildo; turn left into Av Juan B Justo for the warehouses).

Travel into Neighbouring Countries

By Road
Four branches of the Inter-American Highway run from Buenos Aires to the borders of Chile, Bolivia, Paraguay and Brazil. The roads are paved except when otherwise stated.

To Chile via Río Cuarto, Mercedes, San Luis, and Mendoza, Total: 1,310 km paved throughout. (Direct buses to Santiago, 23 hrs, US$70-75, eg Ahumada, El Rápido Internacional and others, 1,459 km; US$70-75 to Valparaíso or Viña del Mar, TAC, Fénix Pullman Norte.) There are also road connections between Catamarca and Copiapó, Bariloche and Osorno and Puerto Montt, and between Salta and Antofagasta.

To Bolivia via Rosario, Villa María, Córdoba, Santiago del Estero, Tucumán, and Jujuy. Total: 1,994 km. There is no direct bus service from Buenos Aires to La Paz but through connections can be booked (Sudamericanos, T 27-6591, goes via La Quiaca–Villazón, US$135, 48 hrs; Atahualpa, T 315-0601, goes via La Quiaca, US$95, or Pocitos, US$91, daily, then a new ticket to La Paz must be bought). If you wish to go part of the way by rail, train/bus combinations are possible via Tucumán.

To Paraguay via Rosario, Santa Fe, Resistencia, Clorinda and Asunción (via toll bridge). Total: 1,370 km. Buses take 20-22 hours, with 11 companies (all close to each other at the Retiro bus terminal). You have choice between *diferencial* (with business class seating, food, drinks, luxury service, US$95) and *común* (without food, but has a/c, toilet, US$60). Also 5 companies to Ciudad del Este, US$45; Caaguazú goes to Villarrica, and Expreso Río Paraná and La Encarnaceña go to Encarnación, US$46. Tickets can be bought up to 30 days in advance.
   Those who wish to drive to Paraguay via Misiones to visit San Ignacio Miní or the Iguazú Falls can take the direct route to Posadas and Iguazú (Route 12), crossing the Río Paraná by the Zárate-Brazo Largo bridges. Alternatively cross the river by the tunnel between Santa Fe and Paraná, or by the bridge between Resistencia and Corrientes and join Route 12. From Posadas cross the river to Encarnación by the bridge and take a good 370-km road to Asunción (see Paraguayan chapter).

To Brazil To the Iguazú Falls, follow route 12 via Posadas (see above under **To Paraguay**). An alternative route to the Brazilian frontier at Paso de los Libres is via the Zárate-Brazo Largo bridges over the Río Paraná, then following Route 14 via Colón and Concordia. Total: 668 km. Direct buses to Brazil via Paso de los Libres by Pluma (T 313-3901): São Paulo, 40 hrs US$145, Rio de Janeiro, 45 hrs, US$163; Porto Alegre, US$71; Curitiba, 38 hrs, US$128; Florianópolis, 32 hrs, US$115. To Rio, changing buses at Posadas and Foz do Iguaçu is almost half price, 50 hrs. A third route across the Río de la Plata and through Uruguay is a bit cheaper, not as long and offers a variety of transport and journey breaks. Tickets from Buen Viaje, Av Córdoba 415 (31-2953) or Pluma, Av Córdoba 461 (311-4871 or 311-5986).

To Uruguay Direct road connections by means of two bridges over the Río Uruguay between Puerto Colón and Paysandú and between Puerto Unzué and Fray Bentos (much slower than the air or sea routes given below). "*Bus de la carrera*" (office 65-67 Retiro, T 313-3695) links Montevideo and Buenos Aires, 8½ hrs, US$25. Departure from each city at 1000, 2200 and 2230 via Zárate-Gualeguaychú-Puerto Unzué-Fray Bentos-Mercedes.

To Peru Ormeño (T 313-2259) and El Rápido Internacional (T 393-5057) have a direct service Buenos Aires-Lima, from Retiro bus station, 3½ days, all meals incl, one night spent in Coquimbo, Chile (if you need a visa for Chile, get one before travelling), the route is: Mendoza, Coquimbo, Arica, Tacna, Nazca, Ica, Lima. El Rápido Internacional, from Buenos Aires bus terminal, ticket office 89, US$160.

Air, River and Railway Services

Brazil Daily air services to São Paulo, Rio de Janeiro and other Brazilian cities. No rail connections. Shipping service between Buenos Aires and Brazilian ports by various transatlantic lines. See *Buenos Aires Herald*, English-language daily.

Chile There are no passenger-train service across the Andes between Mendoza and Santiago, but the train service between Salta and Antofagasta is open again. Bus services are available on both these routes.

Foreign and national lines fly daily between Buenos Aires and Santiago, 1½-2 hrs.

Bolivia As of Mar 1993 there were no passenger rail services from Argentina to connect with the Bolivian lines from La Quiaca to La Paz and Pocitos to Santa Cruz de la Sierra. There are air services to La Paz and Santa Cruz de la Sierra by AR and LAB.

Paraguay There are no Argentine trains to the Paraguayan border. There are daily air services to Asunción by AR. See also Posadas, **p 160**. Occasional river boats to Asunción in May to Oct, 11 days, bed and private bath, food and nightly entertainment, US$400, reported good. Details from Tamul, Lavalle 388, T 393-2306/1533.

Uruguay Tickets heavily booked Dec-Mar, especially at weekends. **NB** No money changing facilities in Tigre, and poor elsewhere. Beware of overcharging by taxis from the harbour to the centre of Buenos Aires. Note: US$6 port tax is charged on all services to Colonia/Carmelo, US$10 on direct services to Montevideo (no tax payable for journeys from Uruguay to Argentina). Do not buy Uruguayan bus tickets in BsAs; wait till you get to Colonia.

Boat connections: 1) From Tigre to Carmelo, boats are operated by 2 companies, Cacciola at 0800 and 1730, 3 hrs, and Delta Nave, Mon-Sat 0830 and 1630, Sun 0830 and 2400, 3 hrs, both services US$11 to Carmelo, US$13 (Delta Nave) and US$18.50 (Cacciola) to Montevideo; tickets at Lavalle 623 and Florida 520, BsAs (T 322-9374/0026) or Estación Fluvial, *local* 13, Tigre. It is advisable to book in advance; connecting bus from Carmelo to Montevideo.

2) Direct to Montevideo, Buquebus, Córdoba 867, T 313-4444/5500, "Avión de Buquebus" 4 times a day, 0730, 1130, 1530, 1930 (Sun 0730, 1530 and 1930), 3 hrs (summer schedule), US$37 one way, vehicles US$90-100, bus connection to Punta del Este.

3) From Dársena Sur to Colonia, services by Ferrytur, Av Córdoba 699, T 394-8412 (port: Dársena Sur, Ribera Este, T 361-4161) at 0800 and 1600 (Mon-Fri), 0830 (Sat), US$18 (plus US$6 seaport tax), US$25 incl bus to Montevideo, 3 hrs to Colonia, total of 6 to Montevideo. Free bus will pick you up 1 hr before departure on Florida y Córdoba. Buquebus' ferry service BsAs to Colonia, plus bus to Montevideo, costs US$29 one way, 4 times a day. Uruguayan immigration officer on ferries. Ferrytur run a catamaran service BsAs-Colonia, with connecting bus to Montevideo, 45 mins, US$27, US$34 incl bus to Montevideo, cars US$70. Sailings may be cancelled in bad weather.

4) Puente Fluvial runs hydrofoils (*aliscafos*) to Colonia 3 times a day (winter) or 4 times a day (summer), 1 hr, US$27 one way, US$34 incl bus to Montevideo, US$42 to Punta del Este. There are also sailings La Plata-Colonia once a day on Fri, Sat and Sun. All tickets from Puente Fluvial, Córdoba 787, T 314 2473/2672/0969, or at dock at Madero & Córdoba, T 311 1346/6160; reconfirm seat in Montevideo.

Several airlines fly from Jorge Newbery Airport (Aeroparque, Puente Aéreo section) to Colonia 12 mins, US$30. Buy tickets directly at the LAPA or AUSA counters shortly before departure (except at weekends when flights are fully booked). Continue by bus to Montevideo (or special car connecting with Lapa flight, US$3-4 to Montevideo. Also from Jorge Newbery, shuttle service to Montevideo, known as Puente Aéreo and run by AR and Pluna, daily 0730 and 0910, 40 mins. Book at Jorge Newbery Airport or T 393-5122/773-0440. Punta del Este, 5 flights daily 15 Dec-1 Mar with AR, 40 mins, or Pluna (out of season, Fri only).

Suburbs of Buenos Aires

Avellaneda, a separate municipality of over 650,000 people, is one of the most important industrial centres in the country; the handling of hides, wool and animal produce is concentrated here. It is 5 km from Plaza Constitución station, on the other side of the Riachuelo river from Boca.

Quilmes (BsAs), with one of the world's largest breweries, an important industrial centre, was given that name because the Quilmes Indians were forcibly moved there in 1665 from the famous Inca site in Tucumán Province (see p 108

The naturalist and writer WH Hudson (1841-1922) was born at Florencio Varela, near Quilmes, about 32 km from Buenos Aires. His birthplace is now a national monument. Hudson's *The Naturalist in La Plata*, reedited by Dover, is very useful on Argentine fauna.

Olivos, on the River Plate coast, 20 minutes by the Bartolomé Mitre Railway or 40 mins by Bus No 60, is a favourite residential district. The presidential residence is there, many foreign residents. Population, about 160,000. (A rec restaurant here is *Grinzing*, Córdoba 2864, European specialities, historical objects in house, garden with swimming pool.)

From Olivos station, walk up Calle Corrientes with its neocolonial architecture and old, shady trees. Taking Corrientes to the river you reach the Puerto de Olivos, mainly used for construction materials, but there are a marina (private yacht club) and several *parrilladas* (popular). On Sat and Sun a catamaran sails to Tigre, 2 hrs, rec trip past riverside mansions, sailing boats and windsurfers.

Martínez, nearby, is an attractive residential area overloooking the Río de la Plata, with an interesting shopping area. Sailing and windsurfing are well represented and river launches and other craft may be hired. At the Panamericana intersection with Edison and Paraná is the giant Unicenter shopping mall and supermarket.

San Isidro, just beyond Olivos, a resort for golf, yachting, swimming, and athletics, is one of the most attractive suburbs on the coast. Fashionable nightlife here, especially along the river bank. There is a magnificent turf racecourse, an attractive central plaza ("hippy" fair at weekends) and fine colonial buildings with a historical museum. Pop: 80,000.

Tigre (pop 40,000) on the delta of the Paraná, is about 29 km (45 minutes) by train from Buenos Aires, US$1.50 one way, every 10 mins during peak hours, otherwise every 15 or 20 mins. Take the 'C' line train from platform 1 or 2 at Retiro station (FC Mitre) to Bartolomé Mitre and change to Tren de la Costa. It can also be reached by bus 60 bajo, which takes a little longer; the 60 alto bus takes a faster road but is less interesting for sightseeing. Regattas are held in Nov and Mar on the Río Luján. There are numerous "recreos" and restaurants on the river front, but sleeping accommodation is not good. There is an excellent fruit market at nearby Canal San Fernando on Sun; craft market is tacky. Inland from Tigre are innumerable canals and rivulets, holiday homes, clubs (some beautiful buildings – the Italian club is in Venetian style) and a profitable fruit growing centre. The fishing is excellent and there is peace on the waterways, apart from motor-boats at week-ends. Regular launch services, each company with its own routes, for all parts of the Delta, including taxi launches—watch prices for these!—leave from wharf opposite railway station. Be warned that if you leave just before lunch the launch crew may stop along the way for a 1-1½ hr lunch break! Another journey through the Delta, with its lush tropical vegetation (even in winter) is fascinating. The option is a 1½-hr ride by catamaran (US$10); they dock on the other side of the bridge from the railway station and leave at 1330 and 1600 Mon-Fri, and hourly from 1300 on Sat and Sun; longer trips (4½ hrs) to the open Río de la Plata estuary are available. The snacks and refreshments on board are expensive: if you sit on the open deck you can eat your own food. Do not confuse the tourist catamarans with the *lanchas* which run regular passenger services between islands and are much cheaper (4 hr trip incl lunch stop, US$3). In the delta is *El Tropezón*, an old inn on Paraná de las Palmas island (the boat crews know it); C pp incl meals, formerly a haunt of Hemingway, now frequented by affluent *porteños*, highly rec despite the mosquitoes. Also rec, *Atelier*, *I'Marangatú* and *Fondeadero*. Delta **Youth Hostel** at Río Luján y Abra Vieja, Canal de San Fernando (take bus 170 from the square outside train station to the river. The YH is on an island. There is no ferry, ring bell on landing stage and wait, or ask a passing boat to take you across (or call Hostel manager who may pick you up), F pp, clean, hot showers, table tennis, volleyball, canoes; ask at Talcahuano 214, Buenos Aires. Bring all food in advance, there are basic cooking facilities. *Restaurant Sagitaria*, near railway station, good, cheap. Direct ferry to Carmelo, Uruguay (see p 82) from opposite railway station. A new rail line is being built out to the delta, 'Tren de la Costa'. Starts from new terminal on Av Maipú. Due to open Sep 1995.

The Museo Naval, Liniers 1264, T 749-6161, is worth a visit (open Mon-Fri 0800-1230, Sat and Sun 1400-1800). It contains models old and new, navigation instruments, flags and banners, and paintings of naval battles. There are also relics of the 1982 South Atlantic war on display outside. The Museo de la Reconquista, Liniers 818, T 749-0900, Wed-Sun 1500-1900, celebrates the reconquest of Buenos Aires from the British in 1806-07.

Martín García island (Juan Díaz de Solís' landfall in 1516) in the Río de la Plata, 45 km N of Buenos Aires, used to be a military base. Now it is an ecological/historical centre and an ideal excursion from the capital, with many trails through the thick cane brakes, trees and rocky outcrops – interesting birds and flowers. Some of the old buildings have a colonial air. Boat trips leave from Tigre at 0800, returning 1600, 3 hr journey. Reservations can be made through Cacciola, Florida 520, 1° piso, Of 113, T 394-4115, who also handle bookings for the inn and restaurant on the island. Excursion costs US$42 with *asado* lunch, US$25 without. For bungalow rental T (0315) 24546.

Other Towns in the Pampas

66 km W of the capital by Sarmiento railway from Once station (1-1½ hours) or by bus from Once station (1 hr) is **Luján** (pop 30,000), a place of pilgrimage for all devout Catholics in Argentina. An image of the Virgin was being taken from church to church in the area in 1630 by ox cart. At a certain spot the cart got stuck, in spite of strenuous efforts by men and oxen to move it. This was taken as a sign that the Virgin willed she should stay there. A chapel was built for the image, and around it grew Luján. The chapel has long since been superseded by an impressive neo-Gothic basilica and the Virgin now stands on the High Altar. 8 May is her day. Each arch of the church is dedicated to an Argentine province, and two of the transepts to Uruguay and Paraguay. Very heavy traffic at weekends.

Museo Colonial e Histórico (The Colonial and Historical Museum), in the old Cabildo building, is one of the most interesting museums in the country. Exhibits illustrate its historical and political development. Open Wed-Sat 1200-1800. No cameras allowed, and nowhere to store them. General Beresford, the commander of the British troops which seized Buenos Aires in 1806, was a prisoner here, and so, in later days, were Generals Mitre, Paz, and Belgrano. There are also museums devoted to transport and to religious ex-votos. The Río Luján is picturesque at this point, a favourite spot for picnic parties.

Hotel *La Paz*, 9 de Julio 1054, T 24034; several others. There are numerous **restaurants**: an excellent one is *L'Eau Vive* on the road to Buenos Aires at Constitución 2112; it is run by nuns, pleasant surroundings.

There are dozens of small, prosperous towns scattered throughout the vast area of the pampas. They serve as clearing centres for the cattle and grain and supply the rural population, which is much denser in the Humid Pampa than elsewhere in rural Argentina. Only the larger towns and resorts are dealt with here.

La Plata (pop 545,000), on the Río de la Plata 56 km SE of Buenos Aires was founded in 1882 as capital of Buenos Aires province after the city of Buenos Aires had become federal capital. Its port is accessible to ships of the largest tonnage. Its major industrial interest is the YPF petroleum refinery; a 72-km pipeline runs to the South Dock at Buenos Aires. Its Museo de Historia Natural is one of the best in Argentina and has several unique exhibits. A motorway is being built to link La Plata with Buenos Aires, via Riachuelo, Avellaneda, Berazategui, Gonnet and Tolosa.

Points of Interest The Museum at La Plata is famous for its collection of extinct animals. Its treasures are largely ethnological and include human skulls, mummies, and prehistoric implements. There are zoological, botanical, geological, mineralogical, palaeontological and archaeological sections, guided tours in Spanish. Highly rec, open daily, 1000-1900, US$3, closed in Jan and on public holidays (T 21-8217). Well laid-out Zoological Gardens; fine racecourse and Observatory. The Museum, Zoological Gardens, and Observatory are all in the public park; park entrance at Calle 1 y 53 (take bus to Plaza Moreno, US$0.50). The Muncipalidad and Cathedral ("a magnificent building with a classical Gothic interior") are in the Plaza Moreno. W of the city is the República de los Niños, an interesting children's village with scaled-down public buildings, built under the first Perón administration; take a green microbus 273 or a red and black 518 to República de los Niños from Plaza San Martín. To the NE are the Islas del Río Santiago, the Yacht Club, Arsenal and Naval Academy. At Punta Lara, an Argentine holiday resort nearby, there is a small, interesting nature reserve, slide show and tour, open to public Sat-Sun, 1000-1300 and 1400-1800.

Local Holiday Foundation of the City, 19 Nov.

Hotels A3 *San Marco*, Calle 54 No 523, T 40456/40923, good; *Corregidor*, Calle 26

BUENOS AIRES & THE PAMPAS

between Av 53 and 54, 4-star, expensive; **D** *Roga*, Calle 54 No 334, close to museum; **D** *Plaza*, Calle 44 y 2, with bath; **D** *Roca*, Calle 1 y 42, with bath.

Restaurants Restaurants rarely open before 2100. *El Fogón*, Av 1, Calle 49; *Ianno*, rec, Calle 46 y 10; *Don Quijote*, Plaza Paso, good value, best in town, can get very crowded; Chinese "tenedor libre" at *Guinga*, Plaza Paso; *La Linterne*, Calle 60 y Av 1, upmarket, good value; *El Chaparral*, good *parrillada*, Calle 60 y Calle 117. Several reasonable restaurants around the bus station (which is in the red light area, though quite safe even at night). Recommended bar, with steak sandwiches, *El Modelo*, Calle 52 and 4. Best *empanadas* at *La Madrileña*, a hole-in-the-wall on Calle 60 between 5 and 6. Best bakery is *El Globo*, Calle 43 y 5.

Entertainments Tango and tropical music at *El Viejo Almacén*, on Diagonal 74, Calle 2. There are free concerts during the summer in the Bosque amphitheatre.

Tourist Office In the old white theatre on the main plaza, also at bus terminal. Turismo San Martín, Calle 51 between 7 and 8, rec.

Buses To Buenos Aires, 1½ hrs, US$3.20, about every half hour, Río de la Plata company (from Retiro in Buenos Aires day and night; from Plaza Constitución, daytime, and Once). **Train** from Constitución station, US$13 1st class, US$17 pullman.

On the coast 400 km S of Buenos Aires, lies Mar del Plata, the most celebrated Argentine seaside resort. The road and rail routes S to it are through Chascomús and Dolores. **Chascomús** (pop 22,200), 126 km from Buenos Aires, is on a wide plain on the shores of Lago Chascomús, which covers 3,000 ha and swells greatly in size during the rains. Its slightly brackish water is an important breeding place for *pejerrey* fish; amateur fishing competitions are held in the winter season. There is a *gaucho* museum, and also a Regatta Club, bathing beaches and 4 campsites including Monte Brown, on the far side of the lake (all nicely located, but poor facilities).

Dolores, 204 km (3½ hrs by bus) from Buenos Aires, has a district population of 30,000; it was founded in 1818, destroyed by Indians three years later, and rebuilt.

It is a grain and cattle farming centre, little changed since the 1940s. The Museo y Parque Libres del Sur, commemorating the revolt of the district against Rosas in the early 19C, is interesting and well displayed. *Hotel Plaza*, very pleasant.

San Clemente del Tuyú, 107 km E of Dolores, is the nearest Atlantic coastal resort to Buenos Aires. A family resort with little nightlife, it is cheaper than the more fashionable resorts further S. Frequent buses from Mar del Plata, with Empresa Costamar, first at 0700, US$11, 5 hrs. To Buenos Aires with several companies, US$15-20. 9 km away at **Punta Rasa**, there are an old lighthouse and a nature reserve owned by the Fundación Vida Silvestre, with interesting birdlife. (**Hotels** many along the promenade, incl C *Aquario*, Calle 15, clean, friendly, incl breakfast; **D** *Splendid*, on main shopping street; *Residencial-Restaurante Cueva*, Calle 4 y Calle 1, not very clean, poor service, but cheap beer; **D** *Residencial Bahía*, Calle 4, entre 1 y 15, breakfast incl, good; several campsites. *Restaurante Yo y Vos*, Calle 4 y Calle 17, large and cheap portions, friendly, good. US dollars can be changed at the Banco de la Provincia de Buenos Aires, Calle 1 y Calle 4, but TCs are not accepted anywhere in town.) 3 km from the centre, near the harbour, is *Mundo Marino*, the largest oceanarium in South America (T 0252-21071), with amusements and shows as well as whales, penguins, etc; open daily from 1000, closes 1530 May-Sep, 1630 Mar-Apr, Oct-Dec, 1800 Jan-Feb. Micro bus 500 goes there.

Pinamar, 89 km S of San Clemente, a resort with a casino, is eclipsing Mar del Plata. The water-skiing is good. Fish, including conger eel (*congrio*) may be bought on the beach from local fishermen. Tourist office, friendly and helpful, is in the main square.

Accommodation Many, from *Arenas*, Av Bunge 700, T 82444, 4 star, to *Berlín*, Rivadavia 326, T 82320, 1 star. All hotels fully booked throughout Jan-Mar (as much as two years in advance!). Houses and apartments can be rented from Dec-Mar: 2-room flats about US$800/month, up to US$5,000 for a mansion. In Mar rates are halved. **Youth Hostel** Nuestras Malvinas y Sarmiento, T 82908, and *Moby Dick* campsite at Ostende, T 86045. Many other campsites close to town.

Villa Gesell (pop 8,700), 22 km further S, is a modern resort with a chocolate factory, fine beaches and over 100 hotels, which has become very popular although less crowded than Mar del Plata. Tourist office at bus terminal. Direct bus service to Buenos Aires (US$29) by Empresas Antón and Río de la Plata (book in advance at weekends).

Hotels *Terrazas Club*, 4 star, suite accommodation, Av 2 between Calles 104 and 105, T 6 2181; *Colón*, 2 star, 3 blocks from beach at Av 4, Calle 104, T 62310, private bath, restaurant; **C** *Hostería Gran Chalet*, Paseo 105 No 447 y Av 4-5, T 62913, clean, rec; **D** *Bero*, Av 4 y Calle 141, T 66077, opposite bus terminal. Many others of all classes within 800m of sea. Many apartments for rent (rates as Pinamar). **Youth Hostel** *Albergue Camping El Coyote*, Alameda 212 y 306, Barrio Norte, T 68448.

Camping Sites Many, a few open all year round.

Air Flights with AR and LAPA, the latter for half the normal tariff.

Mar del Plata, the greatest Argentine resort, built at the turn of the century, is 130 km further S and 400 km from the capital. The normal population is 407,000, but during the summer about two million visitors stay there; there are all classes of apartment blocks, boarding houses and lodgings. It is necessary to book in advance between late Dec and mid-Mar (when the night-life continues all night). For the rest of the year the town is fairly quiet and good value. The city is famous for its casino: the upper floor is open to the public, US$5. Small but pleasant natural history museum in Plaza España off Playa La Perla. Interesting municipal art museum at Villa Ortiz Basualdo, Av Colón 1189. Centro Cultural Victoria Ocampo, Villa Victoria, Matheu 1851 (house prefabricated in England, early 20th century), where the famous author spent her summers until her death in late 1970s.

There are fine squares, especially Plaza San Martín, and eight km of beaches, including fashionable Playa Grande, with its private clubs and the summer estates of wealthy *porteños*; Playa Bristol, where the casino is; and Playa La Perla, with moderately priced hotels. At Punta Iglesia there is a large rock carving of Florentino Ameghino, the palaeontologist who collected most of the fossils in the museum at La Plata. The wooded municipally-owned Parque Camet is 8 km to the N. It has polo grounds and playing fields. For those who do not care for surf bathing, there are salt-water pools. Fishing is good all along the coast and *pejerrey, corvina* and *merluza* (hake) abound; you can charter a private launch for shark fishing.

The port can be reached by bus, 15 mins from bus terminal. There are a large fishing fleet, excursion boats, seafood restaurants and a huge sealion colony (walk along Escollera Sur-Southern breakwater). **Museo de Hombre del Puerto – Cleto Ciocchini**, Fri-Sun 1600-2000, US$1, at Padre J Dutto 383, shows the history of the port and its first Sicilian fishermen.

Visits can be paid to the rocky promontory of Cabo Corrientes to watch the breakers; to Punta Mogotes lighthouse (open Thur 1330-1700); to the Gruta de Lourdes, and the Bosque Peralta Ramos.

Local Holidays   10 Feb (Foundation of City); 10 Nov (Day of Tradition); 22 Nov (St Cecilia). Mar del Plata is known for its hand-finished sweaters.

Hotels   Four-star (category **L2-A1**) incl *Provincial*, 500 rooms, Blvd Marítimo 2500, T 24081/9; *Dos Reyes*, Av Colón 2129, T 28694; *Hermitage*, Blvd Peralta Ramos 2657, T 519081, 150 rooms; *Sasso*, M de Hoz 3545, T 840031 and *Gran Dora*, Buenos Aires 1841, T 25002/6. **L3-A3** *Astor*, Entre Ríos 1649, T 23051/4, small, no credit cards, 3 mins from beach. Among the 3-star hotels (category **A2-A3**) are *Benedetti*, Av Colón 2198, rec, T 30031/2; *Gran Continental*, Córdoba 1929, T 23027; *Presidente*, Corrientes 1516, T 28810. There are scores of other good hotels at reasonable rates eg **B** *O Sole Mío*, Av Independencia 1277, T 26685, half board, Italian run, highly rec; **C** *Boedo*, Almirante Brown 1771 (T 24695), with bath, hot water, clean,   good value, near beaches (open Jan-Feb only); **C** *Europa*, Arenales 2735, 2 blocks from bus station (reductions in low season), clean, quiet, hot water; **D** *Hospedaje Paraná*, Lamadrid 2749, near bus terminal, with bath; **D** *Monterrey*, Lamadrid 2627, clean, good; **D** *Niza*, Santiago del Estero 1843 (E out of season), bath, clean, safe, friendly, rec; **D** *Peley*, on Alberdi near bus station, clean, comfortable, open all year, rec, good value restaurant. During summer months it is essential to book in advance. In the off-season, bargain everywhere. **Youth Hostel**, Tucumán 2728, T 27927, E pp, friendly, clean, only a small discount for YHA card holders. Many hotels and restaurants close when the summer is over; worth looking round the bus-station area out of season for lodging (eg *Little Hotel*) and food.

There are many houses and apartments for rent, built for retired people.

Camping   *Pinar de la Serena* and other sites, reasonable prices. Several on the road S.

Restaurants   *Hostería del Caballito Blanco*, Av Rivadavia 2534, excellent, German decor. *Cantina Capri*, Belgrano 2161 (near Casino), not cheap but excellent value; *La Paella*, Entre Ríos 2025, good; *La Caracola*, Martínez de Hoz y 12 de Octubre, seafood, good but dear; *Tía Teresa*, San Luis, near Colón, fresh pasta dishes, good value; *Lo de Terri*, Gascón y San Luis, parrilla, good *chorizo* and *vacio*; *Raviolandia*, Colón y Las Heras, good, cheap, try the seafood with rice. Vegetarian: *El Jardín*, San Martín 2463, *tenedor libre*, and *La Huerta*, San Martín 2300. Many *tenedor libre* restaurants of all kinds along San Martín. *Los Inmortales*, Corrientes 1662, good, moderately priced. Good value meals at *La Nueva Glorieta*, Alberti 1821, and *El Nuevo Hispano*, Alberti 1933. Best seafood, and cheapest, at Centro Comercial del Puerto (eg *Puerto Gallego*).

Banks and Exchange   Lloyds Bank (BLSA) Ltd, Av Luro 3101. Open 1000-1600. Exchange houses on San Martín and surroundings. **Jonestur**, San Martín 2574, will collect on personal US bank cheques in 15 working days, at 2½% fee. Amex, Colón 2605, does not cash TCs.

Casino   Open Dec to end-Apr, 1600-0330; 1600-0400 on Sat. Winter opening, May-Dec, Mon-Fri 1500-0230; weekends 1500-0300. Entrance US$5.

Cultural Events   Reduced price tickets are often available from *Cartelera Baires*, Santa Fe 1844, local 33 or from *Galería de los Teatros*, Santa Fe 1751.   **La Cultura** (formerly Sociedad de Cultura Inglesa), San Luis 2498, friendly, extensive library.

Post Office   Av Luro 2460. **Telecommunications**   Av Luro y Santiago del Estero.

Tourist Office   Blvd Marítimo, Peralta Ramos 2267, T 41325, nr Casino, open 0800-1900, good information, incl bus routes to all sites of interest.

Immigration Office   Chile y Alberti, open in the morning, allow 2-3 weeks for renewing visas.

Air Services   Camet airport, 10 km from town. Many flights daily to and from Buenos Aires with Austral, Lapa and AR. *Remise* taxi from airport to town, mini bus US$3.50.

Trains   leave Buenos Aires from Constitución, 10 minutes from the centre by any bus marked

"Constitución". Trains (a/c) take at least 5¼ hrs. See under Buenos Aires, **Railways**. Book very early for Dec-Mar trips. Mar del Plata station is at Av Luro 4599, about 13 blocks from centre.

Buses Bus station at corner of Alberti y Las Heras, convenient. Companies from Retiro terminal in **Buenos Aires**: 6 hrs, US$26, Micromar (T BsAs 313-3173), Costera Criolla (T BsAs 313-3580, also has *coche cama* in evening), Empresa Argentina, Chevallier (T BsAs 313-3297). Bus to and from **Miramar** hourly day and night, 45 mins US$4. El Cóndor and Rápido Argentino to **La Plata**, day and night, US$20. La Estrella goes to **San Martín de los Andes**, US$56, and **Bariloche**, US$60 (none direct; change at Bahía Blanca or Tres Arroyos). To **Bahía Blanca**, only Pampa, 6 daily, US$25, 5½ hrs. To **San Clemente del Tuyú**, with Empresa Costamar, frequent service daily, first at 0700, US$11, 5 hrs. To **Puerto Madryn** and **Trelew**, Wed and Sat night. For hitchhiking S, take a colectivo to the monument to El Gaucho.

Outside the city the country is undulating. To the N (34 km) is a lagoon—the Mar Chiquita—joined to the sea by a narrow channel. There is good fishing, yachting, boating and bathing here. Picturesque spots reached from the road inland to Balcarce are (19 km) **Laguna de los Padres** (a **reserva provincial**), and Sierra de los Padres and (32 km beyond) the Laguna La Brava, at the foot of the Balcarce hills.

In these hills, 68 km W of Mar del Plata, is the town of **Balcarce** (pop 28,800), a centre for hill visits to La Brava, above Ruca-Lauquén, and the Cinco Cerros, five hills most strangely shaped. Balcarce is the birthplace of the great racing driver **Juan Fangio**; it has a racing circuit and a motor museum with all Fangio's racing cars and trophies (Calles 17 y 18, open 1100-1800, US$5, rec). Frequent buses from Mar del Plata; excellent *parrilladas* on the outskirts.

Hotel C *Balcarce*, Calle 17, T 22055, good.

Beyond Balcarce Route 226 runs 103 km NW to *Tandil*, at the northern end of the Sierra de Tandil, a ridge of hills which run W from the sea into the pampa for 250 km. Tandil is 390 km by road from Buenos Aires (US$15, 6 hrs) via Azul, 300 km direct. The air is splendidly clear and refreshing, and the Holy Week festivities are outstanding. There is a beautiful lake in the city. Excursions to the Sierra La Aurora. Population: 125,000.

Hotels C *Plaza*, General Pinto 438, T 27160, 3 star, very friendly, clean, comfortable and quiet. **D** *Kaiku*, Mitre 902, T 23114, basic; **D** *Turista*, 14 de Julio 60, T22626, 1 star. *Libertador*, Mitre 545, T 22127, central, good value. Others near railway station. Rec restaurant is *El Estribo*, San Martín 759, friendly, good atmosphere.

From Mar del Plata, along the rocky sea-front to the SW, there is a road (53 km) to *Miramar* (pop 17,500). Like Mar del Plata, this is a resort, but the cliffs backing the beach are higher, the surrounding hills more picturesque, and it is a good deal cheaper. There is a fine golf course at *Hotel Golf Roca* and a casino. Immediately S of the city limits is an extensive forest park on the beach, the **Vivero Dunicola**, whose vegetation stays green and blooming throughout the year, despite winter night-time temperatures below freezing. Fourteen km by road to the S, among dunes and black rocks, is Mar del Sur (*Atlantic Hotel*) with good fishing in a lagoon and bathing on the beach.

Hotels Dozens of hotels and apartments. **C** *Santa Eulalia I*, Calle 26 No 851, T 20808, friendly but run down; **C** *Villa Cruz*, Calle 19, No 864, friendly, clean, near the beach; *Gran*, Calle 29, No 586 esq 12, T 20358, 2 star; *Palace*, Calle 23, No 774, T 20258, 3 star.

Camping El Durazno, 3 km from town, good facilities, shops, restaurant, F pp, take bus 501 marked "Playas". Many sites, reasonably priced.

Exchange None for TCs; must go to Mar del Plata. Try *Ibertur* and *Sastre* property offices.

Tourist Office on central plaza, maps available.

Transport *El Neptuno* train, daily at 1530 from Buenos Aires to Mar del Plata arriving at 2045, continues to Miramar, arriving 2150. **Bus** Buenos Aires-Miramar with Chevallier, Micromar and Costera Criolla (8 a day, US$31). Rápido del Sud from Mar del Plata stops at Calles 34 y 23.

About 110 km further SW along the coast is another famous seaside resort, *Necochea*, 500 km from Buenos Aires. It stands next to Mar del Plata in repute.

The surroundings are picturesque. Visits can be paid to the Paseo del Puente, Punta Negra, the Cascada (or waterfalls) 16 km up the Río Quequén Grande, Los Manantiales, and the Laguna de los Padres. Grain is exported from the port. Urban population: 52,000 including large Danish colony: there are a Danish club and consulate. About 100,000 tourists visit during the season, for the 24-km long beach is one of the best in the country. There is a municipal recreation complex, boasting a large modern casino, various sports facilities, including skating rink, swimming pool, bowling, a cinema and children's play area. The Parque Miguel Lillo (named after the Argentine botanist) faces the beach, comprising 400 ha of conifers, nature park, swan lake with paddle boats, an amphitheatre, museum and go-cart track. The casino is open in summer. Airport.

Hotels The Hotel Association is at Av 79 with Calle 4. Most hotels are in the downtown area from Calle 2 (parallel with beach) N between Av 71-91; there are at least a hundred within 700m of the beach. **C** *Doramar*, Calle 83, No 357, T 25815, family run, friendly, helpful; **D** *Hospedaje Solchaga*, Calle 62, No 2822, T 25584, clean, excellent; **E** *Hospedaje Bayo*, Calle 87, No 363, T 23334.

Camping Beach sites reported expensive in summer.

Restaurants *Rex*, Calle 62, "a trip to 1952 Paris"; *Mi Cantina*, excellent family restaurant. *Parrilla El Palenque*, Av 79 y 6; *Pizzería Kapotte*, Av 79 next beach, both rec.

Language School Instituto Argentino de Idiomas, Galería Monviso, local 8, Calles 62 y 63, rec.

Tourist Office At the bus terminal by the river at corner of Av 47 and Calle 582; also on beach front at Av 79.

Railway Buenos Aires-Necochea (station at Quequén), see under Buenos Aires **Railways**.

Bus Bus terminal at Av 47 y Calle 582, 4 km from the centre. Local bus to centre from outside the terminal. To/from Buenos Aires, US$44, La Estrella, El Cóndor and Costera Criolla. To Mar del Plata US$6, to Bahía Blanca $16.

About 3½ km across the mouth of the river from Necochea is **Quequén**, with an excellent beach, good bathing, and pleasant scenery. The channel to the port has to be dredged daily. **Hotels** *Costa Azul*, *Continental*, *Quequén*; campsites.

Over 320 km W from Necochea by paved road through the coastal area is the port of Bahía Blanca, which can be reached from Buenos Aires by rail (900 km), by air, or by a 688-km paved road (Route 3) through Las Flores (pop 20,200), Azul, Juárez and Tres Arroyos.

Azul, 264 km SW of Buenos Aires, is a cattle centre with an attractive plaza, a French Gothic-style Cathedral and an ethnographic museum. Population: about 45,000. A good stopping place if driving S from Buenos Aires. The river has been dammed to provide a water-sports centre.

Hotels C *Gran Hotel Azul*, Colón 626, T 22011, excellent cafeteria; **D** *Residencial Blue*, Av Mitre 983, T 22742, clean, friendly, near bus station; *Argentino*, Yrigoyen 378, T 25953; *Torino*, San Martín 1000, T 22749. Municipal campsite.

Tres Arroyos (pop 85,000), about 195 km from Bahía Blanca, is a cattle and wheat growing centre of 70,000 people. Many inhabitants are of Dutch origin; there are a Dutch consulate and a primary school named Holanda, supported by funds of the Argentine Dutch. There is also an important Danish colony, with school, club and consulate. A 68-km paved road runs S to the sea at the pleasant little resort of **Claromecó**, with a beautiful beach of dark sand backed by high dunes.

Hotels and Restaurants at Tres Arroyos incl *Parque*, Pellegrini 23, rec (restaurant) and *Andrea*, Istilart 228, good; *Tres Arroyos*, friendly, modest. *Restaurant Di Troppo*, near *Hotel Parque*, good. At **Claromecó D** *Comercio*, good restaurant, pleasant atmosphere; *Pablo Satini's Bar*, on main street, 5 mins from beach, F off season, OK, safe deposit.

Camping at Claromecó Good campsite *Dunamar*, hot showers, fire pits and laundering basins, US$1 a day; also ACA campsite.

Bus Buenos Aires-Claromecó with El Cóndor, US$40. Tres Arroyos-Claromecó twice daily off season, extra buses from mid-Dec in season. Pampa bus to Mar del Plata 0650, 4½ hrs. Modern, efficient bus terminal a few blocks from centre of Tres Arroyos.

Bahía Blanca, population 300,000, the most important centre S of Mar del Plata, stands at the head of a large bay at the mouth of the Río Naposta. The region has over a million people. Bahía Blanca consists of the city itself, built back from the river front, and five ports at various distances from the city strung along the N bank of the Naposta: Arroyo Pareja and the naval base of Puerto Belgrano at the mouth of the estuary; Puerto Ingeniero White, 23 km inland (reached by buses 500, 501, 504 from the plaza), Puerto Galván, 3½ km beyond, and Cuatreros, 8 km upstream. The Barrio Inglés (direction Ingeniero White) is where the foremen and technicians of the port and railway construction teams lived; Brickman St is a row of late Victorian semi-detached houses. Managers lived at nearby Harding Green. Bahía Blanca is also a rail, air and pipeline terminal for the Río Negro valley.

The city has some fine modern buildings and two parks. There is a modest Zoological Garden in Parque Independencia, on the outskirts.

Museums Museo Histórico, Alsina 425, incl interesting photos of early Bahía Blanca; **Museo del Puerto**, Torres y Carrega, Ingeniero White; **Museo de Bellas Artes**, Alsina 65.

To the E of Bahía Blanca is an enormous stretch of sandy beaches, developed for visitors (in the afternoon, it is usually windy). ***Pehuén-Có***, 70 km away (hotel, C, quiet and clean), is an example of the beaches with camping places, well shaded by pine trees (beware of jellyfish when wind is in the S). Signs to it on the main road 24 km from Bahía Blanca. Another fine beach, with hotels and camping places is ***Monte Hermoso***, 106 km, 2 hrs by bus (4 a day in summer, 2 in winter) E of Bahía Blanca. Good cheap meals, several restaurants. (Its hotels are open only Jan-Mar; several campsites – incl *Las Dunas*, 30 mins walk W along the beach, US$3 pp, a friendly spot run by an elderly German couple.)

Local Holidays Sep 24 (Our Lady of Mercy); Nov 10 (Day of Tradition).

Hotels **A1** *Austral*, Colón 159, T 20241, F 553737, restaurant; **A3** *Argos*, España 149, T/F 40001, 3-star; **B** *ACA Motel Villa Borden*, Av Sesquicentenario, entre Rutas 3 y 35, T 40151, F 21098; **B** *Belgrano*, Belgrano 44, T 20240/30498; **B** *City*, Chiclana 226, T 30178; **B** *Italia*, Brown 181, T 20121, simple, clean, restaurant; **B** *Muñiz*, O'Higgins 23, T 20021, friendly, central; **B** *Santa Rosa*, Sarmiento 373, T 20012/3; **C** *Barne*, Hipólito Yrigoyen 270, T 30864/30294; **C** *Bayón*, Chiclana 487, T 22504, friendly, clean, safe; **C** *Victoria*, Gral Paz 82, T 20522, basic, friendly, hot water, rec; **D** *Argentino* (restaurant), Chiclana 466, T 21824; **D** *Del Sur*, 19 de Mayo 75, T 22452, with restaurant, noisy with traffic; **D** *Residencial Roma*, Cerri 759, T 38500, opposite railway station, with private bath, cheaper without; **D/E** *Hospedaje Andrea*, Lavalle, rooms a/c, very friendly. Many other *residenciales* near railway station. **E** *Milano*, 11 de Abril y Estomba, also bar, mainly for "aged bachelors".

Camping Balneario Maldonado, 2 km from centre, next to petrochemical plant, US$0.30 pp; salt water swimming pool, US$0.80, bus 514 along Av Colón every hr but only when beach is open, ie when sunny and not in evening. ACA campsite at Lagoda de Lobos, not rec. Many others.

Restaurants *La Cigala*, Cerri 757, opp railway station, very good; *Il Vesuvio*, San Martín 337, good lunch, cheap; *La Casita de Miguel*, San Martín 510, cheap comedor, good food; *Da Sergio*, Gorriti 61, good food, large portions, very good value. *Café La Bahía*, Chiclana 548, good value, rec; *Bar/Comedor*, Mitre y Casanova, similar. A few good fish restaurants at the harbour, eg *El Royal*. Very good seafood and fish at Ingeniero White.

Banks and Exchange Lloyds Bank (BLSA), Calle Chiclana 102. Citibank, Colón 58. Open 0800-1400 Nov 15-Mar 31, 1000-1600 Apr 1-Nov 14. Amex, Fortur, Soler 38, T 26290, *poste restante*, English spoken. **Casas de Cambio** Pullman, Av San Martín 171, will change US$ cheques into US$ notes, 3% commission on TCs; good rates (closes 1600). **Viajes Bahía Blanca**, Drago 63, good rates. All *casas de cambio* closed at weekends.

Launderette *Laverap*, Estomba 293 and at Colón y Güemes.

Post Office Moreno 43. **Telephones**, O'Higgins 203.

Shopping Good gaucho shop on Soler, nr Fortur (see below), genuine articles.

Tourist Office In town hall on main plaza, Alsina 25, very helpful.

Airport Comandante Espora, 15 km from centre. Austral and Aerolíneas Argentinas flights to **Buenos Aires** daily (except Sun), 0900 and 1745. To **Comodoro Rivadavia**, **Río Gallegos** and **Río Grande**, daily except Sun (Austral).

Trains Station at Av Gral Cerri 780, T 21168. Buenos Aires-Bariloche train passes through; see Buenos Aires **Railways**. To **Cipolletti** (Río Negro, opp Neuquén), daily except Sat, 2130, a/c, bar, video, waitress service.

Buses Terminal is 2½ km from centre at Estados Unidos y Brown, connected by *micro* bus service; no hotels nearby. To **Trelew**, 3 per week, US$32, 734 km. **Río Gallegos** with Don Otto US$80; **Mar del Plata**, with Río Paraná, daily at 2230, US$25, 5½ hrs. **Río Colorado** US$8. To **Buenos Aires** frequent, 8-11 hrs, US$33-49 depending on service (eg Don Otto, T BsAs 313-3580; La Estrella/Cóndor). To **Neuquén**, 6 a day, 9 hrs, US$16, 580 km, one company only. To **Zapala** 3 times daily, a pullman service with food and drinks sold, 15 hrs, US$25 with Alto Valle. To **Viedma** 3 a day, 4 hrs.

Hitchhiking S or W from Bahía Blanca is possible but not too easy. Most southbound traffic takes Route 22 via Río Colorado. N to Buenos Aires on Route 3 is "virtually impossible".

From Bahía Blanca Route 3, a well-built paved highway runs S to Comodoro Rivadavia and Río Gallegos. Another major paved highway, Route 22, runs W to Neuquén and the Lake District. Several routes go North.

Some 100 km to the N is the **Sierra de la Ventana**, a favourite and recommended area for excursions from Bahía Blanca, and a **reserva provincial**, protecting the range's flora and fauna. The small town of *Tornquist*, 32 km N of Bahía Blanca by Route 33, with an attractive church on the central plaza (post and phone office open 0800-1800), is a good starting point (**C Gran Central Hotel**, seedy but friendly; campsite). The town of Pigue is also recommended as a good base. From Route 33 take Route 76 towards the town of Sierra de la Ventana. After 32 km is the entrance to the **Parque Provincial**, with massive ornate gates from the Tornquist family home. From here it's a 3-hr walk to the summit of Cerro La Ventana, which has fantastic views from the "window" in the summit ridge (camping at the base, free, basic facilities, canteen). 5 km further is the forestry station, with audio-visual display, trips to see wild deer, wild horses, guanacos, and on Fri and Sun trips at 0900 to 2 caves, one an Indian cemetery, the other with petroglyphs (US$0.70). Villa Ventana, 10 km further, is a wooden settlement with excellent teashop, *Casa de Heidi*, and wholefood available from *Jardín de Aylem*. Municipal campsite by river with all facilities. The town of *Sierra de la Ventana*, further E, is a good centre for exploring the hills, with hotels **B** *Provincial*, T 915025; **D** *Argentino*, La Perlita; **Youth Hostel** *Albergue Sierra de la Ventana* (sleeping bag necessary) and the excellent *Don Diego* campsite (hot water, open all year round); also **G** pp *Yapay*, Av San Martín near bus terminal, clean, quiet, rec. Excellent tourist information. Tres Picos, rising bare and barren from the rich farmlands to 1,070m, is only 6¼ km away. There is a 9-hole golf course, and good trout fishing in the Río Sauce Grande. All points can be easily reached by bus from Bahía Blanca or Tornquist.

193 km N of Bahía Blanca by road/rail through Saavedra is *Carhué* (pop 18,000). Behind the town hall there is a museum of the wars against the Indians. Tourist information at bus station. Five km away is Lago Epecuén, which covers over 40,000 ha and is over twenty times saltier than the sea. No fish can live in it. These waters are recommended for chronic rheumatism and skin diseases. There are many hotels and *residenciales* at the lake side and the area is a tourist resort. The ghost town of Villa Epecuén, 15 km away, drowned by the lake in 1985, can be visited (unpaved road).

Services *Hotel Shalom*, Belgrano 880, T 2503, C, "eccentric but clean", breakfast extra; restaurant at bus terminal is reasonable. Free camping in the beach area, no facilities. Rotary Club campsite, 2 km from Carhué.

About 38 km by road NE of Carhué, on the Roca Railway, is *Guaminí*, a pleasant summer hill resort of 3,500 inhabitants on the shore of Laguna del Monte, not as salty as Lago Epecuén; *pejerrey* fishing. (**Hotels** *La Aragonesa*, *Roma*; *Camping Municipal* on lake.) From Guamini take routes 65 and 205 back to Buenos Aires, via *Lobos* (excellent ACA campsite at lake 10 km S of Lobos).

Santa Rosa (pop 55,000), capital of the Province of La Pampa, is 332 km NW of Bahía Blanca by road, and 619 km E of Buenos Aires by Route 5, via Chivilcoy (pop 47,500) and Pehuajó (pop 26,800).

Hotels A2 *Calfucura*, Av San Martín 695, T 23608, 4-star, no meals, but excellent steak restaurant round the corner; **C** *Hostería Río Atuel*, Luro 256, opposite bus terminal, T 22597, very good, rec; **D** *San Martín* Alsina 101, clean, restaurant, garage; **D** *Motel Calden*, Route 35, Km 330, T 24311, good restaurant attached, large rooms.

THE CORDOBA REGION (2)

Córdoba, the Republic's second city, has some historic, colonial buildings and is an important route centre, especially for road travel to the NW. The Sierras de Córdoba contain many pleasant, small resorts in the hills.

Córdoba and NW Argentina The pattern of the land in Northern Argentina, from the crest of the Andes in the W to the Río Paraguay in the E, consists of a high, dry Altiplano rising to a Puna cut into on its E face by rivers which flow into the Lowlands. This configuration of the land, similar to Bolivia, is carried S into all the NW provinces of Argentina as far S as Tucumán, but the altitudes in Argentina are not so great as in Bolivia, and the whole area not so large. The E-running rivers born on the Puna flow into the Chaco; their broad valleys, or *quebradas*, make access to the heights comparatively easy. Between the base of the Puna and the Chaco lie a series of front range hogback hills running roughly from N to S; the lowlands between them are known in Argentina as the *valles*. Tucumán is the S boundary of this kind of land. N of Tucumán crops can be grown without irrigation (though there is irrigation where the soil is absorbent) but S of Tucumán is droughty land, with long N-S ranges of low hills such as the Sierras de Córdoba, set in plains which have salt flats and swamps in the depressions.

Settlement and Economy The Puna is windswept, stony and treeless: the only growth is a low, blackish shrub (*tola*), and an occasional cactus. The first Spanish expedition from Bolivia entered Argentina in 1542. A little later a better and lower route was discovered—the main route used today—descending from La Quiaca to Jujuy through the Quebrada de Humahuaca, with rugged and colourful mountain ranges closing in on both sides. Along this new route the Spaniards pressed S and founded a group of towns in the NW: Santiago del Estero (the first) in 1551, Tucumán in 1565, Córdoba in 1573, Salta in 1582, La Rioja in 1591, and Jujuy in 1592. Mendoza (1561), San Juan (1562), and San Luis (1598) were all colonized by people who crossed the passes from Chile. All these colonies were hemmed in by the warlike tribes of the Pampas, and until the war of extermination in 1880 the route from Buenos Aires to Córdoba was often unsafe. The Indians raided frequently for cattle, which they drove S and over the Andes for sale in Chile.

During the whole of the colonial era the trade of the area, mostly in mules, was with Bolivia and Peru rather than with Buenos Aires. The mules were bred mainly in the plains between Rosario, Santa Fe, and Córdoba, and driven finally into Salta for the great fair in Feb and Mar.

Historically, Tucumán was always important, for the two river routes of the Salado and the Dulce across the dry belt forced the mule traffic to pass through Tucumán on the way to Salta. Tucumán still produces most of Argentina's sugar.

Tobacco is a major crop, and an important factor in the North West is the growth of tourism.

In nearly all the provincial towns everything shuts between 1200 and 1600 except restaurants, hotels and post offices. There is nothing to do or see, and we suggest that this is a good time for travelling, although in many places it is also the hottest time of day. (Panamericano and Atahuallpa/Balut buses have been recommended in the NW as clean and with a good service.)

From Buenos Aires to Córdoba

If hitchhiking, take the train from Retiro (San Martín line) to Pilar to reach the main Córdoba highway via Rosario. There are two main road routes: the shorter (713 km) via Rosario and the longer (835 km) via Río Cuarto. The latter goes through **San Antonio de Areco**, 113 km NW of Buenos Aires (bus, 2hrs, US$4, every hour). Here is the Museo Gauchesco Ricardo Güiraldes, on Camino Güiraldes and Aureliano, a typical *estancia* of the late 19th century with manor house, mill, tavern, open Wed-Sun, 1000-1200, 1500-1800 in summer; in winter 1000-1200 and 1400-1700. Check if it is open in Jan-Feb. Güiraldes was a writer who described *gaucho* life; his best-known book is *Don Segundo Sombra*. Visitors can also see over Cina-Cina, a working *estancia*, tour for US$20 includes visit, typical lunch and riding display, rec. Día de la Tradición is a *gaucho* festival with traditional parades, games, events on horseback, music and dance, celebrated in the week up to 10 Nov each year. Accommodation is hard to find at this time.

Many handicrafts are sold, mainly *gaucho* objects, ceramics, silver, leather, colonial furniture. The Argentine artist Gasparini has a museum-school where he sells his drawings of *gauchos* to tourists; Calle de los Martínez, between Bolívar and Rivadavia. There is also a local natural history museum, Parque Metri, on Matheu and Hernández. Sub-Dirección de Turismo at Alsina and Lavalle, T 2101. **Services** C Hotel *San Carlos*, Zapiola y Zerbione, T 22401, clean and friendly, ask in advance for meals; **D** *Residencial Areco*, Segundo Sombra y Rivadavia, T 22166, good, comfortable, clean. Opposite Museo Gauchesco is *Hostería del Palomar*, typical barbecue; *Restaurant La Porteña* on the riverside, typical, very good. Camping near town centre; also *Auto-camping La Porteña*, 12 km from town on the Güiraldes *estancia*, good access roads.

Beyond Pergamino, 146 km, is **Venado Tuerto**, a pleasant town of 58,000 people with a fine Country Club at which race meetings and tournaments are held twice a year (several hotels incl **B** *Touring*, cool, quiet, rec). At **Río Cuarto**, 138,000 people, there is a golf club and a fine old municipal building with a lookout tower worth seeing. In Apr/May one of the country's biggest motor races (*carrera de autos*) is held here.

Hotels C *Gran*, Sobremonte 725, T 33401, 3-star; **D** *Alihué*, Sarsfield 58, good value, very friendly, big rooms. Near bus station on Calle Sobremonte 100-200 block are 3 cheap *residenciales*, *El Ciervo*, *Hospedaje El Bambi*, *Residencial Monge*, all **D**. Municipal campsite, El Verano.

Cafés, bars Many on Calle Sobremonte, particularly *Café Latino* and *Gibbons*.

Exchange *Lucero Viajes*, Constitución 564, T 33656, only place changing TCs, 3% commission. *Coin*, Calle Buenos Aires on main plaza will change sterling.

Buses Buenos Aires, US$34, frequent service. Bus to **Mendoza**, US$24; to **Córdoba** US$10; frequent departures to **Santiago**.

Córdoba is 225 km N of Río Cuarto across flatlands and rolling hills. About half-way between the two, the road runs on the retaining wall of the great Río Tercero dam; the artificial lake here is used for recreation. The town of Río Tercero (several hotels) has gained in importance with the development of groundnut plantations and a local military factory.

Villa María, on the Mitre Railway and at a vital crossroads on the main Buenos Aires-Córdoba road, where it meets the most convenient highway route linking central Chile with Paraguay, Uruguay and Brazil, is a prosperous agricultural town (population 68,000). **Hotels C** *City*, Buenos Aires 1184, T 20948; **D** *Alcázar*, Alvear y Ocampo, T 22445, near bus station, good value.

Córdoba, capital of Córdoba Province and Argentina's second city, has about 1.2 million inhabitants; it stands at an altitude of 440m. The district is well known for its countryside and the city for its buildings; it was founded as early as 1573. The site of the first university in the country, founded in 1613 by the Jesuits, it now has two universities. It is an important industrial centre, the home of Argentina's motor industry. In the heart of the city is Plaza San Martín with a statue of the Liberator. On the W side is the old Cabildo, for many years used as the police headquarters, now a historical museum (see below). Next to it stands the Cathedral, the oldest in Argentina, started in 1697 and finished 1787, see the remarkable cupola. One of the features of this part of the city is its old churches. Near Plaza San Martín at Independencia 122 is the 16th century Carmelite convent and chapel of Santa Teresa, which houses the Museo de Arte Religioso. The church of La Compañía, on Calles Obispo Trejos and Caseros, with a simple façade, dates from about 1650 and is a far better building than the Cathedral; its façade was rebuilt in the 20th century. The barrel vault and cupola of the Capilla Doméstica of this church, built entirely of Paraguayan cedar, are unique. The basilica of La Merced at 25 de Mayo 83, was built in the early 19th century, though its fine gilt wooden pulpit dates from the colonial period. On its exterior, overlooking Calle Rivadavia, are fine murals by local artist Armando Sica. There are some pleasant small 18th century churches with striking bell gables and undulating pediments. The neo-gothic church of the Sagrado Corazón (Sacred Heart), built in 1933, at Buenos Aires e Yrigoyen, is also worth a visit. The Casa del Virrey (Viceroy's House), one block E of the Plaza San Martín, is a fine colonial building housing the Museo Histórico Provincial. Further E, at Blvd JD Perón, is the magnificent Mitre railway station, dating from the late 19th century, with its beautiful tiled *confitería*.

Although Córdoba was once very picturesque, industrialisation and population growth have turned it into a busy modern city with a flourishing shopping centre.

Museums Museo Histórico, in the old Cabildo, Plaza San Martín, free guided tours 1100 and 1700, Tues, Wed and Fri; **Museo Histórico Provincial**, in the Casa del Virrey Marqués de Sobremonte, Rosario de Santa Fe 318; **Museo de Ciencias Naturales**, Av Yrigoyen 115, open Mon-Fri 0800-1900, Sat 0900-1200, good guided tours (in Spanish, entry free, "interesting skeletons of prehistoric glyptodonts"); **Museo de Mineralogía y Geología** of the Universidad Nacional de Córdoba, V Sarsfield 299, open Mon-Fri, 1400-1600; **Museo de Zoología**, same address, open Mon-Fri 0900-1200, Wed-Fri 1600-1800, many birds but poorly displayed with no labels; **Museo del Teatro y de la Música**, in the Teatro San Martín, V Sarsfield 365, open Mon-Fri 0900-1200; **Museo Provincial de Bellas Artes**, Plaza España, open Tues-Fri 0900-1300, 1500-2000; **Museo Municipal de Bellas Artes**, Gral Paz 33, open Tues-Fri 0930-1330, 1630-2030, Sat 1630-2030; **Museo Histórico de la Ciudad**, Entre Ríos 40; **Centro de Arte Contemporáneo**, Parque San Martín; **Museo de Meteorología Nacional**, San Luis 801, open Tues-Fri 0900-1300, 1400-1800, Sat 0830-1230—nearby in Calle Laprida is Argentina's main observatory, open Wed 2000-2200; **Museo de Arte Religioso**, in the convent of Santa Teresa, Independencia 122, Sat 1030-1230.

Local Holidays 6 Jul (Foundation of the City); 30 Sep (St Jerome), 7-10 Oct.

Hotels More expensive hotels, mainly in the centre: **L3** *Crillón*, Rivadavia 85, T 46093, faded glory, very friendly, good restaurant, comfortable; **A2** *Mediterráneo*, Av MT de Alvear 10 T 24-0086; **B** *Cañada*, Av MT de Alvear 580, T 37589, good, incl conference facilities with full technical back-up, a/c, private bath, TV and video, restaurant, laundry, transport; **B** *Sussex*, San Jerónimo 125, T 229071, comfortable, roomy, discounts for ACA members; **B** *Windsor*, Buenos Aires 214, T 224012, comfortable, very good; **B** *Royal*, Blvd JD Perón 180, T 45000; all these have garages. **B** *Del Sol*, Balcarce 144, T 33961, with bath, clean, fan, a/c extra, piped music, rec. More economical: **C** *Garden*, 25 de Mayo 35, central, clean, secure, highly rec.

Hotels between Plaza San Martín and bus terminal, most of them in the cheaper brackets: On Corrientes, **D** *Bristol*, No 64, T 36222, bathroom, a/c, telephone; **D** *Hospedaje Suiza* (No 569), near bus terminal, very friendly but not too clean; **D** *Hospedaje Camacho* (No 519),

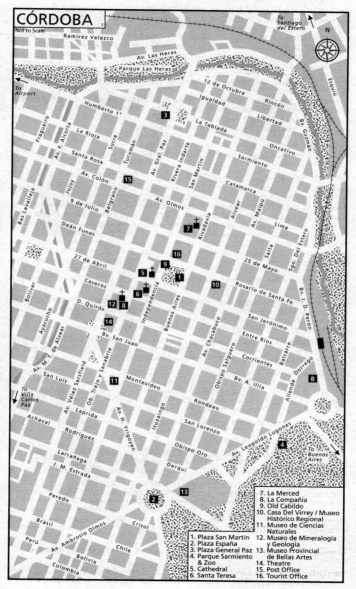

CÓRDOBA

Not to Scale

1. Plaza San Martín
2. Plaza España
3. Plaza General Paz
4. Parque Sarmiento & Zoo
5. Cathedral
6. Santa Teresa
7. La Merced
8. La Compañía
9. Old Cabildo
10. Casa Del Virrey / Museo Histórico Regional
11. Museo de Ciencias Naturales
12. Museo de Mineralogía y Geología
13. Museo Provincial de Bellas Artes
14. Theatre
15. Post Office
16. Tourist Office

clean, quiet, very friendly, rec; **D** *Residencial Mi Valle* (No 586), fan, shared bath, small, clean and nice, family-run, washing facilities, rec; **D** *Residencial Corrientes* (s/n) shared bath, not too clean, washing facilities, pleasant rooms. Plenty of hotels of all classes on San Jerónimo: **B** *Ritz* (No 495), T 45031, "clean but dilapidated"; **C** *Dallas* (No 339), T 46091, rec; **C** *Felipe II* (No 279), T 44752, in new part, **D** in old section, adequate; **D** *Corona* (No 574), T 228789, not incl breakfast, clean, comfortable, friendly. **C** *Roma Termini*, Entre Ríos 687, close to bus terminal, spotless, welcoming; **D** *Florida*, Rosario de Santa Fe 459, T 26373, clean, friendly, rec, some rooms with a/c. On Balcarce: **C** *Mallorca*, No 73, T 39234, quite clean and near bus and railway stations, noisy; **D** *Residencial Plaza*, No 336, 150m from bus station, clean, friendly and quiet.

Near Alta Córdoba station (Belgrano railway): **B** *Yolanda* (opposite station), delightful rooms, friendly, excellent restaurant, highly rec; **C** *Las Colonias*, Cabrera 339; **D** *Italiano*, Cabrera 313; **D** *La Amistad*, Roque Sáenz Peña 1523, T 711943, basic, clean; **D** *Suguía*, Roque Sáenz Peña 1561; **E** *Hospedaje Bontempo*, Cabrera 177. The following offer 10% discount to ISIC card holders: *del Sol*, Balcarce 144 (see above), and on Blvd Pte Arturo Illia, *Damar*, No 518, *del Boulevard*, No 182, *Heydi*, No 615.

A2 *ACA Hotel Dr Cesar C Carman*, Av Sabattini (Ruta 9) y Bajada del Pucará, T 243565, **A1** for non-members, very good.

Camping Municipal site, Gral San Martín, at the back of the Complejo Ferial (bus 31).

Restaurants There are numerous grills of all categories on the outskirts of the city, especially in the Cerro de las Rosas district, for meals out-of-doors when the weather is suitable. Many cheap restaurants along San Jerónimo incl *San Carlos*, No 431, good food and service. *Casino Español*, Rivadavia 63, good; *La Mamma*, Alcorta 270, excellent Italian, pricey; *Il Gatto*, Gral Paz y 9 de Julio, great pasta and pizzas, reasonably priced; *Romagnolo*, Av JD Perón y San Jerónimo, opposite the Mitre railway station, rec. *Betos*, San Juan 454, good *parrilla*, rec, pricey; *Fancy Café*, Andarte 317, good, cheap; *Firenze*, 25 de Mayo 220, busy, pleasant, traditional cafe. Excellent fruit juices (*licuados*) at *Kiosco Americano*, Tucumán 185 and at Gral Paz 242. Good *empanadas* at *La Vieja Esquina*, Belgrano y Caseros; *Empanadería La Alameda*, Obispo Trejo nr University, reasonable food, good student atmosphere, best 2200-2400. Icecream at branches of *Dolce Neve* throughout town; *Soppelsa's* ice cream is also highly rec, with several outlets.

Banks and Exchange Lloyds Bank (BLSA), Buenos Aires 23. **Citibank**, Rivadavia 104, poor rates. **Banco Sudameris** will buy Amex TCs at 1% commission. **Banco Fegin** for Mastercard. **Banco de Galicia** on Sucre for Amex cards. Amex, Simonelli Viajes, Av F Alcorta 50, T 26186. Many *cambios* on Rivadavia just off Plaza San Martín—shop around for best rate.

Cultural Institutes Asociación Argentina de Cultura Británica, Bv San Juan 137, good library, poor reading room. Open Mon-Fri 0900-1200, Mon, Wed, Fri 1600-1945, Tues, Thur 1500-1945. Goethe Institut, Bv Illia 356, open Tues-Fri 1700-2100.

Consulates Bolivia, Castro Barros 783, T 732827; **Chile**, Crisol 280, T 609622; **Paraguay**, 9 de Julio 573, T 226388; **Peru**, Poeta Lugones 212, T 603730. **Austria**, J Cortés 636, T 720450; **Italy**, Ayacucho 131, T 221020; **Germany**, A Olmos 501, T 692269; **Spain**, Bv Chacabuco 875, T 605013; **Sweden**, MT de Alvear 10, T 240094; **Switzerland**, Entre Ríos 185, L-10, T 226848; **Belgium**, F Posse 2533, T 813298; **Finland**, Chacabuco 716, T 605049.

Entertainment Discotheques Several on Av H Yrigoyen, expensive; late night rock music at *Música Pura*, Montevideo 100, Thur-Sat. Folk Music at *Pulpería El Viejo Rincón*, Dumesnil y Mendoza, excellent music till 0500.

Health English-speaking doctor, Ernesto J MacLoughlin, Centro Asistencial Privado de Enfermedades Renales, 9 de Julio 714, home Pérez del Viso 4316, T 814745. Dentist, Dra Olga Olmedo de Herrera, Fco J Muñiz 274, T 804378, her daughter speaks English and will translate.

Language Classes *Comisión de Intercambio Educativo*, San José de Calasanz 151, T 243606, offers classes mainly pre-arranged in Germany. (Contact Kommission für Bildungsaustausch, Wrangelstr 122, DW-2000 Hamburg 20.) *Interswop*, Mariano Fragueiro 2676, B Alta Córdoba, T/F 715442 (or Eppendorfer Weg 287, 20251 Hamburg, Germany, T/F 0049-40-484842) organizes stays abroad and language classes (about US$130/week, 25 hrs of classes) and accommodation at about US$10/day, also exchange programmes for any nationality (write to Hamburg address).

Laundry Chacabuco 32; *Laverap*, Paraná y Rondeau; *La Lavandería*, Avellaneda 182, local 4.

Post Office Parcel Service on the ground floor of the Correo Central, Av Colón 201, beside the customs office, up to 20 kg; wrapping service for small fee. **Telecommunications** Av Gen

Paz 36 and 27 de Abril 27.

Tourist Agencies *Carolina*, San Jerónimo 270, local 13/14, good value excursions but only run with minimum of 6 people; *El Delfín*, Gral Paz 250, local 140, 1° piso.

Tourist Office Dirección Provincial de Turismo, Tucumán 25. Municipal tourist information centre on San Martín at Rosario de Santa Fe 39. Information office also at bus station, has free maps; extensive information on accommodation and camping in the province, helpful. Tourist Office desk at airport often unmanned, but car-hire desks next to it are most helpful. A useful information booklet is the free monthly, *Plataforma 40*, put out by Nueva Estación Terminal de Omnibus de Córdoba (Netoc).

Club Andino, Deán Funes 2100, open Wed after 2100, closed Jan.

Local transport Municipal buses do not accept cash; you have to buy tokens (*cospeles*) or cards from kiosks, US$0.55. Buses No 70, 71 and 73 run between the Mitre Station (and bus terminus) and the Belgrano station at Alto Córdoba.

Car Hire Avis at airport and Corrientes 452, T 227384. A1, Entre Ríos 70, T 224867. Localiza at airport and Castro Barros 1155, T 747747.

Air Pajas Blancas airport, 11 km from the city, is modern and has a good restaurant and a bank (open Mon-Fri 1000-1500). Taxi to airport, US$15. Airport bus leaves terminal opposite railway station; irregular schedule, 30 mins, US$1.50. Alternatively take local bus No 55 from Santa Rosa y Avellaneda (Plaza Colón), allow 1 hr. Several flights to **Buenos Aires** daily, about 1 hr (Austral offering 65% discount on nocturnal flights); to **Mendoza** daily, Austral; to **Tucumán** daily, Austral. To **San Juan**, also daily Austral; to **Salta** Mon AR, Tues-Sun Austral, who fly 5 days a week to **Jujuy**. AR once a week to **Santa Cruz**, Bolivia. Aerolíneas Argentinas, Av Colón 520, T 819676. Austral, Av Colón 678, T 810997. LAB, same location as Alitalia, Av 25 de Mayo 6625, 3rd floor. KLM, Av General Paz 159.

Railways See under Buenos Aires, **Railways** for existing services. A new tourist service, the Tren de las Sierras, runs from Rodríguez del Busto station (15 km out of town) to Capilla del Monte. Dep 0830, returns 1530, Tues, Thur, Fri, Sat, Sun, US$10 one way, incl taxi transfer from main bus terminal to Rodríguez del Busto.

Buses Excellent new bus station at Blvd Perón 300, with Tourist Office, many public telephones, shops incl food supermarket on 3rd floor, bank (does not change cheques), post office, police, restaurants, and showers in bathrooms (about 6 blocks from centre), crowded at weekends. To **Buenos Aires**, Ablo, Costera Criolla, Chevalier or Cacorba, 10 hours, US$39 *común*, US$55 *diferencial*: to **Salta** (US$41) and **Jujuy** (US$45), Panamericano, 4 daily, La Veloz del Norte twice, about 12 and 15 hours. To **Mendoza** (10 hours), 6 a day with TAC, frequent delays and breakdowns, 1 daily with Uspallata US$29; to **Tucumán** US$25, 8 hrs, about 8 a day, Panamericano has more than other companies. To **Posadas** (Expreso Singer) Tues, Thur, Sat, 1730 arrive at Posadas at 1335; Thur and Sat bus continues to Iguazú arriving 1930 next day, no a/c. To **Santa Fe**, frequent, 5½ hrs, US$15. To **La Rioja** 3-4 a day with Cotil and El Cóndor, 6½ hrs; some go on to Catamarca. Córdoba-La Rioja-Aimogasta-**Tinogasta**- **Fiambalá** with El Cóndor, Tues, Thur, Fri; leaves Tinogasta 1140 arr Fiambalá 1240, returns from Fiambalá same day 1445, from Tinogasta at 1600 (**see also p 143**). La Calera bus leaves for **Belén** (Catamarca) on Mon, Wed, Fri, at 2100, arr Belén 1030; return journey, also via **Andalgalá**, Wed, Fri, Sun, dep 1600 arr Andalgalá 1735, dep 1750, arr Córdoba 0055. Cacorba, efficient a/c buses, serve **Villa Carlos Paz** (1 hr, frequent service, every 15 mins or so), **Cosquín** and **La Falda** in the Sierras of Córdoba.

To **Asunción** (Paraguay) direct with Brújula, four times a week, also with Cacorba 19 hrs, US$42. To **Montevideo** (Uruguay), dep 1700, Mon, Wed, Fri and Sun, with Encon, 15 hrs. To **Lima**, Peru, with Colta, dep Fri 2200, via Mendoza, 0700 Sat, arrives Lima Tues am, US$130. To **Pocitos** (Bolivian border) with Panamericano, Agustín Garzón 1229, San Vicente, Córdoba. In general, it is best to travel from Córdoba if you are going N, as at stations in between it may be hard to get a seat; a seat is only guaranteed if one pays US$1 extra.

The ***Sierras of Córdoba***, rising in undulating hills from the pampas, their lower slopes often wooded, particularly in the S, attract each year a large number of visitors. The highest peak, Champaquí (2,975m) has a small lake about 2,550m up. The hills run, roughly, for 500 km from N to S; W of Córdoba they are 150 km wide. There are three ranges of them: the Sierra Grande, the longest, in the middle, with Sierra Chica to the E and Sierra de Guisapampa and its continuation, the Sierra de Pocho, to the W. A network of good roads gives pleasant contrasts of scenery, but there are few footpaths and trails for the walker. The region's climate is dry, sunny and exhilarating, especially in winter.

At the foot of the Sierra Chica are large dams to contain the waters of the Río Primero at Río Molinos (29 km from Córdoba, Route 5, good *pejerrey* and trout-fishing; bus to Villa Carlos Paz), San Roque, and Río Tercero. There are two other large dams in the hills, at Cruz del Eje and La Viña. They provide power and irrigation, and the lakes are in themselves attractive. The Government keeps them stocked with fish. Sailing is popular.

Information can be obtained at travel agencies, at the Dirección Provincial de Turismo or at Casa de Córdoba at Callao 332, Buenos Aires.

Note There are innumerable good hotels and *pensiones* in the Córdoba mountain region; names are therefore not always given. Many services in this area are closed out of season.

The Punilla Valley: *Villa Carlos Paz*, pop 46,000, is 36 km W of Córdoba (buses from Córdoba bus terminal every 15 mins in summer, 36 km, US$1.40; taxi from Córdoba airport, US$10.50; Buenos Aires-Villa Carlos Paz with Ablo, US$26—T BsAs 313-2995; also Cacorba, Chevallier, General Urquiza), on man-made Lago San Roque. It is the nearest resort to Córdoba and is therefore often crowded. Tours possible on amphibian buses which go as far as the two dams on the lake (US$10); launch trips also available. There is a pleasant 5 km walk to the dam from the outskirts of Villa Carlos Paz. At the Casa de Gaspar, Miguel Cané and El Redentor, roller-skating and optical illusions, Fri-Sun 1400-1900 out of season. A chair-lift runs up the slopes to a tearoom and night club overlooking the valley, between 0900 and 1900. Bus tours to areas such as Sierra Chica, for those who like snack bars, fun slides and gravity-defying houses.

Accommodation, Restaurants and Services Plenty of hotels, big and small, eg **B** *El Ciervo de Oro*, Hipólito Yrigoyen 995, T 22498, on the lake, rec; **D** *El Monte*, Caseros 45, T 22001, very good, rec. **D** *Mar del Plata*, friendly, rec; **D** *Villa Carlos Paz Parque*, Santa Fe 50, full board available, rec. Camping at ACA site and several others incl **Las Tolderías** and **Los Pinos**, rec, Curro Enrique y Lincoln (open all year). There are many campsites near the main road through the Punilla Valley, most open Dec-Apr only. Best buys: leather mats, bags, pottery. *Restaurant Carlos Paz* highly rec for food and setting. *Restaurant Pamilla Mingo*, Av Uruguay opp *Hotel Uruguay*, not cheap but good. **NB** Drinking water is not safe. Banco de Córdoba, Av San Martín, will change US$ cash only. Laundry at San Martín y Libertad. Post Office and telephone on Av Gral San Martín. **Tourist office** at bus station, very friendly.

A few km SW of Villa Carlos Paz is the small town at *Ycho Cruz*, by the San Antonio river (bus from Córdoba, with Emp Cotap, US$2; one hotel outside the centre, *Hostería Avenida*, E with bath, usually for air force personnel only, but open to the public if not busy, very clean and pleasant; also several campsites. The *Comedor Familiar* on the main street near the supermarket is rec, good and cheap). Continuing S from Ycho Cruz the road crosses the scenic Pampa de Achala, a huge desert plateau of grey granite, to the small village of El Condor (one bar and a service station, buses from Córdoba, US$5). 7 km N of El Condor is a wide trail leading to Quebrada de los Condoritos (6-7 km), with superb landscape and the chance of seeing condors in their easternmost habitat (thanks for this information to Ortelli Jiri Moreno, Como, Italy).

North of Villa Carlos Paz, on Route 38, a road branches W to Tanti from where local buses go to Los Gigantes, a paradise for climbers, 2-day treks possible. Club Andino has several *refugios*; details in Villa Carlos Paz.

From Villa Carlos Paz Route 38 runs N through the Punilla valley to the following string of resorts: *Cosquín*, 63 km from Córdoba, on the banks of the Río Cosquín, is known as the National Folklore Capital and is the site of the most important folklore festival, beginning last week in Jan. A new arena seating 10,000 spectators has been built and recent reports suggest the festival is becoming commercialized. Museo Camin Cosquín at Km 767, out of town, minerals and archaeology, rec. Bus Córdoba-Cosquín US$2.60, Empresa La Capillense; 1½ hrs, via Carlos Paz or with La Calera via the San Roque dam. Altitude, 720m; pop 16,000. Camping on S bank of river. Tourist office at San Martín 560, **D** *Hotel La Serrana*, P Ortiz 740, near bus station, friendly, good; likewise **D** *Hotel Italia*, across from bus station, rec; **E** pp *Residencial Cosquín*, Tucumán y Sabattini, clean; **E** *Hotel Petit*, Calle Sabattini, 2 blocks from bus station. Take a bus to the Pan de Azúcar hill from where there is a good view over the Punilla valley, at 0930, return 1630 or 2 hrs walk. Chairlift to top (all year round). 19 km N of Cosquín is *Valle Hermoso*, near La Falda (buses from Villa Carlos Paz). Altitude, 850m. Old restored chapel of San Antonio, a little gem. Riding, motoring. Youth hostel, address "Steinhaus", dirty, no heating, very cold, US$2 pp, pay extra for gas. Camping near river,

US$0.60 pp, all facilities, but not too clean.

La Falda (pop 30,000) 82 km from Córdoba, a good touring centre, friendly and peaceful. Bus from Córdoba 2 hrs, US$3. Altitude, 933m. Helpful tourist offices at bus station and in old railway station. Model railway museum at Las Murallas zoo at the end of Av 25 de Mayo. Nearby is the privately run Ambato Archaeological Museum; articles are well displayed, worth a visit, open Thur-Sun and public holidays 0900-2000, US$0.50 entrance. About 30 hotels in all categories, all full in Dec-Feb holiday season (eg **D** *Residencial Atena*, Rosario 329, clean, comfortable, rec), at other times a basic room with bath is in our E range. Houses for rent 1 Mar to 30 Nov on a monthly basis. *Restaurant El Bochín*, Av España 411, good, cheap. Jazz at old *Hotel Eden*; La Falda is visited mostly by the elderly; most hotels belong to pension funds. Tap water is not safe. Bancos de la Nación and de Suquía for exchange. Students of all nations welcome at Córdoba University holiday centre at Vaquerías, 2 km from La Falda. Travel agent Wella Viajes, Av Edén 412, loc 12, T 0548-21380, offers 15% discount to ISIC and youth card holders for trekking, climbing, etc to Cerro Champaquí. Camping near small river. (Bus from Buenos Aires, Cacorba, Cita, US$40.)

Excursions to Quebrada Chica, Cascada del Molino. Extensive hiking in surrounding hills. To La Candelaria, 53 km W along unpaved roads where there is a Jesuit *estancia* and chapel dating from 1693. From La Falda 3½ km N by Route 38 is **Huerta Grande**, at 971m, a resort with good fishing and medicinal waters. Round trip excursion to *Cascadas de Olaén*. Take the road to Valle Hermoso S 10 km towards Cosquín, then follow dirt road about 12½ km to the crossing marked "Cascadas de Olaén"; from here walk 4½ km to the falls: quite spectacular canyon—the water splashes into a small lake full of little fish. Return to the dirt road and 2½ km to a monolith and another dirt road, which leads to La Falda. See the Pampa de Olaén, where there are many quartz mines.

Bus to Asunción, Cacorba, US$69. Connections to Rosario, Mendoza, Catamarca, Santiago del Estero, Tucumán, Salta and Jujuy.

La Cumbre, 12 km N of La Falda. Bus from Córdoba US$4, 2½ hrs. Altitude 1,141m. Trout streams with good fishing from Nov to Apr. Fiesta de la Cerveza Montañesa in Feb, first 3 weeks, beer, meat, hunting and fishing. Swimming, golf, tennis and hang gliding. Has an airport. **C** *Hotel Lima*, swimming pool, quiet, clean. Charming small inn, *Victoria*; *La Cumbre Inn*, large and commercial, good views; **D** *Residencial Peti*, good, friendly. Good restaurants.

Cruz Chica, 2 ½ km N of La Cumbre, altitude, 1,067m, has very English houses and gardens in pine woods. Good English boys' school.

Los Cocos, 8 km N of La Cumbre, is a delightful, extremely popular mountain resort with 3 first rate hotels and many holiday houses. **D** *Hostería Zanier*, full board B, rec. *Blair House*, English-style pub, rec. Hang-gliding nearby at Cuchi Corral.

Capilla del Monte, in the heart of the Sierras, 106 km from Córdoba (bus 3 hrs, US$5.20, from BsAs, General Urquiza, US$35; **C** *Hospedaje Italiano*, clean, showers, opposite bus station; municipal campsite on the way to Cerro Uritorco, G pp, rec, and also 9½ km from Capilla del Monte) . Altitude, 914m. Medicinal waters (good baths at La Toma), rocks and waterfalls and wide views; El Zapato rock is "graffiti–ridden", better are Los Mogotes, 3 km from town, reached through Paseo del Indio. Excursions in the hills, particularly to Cerro Uritorco (1,950m) and to Los Alazanes dam; good path on Uritorco, walk takes 2½ hrs. Permission to walk obtainable from a house beyond crossing (US$3). Many free walks after crossing bridge at La Toma, rec. You can walk on to the direct dirt road to San Marcos Sierra (22 km W); many parakeets and small farmhouses. Along the way you will also get views down to the *Cruz del Eje* dam (**B** *Hotel Posta de las Carretas*, Ruta 38 y R Moyano, T 0549-2517, good, service station and restaurants at the crossroads; camping possible at foot of dam, or stay at friendly, family-run **D** *Hotel España* in village, some private baths; rowboats for rent on dam's lake, where there is good fishing). Cruz del Eje (pop 23,100) is one of two towns with its own "micro-climate" (the other is Merlo in San Luis Province) and own honey production—try that made from carob (*algarrobo*) blossom (1 kg about US$2). Excellent trout fishing at Tío Mayo, an hour from Capilla del Monte by car.

A road runs **North from Córdoba** to *Ascochinga* via pleasant little townships such as Villa Allende, Río Ceballos, Salsipuedes and La Granja. At El Manzano, 40 km N of Córdoba, a road branches W to *Candonga*, altitude 810m. The historic church, now a National Monument, was built in 1730 as an oratory of the Jesuit Estancia of Santa Gertrudis. The arch protrudes to form a porch covering the entrance. 14 km N of Ascochinga is *Santa Catalina*, originally a Jesuit mission founded in 1622 and the most elaborate Jesuit establishment in the hills around Córdoba (no bus from Ascochinga, but 2 a day from Jesús María). (See the church begun in 1754, workshops and stone conduits; the families who now occupy the place as a summer home will show you round.)

Services In Ascochinga: C *Hostería El Cortijo*, full board only, good value, with bath, small swimming pool and river outside, horses for rent, US$1/hr; 5 km walk to Tres Cascadas falls and *balneario*. During winter, open weekends only. Campsite open all year. In **Río Ceballos**: E *Albergue La Gloria*, affiliated to IYHA, warmly rec; 5 campsites. Several campsites also at **Salsipuedes**.

From Ascochinga a road runs E for 20 km to **Jesús María** 51 km N of Córdoba on Route 9. Altitude, 533m (several hotels). Good 18th century Jesuit church and the remains of its once famous winery; in the cloister is an excellent Museo Jesuítico, said to be one of the best on the continent (Mon-Fri 0800-1200 and 1400-1900, Sat and Sun 1600-2000). Each Jan there is a gaucho and folklore festival, lasting 10 nights from 2nd week; very popular. Good trout, *dorado*, and carp fishing in winter. Direct bus from Córdoba, US$2, 1½ hrs. Some 4 km N of Jesús María is **Sinsacate**, with an interesting church. There is also a fine colonial posting inn, now a museum, with long, deep verandah and chapel attached. Route 9, the main road to Santiago del Estero, runs N. Another 132 km to **Villa de María**, the birthplace of Leopoldo Lugones, a poet of country life. His house is a museum. (**D** *Hotel City*, good.)

At Rayo Cortado, 22 km S of Villa de María, a turning leads W to **Cerro Colorado**, 160 km N of Córdoba, the former home of the Argentine folklore singer and composer Atahualpa Yupanqui. His house, now a museum can be visited, US$2 – ask in the village for the curator. There are more than 30,000 rock paintings by the Comechingones Indians in the nearby Cerro Colorado archaeological park and a small archaeological museum (US$1 entry, includes guide in English or Spanish). There is cheap accommodation (eg with Sosa family) and camping. You can stay with Don Elvio, who runs the *pulpería* near the archaeological station. Buses: from Córdoba, Tues, Wed, Thur, Sun, to Santiago del Estero, get off at Santa Elena, hitch from there (11 km); from Jesús María, daily 1610.

Southwest of Córdoba a scenic road climbs from Villa Carlos Paz through the Sierra Grande to another chain of resorts, Mina Clavero, Villa Dolores and Yacanto.

Mina Clavero is 140 km from Córdoba by bus, 6 a day, 4 hrs, beautiful ride through grand lake and hill scenery, and curious palm trees. Three rivers, popular for swimming, pass through the town centre. Altitude, 915m. (**D** *Hospedaje El Clavero*, San Martín 1405, many others; Restaurant: *Rincón Suizo*, Calle Champaquí 1200, T 0544-70447, good pastries.) A good centre for exploring the high *sierra*. No money exchange available. There is a nice church and a most interesting museum, dedicated by a French archaeologist, 13 km S from Mina Clavero and about 5 km from the village of Nono, entrance US$3, called "Rocsen" open 0900 till sunset, with furniture, minerals, instruments, animals, etc.

Villa Dolores, 187 km from Córdoba (bus takes 5 hrs), 48 km SW of Mina Clavero. Altitude, 529m; pop 21,000. The road from Córdoba crosses the two mountain ranges to reach finally the Pampa de Achala (**see p 98**). (Hotels E *Hospedaje Cáceres*, Brizuela 390; E *Residencial Champaquí*, Erdman 162. **Camping** nearest site is Piedra Pintada, 15 min-bus-ride away, pleasant village well situated for walks into mountains.) Bus to San Luis 5¼ hrs.

Champaquí, 2,884m, the highest peak in the Sierras lies E of Villa Dolores. It can be reached from San Javier, 19 km SE of Villa Dolores. For summit, follow path to Capilla La Constancia, set in river valley with pine and nut trees, 2-3 hrs. Take water from here, then cross the river (path), keep left through a pinewood up to a mountain range and follow it up to the top of a huge plateau. Good path, about 4-5 hrs, and then you reach a square enclosure, whence you keep left. Follow stone mounds about 2 hrs until you see the higher of two peaks, which is Champaquí. Lovely views, descent to La Constancia 4 hrs. An alternative route is from Villa de las Rosas, 12 km E of Villa Dolores (several hotels). Neither route should be attempted in misty weather. A good base is *Vai Kunta*, 5885 Villa de las Rosas, run by Rolf Graf (Swiss), rooms for rent, good food, guiding service. Take any Córdoba-Villa Dolores bus to Villa de las Rosas; at bus station look for the *pizzería* where taxis to Los Nolles can be arranged. From Los Nolles it's a 2-hr walk to the house.

2 km S of San Javier, at the foot of Champaquí, in a region of woods and waterfalls is *Yacanto*. Reached by road from Villa Dolores. Curative waters.

A road **South from Córdoba** runs to Alta Gracia and to the Río Tercero dam. **Alta Gracia** (alt 580m; pop 39,000) is 29 km SW of Córdoba beside Lago Tajamar. (Bus ¾ hr, every 15 mins, US$0.75.) Interesting colonial church, finished about 1762,

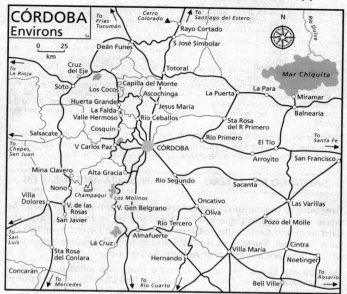

open am and after 1700, and buildings housing Museo del Virrey Liniers, on the Estancia de Alta Gracia, founded in 1588 and taken over by the Jesuits in 1643, open Tues-Fri 0900-1300, 1500-1830, Sat, Sun 0930-1230, 1530-1830, US$1 (all day in summer). There is also the Museo Manuel de Falla on Pellegrini Final, closed Mon, entry US$0.30, where the Spanish composer spent his last years. Take the local bus to La Paysanita or La Serranita for a quiet environment (but no cheap accommodation). Beautiful views from the Gruta de la Virgen de Lourdes, 3 km W of town.

Services *Hostería Reina*, Urquiza 129, good. Two camp sites, one scruffy, the other better and free in winter, which is by golf course. A few reasonably priced restaurants in town centre. Tourist office inside clock tower by Lago Tajamar. Casino.

To the Bosque Alegre and Observatory it is 24 km NW, open Thur 1600-1800, Sun 1000-1200 and 1600- 1800. Good views over Córdoba, Alta Gracia and the Sierra Grande. To the Río Tercero dam (site of a nuclear power staton) is 79 km further S; on the lake is a workers' holiday colony and an ACA *Unidad Turística*.

Villa General Belgrano, 58 km S of Alta Gracia is a completely German town founded by the surviving interned seamen from the *Graf Spee*, some of whom still live in the town. It is a pleasant resort and a good centre for excursions in the surrounding mountains. Beer festival in Oct. If walking between here and La Cumbrecita with Siegfried at *Alta Vista*, E, friendly. **Accommodation B** *Hotel Bremen*, Route 5 y Cerro Negro, T 6133, restaurant, sports facilities; **D** *Allgauer Hütten*, clean, friendly, quiet. There are two *Youth Hostels*, one at Estancia Alta Vista, 14 km from the town, and one, *El Rincón*, D, in beautiful surroundings, cooking facilities, highly rec, in the town (reservations—Patricia Mampsey, Casilla 64, T 6323); both offer discounts to ISIC and youth card holders (25% and 20% respectively). Buses to **Córdoba**, 2 hrs, US$4, 8 a day; to **Mendoza**, US$28; to **Buenos Aires**, Colta (T BsAs 313-0590), 1 a day, US$35.

La Cumbrecita is a German village 30 km W of Villa General Belgrano, reached from General

Belgrano by taxi (US$33, 1-1½ hrs) or by bus, Sun only. Good walking and riding. **Hotels**: **B** *Cascadas*, with pool, tennis etc; **B** *Panorama*, higher up hill (T 98406); three others (B) and **C** *Residencial Casa Rosita*. *Youth Hostel* at Villa Alpina, 17 km from the town.

Some 200 km NE of Córdoba the Río Dulce, flowing in places through salt flats, runs into the shallow *Mar Chiquita* on the S margin of the Chaco and about 320 km SE of Santiago del Estero. People who live in the valley of the Río Dulce are so used to the taste of its water that they often add a pinch of salt to the water they drink when away from home. Mar Chiquita, which is now growing rapidly, is naturally salty, and the water is warm. No river drains it, though two other rivers flow into it from the Sierras of Córdoba in the flood season. There are several islands in the lake. On its S shore is the small town of *Miramar*, which is being gradually overwhelmed by the expanding Mar Chiquita. The area is a very popular resort during the summer months; its salt waters are used in the treatment of rheumatic ailments and skin diseases.

Hotels *Savoy*, cheap, very friendly. **Camping** Autocamping Lilly, Bahía de los Sanavirones.

NB This Mar Chiquita and its town, Miramar, must not be confused with the other Mar Chiquita to the N of Mar del Plata and the seaside resort of Miramar, S of Mar del Plata.

SANTIAGO DEL ESTERO, TUCUMAN, SALTA AND JUJUY (3)

The route to the major tourist centre of Salta, from where trips can be made into Andean regions, the Quebrada de Humahuaca and the Calchaquí and Cachi valleys. There are prehispanic ruins near Tafí del Valle, Quilmes, Santa Rosa de Tastil and others. This is also a region in which there are a number of Amerindian groups.

Santiago del Estero, the oldest Argentine town, was founded in 1553 by conquistadores pushing S from Peru. It is 395 km N of Córdoba and 159 km SE of Tucumán. Population 201,000. On the main square, Plaza Libertad, stand the Municipalidad and the Cathedral (the fifth on the site). The fine Casa de Gobierno is on Plaza San Martín, 3 blocks away. In the convent of Santo Domingo, Urquiza y 25 de Mayo, is a "Holy Shroud", one of two copies of the "Turin Shroud", thought until recently to have covered the body of Christ. This copy was given by Philip II to his "beloved colonies of America". On Plaza Lugones is the pleasant old church of San Francisco, the oldest surviving church in the city, founded in 1565. At the back of the church is the cell of San Francisco Solano, patron saint of Tucumán, who stayed in Santiago in 1593. Beyond the church is the pleasant Parque Aguirre. Several public buildings, including the Casa de Gobierno, were severely burned and damaged in a popular upheaval in 1993 because of low incomes. Airport (Austral flights to Buenos Aires 5 times a week).

Museums Museo Arqueológico, Avellaneda 353, containing a large collection of Indian pottery and artefacts from the Chaco, brought together by Emil and Duncan Wagner, open Mon-Fri, 0800-1300, 1400-1900, Sat, 0900-1200, free; **Museo Histórico**, Urquiza 354, open Mon-Fri, 0830-1230, 1530-1830, Sat 0900-1200; **Museo de Bellas Artes**, Independencia between 9 de Julio and Urquiza, open Mon-Fri, 0900-1300; **Museo Andrés Chazarreta**, Mitre 127, handicrafts.

Festival Carnival in Feb is to be avoided: virtually everything throwable gets thrown by everyone at everyone else.

Hotels B *Gran Hotel*, Avellaneda e Independencia, T 214400, 4-star; *Libertador*, Catamarca 47, T 215766, 3-star; **B** *Residencial Rodas*, Gallo 432, clean, safe, overpriced. **D** *Embajador*, Buenos Aires 60; **D** *Residencial Emausí*, Av Moreno 600 block, with bath, good value. Around the bus terminus are: **D** *Residencial Santa Fe*, Santa Fe 255; *Santa Rita*, Santa Fe 273, clean, basic.

Camping Las Casuarinas in the Parque Aguirre.

Restaurant *Restaurant Sociedad Española*, Independencia 236, popular, good value; *Centro de Viajantes*, Buenos Aires 37, good value lunches; *Mía Mamma*, 24 de Septiembre 16, on Plaza, good restaurant/salad bar, pricey.

Exchange Banco Francés, 9 de Julio y 24 de Septiembre; **Noroeste Cambio**, 24 de

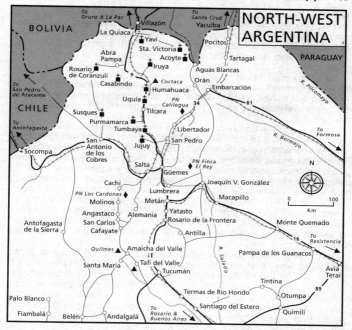

Septiembre 220, good rates. Amex, El Quijote Paladea Turismo, Independencia 342, T 213207.

Tourist Office on Plaza Libertad, very helpful.

Buses to **Resistencia**, 3 a day, 9 hrs, US$25, run by El Rayo company, via Quimili and Roque Sáenz Peña (8 hrs); to **Córdoba**, 12 a day, 7 hrs, US$16; to **Tucumán** (via Río Hondo) US$7. To **Buenos Aires**, several daily, 12 hrs, US$37, Cacorba, La Unión and Atahualpa. Four a day to Salta, US$23, Panamericano, 5½ hrs, and to Jujuy, 7 hrs.

Termas de Río Hondo, 65 km N of Santiago del Estero along the road to Tucumán, is a major spa town, population 25,000. The thermal waters are recommended for blood pressure and rheumatism; good to drink, too, and used for the local soda water. Swimming (free) in a public pool called La Olla near the bridge which crosses the Río Hondo (see **Camping** below). Tourist office at Pasaje Borges, s/n. Frequent buses from Santiago del Estero, 1 hr, US$2 and from Tucumán, 2 hrs, US$4; Chevallier, La Estrella and others from Buenos Aires US$38 (US$75 return). The huge Río Hondo dam on the Río Dulce is close by; it forms a lake of 33,000 ha, used for sailing and fishing.

Hotels There are over 170 hotels, but at national holiday periods, and especially in Aug, accommodation is hard to find, so book well in advance. *Grand Hotel Río Hondo*, Hipólito Yrigoyen 552, T 21185; *Los Pinos*, Maipú 201, T 21175, pleasant; **C** *Ambassador*, Libertad 184, T 21196; *Aranjuez*, Av Alberdi 280, T 21108.

Camping Municipal site, Irigoyen y Ruta 9, near river bank; *La Olla*, left bank of river; ACA 3 km from town; *El Mirador*, Ruta 9 y Urquiza.

Tucumán (properly San Miguel de Tucumán, pop 400,000), capital of its province, is the busiest and the most populous city in the N. It stands on a plain, at 450m, but to the W towers the Sierra de Aconquija. The city was founded by Spaniards coming S from Peru in 1565. There are still some colonial buildings left, and among rows of elaborately stuccoed, spacious, one-storey houses (many of them sadly dilapidated) rise three or four handsome churches with blue and white tiled domes, and the elaborate Italianate Post Office. Summer weather can be very hot and sticky.

Tucumán's main square is Plaza Independencia. On its W side is the ornate Palacio de Gobierno, next is the church of San Francisco, with a picturesque façade. On the S side is the Cathedral, with an old rustic cross, kept near the baptismal font, used when founding the city. There are some unusual modern paintings inside the cathedral.

To the S, on Calle Congreso, is the **Casa Histórica** (see also below) where, in 1816, the Congress of the United Provinces of Río de la Plata met to draft the country's Declaration of Independence. The simple room in which this took place survived the destruction of the original house in 1908 and has now been enclosed in a reconstructed colonial museum. A bas-relief on the museum walls shows the delegates proclaiming independence. Some distance to the W is Plaza Belgrano, with a statue to General Belgrano, who won a decisive battle against the royalists on this site in 1812. Two blocks E is the University, with a grand view from the *vivero*. In the grounds is a good zoo, the Reserva Biológica San Javier. Nightly (not Tues, except in Jul) at 2030, *son et lumière* programme at Casa Histórica, in garden, in Spanish only, adults US$2, children US$1, tickets from tourist office on Plaza Independencia, no seats.

In the large Nueve de Julio park (avoid at night) is the house of Bishop Colombres, who introduced sugar cane to Tucumán in the early 19th century. In the house is his first milling machine. The province of Tucumán is the centre of Argentine sugar production. There are several mills nearby: the easiest to visit is Ingenio Concepción, a modern plant on the outskirts of town, guided tours in Spanish during harvest period only (15 Jul-early Nov), Mon-Sat, 0930 and 1030, no booking required. Take Aconquija bus for Santo Cristo from outside bus terminus in 24 de Septiembre, US$0.40, pay on bus, 15 mins.

Museums Casa Histórica (see above), Calle Congreso, open Tues-Fri 0830-1330, Tues, and Thur, 1700-2000, Sat, Sun 1000-1300, US$0.40. **Museo de Antropología y Etnografía**, 25 de Mayo 265 in University building, fine collection, open Mon-Fri, 0800-1200, 1600-2000. **Museo Folklórico Provincial**, 24 de Septiembre 565, open Mon 1730-2030, Tues-Fri, 0900-1230, 1730-2030, Sat, Sun, 1800-2100, free. **Instituto Miguel Lillo**, San Lorenzo y Lillo (30 mins walk from bus station), associated with the natural sciences department of the University, has a small but well-presented museum containing sections on geology and biology with some stuffed animals and a dinosaur skeleton, open Mon-Fri, 0900-1200, 1500-1800. The Institute also possesses a fine specialist library (not open to the public) which incl an original edition of Von Humboldt's travels in South America. **Casa Padilla**, Plaza Independencia, houses a collection of international art and antiques in the home of a prominent Tucumán family. Near the Casa Histórica at Calle Congreso 56 is the **Museo Histórico de la Provincia** (Casa de Avellaneda) open Mon-Fri, 0900-1230, 1700-2000, Sat-Sun, 1700-2000, closed for reorganization (early 1995); **Museo Iramaín**, Entre Rios 27, a very interesting memorial to the sculptor, open Mon-Fri, 0900-1900. **Museo de Bellas Artes**, 9 de Julio 48, between 24 de Septiembre and Alvarez, open Tues-Fri, 0900-1300, 1630-2100, Sat-Sun, 0900-1200, 1730-2030.

Local Holiday 24 Sep (Battle of Tucumán). 29 Sep, San Miguel. Independence celebrations incl music and speeches at the Casa Histórica on 8 Jul, followed by *gauchos* bringing in the National Flag at midnight. Next day there are markets and music. Also Día de la Tradición, 10 Nov.

Hotels L3 *Grand Hotel de Tucumán*, Av Soldati 380, T 245000, large, new five-star hotel opposite the Parque Centenario 9 de Julio, efficient, outstanding food and service, swimming pool, tennis courts, discotheque; **A1** *Carlos V*, 25 de Mayo 330, T 215042/221972, central, good service, a/c, bar, restaurant, excellent pasta, rec; **A2** *Metropol*, 24 de Septiembre 524, T 311180, good service, worth it; **B** *Gran Hotel Corona*, 24 de Septiembre on corner of Plaza Independencia, good location and facilities, run down; **B** *ACA Motel Tucumán*, Av Salta 2080,

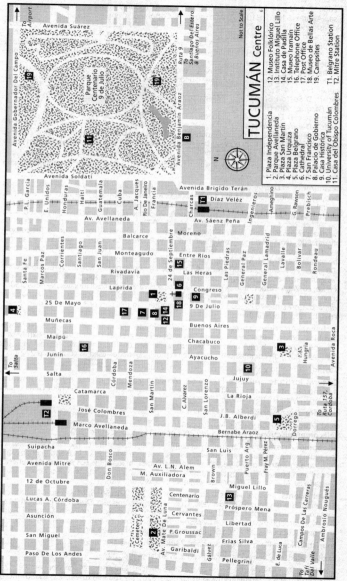

TUCUMÁN Centre

1. Plaza Independencia
2. Parque Avellaneda
3. Plaza San Martín
4. Plaza Urquiza
5. Plaza Belgrano
6. Cathedral
7. San Francisco
8. Palacio de Gobierno
9. Casa Histórica
10. University of Tucumán
11. Casa del Obispo Colombres
12. Museo Folklórico
13. Instituto Miguel Lillo
14. Casa de Padilla
15. Museo Iramain
16. Telephone Office
17. Post Office
18. Museo de Bellas Arte
19. Campsites

T1. Belgrano Station
T2. Mitre Station

Not to Scale

T 266037; **B** *Miami*, Junín 580, T 310265, garage; **B** *Premier*, with a/c, good, friendly, accepts Visa, Alvarez 510, T 310381. Also good: **C** *Congreso*, Congreso 74, T 216025, clean, old-fashioned but rec, with bath, plain, good location; **C** *Plaza*, San Martín 435, T 215502, built round a pretty central courtyard, basic but clean; **C** *Viena*, Santiago del Estero 1054, T 310313; **D** *Tucumán*, Catamarca 573, near Mitre station, clean, OK; **D** *La Vasca*, Mendoza 281, T 211288, with bath, clean, friendly, safe, rec; **D** *Casa de Huéspedes María Ruiz*, Rondeau 1824, clean, safe, rec.

There are hotels near the bus station, eg **B** *Colonial*, San Martín 35, 5 mins from bus station, modern, very clean, private bath, fan, laundry service, breakfast incl, rec; **B** *Mayoral*, 24 de Septiembre 364, T 228351, F 54-81-310080, 20% discount to *South American Handbook* readers; **D** *Boston*, Sáenz Peña, 77, nice courtyards, restaurant, but some rooms are very dirty; **D** *El Parque*, Sgto Gómez 22, across from bus station, fan, clean (though used as a brothel), friendly, safe; **D** *Florida*, 24 de Septiembre 610, T 221785, good value, clean, poorly-lit rooms, helpful; **D** *Independencia*, Balcarce, between San Martín and 24 de Septiembre, with fan, clean, quiet; **D** *Palace*, 24 de Septiembre 233, friendly, rec; **D** *Petit*, C Alvarez 765, T 213902, spacious, friendly, clean, quiet, with bath and breakfast incl, highly rec. Many cheap hotels in streets around General Belgrano station.

Camping Parque Nueve de Julio, 2 sites (US$0.25 per tent, US$0.25 pp). Two roadside camp sites 3 km E and NE of city centre.

Restaurants *El Duque*, San Lorenzo 464, very large, popular, good food, poor service. Good food, poor service in open air at *La Rural* and *Gran Grill* 38, Parque 9 de Julio; there are also several cafés in the park. *Ali Baba*, Junín 380, Arab specialities (Syrian owners), intimate, inexpensive, good, rec, closed lunchtime; *Adela*, 24 Septiembre 358, well prepared food, Arab specialities, good value; *La Leñita*, 25 de Mayo, 300 block, expensive, smart, good meat. *La Parrilla del Centro*, San Martín 381, excellent, reasonable prices; *Farolito Criollo*, Crisóstomo Alvarez 600, regional dishes, very cheap but dirty; *Pizzería La Esquina*, Mendoza y Laprida, good; *Las Gordas*, Plaza Independencia, pleasant, popular with locals, as is *La Plaza*, also on the square; *Las Brasas*, Maipú 740, good but not cheap. Good fast food at *Pic Nic*, San Juan 600 block and Ayacucho 500 block; *Augustus*, 24 Septiembre y Buenos Aires, good café; *Pastísima Rotisería*, Mendoza y Laprida and at San Martín 964, good cheap snacks, take out service; *La Vieja Casa*, Córdoba 680, good, inexpensive set lunch. Set lunches near bus station good value, for instance *Camboriú*, Av Brígido Terán, cheap, clean, and friendly. *Panadería Villecco*, Corrientes 751, good bread, also "integral". In this part of Argentina "black beer" (eg Salta Negra) is available.

Exchange American Express, Chacabuco 38, no longer changes cash or cheques. **Noroeste Cambios**, 24 de Septiembre 549 and San Martín 775, accepts cheques. **Dinar**, San Martín 645 and 742, accepts cash only, and **Maguitur**, San Martín 763, good rates for cash, accepts cheques (with high commission). (See note on provincial bonds used as currency, **p 222**.)

Casino Sarmiento y Maipú, open Fri, Sat, Sun, 2100-0230.

Cultural Institutes Alliance Française, Mendoza 255, free events in French. **Instituto Italiano di Cultura**, Salta 60; **ATICANA** (North American Centre) incl JF Kennedy Library, Salta 581, open Mon-Fri, 0800-1200, 1700-2100.

Laundry *Lava Expreso*, San Martín 929.

Post Office Córdoba y 25 de Mayo, open 0700-1300, 1600-2000 Mon-Fri, 0800-1300 Sat. **Telecommunications** Telecom, Maipú 360, open 24 hrs, best after 1900.

Shopping *Artesanía El Cardón*, Alvarez 427, excellent handicrafts; Mercado Artesanal, at the tourist office in Plaza Independencia, small, but nice selection of lace and leather work. *Librería San Martín* on 24 de Septiembre has English magazines. *Los Primos*, C Muñecas, secondhand books. All shops close 1200-1630. There is a lively fruit and vegetable market, Mercado de Abasto, at San Lorenzo y Miguel Lillo, worth a visit.

Travel Agents *Massini Viajes*, 24 de Septiembre 377, T 215616; *Viajes Ru-Mar*, Alvarez 566, organises day trips to Tafí del Valle, Quilmes etc, Sat, and Sun. *Delfín Turismo*, on 24 de Septiembre, very helpful, good excursions, operates in conjunction with Saltur of Salta. Excursions around the city are run by *Disney Tour*, San Lorenzo 435. Tours may be difficult to arrange out of peak season (eg Sep) owing to shortage of passengers.

Tourist Office in Plaza Independencia at 24 de Septiembre 484, helpful.

Taxis Meters may be rigged, arrange price in advance if possible.

Car Hire Avis, *Hotel del Sol*, Plaza Independencia; Liprandi, 24 de Septiembre 524, T 311210/212665; Movil Renta, San Lorenzo 370, T 218635/310550, F 310080 and at airport; Localiza, San Juan 959, T 311352.

Motorists should not park on the street overnight; pay US$5 for garage parking.

Car Repairs Rubén Boss, Av Aconquija 947, rec esp for Volkswagen.

Air Airport: Benjamín Matienzo, 15 km from town. Bus for each flight, US$1.50, starts from *Hotel Mayoral*, 24 de Septiembre 364. Taxi US$10. Daily flights to Buenos Aires with Aerolíneas Argentinas and Austral, and Lapa 3 times a week. Austral to Córdoba daily, Salta (also Lapa and Ladeco) and Jujuy. AR to Rio de Janeiro once a week.

Rail See under Buenos Aires, **Railways**, for schedules and fares.

N of Tucumán the Belgrano line runs via Rosario de la Frontera to Jujuy, and La Quiaca, on the Bolivian border, 644 km from Tucumán. No passenger service since Mar 1993.

Buses to **Cafayate** (8 hrs, US$17) via Tafí and Santa María (6 hrs) daily at 0600 and 1600. Direct bus in summer to Cafayate Tues, Thur, Sat, 6½ hrs, at 1000 (0600/0700 in winter), US$15. Direct to **Salta** (but not via Cafayate), 4½ hours, several daily, eg La Estrella, Veloz del Norte, US$18 (slow bus 5½ hrs). Plenty of buses to Jujuy, eg Veloz del Norte, 0900, 6 hrs. See note below on routes to Salta.

To **La Rioja**, 7 hrs, US$15. To **Catamarca**, 5 a day with Bosio, plus other lines. To **Santiago del Estero** (US$7), Paraná, Termas de Río Hondo, Orán, Resistencia, 11½ hrs, and Tinogasta. To **Buenos Aires**, Chevallier, La Estrella, Veloz del Norte, 16 hours, all with toilet, a/c, bar, video, 3 stops; book in advance; fares US$48-70.

For those who wish to travel direct from N Argentina to Central Chile, there are daily La Estrella buses (US$40) from Tucumán to **Mendoza**, leaving 1300, 1400 and 2000 (19 hours), via Catamarca, La Rioja, and San Juan. Bus to **Córdoba** 480 km, US$25, 7 hours, many companies (incl Sol and El Tucumano Panamericano). *La Veloz de Norte* serves free coffee, cake and soda. To **La Paz**, take bus to the frontier, then at Villazón, connect with train to Oruro and La Paz. New bus station is on Av Benjamín Araoz beside a huge shopping complex.

Excursions *Simoca*, 50 km S of Tucumán on Route 157, has an authentic Sat morning market, handicrafts and produce, Posta bus, several, 1½ hrs, US$2.50; essential to get there early. West of Tucumán in the Sierras de Aconquija are *Villa Nougués*, 36 km (one of the most interesting tours), the summer residence of the well-to-do Tucumanos (excellent hotel) and San Javier, 34 km (hotel), both reached by San Javier buses, 1200 and 1900. Aconquija park, with glorious trees, is at the foot of the mountains 14 km W of Tucumán. Bus at 1130 (the only one; returns immediately); tours from Terra, 9 de Julio 800. The Quebrada de Lules, the gorge of the Río Lules, is 20 km S of the city. **El Cadillal** dam, in the gorge of the Río Sali, 26 km N of Tucumán, supplies electricity and water for the city and permanent irrigation for 80,000 ha of parched land. There are restaurants, a good ACA campsite, good swimming, and a small archaeological museum at the dam. Reached by Sierras y Lagos buses every 1½ hrs approx, US$1.20, 45 mins, last buses back 1715 and 1945.

North from Tucumán From Tucumán there are 2 routes to Salta. The road via Santa María and Cafayate through the beautiful Quebrada de Cafayate (**see p 108**) is longer but much more interesting than the direct route via Rosario de la Frontera and Güemes. From Route 38 to Tafí del Valle on Route 307 is beautiful semi-tropical jungle with a white-water river. Beyond Tafí del Valle to Cafayate is largely gravel and the area is barren.

From Tucumán to Cafayate 46 km S of Tucumán Route 307 branches NW to *Tafí del Valle* (pop 3,000, 97 km from Tucumán, not to be confused with Tafí Viejo which is 10 km N of the city) known to archaeologists as a holy valley of the precolumbian Indian tribes. 10 km S of Tafí del Valle are Dique El Mollar, formerly La Angostura dam, and nearby the menhir park of *El Mollar*, with 129 standing stones (collected in the early years of this century from various sites) and good views (best to visit in am). Tours to El Mollar and Tafí are available from Travel Agencies in Tucumán, US$15 each for 4 people minimum. Daily bus from Tafí, 1215, 15 mins, US$1. Returns from El Mollar 1330. The Tucumán-Tafí bus stops nearby.

Tafí del Valle and El Mollar are often shrouded in fog because of the dam. Ten mins from Tafí is Capilla Jesuítica y Museo La Banda in the 16th century chapel of San Lorenzo (open 0900-1200, 1400-1800 daily, US$1).

Services B *Hostería ACA*, T 21027, comfortable, good value restaurant, garden; **D** *Colonial*,

T 21067, nr bus station, closed out of season, no singles, friendly, clean; **D** *Hotel Atep*, Los Menhires, nr bus station, E in winter, with bath, clean, friendly, rec; *Pensión*, opp *Colonial*, in billiard hall, ask in advance for hot water; **E** pp *hostal* run by Celia Correa, near church. Hotels and bungalows (C) at El Pinar del Ciervo. 1 km from the town at La Banda is **A+** *La Hacienda Le Pepe*, incl breakfast, English and French spoken, horses for rent. **Restaurants** *El Rancho de Félix*, rec; *El Portal de Tafí*, good, has video room (movies in summer only); *La Rueda*, at S entrance to village, inexpensive, rec; *Los Faroles*, pleasant cafe. **Camping** *Los Sauzales*, very clean, hot showers, rec. Autocamping (US$2 per tent, small cabins for rent, US$10). Try local cheese. For **Tours** throughout the NW from Tafí, contact Margarita and Bruno Widmer, T/F (0867) 21076.

Bus Tucumán-Tafí, with Aconquija, sit on left-hand side, travels through luxuriant gorge with sub-tropical vegetation, 4 a day, 3½ hrs, US$6. On this road at Km 27 there is a large statue of an Indian warrior known as El Indio, picnic area. To Cafayate 4 a day, 4 hrs, US$10. This is a magnificent ride through deep gorges, with giant cacti and bare mountains.

From Tafí the road runs 56 km NW over the 3,040m Infiernillo Pass and through attractive arid landscape to *Amaichá del Valle* (bus from Tucumán, US$7, 0600) which claims 360 sunny days a year, free municipal campsite, *Juan Bautista Alberdi*, 10 min out of town (blue gate) (**C** *Hostería Provincial*, T 21019, full board, showers not always hot, clean and friendly, rec; **E** *Pensión Albarracín*; **E** *Hostería Colonial*, with bath, friendly. **Restaurant** *Parrilla El Quipu*, 50 m from the centre). La Pachamama festival at end of pre-Lent Carnival; also see Sr Cruz' craft workshop.

From Amaicha the road is paved as far as the junction with Route 40 (15 km). A paved road also runs S from Amaicha 22 km to **Santa María**, pop 18,000.

Hotels B *Plaza*, on plaza, clean, small rm, slightly run down; **C** *Provincial de Turismo*, San Martín, friendly, rec, dining room, with bath; **D** *Residencial Alemán*, Quintana 144, small rooms but clean, friendly, quiet; **D** *Residencial Palacios*, Mitre 592, basic, hot water, clean, reasonable and friendly; **E** *Residencial Reinosa*, Av 1° de Mayo 649, good, 2 blocks from plaza, no sign, hot showers, clean, friendly. Municipal **campsite** at end of Sarmiento.

Restaurant *El Cardón*, Abel Acosta 158, cheap and good, regional dishes.

Buses To Tucumán 6 hrs, 0220, 0800, US$8.50. To Cafayate, 4 hrs, daily at 0700 exc Thur at 1030, US$10. Empresa Bosio goes to Catamarca, Sat; via Tucumán Sun at 1230, 9 hrs. Most start from Belgrano 271 on main Plaza; Empresa San Cayetano (600 block of Esquiú) to Belén 4 hrs, Mon, Wed, Fri at 0500.

Excursions to *Fuerte Quemado* (Indian ruins) 15 km N along Route 40, not as impressive as Quilmes (see below); Cerro Pintado, 8 km, coloured sandstone mountains; important ruins of Loma Rica, 18 km; Ampajango, 27 km S off Route 40, important indigenous finds.

Quilmes (Tucumán) 37 km N, with splendid views from the fortifications and interesting cacti, has Inca ruins (dam, village and posting house—*tambo*), sleeping and camping facilities and a guide at the site from 0700 to 1730. Entry US$1.50. There is also a shop selling good indigenous crafts, particularly textiles. It is 5 km along a dirt road off the main Santa María-Cafayate road, and 16 km from Amaicha del Valle. There is also a provincial archaeological museum, plus good restaurant, bar, toilets, camping possibilities. For a day's visit take 0630 Aconquija bus from Cafayate to Santa María, alight at site and take returning bus which passes at 1100. Taxi from Cafayate US$60 return.

From Santa María Route 40 leads N to Cafayate (55 km, see p 115 and S to Belén (176 km, see p 143).

North of Tucumán Route 9 and the Belgrano railway run into the province of Salta. Both Salta and the neighbouring province of Jujuy are home to a number of Indian groups which are either historically indigenous to the area, or which migrated there from other Andean regions, the greater Amazon region, or the Guaraní-occupied territories to the E. The Mataco, Chorote, Chulupi and Toba have retained their own languages, but the Chiriguano language is spoken by the Chiriguano, the Tapiete and the Chane (who belong to the Arawak family of Indians, which originate in the very N of the sub-continent). (We are grateful to John Raspey for this information.) **NB** The best description of the most interesting places and events in NW Argentina is to be found in Federico Kirbus' *Guía de Aventuras y Turismo de la Argentina* (available at Librería La Rayuela, Buenos Aires 96, Salta and El Ateneo, Florida 340, basement, Buenos Aires).

145 km N of Tucumán is **Rosario de la Frontera**, a popular resort from Jun to Sep. Altitude: 769m. 8 km away are sulphur springs. Casino.

Hotels B pp *Termas*, Route 34, T 81004, full board, rambling place, good food but many rooms without private bath (6 km from bus station, taxi US$7). Baths US$1.50. About 1 km from *Hotel Termas* is **ACA motel**, T 81143. Across the road is man-made lake owned by Caza y Pesca Club—ask in your hotel for permission to fish. **D** *Real*, Güemes 185, basic, clean, not all doors close.

Buses To Tucumán, Güemes, Salta and Jujuy, frequent.

Excursions About 20 km N is the historical post house, Posta de **Yatasto**, with museum, 2 km E of the main road; campsite. To **El Naranjo** (19 km) a Jesuit colonial town; church contains images and carvings made by Indians.

About 80 km N of Rosario de la Frontera, at Lumbreras, a road branches off Route 9 and runs 80 km NE to the Parque Nacional **Finca El Rey**, a 44,160-hectare tropical forest and wildlife preserve set among 900-1,500m hills with clear streams (good fishing). It can also be reached from Salta, 196 km, US$50 pp round-trip excursions of at least 6 agencies. There is a Park office in Salta, España 366, 3rd floor (helpful). Check here on timetable for Park truck. From Salta, take bus to Saravia, daily at 1630, 3 hours, US$4.20. Bus drops you at Paso de la Cruz, 38 km from park entrance and 50 km from the park headquarters. No public and little other traffic after this, but you may get a lift with local farm or roadbuilding vehicles. A truck leaves the Park HQ for the main road on Sun, Tues and Fri at 1600 to meet the bus going to Salta at 1825, but it rarely connects with the 1630 coming from Salta. Mosquitoes, ticks and chiggers thrive; take lotion. No accommodation while **Hostería El Rey** is closed (it is due to be transferred to private hands). Camping is free, there are several tent sites, but few facilities. Horseback riding. Landing strip for small planes. The access road is still poor and fords the river 9 times; passable for ordinary cars except in the wet season. Best time to visit is winter (drier).

From Güemes, 148 km N of Rosario de la Frontera, Route 9 runs W through the mountains for 43 km to **Salta**, at 1,190m, 370,000 people, on the Río Arias, in the Lerma valley, in a mountainous and strikingly beautiful district. Situated 1,600 km from Buenos Aires, Salta is now a great tourist and handicraft centre (prices are lower than in Tucumán or Buenos Aires) and the best starting place for tours of the NW. Capital of its province, it is a handsome city founded in 1582, with fine colonial buildings. Follow the ceramic pavement plaques, or get map from Tourist Office, for an interesting pedestrian tour. The Cathedral (open mornings and evenings), on the N side of the central Plaza 9 de Julio, was built 1858-1878; it contains the much venerated images of the Cristo del Milagro and of the Virgin Mary, the first sent from Spain in 1592, and has a rich interior mainly in red and gold, as well as a huge altar baroque altar. The miracle was the sudden cessation of a terrifying series of earthquakes when the images were paraded through the streets on 15 September 1692. They still are, each Sep, when 80,000 people visit the town. On the opposite side of the Plaza is the Cabildo, built in 1783. The Convent of San Bernardo, at Caseros and Santa Fe, was built in colonial style in the mid-19th century; it has a famous wooden portal of 1762. Nuns are still living here so the inside of the convent is not open to visitors. San Francisco church, at Caseros and Córdoba, built in 1882, rises above the city centre skyline with its magnificent façade and red, yellow and grey coloured tower, said to be the tallest church tower in South America (open 0700-1200, 1730-2100, although the times are erratic).

E of the city centre is the Cerro San Bernardo (1,458m), accessible by modern cable car (*teleférico*), functions daily, 1600-2000, US$6 return, children US$3, from Parque San Martín, fine views. Near the *teleférico* station is a lake where rowing boats can be hired (US$3 for 20 mins). It takes about half an hour to walk back down the hill. Very beautifully set at the foot of the hill is an impressive statue by Víctor Cariño, 1931, to General Güemes, whose *gaucho* troops repelled seven powerful Spanish invasions from Bolivia between 1814 and 1821. Nearby, on Paseo Güemes, is the Museo Arqueológico, which contains many objects from Tastil (**see p 118**). A steep path (1,136 steps) behind the museum with Stations of the Cross leads to the top of the hill, where there is an old wooden cross, together with restaurant and artificial waterfalls.

Museums Museo Histórico del Norte, in the Cabildo Histórico, Caseros 549, colonial, historical and archaeological museum, guided tour in Spanish, rec, open Tues-Sat, 1000-1400, 1530-1930, Sun 1000-1400, US$1. **Museo de Bellas Artes**, Florida 20, open Mon-Sat 0900-1300, 1700-2100, Sun 0900-1200, US$0.60 (closed Jan). **Casa Uriburu**, Caseros 421, Tues-Sat, 1000-1400, 1530-1930, US$0.60, has relics of a distinguished *salteño* family. **Museo Folclórico Pajarito Velarde**, Pueyrredón 106. **Museo Antropológico**, behind the Güemes statue, open Tues-Fri 0830-1230, 1430-1830, Sat 1500-1830, Sun 1600-1830, US$1, interesting display. **Museo de Arte Popular y Artesanías Iberoamericanos**, Caseros 476, excellent display of contemporary Latin American handicrafts. **Museo de Ciencias Naturales**, in Parque San Martín, has a full display of over 150 regional stuffed birds and an interesting display of armadillos, rec, open Tues-Sun 1400-2000, US$0.25. **Museo de la Ciudad "Casa de Hernández"**, La Florida 97, Tues-Sat, 0900-1230, 1600-2030. Check opening times in summer at tourist office; many close then.

Festivals 15 Sep, Cristo del Milagro (see above); 24 Sep, commemorating the battles of Tucumán and Salta. On 16-17 Jun, folk music by youngsters in the evening and *gaucho* parade in the morning around the Güemes statue at the foot of Cerro San Bernardo. Salta celebrates Carnival with processions on the four weekends before Ash Wednesday at 2200 in Av Belgrano (seats obligatory at US$2-4); lots of shaving foam (*nieve*) in the early morning; also Mardi Gras (Shrove Tuesday) with a procession of decorated floats and of dancers with intricate masks of feathers and mirrors. It is the custom to squirt water at passers-by and *bombas de agua* (small balloons to be filled with water) are on sale for dropping from balconies on to unwary pedestrians below. Wear a light waterproof!

Hotels Salta is a favourite convention town. Some hotels close for a vacation during the Christmas season until Jan 10, so check. The last two weeks in Jul are often fully booked because of holidays. Accommodation is also very scarce around 10-16 Sep because of the celebrations of Cristo del Milagro. **A2 *Salta***, Buenos Aires 1, in main plaza, T 211011, first class, cash discount, swimming pool, good restaurant on 3rd floor, room security inadequate; **A1 *Portezuelo***, Av Del Turista 1, T 310104/5, F 310133, breakfast extra, some rooms a/c, English, German, French, Italian spoken, swimming pool, clean, helpful, good restaurant, rec, better than the ACA's **A2 *Huaico***, Av Bolivia y P Costas, T 310571; **A2 *California***, Alvarado 646, T 216266, one block from main plaza, singles are small, rec; **A2 *Crillón***, near main plaza, Ituzaingó 30, T 220400, good rooms, noisy a/c, unhelpful, run down; **A3 *Cristal***, Urquiza 616, T 222854, clean, a bit run down, helpful; **A2 *Victoria Plaza***, Zuviría 16, T 211222, expensive but good restaurant, the foyer overlooking the plaza is one of the centres of *salteño* life; **B *Cabildo***, Caseros 527, T 224589, pleasant, a bit run down; **B *Colonial***, Zuviría 6, T 213057, with bath, a/c, rec, but 1st floor rooms noisy; **B *Las Lajitas***, Pasaje Calesto Guana 336, T 234908, modern, clean, good value, ACA reduction, rec. On main plaza is **B *Petit***, H Yrigoyen 225, T 213012, near bus terminus, pleasant, small, friendly, expensive breakfasts, rooms around courtyard with small swimming pool, a/c extra, French spoken; **B *Regidor***, Buenos Aires 10, T 222070, English-speaking owner, avoid 1st floor, good value lunch, clean, comfortable, friendly.

C *Astur*, Rivadavia 752, T 212107, with bath, rec; **C *España***, España 319, T 217898, central but quiet, simple, rec; **C *Florida***, Calle Florida y Urquiza 722, T 212133, with bath, very friendly, clean, will store luggage, rec; **C *Italia***, Alberdi 231, T 214050, next to jazz club/casino, very clean and friendly, rec; **C *Residencial Elena***, Buenos Aires 256, T 211529, clean, friendly and quiet, "charming", safe, try to get there early, even out of season; **C *Residencial Balcarce***, Balcarce 460, T 218023, friendly, clean; **D *Residencial San Jorge***, Esteco 244 y Ruiz de los Llanos 1164 (no sign), T 210443, with bath, parking, safe deposit, laundry and limited kitchen facilities, central heating, homely, guide for climbing, horse-trekking advice by proprietor, Sr. Dejean, also organizes local excursions by car, good value, very popular, highly rec; **C *Residencial Centro***, Alvarado 630, T 211241, same owner as *Crisol*. **Residencial Provincial**, Santiago del Estero 555, friendly, hot water; **Residencial Viena**, Florida 184, small rooms, basic; **Residencial Crisol**, Ituzaingó 166, T 214462, hot water, clean, highly rec.

E *Casa de familia de María del Toffoli*, Mendoza 915 (about 10 blocks from bus station), T 21-7383, nice atmosphere, comfortable, clean, roof terrace, cooking and laundry facilities, discount for ISIC and youth card holders, rec, rooms also at Nos 917 and 919, D, belonging to Sra Toffoli's sisters (reservations at No 917), cosy, highly rec. **E *Hospedaje Doll***, Pasaje Ruiz de los Llanos 1360 (7 blocks from centre), with bath, friendly, safe, rec; **E *Residencial Güemes***, Necochea y Balcarce, near railway station, basic, clean, private bath, laundry service. Many other cheap hotels near railway station (eg **E *Internacional***, Ameghino 651, hot water, basic, with good cheap restaurant), but few near new bus station. **E *Nápoli***, Mitre 1021, fairly near railway, basic, dirty, but café serves good coffee and bread, laundry, not rec. Private house, Pellegrini 408, E pp, not central but clean, peaceful, spacious patio. **Youth Hostel**

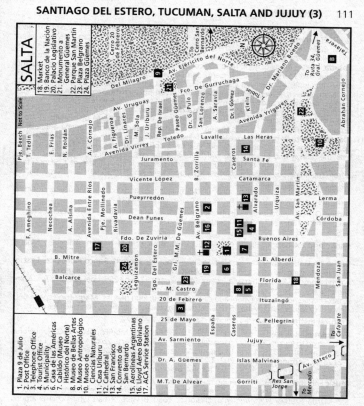

SALTA

Not to Scale

18. Market
19. Banco de la Nación
20. Palacio Legislativo
21. Monumento General Güemes
22. Parque San Martín
23. Plaza Belgrano
24. Plaza Güemes

1. Plaza 9 de Julio
2. Post Office
3. Telephone Office
4. Tourist Office
5. Casa de las Américas
6. Cabildo (Museo Histórico del Norte)
7. Museo de Bellas Artes
8. Museo Antropológico
9. Museo de Ciencias Naturales
10. Casa Uriburu
11. Cathedral
12. San Francisco
13. Convento de San Bernardo
14. Aerolíneas Argentinas
15. Lloyd Aéreo Boliviano
16. ACA Service Station

Backpackers, Buenos Aires 930, T 087-233349, bus 12 from bus terminal or ¹/₂ hr walk, E pp in dormitories, laundry and kitchen facilities, stores luggage, information, bar, clean, hot showers, English, Greek and Hebrew spoken, friendly, frequently rec. *No me Olvides*, Av de los Pioneros, Km 0.800, F pp, shared rooms, cooking facilities, friendly, rec. **NB** Do not be tempted by touts at the bus station offering convenient accommodation.

Camping Casino Provincial municipal grounds, by river, 300 m artificial lake (popular Dec-Feb). Bus 13 to grounds. There is no signposting: leave the city heading S on Calle Jujuy, after 3 km you will see the Coca Cola plant on your left; turn left before the plant and then take the first road right. Charges US$3 per tent plus US$2 pp. Free hot showers available if there is gas (not often), safe, bathrooms run-down, disappointing. Also at *Motel Huaico*, Campo Castañares. *Municipal Campsite* at Campo Quijano, 30 km W of Salta, at the entrance to Quebrada del Toro gorge, hot showers, bungalows, plenty of room for pitching tents, rec, bus from Salta bus terminal. Camping shops: HR Maluf, San Martín y Buenos Aires, and one at La Rioja 995.

Restaurants *El Monumento*, Gurruchaga 20 (opp Güemes monument), good food, slow service, good atmosphere, reasonably priced; *Jockey Club*, Belgrano 366, good; *Maxims*, Mendoza y Florida, good; *La Castiza*, Alberdi 134, huge, little atmosphere, expensive; *Don José*, Urquiza 484, good, cheap, popular, *asado de tira* and grilled kid, warmly rec. *La Posta*, España 476, food and atmosphere both excellent, reasonable prices, highly rec; *El Viejo Jack*, Virrey Toledo 145, good meat dishes, "one of the best steaks in Argentina", huge portions, good value, repeatedly rec; *El Viejo Jack II*, Av Reyes Católicos 1465, gigantic servings of meat, reasonable prices, superb; *Mama Mía*, Las Heras y Virrey Toledo, cheap pasta; *Cantina*.

Caseros y 20 de Febrero, pizzas, steaks, good value; *Las Leñas*, Caseros 444, good beef, good value; *El Arriero*, Caseros 828, good steak and pasta; *9 de Julio*, Urquiza 1020, excellent lunch; *El Rescoldo*, Caseros 427, cheap lunches, rec; *Green Park*, Caseros 529, good snacks, and milk shakes; *El Mesón de Pepe*, Rivadavia 774, fish specialities, good but pricey. *La Posada*, Plaza 9 de Julio, good food and cheap for the location. Pleasant outdoor restaurants in Parque San Martín, at foot of Cerro San Bernardo. *Sociedad Española*, Balcarce 653, excellent cuisine; *JA*, Yrigoyen y San Martín, excellent kid; *Bar Copetín Le Mans*, in parque San Martín, lovely setting by artificial lake; *El Rincón del Artista*, San Martín 1240, cheap, lunch, closed evenings; *de Pablo*, Mitre 399, excellent set lunch; *Alvarez*, Buenos Aires y San Martín, cafetería style, cheap and good. *Casa de Té*, Paseo Alberdi 422, chocolate and cakes; *Pub Yo Juan*, Balcarce 481, popular, live music at weekends; *Café del Paseo* at *Hotel Colonial*, Zuviría 6, open 24 hrs, superb breakfast. *Heladería Gianni*, España 486, ask for *copa dell'Amore* (expensive); excellent coffee served. *Cafe Río*, Mitre 40, good breakfasts for US$1.50; *Time*, Plaza 9 de Julio, good breakfasts, coffee and ice cream. Cheap restaurants near the railway and bus stations, which are also the cheapest places for breakfast. Many restaurants are lunch only, especially on San Martín near the Municipal Market. Cheapest food is from the numerous *superpanchito* stands (huge cheesedogs, US$0.50). Good supermarket, *Disco*, on Alberdi y Leguizamon.

Try local Cafayate wines, such as Michel Torino and Echart Privado, and typical Torrontés-grape wine. The local water also makes excellent beer.

Airline Offices Aerolíneas Argentinas, Caseros 475/485, T 310866; Lloyd Aéreo Boliviano, Buenos Aires 120, T217753 (will hold luggage and schedule a *colectivo* taxi); Austral, Caseros 475, T 310258.

Banks and Exchange Banks open 0730-1300. **Banco de la Nación**, Balcarce y España; **Banco Provincial de Salta**, España 526 on main square, changes TCs, 2.5% commission. **Banco de Galicia** does Visa cash advances without commission. **Banco Noroeste**, Caseros 600-700, Mastercard accepted. **Banco Roberts**, Mitre 143, good rates, changes cheques, 3% commission, rec. Amex, Chicoana Turismo, Av Belgrano y Zuviría 255, does not cash TCs. Many *cambios* on España: **Cambio Dinar**, Mitre 101 (Plaza 9 de Julio and España 609), changes Amex cheques (3% commission) and cash (poor rates), long queues. **Maguitur**, España 666, only cash; **Golden Life**, Mitre 95 (Plaza 9 de Julio), local 1, first floor, best rates for cash.

Cultural Institutes Alliance Française, Santa Fe 20, T 210827.

Consulates Bolivia, Los Almendros 161, T 223377, open Mon-Fri, 0900-1300 (unhelpful, better to go to Jujuy); Chile, Santiago del Estero, T 215757; Peru, 25 de Mayo 407, T 310201; Spain, Las Heras 1329, T 221420; Italy, Alvarado 1632, T 213881; France, Santa Fe 20, T 213336; Germany, Córdoba 202, T 216525, F 311772, consul Juan C Kühl, who also runs *Kuehl* travel agency and photo shop, helpful; Belgium, Pellegrini 835, T 233459.

Music Folk music show and evening meal at *Boliche Balderrama*, San Martín 1126; *Gauchos de Güemes*, Uruguay 750; *Casa Güemes*, España 730. For something less touristy try *Manolo*, San Martín 1296 or *El Monumento*, O'Higgins 1050. Beware of bars which charge around US$7 pp for music, but which don't display charges.

Language School *Academia de Idiomas del Norte*, F Ameghino 426, T/F (087) 211985. Swiss run, branch also in Iquique, Chile.

Laundry *Sol de Mayo*, 25 de Mayo 755, service wash. *Laverap*, Santiago del Estero 363 (open Sun am) good, fast service, US$6 for one load; *Marva*, Juramento 315; *La Baseta*, Alvarado 1170.

Post Office Deán Funes 160, between España and Belgrano *poste restante* charges US$1.15 per letter. **Telephone** office at Av Belgrano 824, 24 hrs, international calls at Av Vicente López 146, 0800-1930.

Immigration Office Maipú 35, 0730-1230.

Shopping Mercado Municipal, corner of San Martin and Florida, for meat, fish, vegetables, *empanadas*, *humitas* and other produce and handicrafts, closed 1200-1700 and Sun. Mercado Artesanal on the outskirts of the city in the Casa El Alto Molino, a late 18th century mansion, at San Martín 2555, T 219195, Mon-Fri 0800-2000, Sat 0900-2000 (sometimes closes in summer) take bus 2, 3, or 7 from Av San Martín in centre and get off as bus crosses the railway line. Excellent range of goods but very expensive (eg poncho de Güemes for US$100 for the heaviest weight, down to US$30). Woodcarvings of birds etc from *Tres Cerritas*, Santiago del Estero 202. *Tiwanaku*, Caseros 424, good selection of local crafts. *Centro de Comercialización de Artesanías*, Catamarca 84, cheaper handicrafts than in tourist shops. For objets d'art and costume jewellery made of onyx, visit *Onix Salta*, Chile 1663. *Feria del*

Libro, Buenos Aires 83; *Librería Rayuela*, Buenos Aires 96, foreign-language books and magazines. Arts and handicrafts are often cheaper in surrounding villages.

Bicycles Shop at Pellegrini 824, Manresa, with imported equipment; helpful mechanic, S Fernández, Urquiza 1051.

Bathing Balneario Municipal, Virgilio Tedín 997, T 231140, on outskirts, reached by bus No 13 from Calle Ituzaingó, entry US$1. Bus fare US$0.50.

Travel Agencies *Saltur*, Caseros 525, T 212012, very efficient and rec for local tours, for instance to Cachi (no English-speaking guides). *Puna Expediciones*, Braquiquitos 399, T 212-797 (well qualified and experienced guide Luis H Aguilar can also be contacted through the *Residencial San Jorge*), organizes treks in remote areas, US$25 a day incl transport to trekking region, food, porters, highly rec. *Hernán Uriburu*, organizes trekking expeditions, Rivadavia 409, T 310605, expensive but highly professional. *Juan Kühl and Elke Schmitt*, Córdoba 202, at Urquiza, tours by light aeroplane, horseback, caravan, boat, German and English spoken, highly rec, also run photographic company. All agencies charge similar prices for tours: Salta city US$15; Quebrada del Toro US$18; Cachi US$45; Humahuaca US$50; San Antonio de las Cobres US$75; two-day tour to Cafayate, Angastaco, Molinos, Cachi, US$80. Out of season, tours often run only if there is sufficient demand; check carefully that tour will run on the day you want. Horse riding, even for the inexperienced, Sibylle and Hansruedi (Swiss), T (087) 921080, see **Excursions** below.

Tourist Office Provincial Tourist Office (Emsatur), Buenos Aires 93 (one block from main square). Open every day, except Sun, till 2100. Very helpful, gives free maps, also a self-guiding tour, Circuito Peatonal, to see important landmarks on foot. David speaks English. Municipal Tourist office, Buenos Aires 61, closed Sun, helpful, free maps. Both offices arrange accommodation in private houses in high season (Jul) and can arrange horse-riding, US$50 full day, US$30 half day incl horses, guide and meals, rec. Office at bus terminal, friendly, no maps.

Car Hire Avis, Alvarado 537, T 216344, rec; Rent A Car, Caseros 489 and 221; local companies reported to be cheaper: ALE, Caseros 753, T 223469; López Fleming, Gral Güemes 92, T 211381, new cars, cheap, friendly; Ruiz Moreno, Caseros 225, in *Hotel Salta*, good cars, helpful; Renta Autos, Caseros 400, also good. It may be cheaper and more convenient to hire a taxi for a fixed fee.

Airport AR to **Santa Cruz** (Bolivia) Mon 1520, and also LAB, US$203 return, dep Wed (which also flies to **Tarija** and **La Paz**, US$182 one-way, change at Santa Cruz). Ladeco flies daily **Santiago (Chile)-Antofagasta-Iquique-Salta**. AR, Austral and Lapa fly to **Bs As** (2 hrs, minimum) and **Córdoba**. Austral to **Bs As**, **Córdoba** and **Tucumán**. Lapa also fly to **Tucumán** and **Bs As**. Special, regular, bus service between airport and Aerolíneas Argentinas office on Caseros, 1 block from Plaza 9 de Julio, US$3; don't be fooled by taxi touts who tell you there is no bus for 3 hours! Taxi from airport to bus station US$7.

Railways As of Mar 1993, no rail services ran to Salta or N of Tucumán, except the Tren a Las Nubes (see below).

To Chile by rail: Argentine railways maintain a train service (freight only), from Salta to Socompa, where tourist cards are available and, with a lot of patience, you may get a train to Antofagasta (**see p 117** for description of line, tourist train to San Antonio de los Cobres, and goods train, and also for road taking similar route.) The surest direct routes Salta-Antofagasta are by air or bus.

Bus Services Bus terminal is 8 blocks E of the main plaza (T 214716 for information). There is a 24 hr Shell station behind bus terminal serving cheap snacks, friendly. To **Córdoba**, 4 a day, 12 hrs, US$41, with Expreso Panamericano (T 212460), luxury service with hostess, twice daily with Veloz del Norte. To **Bs As**, several daily, US$77, 19 hrs (Atahuallpa, La Estrella, incl snacks, dinner and breakfast in restaurant, comfortable, rec. 4 daily Veloz del Norte, US$84 with La Veloz del Norte, dep 1030. To **Puerto Iguazú**, via Tucumán, US$100. To **Mendoza** via Tucumán, several companies, daily, US$52, 20 hrs; the Andesmar Mon bus continues all the way to Río Gallegos, arriving Thur 1430, the other Andesmar services continue as far as Comodoro Rivadavia. To **Santiago del Estero**, 6 hrs, US$22. To **Tucumán**, 4 hrs, several firms (La Veloz del Norte rec, La Estrella), US$18. To **Embarcación** daily with Atahualpa at 0700, US$14.50. To **Jujuy**, Balut Hnos, or Atahualpa hourly between 0700 and 2300, "directo", US$7, 1¾ hrs along new road, 2¾ hrs along old road; to **La Rioja**, US$33; to **La Quiaca**, 11 hrs (see below). To **Belén**, Wed, US$26.

To **Cafayate**, US$10, 4 hrs, three a day, with El Indio at 0700, 1130 and 1800; to **Santa María**, El Indio, 6½ hrs, 0700. To **Cachi** (5 hrs, US$12), **Angastaco** (dep Thur 1300) and **Molinos** (7 hrs) Marcos Rueda daily (except Tues, Thur) at 1300, unreliable on Sun (sit on left). To **Rosario de la Frontera**, US$5, 2½ hrs, stewardess service, very pleasant trip. To **San**

Antonio de Los Cobres, 5½ hrs, El Quebradeño, Sun 1910, Mon, Tues, Sat 1530, Thur, Fri 1010, US$14. The Thur service runs up to the Tincalayu mining camp (arrives 2140), returning to Salta on Fri 1010, passing San Antonio at 1600. This bus is the only public transport going further into the puna than San Antonio.

To **Paraguay**: there is no direct bus from Salta to Asunción, but Salta provides the most reliable cheap land connection between Bolivia and Paraguay. Buses daily 1700, US$49 with La Veloz del Norte (20% reduction for students), Saenz Peña or Panamericano, 13 hrs to **Resistencia**, for crossing into Paraguay (take warm clothing for over-efficient a/c); for description of road, **see p 147**. Salta-**Formosa** with Atahualpa, which provides the quickest route to Asunción (change at Orán), operates only twice weekly because of the state of the road—Wed and Sun at 0630, 12 hrs, US$40. To **Chile**: Services to Calama, San Pedro de Atacama (both US$45), and Antofagasta are run by Géminis (behind bus terminal), Sat 1600 all year round, US$50, 20 hrs to Antofagasta, 14 hrs to Calama. Bus can be caught in San Antonio de los Cobres, book ahead and pay full fare. Atahualpa and Tramaca also have services to Calama (US$50), the latter offers meals and even a couple of rounds of Bingo! Book well in advance, may be difficult to get a reservation, so try at 1000 on day of departure for a cancellation. (Book tickets at Boletería Basio in terminal, T 313887.) Take warm clothes (at night ice sometimes forms on the insides of bus windows), a sheet to protect luggage against dust and food (NB Chilean customs will not allow fruit in). This route is usually closed for at least part of the winter and is liable to closure at other periods of the year.

Routes to Bolivia To La Quiaca, on Bolivian frontier, about 10 buses daily, Atahualpa (US$27), 11 hrs (via Jujuy, prolonged stop), can be very cold, dusty, not rec; best change to Panamericano in Jujuy. Buses also NE to Orán, 6 hrs, for connection with Tarija, Bolivia, which can involve taking overnight bus (Atahualpa, 7-10 hrs) to Aguas Blancas at 2200 (road now paved), arriving before dawn—cold—then crossing river in motor boats to Bermejo, Bolivia and the next bus out is often full. Spectacular 8 hr mountain ride alternative to the latter in open-air pick-up: hair-raising! Also to Yacuiba, via **Pocitos** (Bolivian frontier), for Santa Cruz, Bolivia. US$17 with Atahualpa to Pocitos, 7-10 hrs, very full, with passengers standing, can be uncomfortable, but road now paved. Customs at Pocitos not to be trusted—beware of theft; and overcharging for "excess baggage" (on bus), for which there is no official limit written up anywhere. (Hotel at Pocitos, **E** *Buen Gusto*, just tolerable.) Two trains Yacuiba-Santa Cruz per week. **See also p 126** on the route via Orán.

Excursions   For routes to San Antonio de las Cobres incl the Tren a las Nubes, see below, **p 118**. Cabra Corral, one of the largest artificial lakes in Argentina, 81 km S of Salta via Coronel Moldes; water skiing, fishing, no hotels, just a camping site, restaurant and sailing club; the **B** *Hostería Cabra Corral*, T 231965, is 4 km from the lake, Route 68, half board, swimming pool, "delightful", rec. Paved road ends at the Presa General M Belgrano, impressive views of the bridge across the lake. 11 km NW of Salta is the wealthy neighbourhood of San Lorenzo (new restaurant in high tower, *El Castillo*, owned by John Johnston (US), good food and music, closed Mon, T 921052 for free taxi, 4-6 people); **A2** *Hostal Selva Montaña*, Calle Alfonsina Storni 2315, T 087-921184, luxurious, highly rec; camping and picnicking beside rocky stream and natural woodland. Sibylle Oeschger and Hansruedi Hintermann rent one rm (E pp) and offer horseriding tours, US$44 pp ½ day, incl dinner, or US$28 with coffee and biscuits, T 921080, they live at Villa San Lorenzo, 14 km from Salta (bus from terminal platform 15, hourly, ½ hr, US$1, get off 2 stops before the Quebrada). There is a frequent bus service to San Lorenzo, US$0.90 (about ½ hr). Bus stops in front of *Quebrada* restaurant (good food, friendly, quite expensive). Last bus back about 2330. To Jujuy and Humahuaca, day trip through many agencies, incl lunch. Ask the driver to return by the old Ruta 9, also called Camino de la Cornisa, a beautiful road, through jungle vegetation (huge trees and unexpected plants), a wonderful contrast to the desert all around. To Cuesta del Obispo and the Forgotten Valley, on return, with Saltur day trip, superb. To Cafayate (see below). The Finca El Rey National Park **(see p 109)** is about 200 km E of Salta, at junction of Chaco and pre-Andean regions.

At El Bordo, 45 km E of Salta, Sr de Arias offers luxury accommodation on his finca, L3 pp full board; excursions also arranged. Contact: *Finca El Bordo De Las Lanzas*, 4432 El Bordo, Salta, T 911788/310525.

A magnificent round trip of about 520 km can be taken going SW from Salta to Cafayate (well paved), then N through the Valles Calchaquíes and Cachi, and back E to Salta. (Most travel agencies in Salta offer the round trip, no student discounts, 12 hrs, includes a visit to a *bodega*.) The first part of this trip, S from Salta, goes through El Carril (30 km) where a road from Cachi intersects; continuing S for 25 km Coronel Moldes is reached. Here, a side road to the left goes to Embalse Cabra

Corral (see above). South of Coronel Moldes, Route 68 goes through the gorge of the Río de las Conchas (known as the **Quebrada de Cafayate**) with fascinating rock formations of differing colours, all signposted: Anfiteatro (a gorge), El Sapo, El Fraile, El Obelisco, Los Castillos. The road goes through wild and semi-arid landscapes with many wild birds, including *ñandúes* (rheas). The best place for lunch is at the *Hostería Talapampa* in Talapampa, approx 85 km S of Salta.

Cafayate (altitude 1,660m, population 8,432) is a clean, increasingly popular, little town, with low rainfall (none Mar-Oct), lying between two ranges of Andean foothills and surrounded by vineyards. A walk to La Cruz (3 hrs) takes you to a view of the Aconquija chain in the S to Nevado de Cachi in the N. Cafayate is much frequented by Argentine tourists and accommodation is hard to find at holiday periods (especially for a single person).

Cafayate is an important centre of wine production and home of several renowned *bodegas*. La Rosa owned by Michel Torino can be visited, Mon-Fri, 0800-1230, 1500-1830, weekends am only, no need to book, 30 min tours and tasting, reached by turning right 500m past the ACA *hostería*; Etchart, 2 kms on Ruta 40 to Tucumán, also has tours (T 21310/2), Mon-Fri 0800-1200, 1530-1830, weekends 0800-1200. La Banda, the oldest *bodega* in the valley (next to ACA *hostería*), is interesting because it is more primitive. The Museo de la Vid y el Vino in an old *bodega* is on Av Güemes, 2 blocks S of the plaza, US$0.50, very well laid out. Locally woven tapestries are interesting, and very expensive; visit the Calchaquí tapestry exhibition of Miguel Nanni on the main square. Also Platería of Jorge Barraco, Colón 147, for silver craft work. Oil paintings, woodcarving, metalwork and ceramics by Calixto Mamani can be seen in his art gallery at Rivadavia 452, or contact him at home at Rivadavia 254. Handicrafts in wood and silver by Oscar Hipaucha on main plaza. Pancho Silva and his family have a workshop at 25 de Mayo selling and displaying their own and locals' handicrafts. Souvenir prices are generally high. Local pottery in the Mercado Municipal de Artesanía on the main plaza.

Hotels B *Briones*, on main square, T 21270, clean and comfortable, with bath and hot water, accepts Amex card; **B** *Asembal*, Güemes y Almagro, T 21065, nice rooms with bath, good; **B** *Asturias*, Güemes 158, T 21328, rec; **C** *Hostería Cafayate* (ACA), T (0868) 21296, on N outskirts, modern, quiet (but cold), colonial-style, covered parking, unfriendly, good food, but restaurant may be closed; **C** *Gran Real*, Güemes 128, T 21016, pleasant, clean, rec; **D** *Colonial*, Almagro 134, charming patio; **D** *Confort*, Güemes 200 block, with bath, clean, comfortable. **D** *La Posta del Rey*, Güemes 415, T 21120, clean; **D** *Güemes*, Salta 13, one block off main plaza; **D** *Pensión Arroyo* (no sign), Niño 160, highly rec, friendly, clean; **D** *Hotel Tinkunaku*, Diego de Almagro 12, 1 block from plaza, with bath, clean, friendly; **D** *Vicano*, Toscana 273, clean, rec; *Residencial Familia Herrero*, cheap, clean. Accommodation in private houses is available. Municipal **campsite** Lorohuasi at S access to town, hot water, swimming pool, well maintained, bungalows for rent, D for 4 people; private campsite to N of town, opposite ACA *hostería*. Municipal campsite also at Animaña, 15 km N on Route 40.

Restaurants On the main plaza are *Cafayate*, simple, good regional dishes and nice atmosphere; *Confitería La Barra*, rec. *La Carreta de Don Olegario*, spotless but rather expensive; *El Gordo*, San Martín y Güemes, main plaza, excellent regional dishes, good local wines, friendly, reasonable prices, highly rec; *El Criollo*, Güemes 254, clean, pricey, rec; *La López Pereyra*, Güemes 375, good food, friendly. Several *comedores*, incl *Comedor Juli*, along Rivadavia (2 blocks N of Plaza), where the locals eat. Only the more expensive restaurants are open late. Try excellent *pan casero* (local bread).

Exchange 2 banks, incl Banco de la Nación, main plaza, for cash, TCs and credit cards.

Tourist Office Kiosk on the main plaza. Bike hire from Rentavel, Güemes 175. Horses can be hired from La Florida, Bodega Etchart Privado (2 km from Cafayate on road to Tucumán).

Bus Aconquija bus to **Tucumán** daily at 0630, 8 hours, US$17, also Sat 1500. Alternatively go to Santa María with 1100 El Indio bus, or 0530 Aconquija bus (2 hrs) over good dirt road, US$10, and then take bus to Tucumán. El Indio bus to and from **Salta** via the Quebrada de Cafayate, dep 0700, 1130 and 1800, 4 hrs, US$12.60 (worth travelling in daylight through beautiful views of yellow and red rock formations). To **Angastaco** (El Indio) 1100 daily except Sun, US$4, sit on the right, leaves Angastaco for the return journey at 0630.

One way of seeing the spectacular Quebrada de Cafayate (see above) is by taking the El Indio bus for Salta as far as Los Loros, Km 32. From here you can walk back (and catch a returning bus from Salta); alternatively hire a bike in Cafayate and take it on the early morning El Indio bus as far as Alemania (84 km) and then cycle back. **NB** The sun is very hot, take lots of water.

Continuing S from Cafayate, Route 40 goes to Santa María (**see p 108**), and SE to Tafí del Valle and Tucumán.

N of Cafayate Route 40 runs 160 km through the Valles Calchaquíes to Cachi. The road is mainly gravel and can be very difficult after rain, but the views, of the Andean-foothill desert country with its strange rock formations and unexpected colours, are fascinating. The population is largely Indian. Salta and the Valles Calchaquíes are the centre for US archaeologist John Hyslop's study of Inca roads in the Andes.

About 24 km N of Cafayate is **San Carlos** (altitude 1,710m), a small settlement destroyed four times by Indians. It has a pleasant white church completed 1854, a small archaeological museum, as well as a municipal campsite. **D** *Hostería*, T 218937. Artisans' shops and workshops, craft market near church: reasonable prices, limited variety.

Bus The El Indio bus on the Salta-Cafayate-Angastaco run arrives in San Carlos by noon and on the return journey at 0745.

N of San Carlos Ruta 40 enters the Calchaquí valley and climbs to **Angastaco**, 50 km from San Carlos, 2 km off the main road. The road passes through the spectacular **Quebrada de las Flechas**, remarkable for its formations and colours, 5-10 km S of Angastaco. This small town, expanding rapidly, is surrounded again by vineyards. You can sample the local Vino Patero, red or sweet white, in a house close to the river bridge; apparently *bodegas* can be visited, *vino patero* is supposed to be made by treading the grapes in the traditional manner. The Fiesta Patronal Virgen del Valle is held on the second weekend of Dec, with processions, folk music, dancing, many gauchos and rodeos.

Lodging and Transport D *Hostería*, T 222826, negotiable in low season, good, cheap and delicious meals on request, pool (empty), has its own small but informative archaeological museum. **F** pp *Residencial El Cardón*, good, clean, comfortable. Cheap restaurant (no sign) near the *hostería*. Buses: to Cachi and Salta, Fri, 1100 only; daily bus to San Carlos and Cafayate 0545 (Sat and holidays 0630). Taxi to Molinos US$15.

From the Angastaco turn-off it is 40 km on a winding road through beautiful and desolate rock formations to **Molinos**. The church, with its fine twin-domed bell-towers, built about 1720 and now covered in a yellowish paste to preserve it, contains the mummified body of the last Royalist governor of Salta, Don Nicolás Isasmendi Echalar. To protect it from visitors plucking its hair, this relic can no longer be viewed by the public. The priest is very knowledgeable about local history. A pleasant walk is down from the church, crossing a creek and then climbing a gentle hill, from which there are good views of Molinos and surrounding country.

Lodging and Transport   A3 *Hostería Molinos*, T 214871, rec, new owner reported as unreliable with reservations, with breakfast, good meals, in Casa de Isasmendi, which also contains a small museum. Sra de Guaymas (known as "Sra Silvia") runs a restaurant and rents rooms, **E**, double only, basic, clean; there are other rooms to rent around the main square. Bus to Salta via Cachi, Thur, Fri, Sat, Mon at 0645, also Mon, Wed, Thur, Sat at 1315 with Marcos Rueda; 2 hrs to Cachi, US$4.50, 7 hrs to Salta. To Angastaco, Thur morning.

From Molinos it is 46 km to **Cachi** (Quechua for "salt"), a beautiful little town renowned for its weaving and other crafts; the natives claim people die only of old age, because the climate is very invigorating; altitude 2,280m. The church's floor, roof and confessional are made from the wood of the *cardón* cactus. The Museo Arqueológico (open Mon-Sat, 0800-1800, Sun, holidays 0900-1200) presents a small but interesting survey of pre-colonial Calchaquí culture, US$1.

Lodging and Transport   B *ACA Hostería Cachi*, T 210001, on hill above the town, good, clean, pleasant; **E** *Albergue Municipal*, also has good municipal campsite with swimming pool and barbecue pits, on hill at S end of town. Restaurant in bus station is good, but avoid eating when buses arrive. **Buses** to Salta, 1400 daily (except Wed) at 0900 Thur, Fri, Sat, Mon, 5 hrs, US$12; to Molinos 1200 daily; El Indio from Cafayate Thur am only, returning Thur pm.

At Cachi Adentro, 6 km W of Cachi, is the **C** *Hostal Samay Huasi*, a restored *hacienda*, pleasant and helpful owners, heating and hot water at all times; **A1 Finca El Molino de Cachi Adentro**, a restored working mill, beautiful views, horse riding, rec, min stay 3 days, book in advance, T 8039339, F 4762065 (Bs As), T 213968, F 233122 (Salta); 3 buses a day from Cachi. Hire horses in the village, US$5 per hour. Fishing is also possible.

A trip to the Indian ruins at **Las Pailas**, 18 km W of Cachi, provides a fine 4 hrs walk (one way) in splendid surroundings. Take the 0730 or 1230 bus from Cachi to the school at Las Pailas, walking from there on a track towards the mountains. After 30 mins cross the river and ask at the house there for a guide to take you to the ruins. The ruins themselves are barely excavated and not especially impressive but the view is breathtaking, with huge cacti set against snow-topped Andean peaks. The walk back to Cachi is downhill; return bus to Cachi at 1900.

From Cachi, you follow Route 40 for 11 km N to Payogasta (new *Hostería*, clean), then turn right to Route 33. This road (gravel) climbs continuously up the Cuesta del Obispo passing a dead-straight stretch of 14 km known as La Recta del Tin-Tin with magnificent views of the **Los Cardones National Park** with the huge candelabra cacti, which grow up to 6m in height. (Elsewhere there are not many cacti left as they are used to make furniture.) It reaches the summit at Piedra de Molino (3,347m) after 43 km. Then it plunges down through the Quebrada de Escoipe. The road rejoins Route 68 at El Carril, from where it is 37 km. back to Salta.

N of Cachi Route 40 continues to **La Poma**, 54 km (altitude 3,015m) a beautiful hamlet (*hostería*, F, try bargaining). Marcos Rueda bus service from Salta, Tues, Thur and Sat, 1300 (via Cachi 1750), arrives La Poma 1945, departing next day 0645 and 1315. From La Poma the road runs N over the Paso Abra de Acay (4,900m—the highest pass in South America negotiable by car, often closed in summer by landslides) to San Antonio de los Cobres (see below). This road is in very poor condition (no buses). Don't go further than La Poma without finding out about road conditions. If you inform the Gendarmería Nacional, they will search for you if you don't arrive.

There is a 900 km long metre-gauge railway from Salta through the little town of **San Antonio de los Cobres** to Antofagasta, in N Chile (through trains only as far as Socompa, on the Chilean frontier). The Argentine section was engineered by Richard Maury, of Pennsylvania, who is commemorated by the station at Km 78 which bears his name. This remarkable project was built in stages between 1921 and 1948, by which time developments in road and air transport had already reduced its importance. No racks were used in its construction. The line includes 21 tunnels, 13 viaducts, 31 bridges, 2 loops and 2 zig-zags. From Salta the line climbs gently to Campo Quijano (Km 40, 1520m), where it enters the Quebrada del Toro, an impressive rock-strewn gorge. At El Alisal (Km 50) and Chorrillos (Km 66) there are zig-zags as the line climbs the side of the gorge before turning N into the valley of the Río Rosario near Puerto Tastil (Km 101, 2,675m), missing the archaeological areas around Santa Rosa de Tastil. At Km 122 and Km 129 the line goes into 360 degree loops before reaching Diego de Almagro (3,304m). At Abra Muñano (3,952m) the road to San Antonio can be seen zig-zagging its way up the end-wall of the Quebrada del Toro below. From Muñano (3,936m) the line drops slightly to San Antonio, Km 196.

San Antonio is a squat, ugly mining town on a bleak, high desert at 3,750m, pop: 2,200, only of interest if you want to visit the copper, zinc, lead and silver mines, truck from La Concordia company office, about 20 km. From the mine you can walk to La Polvorilla viaduct, 20 mins, vicuñas and condors en route. **A3 Hostería de las Nubes**, edge of town on Salta road (T 087-909058, or Bs As 326-0126), modern, incl breakfast, spacious, rec; **F Hospedaje Belgrano**, painted blue, no heat, basic, expensive restaurant; **D pp Hospedaje Los Andes**, breakfast extra, very basic, but very friendly, both on main street. Accommodation may also be available in the school.

The spectacular viaduct at La Polvorilla is 21 km further at 4,190m, just beyond the branch line to the mines at La Concordia. The highest point on the line is reached at Abra Chorrillos (4,475m, Km 231). From here the line runs on another 335 km across a rocky barren plateau 3,500-4,300m above sea level before reaching Socompa (3,865m). The inhabitants of this area are Coya Indians who bear a far closer resemblance to their cousins in Bolivia then to the Salteño lowlanders. **NB** On all journeys on this line beware of *soroche* (altitude sickness): do not eat or drink to excess.

The *Tren a las Nubes* (Train to the Clouds) runs between Salta and La Polvorilla viaduct. The service operates every other Sat from Apr to Oct, weather permitting, and on additional days in the high season (Jul/Aug), depart 0700, return to Salta 2215, US$95, no discounts, credit cards not accepted (without meals, first class only, US$250 from Buenos Aires). The train is well-equipped with oxygen facilities and medical staff as well as a restaurant car and snack bar and explanations are available in English, Spanish, French and Italian. This service is operated privately and cannot be booked through Ferrocarriles Argentinos. Book in advance (especially in high season) through Movitren, Caseros 441, Salta, T 216394, F 311264, Operatur, Av Corrientes 534, 10th floor, Bs As, T 394-5399/4199/4668, or through any good travel agency. It can be very difficult get on the train from Salta as it is often booked up from Buenos Aires.

Freight trains still run on this line: a goods train to San Antonio with one passenger coach leaves Salta Wed only at 1015, 12 hrs, US$6.50, good cheap food available; return journey from San Antonio 1800. In practice this usually leaves several hours late so you see little on the journey. A goods train to Pocitos, beyond San Antonio, leaves Salta on Mon. On Wed a goods train with two passenger coaches leaves for Socompa at 1030, arriving at San Antonio 1530 and Socompa 1230 Thur, returning Fri 1600. Buy ticket 1 hr before departure, US$18.40 single, first class carriage has dining car (and heating if you're lucky) and is the same price. Long delays are common on this route and you may do the entire journey in the dark. Make friends with the guards by offering cigarettes and you may be able to sleep in their warm wagon.

Goods trains run from Socompa to Augusta Victoria and Baquedano (Chile) on Mon and Tues: officially the Chilean railway authorities do not permit passengers to travel on this line, but some travellers have managed to do so. There is also irregular service Socompa-Antofagasta. Chilean trains do not connect with trains from Salta and you may have to wait several days for a lift in a truck. There is no food or accommodation, but you may be able to sleep on the floor in the Chilean customs building.

Timetables for these services are meaningless—the line is single-track and goods trains are delayed for loading and unloading. Reliable information about departures from Salta can only be obtained from the Oficina de Trenes at the station (T 212641) and they will often not know until 2 hrs before departure. To secure seats get on the train while it is loading in the goods depot, about 400m down the line. Take plenty of food, water, camera film and warm clothing.

San Antonio can also be reached by Route 51 from Salta. This road is being upgraded as part of a new Brazil-Argentina-Chile route. From Campo Quijano it runs along the floor of the Quebrada del Toro (fords) before climbing the Abra Muñano in a long series of steep zig-zags. Buses to Salta, El Quebradeño, daily except Thur and Sat, 5½ hrs, US$14.

On a day trip from Salta by minibus, stop at Santa Rosa de **Tastil** to see Indian ruins and a small museum (US$0.50), rec. Alternatively, take the Empresa Quebradeño bus, Thur 1010 only, arriving 1600 at Tastil, which leaves you 4 hours at ruins (plenty of time) before catching the bus (1955) on its way back from San Antonio de los Cobres. A third alternative is to share a taxi. Basic accommodation next door to the museum, no electricity or heating, take food, water and candles. Try the *quesillo de cabra* (goat's cheese) from Estancia Las Cuevas. If hiking, take your own water, there is none in the mountains.

The road from San Antonio de los Cobres over the pass of Huaytiquina (4,200m) to San Pedro de Atacama is no longer in use. At its highest, this road is 4,560m, but it has been replaced by the less steep Sico Pass, which runs parallel to Huaytiquina. Fork left just before Catúa, cross the border at **Sico** (4,079m) and continue via Mina Laco and Socaire to Toconao (road very bad between these two points) where the road joins the Huaytiquina route. It is a very beautiful trip: you cross salt lakes with flamingoes and impressive desert. The road on the Argentine side is very good (although the section between Santa Rosa de Tastil and *Restaurancito Alfarcito* is very steep, not suitable for long vehicles). Gasoline is available in San Pedro and Calama. Because of snowfalls, this route may be closed 2-3 times a year, for 2 or 3 days each time. A car must be in very good condition to cope with the heights. Ask the *gendarmes* in San Antonio de los Cobres about road conditions, and complete exit formalities there; entry formalities must also be carried out at San Antonio (no facilities at border). **NB** Hitchhiking across the Andes from here is not recommended.

The direct road **from Salta to Jujuy**, Route 9 via La Caldera and El Carmen, is picturesque with its winding 92-km subtropical stretch, now paved, known as *la cornisa* (lush vegetation). Be careful as the road is very narrow and often wet. The longer road, via Güemes, is the better road for hitchhiking.

Jujuy (pronounced Hoo-hooey), formally San Salvador de Jujuy and often referred to by locals as San Salvador, is the capital of Jujuy province and stands at 1,260m, completely surrounded by wooded mountains. The city was founded first in 1561 and then in 1575, when it was destroyed by the Indians, and finally established in 1593. Population 230,000. In the eastern part of the city is the Plaza Belgrano, a fine square lined with orange trees. On the S side of the plaza stands the Casa de Gobierno, an elaborate French baroque-style palace (open Mon-Fri, 0800-1200, 1600-2000, but not always). On the W side is a colonial Cathedral with very fine 18th century images, pulpits, walls and paintings finished about 1746. It has been heavily restored, but in the nave is a superb wooden pulpit, carved by Indians and gilded, a colonial treasure without equal in Argentina. On Calle Lavalle you can see the doorway through which General Lavalle, the enemy of Rosas, was killed by a bullet in 1848, but the door is a copy; the original was taken to Buenos Aires. The Teatro Mitre (worth a visit) is at Alvear y Lamadrid. In the western part of the city are the Parque San Martín and an open space, La Tablada, where horses, mules and donkeys used to be assembled in caravans to be driven to the mines in Bolivia and Peru. See the Palacio de Tribunales near the river, one of the best modern buildings in Argentina. Streets are lined with bitter-orange trees. The scenery is varied and splendid, although the city itself has become a little shabby.

History   The province of Jujuy bore the brunt of fighting during the Wars of Independence: between 1810 and 1822 the Spanish launched 11 invasions down the Quebrada de Humahuaca from Bolivia. In Aug 1812 Gen Belgrano, commanding the republican troops, ordered the city to be evacuated and destroyed before the advancing Spanish army. This event is marked on 23-24 Aug by festivities known as El Exodo Jujeño with gaucho processions and military parades. As a tribute to the city for obeying his orders, Belgrano donated a flag which is displayed in the Sala de la Bandera in the Casa de Gobierno.

Museums   **Museo Histórico Provincial**, Lavalle 250, open daily 0830-1230, 1500-2000; **Museo de Paleontología y Mineralogía**, part of the University of Jujuy, Av Bolivia 2335, open Mon-Fri 0800-1300. **Museo de Bellas Artes**, Güemes 956, open Mon-Fri, 0800-1200, 1700-1900. **Police Museum**, in the Cabildo, open Mon-Fri 1000-1300, 1500-2100, Sat 1030-1230, 1830-2100, Sun 1830-2100; **Museo de la Iglesia San Francisco**, Belgrano y Lavalle, incl 17th century paintings from Cuzco and Chuquisaca. The **Estación Biológica de Fauna Silvestre**, Av Bolivia 2335, is open to the public on Sun (for private tours on other days, contact Dr Arturo A Canedi, T 25617-25845), very interesting.

Public Holidays   6 and 23-24 Aug (hotels fully booked). Festival on 6 Nov.

Hotels *Panorama*, Belgrano 1295, T 30183, 4-star, highly-regarded; **A2** *Augustus*, Belgrano 715, T 22668, 3 star, modern, comfortable but noisy. **A2** *Internacional*, Belgrano 501 (main square), T 22004; **A3** *Fenicia*, on riverside at 19 de Abril 427, T 28102, quiet. **B** *Avenida*, 19 de Abril 469, T 22678, on riverside, with good restaurant (C off season, cafeteria only); **B** *Hostería Posta de Lozano*, Route 9, Km 18, friendly, clean, good restaurant, pools with fresh mountain water, covered parking; **B** *Motel Huaico*, Route 9, just N of town, T 22274, good; **B** *Sumay*, Otero 232, T 22554, central, clean. **B** *Alto* **C** *La Viña*, Route 56, Km 5, T 26588, attractive, swimming pool, bus US$0.35 from town. **C** *Residencial Los Andes*, Siria 456, T 24315, clean, hot water, a bit prison-like. Across the street is **C** *Residencial San Carlos*, Siria 459, T 22286, modern, friendly, some rm a/c, others poorly ventilated, locked parking; **D** *Belgrano*, Belgrano 627, T 26459, old fashioned, hospitable, clean, walls thin so can be noisy, mixed reports but mostly rec; **D** *Chung King*, Alvear 627, T 28142, friendly, dark, very noisy, many mosquitoes, good restaurant. Near the bus terminal only **D** *San Antonio*, Lisandro de la Torre (opposite), modern, clean, quiet, highly rec. Several cheaper places near railway station: **E** *El Aguila*, Alvear 400, opp station, basic; **E** pp *Residencial Norte*, Alvear 446, without bath, basic, unfriendly; **E** *Residencial Río de Janeiro*, Av José de la Iglesia 1536, very basic, clean, close to bus station, bit run down.

Camping   *Autocamping Municipal*, US$2.40 per tent, ask for a cheaper rate for one person. 14 km N of Jujuy on Humahuaca road, also *Autocamping*, 3 km N outside city at Huaico Chico, US$4 per tent, motel opposite. Buses 4 or 9 frequent. Hot showers (if you remind the staff), clothes washing facilities, very friendly.

Restaurants   *El Cortijo*, Lavalle y San Martín, interesting salads, good vegetarian food, reasonably priced; *Restaurant Sociedad Española*, Belgrano y Pérez, elegant setting; *Bar La Royal* on Belgrano (near Lavalle), good but expensive; *Bar-Restaurant Sociedad Obrera*, Balcarce 357, for cheap food, but not attractive. *Chungking*, Alvear 627; *Restaurant Sirio Libanesa*, Lamadrid 568 (don't be put off by the uninviting entrance). *La Victoria*, Av El Exodo

642, away from centre, good; *Confitería Carena*, Belgrano 899, old-fashioned, good for breakfast; *La Ventana*, Belgrano 751, good cheap menu, good service, à-la-carte menu is expensive. *La Rueda*, Lavalle 320, good food and service, very popular, expensive; *Krysys*, Balcarce 272, excellent atmosphere but now expensive; *La Pizzería*, Alvear 921, warm welcome, pleasant atmosphere; *Ruta 9*, Costa Rica 968, Barrio Mariano Moreno (take taxi), good local food, Bolivian owners. Cheaper places behind bus terminus on Santiago del Estero and Alem. Very good ice cream at *Helados Xanthi*, Belgrano 515, made by Greek owner. *Opus-Café*, Belgrano 856, good coffee, music and atmosphere. Good bread and cake shop at Belgrano 619. Good sandwiches at *Rada Tilly*, 2 locations on Belgrano (one next to *Hotel Avenida*).

Banks and Exchange At banks; **Banco de la Provincia de Jujuy**, Lavalle, gives cash against Mastercard, no commission, also changes dollars; **Banco de Galicia**, US$10 commission on Amex TCs; **Horus**, Belgrano 722, good rates for cash, no cheques; **Dinar**, Belgrano 731, 4% commission on TCs. Travel agencies on Calle Belgrano also change cash and dollar TCs. Thomas Cook cheques cannot be changed. If desperate, ask the *dueña* of the *confitería* at bus station, rates not too unreasonable. (See note on provincial bonds used as currency, p 222).

Consulates **Bolivia**, Patricinio Argentino 641, T 23156, price of visa should be US$5, pay no more; **Spain**, R de Velasco 362, T 28193; **Italy**, Av Fascio 660, T 23199; **Paraguay**, Tacuarí 430, T 28178.

Laundry *Laverap*, Belgrano y Ramírez de Velazco.

Post Office at Independencia y Lamadrid, in Galería Impulso, Belgrano 775, and at bus terminal. **Telecom**, Senador Pérez 18 and Alvear, open 0700-0100.

Shopping Handicrafts are available at reasonable prices from vendors on Plaza Belgrano near the cathedral; *Regionales Lavalle*, Lavalle 268; *Centro de Arte y Artesanías*, Balcarce 427. *Librería Rayuela*, Belgrano 636; *Librería Belgrano*, Belgrano 602, English magazines and some books. *Farmacia Avenida*, Lavalle y Av 19 de Abril, 0800-2400.

Travel Agencies Many along Belgrano; *Alicia Viajes*, No 592, T 22541; *Giménez*, No 775, T 2924; *Turismo Lavalle*, No 340. All offer tours along the Quebrada de Humahuaca, 12 hrs, US$25. *Be Dor Turismo*, No 860 local 8, 10% for ISIC and youth card holders on local excursions.

Tourist Office Belgrano 690, T 28153, very helpful, open till 2000.

For information on bird watching, contact Mario Daniel Cheronaza, Peatonal 38, No 848-830, Viviendas "El Arenal", Jujuy.

Migración, Belgrano 499.

Airport El Cadillal, 32 km SE, T 91505; Tea Turismo vans leave *Hotel Avenida* to meet arrivals, US$4.50. Service to **Buenos Aires** by Austral, 1 flight a day direct with bus connection to Tartagal (in the NE of the province) via San Pedro and Embarcación. Austral also flies to **Salta**, **Santiago del Estero**, **Tucumán** and **Córdoba**. Bus from airport to Jujuy takes 1 hr, US$4.

Train No passenger services as of Mar 1993.

Buses Terminus at Iguazú y Dorrego, 6 blocks S of centre. Young boys charge US$1 for loading luggage. To/from **Buenos Aires**, US$89, several daily with Balut Hnos (T Bs As 313-3175) and La Internacional. Via Tucumán to Córdoba, with Panamericano T 27281/27143 and La Veloz, daily, **Tucumán** 5 hrs, US$25, and **Córdoba**, 14 hrs US$45; to **Puerto Iguazú**, 2 a week, US$80, 30 hrs. To **Salta** hourly from 0700, 2¾ hours, US$7. To **La Quiaca**, 6½ hrs (many passport checks), Panamericano (best) and Atahuallpa, US$21.50. Road paved only as far as Humahuaca, reasonably comfortable, but very cold. To **Orán** daily at 1700; to **Humahuaca**, US$7, 3 hrs, sit on left side. To **Embarcación**, US$7 with Agencia Balut, via San Pedro and Libertador San Martín. Jujuy-**Purmamarca-Susques**, leaves Purmamarca at 1330 on Wed and Sat, returning Thur and Sun, crossing the Abra Potrerillos (4,164m) and the Salinas Grandes of Jujuy. To **Tilcara** 1½ hrs, US$4.

To Chile: in 1991, the Jama pass was opened for traffic between Jujuy and Antofagasta, and is suitable for all traffic. Bus to **Calama**, via San Pedro de Atacama (15 hrs), Fri 1700, with Tramaca, US$39 incl cold dinner, breakfast, and bingo entertainment; to **Iquique** on Wed and Sat, Panamericano, US$55. Check weather conditions in advance.

Drivers should stock up with fuel here if taking the Purmamarca route to San Antonio de los Cobres.

19 km W of Jujuy is *Termas de Reyes*, where there are hot springs. This resort, with the *Gran Hotel Termas de Reyes* (B with breakfast, A3 half-board, A2 full board, refurbished, restaurant, friendly, T 0882-35500), is set among magnificent mountains 1 hr by bus from Jujuy

bus terminal or Av 19 de Abril, 6 times a day between 0630 and 1945, returning 0700-2040, US$1. US$3 to swim in the thermal pool at the hotel; municipal baths US$1, open daily 0800-1200 and 1400-1700 (Thur 1400-1700 only). It is possible to camp below the hotel free of charge. Cabins for rent beside river, F pp, shower and thermal bath.

North from Jujuy Lovers of old churches will find Salta and Jujuy excellent centres. Franciscan and Dominican friars arrived in the area from Bolivia as early as 1550. The Jesuits followed about 1585. Along both the old Camino de los Incas (now non-existent) and the new route through the Quebrada de Iturbe the padres, in the course of two centuries, built simple but beautiful churches, of which about 20 survive. They are marked by crosses on the map on **p 103**. All of them can be visited by car from Salta or Jujuy, though some of the roads are very rough. A spare fuel can and water should be carried because service stations are far apart. (There are ACA stations at Jujuy, Humahuaca and La Quiaca, and YPF stations at Tilcara and Abra Pampa.)

One group, in the Puna de Atacama, on the old Camino de los Incas, can be reached by the road which runs W from Salta through the picturesque Quebrada del Toro to San Antonio de los Cobres (**see p 117**). The road S from San Antonio to Antofagasta de la Sierra (235 km) is pretty severe going. The road N to **Susques** (105 km) is comparatively comfortable, but runs through utter desert. There is poor lodging at Susques and an interesting 16th century chapel. Close to the Bolivian and Chilean frontier is El Toro, lovely ride through *altiplano*, past Laguna Turilari, mining territory, bizarre rock formations. Lodgings may be available in first-aid room, ask nurse, Don Juan Puca. From El Toro on to Coranzulí is very rough.

The second group can be reached from the road N from Jujuy to La Quiaca through the **Quebrada de Humahuaca**, which is itself beautiful, with a variety of rock colours and giant cacti in the higher, drier parts; Route 9, the Pan-American Highway through it has been paved as far as Iturbe. In the rainy season (Jan-Mar) this road is sometimes closed by flooding. After heavy rains ask the highway police before using minor roads.

Beyond Tumbaya, where there is a church originally built in 1796 and rebuilt in 1873, a road runs 5 km to **Purmamarca**, a very popular, picturesque village overlooked by a mountain: 7 colours can be distinguished in the rock strata (arrive before noon when sun is in the E); **E** pp *Ranchito del Rincón*, Sarmiento, new, clean, owners Yolanda and Zulma are friendly and helpful, highly rec; also 2 rm in shop, F pp, friendly, ask at the police station for the address, *comedor* on main square has good, cheap, local food. At the entrance to Purmamarca a right turn leads to a new gravel road, which leads through another *quebrada* over a 4,170-metre pass to the Salinas Grandes salt flats at 3,500m on the Altiplano (fantastic views especially at sunset). In the winter months, on both sides of the road, three different ancient types of salt mining by hand can be seen. Look out for the spectacular rock formations on the road W from Purmamarca.

About 10 km N of the turn, on the Pan-American Highway, is **Maimará** (**D** *Pensión La Posta*, clean and friendly, the owners' son is a tourist guide and has helpful information, 5 km from Maimará). 3 km S of Maimará is a new folk museum called Posta de Hornillos in a recently restored colonial posting house, of which there used to be a chain from Buenos Aires to the Bolivian border (open, in theory, Wed-Mon 0900-1800, free).

22 km N of Purmamarca is *Tilcara*, where there is a reconstruction of a *pucará*, or Inca fortified village, set in botanical gardens containing only high altitude and Puna plants. Beautiful mountain views, rec. The Museo Arqueológico, attached to the University of Buenos Aires, contains a fine collection of precolumbian ceramics from the Andean regions of present day Argentina, Chile and Peru, open Tues-Sun 0900-1200, 1500-1800, highly rec, US$2, free entry Tues (admission incl botanical gardens and *pucará*, which is about 2 km from the museum). *Fiestas* on weekends in Jan. There are excellent craft stalls and shops around the main square, selling ponchos, sweaters and wooden items (dollars accepted). A rec art shop is near *Hotel El Antigal*.

Lodging and Food C *Hotel de Turismo*, Belgrano 590, swimming pool, usually dry; **D** *El*

Antigal, pleasant, good restaurant, colonial style, stores luggage, rec; **E** *Residencial Edén*, dirty but one of cheapest; **E** *Hostería La Esperanza*, spacious rm, arranges walking tours; **E** *Residencial Frami*, near hospital. Private houses: **E** Peter Edmonds, Padilla 690, breakfast extra, guided tours; **E** Juan Brambati, San Martín s/n, comfortable, hot water, meals, highly rec, also does tours. Also at Radio Pirca, **E** pp, 3 blocks from plaza, use solar energy. Municipal campsite, dirty; *Camping El Jardín*, US$5, clean, hot showers. *Restaurant Pucará*, good value. *Café del Museo*, good coffee.

The churches of Huacalera, **Uquía**, and Humahuaca are on the main road. At **Huacalera** is the **C** *Hotel Monterrey*, friendly but run down. Two km S of Huacalera, a sundial 20m W of the road gives the exact latitude of the Tropic of Capricorn. At Uquía (church built 1691, with *cuzqueño* paintings), the walls of the naves are hung with 17th century paintings of winged angels in military dress: the so-called *ángeles arcabuceros*. Cactus-wood decoration is found in many local churches.

Both in Tilcara and Humahuaca there are displays of pictures of the Passion made entirely of flowers, leaves, grasses and seeds at Easter and a traditional procession on Holy Thursday at night joined by thousands. No beef is sold during Holy Week in shops or restaurants. All along the Quebrada de Humahuaca the pre-Lent carnival celebrations are picturesque and colourful.

Humahuaca, altitude 2,940m, 129 km N of Jujuy (by bus 3 hrs, US$7), dates from 1594 but was almost entirely rebuilt in the mid 19th century. Population 4,000. Until the arrival of the railway in 1906, Humahuaca was an important trading centre. Today it is an attraction for coach trips from Salta and Jujuy; few tourists stay for more than a couple of hours, but it is an attractive and peaceful centre from which to explore the Quebrada de Humahuaca. The church, originally built in 1631, was completely rebuilt in 1873-80, it has a bell from 1641. A mechanical figure of San Francisco Solano blesses the town from the neo-colonial town hall at 1200. Overlooking the town is the massive Argentine National Independence Monument, built in 1924 and sited here because the valley was the scene of the heaviest fighting in the country during the Wars of Independence. There is a good Feria Artesanal on Av San Martín (on the far side of the railway line), but avoid the middle of the day when the coach parties arrive. Candelaria, Feb 2, is the town's main festival.

Museums Museo La Casa, Buenos Aires 296, next to the post office, open daily 1000-2000, US$3, guided tours in Spanish only, offers a fascinating insight into social customs in the mid-nineteenth century, rec; **Museo Ramoneda**, Salta y Santa Fe, private collection of contemporary art (hours unknown); **Museo Arqueológico Municipal**, at one side of Independence monument, Mon-Fri 0800-1200, 1400-1700, US$0.25; **Museo Nicasio Fernández Mar**, Buenos Aires, opposite *Hotel de Turismo*, memorial to the sculptor, open daily, free. **Museo Folklórico Regional**, Buenos Aires 435, run by Sixto Vásquez, US$10 incl guide.

Hotels D *Provincial de Turismo*, Buenos Aires 650, T 12, run down, swimming pool dry even in summer, poor service, modern building is sadly out of keeping with surroundings; **D** *Residencial Humahuaca*, Córdoba y Corrientes, one block N of bus station, some a/c, traditional, clean, friendly, rec. **D** *Residencial Colonial*, Entre Ríos 110, near bus terminus, T 21007, with bath, some windowless rooms, clean, laundry facilities. Youth Hostel, *Albergue Humahuaca*, Buenos Aires 435, clean, laundry and very limited cooking facilities, run down, cold, F pp, special price for ISIC and youth card holders.

Camping Across bridge by railway station, small charge incl use of facilities.

Restaurants Most restaurants open only during the day, difficult to find breakfast and the mediocre restaurant at the bus terminal is often the only place open in the evenings. *La Cacharpaya*, Jujuy 295, excellent, pricey; *Humahuaca Colonial*, Tucumán 22, good regional cooking, good value, but invaded by coach parties at midday; *El Rancho*, Belgrano s/n, just around the corner from market, lunches only, where the locals eat.

Exchange Bank. Try the handicraft shops on the main plaza, or the *Farmacia* at Córdoba 99; better rates at Youth Hostel, but best to change before you go. Credit cards are not accepted anywhere.

Tourist Office Kiosk in main plaza in high season. Sr Carlos Gómez Cardozo, Director of the Museo La Casa, is a mine of information on the area and may be able to arrange English-speaking guides at weekends.

Excursions To **Coctaca**, 10 km NE, where there is an impressive and extensive series of pre-colonial agricultural terraces, covering 40 ha. To the mine at El Aguilar (see below), trucks leave Humahuaca early am.

20 km N of Humahuaca along Route 9, an unpaved road runs NE 8 km to Yrigoyen (railway station called Iturbe) and then over the 4,000m Abra del Cóndor before dropping steeply into the Quebrada de Iruya. **Iruya**, 66 km from Humahuaca, is a beautiful walled village wedged on a hillside at 2,600m. It has a fine 17th century church and Rosario festival on first Sun in Oct. Accommodation at **F** pp **Albergue Belén**, very basic. The trips to Iruya offered by *pensiones* in Humahuaca, or even by people in the street, are overpriced. It is worthwhile staying in Iruya for a few days; it makes an extremely pleasant and friendly centre for horseback or walking trips (take sleeping bag). At Titiconte 4 km away, there are unrestored pre-Inca ruins (take guide). Puna Expediciones (**see Salta p 113**) runs a 7-day trek, Salta-Iruya-Nazareno-La Quiaca, walking between Iruya and Nazareno on small, remote paths where there are no tourists or motor vehicles, sleeping in local schoolhouses; rest of route is by truck.

Transport Daily bus service from Jujuy and Humahuaca to Yrigoyen by Panamericano, 1400 and 1900, 45 mins; in **Yrigoyen** (**F Pensión El Panamericano**, basic) you may be able to get a seat on a truck. Empresa Mendoza bus from Humahuaca, 0800, Wed and Sat 3½ hrs journey, US$7 one way, waits 2-3 hrs in Iruya before returning; service varies according to time of year and is suspended in rainy season (esp Feb and Mar), one report says this journey can be dangerous as an overloaded bus follows a riverbed after the road ends, details from *Almacén Mendoza*, Salta y Belgrano, Humahuaca.

A pretty walk in Yrigoyen: "cross the bridge and go straight on until you reach a hairpin bend by some white rocks. A small path on the left of the bend follows a gorge to the top of the ridge. From here go straight ahead and turn right at the "crossroad" to a small ridge for panoramic views." (M Powell)

From Humahuaca to La Quiaca on the Bolivian border, Route 9 is unpaved and runs across the bleak and barren *puna*. At Tres Cruces, 62 km N of Humahuaca, a paved road runs S for 46 km to the mine at El Aguilar. **Abra Pampa**, an important mining centre, population 4,000, is further N at Km 91 (**F** pp **Residencial El Norte**, Sarmiento 530, shared rm, clean, hot water, good food). From here an unpaved road leads NW to Laguna Pozuelos and on to the Rinconada gold mine. **Laguna Pozuelos**, 3,650m, 50 km from Abra Pampa, is a flamingo reserve and natural monument. Bus daily at 1030 exc Sun via the mines at Pan de Azúcar and Rinconada, 4 hrs, US$3, dropping you at the park ranger station. If driving, the Laguna is 5 km from the road; walk last 800m to reach the edge of the lagoon. Temperatures can drop to -30°C in winter; if camping warm clothing, drinking water and food are essential. By car it is possible to drive N along the E side of the Laguna via Cienaguillas to reach La Quiaca. 15 km from Abra Pampa is the vicuña farm at Miraflores, the largest in Argentina. Information offered, photography permitted; colectivos go am Mon-Sat from Abra Pampa to the vicuña farm.

From a point 4 km N of Abra Pampa roads branch W to Cochinoca (25 km) and SW to **Casabindo** (62 km). "On 15 Aug at Casabindo, the local saint's day, the last and only *corrida de toros* in Argentina is held amidst a colourful popular celebration. The event is called "El Toreo de la Vincha"; in front of the church a bull defies onlookers to take a ribbon and medal which it carries. The Casabindo church itself is a magnificent building, being called "the cathedral of the Puna". (Federico Kirbus).

Yavi, with the fine church of San Francisco, which has magnificent gold decoration and windows of onyx (1690), is 16 km E of La Quiaca, reached by a good, paved road; taxi available – US$25 return fare, including one hour wait. (Find the caretaker at her house and she will show you round the church, open Tues-Sun 0900-1200 and Tues-Fri 1500-1800.) Opposite this church is the house of the Marqués Campero y Tojo. Only a precarious road for trucks and pick-ups leads on to the two churches of Santa Victoria (a forlorn Indian village in a rain forest valley) and

Acoyte. At **Santa Catalina**, 67 km W of La Quiaca, along a poor road, there is also a 17th century church. (Bus from Jujuy to La Quiaca, 8 hrs, and Santa Catalina, 19 hrs, Mon and Fri.)

La Quiaca, 292 km from Jujuy at an altitude of 3,442m, is joined to its Bolivian neighbour, Villazón, by a concrete bridge. Warm clothing is essential all year round, but particularly in winter when temperatures can drop to -15°C. At the same time, care should be taken against sunburn during the day. On the third Sun in Oct the Manca Fiesta, or the festival of the pots, is held here, and the Colla Indians from Jujuy and the Bolivian *altiplano* come, carrying all sorts of pots; local food is eaten. Most commercial activity has moved to Villazón because everything is much cheaper in Bolivia.

Hotels C *Turismo*, Siria y San Martín, T 2243, rec, clean, modern, comfortable, hot water 1800-2400, heating from 2030-2400 in winter, restaurant; **D** *Cristal*, Sarmiento 543, T 2255, clean and comfortable, with café and bus office adjacent. **D** *Victoria*, opp railway station, clean, good hot showers; *Alojamiento Pequeño*, Av Bolívar 236, friendly, cheap, clean. **D** *La Frontera* hotel and restaurant, Belgrano y Siria, downhill from Atahuallpa bus stop, good; **E** *Residencial Independencia*, rec, near railway station and church, hot water but no room heating even in winter. *Restaurant Sirio-Libanesa*, near *Hotel Frontera*, good, cheap set meal.

Camping is possible near the control post on the outskirts of town; also at the ACA service station about 300 m from the border on the left (entering Argentina).

Exchange No facilities for changing cheques. There are several *cambios* in Villazón (open on Sun) which accept cash only and sell pesos as well as bolivianos. Rates are better in Villazón.

Medical There are a good hospital in La Quiaca and a doctor in Villazón. *Farmacia Nueva*, ½ block from Church, has remedies for *soroche* (mountain sickness).

Transport Difficult to obtain information in La Quiaca about buses leaving Villazón for points in Bolivia (see Bolivia, **South from La Paz** for Villazón), though Bolivian buses tend to be more reliable than Bolivian trains. New bus station in La Quiaca at Av España y Belgrano, 4 blocks from railway station; all bus companies have offices here, payment accepted in US$. 6-8 buses a day to **Salta** (US$27) via Humahuaca and Jujuy, US$22 with change of bus in Jujuy (5 hrs to Humahuaca, 6 hrs to Jujuy, 10 hrs to Salta). Panamericano has 5 buses a day to **Jujuy**, US$21.50, 6½ hrs. Some meal breaks, but take own food, as sometimes long delays. Buses may be stopped and searched for coca leaves. Bus to **Buenos Aires**, via Jujuy, US$89 incl meals, 28 hrs. As of Mar 1993, no passenger trains were running S of La Quiaca.

Entering Bolivia The frontier bridge is 10 blocks from bus terminal, 15 mins walk (taxi US$0.50).

Warning Those travellers who need a visa to enter Bolivia are advised to get it before arriving in La Quiaca because the consular staff there try to charge US$15 per visa; pleading may reduce the charge.

Motorists should visit the Servicio Nacional de Turismo to obtain the Hoja de Ruta, which all motorists must have. It is not restrictive in any practical sense; just a nuisance!

If leaving Argentina for a short stroll into Villazón, show your passport, but do not let it be stamped by Migración, otherwise you will have to wait 48 hrs before being allowed back into Argentina.

Entering Argentina Argentine immigration and customs are open 0800-2000 (signature needed from customs officer, who may be out for lunch); on Sat, Sun, and holidays there is a special fee of US$3 which may or may not be charged. Buses arriving outside these hours will have to wait, so check before travelling. You can cross the border at night, without luggage, and your passport will not be stamped. Formalities are usually very brief at the border but very thorough customs searches are made 100 km S of the border at Tres Cruces; be prepared for camera search.

NB Bolivian time is one hour earlier than Argentina. The Argentine frontier opens at 0800, the Bolivian at 0700.

North-East from Jujuy 63 km from Jujuy is **San Pedro de Jujuy**, a sugar town of 60,000 people. The Ingenio La Esperanza, on the outskirts, is a sugar-mill with hospital, housing and a recreation centre, formerly owned by the English Leach brothers. **C** *Hotel Alex 2*, R Leach 467, T 20269, private bath, fan, clean; *Alex I*, Tello 436, T 20299; **E** *Vélez Sarsfield*, V Sarsfield 154, T 20446; excellent restaurant at *Sociedad Sirio-Libanesa* on the plaza. Bus to Jujuy, US$2.50, 1½ hrs; to Embarcarción, Atahuallpa, US$6.50, 2½ hrs.

Libertador (formally Libertador General San Martín), another sugar town 50 km N of San Pedro, is a base for exploring the **Parque Nacional Calilegua**, an area of peaks and sub-tropical valleys, reached by dirt road from just N of the town. Camping site near the first ranger house, at Agua Negra. Drinking water from river nearby, and some cooking facilities and tables. The ranger, Angel Caradonna, and his wife, Mony, are very friendly and knowledgeable. Mony sells hand-painted T-shirts featuring the park's wildlife. There are over 200 species of bird here including the very rare black and chestnut eagle and the red-faced guan. There are 60 species of mammal including tapir, puma, deer and otters. 13 km further along the trail is the 2nd ranger house, at Mesada de las Colmenas (ask permission at the 1st ranger house to camp here). 10 km from here is the N boundary of the park, marked by an obelisk, and where the most interesting birds can be seen. An all-weather track leads from the village of San Francisco to Alto Calilegua (10 hrs walk), overlooked by the 2 highest peaks in the park – Cerro Amarillo (the tallest at 3720 m with Inca ruins at the top) and Cerro Hermoso. Condors and taruca deer may be seen. (Thanks for park information to Ortelli Jiri Moreno, Como, Italy.) The park entrance is 10 km along the dirt road (hitching from Libertador possible), which climbs through the park and beyond to Valle Grande (no accommodation, basic food supplies from shops), 90 km from Libertador. From here it is possible to walk to Humahuaca and Tilcara (allow at least 3 days; these walks are described in *Backpacking in Chile and Argentina* by Bradt Publications). Trucks run by Empresa Valle Grande, Libertad 780, leave Libertador, Tues, and Sat, 0730, 6 hrs if road conditions are good, very crowded, returning Sun and Thur 1000. Check with Sr Arcona (the driver, everyone knows him) who lives opposite the railway station, if the truck is going. Weather is unpredictable. Or contact Gustavo Lozano at Los Claveles 358, Barrio Jardín, T 21647, who will contact the ranger, Angel Caradonna to pick you up. Park headquarters are on San Lorenzo s/n, in Calilegua, 4 km from Libertador. T (0886) 22046.

Services at Libertador: **E** *Residencial Gloria*, Urquiza 270, clean, hot water; **E** *Ledesma*, Jujuy 473 just off plaza, friendly, large rooms but no keys, local radio station opposite so can be noisy; *Restaurant Sociedad Boliviana*, Victoria 711, where the locals eat. On Plaza San Martín, **Banco Roberts** changes dollars at a good rate. The tourist office in the bus station is unhelpful.

From Libertador, Route 34 runs NE 244 km, to the Bolivian frontier at Yacuiba (see **Eastern Bolivia** section), via Embarcación (Km 101) and Tartagal. **See p 114** for Pocitos border crossing.

Embarcación (pop 24,000) has several hotels (**D** *Punta Norte*, España 277, clean, a/c, friendly; Sr Sarmiento's Hotel; *Universal*, hot water), of which the cheaper are near the railway station. Restaurant of *Sociedad Sirio-Libanesa*, H Irigoyen and 9 de Julio, cheap and good. 2 km from Embarcación you can walk to the Loma Protestant mission for Mataes and Toba Indians, who sell unpainted pottery there. Buses go to Orán, 1 hr, US$1.70 on a paved road. Buses Embarcación-Pocitos (change at Tartagal, making sure your ticket is stamped with the next bus time or you won't be allowed on it); bus Buenos Aires-Pocitos US$91. Bus Embarcación-Salta US$14.50, 3 a day. Regular bus scheduled to run daily at 1300, 17 hrs, US$40, Atahuallpa, but frequently cancelled. Alternatively take bus to Pichanal, US$1.25, several, another bus to JV Gonzales, US$10, 1600, and change again for Resistencia, 2215. From here there are buses to Formosa and Clorinda.

Tartagal, 74 km N of Embarcación, pop 70,000, is an agricultural centre with a small museum featuring displays on animals of the Chaco and regional folk art. The director, Ramón Ramos, is very informative about the region. Animal masks and pottery are made by Indians nearby at Campo Durán. **Hotels**: *Argentino*, San Martín 54, T 21327, 3-star; *Espinillo*, San Martín 122, T 21007; *Residencial*

City, Alberdi 79, T 21558.

Another route to Bolivia is via **Orán**, 110 km N of Libertador on Route 50, an uninteresting place, pop 34,000. (**D** *Residencial Centro*, Pellegrini 332; **D** *Residencial Crillon*, 25 de Mayo 225, T 21101, dirty; **C** *Gran Hotel Orán*, Pellegrini 617, T 21214; **D** *Residencial Crisol*, López y Planes, hot water, friendly, rec.)

   Buses, 6 daily to **Salta**, 7-10 hrs; direct bus to **Tucumán** at 2130, connecting for Mendoza bus which leaves at 1300. Bus to **Tartagal** daily at 0630 and 1800; to **Jujuy** at 1200 daily; to **Formosa**, US$28, 14 hrs, leaving Tues, Thur, Sat at 0930; to **Embarcación**, US$1.70. To **Resistencia**, Atahualpa buses every 2 hrs or so, 5 hrs, US$12.

   There are frequent bus services to **Aguas Blancas** (45 mins, US$2, luggage checks on bus), on the frontier. There is nowhere to stay at Aguas Blancas nor anywhere to change money, but there are restaurants (*El Rinconcito de los Amigos*) and shops. The passport office is open from 0700 to 1200 and 1500 to 1900. Insist on getting an exit stamp. There is no exit tax. Buses run twice daily from Bermejo, across the river (ferry US$0.50), to Tarija (10 hrs).

   If entering Argentina spend your remaining Bolivian money here, not accepted in Orán; buses to Orán every 45 mins to Güemes, 8 a day, US$10; through buses to Salta, Veloz del Norte and Atahuallpa, 3 daily each, US$17.50.

   There is no direct bus from Orán to Asunción, Paraguay; take bus to Embarcación, from there bus to Formosa, then bus to Asunción.

THE CUYO REGION: OVER THE ANDES TO CHILE (4)

From the pampa to the heights of Aconcagua and the Uspallata Pass, en route to Santiago. Mendoza is a centre of wine making, fruit growing, winter sports (several ski resorts nearby) and climbing.

In the Cuyo region, in the W, there is little rain and nothing can be grown except under irrigation. On the irrigated lands grapes and fruit are possible, and alfalfa takes the place of the maize grown in the N. The two most important oases in this area of slight rainfall are Mendoza itself and San Rafael, 160 km to the S.

   Of the 15 million hectares in Mendoza Province, only 2% are cultivated. Of the cultivated area 40% is given over to vines, 25% is under alfalfa grown for cattle, and the rest under olive groves and fruit trees. Petroleum is produced in the Province, and there are important uranium deposits.

NB No fresh fruit, vegetables or cold meats may be brought into the provinces of Mendoza, San Juan, Río Negro or Neuquén.

The Transandine Route Travelling from Buenos Aires westward across the pampa, one comes first to **Mercedes**, in Buenos Aires Province, a pleasant city with a population of 47,850. It has many fine buildings. (Not to be confused with Villa Mercedes in San Luis Province—see below.) Tourist Office on plaza, very friendly.

Hotels D *Loren* (no sign), Salta 228, friendly, clean, parking; **D** *Aragón*, ½ block from Plaza, friendly, hot water. **D** *Libertador*, opp bus station, good.

Junín, 256 km from Buenos Aires (Eva Perón was born near here) is close to lagoons from which fish are taken to the capital. Population, 63,700.

Accommodation   A2 *Copahue*, Saavedra 80, T 23390, F 29041, faded, ACA discount; *Embajador*, Sáenz Peña y Pellegrini, T 21433. **Restaurant** *Paraje del Sauce*, Km 258 on Route 7, picturesque, good food but "don't stop there if you are in a rush". *El Quincho de Martín*, B de Miguel y Ruta 7, good.

At Rufino (pop 15,300), on Route 7, 452 km from Buenos Aires, is the rec **L3** *Hotel Astur*, Córdoba 81, C with ACA discount; also at **Laboulaye**, on Route 7, 517 km from Buenos Aires, there are several good and cheap hotels, eg *Victoria*, and **C** *Motel Ranquel Mapu*, Km 489, very good, but drinking water is a problem, bottled water supplied.

At **Villa Mercedes** (San Luis Province, pop 77,000), 693 km from Buenos Aires (where the old municipal market is now an arts and community centre), Route 8 runs NE to (122 km) Río Cuarto (pop 110,000). About 65 km beyond Villa Mercedes, the rolling hills of San Luis begin; beyond there are stretches of woodland.

Hotels ACA hotel **C** *San Martín*, Lavalle 435, T 22358, restaurant, garages, clean, friendly; the ACA restaurant at the service station on Route 7, outside town (just before junction with Route 8), is very good value. *Centro*, Junín 40, T 21212. Cheaper places on Mitre, eg: **D** *Residencial Cappola*, No 1134, clean, rec.

Air Airport: Villa Reynolds, 10 km from Villa Mercedes.

Bus Villa Mercedes—Buenos Aires US$28.

Merlo, some 150 km N of Villa Mercedes, is a small town on the western slopes of the Sierra de Comechingones. At 700 m above sea level it enjoys a fresher climate than the pampas in summer, and the area is being promoted for its rich wildlife, particularly birds. One hotel rec is the *Rincón del Este* (no price given), 5-6 km from the centre, and nearby are three camping sites. The tourist office is on the main plaza and the bus station 3 blocks away; frequent buses to and from **San Luis**, TAC to **Buenos Aires** at 1800.

Mac McCreadie from Villa Mercedes, recommends the following walks: Behind the *Hotel Rincón del Este* it is possible to climb the rocky watercourse above the *guardaparque's* cottage to a cross on a hill-top 1500 m above the plain. This is an energetic scramble and takes $1\frac{1}{2}$-2 hrs, probably longer and tougher in the wet months. It is a further 500 m to the hill-crest at Cerro Linderos Alto over steep rocky ground. Few tracks exist. You have to select you route through spiny vegetation and over boulders. A sure footing and appropriate clothing will help. Stunning views W over the pampas towards the Sierras de San Luis and S towards peculiarly shaped hills near La Toma.

Lower down, again starting near the *guardaparque's* house, is a good walk of 3 to 4 hrs called El Circuito de Damiana Vega. This is less demanding but takes in the lushly wooded slopes along a 'ripio' (gravel road), negotiable by vehicles. The Circuito is named after a woman from the Comechingones indigenous people, who lives in a small house by the 'ripio'. In 1993 Damiana Vega was 110 years old, she welcomes visitors and likes to talk about the region.

8 km N of Merlo is *Piedra Blanca*, a small settlement in attractive surroundings, with several hotels. South of Merlo is a string of pretty villages along a scenic road running parallel to the main route (Ruta 148), S to Villa Larea, including the Carpintería, Cortaderas, and Villa Larea.

San Luis, 98 km from Villa Mercedes, is the capital of the Province of San Luis. It stands at 765m at the S end of the Punta de los Venados hills. It was founded by Martín de Loyola, the governor of Chile, in 1596, and is still faintly colonial. The area is rich in minerals and an onyx quarry is worked. Visit the Centro Artesanal San Martín de Porras, run by the Dominican fathers, on 25 de Mayo, opp Palacio de Gobierno, where rugs are woven. Open 0700-1300 exc Sat and Sun. Population: 150,000. San Luis to Mendoza is 264 km.

A "Via Crucis" sculptured in white marble skirts the mountainside at Villa de la Quebrada, 35 km N. Beyond Salto Grande, Salto Colorado and the Gruta de la Virgen de las Flores is El Volcán (12 km; *balneario*, walks, picnics; *Hotel Andrea*) in whose neighbourhood is Cruz de Piedra dam (drives, fishing), and Carolina (placer gold mining, riding and fishing). Hotels and inns along the road.

Hotels Several on Av Pres Illia: *Quintana*, No 546, T/F 29548, best; **A2** *Aiello*, No 431, T 25644, F 25694, a/c, private bath, garages, rec. *Gran San Luis*, No 470, T 22881, pool, 50m from ACA; *Gran Hotel España*, No 300,T 25051; also *Novel*, Junín 748, all categories **B-C**. Others on Rivadavia, eg **B** *Gran Palace*, No 657, T 22059; *Intihuasi*, La Pampa 815 (behind Casa de Cultura), spotless, very friendly, TV, lounge, highly rec (price unknown). **D** *Rivadavia*, Estado de Israel 1470, T 22437, with bath, hot water, friendly, opp bus station; next door is *17 de Octubre*, which should be avoided, basic, dirty.

Camping Rio Volcán, 4 km from town.

Restaurants The majority close at weekends; hotel restaurants are closed Sun, *San Luis'* closes Sat too. *El Cantón de Neuchatel*, San Martín 745, opp Cathedral on main square, is open Sun, modest. *Michel*, Lafinur 1361, good food and service.

Exchange Very difficult to change TCs, try **Banco de Galicia**, Rivadavia y Belgrano, 1.5% commission.

Tourist Office Junín, opp Post Office, excellent.

Bus station at Viá España between San Martín y Rivadavia. **Train** Passenger services suspended.

16 km from San Luis is **L3** *Hotel Potrero de los Funes*, T (0652) 30125/20889, F 23898 or

BsAs 313-4886, F 312-3876 (25 de Mayo 516, piso 11), a luxury resort and casino on lake of the same name, which has its own microclimate (sports and watersports, lovely views but upkeep a little lacking). Route 146 runs N from San Luis towards Córdoba through Villa de la Quebrada, San Francisco del Monte de Oro, Luján and Villa Dolores. An alternative is to take Route 9 via Trapiche (**A2 Hostería Los Sauces**, bus from San Luis, US$4 return) to Carolina. A disused goldmine can be seen at Carolina, allegedly put out of action deliberately in the 1970s, in an attempt to force up the world price of gold. A statue of a gold miner overlooks the main street of what has become a ghost town. Near Carolina, at Gruta de Intihuasi, a natural arch forms a cave in which the mummified body of a child was found, estimated to be 8,500 years old. 4WD vehicles can drive up Tomolasta mountain (2,000m) to see typical San Luis landscapes. From this road the Cuesta Larga descends to San Francisco. At Luján a road heads W to meet the San Luis-San Juan road (Route 147) at La Tranca.

70 km NE of San Luis is **La Toma** (**D Hotel Gran Italia**, hot showers; **Residencial Days**, P Graciarena 158, private bath) the cheapest place to buy green onyx—about 20 shops. From here you can make an excursion to Cerros Rosario, interesting hills and rock scenery, 10 km NW; and San José del Morro, a group of mountains which were originally volcanoes (there is a model in the Museo de Ciencias in Buenos Aires). You will find a lot of rose-quartz.

Beyond San Luis Route 7 climbs to a height of 460m and descends and crosses the valley of the Río Desaguadero, which forms the provincial boundary with Mendoza. At **San Rafael** (273 km SW of San Luis, 242 km S of Mendoza), at the foot of the Andes, irrigation makes it possible to grow fruit in large quantities. 2 bodegas to visit, Suter and Bianchi (Monte Caseros y E Civit, rec). The town—there are some oil wells near—has a population of 72,200. There is a small but interesting natural history museum 6 km SE of town at Isla Río Diamante (Tues-Sun 0800-1200, 1500-1900, free; Iselin bus along Av JA Balloffet); zoo nearby. A road runs W over El Pehuenche pass to Talca (Chile). Bus to Mendoza, frequent, US$9. Bus to Neuquén, US$20.

Hotels C *Rex*, Yrigoyen 56, T 22177; **D** *Kalton*, Yrigoyen 120, T 22568/30047, excellent, clean, safe, good value; **E** *Martínez*, 30m from bus station, good, also cheap meals.

Campsites 2 sites (one of them ACA) at Isla Río Diamante, 6 km SE.

Tourist Office Av H Yrigoyen y Balloffet, very helpful. Ask for Aldo or Hector Seguín at España 437 for trekking and climbing information.

Above the town, up the Río Atuel valley, there is beautiful scenery in the **Valle Hermoso** up to the 3 dams of El Nihuil which provide irrigation water and hydroelectric power to Mendoza. There is fishing in the reservoir above the highest dam. In the Río Atuel canyon there are polychrome rocks in the spectacular gorge. 3 buses a day go to Valle Grande at the end of the canyon, US$3. Plenty of hotels and campsites, river rafting and horse riding. Good skiing at **Las Leñas**, 2,250m at the end of Valle Los Molles, a new resort with 33 pistes, three T-bars, three ski-lifts (US$35-45/day; equipment hire US$11-18). It claims to be the foremost ski resort in the S hemisphere. (Buses from Buenos Aires, 15 hrs, in skiing season only.) Three stonebuilt hotels: *Escorpio*, *Acuario* and *Gemini*, T for all 71100, and a disco, shop renting equipment and expensive restaurant. All the hotels are L2; for cheaper accommodation you have to stay in Los Molles (bus from San Rafael US$5.30, colectivo US$20; from Las Leñas US$0.70) where there is **B** *Hotel La Huenca*, a/c, clean. There is an airport in **Malargüe**, pop 8,600 (**B-C** *Hotel del Turismo*, San Martín 224, T 71042, quiet, rec; **C** *Hotel-Restaurant El Cisne*, Villegas 278, T 71350, clean, rec; *Portal del Valle*, T 71536, provides multilingual tour guides; several others) 70 km from Las Leñas, with flights to Buenos Aires. This area is developing as a tourist centre. Ask at the tourist office for information on Cavernas de Brujas and Pozos de Animas, both worth visiting.

Mendoza, at the foot of the Andes, 1,060 km from Buenos Aires, is linked to it by air, the San Martín railway and a paved road, which continues across the Andes to Chile. (No rail service now between Mendoza and Buenos Aires or Chile.)

Mendoza (756m) is an expanding and very pleasant city. Rainfall is slight, but irrigation has turned the area into an oasis of fruit trees and vineyards. The city was colonized from Chile in 1561 and named in honour of the then governor of Chile. It was from here that the Liberator José de San Martín set out to cross the Andes, to help in the liberation of Chile. Mendoza was completely destroyed by fire and earthquake in 1861, so today it is essentially a modern city of low dwellings (as a precaution against earthquakes), thickly planted with trees and gardens. The main street is Avenida San Martín, which runs S to N parallel to the San Martín railway line. Population of city 148,000, but with suburbs included, it is about 600,000.

See the Cerro de la Gloria, a hill above the great Parque San Martín on the W side of the city, crowned by an astonishing monument to San Martín. There is a great rectangular stone block with bas-reliefs depicting various episodes in the equipping of the Army of the Andes and the actual crossing. In front of the block, San Martín bestrides his charger. In the park at the foot of Cerro de la Gloria steep and twisting paths run to the Jardín Zoológico (US$1). Nearby in the park there are watercourses and a 1 km-long artificial lake, where regattas are held, and views of the Andes (when the amount of floating dust will allow) rising in a blue-black perpendicular wall, topped off in winter with dazzling snow, into a china-blue sky. The entrance to the Parque San Martín is ten blocks W of the Plaza Independencia, reached by bus 110 from the centre. An hourly bus ("Oro Negro") runs to the top of the Cerro de la Gloria from the E end of the park, on Av Libertad— it's a long walk (45 mins).

The best shopping centre is Avenida Las Heras, where there are good souvenir and handicraft shops; leather goods are cheaper here than in Buenos Aires. The municipal market is clean and well-stocked; worth a visit. Plaza Pellegrini (Av Alem y Av San Juan) is a beautiful small square where wedding photos are taken on Fri and Sat nights. The wine vintage festival, Fiesta de la Vendimia, is held in the amphitheatre of the Parque San Martín at the end of Mar. There is a wine museum (Av Peltier, at the Giol *bodega*—see below), with good guides and wine tasting, just behind the Palacio de Gobierno, opening hours from the tourist office. Outside Mendoza, about 40 km due E, there is a modern satellite town called San Martín. **NB** Official tours of the city are a waste of time and money; a large sign in Plaza Independencia shows a walking tour which takes about 2 hours. Beware theft in pedestrian areas.

Museums Museo Histórico San Martín, Av General San Martín 1846, seven blocks N of the Tourist Office, open Mon-Fri, 0900-1200, 1700-2000, US$1; **Museo del Pasado Cuyano**, Montevideo 544, beautifully furnished, with a collection on San Martín and history of Mendoza, open Mon-Fri 0930-1230, Tues and Thur, 1600-1730, but times vary, US$0.50; **Museo de Historia Natural**, in Parque San Martín, open Tues-Fri 0900-1200, 1600-2000, Sat, Sun 1600-2000; **Museo de Ciencias Naturales y Antropológicas**, Playas Serranes, Parque Gral San Martín, Tues-Fri 0900-1200, 1400-1800, Sat-Sun 1500-1900; **Museo Municipal de Arte Moderno**, underground (subsuelo) in Plaza Independencia, US$1.50, very small unless there is a special exhibition. The **Acuario Municipal** is underground at Buenos Aires e Ituzaingó, small but worth a visit, US$0.50, open Mon-Fri 1000-1200 and 1530-2000, Sat and Sun same times am. The **Museo Arqueológico** and the **Museo de Ciencias Naturales** are both in the Ciudad Universitaria—ask at Tourist Office for details. Worth seeing, also, are the ruins of the **San Francisco church** at Ituzaingó y Beltrán. Next to the ruins is a **Museo del Area Fundicional**, Alberdi y Videla Castillo, history of Mendoza, Tues-Sat 0800-1400, 1630-2230, Sun pm only, rec; in front of the museum are the ruins of the Jesuit church of San Francisco, part destroyed in the 1861 earthquake. **Acuario Municipal**, Buenos Aires e Ituzaingó; Serpentarium opposite (US$2).

Wine Wine *bodegas* (wine-making season Mar/Apr) and fruit preserving; visiting times available from Tourist Office. To the *Giol* winery, one of the world's biggest, take 150 or 151 bus marked "Maipú" (every hour, 0900-1230, 1500-1800), but check if winery is open before going, T 972090. The tour is rec in season (mid Mar to mid April). Also in Maipú district is *Peñaflor*, on Mitre, bus 17, good visit and generous tasting. *San Felipe* (Bodega La Rural), C Montecaseros, Coquimbito, Maipú, T 972013, a small bodega, is worth visiting, bus 170, tours 0900-1100, 1600-1800, tasting, Museo del Vino (fascinating), open Mon-Fri 0800-1100, 1500-1800. (In Maipú itself see the lovely square and eat at the *Club Social*, good simple food.) *Bodega de Arizu* is open 0900-1600, bus No 7 from city centre; many of the others also admit visitors, and offer you a glass after the visit. Try *Bodega Escorihuela* (bus 15 from centre Belgrano 1188, T 220215) if you are more interested in the information than the wine-tasting. The *Toso* bodega at JB Alberdi 808, T 380244, is small, old-fashioned, has excellent wines and an interesting, free guided tour, some tasting, highly rec. The *Orfila* bodega in San Martín, 40 km E, located in the house of the Liberator, also has a wine museum. Prices at the bodegas have roughly a 100% mark-up from supermarket prices. Recommended: Cruz del Sur from Bodega Arizu, Cuesta del Parral, Valroy-Borgoña, Valroy-Cabernet Sauvignon, Viejo Toro, Trapiche from Bodega Peñaflor, and Vino de Mesa Arizu Tinto Seco. Many tourist agencies incl the bodegas in their half-day or day-long tours (US$4-8 but these visits are too short, with too few guides and little tasting—only of the cheaper wines, usually in plastic cups).

All Mendoza restaurants offer a tourist special of a bottle of wine for US$1.50.

Local Holidays 18 Jan (Crossing of the Andes); 25 Jul (St James); 8 Sep (Virgin of Carmen de Cuyo). Annual wine festival during the final week of Mar, when hotels fill up fast; book ahead! Prices rise at this time, and in Jul (the ski season) and Sep (the spring festival).

Hotels L3 *Aconcagua*, 4 star, comfortable, San Lorenzo 545, T 243321/243833, good but expensive restaurant, pool, disappointing tourist advice and bookings available. In our **A2-3** range: *Crillón*, Perú 1066, T 245525, small, clean but overpriced. *Plaza*, Chile 1124 on main plaza, T 233000, not too clean, but obliging; **A2** *Nutibara*, Bartolomé Mitre 867, T 245747/244658 (discounts for cash), central, colour TV, a/c, parking, no breakfast, modern swimming pool, rec; *Palace*, Las Heras 70, T 234200, a/c, bath, incl breakfast, central; *San Martín*, Espejo 435, T 380677, rec; *Vecchia Roma*, España 1619, T 231515 (next door to restaurant of same name), comfortable, safe. **B** *Balbi*, Las Heras 340, T 233500, small swimming pool, a/c but you must phone to have it turned on each time you return to your room, nice rooms; **B** *Argentino*, Espejo 455, Plaza Independencia, T 254000, good, breakfast incl (poor), quite comfortable. **B** *1 de Mayo*, Garibaldi 80, T 248820, highly rec, breakfast incl, 0800 checkout time; *Royal*, Las Heras 145, T 380522/380675, breakfast incl, friendly, clean, a/c, rec; *Center*, Alem 547, with bath, very clean; *Imperial*, Las Heras 84, T 284671, washing facilities, friendly, rec, may offer cheaper price.

In our price range **C**: *City*, Gen Paz 95, T 251343, clean, helpful; *Monterrey*, Gen Paz 360, good; *Gran Ritz*, Perú 1008, T 248506, clean, modern, good; *Vendimia*, Godoy Cruz 101, T 250675/233099, good; *Petit*, Perú 1459, T 232099, without breakfast, 1½ blocks from railway station, clean, friendly, rec; *Pacífico*, San Juan 1407, T 256286, modern, comfortable, clean; *Milena*, Pasaje Babilonia 17 (off San Juan nr Don Bosco), T 240284, 2 star, clean, nice atmosphere; *Messidor*, Alberdi 690, T 314013, reasonable, friendly, clean, comfortable, arranges tours; *Balcarce*, San Martín 1446, T 252579, clean, safe, very friendly, incl breakfast; *El Libertador*, España 247, T 290921, good; *Las Viñas*, Av Martínez de Rosas, clean.

The following are in our **D** range: *Galicia*, Av San Juan 881, near Av LM Alem, T 249619, very clean, hot water, use of kitchen, rec; *San Remo*, Godoy Cruz 477, T 234068, clean, quiet, central, stores luggage, secure parking, highly rec; *El Piño Azul* apartments, San Martín 2872 (T 304593); *Savoy*, Belgrano 1377, good, clean, some rooms without window, tours offered at 20% discount; *Mayo*, 25 de Mayo 1265, incl breakfast, good value. On Calle Juan B Justo: *Penitentes* (No 67), T 230208, with bath, a/c and heating, good, snack bar; *Ideal* (No 270, T 256842), transport to bus station. On Perú: *Zamora* (No 1156), T 257537, reasonable and friendly, converted house; *Residencial D'Amore* (No 1346), clean, no fans, good bathrooms, use of kitchen; *España* (No 1535), run down, basic, safe; *Dardex* (No 1735), 2 blocks from railway station, friendly. On General Paz: *Alcor* (No 86), T 380100/234800, central, good; *Gran Marta* (No 460), clean, but only cold showers, rec; *El Descanso* (No 464), basic; *Necochea*, Necochea 541, T 253501, pleasant, cheerful, English spoken; *Vigo*, Necochea 749, T 250208, good value, dark, good *comedor*; *Residencial Alberdi*, Alberdi 51, T 234110, family run, friendly, clean; *El Rosario*, Chile 1579, T 254765, good, clean, hot water, rec; *Quijote*, Av San Juan 1407, clean, friendly, restaurant; *Escorial*, San Luis 263, T 254777, very friendly and clean, rec. *Residencial Betty*, Güemes, cheap, good value. **E** *Gotelcas*, Juan B Justo 67, good, also acts as youth hostel.

Youth hostel *Tirasso* 2170, T 263300, E, take bus 20, "B Paraguayo", takes 20 mins, ask driver.

Camping In Parque General San Martín permitted, free, in cars, but not in tents. Three campsites at El Challao, 6 km W of the city centre, reached by colectivo No 11 leaving every hour, *Atsa*, friendly, swimming pool, good service, caters for families; noisy at weekends from disco. *Camping Suizo*, modern with pool, barbeques, hot showers, friendly, rec. *Saucelandia*, at Guaymallén, 9 km E of Mendoza. Mendoza is reportedly a good place to sell off camping equipment. White gas (*bencina blanca*) can be bought at *Ferretería Alsina*, Catamarca 37.

Restaurants *Trevi*, Las Heras 68, good food and service, rec. *Bárbaro*, San Martín 914, English spoken, speciality is roast kid, pricey but good. *Tristán Barraza*, Av Sarmiento 658 (*parrilla*), good. *Parrillada Arturito*, Chile 1515, good steak, popular with locals; *Montecatini*, Gral Paz 370, wide variety, good food, good value, rec; *Parrilla 14*, San Lorenzo

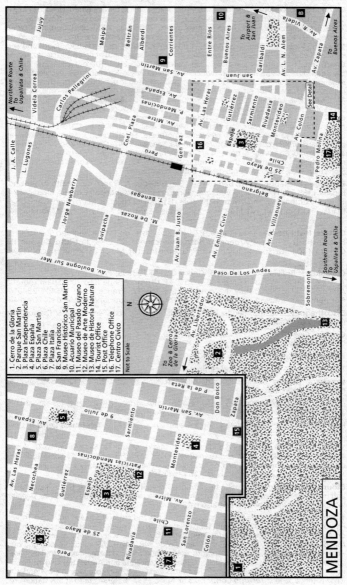

MENDOZA

1. Cerro de la Gloria
2. Parque San Martín
3. Plaza Independencia
4. Plaza España
5. Plaza San Martín
6. Plaza Chile
7. Plaza Italia
8. San Francisco
9. Museo Histórico San Martín
10. Acuario Municipal
11. Museo del Pasado Cuyano
12. Museo de Arte Moderno
13. Museo de Historia Natural
14. Tourist Office
15. Post Office
16. Telephone Office
17. Centro Cívico

Not to Scale

65, good meat, rec; *Don Angelo*, Lavalle 150, cheap set meal; *Club Alemán*, Necochea 2261, Godoy Cruz, rec; *Club Sociedad Libanesa*, Necochea 538-42, good value; *Govinda*, Salta 1538, vegetarian, good and cheap set meal, open 1200-1600, 1900-2200; *Comedor Línea Verde*, Montecaseros 1177, vegetarian, *tenedor libre*; *El Dragón de Oro*, Chinese, 25 de Mayo 1553 (near Las Heras), very good; *Cervecería Zurich*, Las Heras 530, good food and service, cheap, rec. Ice cream at *Soppelso*, Las Heras y España and at Paseo Sarmiento, rec. *Sr Cheff*, restaurant/confitería at *Hotel 1 de Mayo*, Garibaldi 80. *Il Tucco*, Emilio Civit 556 (nr park gates), also same name and owner in centre at Paseo Sarmiento 68, excellent Italian restaurants, reasonable prices. Good value, and big "super pancho" sandwiches in many places, incl *Pizzería Seb*, Alem 431, only US$1.50 incl a glass of red or white wine; *Pizzería Mi Querencia*, Las Heras 519, very good pasta dishes. Huge sandwiches in *Belgrano*, on street of same name, crowded with locals, highly rec. Several places with cheap 3-course menus on San Juan, 1300 and 1400 blocks. *Aranjuez*, Lavalle y San Martín, nice cafe, good meeting place. *Mankie Snack Bar*, Las Heras y Mitre, excellent breakfasts; *Café de la Gente*, café/bookshop at Rivadavia 135, pleasant atmosphere. Several good snack bars (known as *carrito* bars): *Tío Paco*, Salta y Alem; *Torombola*, San Juan 1348; *Don Claudio*, Perú y Godoy; *El Gran Lomo*, Rivadavia 56, open 24 hrs, rec. There is a good, cheap café (excellent ice creams) next to the bus station, past the underground walkway. Out of town, *Lomo Loco*, a few km S on Luján road, locals' favourite *parrilla* but not cheap.

Banks and Exchange Lloyds Bank (BLSA), Gen Gutiérrez 72. **Banco de Crédito Argentino**, España 1168, cash advance on Visa card, high commission. **American Express**, Rivadavia 24, T 290374 **Citibank** Av San Martín 1099, gives US$ cash for cheques. Many *cambios* along San Martín, incl **Exprinter**, No 1198, best for cheques; **Santiago** No 1177, rec; **Maguitur**, No 1203. *Casas de cambio* open till 2000 Mon-Fri, and some open Sat, am.

Cultural Institutes Alianza Francesa, Chile 1754; **Instituto Dante Alighieri** (Italy), Espejo 638; **Instituto Cultural Argentino-Norteamericano**, Chile 985; **Instituto Cuyano de Cultura Hispánica** (Spain), Villanueva 389; **Goethe Institut**, Morón 265, Mon-Fri 0800-1200, 1600-2230.

Consulates Bolivia, Azopardo 276, Godoy Cruz, T 223893; **Peru**, Perú 8185, Carrodilla, T 390863; **Chile**, Av Emilio Civit, 296, T 255024; **Uruguay**, 9 de Julio 200. **Spain**, Agustín Alvarez 455, T 253947; **Italy**, Necochea 712, T 251886; **France**, Chile 1754, T 234614; **Germany**, Montevideo 127, 1° Piso D6, T 242539; **Finland**, Boulogne Sur Mer 631, T 973844.

Discothèques *Saudades*, Barraquero y San Martín; *Kalatraba*, Perú 1779; *El Diablo*, Ruta Internacional Vistalba Luján.

Cinema *Cine de Arte Eisenchlos*, 9 de Julio 500, Thur-Sun 2200. Free film shows at *Salón Cultural Rivadavia*, José V Zapata 349.

Casino 25 de Mayo 1123, daily 2100-0300.

There is a private **gynaecological clinic** at Gral Paz 445; helpful and relatively inexpensive.

Language Classes Sra Inés Perea de Bujaldon, Rioja 620, T 290429, teaches Spanish to German speakers, rec.

Coin-operated **laundromat**, Colón 543, also on Garibaldi near La Rioja, on Salta near San Luis, and at corner of San Juan and Rondeau. *Laverap*, Av Colón 547.

Post Office Av San Martín y Av Colón, unreliable *poste restante*. **Telefónica Central**, Chile 1574.

Shopping Leather goods good and cheap; try *Alain de France*, San Martín 1070, also at Andrade 147. Books (English and German selection) from *Historias* on Av San Martín and *Centro Internacional del Libro*, San Juan. English language magazines and *Buenos Aires Herald* usually available from kiosks on San Martín.

Mountain Climbing Information from Tourist Office. There is a three-day (Thur-Sat) climbing and trekking expedition via Godoy Cruz and Cacheuta to Cerro Penitentes (4,351m), sleeping in mountain refuge, food incl. See also p 135.

Travel Agencies Lots, especially in Las Heras, between Perú and San Martín. *Cuyo Travel*, Paseo Sarmiento 162, 10% discount for ISIC and youth card holders for trekking and climbing on Aconcagua. *Servicios Especiales Mendoza*, c/o Annette Schenker, Amigorena 65, 5500 Mendoza, F (061) 244721, 240131, or Radio, code 548, 242162/244505 (day or night, only Spanish spoken), run by Bernard Klapproth, guided tours around all Argentina, many languages spoken, waterskiing on El Carrizal lake, climbing Aconcagua and Andes, trekking and many other specialist programmes, access to Red Cross and Police, only company to cross Andes to Chile without papers. *Turismo Cóndor*, 25 de Mayo 1537, T 259341 (also at bus station), rec for tours in and around the city, and to El Cristo Redentor statue, good guides, Spanish only; *Mylatours*, Paseo Sarmiento 23, T 254516, rec. *Turismo Sepeán*, San Juan 1070, friendly and helpful, have branch in Santiago. *Turismo Cultural*, Rivadavia 211, T 242579, helpful. *Ibiza*, Espejo 217, T 258141, helpful and efficient. *Hunuc Huar Expediciones*, Av España 1340, 8 piso, oficina 7, and *Huera Pire*, Emilio Civit 320, specialize in assistance to climbers, especially on Aconcagua. *José Orviz*, Juan B Justo 550/536, T/F 256950/380085, guides, mules, transportation and hire of mountain trekking equipment.

Tourist Offices   at airport, T 306484, helpful (frequently closed), at the bus terminal (helpful but limited English spoken), T 259709, at Municipalidad on Av España, at San Martín 1143 (evening city walks, US$1), at San Martín y Garibaldi, and at Mitre y Las Heras. They have a list of reasonable private lodgings and a hotel booking service (**C** range and upwards), and other literature incl lists of *bodegas* and an excellent free town and province map; the latter is also available at most kiosks. *Recreación*, leaflet lists all museums.

Car Hire   Avis, Espejo 228; **Lis Car**, San Lorenzo 110, T 291416; **AS Rent-a-Car**, Garibaldi 186, T 248317; **Localiza**, at airport and Gutiérrez 453, T 254105. **Motorcycle repairs** César Armitrano, Rubén Zarate 138, 1600-2100, highly rec for assistance or a chat; he will let you work in his workshop.

Airport   Plumerillo, 8 km from centre, reached by *remise* taxis (US$9, incl US$1 to enter airport grounds) and bus No 68 from the corner of San Juan and Alem which takes you close to the terminal (10 mins walk); make sure there is an "Aeropuerto" sign on the driver's window. Flying time from Buenos Aires: 1 hr 50 mins. AR flies 3 times a day (once on Sat); Austral twice a day (once on Sat), Lapa (not Sat). Austral offer a 65% discount on nocturnal flights. AR and Ladeco to **Santiago**, daily. Daily flight to **Córdoba** with Austral, AR fly to **San Juan** (Sun only). TAN flies to **Neuquén**. Aerolíneas Argentinas, Paseo Sarmiento 74, T 340170/100; Austral, Av San Martín 921, T 340088.

Buses   Terminal on E side of Av Videla, 15 mins walk from centre. To **Bariloche**, Andesmar daily, TAC, 3 a week, US$70, on a mostly paved road, about 22 hrs, book well ahead; to **Córdoba**, TAC 5 daily, 9 hrs, US$29; to **San Rafael**, many daily, US$9; to **San Juan** at least every 2 hours, US$11, 2 hrs (several companies, incl TAC, El Cumbre and Villa del Sur y Media Agua). To **La Rioja** US$25, 10 hrs, 5 a day, 3 companies; similarly to **Catamarca**, 12 hrs, daily, US$20. 6 daily to **Tucumán**, US$40; to **Salta**, Andesmar daily (via Tucumán) at 1300 and 2130, 20 hrs, US$54 (plus 4 other companies). To **Puerto Iguazú** at 1930, Mon, Wed, Sat with Cotal, US$70, 38 hrs; alternatively take daily Villa Marta bus to Santa Fe and change for Iguazú bus, about 40 hrs incl waiting time. To **Comodoro Rivadavia**, daily with Andesmar, at 2000, US$100, 32 hrs incl 4 meal stops; the Tues and Sat departures continue to Río Gallegos, arriving 1450 Thur. To **Rosario**, US$40, 12 hrs. To **Buenos Aires** via Route 8, 2nd class US$54 (cheaper in winter), 1st class daily, US$60 (lines incl Chevallier, TAC Coop, Jocoli); luxury service daily at 1800 (Chevallier), 32 hrs incl meals; via Route 7 (Junín-Mendoza) at 2020, arrive 1205. Dull scenery, and very cold across the Pampas at night. 20% student discount on some routes (eg Comodoro Rivadavia). A US$1 tip is expected for removing luggage from buses.

International Buses   For services to **Santiago** see p 137. To **La Serena**, Dec-Mar only. To **Lima**, El Rápido Mon, Wed, Sat 0900. To Montevideo, El Rápido, Tues.

Hitchhiking   between Mendoza and Buenos Aires is quite easy. If hitching to San Juan, take bus No 6 to the airport near the highway. Hitching from Mendoza to Los Andes (Chile) is easy; go to the service station in Godoy Cruz suburb (also bus No 6), from where all trucks for Chile, Peru and elsewhere leave.

Excursions   If driving in mountains remember to advance the spark by adjusting the distributor, or weaken the mixture in the carburettor, to avoid the car seizing up in the rarified air. Ask in agencies about river rafting, popular and fun. TAC and Uspallata buses run to the hot springs at *Cacheuta*, US$3.15 round trip, US$8 entry (indoor thermal baths for a variety of ailments, for residents only), 45 km to the SW (**L Hotel Termas**, T 259000/230422, full board; other hotels not rec, campsite). About 50 km N of Mendoza are the hot springs at Villavicencio, visited by many tourists. Pleasant walks in the area. The charming resort of *Potrerillos* is 13 km from Cacheuta, with ski slopes not far away and excellent birdwatching in summer. **A1 Gran Hotel**, T 233000, with meals; ACA campsite. *Restaurant Armando* rec. In summer, you can hike 20 km from Potrerillos to Vallecito, a closed ski resort, taking two days. On the first you will see desert scenery, blooming cactus flowers, birds and an occasional goat or cow. The second you walk surrounded by peaks, a steep but not difficult climb to the San Antonio refuge, usually open with beds and meals. Two other popular resorts within a few km of the Mendoza are Barballón, to the NE, and Challao, to the NW.   The small ski resort of Los Penitentes, 170 km away, can be reached by bus, 4 hrs (**see p 135**), equipment hire US$5 a day, lift ticket for a day US$9. The best skiing is at (2,250m) Valle de las Leñas, S of San Rafael in the Valle Hermoso (see p 128). Excursions also to the dam at El Nihuil, with artificial lake, and to the Río Atuel canyon, superb rock scenery (although the 16 hour round trip from Mendoza can be uncomfortable in hot weather, better to visit the canyon from San Rafael). On the road to Luján de Cuyo (buses go every 15 mins from near bus terminal) is an excellent fine arts museum dedicated to Argentine artists, surrounded by sculpture in gardens, admission US$1.50, open Tues-Fri 0930-1330, 1500-1900, Sat, Sun 1630-2030 (Museo Provincial de Bellas Artes Emiliano Guiñazu, **Casa de Fader**), worth visiting.

NB It is no longer possible to go from Mendoza to Santiago via the statue of El Cristo Redentor (Christ the Redeemer) at 3,854m. All buses and cars go through the tunnel to Chile, leaving the statue unseen above. To see the statue you must go on a 12 hr excursion from Mendoza (weekends early am, all travel agencies, highly rec) since the Chilean side of the frontier at the statue is closed. The excursion also includes Puente del Inca (see below).

Over the Andes to Chile

The route to Chile is sometimes blocked by snow in winter: if travelling by car in Jun-Sep enquire about road conditions from ACA in Mendoza (San Martín y Amigorena).

NB No visas into Chile are available at the border, so if you need one and haven't got it, you will be turned back. Tourist cards are given out on international buses.

There are 2 alternates of Route 7, which meet at **Uspallata**, the only settlement of any size between Mendoza and the Chilean frontier. The fully-paved S branch, via Cacheuta and Potrerillos, is wider and better than the N branch, which goes via Villavicencio with a stretch of one-way traffic just beyond the resort, where the road leads up spectacularly to the 3,050m high Cruz del Paramillo. This N branch is still unpaved. Near Uspallata are the ruins of Las Bóvedas, built by the Huarpe Indians under the Jesuits, and an Inca *tambería*; there is a small, interesting museum. They are just off the road which leads to Barreal and Calingasta (see p 140), unpaved for its first part and tricky when the snow melts and floods it in summer.

Hotels A2 *Valle Andino*, Ruta 7, T (0624) 20033, good rooms and restaurant, heating, pool, incl breakfast, ACA discount; **B** *Hotel Uspallata*, T 20003, dinner at 2100; payment for meals and drinks in cash, bowling alley, nice location, but hotel run down, service friendly, but vast herds of people get driven through it. **D** *Hostería Los Cóndores*, T 20002, clean, friendly.

Camping There is a run down ACA site at Uspallata, US$3 per head, full washing facilities, hot water.

The crossing of the Andes taken by San Martín is the old mountain trail the Spaniards named the Camino de los Andes. Beyond Uspallata is a vast, open, undulating plain, wild and bare. On all sides stand the grey, gaunt mountains. On the far side of this plain the valley narrows till Río Blanco is reached, and there the mountain torrents rush and froth into the river. At Punta de Vacas, look left up the Tupungato Valley at the majestic cone of **Tupungato**, one of the giants of the Andes, mass of 6,550m. An equally majestic mass of pinnacled rocks, Los Penitentes, is passed on the left; they are about 7 km away. The climber to their base (an easy task from Puente del Inca with a guide) sees a remarkable sight. The higher rocks look like a church and the smaller, sharper rocks below give the impression of a number of cowled monks climbing upwards. Walking tours in the Tupungato area can be arranged by Quinche Romulo, Alte Brown, Tupungato, T 0622-88029.

Puente del Inca, 2,718m above sea level, 72 km W of Uspallata, is a sports resort set among mountains of great grandeur. Good views of Aconcagua can be had from above the village or by walking W along the old railway line. (**B-C** *Hostería Puente del Inca*, T 380480, less off-season, very pleasant atmosphere, but overpriced and poor service, more expensive if booked in Mendoza.) Camping possible next to the church, if your equipment can withstand the winds. 5 km from Puente del Inca on the road to Mendoza is a ski club, **E** *Cruz de Caña*, only open in season, friendly, with comfortable dormitories (**C** with 2 meals), and a good restaurant. The owner organizes trekking expeditions to Plaza de Mula; prices:

US$50 a day full board during expedition, and US$20 per mule.

The natural bridge after which Puente del Inca is named is one of the wonders of South America; it crosses the Río Mendoza at a height of 19m, has a span of 21m, and is 27m wide, and seems to have been formed by sulphur-bearing hot springs. Watch your footing on the steps; extremely slippery. There are not thermal baths just under the bridge, a little dilapidated but a great place to soak. Puente del Inca is the best point for excursions into the higher Andean valleys or for a visit to the base of Aconcagua, which was first climbed by Zurbriggen of the Fitzgerald Expedition in 1897. Visits can be made on horseback from Puente del Inca to **Los Penitentes** (**A3-C** *Hotel Ayelén*, in middle of village, T 259990, price depends on room, clean, comfortable, pricey but the cheapest; **D** *La Taberna del Gringo*, Km 151, Villa Los Penitentes, rec, and others). Ski hire is US$35 a day; it may be cheaper to hire it in Mendoza. Lift pass is US$28 a day. Skiing is good with few people on slopes. A visit on foot to the green lake of Laguna de los Horcones is worthwhile (walk along road towards Chile, then after 1 km follow signs to mountain, excellent views of Aconcagua, especially am). Go by car (only with a well regulated engine) or bus or on horseback to the statue of El Cristo Redentor set above La Cumbre (or Uspallata) pass on the frontier at an altitude of 3,854m. It was erected jointly by Chile and Argentina in 1904 to celebrate King Edward VII's decision in the boundary dispute of 1902. It is, unfortunately, somewhat disappointing from the road, for it is completely dwarfed by the landscape. (The road from the tunnel to the statue is closed for the season after the first snowfall in Apr.)

Local bus (Expreso Uspallata) from Mendoza for Uspallata and Puente del Inca, US$8, 4 hrs, 0600 and 1000, returning from Puente del Inca 1200 and 1615; local buses also go on from Puente del Inca to Las Cuevas, Expreso Uspallata, US$12 return (**NB** take passport). Also note that buses from Mendoza through to Santiago de Chile do not stop here.

W of Puente del Inca, on the right, there is a good view of Aconcagua (6,959m), sharply silhouetted against the blue sky. In 1985, a complete Inca mummy was discovered at 5,300m on the mountain.

Best time for climbing **Aconcagua** (the highest peak in the Americas and a **national park**) is from end-Dec to Feb. For trekking or climbing it is first necessary to obtain a permit: 3-day trekking US$15, 5 days' trekking US$30. For climbing a 20-day permit is required. (Argentines US$40, foreigners US$80). Permits are sold only at Dirección de Recursos Naturales Renovables, address below. From Mendoza take a bus or colectivo to Puente del Inca. From here mules are available but cost US$25 per mule per day, with extra charges according to the weight of your pack (more economical to travel with a group); you have to pay for 3 days there and back (1 day rest) and for the muleteer and his wages (US$30 for more than 3 days). This only takes you to the base camp at Plaza de Mulas (4,200m), where there is now, nearby, the highest hotel in the world, *Refugio Plaza de Mulas* (see below), and a rescue patrol, crowded in summer. Also at 4,200m is Plaza de Francia, facing the south face, less crowded in summer. Plaza de Francia is about 25 km from Puente del Inca and can be reached in 2 stages via Confluencia (camping also available here, rec if pacing yourself). Of the huts above this height only La Libertad (Berlín) hut at about 6,000m is in serviceable condition. Both huts are small with no facilities. Take a tent able to withstand 100 mph + winds, and clothing and sleeping gear for temperatures below -20C. Allow at least one week for acclimatization at lower altitudes before attempting summit (4 days from Plaza de Mulas). Treks and climbs organized by Sr Fernando Grajales, the famous climber, in *Hostería Puente del Inca*, or at JF Moreno 898, 5500 Mendoza, Telex 55-154. Information also from Eduardo Enrique Esteban, Emilio Civit 320, Maipú, Mendoza, CP 5515, T/F (61) 973393 and Carlos and Amalia Cuesta, *Los Geteados*, nr Cementerio de los Andinistas, 1 km before Puente del Inca (Dec-Feb, or T Mendoza 391080/290410), rec for details on mules, trekking and climbing. Other guides can be found at the airport in Mendoza and further information from **Dirección de Recursos Naturales Renovables**, Parque Gral San Martín, Mendoza, T 252090 (see also under Mendoza: **Travel Agencies**).

Refugio Plaza de Mulas, US$140 pp full board, double rooms with bath, and dormitories for 10, US$30 pp without meals, good food, information, medical treatment, rec, also camping area. Altitude 4,370 m. In Mendoza you can book *refugio* reservations and programmes which incl trekking, climbing to the summit, with hotel accommodation or camping, prices from US$990 to US$1,890 for 10 days, T/F Mendoza 61-380383, Nueve de Julio 1126.

The Chilean frontier is beyond **Las Cuevas**, a neat, modern settlement being developed as a ski-ing resort (though there is no ski-lift as yet), but recently damaged by landslides and a fire. It is wise to take snow chains from Jun to Oct. Officially, driving without chains and a shovel is prohibited between Uspallata and the border, but this can be resolved in a friendly way with border police. Both ACA and Chilean Automobile Club sell, but do not rent, chains, but ask at YPF station in Uspallata about chain rental.

Hotel *Hostería Las Cuevas*, only one, poor food, no heating in annex. Food available at kiosk at Expreso Uspallata bus terminal point.

Beyond Las Cuevas, the road, completely paved, goes through the 4-km El Libertador-Las Cuevas toll road tunnel (US$2 for cars and VW buses). The old road over La Cumbre pass is now closed to through traffic; the famous statue of Christ

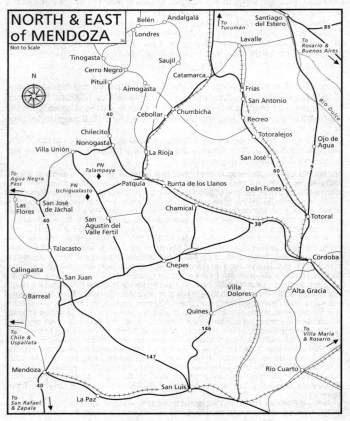

can be visited only by excursion from Mendoza (see above).

Giuliano Sargenti of Quartino, Switzerland, recommends taking the 0600 bus from Mendoza to Las Cuevas (arrives 1030, or 1000 at Puente del Inca), walk 3 hrs to the Cristo Redentor, great views, then return to Las Cuevas in time for 1600 bus back to Puente del Inca or Mendoza.

Transport to Chile Turismo cars (Chi-Ar—some adverse reports—and Nevada) carrying up to 11 passengers (US$27, 5 hrs) and minibuses (5½-6 hrs) do the trip to **Santiago** daily. When booking, ensure that the car will pick you up and drop you at your hotel; have this written on your receipt, if not you will be dropped at the bus station. If travelling by bus from Mendoza to Santiago take a direct bus as it is not possible to walk across the border. Buses Mendoza to Santiago daily at 0600-1430; several companies, El Rápido, Tur Bus and TAC, rec; mixed reports on El Rápido and adverse reports on Chile Bus and Nevada Tours. Most buses are comfortable and fast (6½-8 hrs) and charge US$15-20, those with air-conditioning and hostess service (incl breakfast) charge more (US$25, TAC), worth it when crossing the border as waiting time can be a matter of several hours. Also 3 buses daily to Viña del Mar and 2 to Valparaíso, US$20-25. All companies in same part of Mendoza bus station: you can easily shop around. Children under 8 pay 60% of adult fare, but no seat; book at least one day ahead. If all seats booked try CATA, its service is reportedly less good than others thus it usually has some empty seats. Passport required, tourist cards given on bus. The ride is spectacular. Information at main bus station. If you want to return, buy an undated return ticket Santiago-Mendoza; it is cheaper. A taxi Mendoza-Santiago costs about US$90 for 4-5 people. For Chilean side, see Chile, **Santiago and the Heartland** (Section 3), To Buenos Aires across the Andes.

All Argentine entry and exit formalities are now dealt with at Punta de Vacas, 30 km E of Las Cuevas (entering Argentina by taxi, expect to be stopped and searched). A new customs post, Ingeniero Roque Carranza has been built near Laguna Los Horcones, nearer Las Cuevas. Car drivers can undertake all formalities in advance at Uspallata while refuelling. One can hitchhike, or possibly bargain with bus drivers for a seat, from Punta de Vacas to Santiago, but if one is dropped at the entrance to the tunnel in winter, one cannot walk through. Travellers report that customs men may help by asking motorists to take hitchhikers through to Chile. Chilean migration and customs check is W of the tunnel—searches for fruit, meat, vegetables, which may not be imported into Chile, in a new building with the bus parked inside. All luggage is X-rayed. Remove all camera film before boarding bus as hand-luggage isn't x-rayed. Customs at the frontier are closed 1200-1400. Members of ACA need only the *Libreta de Pasos por Aduana*, otherwise you need the *Documento de Exportación* to enter Chile. Good food at frontier hotel, and there is an excellent motel on the Chilean side about an hour down.

NORTH OF MENDOZA (5)

The oases of San Juan, La Rioja and Catamarca between the plains and the Andes. Interesting natural rock formations can be seen, especially Valle de la Luna and Puerta de Talampaya.

Of the three oases in the more arid zone N of Mendoza, San Juan is the most prosperous, wine and olives support La Rioja, but Catamarca is economically depressed. The first, 177 km from Mendoza by paved road, is

San Juan pop 122,000 at 650m, founded 1562 by Don Juan Jufré de Loaysa y Montese and capital of its namesake province. The city is proud of its sunny climate and clean, tree-lined streets. Nearly destroyed by a 1944 earthquake, the centre is well laid-out, with a modern cathedral. The birthplace of Domingo Sarmiento (President of the Republic, 1868-1874, also an important historian/educator) is a museum. The area is famous for its wine, "to be between San Juan and Mendoza" is an Argentine expression for having drunk too much. One of the country's largest wine producers, Bodegas Bragagnolo, on the outskirts of town at Route 40 y Av Benavídez, Chimbas, can be visited (bus 20 from terminal; guided tours daily 0830-1330, 1530-1930, not Sun). **Escuela de Fruticultura y Enología**, Sarmiento 196 (bus going W on Av San Martín), students show visitors round.

Museums Museo Casa de Sarmiento, Sarmiento y San Martín, open Tues-Sat 0830-1900;

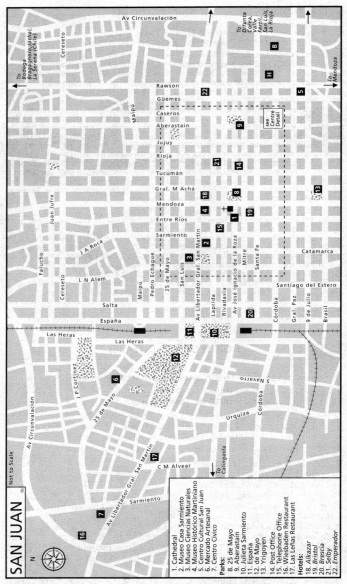

SAN JUAN

N

Not to Scale

Av Circunvalación

To Bodega Jáchal, Bregango, La Serena (Chile)

Av Circunvalación

Av Circunvalación

To Difunta Correa, Valle Fertil, San Luis, La Rioja

To Mendoza

Rawson

Güemes

Caseros

Aberastain

Jujuy

Rioja

Tucumán

Gral. M Achá

Mendoza

Entre Ríos

Sarmiento

see Centre Detail

Catamarca

Santiago del Estero

España

Las Heras

Las Heras

To Calingasta

C M Alvear

Sarmiento

1. Cathedral
2. Museo Casa Sarmiento
3. Museo Ciencias Naturales
4. Museo Histórico Martiniano
5. Centro Cultural San Juan
6. Mercado Artesanal
7. Centro Cívico

Parks:
8. 25 de Mayo
9. Aberastain
10. Julieta Sarmiento
11. España
12. de Mayo
13. Yrigoyen
14. Post Office
15. Telephone Office
16. Wiesbaden Restaurant
17. Las Leñas Restaurant

Hotels:
18. Alkazar
19. Bristol
20. Brescia
21. Selby
22. Emperador

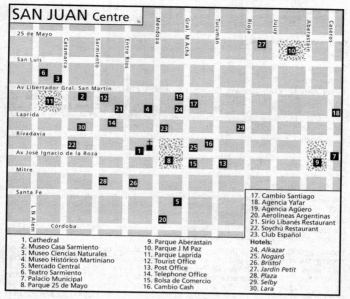

SAN JUAN Centre

1. Cathedral
2. Museo Casa Sarmiento
3. Museo Ciencias Naturales
4. Museo Histórico Martiniano
5. Mercado Central
6. Teatro Sarmiento
7. Palacio Municipal
8. Parque 25 de Mayo
9. Parque Aberastain
10. Parque J M Paz
11. Parque Laprida
12. Tourist Office
13. Post Office
14. Telephone Office
15. Bolsa de Comercio
16. Cambio Cash

17. Cambio Santiago
18. Agencia Yafar
19. Agencia Agüero
20. Aerolíneas Argentinas
21. Sirio Libanés Restaurant
22. Soychú Restaurant
23. Club Español

Hotels:
24. Alkazar
25. Nogaró
26. Bristol
27. Jardín Petit
28. Plaza
29. Selby
30. Lara

Museo de Ciencias Naturales, Av San Martín y Catamarca, incl fossils from Ischigualasto Provincial Park (see below), open Mon-Sat, 0830-1230, 1630-2030, Sat 0900-1200, US$0.50; **Museo Histórico Sanmartiniano**, Laprida 96 Este, incl the restored cloisters and two cells of the Convent of Santo Domingo. San Martín slept in one of these cells on his way to lead the crossing of the Andes, closed Sun, US$0.40.

Hotels **A1** *Alkazar*, Laprida 82 Este, T 214965, F 214977, incl breakfast, garage, new, good; **A2** *Hotel Nogaró*, de la Roza 132 Este, T 227501/5, pool, a/c, central, TV, in need of maintenance (1994), car park US$4 (ACA and US AAA discounts); **B** *Bristol*, Entre Rios 368 Sur, T 222629, a/c, hot water, clean, rec; **B** *Central*, Mitre 131 Este, T 223174, very clean and quiet, good beds, friendly owner; **B** *Jardín Petit*, 25 de Mayo 345 Este (ACA discount with cash), T 211825, hot water, pricey, parking lot next door US$5; **C** *Brescia*, España 336 Sur, near train station, T 225708; **C** *Plaza* Sarmiento 344 Sur, T 225179, friendly, noisy disco behind; **C** *Selby*, Rioja 183 Sur, T 224777. **B** *Embajador*, Rawson 25 Sur, T 225520, large rooms, clean, pleasant, café, good value; **C** *Residencial Hispano Americano*, Estados Unidos 381 Sur, T 221477, poor. Better cheaper hotels: **D** *Jessy-Mar*, Sarmiento 8 Norte, T 227195, small rooms, noisy; **D** *Residencial 12 de Diciembre*, Sarmiento 272 Norte, clean; **D** *Lara*, Sarmiento y Rivadavia, basic but clean, good value, rec. Several residenciales (**C**) along Av España, blocks 100-600 Sur.

Camping At Chimbas, 7 km N; 3 sites at Rivadavia, 8 km W.

Restaurants *Wiesbaden*, Circunvalación y San Martín, German-style, pleasant setting; *Soychú*, de la Roza 223 Oeste, excellent vegetarian food; *Club Sirio Libanés "El Polito"*, Entre Rios 33 Sur, pleasant decor, good food; *El Castillo de Oro*, de la Roza 199 Oeste, central, reasonable; *Comedor Central*, de la Roza 171 Este, not luxurious but good *locro* (stew) and *chivito* (goat). *Parrilla Bigotes*, Las Heras e Ignacio de la Roza, inexpensive "all you can eat" meat, chicken, salads. *Club Español*, Plaza 25 de Mayo, more expensive, large portions of mediocre food. Many *pizzerías*, *confiterías*, and sidewalk cafés, incl *Café Amadeus* and *Café del Aguila*. *Lomoteca San José*, San Martín 179, grills, inexpensive, late night music at weekends; *El Clavel de Oro*, Santa Fe y Entre Ríos, snacks, drinks; *Marilyn Bar*, San Martín y Mendoza, late night drinks. Eat under thatched shelters (*quinchos*) at *Las Leñas*, San Martín, 1600 Oeste.

Banks and Exchange Good rates at **Cambio Santiago**, Gral Acha 52, weekdays until 2000, Sat am. **Cambio Cash**, Tucumán 210 Sur; **Montemar**, Laprida 133 Sur; **Multicrédito**, Laprida y Mendoza; **Bolsa de Comercio**, Gral Acha 278 Sur.

Centro Cultural San Juan, Gral Paz 737 Este, concerts and other events.

Laundry *Marva*, San Luis y Av Rioja.

Shopping **Mercado Artesanal** at Av España y San Luis worth a visit.

Bicycle Repairs Ruedas Armado, San Martín y La Rioja, helpful.

Travel Agents *Yafar Turismo*, Caseros y Laprida, T 214476 (no tours); *Mario Agüero Turismo*, Gral Acha 17 Norte, T 220864, tours to Ischigualasto subject to demand, US$50 pp plus US$3 National Park entry fee. *Dante Montes*, Santa Fe 56 Este. *Almen Tours*, San Martín 149 Este, T 211006. For mountain climbing contact Pablo Schlögl, 543 Haité Este, T 225132, rec as probably the most experienced mountaineer in Argentina.

Tourist Office, Sarmiento y San Martín, helpful, good brochures, open Mon-Sat, 0900-1330, 1430-2100, Sun 0900-1300; also at bus terminal. Arranges tours in summer only. Large-scale provincial maps available at bookshops. For information on Difunta Correa, consult Fundación Vallecito at Caucete. **ACA**, 9 de Julio 802 Este, useful information on routes, helpful. The **Diario de Cuyo** published a *Guía de Turismo* for San Juan province in Oct 1993 (similar to Chile's *Turistel* guides), very informative.

Car Hire **Parque Automotor**, España y San Martín, T 226018. Cash discount on request. Localiza, España 274 (Sur), T 229243.

Air Chacritas Airport, 14 km SE. From Buenos Aires with AR daily; AR once a week from Mendoza (Sun, 0855). Ladeco from Santiago 3 times a week; Mon, Wed, Sat Ladeco flies to/from La Serena, summer only (Dec-Feb).

Buses Terminal at Estados Unidos y Santa Fe, 9 blocks E of centre (buses 33 and 35 go through the centre). Long distance services to **La Rioja** (550 km, 9 hours, US$19), or go via Chepes, 0900 daily US$6, with connecting service from Chepes, Mon, Wed, Sun at 1600, 4 hrs, US$10. **Catamarca** (660 km over secondary roads, US$17, with connection to Salta, US$29). **Tucumán** (3 a day, 13 hrs, Libertador is cheapest), Córdoba, Santa Fe, Mar del Plata, Bahía Blanca and BsAs (Autotransporte San Juan, US$47). To **San Agustín** at 1800, US$11. Fifteen departures daily to and from **Mendoza** with TAC and El Cumbre, 2 hrs, US$11, try to sit in the shade (on W side in am, E in pm). Also service to provincial tourist destinations.

To Chile: only connection with **Santiago (Chile)** is via Mendoza; catch the TAC bus at 0600, arrives in Mendoza 0830 in time for bus to Santiago.

The Agua Negra pass (4,600m) has been reopened after having been closed in 1978. Cars can now cross the Andes over this spectacular high point, but it is only open Jan to early Apr; in winter it is closed by snow, in summer it may be closed by rain. No buses take this route. ACA, customs and immigration at Las Flores (see below) informs all the ACA stations in the country of road conditions. It takes approx 6 hrs from Las Flores in Argentina to Rivadavia in Chile (where the first service station can be found).

From San Juan Hitchhiking to La Rioja, take route 141 to Chepes (ACA *Hostería*), then N to Patquia; more traffic on provincial route 29, a well paved, but less interesting road than that via San Agustin or Jachal (see below).

Excursions To the Museo Arqueológico of the University of San Juan at La Laja, 20 km N, open Mon-Fri, 0900-1900, Sat, Sun, 1000-1300, US$2, which contains an outstanding collection of prehispanic indigenous artefacts, incl several well-preserved mummies. Inexpensive thermal baths nearby. Bus No 20 from San Juan, 2 a day, but you need to take the first (at 0830) to give time to return. To *Vallecito*, 64 km E, to the famous shrine to the **Difunta Correa**, an unofficial saint whose infant (according to legend) survived at her breast even after the mother's death from thirst in the desert. During Holy Week, up to 100,000 pilgrims visit the site, some crawling 100m on their knees. See the remarkable collection of personal items left in tribute, incl number plates from all over the world and even one policeman's detective school diploma! (*Residencial Difunta Correa*).

Along scenic provincial route 12 (open westbound mornings, eastbound afternoons), 135 km W of San Juan, lies *Calingasta*, in the valley of same name (annual simple festival in Apr). (**Hotels**: **C** *Calingasta*, T 22014, remodelled, swimming pool, full board available; **D** *La Capilla*, T 21033, incl breakfast, basic but very clean, family run and friendly, the family also sells the TAC bus tickets, and has the only public telephone in the village.) 40 km S on the road to Uspallata is *Barreal* (**Hotel Barreal**, T 0648-41000, good, also good value in restaurant;

Cabañas Doña Pipa, see below; also **E** *Hotel Jorge*, clean, very simple. *Posada San Eduardo*, small, quaint, few rooms with bath, open summer only; accommodation with Sr Patricio Sosa or Sr Cortez. *Restaurant Isidoro*, owned by local baker and sandyacht champion, reasonable, ask waiter for the day's recommendation; food also available at *Mama Rosa*). Tours of observatory at El Leoncito (at 2,348m), 26 km from Barreal (no public transport) can be arranged from San Juan. Bus El Triunfo San Juan-Barreal daily 0700, plus Mon, Wed, Fri, Sun at 2030 (return Mon, Wed, Fri, Sun 1330, 1600, Tues, Thur 1400, Sat 1600), 5 hrs, US$11. *Remise* service San Juan-Barreal, US$16 pp, T 211729, at Mendoza 416 Norte, San Juan, T 41023, Sr Pachá, *Restaurante Isidoro*, Barreal; leaves San Juan 0900, or 1000, leaves Barreal 1430. Omnibus Vitar from Mendoza (Las Heras 494, T 232876) Thur and Sat via Uspallata, continuing to Tamberías and Calingasta (return Fri and Sun); fare Barreal-Calingasta US$7. The road Uspallata-Barreal is bad (like a washboard on the gravel section in Mendoza province, broken pavement in San Juan province). Rafting trips can be arranged in Barreal, contact Sr Eduardo Conterno.

Sr Ramón Luis Ossa, physical education teacher at Barreal's high school, runs mule treks into the Andes, crossing the foothills in summer, from 10 to 21 days between Nov and April; he can be reached at *Cabañas Doña Pipa*, Mariano Moreno s/n, 5405 Barreal, Pcia San Juan, T (0648) 41004. The *cabañas* sleep 5, with bath, kitchen, sitting room, comfortable. We are grateful to Herbert Levi for a detailed account of Sr Ossa's treks (not printed for lack of space). In addition to the organizer's list of essentials, Sr Levi recommends the following on any Andean trip: metal drinking mugs, metal containers to prevent tubes of toothpaste etc emptying themselves in mule packs, long underpants to protect against chafing, woollen cap, insect repellent, sunburn cream, laxatives, soap, nylon groundsheet for sleeping bag (depending on weather), portable tent for privacy, and fishing gear for those who prefer catching their own meals (No 3 spoons best for Andean streams--permit required).

Climbing *Mercedario* (also El Ligua), 6,770m. No authorization is required, but it is advisable to inform the Gendarmería Nacional at Barreal. From Barreal go to Casas Amarillas on the Río Blanco, about 100 km on a gravel road. It may be possible to hire a Unimog 4 x 4 from the Gendarmería Nacional; guides (*baqueanos*) may also be hired, they can provide mules if necessary. The best time is mid-Dec to end-Feb; the types of terrain encountered are gravel, snow and rock. There is no rescue service. Nearby peaks incl Pico Polaco (6,050m), La Mesa (6,200m), Alma Negra (6,120m) and Ramada (6,410m). More information is available from Club Andino Mercedario, 9 de Julio 547 Este, 5400 San Juan, or Antonio Beorchia Nigris, director, Ciadam (Research Centre for Andean Archaeology), República del Líbano 2621, 5423 San Juan. **NB** Do not enter this region from Chile, it is illegal.

Route 40, the principal tourist route on the E Andean slope, heads N toward Cafayate and Salta, via San José de Jachal. At Talacasto, 55 km from San Juan, route 436 branches toward Las Flores (Km 180) and the Chilean border at Agua Negra pass (4,600m—see under **Buses** above). Alternatively Route 141 runs directly N from Calingasta to Las Flores, a dirt road via Villa Nueva and Tocota, reported scenic but lonely.

At *Pismanta*, 5 km N of Las Flores, the **C** *Hotel Termas de Pismanta*, T 227501, has rooms for 120 guests, thermal baths between 38° and 44°C, a large swimming pool, medical attention, bowling, bingo occasionally, covered parking, well-maintained. Reservations in Buenos Aires (Maipú 331) and San Juan (San Martin y Sarmiento). From San Juan, two buses daily with TAC, four weekly with Empresa Iglesia, also from Mendoza. 22 km further N, in Rodeo, Ing Meglioli raises guanaco and vicuña, and sells local produce and crafts. From here, a scenic road, with several tunnels, follows the Rio Jachal 61 km E to *San José de Jachal*, a wine and olive-growing center (pop 15,000), with many adobe buildings. Expreso Argentino bus from San Juan at 0730 arrives at 0940.

Services **D** *Plaza*, San Juan 545, T 20256; *San Martín*, Juan de Echegaray 387, T 20431; *El Chato Flores* restaurant, good. Camping.

From Jachal, route 491 offers a scenic alternative to Villa Unión (see below), but buses now take new route 40 via Huaco. The undulating road, paved to the La Rioja border, crosses dozens of dry watercourses.

East of San Juan, one can make a loop via San Agustín del Valle Fértil and Villa Unión (La Rioja province). Turn off route 141 at Marayes (133 km), from which paved route 510 (poor) goes N 114 km to *San Agustín del Valle Fértil*. Pensiones

(*Andacollo*, *Los Olivos*; ask at bus station for family *Hospedaje Romero*, D) and private houses also provide lodging. There is a municipal swimming pool, and a lake with fishing. Tourist information on the plaza. Local weavers offer ponchos and blankets. Bus from San Juan US$9; San Juan-La Rioja bus stops in San Agustín about midnight, leaves at 0300, 4 hrs, US$9.50.

North of San Agustín, at a police checkpoint, 56 km by paved road, a side road goes NW for 17 km to the 62,000-ha *Ischigualasto* Provincial Park, also known as *Valle de la Luna* for its exotic desert landforms, entrance US$5. Here the skeletons of the oldest known dinosaurs have been found (230 million years). All private vehicles must be accompanied by rangers whose knowledge and interest vary greatly; fee US$2 pp. The circular tour, on an unpaved road, lasts 2-3 hours. Local bus from San Juan Mon and Fri to police checkpoint and on Sat afternoon, if demand is sufficient. Tours from San Juan, US$50 (not incl lunch); from San Agustín US$18 for a guide, ask at tourist office on plaza. Rec guide is Barros Lito, US$40 for full day tour of Valle and Talampaya in private car. Taxi to park US$55 (rec if there are 4-5 people).

Just beyond the police checkpoint, near Los Baldecitos, paved route 150 heads E to Patquia and then to La Rioja or Chilecito, while provincial route 26 heads N. 58 km N of the junction a paved road goes E to **Puerta de Talampaya** Provincial Park (open 0800-1630, entrance US$3), another collection of spectacular desert landforms (*Refugio* near the entrance, sleeping bag essential). Tours follow the dry bed of the Río Talampaya in four-wheel drive vehicles operated by park rangers (US$35 for 2-hr tour for 4-8 people, longer tours US$70 and US$110, rec). Herbert Levi writes "There are 6,000 year old petroglyphs with pictures depicting animals. The whole area is said to have been covered with water long ago; now there are two visible strata, the *tarjado* and the *talampaya*. After that one enters a canyon with "balconies", sheer overhanging walls. Coming out of the canyon there are rocks shaped like a cathedral, a bird, a castle, a chessboard, a monk, and three kings on a camel". Better to visit park in the morning and avoid strong winds in the afternoon. Tours, arranged through Dirección Provincial de Turismo in La Rioja, or Sr Furlin, park director, in Pagancillo, who can also arrange accommodation in the village (eg with Familia Flores, D pp, incl breakfast and dinner). Chilecito-San Juan buses pass Talampaya, drop off at Km 144. Patquia-Villa Unión buses pass Pagancillo.

From the park junction route 26 continues to **Villa Unión** (**C** *Hostería Provincial*, Dávila 61, T 7271, simple, rec; **E** *Hospedaje Paola*, main street opp police station, basic; next door is **E** *Hospedaje Changuito*, restaurant). Bus station behind plaza. Jeep excursions can be made to Ischigualasto and Talampaya, Laguna Verde and Laguna Veladero. The remains of a huge volcano crater, La Caldera del Inca, can also be visited from here. It spans 40 km across, between the peaks Pissis (6,882m) and Bonete (6,872m). The bottom of the crater is desert-like but with glaciers beneath the sand in parts, and with a lake frequented by flamingos and other birds. A fascinating area, but hard to reach. Ask for Werner Lorenz in the town for directions, or for organizing an expedition. The tourist office in Chilecito (below) may be able to help, or, in the same town, Jorge Llanos hires out vehicles.

From Villa Unión, partly paved route 40 crosses the Cuesta de Miranda, dropping through a deep narrow canyon in a series of hairpins. This beautiful canyon is not rec to drive through after rains, deep river crossings, even in 4WD. Ask about road conditions at the ACA service station in Villa Unión, or at the police checkpoint there. After 92 km, it intersects the paved Patquia-Chilecito road.

18 km N of the junction is **Chilecito**, La Rioja province's second town, pop 20,000. Founded in 1715, it has good views of Sierra de Famatina, especially from the top of El Portezuelo, an easy climb from the end of Calle El Maestro. At Los Sarmientos, 2 km N of town, is the Santa Clara church, dating from 1764. The region is famous for its wines, olives and walnuts.

Museums Samay Huasi, 3 km S of town, the house of Joaquín V González, founder of La Plata University, open 0800-1200 and 1500-1800, contains the **Museo de Ciencias Naturales, Mineralogía y Arqueología**, pleasant gardens, and good views of Chilecito, the Famatina ridge and connecting valley. **Molino San Francisco y Museo de Chilecito**, at J de Ocampo 63, has archaeological, historical and artistic exhibits, open Mon-Fri 0800-1300, 1400-1900.

Hotels B ACA Chilecito, Dr L Martínez y 8 de Julio, T 2201/2, good, clean, friendly, no credit cards, safe parking, pool, good restaurant; **C** Riviera, Castro Barros 133, rec, clean, hot showers; **D** Belsavac, 9 de Julio y Dávila, T 8277, good but paperthin walls; **D** Wamatinag,

Galeria Victoria, W side of Plaza Sarmiento, clean, pleasant, best value in town; **D** *Americano*, Libertad 68, T 8104, unfriendly; **D** *Bellia*, El Maestro y Libertad. The Tourist Office has a list of families offering accommodation, but not for singles.

Camping at Santa Florentina, 6 km NW of Chilecito and Las Talas, 2 km beyond.

Restaurants *El Gallo*, Perón e Illia, excellent; on Plaza Sarmiento are: *Chaplin*, best in town; *Robert Snak Bar*, light meals and drinks; *Vanesa*, good home-made ice-cream; *Toscanini*, Fátima y San Martín, good Italian food, inexpensive; *Ferrito*, Av Luna 661, pricey.

Tourist Office Libertad e Independencia, T 2688, very helpful.

Transport Líneas Aéreas Riojanas fly **La Rioja**-Chilecito, 20 min. Buses: to **San Juan**, Tues, Thur, Sat at 2200, arr 0705; to **Tinogasta** (Catamarca), Mon-Fri, direct at 0700 via route 11, returning same day at 0600; to Tinogasta Mon and Thur 0600, returning 1330 the same days; to **La Rioja**, 3 times daily with Cotil, to **Villa Unión** daily at 1345 with Cotil. Connections with Catamarca and **Córdoba** via La Rioja only.

Excursions La Mejicana mine via Santa Florentina road: a cable car system (built 1903) which brought ore 39 km to the railhead at Chilecito is now out of use, although it runs on some weekends between stations 1 and 3. For treks, and trips to see gold washers at Famatina or to Talampaya, ask for Carlos de Caro, or enquire at tourist office. To Famatina, a sleepy hamlet amid nut plantations, *hostería*, restaurants.

With construction of an excellent new road, route 40 now goes via Salicas, since the Cuesta de Zapata, N of Tinogasta, was closed after 1981 floods. 21 km N of Chilecito, the old road (now route 11) goes via Famatina to **Tinogasta**, a half-Indian former-copper mining town in an oasis of vineyards, olive groves, and poplars (pop 9,000).

Hotels B *Provincial de Turismo*, Romero y Gordillo, T 23911, clean but run down, restaurant; *Hostería Novel*, near airport.

Restaurants *Persegani*, Tristán Villafañe 373; *Rancho Huairapuca*, on Moreno.

Transport Buses: to **Tucumán**, Empresa Gutiérrez, Tues, Fri, Sun 1700, Mon, Tues, Fri, Sun 0615, Fri 0845, US$22; return Tues, Fri, Sun. To **Catamarca** 1700 and 0030 daily; to **La Rioja** 0930, El Cóndor, US$11. Services to **Chubut**, **Comodoro Rivadavia**, and **Caleta Olivia**, with Empresa Ortiz, reflect that this is the source region for labour in the Patagonian oilfields. To **Puerto Madryn** and **Comodoro Rivadavia**, Empresa Robledo, Tues and Fri at 1600. To **Copiapó**, Chile, in summer, an excursion bus crosses the San Francisco pass, Adbeca, T (0836) 30725, 3 day tour, US$220. For air services, see under Catamarca.

Mountaineering Tinogasta is the starting point for expeditions to the second highest mountain in South America. Most recent cartography has allowed for some corrections in altitude so that *Pissis* has been confirmed, at 6,882m, as higher than Ojos del Salado (6,879m). To get there take Route 60 which crosses Tinogasta in the direction of the San Francisco pass. Everyone has to register at the police station outside Fiambalá, take passport. Expeditions organized and horse riding with Omar Monuey, La Espiga de Oro, 25 de Mayo 436.

Fiambalá is 49 km N of Tinogasta. **C** *Hotel* with restaurant, and small, basic *pensión* (unsigned – ask), near which is a good restaurant. There is also a clean *hostería*. Drive or take a taxi from here to *aguaditas*, hot springs, US$1 entry, temperatures from 30°C to 54°C (make sure taxi fare includes wait and return). The entire province is rich in thermal mineral waters. There are vineyards in the valley. Empresa Gutiérrez daily at 1345 to Catamarca via Tinogasta (1500) and Cerro Negro junction (1610), connect with Coop Catamarca bus to Belén (from Catamarca), about 2 hrs by bad road. Also 0530 departure from Fiambalá. 4WD vehicles may be hired for approaching the Pissis-Ojos region; ask at the Intendencia. For transport into the *puna* ask for Sr Jonson Hugo Reynoso (check state of vehicles). 36 km beyond Fiambalá is Palo Blanco, in the *pre-puna* foothills.

From Chilecito, new route 40 goes to Pituil, where the paved section ends, and on to Salicas and Cerro Negro junction (59 km) with route 60, the Tinogasta-Aimogasta road. Turning left at Cerro Negro for 2 km, paved route 40 heads N to **Londres**, founded in 1558 and the second-oldest town in Argentina, named in honour of the marriage of Mary Tudor and Philip II. The town hall displays a glass coat-of-arms of the City of London and a copy of the marriage proposal. 15 km further (paved) is **Belén**, pop 8,800 (**B** *Hotel Samai*, Urquiza 349, clean, friendly, rec; **D** *Hotel Turismo*, cheap and good, with bath; *Hotel Provincial*, dilapidated. Good breakfast at bus terminal; *Restaurant Dalesio*, near YPF gas station, excellent and cheap; *El Amigazo*, behind church, good). The whole district is famous for weavings, ponchos, saddlebags and rugs. There are good views from the new statue of Virgin of Belén at the summit of the path beginning at Calle General Roca, and an interesting archaeological museum, Condor Huasi. Folklore festivals Oct and Christmas. Belén is encircled by mountains, except to the SE; lush vegetation along Río Belén. N of Belén Route 40 runs another 176 km, largely unpaved, to Santa María at Tucumán provincial border (**see p 108**), and on to Cafayate (**p 115**).

Transport Belén-Villavil (thermal springs – open Jan-April), incl side trip to Corral Quemado and end of line at Barranca Larga, 19 km N of Villavil, Tues, Thur, Sun at 0800, returns from Villavil at 1830. (Villavil may have to be abandoned, under threat of seismic collapse.) Sit on right-hand side for best views of impressive canyon and Río Bolsón reservoir. Belén-Santa María Tues 1330, Fri and Sun 2020; return Tues and Thur 0930, Sun 1945. Belén-Salta via Hualfín (mineral hot springs), Santa María, Cafayate Thur 0600.

From Cerro Negro it is 38 km SE to Aimogasta (national olive festival in May) and another 30 km to turnoff to Termas Santa Teresita. 15 km E on route 60 a good new road branches N to Saujil (60 km) and *Andalgalá* (130 km, pop 7,800), a beautiful town renowned for strong alcoholic drinks (*Hostería Provincial*, often full; *Residencial Galileo*; 3 bus lines to Catamarca). The road parallels the Salar de Pipanaco on the W and Sierra de Ambato on the E. At Minas Capillitas, rhodochrosite, Argentina's unofficial national stone is quarried; it can be bought at shops around the plaza in Andalgalá. Beyond Andalgalá, there is no public transport on the difficult but beautiful road to Santa María over the Cuesta de Capillitas, although trucks go weekdays to the mines just beyond the pass.

An alternative route to Salta is along Route 53 (43 on some maps), which branches W off Route 40 at a point 52 km N of Belén and runs via Antofagasta de la Sierra and San Antonio de los Cobres (petrol available—**see p 117**). This route is almost impassable in passenger cars after heavy rains, and requires enough fuel for 600 km at high altitudes on unmaintained roads (fill up at Hualfín, 10 km past turnoff to Route 53). Also, the stretch beyond the right turn at Puerto de Corral Quemado is very difficult (37 km of fords), to be avoided in summer rainy season. At Km 87 is Cerro Compo (3,125m), magnificent descent; at Km 99 the road turns right to Laguna Blanca, where there is a small vicuña farm (don't go straight at the junction). *Antofagasta de la Sierra* (260 km) can be reached by colectivo from Belén on Fri about 1000, arriving 2200, returning Mon 0700, or by hiring a pickup or hitching, or by plane, inquire at Dirección de Aeronáutica, Aerodromo de Choya (10 km from San Fernando del Valle de Catamarca), T 24750, bus L22 from airfield to centre (**C** *Pensión Darío*, blue door just off main square; *Almacén* **F** *Rodríguez*, Belgrano y Catamarca, serves meals, incl breakfast). No petrol station, but fuel obtainable from *intendencia*. Together with El Peñón and Laguna Blanca in the *puna*, and Villavil and La Hoyada in the *pre-puna*, this is the main township of NW Catamarca. La Hoyada can be reached from Santa María in the NE via provincial Route 118. There are lunar landscapes, with salt lakes, around Antofagasta, and many peaks over 5,000m. Deposits of marble, onyx, sulphur, mica, salts, borates, and gold are present. Wildlife in the sparsely populated region incl vicuña, guanaco, vizcacha, flamingoes, foxes and ostriches. **NB** Petrol/gasoline is rarely available in this region; remember that in the *puna* fuel consumption of carburettor engines is almost double that in the lowlands.

La Rioja, founded 1592, 106,000 people, is capital of its province, which is home of Argentine president Carlos Menem (he comes from Anillaco). Some colonial buildings survive, despite a major earthquake in 1894. The Convent of San Francisco, 25 de Mayo/Bazán y Bustos, contains the Niño Alcalde, a remarkable image of the infant Jesus as well as the cell (*celda*) in which San Francisco Solano lived and the orange tree, now dead, which he planted in 1592. To visit the tree when the church is closed, ring the bell at 25 de Mayo 218 next door. A visit may also be made to Los Padrecitos, 7 km from town, where a stone temple protects the remains of the 16th century adobe building where San Francisco converted the Indians of the Yacampis valley. The Convent of Santo Domingo, Luna y Lamadrid, is the oldest surviving temple in Argentina, dating from 1623. The Casa González, a brick "folly" in the form of a castle, is at Rivadavia 950.

La Rioja is known as "City of the Orange Trees," but there are also many specimens of the contorted, thorn-studded *palo borracho* tree, whose ripened avocado-like pods release large brown seeds in a kapok-like substance. It is also a common ornamental in Buenos Aires.

Museums Museo Folklórico, P Luna 811, Tues-Fri, 0900-1200, 1600-2000, Sat, Sun, 0900-1200, US$1.50; Museo Arqueológico Inca Huasi, Alberdi 650, owned by the Franciscan Order, contains a huge collection of fine Diaguita Indian ceramics, open Tues-Fri, 0800-1200, 1500-1900, US$1. Museo Histórico de la Provincia, Dávila 87, opening hours variable. Museo Municipal de Bellas Artes, Copiapó 253, works by local, national, and foreign artists.

NB Avoid arriving on Sat night as most things are shut on Sun.

Hotels Accommodation can be difficult to find, particularly in the lower price ranges. A2 *Plaza*, San Nicolás y 9 de Julio, T 25215, rec but street noisy; *International Sussex*, Ortiz de Ocampo 1551, T 25413; *King's*, Quiroga 1070, T 25272; *Libertador*, Buenos Aires 253, T 27474, good value. *Talampaya*, Perón 951, T 24010; *Hotel de Turismo*, Perón y Quiroga, T 25240, offstreet parking, no breakfast; all **B**. **C** *Imperial*, Moreno 345, T 22478, clean, helpful; **C** *Residencial Petit*, Lagos 427, basic, friendly; **D** *Savoy*, Roque A Luna 14, T 26894, excellent value, hot shower. **D** *Pensión 9 de Julio*, Copiapó y Vélez Sarsfield, rec. Best of the *residenciales* is **D** *Sumaj Kanki*, Castro Barros y Lagos; **D** *Residencial Florida*, 8 de Diciembre 524, clean, basic, cheap. At Anillaco, on Highway 75 between La Rioja and Aimogasta, there is an *ACA Hostería*, T (0827) 794064, **E**, mixed reports. Tourist Office keeps a list of private lodgings, such as Sra Vera, Dávila 343.

Camping at Balneario Los Sauces, 13 km W.

Restaurants *Café Corredor*, San Martín y Pelagio Luna, good, cheap; *La Cantina de Juan*, Yrigoyen 190, excellent food, inexpensive; *Il Gatto*, Plaza 25 de Mayo, good pastas and salads; *Club Atlético Riojano*, Santa Fe between 9 de Julio and Buenos Aires, no atmosphere but cheap; good open air *churrasquería* next to *Hotel de Turismo*; *La Casona*, Rivadavia 449, very good and reasonably priced, rec; *Taberna Don Carlos*, Rivadavia 459, good fish and service; *Comedor Sociedad Española*, 9 de Julio 233, excellent pastas, inexpensive; *La Pomme*, Rivadavia y San Martín, open-air terrace, popular meeting place.

Banks and Exchange US$ cash changed at Banco de Galicia, Plaza 25 de Mayo (no commission on Visa cash advance), and Banco de Crédito, San Nicolás 476. Cheques difficult to change—try Banco de la Provincia, Bazán y Bustos, commission 8%. Better to change plenty before arriving (see note on provincial bonds used as currency, p 222).

Laundry *Laverap*, Av Perón 944.

Post Office Av Perón 258. **Telecommunications**, Perón 764.

Travel Agent *Zu Tours*, runs tours of Talampaya and Valle de la Luna, rec.

Tourist Office at Perón y Urquiza, T 28834.

Transport By air: Aerolíneas (T 27355) daily except Sun, at 0630, from Bs As; Líneas Aéreas Riojanas to Catamarca (0800 and 1330 weekdays), Chilecito.
   Buses: Terminal 7 blocks S of the Cathedral at Artigas y España. To Buenos Aires with General Urquiza, US$47, combination Ablo, via Córdoba. To Mendoza (US$25) and San Juan (US$19), night service with La Estrella or Libertador, with Andesmar, 1000, 8 hrs. To travel to San Juan by day (good scenery), take 0715 Cotil bus to Chepes (new bus station and ACA motel), then Cotil again next day to San Juan at 0900 or 20 de Junio bus at 1000 for San Juan or 1230 to San Luis. To Tinogasta, 0620, 2200, daily, US$11. To Tucumán (US$15), with Bosio and La Estrella. To Salta, Andesmar, 2100, arr 0700, US$33, video, sandwich, juice, coffee free, rec. Also provincial services.

Excursions To Ischigualasto and Talampaya (via Nonogasta, Cuesta de Miranda and Villa Unión, by private car with guide), costs US$190 for up to 5 people plus entrance fees, departs 0900. To Samay Huasi (see Chilecito, p 142). Fishing at El Portezuelo dam (see below). Swimming and fishing at Los Sauces dam, 15 km W; beyond Los Sauces is Sanagasta, El Cóndor buses, 45 mins, times vary. Good views of La Rioja from Cerro de la Cruz (1,680m), 12 km W, now a centre for hang-gliding, where condors and falcons may be sighted. Two hours to thermal springs at Santa Teresita.

A paved road runs to the third oasis, **Catamarca** (San Fernando del Valle de Catamarca), population 89,000, capital of its province, at 490m on the Río del Valle, between two S slopes of the Sierra de Aconquija, about 240 km S of Tucumán. Cattle, fruit, grapes and cotton are the main agricultural products, but it is also renowned for hand-woven ponchos and fruit preserves (try Casa Valdés, Sarmiento 586). Pilgrimages to the church of the Virgen del Valle. Therapeutic mineral springs. There are traces of Indian civilizations, including extensive agricultural terraces (now mostly abandoned), throughout the province. The *Zonda*, a strong dry mountain wind equivalent to the European *Föhn* or North American chinook or Santa Ana, can cause dramatic temperature increases. In Jul, regional handicrafts are sold at Festival del Poncho, a *feria* with four nights of music, mostly folklore of the NW.

Museums Instituto Cultural Esquiú, Sarmiento 450, incl important archaeological section, open Mon-Fri 0700-1300, 1430-2000, Sat, Sun, am only; **Museo Folklórico**, underground (subsuelo), Paseo Gral Navarro.

Hotels **B** *Ancasti*, Sarmiento 520, T 25001/4, restaurant; **C** *Inti Huasi*, República 297, T 24664; **D** *Colonial*, República 802, T 23502, no food, rec, clean, welcoming, good value; **D** *Delgado*, San Martín 788, basic, friendly; **D** *Suma Huasi*, Sarmiento 547, avoid TV lounge and rooms above it; **C** *Centro*, Rosas y 9 de Julio, basic; **E** *Las Cumbres*, Plaza 25 de Agosto. Many *residenciales* around Avenida Güemes. Discounts to ACA members at *Ancasti*, *Inti Huasi*, and *Suma Huasi*. Provincial tourist office has a list of families who rent rooms.

Restaurants *Sociedad Española*, Urquiza 703; *La Cabaña*, Tucumán 1115, has folk dancing. *La Tinaja*, Sarmiento 500 block, excellent, pricey, live music, warmly rec; *Pizzería Maryeli*, Esquiú 521, basic (but good *empanadas*). *Sociedad Italiana*, M Moreno (off Paseo Gral Navarro), pastas, inexpensive; *Comedor Unión Obrera*, Sarmiento 857, good value, speciality *cabrito*; *Parrilla de Adrián*, Av Güemes block 500, good *asado*; *Montmartre*, Paseo Gral Navarro, good food, reasonably priced; *Marco Polo Bar*, Rivadavia 916, drinks, snacks. Many cheap restaurants along Av Güemes, bars and cafés along Rivadavia (pedestrian street).

Banks and Exchange Banco de Catamarca, Plaza 25 de Mayo, changes US$ cash but not cheques. Banco de Galicia changes cheques, US$10 commission.

Post Office San Martín 753, slow, open 0800-1300, 1600-2000. **Telephones**, Rivadavia 758, open 0700-2400, daily.

Shopping Catamarca specialities from: *Cuesta del Portezuelo*, Sarmiento 575; *Maica Regionales*, next to Aerolíneas Argentinas; and *Suma Regionales*, Sarmiento y Esquiú. **Mercado Artesanal**, Urquiza 945, wide range of handicrafts, open 0700-1300, 1400-2000, reached by infrequent colectivo 23 from centre.

Tourist Office Urquiza y Mota Botella, open 0800-2000, helpful. In small surrounding towns, go to municipal offices for information and maps.

Air Cooperativa de Transportes Catamarca, less dependable than Aerolíneas Riojanas, twice weekly Tinogasta to Belén. Officially departs Tinogasta 0810, but one is told to appear at municipal building at 0815 to be at plane at 0830. Route is circular: Catamarca-Tinogasta-Belén-Andalgalá-Catamarca, in small Piper or Cessna. AR offices on Sarmiento, next to *Hotel Suma Huasi*, T 24450/24460.

Buses Good bus information at bus terminal. To **Tucumán**, 4-5 daily with Bosio, 4½ hrs, US$10, several other companies; road paved, in good condition except for rough stretch at provincial border (Cuesta del Totoral has steep gradients, hairpins, potholes). To **BsAs**, US$50, 2nd class at 2200, 1st class at 1900, daily. To **Belén** via Cerro Negro with Coop Catamarca, returns from Belén daily 1300 (**see p 143**). Also Belén-Catamarca via Andalgalá; Coop Catamarca via Saujil, Poman, Chumbicha, Tues, Thur 1000, Fri, Sun 1300, about 8 hrs. Catamarca-El Rodeo-Las Juntas daily at 1300, returns from Las Juntas 1700. Five buses daily to **Córdoba**. To **Santiago del Estero**, 1630, US$12. There are several buses daily to Mendoza.

To **Copiapó**, Chile: weekly tourist buses, leaving Tinogasta on Fri to cross the San Francisco Pass, 3 days all incl, US$220 pp, run by AdBeCa, Catamarca, T 0833-30725/0836-2991, Dec to Feb only. Tours from Catamarca run to Chile.

Excursion To Dique Las Pirquitas, 3 hrs with local bus 1A from bus station. Bus stops at *Hostería de Turismo* (with restaurant) at Villa Pirquitas, about 45 min walk. Five morning buses from 0700, last returns at 2200. Opening hours Mon-Fri 1000-1900, Sat, Sun and holidays 0830-1900.

A road runs NE to **Lavalle** (towards Santiago del Estero). This 116 km run over the **Cuesta El Portezuelo** (1,980m), is scenic, but steep and difficult (to be paved, 1995). No bus service over Portezuelo to Lavalle, but a service to Frías, E, and also in Santiago del Estero province—No 9 and not No 18 (which crosses the Totoral), run by Coop de Transportes de Catamarca. Leaves 0500 Tues, Thur, Fri and Sat, arrives at Frías 1000, returns 1400, arrives in Catamarca 1900. From Frías travel to Lavalle.

Catamarca-Frías via Totoral, No 18 Mon, Wed, Fri, Sat 0500, arrives 1030, return 1330, arrives Catamarca 1900. No 14 via El Alto, longer trip, arrives Frías 1045. Catamarca-Lavalle via Totoral, same No 18, leaves Tues, Thur, and Sun 1100, arrives Lavalle 1510.

THE CHACO (6)

A sprawling alluvial lowland, rising gradually toward the W, covered by palm savanna and sometimes impenetrable thorn scrub; the birdlife is abundant and interesting.

Between the NW highlands already described and the Río Paraná to the E lies the Argentine Chaco, comprising the entire provinces of Formosa and Chaco, parts of Salta, Santiago del Estero and Santa Fe, and a tiny corner of the province of Córdoba. Its S limit is the Río Dulce valley, which forms a segment of the border between Santiago del Estero and Córdoba provinces. South America's highest temperatures, exceeding 45°C, have been recorded here, but winters are mild, with an occasional touch of frost in the S. Rain falls mostly in summer, decreasing from E to W. Numerous Indian peoples, who call themselves Wichi, inhabit the Chaco, including the Toba, Mataco, Mocoví, Pilagá, and some immigrant Mapuches from the S.

Communications Before the recent advent of modern highways, the Belgrano railway provided the only all-weather routes. There are two main N/S lines from Buenos Aires: the international route to La Paz and the line through Rosario and Santa Fe to Resistencia. Regular passenger rail services across the Chaco, N/S and from Resistencia to Metán have been suspended; determined train buffs may still be able to wangle a passage on a freight. Buses and planes provide the main means of transport.

Route 16, the main road across the Chaco runs NW from Resistencia to connect with Route 9, N of Metán and Rosario de la Frontera and provides the quickest route between Paraguay and NW Argentina. It is mostly paved and passes through **Pampa del Infierno** to the Santiago del Estero border. In Santiago province the road is good to Los Tigres, then less good to the Salta border. From this border to **Macapillo**, it is straight, well-paved. After Macapillo you can turn left, just before a railway crossing onto a dust road to Corral Quemado. At the T junction turn right and follow a dust road in reasonable condition for 50 km (50-60 kmph possible) to rejoin Route 16 at El Tunal. Turn left; the asphalt is good for a while then deteriorates to Route 9. Alternatively, after Macapillo, continue on Route 16 to **Joaquín V González**, around which the road is appalling and difficult after rain, then to Ceibalito, El Tunal and on to Route 9. At González, sidewalk **Restaurant Santa Cecilia** is good value. At Ceibalito, 18 km beyond González, an excellent lateral detour leaves Route 16 to connect with provincial Route 5 (passing Parque Nacional Finca El Rey, see p 109) and major N/S national Route 9 (at Lumbreras). This is a shorter, quicker route to Salta than via Rosario de la Frontera, but be sure to fill your tank in González, since there is no more petrol until General Güemes.

There are service stations at Roque Sáenz Peña, Pampa del Infierno (ACA *Hostería*), Pampa de los Guanacos (good hot, clean and free showers at the YPF station, and good value set dinner at the *comedor* next door), **Taco Pozo** (basic *hospedaje* ½ block from ACA station) and **El Quebrachal** (gaucho festival in late Nov), but during frequent power cuts they cannot pump fuel. In general, Chaco roads are poor, but provincial Route 94 from **Avia Terai** to General Pinedo, which continues as national Route 89 to Quimilí and Santiago del Estero, has an excellent paved surface. At the Avia Terai junction, it is easy to follow this route mistakenly rather than continue on Route 16 across the Chaco.

Tannin and cotton are the traditional great industries of the Chaco, although acreage planted to sunflowers has increased dramatically in recent years, along with maize and sorghum. The iron-hard *quebracho* (axe-breaker) tree, which grows only in the Argentine and Paraguayan Chaco, is the purest known source of tannin. The industry is struggling against competition from synthetic tannin and the huge mimosa plantations in South Africa. The more accessible eastern forests have nearly disappeared; deforestation of all species is proceeding rapidly in the N and W of the province, which produces charcoal for a military steel foundry in Jujuy. Small roadside factories also produce custom furniture.

Roque Sáenz Peña (population 75,000), 160 km NW of Resistencia on Route 16, offers almost no shade for relief from the overpowering summer heat. Its zoo, populated mostly with animals native to the region, is one of the country's best.

Hotels **A2** *Gualok*, San Martín 1198, T 20521, incl use of thermal baths (also available to non-residents for a small charge); **B** *Augustus*, Belgrano 483, T 20068, a/c; **C** *Orel*, San Martín 130; *Residencial Asturias*, Belgrano 402, fair; *Residencial Sáenz Peña*, Subpalmira 464, T 20320, near bus station, cheap, clean, friendly.

Buses To **Buenos Aires**, daily 2000, US$40 (from Buenos Aires also daily 2000), La Estrella and La Internacional alternate days; to **Santiago del Estero** and **Tucumán**, Empresa El Rayo daily; to **Resistencia** (connection for Salta 1700 daily), 2 hrs, US$4.

Central Sáenz Peña has buses at 1100, 1530 and 2000 to the village of *Castelli* (tap water is suspect due to drought), about 100 km N, which has a large Toba Indian community and an *artesanía* shop (**E** *Hotel Guc*, basic). On route 16, 23 km E of Sáenz Peña, is Quitilipi, a Toba community with a free municipal campsite.

Between Resistencia and Sáenz Peña is **Parque Nacional Chaco**, an ecological island which preserves some of the last remaining eastern Chaco forest and savanna, and which is a good place to see the region's abundant bird life. The friendly park keeper will take you on a 1-2 hr walk, explaining about plants, animals and the region, rec. There are good free camping facilities, with cold showers, but the nearest supplies are in Capitán Solari, 6 km from the park entrance. From Resistencia, several buses go daily to Capitán Solari, but there is no public transport direct to the park. The rest of the Chaco is mostly cattle country, consisting of large estancias with low stocking rates.

Towns of the Chaco The most important ones—Resistencia and Formosa—are on the W bank of the Paraná and Paraguay and will be described, for convenience's sake, under Argentine Mesopotamia. Apart from Roque Sáenz Peña, the only other town of any importance is Santiago del Estero, on the W boundary of the Chaco.

Federico Kirbus tells us that on the border of Chaco and Santiago del Estero provinces is *Campo del Cielo*, a meteorite impact field about 15 km by 4 km where about 5,000 years ago a planetoid broke before landing into 30 main pieces. Some of the meteorites are on display in Buenos Aires (the Rivadavia Museum and the Planetarium), but the largest, "El Chaco" (33.4 tonnes), is on display at the Campo. Access from Route 89 (between Resistencia and Santiago del Estero) at Gancedo, where you travel 15 km S to Las Víboras (many buses).

MESOPOTAMIA (7)

This section begins at the Río de la Plata and ends at the magnificent Iguazú Falls on the Brazilian border. Two routes are followed, the Ríos Uruguay and Paraná, describing the river towns and beaches, and the Jesuit missions near Posadas (in particular San Ignacio Miní). Crossings to Uruguay and Paraguay are also given.

Between the Ríos Uruguay and Paraná lies Argentine Mesopotamia: the provinces of Entre Ríos, Corrientes, and Misiones. The distance between the rivers is 390 km in N Corrientes, but narrows to about 210 km in the latitude of Santa Fe. Mesopotamia was first colonized by Spaniards pushing S from Asunción to reoccupy Buenos Aires; Santa Fe was founded in 1573, Corrientes in 1588. From about 1880 there were Jewish agricultural settlements in Entre Ríos, promoted by Baron Hirsch for victims of pogroms in the Czarist empire (see "Los gauchos judíos" by Alberto Gerchunoff). Vestiges of these settlements remain at Domínguez (museum) and Basavilbaso, and across the river in Moisesville (Santa Fe).

Much of Entre Ríos and Corrientes is still pastoral, a land of large *estancias* raising cattle and sheep. Maize (a gamble in the N) is largely grown in southern Entre Ríos, which is also the most important producer of linseed, citrus fruit and poultry in Argentina. In Corrientes, along the banks of the Paraná between the cities of Corrientes and Posadas, rice and oranges are grown.

The province of Corrientes, in the N, is marshy and deeply-wooded, with low grass-covered hills rising from the marshes. The normal rainfall is about 2,000 mm, but the rains are not spread uniformly and drain off quickly through the sandy soil. Entre Ríos, to the S, has plains of rich pasture land not unlike those of Uruguay. Winters in Mesopotamia are mild; summers are hot with rain falling in short, sharp storms. Both Entre Ríos and Corrientes often suffer from summer drought.

Misiones Province, in the far NE, was first occupied by the Jesuit Fathers fleeing from the Brazilian Alto-Paraná region with their devoted Indian followers before the slave-hunting Bandeirantes. These missions and their history are described under Posadas (**see p 160**). Misiones is a hilly strip of land between the Uruguay and the Alto Paraná rivers, 80-100 km wide and about 400 km long; its capital is the river port of Posadas. Its boundary to the N is the river Iguazú, which here tumbles over the great Iguazú Falls. Misiones is on the Paraná Plateau; much of it is covered with forests of pine and cedar and broad-leaved trees, and the land, with its red soil, is reminiscent of Brazil. Here too the rainfall is heavy: twice as heavy as in Entre Ríos. The days are hot, and the nights cool.

It was the Jesuits who first grew *yerba mate* in plantations; Misiones has always been a large producer of this leaf, and also of citrus, tobacco, timber and tung oil. The province has attracted immigrants from Eastern Europe, from Paraguay and from the rest of Mesopotamia. There is good fishing in many of the small river-towns. In NE Corrientes and in Misiones more Indian tea is now grown than can be absorbed by the internal market.

The Indian-tea industry was started by Sir Herbert Gibson, who sent for seed from Assam in 1929; it was sown in Playadito, Corrientes province. Six seeds developed into sturdy bushes. Year after year their seed was given to anyone interested. All Argentina's tea plantations today have their origin in Sir Herbert Gibson's enterprise.

Communications in the area are by road (now greatly improved) and by the two rivers, the Uruguay and the Paraná, which bound it to E and W. Neither river is very good for navigation. Bridges between Fray Bentos (Uruguay) and Puerto Unzué, near Gualeguaychú, and between Paysandú (Uruguay) and Colón were opened in 1976, and there are a road and railway over the Salto Grande dam, near Concordia.

Up the Río Uruguay

The Río Uruguay is the eastern boundary of Mesopotamia and forms the western border of the Republic of Uruguay. There are no regular passenger shipping services.

Boats leaving Buenos Aires go past Martín García island, and enter the wide estuary. At 193 km from Buenos Aires, the Uruguayan town of Fray Bentos is to the right; there is a bridge (toll US$1) between Fray Bentos and the Argentine town of **Puerto Unzué**, near Gualeguaychú, but pedestrians and cyclists cannot cross it other than on motor vehicles; officials will give lifts on either side (customs formalities take about 10 mins). The river now becomes braided into channels and

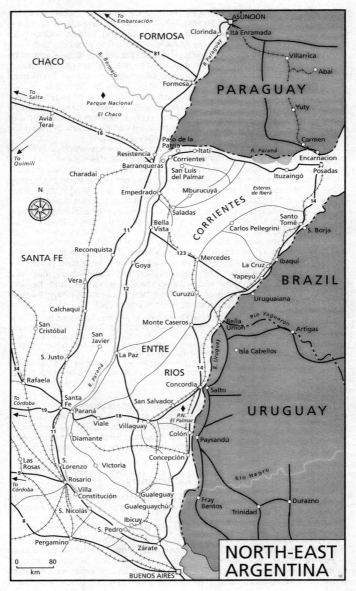

NORTH-EAST ARGENTINA

0 — 80
km

islands. Opposite Fray Bentos, on the left, is the mouth of the Río Gualeguaychú; 19 km up is **Gualeguaychú**, a very pleasant town with a river promenade, an open-air railway museum (in the old railway station) and an attractive cathedral (1863). Lively pre-Lenten Carnival. Population, 80,000, with quite a large German contingent. Since the opening of the bridges between Zárate and Brazo Largo, the journey time from Buenos Aires, 248 km S, has been reduced and Gualeguaychú has become a popular weekend resort for *porteños*. Airport.

Hotels Accommodation is scarce at weekends and during carnival. The tourist office has a list of families. **B** *Embajador*, San Martín y 3 de Febrero, T 24414, casino; **D** *Entre Ríos*, Andrade 1009, T 27214; **D** *Alemán*, Bolívar 535, T 26153, friendly, German-speaking, rec; **D** *París*, Bolívar y Pellegrini, T 26260; **D** *Mayo*, Bolívar 550, T 27661, uncomfortable beds, noisy.

Camping *La Delfina* in the Parque Unzué; *Puerto del Sol* and *Playa Chica*, near the river; *Ñandubaysal*, 15 km E, best.

Exchange Banco Internacional Cooperativa, 25 de Mayo y Perón, changes cash; *Casa de Cambio*: Daniel, 3 de Febrero 128.

Tourist Office Av Costanera y 25 de Mayo, open 0800-2000.

Buses Terminus in centre at Bolívar y Chile. To Fray Bentos, 1 hr, US$3, 4 a day, ETA. To **Mercedes**, 1½ hrs, US$4, 2 a day, ETA; to **Concepción del Uruguay**, **Colón** and **Concordia**; to/from Buenos Aires US$9; companies running these routes are Tigre Iguazú (T Bs As 313-2355), Tata Rápido (T Bs As 313-3836), Singer (T BsAs 313-3915).

Concepción del Uruguay (known locally as Concepción), the first Argentine port of any size on the river, is 74 km N of Gualeguaychú. Founded in 1783, it was until 1883 capital of Entre Ríos province. Population 50,000. Overlooking the main plaza is the church of the Immaculate Conception which contains the remains of Gen Urquiza, whose former residence, the Palacio San José, 35 km W of the town, is now a museum, open daily 0900-1300, 1500-1900, US$1.50 (buses to 3 km from the Palacio), highly rec.

Hotels D *Gran Hotel*, Rocamora y Colón, T 22851; **D** *Virrey*, Aceso Ruta 131 y 15 de Oeste, T 25017; **D** *Ramírez*, Blvd Martínez 50, T 25106; **E** *Hospedaje Los Tres Trenes*, Galarza 1233, clean, friendly. Many hotels of all classes by the bus station.

Restaurants *El Canguro*, opposite bus terminus, good food, reasonably priced; *Rocamora*, Rocamora y Millán.

Tourist Office 9 de Julio 844, T 25820.

Colón (pop 17,000), 350 km from Buenos Aires, is 45 km N of Concepción del Uruguay. The river is more picturesque here with sandy beaches, and cliffs visible from a considerable distance; a road bridge now links Colón and Paysandú. (Toll for cars US$1.40. All border formalities, incl stamping of vehicle carnets, are conducted at both ends of the bridge, easy crossing.) The town is known for *artesanía* shops down San Martín, the main street, and there is a large handicrafts fair at Carnival time (Feb). Tourist office Av Quirós y Gouchón (very helpful).

Hotels L3 *Quirinale*, Av Quirós s/n, T 21978, 5-star, (with casino); **C** *Nuevo Hotel Plaza*, 12 de Abril y Belgrano, T 21043; **C** *Palmar*, Blvd Ferrari 285, T 21952, good; **D** *Holimasu*, Belgrano 28, T 21305; **D** *Vieja Calera*, Bolívar 344, T 21139; **C** *Res Aridan*, Alvear 57 y San Martín, T 21830, clean, hot water; **D** *Ver-Wei*, 25 de Mayo 10. Many families rent rooms—the Boujon family, Maipú 430, E, good breakfast, have been rec. Apartments for rent from Sr Ramón Gallo, Av Paysandú, T 472 3280, with kitchen, bathroom, hot showers, close to bus terminal. Several **campsites** along river bank (municipal site, excellent facilities, cheapest).

Restaurant *Comedor El Rayo*, Paysandú 372; *Pizzería Luisa*, San Martín 346; *La Rueda*, San Martín y 3 de Febrero; *Marito*, Gral Urquiza y Andrade.

Buses Bus terminal on outskirts, but buses also call at bus company offices in town. To **Paysandú**, US$2, 45 mins, but none 1145-1645 and none Sun. To **Buenos Aires**, 4 a day, US$18, 5 hrs, to **Concordia**, US$6 (2½ hrs) and **Paraná** daily. To **Córdoba** 4 a week.

Parque Nacional El Palmar (8,500 ha), 44 km N of Colón off the Ruta Nacional 14. Buses from Colón, 40 mins, US$2.50, will drop you on the road and it is easy to hitch the last 6 km to the park administration. There are camping facilities (US$3 pp, electricity, hot water), a small hotel 8 km N of the Park, with restaurant opposite, and a small shop. The Park (entrance US$2) contains varied scenery with a mature palm forest, sandy beaches on the Uruguay river, Indian tombs and other remains, a good museum and many rheas and other birds. The Yatay palms grow up to 12 m and some are hundreds of years old. It is best to stay overnight as wildlife is more easily seen in the early morning or at sunset. Very popular at weekends in summer.

Concordia, 104 km N of Colón, a little downriver from Salto, Uruguay, is a prosperous city, with a population of 93,800, which has some fine public buildings, a racecourse, rowing clubs, and a 9-hole golf club. Paved roads to Buenos Aires, Paraná and Posadas.

Park, Museums 5 km out is Parque Rivadavia, with a circular road used occasionally as a motor-racing track; there are pleasant views of the river and in the centre of the park is the Palacio San Carlos, inhabited briefly by Antoine de Saint-Exupéry. To get to the park, take colectivo No 2, 1 block from Plaza 25 de Mayo, to corner of Av Justo and Av Salto Uruguay, beyond bus terminal; entrance is 1 block from here. The Regional Museum on Plaza Urquiza is worth a visit; local and natural history collections, entry free.

Hotels A1 *Salto Grande*, Urquiza 575, T 213916; **B** *San Carlos*, Parque Rivadavia, T 216725; **C** *Colón*, Pellegrini 611, T 215510, simple, unusual but run down; **C** *Embajador*, San Lorenzo 75, T 213018, nr bus station, neat and clean; **C** *Palmar*, Urquiza 517, T 216050; **D** *Central*, 1° de Mayo 148, T 212842, reasonable, but shared bathrooms not too clean; **D** *Victoria*, Urquiza next to Esso, 2 blocks from terminal, quite good.

Camping *La Posada de Suárez—Club Viajantes* on Av Costanera near the park, warmly rec, with good *parrillada* alongside.

Restaurants *La Estancia*, good value, and *Gran Mary* (1st floor), both on plaza; *El Abrojito*, Pellegrini 1203, rec. *Comedor Las Dos Naciones*, Plaza 25 de Mayo and Av 1° de Mayo, good, moderate prices, large portions; *Mafalda*, corner of Plaza Urquiza and Av Entre Ríos, very good home made ice cream and cakes.

Services Exchange Banco Río de la Plata, on plaza, no commission on Visa advances; Casa Julio, 1 de Mayo, ½ block from plaza; *Casa Chaca*, on plaza; *Tourfé* on Mitre. **Post Office** La Rioja y Buenos Aires. **Telephone** 700 block of San Luis (24 hrs).

Tourist Office Plaza 25 de Mayo, open 0700-2400 daily, very friendly; kiosk at bus terminal, lousy map.

Buses Bus terminal 2 km from centre. No 2 bus goes to main plaza. To **Buenos Aires**, 6 daily, US$17, 6½ hrs; to **Córdoba**, US$25 with Expreso Singer, at 2200 and 0300, 9 hrs; to **Paraná** 5, to **Posadas** at 1800 and 2300, with Expreso Singer (8½ hrs, US$32), to **Iguazú** one (1810, 13½ hrs), to **Corrientes** US$11. Bus to **La Paz** (Entre Ríos)—see p 156, 1100, US$10.50, 8 hrs. To **Paso de los Libres** direct, 2300 or take 0755 Empresa Gualeguaychú bus to Curuzú Cuatiá and catch connecting service. Possible to sleep overnight on benches in bus terminal.

The river is impassable for large vessels beyond the rapids of Salto Chico near the town, and Salto Grande 32 km up-river, where there is a large international hydro-electric dam, providing a route for an international road and railway. Above Salto Grande the river is generally known as the Alto Uruguay. There is excellent fishing in the artificial lake. Before Salto Grande lake was filled, the town of Federación (pop 7,000) had to be relocated to higher ground.

To Uruguay Take No 2 or 4 bus from Concordia bus terminal marked "Puerto", for ferry crossing to Salto US$2.50 (tickets obtainable at a small kiosk, which shuts 15 mins before departure, outside customs) departures 0900, 1000, 1200, 1430, 1600, weekdays, 0900, 1200, 1500, Sat but none Sun; takes 15 mins, passengers only.

About 153 km upstream from Concordia lies the small port of *Monte Caseros* (pop 18,400), with the Uruguayan town of Bella Unión, on the Brazilian border, almost opposite (**Hotels** *Paterlini*, Colón y Salta, T 219; *Conte*, Salta 463; *Cortez*, 2 de Febrero 1663).

Above Bella Unión, the **Alto Uruguay** is the boundary between Argentina and Brazil. Ninety-six km above **Monte Caseros** is *Paso de los Libres* (pop 25,000), with the Brazilian cattle town of **Uruguaiana** opposite: a bridge joins the two. No bus service on Sun – taxi charges US$20. From Uruguaiana into Brazil the buses are much quicker than trains, though there is a comfortable railway service to Porto Alegre. Paso de los Libres was founded in 1843 by General Madariaga; it was here that he crossed the river from Brazil with his hundred men and annexed Corrientes province for Argentina. Road (paved) to Paraná.

Hotels C *Alejandro* I, Coronel López 502, T 21000, best; *Uruguay*, Uruguay 1252, T 21672.

Transport Líneas Aéreas Entre Ríos (LAER) flies from Aeroparque, Buenos Aires to Paraná, Gualeguaychú and Concordia with very low fares; enquire at Puente Aéreo desk at Aeroparque.

58 km N of Paso de los Libres, on the road to Alvear, is **Yapeyú**, the site of a Jesuit mission and famous as the birthplace of the liberator, José de San Martín. Part of the house where he was born is well preserved, and there is an interesting Jesuit Museum. (**D** *Hosteria ACA*, T 93020; the Carillo family on the main plaza rent rooms, E, good; *cabañas* on the outskirts of town; camping by the river.)

Up the Río Paraná

Navigation River boats carry passengers along various stretches of the river, but there are no long-distance passenger services up the river from Buenos Aires, except those to Asunción, Paraguay. Depending on the tide, boats enter the Paraná river by either the Las Palmas reach of the delta, on which is Zárate, or the Paraná-Guazú reach, on which is Ibicuy.

Most of the important towns of Mesopotamia lie on the E bank of the Paraná, or the S bank of the Alto Paraná.

Zárate, 65,000 inhabitants on the W bank 90 km N of Buenos Aires, is industrially important, with large *frigoríficos* and paper works (**C** *Hotel San Martín*, Ameghino 773, T 2713, clean; *Restaurant La Posta de Correa*, cheap, good service). Along the waterfront are many *parrillas* and restaurants; trips to Palmira in Uruguay are arranged here, 2½ hrs, US$11. There are 2 museums: in the old Urquiza station, local history, and a Boy Scout museum. In Plaza Italia a handicraft market is held on Sun and holidays. It is served from Buenos Aires by bus (US$3, every 30 mins from Plaza Once) and two railways: the Mitre and the Urquiza. Urquiza trains used to be ferried 84 km across the river, but a link including two large and beautiful bridges have been built between Zárate and Brazo Largo, accelerating rail and road journeys alike (the bridge toll is US$6). The picturesque Ibicuy Islands can be visited by boat. About 50 km N of Zárate is **San Pedro** (pop 28,000) where fine riverfront camping can be had at either the *Centro Turístico*, *Club Pescadores* or *Camping Municipal*.

About 108 km N of Ibicuy, on the E bank, is **Gualeguay**, with a population of 26,000. It is the centre of one of the richest cattle and sheep ranching regions in Entre Ríos. The house in which Garibaldi was tortured by the local chief of police in 1837, in the time of Rosas, still exists. Eight km S is its river port, Puerto Ruiz. The road from Gualeguay N along the E bank of the Paraná is paved most of the way to Posadas.

Hotels B *Gran Hotel Gualeguay*, Monte Caseros 217, T 23085; **E** *Italia*, Palacios 1, T 24575, with bath, friendly. There is a municipal **campsite**. In the centre there are practically no **restaurants**, but the *Jockey Club* and the *Club Social*, both on the main square close to the *Gran Hotel Gualeguay*, cater also for non-members. The *Club Social* has a very nice atmosphere, good food, and you might be invited to see films on certain nights.

On the way upstream to Rosario, on the W bank, are two ports which export grain: *San Nicolás* (pop 97,000), 80 km below Rosario, and *Villa Constitución* (pop 34,000), 37 km below Rosario. Both are served by a railway from the capital. At San Nicolás is the General Savio steel plant. *Pergamino*, an important road/rail junction in the pampas, is 72 km S by road or rail.

Rosario, chief city of the province of Santa Fe, 320 km N of Buenos Aires, is the third city of the republic, with a population of well over a million. It is a great industrial and export centre. The streets are wider than those of Buenos Aires, and there are fine boulevards, handsome open spaces and good shopping facilities. In recent years the city has been developing a lively cultural scene. It is the home of many popular rock musicians and modern artists and there are good discothèques and theatres. From Oct to early Mar it is warm, and from Dec to the end of Feb uncomfortably hot. Changes of temperature are sudden.

Points of Interest Monument of the Flag, a memorial on the river bank in honour of General Belgrano, designer of the Argentine flag, who raised it on this spot for the first time (lifts go to the top); **Parque Independencia** (Rose Garden): Boulevard Oroño; **Cathedral** in Calle 25 de Mayo; **St Bartholomew's Church** (Anglican), Calle Paraguay; racecourse, the Alberdi and Arroyito boat clubs, and Saladillo Golf Club, with its own Links station on the Mitre line. The Aero Club is in the suburb of Gral Alvear. The **Museo Histórico Provincial** (open Thur and Sat 1500-1800, and Sun 1000-1200, 1500-1800) is in Parque Independencia. Two art museums: **Museo Municipal de Bellas Artes Juan B Castagnino**, Av Pellegrini 2202, 1,500 paintings, among them El Greco, Goya and Titian; **Museo Municipal de Arte Decorativo Firma y Odilio Estévez**, Santa Fe 748, has some Caravaggios, Goyas and Murillos. A rec pedestrian tour called "**Paseo Centenario**" around Calle Córdoba touches on the interesting buildings and monuments of the "Golden Days of Rosario" (1880-1950). There are explanation signs now installed. Swimming at sandy **Florida beach**, about 8 km N of Rosario.

Local Holiday 7 Oct (Foundation of the City).

Hotels A1 *Riviera*, San Lorenzo 1460, T 213481, a/c; **B** *Presidente*, Av Corrientes 919, T 242545, good; **B** *Plaza*, Barón de Mauá 26, T 47097; many **C** hotels opp bus station (*Embajador*, *Micro*, *Nahuel*, shabby); **D** *La Paz*, Barón de Mauá 36, T 210905, clean, quiet, friendly, rec; **E** *Río*, Rivadavia 2665, T 396421, opp railway station, clean, friendly.

Camping La Florida, near the river.

Restaurants *Don Rodrigo*, Sante Fe 968, and *Fénix*, Santa Fe next to Citibank, are both very good. *Doña María*, Santa Fe 1371, does good Italian food; *Casa Uruguaya*, Alvear 1125 (T 69320), away from centre, good. *Marialronn*, Santa Fe y Pres Roca, rec for dancing. Along the river are good cheap restaurants and fishing club barbeques, good atmosphere.

Exchange Lloyds Bank (BLSA), Calle La Rioja 1205; **Citibank**, Santa Fe 1101; **First National Bank of Boston**, Córdoba esq Mitre. Open 1000-1600. Most banks charge 2% commission on cheques and cash. Amex, Grupo 3 de Turismo, Córdoba 1147, T 244415. *Casas de Cambio*: *Transatlántica*, Córdoba 900; *Carey*, Corrientes 802; *Carbatur*, Corrientes 840.

Laundry Santa Fe 1578.

Post Office Córdoba y Buenos Aires. **Telecommunications** San Luis, between San Martín and Maipú.

Tourist Office At Monument of the Flag, helpful but information inadequate.

Airport at Fisherton, 8 km from centre. Taxi charges vary. Several flights daily to Buenos Aires with AR, 3 a week with Austral.

Buses Bus terminal expanded 1994. There are regular bus services to Arroyo Seco, Casilda, Cañada de Gómez, San Lorenzo and other important centres up to 80 km from the city. To **Buenos Aires**, via San Nicolás on Route 9 (4 hrs) or via Pergamino, less frequent on Route 8 (Chevallier bus every hour, US$20; also Ablo, General Urquiza, La Unión), NW to **Córdoba** and **Tucumán**. To **Santa Fe**, US$10. To **Mendoza**, US$40. To **Puerto Iguazú**, US$50.

Rosario can be reached from Buenos Aires by Route 8 (marked Córdoba) to Pergamino, and then, following signs, by Route 188, and then 178 to Rosario. This is a better way than lorry-packed Route 9. Hitching to Salta along Route 34 is possible.

Ferries to Victoria, in Entre Ríos, which has a municipal **campsite**.

Above Rosario the river is very braided and islanded. Boat trips to river islands can be made at weekends (eg *Ciudad de Rosario* from Estación Fluvial by the Monument of the Flag, Sat 1730, Sun 1600, 1830), or from Florida beach at any time. Canoes can be hired. Some 23 km N of Rosario is *San Lorenzo* (pop 28,700), with one of the largest chemical works in Argentina. See the restored San Carlos monastery on the river bank, where in 1813 San Martín won his first battle in the War of Independence. Visitors are shown a pine tree grown from a cutting of the tree under which the Liberator rested after the battle.

Some 180 km above Rosario, on the E bank, is *Paraná*, capital of Entre Ríos (pop 210,000), founded in 1588. From 1853 to 1862 the city was the capital of the Republic. The centre is situated on a hill offering fine views over the river and beyond to Santa Fe. There are many fine buildings; in the centre is the Plaza Primero de Mayo, where there are fountains and a statue of San Martín. Around the Plaza are the Municipalidad, the Cathedral, notable for its portico and its interior, and the tourist information office. The Casa de Gobierno at Santa Fe y Laprida has a grand façade. The city's glory is Parque Urquiza, to the NW. It has an enormous statue to General Urquiza, and a bas-relief showing the battle of Caseros, at which he finally defeated Rosas; also an open-air theatre. There are pleasant walks along the river bank and around the fishing *barrio* of Puerto Sánchez. Boats sail along the river from near the tourist office.

Museums Museo de Bellas Artes, Buenos Aires 355; **Museo Histórico**, Buenos Aires y Laprida, open Mon-Fri, 0800-1200, 1500-1800, Sat, 0900-1200, 1600-1900, Sun, 0900-1200.

Hotels There is a shortage of hotel space, especially at peak periods (Semana Santa and Jul), when the tourist office arranges accommodation with families. There is a greater selection of hotels—at lower prices—in Santa Fe. **A1** *Mayorazgo*, Etchevehere y Córdoba, on Costanera Alta, T 216111, 5-star, with fine view of park and river, has casino and swimming pool; **C** *Gran Hotel Paraná*, Urquiza 976, T 223900; **C** *Super Luxe*, Villaguay 162, T 212373; **D** *Almafuerte*, Av Almafuerte 1295, T 240644. Cheap hotels near railway station, incl **E** *City*, basic, rec, and **D** *Bristol*, Alsina 221, T 213961, close to the bus terminal, good quality, refurbished rm, and **D** *Plaza*, San Martín 915, T 210122.

Laundry *Laverap*, Belgrano 650.

Tourist Office 25 de Mayo 44, T 221632.

Air Service Airport: General Urquiza, 12 km from town.

Bus E across Entre Ríos to Concordia on Río Uruguay, 5 a day, 5 hours. To/from Buenos Aires, US$18.

Travelling Between Santa Fe and Paraná The 2 cities do not face one another, but are 25 km apart and are separated by several islands. From Paraná the Hernandarias tunnel, toll US$2 per car, passes under the river to connect with the W bank; from here a road runs 23 km W to Santa Fe across two islands and bridges. Trucks with dangerous loads cross the river by a launch which also carries pedestrians and operates Mon-Sat, 0600-2100, 20 mins journey, frequency depending on demand from trucks. Frequent bus service between the 2 cities by Etacer and Fluviales del Litoral, US$2, 1 hr.

Santa Fe, a larger city of some 400,000 inhabitants, is the capital of its province and the centre of a very fertile region (160 km from Rosario). It was founded by settlers from Asunción in 1573, though its present site was not occupied until 1660. It was in its Cabildo (town hall) that the Constitution of 1853 was adopted. The oath of allegiance was taken before the crucifix in the sacristy of the church of San Francisco, built in 1680 from materials floated down the river from Paraguay; this old colonial church has been tampered with but is still fine, especially the carved wooden ceilings, which were fitted without nails.

Most of the best buildings are in the E part of the city near the Plaza 25 de Mayo. On the Plaza itself are the **Cathedral**, the church of **Nuestra Señora de los Milagros** and the majestic **Casa de Gobierno**. The church and convent of **San Francisco** (see above) are a block SE of the Plaza. Opposite it is the **Museo Histórico Provincial**. The **Convent of Santo Domingo**, a block W of the Plaza at 3 de Febrero y 9 de Julio, has a fine patio and museum. In Calle General López is the **Museo de Bellas Artes Rosa Galisteo de Rodríguez**, where local painters hold their exhibitions. The church of **Nuestra Señora de Guadalupe**, with beautifully painted glass windows, is at Javier de la Rosa 623 and may be reached by bus 8, 14 or 16 from the centre. Twice weekly boats from Buenos Aires, 483 km to the south; regular only in winter.

Local holidays 30 Sep (St Jerome); 15 Nov (Foundation of City).

Hotels A2 *Río Grande*, San Gerónimo 2586, modern, rec; **B** *Bertaina*, H Irigoyen 2255, may negotiate; **B** *Corrientes*, Corrientes 2520, T 40126; **B** *El Conquistador*, 25 de Mayo 2676, T 51195; **B** *Hostal de Santa Fe de la Vera Cruz*, San Martín 2954, T 51740, best, genial, well-kept and run; **C** *Avellaneda*, Av Oro Blanco 765, Ruta 11, Km 792, suburban, T 81187, good; **C** *Colón*, San Luis 2862, T 45167, with bath, D without, pleasant, large and clean rooms; **C** *Niza*, Rivadavia 2755, T 22047, very clean, friendly; **C** *Royal*, Irigoyen Freyre 2256, clean, private bath, opp bus station; **C** *Suipacha*, Suipacha 2375, T 21135, clean, safe, rec; **C** *Brigadier*, San Luis 3148, T 37387, two blocks from bus station, good, clean, friendly, 50 rooms, a/c extra but rec if the river is in flood and there are lots of mosquitoes, some English spoken, private parking; **D** *Carlitos*, Irigoyen Freyre 2336, T 31541, clean, friendly; near the bus terminal is **E** *Apolo*, Belgrano 2821, clean, basic.

Camping Possible in free municipal site near town centre, Parque del Sur, bus No 5; beware ferocious mosquitoes. Several sites on the lakes and rivers outside town incl: *Luz y Fuerza*, 7 km N near Lago Guadalupe; *Cámara del Hogar*, 4 km E on Route 168; 2 sites on Río Colastine, 15 km E on Route 168.

Restaurants Many good ones, offering excellent meals with good wine. *El Quincho de Chiquito*, Obispo Príncipe y Almte Brown, excellent and good value, classic fish restaurant, huge helpings. Excellent grills incl *surubí* (local fish) at *Gran Parrillada Rivadavia*, Rivadavia 3299. *Surubí* also at *España*, San Martín 2644. Several good cafeterias around San Martín y 25 de Mayo, incl *Café de la Paix*, San Martín y Santiago del Estero; *Comedor Porky*, Gálvez 2345, eat all you want. *Nochera Española*, opposite railway station.

Exchange Lloyds Bank (BLSA), Calle 25 de Mayo 2501, open 0715-1315; *Citibank*, San Martín 2609. **Amex** representative, Vacaciones Felices, San Martín 2347. *Casas de Cambio*: *Camsa*, 25 de Mayo 2466; *Carbatur*, San Martín 2520; *Tourfé*, San Martín 2901, changes TCs.

Laundromat *Servi Rap*, Rivadavia 2834 (open Sat 0800-1300); *Laverap*, San Martín 1687.

Swimming On river at Guadalupe beach; local bus.

Tourist Office at the conveniently situated bus terminal: maps, friendly.

Airport At Sauce Viejo, 17 km from the city. Two daily AR flights (1 on Sat and Sun) to and from Buenos Aires, T 20713.

Roads and Buses Fully paved to Rosario, 160 km (3 hours by bus); to Formosa, 894 km; to Roque Sáenz Peña, with spurs S to Villa Angela and General Pinedo and N to San Martín. Large and modern bus terminal. Bus for **Asunción** (Paraguay), La Internacional, express at 0100, 12 hrs, US$45, *convencional* at 1925, 13 hrs, US$32. To **Córdoba**, US$15, 5 hrs. Many buses to **Buenos Aires** (US$25, La Internacional, Tata), **Paraná** and **Rosario**; daily to **Mendoza** (2100) and **Santiago del Estero/Tucumán** (2010).

Upstream from Santa Fe the Paraná rapidly loses depth and is navigable only by river boats and small coastal vessels.

Between Paraná and Goya, on the left bank, is **La Paz (Entre Ríos)**, a small port (pop 15,200) with regional museum, riverside park and golf club. Buses to Buenos Aires, Rosario and Concordia.

Hotels *Milton*, Italia 1029, T 22232, modern; *Plaza*, main square, T 21208; *Rivera*, San Martín 367, T 21032. Small **restaurants** in port and near bus station.

Between Santa Fe and Corrientes the boat calls at several river ports, incl La Paz, Goya and Empedrado. **Goya** (airport 7 km from centre), on the E bank, the second town of the Province of Corrientes, is near the junction of the Paraná with the Santa Lucía river. It is a large tobacco centre on the Urquiza railway, with a population of 47,000. There is a vehicle-ferry service across the river to **Reconquista** (34,800 people). The road N from Goya to Empedrado and Corrientes is paved; many buses. Some stop at Bella Vista where a river crossing is possible at the port 5 km away, US$1.50, closing times unknown. Bus Reconquista-Santa Fe 6 hrs, US$12.

Hotels at Goya *Hotel de Turismo*, Mitre 880, T 22560, modern, rec. *Cervantes*, JE Gómez 723, T 22684; *Goya*, Colón 929, T 22354; **D** *España*, España 345, clean, hot water, friendly, near bus station. *Hoguimarsa*, B Mitre 880/90 (the last-named also has establishments at Curuzú Cuatiá, Empedrado and Mercedes, in Corrientes province). *Restaurant El Colonial* said to be the best, near bus station at Loza 415.

Hotels at Reconquista B *Grand*, Obligado 8083, T 20010; **C** *Magui I*, H Yrigoyen 755, T 21470, adequate, excellent restaurant. **C** *Motel Hostal del Rey*, located on the edge of town, clean, with bath. Many around bus station, eg **D** *Olessio*, opposite bus terminal. **D** *Residencial San Martín*, with bath, on B Mitre y Bolívar.

140 km E of Goya is **Mercedes (Corrientes** – pop 20,750) (*Hotel de Turismo*, Caaguazú y Sarmiento, T 317; *Hotel Plaza*, San Martín 699, T 13, E, cheapest), a good base from which to visit the *Iberá marshes*. The marshes are a nature reserve containing more species, it is claimed, than the Pantanal in Mato Grosso, Brazil. Among the species are the endangered aguará-guazú (maned wolf), deer, otters, the Juan Grande stork, kingfishers, snakes, etc. At *Carlos Pellegrini*, 110 km NE of Mercedes (3 buses a week), a new visitors centre to the marshes has been opened (take food, sleeping bag, light, binoculars). Workers at the visitors

centre take boat trips in small punts, a recommended way of discovering the wildlife quietly, or tours can be arranged in Mercedes or Corrientes. The tap water here is not drinkable, but bottled water is sold at the main store in the village.

27 km S of Mercedes are the strange Ita Pucú rock formations, remnants of a mountain massif long disappeared.

Empedrado, further up the river on the E bank, has a population of 5,000. It is on the railway line between Buenos Aires (1,014 km) and Corrientes. Oranges and rice are grown in the neighbourhood. **Hotels** *Turismo*, with swimming pool and fine views; *Rosario*. **Campsite**.

About 600 km upstream from Santa Fe, on the W bank, is the little port of *Barranqueras*, served also from Santa Fe by railway (17 hours). It is on a steep bluff overlooking the Paraná. A paved road connects it with *Resistencia*, the bustling, hot and energetic capital of the Province of Chaco, a galaxy of neon after dark, 6½ km up the Barranqueras stream. Pop 218,000. The road N from Resistencia to Formosa (200 km) and on to Puerto Pilcomayo (137 km) is paved.

In the streets there are many modern statues, promoted by the **Fogón de los Arrieros**, Brown 350, between López and French, a famous club frequented by local artists and full of local art and "*objets*" from abroad. Open to non-members Mon-Sat, 0800-1200, Tues, Wed, Thur only, 2130-0100. Entry US$2. Good place to meet local people.

Museums *Museo Histórico Regional*, Donovan 475, open Mon-Fri, 0800-1200, 1400-1700, traces the development of the city; **Museo de Ciencias Naturales**, Oturo Illia 658, open Mon-Fri, 0700-1200, 1700-2000, Sat 0900-1200; **Museo de Bellas Artes**, Mitre 163, open Mon 1600-2200, Tues-Fri, 0900-1300, 1600-2200, Sat/Sun 1900-2200, collection of 19th and 20th century local works; **Museo Regional de Antropología**, Las Heras 727 in the Universidad Nacional del Nordeste.

Area Products Cotton, *quebracho*, cattle.

Hotels Many accept Visa cards. **B** *Colón*, Sta María de Oro 139, T 22861, friendly, clean, rec; **B** *Covadonga*, Güemes 182, T 22875, small rooms, clean, a/c, *Tabaré* snack bar; **C** *Esmirna*, H Irigoyen 83 on corner of Plaza, T 22898, with bath, good; **C** *Sahara*, Güemes 169, T 22970. **D** *Celta*, Alberdi 210, T 22986; **D** *Residencial San José*, Rawson 304, clean, decent. Several cheap ones near bus station, eg **D** *Aragón*, Santiago del Estero, 154; **D** *Residencia Alberdi*, Av Alberdi 317, one block from bus station, basic but clean, restaurant, friendly owner, rec.

Camping *Parque Dos de Febrero*, very pretty, near artificial lake, tent US$3, take bus 5 or 9 one block from terminal; adequate free site nearby. *Parque Mitre*, showers and toilets. There is another site, shady but no facilities, NW of Resistencia on Route 16.

Restaurants *Círculo Residentes Santafecinos*, Vadia 150, tasty meals, family style. Try *chupín de surubí*, a sort of bouillabaisse, delightful. *Parrillada Clemente*, Santa María de Oro 399 opp bus station. *Restaurant Sociedad*, *Italiana*, Yrigoyen 204, excellent cuisine, smart, pricey; *Charly*, Güemes 215, snacks, good breakfast.

Banks and Exchange Banco del Chaco, Güemes on main plaza, cash only; Banco de Crédito, Justo 200 block, cash advance on Mastercard. Banco de Iberá changes TCs (3% commission). It can take a long time to change TCs on Mon as locals queue for money; Cambio Dorado, Güemes, changes TCs at reasonable rate. Try also the *Hotel Sahara* (cash only).

Laundry *Tokio*, Güemes y Brown.

Post Office Plaza 25 de Mayo, Mon-Sat, 0700-1200, 1500-2000. **Telecommunications**, Justo y Paz.

Shopping Sculptured Chaco woods from Domingo Arenas, cubist-type wood-statues. Regionales Pompeya, Güemes 154, sells local handicrafts and has an Indian handicraft display. Excellent leather goods at CHAC, Güemes 160.

Tourist Office Justo 135; kiosk in Plaza 25 de Mayo, very little info.

Car Hire Avis, French 701 and at airport. Localiza, Julio A Roca 460, T 39255.

Air Airport 8 km from town (no bus). AR (T 22859/25360) 3 and Austral 4 times a week to Buenos Aires.

Buses Buses leave every 15 mins to **Corrientes** over the Río Paraná bridge, 40 mins, US$0.55, the Resistencia terminal is on Sta María del Oro, 3 blocks from main plaza. 3 *especiales* a day to **Buenos Aires** (US$47) 14 hrs, 3 *comunes* a day (US$40), 17 hrs La Internacional, El Norte Bus; bus to **Santa Fe** (US$18). 8 a day to **Formosa** (2½ hrs, US$9) and **Puerto Pilcomayo**,

6-7 hrs. To **Iguazú** (US$40), 0700, 2300. To **Posadas**, 1230, 1300, 5½ hrs (good road), US$15, 4 a day, hot journey with lots of stops. Veloz del Norte and Saenz Peña direct to **Salta** (US$49) at 1700, 13 hrs. To Bolivian border at Aguas Blancas/Bermejo, take bus for Salta, change at Güemes, for direct connection to Orán (5 hrs, US$12, Atahuallpa buses every 2 hrs or so), from where it is a 45 min ride to border. El Rayo to **Tucumán** at 1930 and 2200, 12 hrs, US$21. Bus to **Rosario**, daily, 2015, US$21. Bus to **Clorinda** and Paraguayan border US$13, 5 hrs (walk across bridge then take taxi to Asunción, US$20 per vehicle). Many searches, watch your belongings and make sure everything is there afterwards. Also to **Asunción** daily, via Formosa, with Godoy (at 0300, 0600, 1400) and Brújula, 6½ hrs, US$18. Easy border crossing. Possible to change money.

Excursion To El Chaco National Park, camping possible, see p 148.

On the other side of the river from Resistencia (25 km) is **Corrientes**. The 2¾-km General Belgrano bridge crosses the river (toll US$1 per car); the best view of it is from the Corrientes side. The city, site of Graham Greene's *The Honorary Consul*, is the capital of Corrientes Province. The river can make the air heavy, moist and oppressive, but in winter the climate is pleasant. Population, 200,000. The city was founded in 1588. The church of La Cruz de los Milagros (1897) houses a miraculous cross placed there by the founder of the city, Alonzo de Vera—Indians who tried to burn it were killed by lightning from a cloudless sky. The Cathedral is in the renaissance style. Plaza Sargento Cabral has a statue to the sergeant who saved San Martín's life at the battle of San Lorenzo. A beautiful walk eastwards, along the Av Costanera, beside the Paraná river leads to Parque Mitre, from where there are good views of sunsets over the river. Up river from the bridge to Resistencia, is a zoo with animals of the region. Calle Junín is pedestrianized, with restaurants and shops, crowded at night. Swimming pools in town are open to members only.

Museums Museo Histórico Regional, 9 de Julio 1044; Museo de Bellas Artes, San Juan 634, open Tues-Fri, 0800-1200, 1600-2100, Sat, Sun, 0900-1200, 1800-2000; **Museo de Ciencias Naturales**, San Martín 850, a once famous collection now sadly neglected; **Museo de Artesanía**, Quintana 905, Mon-Fri, 0730-1200, 1500-2000, Sat 0900-1200, 1600-1900.

Hotels More expensive than Resistencia, **B** *Gran Hotel Guaraní*, Mendoza 970, T 23663/23090, very good a/c restaurant; **C** *Corrientes*, Junín 1549, T 65025; **C** *Gran Hotel Turismo*, Entre Ríos 650, T 23841, pool US$3 a day to non-residents; **C** *Orly*, San Juan 861, T 27248; **D** *Sosa*, España 1050, T 62151, a little overpriced; **D** *Robert* on La Rioja, nr *Colón* (No 437), basic, clean; **D** *SOS*, Irigoyen 1750, friendly, but noisy.

Camping Near bus terminal and railway station is *Camping-club Teléfono*, hot showers or bath, friendly. There is another campsite on the riverbank, go up through Parque Mitre and continue along the road closest to the river; the site is just past the water works.

Restaurants *El Recreo*, Pellegrini 578, good, reasonable prices, popular with locals. Many others, incl *Raviolandia*, Nueve de Julio 652; *Che Camba*, Av Independencia 1173; and various *pizzerías*. Ice creams at *Italia*, Nueve de Julio 1301 and *Verona*, Av Ferré 1750. Several tea rooms on San Juan, eg *Confitería Viki*, San Juan 721 y Maipú 1198 and on Junín. Try local, baked delicacy called *chipa*.

Banks and Exchange Banco de la Provincia, 9 de Julio y San Juan, cash advance on Mastercard; **Banco de Crédito**, Junín 1326, cash accepted only; street money-changers at SW corner of Plaza Cabral.

Nightclubs *Metal*, Junín y Buenos Aires; *Savage*, Junín y San Lorenzo.

Travel Agency *Turismo Aventura 4WD*, Galería Paseo del Sul, Junín 1062, T 27698, Amex. *Quo Vadis*, Carlos Pellegrini 1140, T 23096.

Tourist Office Plaza Cabral; lots of information about fishing.

Car Hire Avis at *Gran Hotel Guaraní* and airport; only credit cards accepted from foreigners.

Airport Camba Punta, 10 km from city. (Bus No 8 from urban bus terminal at river end of La Rioja) Aerolíneas Argentinas T 27442; Austral, Junín 1301, T 23850. Austral flights to and from Buenos Aires daily.

Bus Terminal 5 km from centre; bus No 6 from terminal to town centre (US$0.20). Corrientes-**Posadas** US$15, 5½ hrs, road paved. Buses to **Resistencia** US$0.55, Cota, every 15 mins, 40 mins journey, labelled "Chaco", leave from harbour; **Buenos Aires**-Corrientes,

US$50, Chevallier; Tata Rápido; there are many more buses to Buenos Aires, Rosario and Santa Fe from Resistencia than from Corrientes.

At 20 km along Route 12 from Corrientes is **Santa Ana de los Guacaras**, a 17th-century settlement with attractive colonial architecture. To the N of Corrientes is the small town of **Paso de la Patria** (38 km, Route 12), a paradise for *dorado* fishing, with plenty of bungalows to stay. (**B** Hostería Don Julián, T 94021, full board.)

A tiny port on the Alto Paraná, **Itatí** (pop 5,700), is reached by bus (73 km on Route 12). Here, on 16 Jul, is held a festival which celebrates jointly the crowning of the Virgin of Itatí (housed in a sanctuary built 1638), and St Louis of France. Thousands of pilgrims arrive on the 16th (when the religious ceremonies begin) from San Luis del Palmar (pop 15,000) in picturesque procession. *Hospedajes* incl **Antártida, El Promesero, El Colonial**.

Some 250 km E of Corrientes is **Ituzaingó**, pop 10,000, a rapidly growing town serving the Yacyretá-Apipé hydroelectric project (all turbines due to be in place by 1998). Buses run to the Relaciones Públicas centre (free, no stops en route), where a video film is shown and other information given. Several hotels, eg **E** *Hospedaje Dos Hermanos*, Pellegrini y Posadas, clean, friendly.

About 15 km W of Ituzaingó on Ruta Nacional 12, Km 1237, is *Estancia San Gará*, "the perfect place to relax and experience the typical Gaucho life" (Thomas and Petra Sbampato, Switzerland), US$80 pp in double bedroom with rm service, or US$30 pp in dormitory with hammock-style accommodation. Price incl 4 good meals, use of pool and all excursions into the Iberá marshes, by boat, jeep or on horseback (highly rec); a lovely place with extraordinary hospitality. Book in advance: T 0786-20550, in Posadas 0752-27217, in Buenos Aires, 01-811-1132, F 476-2648 (office at Av Alvear 1668, 5 piso); always ask for owner Sr Pablo Prats. Ask to be let off any bus going to or from Posadas via Ituzaingó at the turn-off (drivers know it) and walk 1.5 km to the *estancia*.

210 km SE of Corrientes, on the edge of the Iberá marshes (**see p 156**), is the Estancia of **San Juan Poriahú** (16,500 ha), a wildlife reserve with a superb array of animals and birds. Visitors can explore the estancia on horseback, or in pick-ups or tractors.

Corrientes is 40 km below the confluence of the Paraguay and Alto Paraná rivers. Up the former are Formosa and Asunción; up the latter are Posadas and Iguazú.

The only Argentine port of any note on the Paraguay river is **Formosa**, 240 km above Corrientes. It is the capital of Formosa Province, and has a population of 95,000. There is a colonial museum in the town centre. The surroundings are flat and swampy, the climate and vegetation tropical. From the port a trip can be made to Isla Alberdi, a Paraguayan duty-free spot; no possibility of continuing into Paraguay, and can only be done if you have a multiple entry visa. By road from Buenos Aires; 1,365 km. Airport (5 Austral flights a week).

Hotels A2 *Turismo*, best, San Martín 759, T 26004; **C** *Colón*, Belgrano 1098, T 26547, noisy, a/c, colour TV, spacious, 1st floor, B 2nd floor, good; **C** *Plaza*, J.M. Uriburu 905, T 26747. Several others on San Martín, eg **D** *Rivas*, Belgrano 1395, T 20499, ½ block from old bus station, with bath (E without), cold water, basic, run down, friendly. **D** *Colonial*, San Martín 897, T 26345, near railway station, with private bath (E without), clean, a/c, basic but good value, private parking available. **D** *Casa de Familia*, Belgrano 1056, friendly, good. Many more along Belgrano.

Camping Possible on the river about 2 km from the centre along a dirt road, upstream and over the railway lines.

Restaurant *Ser Bran*, near bus terminal, cheap and good; several others opp bus terminal, eg *17 de Agosto*, good, cheap. *El Alamo*, Av 25 de Mayo 65, good *parrillada*; *Latino American Bar*, 25 de Mayo 55, good Italian food, nice atmosphere, expensive. On same road *Italiano*, excellent food, friendly, reasonable prices, and *Raíces*, good.

Exchange Banks close at about noon and there are no exchange shops; buy pesos in Asunción or Clorinda if en route when they're closed. **Banco de la Provincia de Formosa** changes TCs, but very high commission.

Tourist Office *Hotel Internacional*, San Martín 759. Also at new bus terminal very helpful.

Roads S to Resistencia (200 km); N to Clorinda and Asunción, paved, 150 km, via new toll bridge. Direct road to Salta very bad.

Bus To Asunción, 0400, 0800 and 1730, 3 hrs, US$10.50, delays at frontier common. Easier to go to Clorinda on the border (US$6.50) and then take a micro to Asunción. To Puente Loyola,

US$5, Empresa Godoy, Mariano Moreno 1050 (surcharge for every 5 kg of luggage). Six a day to **Resistencia**, US$9. To/from Buenos Aires US$41, La Internacional.

Bus services to **Embarcación** are frequently cancelled (scheduled daily 1200; do not rely on this as a route to Bolivia, better to go from Resistencia to Salta and then N).

Excursions To nature reserve (flora and fauna) at Guaycotea, incl zoo with animals badly neglected in small cages, 6 buses a day from Formosa, ¾ hr, US$2. To Estancia Bouvier, 70 km N, an 80,000 hectare estate which incl a wildlife reserve. Accommodation available on the Estancia which is accessible only by motorboat. Details: Santiago de la Vega, T 795-1727.

137 km N of Formosa, almost opposite Asunción (Paraguay), is *Clorinda* (pop 21,200), whence the new Loyola bridge crosses to Puerto Falcón, Paraguay. Border crossing is easy. Many buses from Argentine end of bridge: to Formosa (10 a day), Resistencia (4) and Santa Fe/Rosario/Buenos Aires (3). Clorinda has a banana festival in early Oct. Street money changer at Clorinda bus station gives good rates pesos/guaraní. From Puerto Pilcomayo, close to Clorinda (bus US$0.40) one can catch a ferry to Itá Enramada (Paraguay), a US$0.65 five-minute journey every 20 minutes. Argentine migration office at Puerto Pilcomayo is open 7 days a week.

Hotels C *Embajador*, San Martín 166, T 21148; **D** *Helen*, San Martín 320, T 21118; **E** *Residencial 9 de Julio*, San Martín y R Sáenz Peña, T 21221; *Residencial San Martín*, 12 de Octubre 1150, T 21211.

At the confluence of the two rivers above Corrientes the Río Paraguay comes in from the N, the Alto Paraná from the E. The Alto Paraná is difficult to navigate; it is, in parts, shallow; there are several rapids, and sometimes the stream is braided, its various channels embracing mid-stream islands. Much rice is grown on its banks. The shortest and least crowded route from Buenos Aires to the Alto Paraná is along Route 14 from Zárate which follows the Río Uruguay and avoids the main population centres.

The main Argentine port, on the S bank of the Paraná, is **Posadas**, capital of the province of Misiones, 377 km above Corrientes, and very hot in summer. Population 141,000. A good way of seeing the city is to take the No 7 bus ("Circunvalación") from Calle Junín. There is a good Mercado Artesanal at Alberdi 602 in the Parque Río del Paraguay (Mon-Fri, 0800-1200). Yerba mate, tea and tobacco are grown in the area. **NB** All street numberings have been changed: buildings now have both new and old numbers.

Museums Museo Regional, Alberdi 606 in the Parque Río del Paraguay, open 0800-1200, 1400-2000, rather neglected; **Museo del Hombre**, Gen Paz 1865, open Mon-Fri, 0700-1300, 1400-1900, housing archaeological pieces from the areas to be flooded by the Yacyretá hydroelectric project and a section on the Jesuit missionary era; **Museo de Ciencias Naturales**, San Luis 384, open Tues-Sun, 0800-1200, 1500-1900, incl artefacts from San Ignacio Miní; **Museo de Bellas Artes**, Sarmiento 317, open 0700-1230, 1400-1830.

On the opposite bank of the river lies the Paraguayan town of Encarnación (with buses to Asunción): a bridge links the two towns, no pedestrians or bicycles allowed across. Buses every 15 mins from opposite bus terminal, US$1; bus will not wait at frontier so keep your ticket (and your luggage) and catch next bus. A ferry service still runs, apparently for Argentines only. Pesos are accepted in Encarnación, so no need to change them back into dollars.

Hotels Best is **A1** *Libertador*, San Lorenzo 2081, T 37601; **A2** *Continental*, Bolívar 314, T 38966, comfortable, but noisy, reasonable breakfast; **A2** *Posadas*, Bolívar 272, T 30801, with bath and breakfast, good service, snack bar, laundry, highly rec; **C** *Familiar*, Mitre 58; **C** *Turismo*, Bolívar 171, T 32711, modern but poor maintenance; **C** *City*, Colón 280, T 33901, shower, a/c, clean and reasonable, good restaurant (colectivo bus service from airport to this hotel); **C** *Residencial Colón*, Colón, 2169, good and clean; **C** *Horianski*, Líbano 2655, T 22675, with bath, garage, family atmosphere but poor value; **C** *Residencial Córdoba*, Santiago del Estero 171, T 35451; **C** *Residencial Misiones*, Azara 382, simple but good value, bugs; **C** *Residencial Marlis*, Corrientes 234, T 25764, clean, German spoken, highly rec. Many adequate *residenciales* in the centre. **D** *Residencial Andresito*, Salta 1743, T 23850, youth hostel style, clean, noisy.

Camping Municipal camping ground on the river, off the road to San Ignacio Miní, electric showers, dirty, shop, reached by buses 4 or 21 from centre.

Restaurants *El Tropezón*, San Martín 185, good, inexpensive; *El Encuentro*, San Martín 361, good value; *La Ventana*, Bolívar 1725, excellent; *Restaurant de la Sociedad Española*, La Rioja 1848, good food, popular lunches; *El Estribo*, Tucumán y Ayacucho, good cooking in attractive atmosphere, rec; excellent buffet on ground floor of *Hotel Savoy*. There is an excellent restaurant *La Querencia*, Bolívar 322, on Plaza 9 Julio, good value, rec; *Pizzería Los Pinos*, Sarmiento y Rivadavia, excellent and cheap; *Pizzería La Grata Alegría*, Bolívar y Junín, good. *Sukimo*, Azare near San Martín, good for breakfast. The restaurant at San Martín 1788 serves excellent meals, good value. Several cheap places on Av Mitre near the bus terminus, near the market and on the road to the port.

Banks and Exchange Difficult to change cheques. Only **Banco de Iberá**, Bolívar 1821 (main square), changes Amex cheques (4-5% commission). **Banco de La Nación**, Bolívar 1799. Opens very early, 0700-1215. **Banco Francés**, San Martín y San Lorenzo, Visa cash advance (am only) also **Banco Río**, Colón 1950. *Cambio Mazza*, Bolívar 1480 and Buenos Aires 1442. Street money changers on SW corner of Plaza 9 de Julio. If stuck when banks and *cambios* are closed, cross the river to Encarnación and use the street changers.

Paraguayan Consulate San Lorenzo 179. **Brazilian Consulate** Mitre 631, T 24830, 0800-1200, visas issued free, photo required, 90 days given.

Discos on Bolívar between 3 de Febrero and 25 de Mayo (*Power*) and at San Martín y Jujuy, open 0100-0500 Thur-Sun.

Post Office Bolívar y Ayacucho.

Travel Agent *Viajes Turismo*, Colón 1901, ask for Kenneth Nairn, speaks English, most helpful, good tours to Iguazú and local sights. Amex agent, *Express Travel*, Félix de Azara 2097, T 237687.

Tourist Office Colón 1985 y La Rioja, T 24360, helpful, open Mon-Fri, 0630-1230, 1400-2000, Sat/Sun, 0800-1200, 1600-2000; maps and brochures in English of Posadas, Formosa and Iguazú Falls. Hotel listings for Misiones province.

Airport General San Martín (12 km), reached from Posadas by Bus Nº 8 or 28 from near bus terminal (ask at kiosk opp terminal) in 20 mins, US$0.45, taxi US$13. Daily from **Buenos Aires** with Austral, Ayacucho 264, T 32889/35031, Mon-Fri via Corrientes.

Buses Terminus at Av Uruguay y Av Mitre on W side of town. From **Buenos Aires**, US$40-80, 15 hrs; Expreso Singer and Tigre-Iguazú each have several buses a day: *común* US$47.50, *diferencial* US$58, *ejecutivo* (with hot meal) US$70. Some go via Resistencia, some via Concordia. Expreso Singer (Av Mitre 2447, T 24771/2) and Tigre bus terminal is 5 mins walk from the main bus terminal. From the Argentine side of the international bridge bus tickets to Buenos Aires are sold which incl taxi to bus terminal and breakfast. Frequent services to San Ignacio Miní (1 hr), US$5 and Puerto Iguazú, *servicio común* US$19 (20% student discount), 7 hrs, *expreso*, US$23, 5 hrs. To **Córdoba** with Singer and Litoral on alternate days at 1200, arrive at 0735 next day. To **Corrientes** US$15; to **Formosa**, US$8. La Estrella bus to **Tucumán**, Tues, Thur, Sun at 1720, 16 hrs, US$28. To **Resistencia**, 6-7 hrs, US$15. To **Concordia** (Expreso Singer) US$32, 2100 daily, 10 hrs. To **Concepción del Uruguay**, Singer, US$29, 11 hrs.

International To **Asunción** (Expreso Singer, daily 1400, 7 hrs, and Empresa Godoy), US$14. To **Montevideo**, a roundabout journey because the main Asunción-Montevideo route passes through Corrientes. One can take Expreso Singer bus to the junction for Colón, at Villa San José (ACA hostel, C), local bus to Colón; two local buses over the bridge to Paysandú (US$3), then plenty of buses to Montevideo. If going to Brazil (Uruguaiana) there are 3 daily buses (Singer) to **Paso de los Libres** for Puente Internacional—Argentine customs—the bus from here to the Brazilian border on the other side of the Río Uruguay costs US$0.50. Expreso Singer bus to **Porto Alegre** (via Oberá, Panambí, Santo Angelo and Carazinho), Tues, Thur, Sun at 1400, arriving 0345 next day. If the bus is full it is possible to buy a ticket (without a seat) in Oberá. The bus usually empties before long and you can get a seat.

Excursion To *San Miguel Apóstoles*, 65 km S, a prosperous town founded by Ukrainian and Polish immigrants, where a maté festival is held in Nov (**E** *Hotel Misiones*, clean).

From Posadas a visit should be paid to the impressive ruins of Jesuit settlements and to the magnificent Falls of Iguazú.

Not far from Posadas are the ruins of several old Jesuit missions among the Guaraní Indians, from which the province of Misiones derives its name. On Ruta 12, 25 km E of Posadas, is Candelaria, the oldest Jesuit village in Misiones (not signposted, in grounds of the prison, ask permission to visit). 16 km before San

Ignacio Miní (the best-maintained – see below) are the impressive ruins of **Santa Ana**, more extensive in area than San Ignacio. The turn off to the ruins (signed) is 1 km from the town of Santa Ana; they lie about 15 mins walk off the main road along a path. **Loreto** (not restored) can be visited from San Ignacio. The ruins are 5-6 km before San Ignacio (coming from Posadas), 3 km down a dirt road; there is a sign post. Little remains standing, other than unconnected walls, of a once substantial establishment. Note the number of old trees with stones encased between their buttresses and main trunk.

At **San Ignacio Miní**, founded on its present site in 1696, the grass-covered plaza, a hundred metres square, is flanked N, E and W by 30 parallel blocks of stone buildings with ten small, one-room dwellings to the block. The roofs have gone, but the massive metre-thick walls are still standing except where they have been torn down by the *ibapoi* trees; each block was surrounded by a roofed gallery. The public buildings, some of them still 10m high, are on the south side. In the centre are the ruins of a large church finished about 1724. To the right is the cemetery, to the left the school and the cloisters of the priests. Beyond are other buildings which were the workshops, refectory and storerooms. The masonry, a red or yellow sandstone from the Paraná River, was held together by a sandy mud. There is much bas-relief sculpture, mostly of floral designs. Now maintained by UNESCO as a National Monument (open 0700-1900, entry US$2.50, includes "Museo Vivo", see below – US$10 with guide, tip appreciated if the guards look after your luggage; you have to pay to park by the ruins' fence; park on the other side of the street, it's free!). Opposite the entrance is a shop selling massive homemade ice creams for US$2.50. Allow about 1½ hrs for a leisurely visit. There are heavy rains in Feb. Mosquitoes can be a problem. Go early to avoid crowds; good birdwatching.

The Jesuits set up their first missions among the Guaraní Indians about 1609, in the region of Guaíra, now in Brazil. The missions flourished: cotton was introduced, the Indians wove their own clothes, dressed like Europeans, raised cattle, and built and sculpted and painted their own churches. But in 1627 they were violently attacked by the slave-hunting Bandeirantes from São Paulo, and by 1632 the position of the missions had become impossible: 12,000 converts, led by the priests, floated on 700 rafts down the Paranapanema into the Paraná, only to find their route made impassable by the Guaíra Falls. They pushed for eight days through dense virgin forests on both sides of the river, then built new boats and continued their journey; 725 km from their old homes they founded new missions in what is now Paraguay, Argentine Misiones, and Brazilian Rio Grande do Sul. By the early 18th century there were, on both sides of the river, 30 mission villages with a combined population of over 100,000 souls. Only four of these show any signs of their former splendour: San Ignacio Miní, São Miguel (Brazil), and Jesús and Trinidad (Paraguay). (Note Trinidad can also be visited by bus from Posadas. See Paraguay section for details.) At the height of its prosperity in 1731 San Ignacio contained 4,356 people. In 1767, Charles III of Spain expelled the Jesuits from Spanish territory; the Franciscans and Dominicans then took over. After the Jesuits had gone, there was a rapid decline in prosperity. By 1784 there were only 176 Indians at San Ignacio Miní; by 1810, none remained. By order of the Paraguayan dictator Francia, all the settlements were evacuated in 1817, and San Ignacio was set on fire. The village was lost in the jungle until it was discovered again in 1897. In 1943 an agency of the Argentine Government took control. Some of the craft work produced at the settlement can be seen at two museums in Buenos Aires: the Museo Colonial Isaac Fernández Blanco and the municipal Museo de Arte Colonial. 200m beyond the entrance to the ruins is the Centro de Interpretación Jesuítico-Guaraní, generally known as the "Museo Vivo", with sections on the lives of the Guaraníes before the arrival of the Spanish, the work of the Jesuits, the consequences of their expulsion and a fine reconstruction of the ruins, well laid out, rec before going on to ruins. Son-et-lumière show at the ruins, 2000 (not Mon or Tues) US$2.50, weekends only out of season, cancelled in wet weather, Spanish only, tickets from museum. Festival Jul 30-31.

Accommodation B ACA *Hostería*, good, lunches available; **C** *Hotel San Ignacio*, friendly, good, clean, restaurant with light meals, *cabañas* (closed in Aug/Sep); **D** *Hospedaje El Descanso*, Pellegrini 270, clean, modern, quiet, owner speaks German, rec, signposted from the main road, also has excellent camping, US$4 pp; **D** *Albergue Municipal*, San Martín 4040. **E** *Hospedaje Alemán Los Salpeterer*, Sarmiento y Centenario, 100 m from bus station, kitchen, nice garden, a bit run down, "pool", camping, rec, English and German spoken, owner Peter Sutter is helpful and has good travel information. Gerardo, owner of *Caño 14* restaurant, on left between exit and entrance to ruins, offers cheap lodging, or camping in garden, good. *Hospedaje de la Selva*, 5 km NE on Route 12, D pp with meals, also cabins, horse riding, canoeing and ecological tours, English and German spoken, a good way to experience life on a farm. Ask at *Rest Artemio* (see below) and you will be given a lift there, rec. *Restaurant Artemio I*, good and cheap lunches, open evenings in high season, weekend evenings otherwise (accepts all local currencies, US$ and D-mark, good exchange rate too). There are two *comedores* (lunch only) opposite the entrance to the ruins.

Camping outside the ruins in municipal site; cold showers and toilets. Two pleasant sites by small lake about 5 km S of San Ignacio, on Route 12, cold showers only.

Buses To/from **Posadas** every ½ hr-1 hr, US$5, last return bus at 2100; to Puerto Iguazú, dep 0915, arr 1500, US$14; to **Buenos Aires**, US$35 incl dinner, 24 hrs, dep 1800 or 1900, tickets from restaurant at entrance to town.

Excursions To the house of Horacio Quiroga, the Argentine writer, 2 km outside town. To the Peñón Teyu-Cuare, 11 km S, a 150m high hill overlooking the Río Paraná offering panoramic views. Tours and excursions on foot, on horseback and by canoe are offered by Dante and Eva Perroue, details from tourist information.

At Jardín América, 48 km N of San Ignacio, there is an excellent municipal campsite 2 km off Route 12. Flights can be taken over Misiones province for US$50. At *Capiovi* there is a restaurant (*Salto*) and campsite, with a room with beds for budget travellers, pleasant, near Capiovi Falls; owner speaks German and English. At **Puerto Rico**, 21 km N of Jardín América, there is a good hotel, *C Suizo*; campsite at Club de Pesca; rec restaurants are *Don Luis* and *Churrascaria Flach*, both on main street. In **Montecarlo**, 38 km further N, there is a zoo (ACA *hostería*, T 97023, highly rec; *Hotels Ideal* and *Kayken*, both F, clean, friendly).

The most successful colonization in Argentina of late years has been at **Eldorado** (pop 14,440), 16 km further N. This prosperous small town is surrounded by flourishing *mate*, tung, citrus, eucalyptus and tobacco plantations. There are tung oil factories, sawmills, plywood factories, *mate* drying installations and a citrus packing plant. The ACA office is very helpful and has a large illuminated map of Eldorado and its surroundings. For information on the **Misiones Rainforest Reserve**, contact Daphne Colcombet, T (0751) 21351.

Hotels at Eldorado B *Hostería ACA*, T 21370, pool, good facilities; *C Alfa*, Córdoba y Rioja, T 21097; *D Atlántida*, San Martín 3087, T 2441, a/c, pool, parking, good restaurants, friendly, rec; *D Esmeralda*, Av San Martín, Km 8; *D Ilex*, Av San Martín, Km 9, clean, safe; *Gran Riojano*, Av San Martín 314, T 22217, very friendly, 5 min walk from main road crossing, with restaurant; *E Ideal*, clean, safe.

Camping Municipal site in Parque Schweim, Av San Martín, Km 1, T 0751-2154, free, good.

Exchange *Cambio Fonseca*.

Near **Wanda**, 42 km further N, there are at least two open-cast amethyst and quartz mines which sell gems, but they are much more expensive than in Brazil. There are free guided tours to one of them, Salva-Irupé, daily, worthwhile. Nearby at **Puerto Esperanza** is the *D pp Hotel Las Brisas*, Swiss owned, English and German spoken, discount for Swiss nationals. (Buses between Posadas and Puerto Iguazú stop near the mines and the hotel.) From Eldorado, an interesting trip, especially for lovers of flora and fauna, can be made by following Route 17 W (buses 0800 and 1530), paved to **Bernardo Yrigoyen**, a nice village, lovely vegetation en route (*D ACA Motel*, T 0751-92026, Ruta Nacional 14, Km 1435, clean, friendly). The direct (dirt) road from Puerto Iguazú to Bernardo Yrigoyen crosses the National Park of Iguazú, passing Andrecito (*D Residencial Los Robles*, clean, quiet, nice), Cabuneí and San Antonio. Local buses ply the route if the weather is dry. From B Yrigoyen follow Route 14 to Tobuna, where you will see the Alegría falls. At **Palmera Boca**, 3 km from San Pedro, SW of Tobuna, is *D Posada Itaroga*, T 0751-70165, a family farm with log houses beside a lake, swimming and rowing boats, breakfast incl in price, cooking facilities, peaceful, relaxed and friendly, rec. Continue on Route 14 to the small village of Paraíso, see Moconá falls 82 km from there, then Dos de Mayo (*D Hotel Alex*, clean, friendly). Pass through **Oberá**, pop 42,000, the second largest town in Misiones (*Hotel Cuatro Pinos*, Av Sarmiento 853, T 21306, good value; *D Hotel Real*, opp bus terminal, basic, hot showers; many others; cheap accommodation at Centro Deportivo; campsite 6 km outside town on road to Santa Ana, with swimming pool and waterfall nearby; *EnQüete* restaurant, Cabeza de Vaca 340, good, excellent *empanadas* at *Bar Terminal* next to bus terminal), and follow Route 103 W to Santa Ana, and the main Puerto Iguazú-Posadas road. In Oberá, there is a Parque de Naciones, with houses to commemorate the nationalities of all the immigrants who founded the town. In the first week of Oct is a Fiesta del Inmigrante; there are about 14 groups of immigrants. Places of interest: Museo de Ciencias Naturales; ceramics workshops; Criadero de Pájaros Wendlinger (with birds of the region); Serpentario, Calle La Paz (with snakes of Misiones), best visited 1000-1200; and the many tea and maté-leaf drying factories can be visited. Tourist information centre at Plazoleta Güemes, close to San Antonio church, open 0700-1900, Sat 0700-1300, very helpful, lots of maps. Bus to Posadas, 2 hrs, US$5.50, Expreso Singer; once a day to/from Iguazú, 5 hrs.

THE IGUAZU FALLS (8)

For specific references to the Brazilian side of the Falls, with accommodation and transport links, see Southern Brazil section, the Paraná River. For a general description, local transport arrangements, and specific Argentine references, see below.

The **Iguazú Falls** are the most overwhelming falls in South America. They lie about 350 km upstream from Posadas where, 19 km above the confluence of the Iguazú with the Alto Paraná, the waters fall thunderously in virgin forest bright with orchids and serpentine creepers festooning the branches. Above the impact of water on basalt rock hovers a perpetual 30-metre high cloud of mist in which the sun creates blazing rainbows. The Río Iguazú (Guaraní for great waters) rises in the Brazilian hills near Curitiba and receives some 30 streams on its course across the plateau. Above the main falls the river, sown with wooded islets, opens out to a width of 4 km. There are rapids for $3^1/_2$ km above the 60-metre precipice over which the water plunges in 275 falls over a frontage of 2,470m, at a rate of 1,750 cubic metres a second. Their height is greater than Niagara's by 20m or so and their width by one half, but most of the falls are broken midway by ledges of rock. Viewed from below, the tumbling water in its setting of begonias, orchids, fern and palms with toucans, flocks of parrots and cacique birds, swifts (*vencejos*) dodging in and out of the very falls, and myriads of butterflies (at least 500 different species), is majestically beautiful, especially outside the cool season (when the water is much diminished, as are the birds and insects). The first European visitor to the falls was the Spaniard Alvar Núñez Cabeza de Vaca in 1541, on his search for a connection between the Brazilian coast and the Río de la Plata.

Visitors to the Falls should note that the Brazilian side (best visited in the morning because the light then is better for photography) shows the best panorama of the whole falls and should therefore be preferred if your visit is limited to, say, half a day, but the Argentine side (which needs a day or more to explore properly: the area is much greater) shows more close detail of the individual falls and is much more interesting from the point of view of seeing the forest with its wildlife and butterflies. There is a bird hide overlooking a marsh (Bañado), a 4 km-long interpreted (Spanish) nature trail (Macuco) in the jungle, $1^1/_2$ hrs, US$25, a self-guided trail around the *Circuito Inferior*, and a tour of the jungle by jeep, 1030 and 1500 daily, US$30 (Spanish only), "good fun but not a serious nature experience". There is a natural pool, El Pozón, at the end of the nature trail, fed by a waterfall, and good for swimming (peccaries have been spotted here). Another nature trail leads from the old airstrip, near the start of the Macuco trail, and follows the route of the old dirt road to Puerto Iguazú. The whole park on both sides of the border is an excellent place for seeing birds and wildlife, but to appreciate this properly you need to get well away from the visitors' areas. Many of the roads and trails on both sides need permission to enter. A company like Focus (T Belo Horizonte, Brazil, 031-223-0358, USA 612-892-7830) can arrange guided tours on foot (full details under Belo Horizonte **Travel Agents**). (An advantage in visiting the Argentine side first is that the information provided at the Visitors' Centre is far superior to anything offered in Brazil.) One cannot cross the river at the Falls themselves; this can only be done by bridge between Porto Meira and Puerto Iguazú.

The Devil's Throat, the most spectacular fall, is best seen from Puerto Canoas, to which buses run (see below), or you can drive (parking US$1). On the Argentine side the upper series of catwalks on the river, *Circuito Superior*, are periodically destroyed by floods (they were open in late 1993/1994). Boats from Puerto Canoas to the Devil's Throat catwalk charge US$5, "breathtaking". Recommended in the evening when the light is best and the swifts are returning to roost on the walls, some behind the water. There are no boats when the water level is low.

To walk along the lower series of catwalks, at the level of the midway ledge,

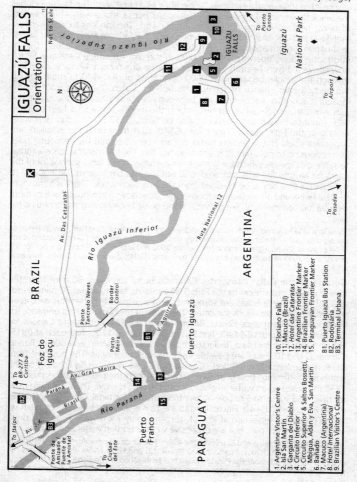

IGUAZÚ FALLS
Orientation

1. Argentine Vistor's Centre
2. Isla San Martín
3. Garganta del Diablo
4. Circuito Inferior
5. Circuito Superior & Saltos Bossetti, Mbigua, Adán y Eva, San Martín
6. Bañado
7. Macuco (Argentina)
8. Hotel Internacional
9. Brazilian Visitor's Centre
10. Floriano Falls
11. Macuco (Brazil)
12. *Hotel das Cataratas*
13. Argentine Frontier Marker
14. Brazilian Frontier Marker
15. Paraguayan Frontier Marker

B1. Puerto Iguazu Bus Station
B2. Rodoviária
B3. Terminal Urbana

waterproof coats or swimming costumes are advisable but not absolutely necessary. Wear shoes with good soles when walking around, as the rocks are very slippery in places. Put your camera in a plastic bag. Take bathing gear in summer to cool off. A trail starting behind the *Hotel Internacional* leads down to the Río Iguazú ferry to Isla San Martín; ferry leaves on demand, takes 2-3 mins, US$5 return (no charge in low season, early 1995); bathing is possible from Isla San Martín, and a circuit of paths gets very close to some of the less-visited falls; well worth the effort but waterproofs essential. The boat trip, Aventura Náutica or Adventurama, is good (US$25); it goes over the rapid water, under a couple of falls, 10-15 mins, life jackets are provided and be prepared to get drenched.

The Argentine Iguazú National Park embraces a large area. The fauna includes the black howler monkey, capybara, jaguar and puma, along with a huge variety of birds; neither hunting nor fishing are allowed. The months to avoid are Jul (holidays) and Dec-Mar (hot); at any time of year the Falls are a very popular tourist destination. Information and permits can be got from the Visitors' Centre information desk, open daily 0800-1200 in the old, Argentine Cataratas Hotel, now converted (very helpful). The Visitors' Centre organizes a 4-hour walk (8 km) through the jungle, beginning at 0900 daily; fixed price US$40 to share among the party (better chance of seeing wildlife, rec). Catch 0825 bus from Puerto Iguazú. It also runs night-time walks between *Hotel Internacional Iguazú* and the falls when the moon is full; on clear nights the moon casts a blue halo over the falls. Mountain bikes and boats can also be hired, US$2.50 an hour. Helicopter rides over the Falls, about 7 mins for US$40, start from both the Brazilian and Argentine sides. The Argentine National Park keepers regard the helicopter rides as a serious noise pollutant. It is also reported that the helicopter noise is a threat to some bird species which are laying thinner-shelled eggs. Also, sadly, a lot of the parkland around the falls is littered, and not a waste bin in sight. Do not add to the rubbish that has to be dredged from the falls each week. There is a museum of local fauna and an auditorium for periodic slide shows (on request for 8 or more people), no commentary, just music. A good guide book on Argentine birds is for sale.

There is a US$3 charge which allows one-day entry to the Argentine Park; pay in pesos or dollars only (guests at *Hotel Internacional* pay and should then get their tickets stamped at the hotel to avoid paying again). Entry is free before 0800 and after 1800. Tenders are out for the private operation of tourist services in the park (mid-1994); if awarded, facilities may alter greatly.

Getting to the Falls Transportes Cataratas buses run every 30 mins from the Puerto Iguazú bus station to the Falls (US$4 return), taking about 30 minutes for the 22½ km. These buses are sometimes erratic, especially when it is wet, even though the times are clearly indicated. They stop at the National Park entrance for the purchase of entrance tickets. Return fare to the Falls and Puerto Canoas for Garganta del Diablo, US$4.40; first bus at 0640, last at 1700; first back at 0915, last at 1900. Inclusive fare, including boat to Isla San Martín and bus to Puerto Canoas is US$10. Fares are payable in pesos, dollars or reais. The bus runs from the Park Administration to Puerto Canoas (for Devil's Throat), US$1, hourly on the half-hour; returning, hourly at twenty-minutes-past-the-hour, but the bus is at 1750 (no buses when water level is low, but hitching is easy). There are fixed rates for taxis, US$30, up to 5 people. A tour from the bus terminal, taking in both sides of the Falls, costs US$40. Hitchhiking to the Falls is difficult, but you can hitch up to the Posadas intersection at Km 11, then it is only 7 km walk. Food and drink are available in the park but are expensive so take bottled water and a snack.

Travel between Argentina and Brazil is by the 480m Puente de la Fraternidad/Ponte Presidente Tancredo Neves, which joins Puerto Iguazú (Route 12) and Porto Meira (BR-469). Buses run every 20 mins (US$3) from the Puerto Iguazú bus terminal on Av Córdoba to Foz do Iguaçu, pausing at the border but not stopping long enough for passport controls; if you want to stay in Brazil, you have to buy a transfer ticket and wait for the next bus after getting your passport stamped (keep the ticket so as not to pay twice). Pluma bus company have been rec. Some companies have a mechanical turnstile and you have to pay again if you get off the bus. On the other hand if you are simply crossing to see the other side of the Falls and returning the same day, just stay on the bus. There is a new free zone being created round the falls so that tourists can tour the Brazilian and Argentine sides without having to worry about border crossings. Note that the Terminal Urbana is not the bus' final destination in Foz, it continues to the Paraguay border bridge; ask for the terminal if you want to alight there. The last bus leaves Puerto Iguazú at 1850. Motorists visiting the Argentine side from Brazil can park overnight in the National Park, free. Taxis between the border and Puerto Iguazú cost US$15 and between the border and **Hotel Internacional Iguazú** cost US$35. Between Oct and Feb (daylight saving dates change each year) Brazil is one hour ahead of Argentina.

Change some money into reais before going into Brazil: they try to charge you triple the true cost if you use Argentine money. Foz do Iguaçu being much the larger town, tends to be cheaper, with more choice than Puerto Iguazú for hotels and food.

It is not possible to go direct by road to Puerto Franco (Paraguay) from Puerto Iguazú; one must go through Brazil. If passing through Foz do Iguaçu en route from Puerto Iguazú to Paraguay, make sure that Brazilian officials stamp your passport. "Ponte-Ponte" buses ply between the Brazilian ends of the bridges into Argentina and into Paraguay, via Foz do Iguaçu. However, there are launches plying on the rivers Paraná and Iguazú between Puerto Franco and Puerto Iguazú: every 2 hours or so. The customs office only opens am on Argentine side.

On the Argentine side is **Puerto Iguazú**, a small modern town above the river (pop 19,000). There is a helpful tourist office (English spoken) at Av Victoria Aguirre and Brasil, open 0800-1200, 1500-2000 Mon-Fri, 0800-1200, 1630-2000 Sat and Sun (also a small office at the bus terminal). At the far end of the Av Tres Fronteras there is a mirador overlooking the confluence of rivers Iguaçu and Alto Paraná, with several tourist souvenir and crafts stalls.

Hotels Crowded during summer (Jan-Feb), Easter and Jul holiday periods and busy at other times of the year. Accommodation is generally expensive and in 1994 it was much cheaper to stay in Foz do Iguazu. Outside the high season be prepared to shop around and to bargain. **L2-L3** *Internacional Iguazú*, T 20748, F 20311, five-star, pool, casino, good restaurants, business facilities, overlooking the falls, rooms with garden views cost less, excellent, check-out can take ages. Reservations at Av Eduardo Madero 1020 (T 3114259, or 3136292), Buenos Aires (in UK through Utell Internacional). **A1** *Esturión*, Av Tres Fronteras 650, T 20020, clean, comfortable, swimming pool, good restaurant, reservations at Belgrano 265, 10th floor, Buenos Aires. **A2** *Saint George*, Av Córdoba 148, T 20633, with breakfast, comfortable, pool and garden, good, expensive restaurant, B in low season, highly rec; **B** *La Cabaña*, Av Tres Fronteras 434, T 20564, with shower and breakfast, a/c, good, clean and friendly, with an older part and a new annexe, swimming pool, rec; **B** *El Tropical*, Av Aguirre, out of town, breakfast incl, pool, rec; **B** *Libertador*, Bompland 110, T 20416, modern, central, helpful, large bedrooms and public rooms, rooms at back have balconies overlooking garden and swimming pool, no credit cards; **B** *Alexander*, Córdoba 456, T 20249, opp bus station, incl meagre breakfast, swimming pool; **B** *Las Orquídeas*, Ruta 12, Km 5 (T 20472), very comfortable, clean, set right in the jungle outside Puerto Iguazú, restaurant; **C** *Hostería Casa Blanca*, Guaraní 121, T 21320, 2 blocks from bus station, with breakfast, fan, immaculate rooms with phone, friendly, rec. Behind *Saint George* is **C** *Hostería Los Helechos*, Amarante 76 (off Córdoba), 100 m from bus station, T 20338, with bath and breakfast, owner speaks German, clean, pleasant and friendly, fan, motel-style accommodation, 10% discount for ISIC and youth card holders in high season; **C** *Residencial Gloria*, Av Uruguay 344, with bath (electric showers) and fridge, pool, clean, quiet, friendly; **C** *Residencial Lilian*, FL Beltrán 183, 2 blocks from bus terminal, with bath, clean, helpful, safe, rec; **C** *Residencial Paquita*, Av Córdoba 158, T 20434, opp bus terminal, clean, friendly, nice setting, some rooms with terrace rec; **C** *Residencial Río Selva*, San Lorenzo 147, T 21555, clean, friendly, laundry facilities, large garden, use of swimming pool, communal barbecue, highly rec. **C** *Residencial San Fernando*, Córdoba 693, close to bus station, with bath, clean, popular, D in low season. Two blocks uphill to left of bus station is **C** *Residencial San Diego*, with shower and breakfast, clean, friendly, rec. **D** *Tierra Colorada*, Av Córdoba y El Urú 265, T 20649, very good, clean, with fan and bath, nice restaurant, trips arranged; **D** *Residencial Arco Iris*, Curupy 152, with private shower, basic, cooking facilities, clean; **D** *El Descanso*, Curupy 160, T 20758; **D** *King*, Aguirre 209, T 20917, pool, hot showers, good value; **D** *Misiones*, Aquirre opp Tourist Office, clean, friendly and less busy than many other hotels. **E** *Hospedaje Uno*, Beltrán, T 20529, toilet and electric shower in all rooms,

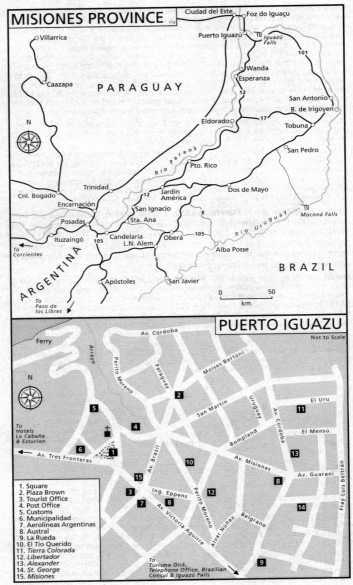

MISIONES PROVINCE

Villarrica

Caazapa

PARAGUAY

Ciudad del Este — Foz do Iguaçu

Puerto Iguazú — *Iguazú Falls*

11a

101

Wanda

Esperanza

12

San Antonio

B. de Irigoyen

Eldorado

17

Tobuna

Río Paraná

San Pedro

Pto. Rico

Trinidad

12

Jardín América

Dos de Mayo

Cnl. Bogado

Encarnación

San Ignacio

Sta. Ana

8

Río Uruguay

Moconá Falls

Posadas

Candelaria

L.N. Alem

Oberá

105

Ituzaingó

105

Alba Posse

B R A Z I L

To Corrientes

A R G E N T I N A

Apóstoles

San Javier

5

0   50

km

To Paso de los Libres

PUERTO IGUAZU

Not to Scale

Ferry

Av. Córdoba

Arroyo

Perito Moreno

Paraguay

Moises Bertoni

San Martin

Uruguay

Av. Córdoba

El Uru

11

El Mensú

2

5

4

13

Bompland

Av. Misiones

To Hotels La Cabaña & Esturión

6

1

Av. Guaraní

Av. Tres Fronteras

10

B

Fray Luis Beltrán

15

Av. Brazil

3

Ing. Eppens

12

7

8

Perito Moreno

Av. Victoria Aguirre

Belgrano

14

Alvar Núñez

1. Square
2. Plaza Brown
3. Tourist Office
4. Post Office
5. Customs
6. Municipalidad
7. Aerolíneas Argentinas
8. Austral
9. La Rueda
10. El Tío Querido
11. *Tierra Colorada*
12. *Libertador*
13. *Alexander*
14. *St. George*
15. *Misiones*

9

To Turismo Dick, Telephone Office, Brazilian Consul & Iguazú Falls friendly, clean, rec. The Tourist Office has a list of *Casas Familiares* (F pp), though it may be reluctant to find private accommodation unless the hotels are full.

Camping Free site 600m past parking area at Puerto Canoas. Tables, but no other facilities. Camping sometimes permitted at the school just inside the Park entrance. Municipal campsite in Puerto Iguazú reported "grim". Camping El Pindó at the edge of town, charges US$1.60 pp, plus charge for tent and for use of pool, friendly, but very run down. There are also facilities at Complejo Turístico Americano, Km 5, Route 12, T 2782 incl pool (open to non-guests, US$2.50) in pleasant, wooded gardens, but no food; US$3 pp, US$3/car, US$3/tent.

Restaurants *La Rueda*, Av Córdoba 28, good food at reasonable prices; *Pizzería Ser*, Victoria Aguirre 453, good pizzas; *Charo*, Córdoba 106, good food, popular with locals, no credit cards; *Don Nicola*, Bompland 555, good. *El Criollito*, Av Tres Fronteras 62, rec; *Casa de Comercio*, Aguirre 327. Good meals in the bus terminal restaurant, *Toma's*, open 24 hrs. *Bar La Plaza*, Av Aguirre, outdoor tables, music, cheap and pleasant. *Chapa*, behind bus station, cheap, highly rec. *Fechonas*, Ing Eppens, good *empandas*.

Exchange Banco de la Nación, Aguirre, cash only, am only. 3 *casas de cambio* opposite the tourist office (rates may vary between the *casas*; shop around!), only one, **Dick**, Av Aguirre, on outskirts of town towards the falls, changes TCs, with half commission (up to 10%). Kiosk at the bus terminal accepts cheques (high commission). Several *casas de cambio* also on the outskirts of town towards the falls. Alternatively change dollars in Foz do Iguaçu and buy pesos in Puerto Iguazú. Bad rates at bus station.

Brazilian Vice Consulate Aguirre 77, 0800-1200, arrive early with onward ticket and 1 photo for a free, 90-day, multiple entry visa (check Brazil chapter, **Documents** section). Without ticket, only 15 days given. Supplies useful maps of Foz do Iguaçu.

Car Hire Avis at airport. Localiza, at airport and Victoria Aguirre 279, T 20975. Cars may be taken to the Brazilian side for an extra US$5.

Travel Agents *Turismo Dick*, Aguirre on outskirts of town towards the falls, also in Foz do Iguaçu; does not close at lunchtime; *Reinhard Foerster*, Privat Servis, Av Tres Fronteras 335, T 2774, offers naturalists' and birdwatchers' programmes. *Turismo Caracol*, on Aguirre, T 2124, does all-day tour of both sides of falls, incl good meal in Brazil, but mainly for "non-English speaking clients with an interest in shopping". *Turismo Cuenca del Plata*, Paulino Amarantes 76, T 20338, offers 10% discount to ISIC and youth card holders on local excursions. Recommended taxi-guide, Juan Villalba, T 20973 (radiotaxi 044), good value, speaks basic English. Agencies arrange tours to the Brazilian side, lunch in Foz, Itaipú and Ciudad del Este (US$45), or to a Wanda gem mine, San Ignacio Miní and a local zoo (10 hours driving time, US$25, not incl entry fees, may be cheaper for more than 2 in a taxi or hired car). *Africana Tours*, Esmeralda 358, Buenos Aires T/F 394-1720, are rec for their complete package, by plane or bus, incl all tours, hotels and half-board (US$167-598 depending on hotel). Many agencies run tours from Buenos Aires, starting at US$75 for 1-day (Flyer Turismo, T 312-9194).

Airports There is an Argentine domestic airport near the Falls, and a Brazilian international airport about half-way between Foz do Iguaçu and the Falls. Taxi between the two airports over the bridge costs US$25. Expreso A del Valle buses (T 20348) run between Argentine airport and hotels, about 2 hrs before plane departures, US$3; it stops at the bus terminal, check times at Aerolíneas Argentinas office in Puerto Iguazú (Brasil y Aguirre, T 20237/20168, open Mon-Sat until 2000 and on Sun am). (Austral office is at Aguirre 429.) A bus meets each flight on arrival; tickets US$3. Taxis charge US$10 to *Hotel Internacional* and at least US$18 to Puerto Iguazú and US$14 to Foz do Iguaçu.

Air Transport By Boeing 737 (Aerolíneas Argentinas and Austral) from Buenos Aires, mostly direct (1 hr 50 mins), several daily, US$175. Lapa Buenos Aires-Iguazú; Thur and Sun. For best view on landing, sit on left side of aircraft. Flights back to **Buenos Aires** are very crowded.

Road Transport From **Buenos Aires** crossing the Paraná at Santa Fe or Resistencia, taking the paved road to Posadas, and on to the falls, or the more direct run via Zárate and Concordia. Direct buses take some 21 hours, leaving at 1130 (returns at 1200), with Singer (Av Perito Moreno 366, T 2581) no a/c, and Buenos Aires-Posadas-Iguazú (returns at 1600 to Buenos Aires) Expreso Tigre-Iguazú, daily at 1500 and 1945, offices at Plaza Once, Buenos Aires leaving from Retiro terminal (US$56 cheapest fare). Expreso Iguazú and other companies offer discounts to students. From Iguazú to Buenos Aires, it is cheaper to take a local bus to Posadas, and then on from there. To **Santiago del Estero**, Wed and Sat at 0130 (20 hours) with Cotal, gives student discount. To **Córdoba**, daily at 1130, via Posadas 26 hrs, US$40, with Singer or El Litoral. To **Rosario** daily except Thur, 24 hrs, US$50. To **Posadas**, stopping at San Ignacio

Mini, frequent, 5 hrs, US$23, *expreso*, 7 hrs, US$19 *servicio común*. To **San Ignacio Mini**, US$14 *servicio común*, US$17 *rápido*. To **Resistencia** daily 1430 and 2200, 11 hrs, US$40; change there for Bolivian border at Aguas Blancas/Bermejo, via Güemes and Orán. Puerto Iguazú to **Eldorado**, 2 hrs, US$5 with Cotal. To **Salta**, via Tucumán, Tues, Thur, Sun at 1100, 12 hrs, US$80, with Itatí.

THE LAKE DISTRICT (9)

The **Lake District** contains a series of great lakes strung along the foot of the Andes from above 40° South to below 50° in the Los Glaciares National Park area. In the N the W ends of these lakes cut deeply into the mountains, their water lapping the forested skirts of some of the most spectacular snow-capped peaks in the world; their eastern ends are contained by the frontal moraines deposited there by the ancient glaciers which gouged out these huge lakes. The water is a deep blue, sometimes lashed into white froth by the region's high winds. The area is good for fishing, water-sports, walking, climbing and skiing.

Northern Patagonia has two railway lines. The more northerly runs W from Bahía Blanca to Neuquén and Zapala; the southern line runs from Bahía Blanca southwards across the Colorado to Viedma and then W through San Antonio Oeste to Bariloche and the Lake District. The roads along which buses ply and airlines are mentioned in the text. See the Chilean chapter, section 5 **The Lake District**, for map and details of the system of lakes on the far side of the Andes. These can be visited (unpaved roads) through various passes. The Puyehue route is given on p 182, with an alternative in the Chilean section.

NB Off season, from mid-Aug to mid-Nov, many excursions, boat trips, etc, run on a limited schedule, if at all. Public transport is also limited.

Fishing The 2 main areas in this region are Junín de los Andes (from Lago Aluminé south to Bariloche), and around Esquel (from Lago Cholila in the N to Río Grande in the S to Río Arroyo Pescado in the E). The latter is the most scenic area. The lakes are full of fish, and the best time for fishing is at the beginning of the season, that is, in Nov and Dec (the season runs from early Nov to the end of Mar). Among the best are: Lagos Traful, Gutiérrez, Mascardi, Futalaufquen (in Los Alerces National Park), Meliquina, Falkner, Villarino, Nuevo, Lacar, Lolog, Curruhué, Chico, Huechulafquen, Paimún, Epulafquen, Tromen (all in Lanín National Park), and, in the far N, Quillén. In the far S, the fishing in Lago Argentino is also good. The Río Limay has good trout fishing, as do the rivers further N, the Quilquihue, Malle, Chimehuin, Collón-Curá, Hermoso, Meliquina and Caleufú. All rivers are "catch and release". They are all in the neighbourhood of San Martín de los Andes. See **Fishing**, p 229.

To the northern lakes: From Bahía Blanca, Route 22 cuts across the southern tip of La Pampa to Río Colorado (campsite with all facilities), on the river of the same name. (Bus to Buenos Aires 0100, 11 hrs, US$30.) It then runs through N Río Negro to *Choele Choel* on the Río Negro itself, 308 km from Bahía Blanca. (**C** *ACA Motel* on edge of town, T/F 0946-2394, Ruta Nacional 22, Km 1006, with bath, good restaurant at bus station, and fine modern *Hotel Choele Choel*; several other hotels; free municipal campsite beside Río Negro, shady, excellent, no showers.) The railway line from Buenos Aires follows the Río Colorado for some distance, then crosses it into the valley of the Río Negro where large fruit growing areas at Choele Choel and Villa Regina (en route to Neuquén) are irrigated from the Río Negro dam. An unbroken series of groves of tall trees shelter the vineyards and orchards.

Neuquén, capital of Neuquén Province, was founded 1904 on the W side of the confluence of the Ríos Limay and Neuquén (223 km from Choele Choel by Route 22). It is a pleasant, clean industrial city of 90,000 people. A major stop on paved

Highway 22, 540 km from Bahía Blanca and 474 km NE of Bariloche, it serves the rich oilfields to the W with heavy equipment and construction materials, and the irrigated fruit-producing valley to the E. There are also many wine *bodegas* nearby. Much farm machinery is sold to the orchards where apples, pears, grapes, hops and plums are grown. At the Parque Centenario is a *mirador* with good views of the city and the confluence of the rivers, where they become the Negro (be sure *not* to take the bus to Centenario industrial suburb). Facing Neuquén and connected by bridge is Cipolletti, in Río Negro province (pop 43,600) a prosperous centre of the fruit-growing region. The Museo Provincial Carlos Ameghino, Yrigoyen 1047, is modest but interesting.

Museums Museo Histórico Provincial, Santa Fe 163; **Museo de Ciencias Naturales**, at entrance to airport (as is the Casino).

Hotels A3 *del Comahue*, Av Argentina 387, T 22439, 4-star, very good; **C** *Apollo*, Av Olascoaga 361, T 22334, very good; **C** *Cristal*, Av Olascoaga 268, T 22414, adequate; *ACA Cipolletti*, Ruta Nacional 22 y Av Luis Toschi, just outside Neuquén, T 71827; **C** *Hospedaje Neuquén*, Roca 109, T 22403, overpriced; other *Hospedajes* on San Martín, mostly **D**. 13 km S on Zapala road is *Hostal del Caminante*, T 33118, with pool and garden, popular. Municipal camping site near river, free, local police warn that it's dangerous.

Restaurants *Las Tres Marías*, Alberdi 126, excellent. Pleasant bars on Av Argentina; cheap places on Av Mitre opp bus station.

Exchange *Pullman*, Alcorta 163, T 22438.

Tourist Office Félix San Martín y Río Negro. **Post Office** Rivadavia y Santa Fe.

Car Mechanic Normando Toselli, Mitre 801, Neuquén 8300 (former South American superbike champion), for cars or motorbikes, highly rec.

Air Airport 7 km from centre. Taxi US$8. 3 daily flights to and from Buenos Aires, one with AR (T 30841), and 2 with Austral; also Lapa 5 a week. Connecting flights to **San Martín de los Andes** with TAN, Av Argentina 383, T 23076/24834 (30096 at airport), who also fly to **Mendoza** 7 times a week, Córdoba, Bahía Blanca (3 a week each), Comodoro Rivadavia (6 a week), **Bariloche** (8 a week) and **Puerto Montt** and **Temuco** in Chile. Ladeco flies to Temuco and Santiago 3 times a week.

Rail From Cipolletti to **Bahía Blanca** daily except Sat, 1240, a/c, bar, video, waitress service.

Buses La Estrella/El Cóndor (La Estrella), El Valle and Chevallier bus **Buenos Aires**-Neuquén, daily US$44, 18½ hours; paved road throughout. Connections with **Copahue** and **Córdoba**; also with **San Rafael** (US$20) and **San Martín de los Andes** (US$22, 4 hrs). Bus to **Zapala** daily, 7 hours. To **Mar del Plata**, US$40, 12 hrs. To **Bariloche**, take La Estrella or Chevallier (not El Valle as it stops too often), and sit on left. Bus La Unión del Sud to **Temuco** (Chile) via Zapala all year three times a week each way, and Ruta Sur twice a week, US$30, 16 hrs.

Roads If driving from Neuquén to Buenos Aires on Routes 151 and 21, via *Catriel* (rather than on Route 22), fill up with fuel here because there is no other fuel for 323 km of desert before **General Acha**. Driving from Neuquén to **Bariloche**, go via El Chocón hydroelectric lake, Junín and San Martín (both "de los Andes"), taking Routes 237, 40 and 234; route more attractive than that via Zapala. The most direct road to Bariloche (426 km) is by Route 237, then Route 40, missing Junín and San Martín. The road is fast, skirting the entire length of the reservoir formed by the Ezequiel Ramos Mejía dam. Then it drops over an escarpment to cross the Collón Curá river before following the Río Limay valley to Confluencia (see p 174) and the Valle Encantado.

Excursions Paved roads lead 33 km N to the artificial and natural swimming pools at the Ballester dam (take bus marked "Banda del Medio" from terminal); nearby is artificial Lago Pellegrini, where watersports are held. A narrow-gauge railway runs with sporadic services via Cipolletti to Contralmirante Cordero, 7 km from the dam. Extensive irrigation has turned the Río Negro valley into a major fruit-producing region, with apples the principal crop. All the towns in the valley celebrate the Fiesta Nacional de la Manzana in the second half of Mar.

Route 22 and the railway go W from Neuquén to **Zapala** (179 km, pop 20,000) through the oil zone at Challacó, Cutral-Có and Plaza Huincul (at the local Carmen Funes municipal museum, there are the vertebrae of a dinosaur, Argentinosaurus Huinculensis, believed to be the largest that ever lived on Earth; its vertebra are estimated to have weighed 70 kg each; a recovered tibia is 1.60m in length). There is an excellent geology museum in Zapala, visited by specialist groups from all over the world (open only to 1300, entry free, closed weekends). Among the collections of minerals, fossils, shells and rocks, is a complete crocodile jaw, believed to be 80 million years old. There is an airport and an ACA service station.

Accommodation and Food A3 Hue Melén, Almte Brown 929, T 22407, good value, restaurant; **C** Coliqueo, Etcheluz 159, T 21308, opposite bus terminal, good; **C** Nuevo Pehuén, Vidal y Etcheluz, 1 block from bus terminal, T 21360, rec; **D** Huincul, Roca 313, restaurant. **D** Odetto's Grill, Ejército Argentino 455, 2 mins from bus terminal, OK. There is a municipal camping site.

Buses A Pullman bus, with hostess service, plies 3 times daily between Bahía Blanca and Zapala (15 hrs, US$25 with Alto Valle). El Petróleo bus leaves Zapala 0230 and 1630 for **San Martín de los Andes** (5½ hrs) via Junín de los Andes. In winter the direct route from San Martín de los Andes via the lakes may be impassable, so a bus must be taken back from San Martín to La Rinconada and then round to Bariloche (4 hrs). There is also an overnight (at 2200) Neuquén-Zapala-San Martín bus that comes through Zapala at 0230; same service at 0915 (US$23). From Zapala to **Bariloche** there are direct buses about twice a week. Zapala-**Temuco** (Chile) all year with La Unión del Sud and Ruta Sur, at 0500, US$22, 10-12 hrs, as under Neuquén (see above). Also with Igi-Llaimi Wed and Fri at 0530, return 0330, twice weekly. Buy Chilean currency before leaving.

North of Zapala on the Chilean border is the Copahue National Reservation, best-known for its thermal baths and volcano of the same name. At 1,980m above sea-level in a volcanic region, **Copahue Termas** are enclosed in a gigantic amphitheatre formed by mountain walls, with an opening to the E (several hotels in the town of Copahue, 15 km from the Termas). Near Copahue, Caviahue is being developed; accommodation is available in prettier surroundings (there are trees), and a bus service connect the two. There are bus services from Neuquén (5 hrs) and Zapala to Copahue, which may also be reached by road from Mendoza. TAN flies daily Neuquén-Copahue. The **Laguna Blanca National Park** 35 km SW of Zapala is known for its animal and bird life (notably black-necked swans). The park has not yet become a tourist centre. It can be reached by an unmarked turning off Route 40 about 10 km S of Zapala. The park entrance is 10 km from this turning, and the lagoon lies amid flat and scrubby land 4-5 km beyond. No public transport and little traffic makes hitchhiking difficult. Advice may be available at the park warden's (guardia fauna) office on Vidal, next to Hotel Pehuén, in Zapala.

Hotels N of Zapala incl those at Churriaca (131 km), Chos Malal (202 km) and Río Barrancas (at 340 km). The road via Las Lajas is paved as far as **Chos Malal**, founded as a military fort in 1889 (restored as a historic monument, with Museo Histórico Olascoaga). ACA service station and hotels (Chos Malal, San Martín 89, T 21469; Hostería El Torreón, T 21141; Hospedaje Baal Bak, T 21495; Hospedaje Lavalle, T 21193). Routes 143 and 151 from Neuquén to Mendoza via San Rafael are almost fully paved (apart from 40 km around Santa Isabel) and provide faster, though less scenic alternatives to Route 40 via Zapala, Chos Malal and Malargüe.

Bariloche is 418 km S of Zapala by a road through **Junín de los Andes** and San Martín de los Andes. Junín, known as the trout capital of Argentina, is famous for salmon and rainbow trout. A short detour from Junín leads to the very beautiful lake of Huechulafquen (bus, Kiko, US$6 one way, arrange return journey with driver); from Junín, too, a road runs W over the Tromen Pass through glorious scenery to Pucón (135 km) on Lago Villarrica, in Chile; on the way there are splendid views of Lanín volcano. Between Junín and San Martín is Chapelco civil airport, served by AR and TAN, the provincial airline of Neuquén.

Hotels and Food B Hostería Chimehuín, Suárez y 25 de Mayo, T 91132, fishing hostelry; **C** Alejandro I, on edge of town, T 91184; **D** Residencial Marisa, Rosas 360, cheapest; **D** Residencial El Cedro, Lamadrid 409, T 91182, with bath, gloomy. Posada Pehuén, Coronel Suárez 560, clean, good value, charming owners, Rosi and Oscar Marconi, rec. Estancia Huechahue (reached from the Junín-Bariloche bus), T 0944/91303, run by Jane Williams (English), comfortable, friendly, farmhouse accommodation, horseriding, fishing, river trips, rec. **Restaurant Ruca Hueney**, main plaza, good trout and pasta dishes, friendly service, rec. Municipal campsite. 30 km N of Junín is the ACA **Las Rinconadas**.

The Tromen (Chileans call it Mamuil Malal) pass route between Argentina and Chile is much less developed than the Puyehue route, and definitely not usable during heavy rain or snow (Jun to mid-Nov). Parts are narrow and steep. Argentine customs are at the pass. The Chilean *aduana* is at Puesco, 58 km SE of Pucón and 16 km from Tromen. Ferry at Lago Quilleihue, which is halfway between the posts, has been eliminated by a road blasted across cliffs. It is possible to camp in the area (though very windy), but take food as there are no shops at the pass. From the border, it is 24 km to Currarrehue, from where several buses a day go (either at 0600 or at the latest at 1400) to Pucón. The international bus will officially only pick up people at Tromen but at the discretion of the driver can pick up passengers at Puesco (no hotel) at 0900 and Currarehue stops. Hitchhiking over to the Tromen Pass is difficult.

Lanín Volcano   at 3,768m high, is extinct and one of the world's most beautiful mountains. Geologically, Lanín is one of the youngest volcanoes of the Andes. Special permission to visit is not needed; from Junín, during the summer season, trucks carry hikers to Paimún for US$1. A 4-hour hike from the Argentine customs post at Tromen pass (speak to the *guardaparque* at the border) leads to the *refugio* at 2,400m. The climb from *refugio* to summit is easy but crampons and ice-axe are needed. Dr González, President of the Club Andino in Junín, can arrange guides and equipment hire.

San Martín de los Andes, 40 km S of Junín (paved road), and 196 km from Zapala, is a lovely but expensive little town, population 14,000, at the E end of Lago Lacar; Mirador Bandurrias above town for views. It is the best centre for exploring **Lanín National Park**, with its sparkling lakes, wooded mountain valleys and the snow-capped Lanín Volcano (Park Administration on main plaza, helpful but maps poor; entry US$3). The numerous deer in the park are the red deer of temperate Europe and Asia. There is excellent ski-ing on Cerro Chapelco, to which there is a road, and facilities for water ski-ing, windsurfing and sailing on Lago Lacar.

Hotels   Single accommodation is scarce. Motel, **L2-L3** *El Sol de los Andes*, very expensive and nice, set above the town (Cerro Cnl Díaz), T 27460, 5-star, shopping gallery, swimming pool, sauna, night club, casino, regular bus service to centre of town. In our **L3-A1** range: *Alihuen Lodge*, Ruta 62, Km 5 (road to Lake Lolog), T 26588, F 26045, incl breakfast, other meals (very good) available, lovely location and grounds, very comfortable, highly rec (owners Tomás Alfredo Sinclair and Barbara Marggraf); *El Viejo Esquiador*, San Martín 1242, T 27690, clean, friendly, rec. *La Cheminée*, Roca y Moreno, T 27617, very good, breakfast incl, but no restaurant; *La Masia*, Obeid 811, T 27688, very good. **A2** *Turismo*, Mascardi 517, T 27592, rec. *La Raclette*, Pérez 1170, T 27664, 3-star, charming, warm, excellent restaurant, rec; *Posta del Cazador*, San Martín 175, T 27501, very highly rec; **B-C** *Curra-Huinca*, Rivadavia 686, T 27224, clean, modern, rec; **B** *Hostería Los Pinos*, with breakfast, Almte Brown 420, T 27207 (cheaper low season), German-run, with a/c and heating, clean, friendly, lovely garden; **B** *Hostería Anay*, Cap Drury 841, T 27514, central, good value, rec; **B** *Hostería Las Lucarnas*, Pérez 632, T 27085/27985, English and French spoken; **B** *Residencial Peumayén*, Av San Martín 851, T 27232, very clean, with bath and breakfast. Also good, **C** *Casa Alta*, Gabriel Obeid 659, T 27456, chalet in rose garden, "beyond comparison and fantastic"; **C** (low season) *Hostería Cumelén*, Elordi 931, T 27304 (or BsAs T 502-3467), B high season, with bath, hot water, breakfast, nice lobby with fireplace, rec; **C** *Cabañas del Sur*, on main road out of town towards Junín, sleeps up to 6 in comfortable cabin, price per cabin, rec; **C** *Casa del Amigo*, Obeid y Cnl Pérez, very friendly. Consult tourist office for other private addresses, but these are only supplied in high season. Cheapest is **E** pp *Posta del Caminante*, Caballería 1164, summer only, basic, friendly, good atmosphere, noisy. The following offer discounts to ISIC and youth card holders: **D** pp *Hospedaje Turístico Caritas*, Capitán Drury 774, T 27313, shared rooms, run by church, friendly, clean, also floor space for sleeping bags in summer; *Albergue Universitario Técnico Forestal*, Pasaje de la Paz s/n, T 27618, youth hostel style, and *Hostería Los Pinos* (see above).

Camping   ACA Camping with hot water and laundering facilities, F pp. *Camping Los Andes*, Juez del Valle 611, other side of bridge, accommodation, D, clean, bunk beds, shared bath. Pleasant site by the lake at Quilaquina, 27 km from San Martín, with beaches, and another on the lake at Catritre, just 6 km from town.

Restaurants   Try smoked venison, wild boar or trout, at *El Ciervo*, Villegas 724; *Piscis*, Villegas y Moreno, *Betty*, San Martín 1203, and *El Peñón*, Calderón, all good. *La Tasca*, Moreno 866, excellent trout and venison, home-baked bread, rec; *Parrilla La Tranquera*, Villegas 965, good value; and *Parrilla del Esquiador*, Belgrano 885, reasonable home-cooked food. *Mendieta*,

San Martín, *parrillada*, popular; *Paprika*, Villegas 568, venison and trout, excellent, highly rec; *Jockey Club*, Villegas 657, also good. It is difficult to get dinner before 2200, but there are various good restaurants in the area. *Pizzería La Strada*, San Martín 721, good; *Fanfani*, Rodhe 786, has good pasta.

Exchange Banco de la Nación, San Martín 687, exchanges cash only; **American Express** office on San Martín, 1 block from tourist office; **Andino Internacional**, San Martín 876, Piso 1, only place to change cheques, commission 3%.

Laundry *Laverap*, Drury 878, 0800-2200 daily and Villegas 986, cheaper, 0900-1300, 1600-2130 Mon-Fri, 0900-1300 Sat.

Travel Agency *Tiempo Patagónico*, Av San Martín 950, T 27113, excursions and adventure tourism, 10% discount to ISIC and youth card holders; also *Pucará Viajes*, Av San Martín 943.

Tourist Office at Rosas 790, on main square, corner of San Martín, open 0800-2200, very helpful. **Police station** at Belgrano 611.

Car Hire Avis office, San Martín 998. Localiza, at airport and Villegas 977, T 28876.

Air There are 5 flights a week from Buenos Aires with Austral (San Martín 890, Chapelco, T 0972-27003) to Chapelco Airport, 20 km from San Martín, and daily flights except Mon and Thur with TAN from Neuquén. TAN also to Bariloche, and Puerto Montt.

Buses Station at Gral Villegas 251, good toilet facilities. **Buenos Aires**-San Martín, US$60, daily at 1240 (Chevallier) and 2100 with El Valle. To **Bariloche**, Ko Ko, 3 days a week, 0800, 4 hrs, US$22.50. To Villa La Angostura via Seven Lakes, 3 days a week with La Petroule.

Excursions The most popular trips by car are to Lagos Lolog, Alumine, Huechulafquen and Paimún, to a campsite in the shadow of Lanín Volcano. Shorter excursions can be made on horseback or by launch. A small road runs W from San Martín along the S edge of Lago Lacar for 10 km to Quila Quina, where there are Indian engravings and a lovely waterfall. Boat trip on Lago Lacar from San Martín to Quila Quina, 45 mins one way, US$10 return.

Activities Skiing There are several chair-lifts of varying capacity on Cerro Chapelco and a ski-tow higher up. Bus from San Martín to slopes, US$7 return. Very good slopes and snow conditions. As yet uncrowded. Lift pass US$25, ski hire US$5 a day from *Hostería Villa Lagos*. At the foot of the mountain are a restaurant and base lodge. There are three more restaurants on the mountain and a small café at the top. For information on trout **fishing** or duck and geese **shooting**, contact Logaine and David Denies at Trails, Pérez 662, San Martín.

To Chile 1) To Panguipulli via the frontier at Hua-Hum: boat leaves San Martín for Hua-Hum at the W end of Lago Lacar, at 0930, returns 1800, US$20 (T 27380). Camping with shop at Hua-Hum. There is now a road between San Martín and Puerto Pirehueico (Chile). Buses daily at 0800, US$6, 2 hr journey through Lanín National Park. For connections from Puerto Pirehueico to Panguipulli and beyond, see Chile chapter, **Section 5**. This route is open all year round and is an alternative to the route via the Tromen Pass (see above).

2) To Pucón and Temuco via Junín de los Andes and the Tromen Pass: mid-Nov to May Empresa San Martín Mon, Wed and Fri, at 0700, returns from Temuco the following day at 0500, Igi-Llaimi Tues, Thur and Sat at 0700, returns next day at 0630, US$25, 7 hrs, rough journey. When the pass is closed buses go via Hua-Hum and do not pass through Pucón—Empresa San Martín switches its return and forward journey days but not the times. Igi-Llaimi goes Wed and Fri only at 0500, returning from Temuco Tues and Thur at 0330. For Pucón change to JAC bus in Villarrica. JAC also runs a service between Temuco and San Martín, via Junín de los Andes and continuing to Neuquén. The companies will not give information about each other, and do not run buses in winter when the pass is blocked.

There are 2 routes S to Bariloche: one, via Lago Hermoso and Villa La Angostura, known as the "Seven Lakes Drive", is very beautiful. (National Park permit holders may camp freely along this route). On this route, from a bridge 7 km S of San Martín, you can see the Arroyo Partido: at this very point the rivulet splits, one stream flowing to the Pacific, the other to the Atlantic. Some bus services, however, take a rather less scenic route following Río Traful, then Lago Lanín and joining the paved Bariloche highway at **Confluencia** (ACA station and a hotel, also motel *El Rancho* just before Confluencia). El Valle buses, 4 a week, take this latter route; Ko Ko buses, don't follow the Seven Lakes Drive either. Round trip excursions between San Martín along the Seven Lakes Drive, 5 hrs, are operated by several tour companies.

Villa Traful, beside Lago Traful about half-way between San Martín and Bariloche on a side road, is described as a "camper's paradise". Marvellous views, fishing (licence needed) excellent. All roads are dirt; drive carefully, avoiding wild cattle! **D** pp *Hotel Pichi Traful*, and *Hostería Traful* provide accommodation.

National Park Lago Nahuel Huapi with its surroundings, an area of 7,850 sq km, was set aside in 1903 as a National Park. It contains the most diverse and spectacular natural phenomena: lakes, rivers, glaciers, waterfalls, torrents, rapids, valleys, forest, bare mountains and snow-clad peaks. Most of the area is covered with abundant vegetation, though it is notably more abundant on the Chilean side, which gets more rain. Many kinds of wild animals live in the region, but they are extremely shy and seldom glimpsed by the explorer. Bird life, on the other hand—particularly swans, geese and ducks—is seen at any time and everywhere in large flocks.

The outstanding feature of this National Park is the splendour of the lakes. The largest is *Lago Nahuel Huapi*, 531 sq km and 460m deep in places. It is 767m above sea level, in full view of the snow-covered peaks of the Cordillera and of the forests covering the lower slopes. Towering over the scene is Cerro Tronador. Some 96 km long, and not more than 12 km wide, the lake is very irregular in shape; long arms of water, or *brazos*, reminiscent of the Norwegian fjords, stretch far into the land. There are many islands: the largest is *Isla Victoria*, on which stands the forest research station where new species of vegetation are acclimatized. The Zoological Board is adding to the indigenous fauna; the trout and salmon of the lakes, for instance, have been introduced from abroad. Lago Nahuel Huapi is drained eastwards by the Río Limay; below its junction with the Río Neuquén it becomes the Río Negro, Argentina's second largest river.

A mere sand bar in one of the N *brazos* separates Lago Nahuel Huapi from Lago Correntoso, which is quite close to Lago Espejo. Lago Traful, a short distance to the NE, can be reached by a road which follows the Río Limay through the Valle Encantado, with its fantastic rock formations. S of Nahuel Huapi there are other lakes: the three main ones are Mascardi, Guillermo, and Gutiérrez. There is the luxury *Hotel Tronador* on Lake Mascardi, beautiful setting, highly rec, also camping *La Querencia*. On the shore of Lago Gutiérrez, in a grotto, is the Virgen de las Nieves (Virgin of the Snows). There is a road to these lakes from Bariloche.

Bariloche (San Carlos de), on the S shore of Lago Nahuel Huapi, founded 1898, is the best centre for exploring the National Park. Renowned for its chocolate industry, it is a beautifully-situated, Swiss-looking town of steep streets, its wooden chalets perched upon a glacial moraine at the foot of Cerro Otto. To the S lie the heights of the Ventana and the Cerro Colorado (2,135m). The place is full of hotels and *hosterías*. The cathedral, built in 1946, dominates the town; interior unfinished. There is a belvedere at the top of Cerro Otto with wide views of lake and mountain. The main road into Bariloche from the E is paved and in good condition. The town has experienced phenomenal growth and can be very busy. The best time to visit it is out of season either in the spring or autumn, although the weather is unpredictable (the forest is particularly beautiful around May). Mainly in Jul, Bariloche is a major destination for secondary school students, who come to complete courses, ski and enjoy themselves in the evening. The 24 km road to Llao-Llao (bus No 20, ¾ hr) is ribbon-developed, except near Cerro Catedral. Population, over 70,000. Lido swimming pool on the lake shore is beautifully sited but somewhat run down.

Museums The **Museo de La Patagonia** in the Civic Centre, has a nice collection of stuffed animals, also well worth seeing for its collection of Indian artefacts, open 1000-1200, 1400-1900 Tues-Fri, 1000-1300, Sat US$2.50; the attached **Biblioteca Sarmiento** is open Mon-Fri, 1100-2200. The clock in the Civic Centre has four figures which rotate at noon; photos with St Bernard dogs (incl brandy keg) may be taken in the Civic Centre square and on 12 de

Octubre above the Lido.

Hotels The most complete listing with map is published by the Oficina Municipal de Turismo, which you are advised to consult if you arrive in the high season without a reservation. It also has a booking service at Florida 520 (Galería), room 116, Buenos Aires. Out of season, prices are most reasonable, in all ranges, but in season everything is very expensive. Most hotels outside the town incl half-board, and those in the town incl breakfast. Hotels with lake views normally charge US$3-4 extra, per room per day, for the view in high season; we give lake-view high-season prices where applicable. The best outside town are: *Huemul* (road to Llao-Llao, 1.5 km, T 22181); *Apart-hotel Casablanca* (same road, 23.5 km), T 48117, good, on a peninsula between Lagos Nahuel Huapi and Moreno, both **L2**. Also at Llao-Llao, 24 km from Bariloche, is **L2** *Tunquelén*, T 48233. *Hotel Llao-Llao*, reopened after complete redecoration, run by a US company, visitors welcome. **C** *La Caleta*, Km 5 on Llao-Llao road, bungalows run by Neil Callwood, price for an apartment sleeping 4, shower, open fire, excellent value, self-catering, rec, T 25650. *Pájaro Azul*, Km 10.8 Ruta Llao-Llao, 4 rooms, friendly, bus No 20 passes the door. **A1** *La Cascada*, Av Bustillo Ku 6, T 41046, La Cascada district, 5-star, rec.

In the town are the following: **L2** *Bariloche Ski*, San Martín 352, 4-star, T 22913, Telex 18273, good; **L2** *Edelweiss*, Av San Martín 232, 5-star, T 26165, modern, spotless, excellent food, enclosed pool, highly rec; **L2** *Interlaken Palace*, VA O'Connor 383, T 26156, lake view, 4-star, small rooms, noisy; **L2** *Lagos de la Patagonia*, San Martín 536, T 25846, 5-star, heated swimming pool; **A3** *Tres Reyes*, 12 de Octubre 135, T 26121, F 24230, lake view, 4-star. First class: **A2** *Bella Vista*, Rolando 351, T 22435, with breakfast, large well-appointed rooms with lake view, 2 good restaurants; **A2** *Italia*, Tiscornia 892, new, clean, friendly, good breakfast; **B** *Aguas del Sur*, FP Moreno 353, T 22995/24329, incl excellent 4-course meal and breakfast; **B** *Colonial*, Quaglia 281, T 26101, clean, helpful, lake views; **B** *Concorde*, Pasaje Libertad 131, T 24500, 4-star, parking; **B** *Internacional*, Mitre 171, T 25938, F 20072, clean, reduction for ACA members; **B** *La Pastorella*, Belgrano 127, T 24656, with bath and breakfast, English and French-spoken, central, rec; **B** *Nevada*, Rolando 250, T 22778, with shower, and heating, breakfast incl, nice rm; **B** *Hostería Tirol*, Pasaje Libertad 175, T 26152, clean, friendly, good, German spoken; **B** *Ayelén*, same street, No 157, T 23611, 3-star, comfortable, TV, restaurant, rec; **C** *Fontán*, Palacios 200 block, pleasant, friendly, family-run, new; **C** *Millaray*, No 195, good, shower, closed off season; **C** *Casita Suiza*, Quaglia 342, T 23775/26111, comfortable, rec; **C** *Hostería Ruca Cheli*, 24 de Septiembre 265, T 24528; **C** *Residencia Elisabeth*, JJ Paso 117, central, clean, quiet, safe; **C** *Residencial Premier*, Rolando 263, T 23681, ½ block from main street, incl breakfast, clean, hot showers, English and German spoken, small and basic rm, rec; **C** *Residencia La Sureña*, San Martín, 500m W of Civic Centre, friendly, clean, helpful; **C** *Hostería Sur*, Beschtedt 101, T 22677, excellent value, with bath and breakfast, gives 10% discount to ISYC and youth card holders; opp is **D** *Residencial Piuké*, Beschtedt 136, incl breakfast (A in skiing season), clean, friendly, rec. **C** *Pucón*, Rolando y Mitre, T 26163, clean, helpful, rec; **C** *Residencial Adquintue*, VA O'Connor 776, T 22084, clean and comfortable; **C** *Hostería El Ñire* (T 23041), John O'Connor 94, hot showers, clean, very pleasant, good location, heated, Sr Golisch speaks English, prefers longer-stay visitors, highly rec; **C** pp *Hostería El Radal*, 24 de Septiembre 46, T 22551, clean, comfortable, warm, English spoken, breakfast incl, D pp in low season; **D** *Hotel Le Montague*, Elflein 49, T 22500, comfortable, clean, friendly, restaurant, gives 10% discount to ISYC and youth card holders; **D** *Punta Nevada*, Onelli 347, rec; **D** *Venezia*, Morales 446, T 22407, clean, rec; **D** *Victoria*, price per person, shared rm Mitre 815, friendly, information service helpful. Also rec, **D** *Hostería Güemes*, Güemes 715, T 24785, with breakfast, helpful; **D** pp *Residencial Puyehue*, Elordi 243, T 22196, clean, friendly, incl private bath and breakfast, discount for SAH users; **D** *pensión* of Sra Carlota Baumann, Av de los Pioneros 860 (T 29689), follow 20 de Febrero uphill for 10-15 minutes, kitchen, bath, hot water, laundry service, friendly, Sra Baumann speaks English and German, charges US$1.50 to be collected from bus station. **E** *Godec*, 24 de Septiembre 218, T 23085, run down but good value, restaurant (reservations in Buenos Aires T 751-4335); **E** pp *Residencial No Me Olvides*, Av Los Pioneros Km 1, T 29140, half hour walk from centre or Bus 50/51 to corner of Calle Videla then follow signs, nice house in quiet surroundings, friendly, clean, use of kitchen, camping US$5 pp, highly rec; **E** *El Mirador*, Moreno 652-76, price per person, hot water, owner speaks German, very pleasant, rec; **E** pp *Residencial Rosán*, Güemes 691, T 23109 (Sra Arco), strongly rec, English and German spoken, cooking facilities, clean, helpful, US$5 to put up tent. Many private homes also offer accommodation, the tourist office keeps a list. Among those rec are: **D/E** *Familia Dalfaro*, Rolando y Tiscornia (SW corner), clean, quiet, breakfast served in your room US$2, rec; **E** *Pensión Venus*, Salta 571, heating, clean, cooking facilities; **F** *Casa Diego*, Elflein 163, T 22556, price pp in dormitory, kitchen facilities, clean; **E** *Pire-Cuyen*, Anasagasti 840, clean, doubles only; **E** *Frey* 635, clean, dormitory accommodation, cooking and laundry facilities, motorcycle parking; **E** *Anasagasti* 348, friendly; **E** pp Sra Iris, Quaglia 526, with bath, rec; **E**

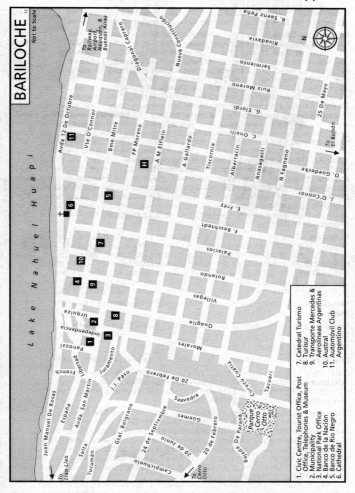

Eloilsa Lamuniere, 24 de Septiembre 71, homely, helpful, cooking and washing facilities; **E** pp *Casa Nelly*, Beschtedt 658, T 22295, hot showers, kitchen, camping possible, friendly; **E** Mariana Pirker, 24 de Septiembre 230, T 24873, two 3-bedded apartments with bath and kitchen. Apartments and chalets—may also be rented—prices vary enormously according to the season.

Youth Hostels: *Los Andes*, FP Moreno 594, T 22222 (not IYHA affiliated), D pp, cold, gloomy, overpriced; *Alaska*, T 61564, on the road to Llao-Llao, Km 7.5 (buses 10, 20, 21, get off at La Florida), IYHA-affiliated, E pp, good atmosphere, cooking and washing facilities, mountain bikes, pleasant location, English spoken, good information on local treks, highly rec; both offer 10% discount to ISYC and youth card holders.

Camping List of sites from Tourist Office. Two sites on road to Llao-Llao: *El Yeti*, Km 5.6, good, rec; *Petunia*, Km 14.9, well protected from winds by trees, hot showers, well-stocked shop, rec.

Restaurants *Casita Suiza*, Quaglia 342, excellent but expensive, poor service; *La Marmita*, Mitre 329, small, cosy, excellent mixed fondues particularly rec; *El Mundo*, Mitre 700, excellent, good value; *El Viejo Munich*, Mitre 102, good meat and fish, rec; *La Andina*, Elflein 95, specializes in inexpensive but good "fast food", rec; *Caza Mayor*, Quaglia y Elflein, game and fish, good but expensive; *La Montaña*, Elflein 49, very good value; *Kandahar*, 20 de Febrero 698, T 24702, excellent, run by Argentine ski champion Marta Peirono de Barber; *Parrilla 1810*, Elflein 167, T 23922, good meat, rec; *Parrilla La Vizcacha*, Rolando 279, good value, rec; *Parrilla Los Pioneros*, Quaglia 259, pleasant, historical photographs of Bariloche; *El Rincón*, Villegas 216, good service, cheap, rec; *Lennon*, Moreno 48, small, good food, reasonably priced, English spoken; *La Jirafa*, Palacios 288, good food, good value; *Familia Weiss*, also on Palacios (with delicatessen round corner on Mitre), excellent local specialities. Good pastries and hot chocolate at *Hola Nicolás*, Moreno 66 y Urquiza (see the graffiti-graven tables). *La Rondine*, San Martín 536, Italian, luxurious, good (above *Hotel Panamericano*). *Jauja*, Quaglia 370, good local dishes; *El Ahumadero*, Palacios, good meat and fish; *La Andinita*, Mitre 56, rec, pizzas, reasonable, friendly; *Cocodrilo*, Mitre 5, big choice of good pizzas, good value, take-away service; *Pizzaiola*, Pagano 275, good pizzeria; *La Nueva Estancia*, Elflein 401, good meat and trout, occasional live entertainment. *La Alpina Confitería*, Moreno 98, open fire, good food, reasonably priced, cheese fondue rec, very popular. *Ermitage*, tea rooms, on road to Llao-Llao at Km 18, owner speaks Slovene. Many good delicatessens in the area with take-away food, incl chicken pizzas and cheeses, for picnics.

On Av Bustillo (the road to Llao-Llao), Km 10, is *La Posta del Río*, reasonable, and *La Glorieta*, Av Bustillo, Km 3.8, good.

Exchange There are several banks and exchange shops, which buy and sell virtually all European and South American currencies, besides US dollars; Sat is a bad day. *Kiosko Anri*, Mitre 339 (rear of Galería Arrayanes), US\$ cheques and Chilean pesos accepted. *Olano*, Quaglia 238, 2% commission on TCs. *American Express*, B Mitre 387, will not change money and sends you to the **Banco Nación**, Mitre y Villegas, to buy TCs, but does have emergency cash service. **Banco Quilmes**, Mitre 300 block, cash advances on Visa. Beware forged Argentine banknotes. If everything closed try *Kiwanis* (boot rental), Mitre 210, 3% commission.

Consulates Chilean JM de Rosas 180, friendly, helpful; **German**, Ruiz Moreno 45, T 25695; **Swiss**, Quaglia 342, T 26111.

Cinemas Arrayanes, Moreno 39; Cine Club, Tues 2115 only, Biblioteca Sarmiento in the Centro Cívico.

Clinic Cruz Azul, Capraro 1216.

Laundry Laundromats on Palacios, San Martín, Quaglia, and on Villegas nr Mitre.

Post Office Centro Cívico (same building as tourist office). *Poste Restante* US\$2.50 per letter. **Telecommunications** San Martín e Independencia and Elflein y Frey (3 min minimum charge); cheaper from *Hotel Bariloche*, San Martín 127. Outside the phone office is a telephone with links to several countries (eg UK, Chile, Japan).

Shopping Woollen goods, eg at *Arbol* (expensive) on Mitre. The products of the local chocolate industry are excellent: *Fábrica de Chocolate Cerro León* on Av 12 de Octubre, near railway station. You can watch chocolates being made at *El Turista*, San Martín 252. One block away is *Mamushka*, excellent. Very good chocolate at *Estrella Alpina*, Villegas 216 or Albarracín 146, and *Gallardo*, *Benroth*, Beschtedt 569, and at *Abuela Goye*, Albarracín 157. Smaller shops reported to be better value. Try "Papas de Bariloche", the local chocolate speciality. Local wines are also good. Handicraft shops all along San Martín; some will change money. Artesanía cooperative on Moreno y Rolando, rec. *Burton Cerámica*, 2/3 km on Llao Llao road, Av E Bustillo 4100, T/F 41102, makes and sells "Patagonian pottery". Winter clothing at *Flying Patagonia*, Quaglia between B Mitre and VA O'Connor. **Bookshop** *Cultura*, Elflein 78, has a good range of technical books, some in English and German.

Bicycles may be hired beside the lake in high season (eg A Carlucci, Mitre 723, US\$20 full day). Mopeds from Vertigo Rental, San Martín 594.

Tourist Agencies Tour buses pick you up from your hotel. *Catedral Turismo*, Mitre 399, T 25443/5, runs boats to Chile for Peulla-Puerto Montt trip, US\$65 one way, rec (10% discount for ISIC and youth card holders on lake crossing to Chile and local excursions); *Turisur*, Quaglia 227, T 26109, organizes trips on lake and on land. *Limay Travel*, VA O'Connor 710, English and German spoken; Hans Schulz, Casilla 1017, T 23835/26508 (speaks Spanish, German and English) arranges tours and guides, highly rec. Arrange trekking with Sr Daniel José Gorgone,

San Martín 127, DT 0706, T 26181. Also rec, *Cumbres y Lagos*, Villegas 222, T/F 23831, skiing, mountain biking, trekking and excursions. Rec guide *Daniel Feinstein*, T/F 42259, speaks fluent English, naturalist and mountaineer, very experienced in both Argentina and Chile. **NB** Check what the cost of your tour incl; funicular rides and chair lifts are usually charged as (expensive) extras.

Tourist Office Oficina Municipal de Turismo in Centro Cívico, open in skiing season Mon-Fri 0800-2000, Sat 0900-1900. Daily at those times in summer but check times out of season (Apr, Oct-Nov) when closed at weekends. Has full list of city buses, and details of hikes and campsites in the area and is very helpful in finding accommodation. The book, *Guía Busch, Turismo y Comercio*, useful, is available free at the Río Negro or national tourist offices in Buenos Aires, but is not free in Bariloche. Also on sale is *El Sur* (Guías Regionales Argentinas, T 61478) which covers the lake district and neighbouring parts of Chile. National Park information (scanty) at San Martín 24, open 0800-2000. Information also from Sociedad Profesional de Guías de Turismo, Casilla de Correo 51, 8400 SC de Bariloche (President: Ama Petroff).

Immigration Office Next to *Hostería Tirol*, Libertad 175.

Taxis Remise Bariloche, T 30222; Auto Jet, T 22408. Some drivers speak English or German.

Car Hire Hertz, Avis, and A1 International, at airport and in town (latter at Bartolomé Mitre 26, T 24869, 22038); no flat rates. **Guíñazó del Campo**, Libertad 118, good cars, English spoken, no office at airport but arranges transport to meet flights. **Chapis Car**, Libertad 120, and **Carro's SACI**, Mitre 26, T 24826 (out of season open Mon-Fri, am only) are both said to be cheaper. **Localiza**, at airport and San Martín 570, reliable, helpful, competitive, better km allowance than others. To enter Chile a permit is necessary, US$50, allow 48 hrs.

Car mechanic Auguen SA, VA O'Connor 1068, fast, reasonable, highly rec.

Air Services Airport, 15 km from town. Many flights to **Buenos Aires**, twice a day with AR (Mitre 119 y Villegas, T 23759/23161) and daily with Austral (Mitre 185, T 22591), and Lapa 3 a week. LADE to **Trelew** and Comodoro Rivadavia, Fri and Mon. Flights, with LADE to **Esquel**, twice a week, and Austral, once. LADE also has other services in the Lake District. (It is reported that it is difficult to obtain LADE flights from Bariloche now, especially the cheaper night flights to Buenos Aires.) TAN (Villegas 142, T 27889) flies to **Puerto Montt** (Chile), twice a week, summer only, and to destinations S of Neuquén. Ladeco also flies to Puerto Montt, and to Temuco and Santiago. Taxi to or from airport, US$12; bus US$3 from Austral or Aerolíneas office.

Rail Services The railway station is 5 km E of centre (booking office closed 1200-1500 weekdays, Sat pm and all Sun), reached by local buses 70 and 71 (US$0.25), taxi US$5-6. Information from the Tourist Office; tickets also available from *Hotel Pagano y Pamozzi*, 3 blocks from Centro Cívico. See under Buenos Aires, **Railways**, for schedule and fares. The train goes via **Bahía Blanca** (about 24 hrs Bariloche-Bahía Blanca). Trip can be extremely dusty, take a wet towel in a plastic bag for face and hands. Scenery only interesting between Bariloche and Jacobacci, (**see p 185**) 4½ hrs. Food on board reasonable (US$7.50 for 3 courses), but not always available and water sometimes runs out.

Buses Buses stop at railway station. Paved road from Buenos Aires via Neuquén, 1,600 km. Chevallier (rec), **Buenos Aires** to Bariloche, daily, 22½ hrs, US$80, incl meals. Also La Estrella daily and El Valle via Neuquén, US$57 (not rec), all have toilet, a/c, video and bar. For **Mar del Plata**, take Buenos Aires bus and change at Bahía Blanca or Tres Arroyos (eg La Estrella, 1500, arrive Tres Arroyos 0555, US$60). To **Mendoza**, TAC (Mitre 86), Tues, Thur and Sat, US$70, 22 hrs, on a paved road via Zapala, Buta Ranquil and San Rafael. To **Córdoba**, TUS, 25 hrs, 4 a week, US$70. To **El Bolsón**, Don Otto (San Martín 283) or Mercedes, daily except Sun, 3½ hrs, US$10. To **Esquel**, Don Otto, daily, 6 hrs, US$30 (direct along Route 40) or Mercedes, US$28.50, 7 hrs (more scenic route through Los Alerces National Park, though the bus may get stuck after rainfall, sit on the right, rec). The Don Otto service continues 4 times a week to Comodoro Rivadavia, US$55. To **Puerto Madryn**, 24 hrs via Esquel (7 hr wait), and Trelew, US$60. To **San Martín de los Andes**, Ko Ko, Moreno 107, daily except Wed and Sun, 1430, US$22.50, 4 hrs. To **Neuquén** (550 km) US$18 by Transportes Mercedes on Bartolomé Mitre or daily with La Estrella, Palacios 246 at 1415, 6½ hrs (a dull journey). (No direct bus to Río Gallegos; you have to spend a night in Comodoro Rivadavia en route. Don Otto fare to Río Gallegos US$88. If heading for Punta Arenas it may be better value to go to Puerto Montt and take a Chilean bus from there.) To **Santiago** (Chile), Tues, Fri and Sun, 24 hours with tea and breakfast served en route. To **Puerto Montt**, see the route to Chile from Bariloche, **p 182**.

Activities Apart from sailing and boating, there are golf, mountaineering, walking, birdwatching, skiing, and fishing (for which you need a permit). Racquet Club, Ruta Llao-Llao,

Km 13.5, tennis and squash, snack bar. Before going hiking you are rec to buy moisturizing creams for exposed skin areas and lips. Club Andino has sketch maps of hikes, some out of date and incomplete. Excellent trout fishing Nov-Mar; boat hire arranged with tackle shops. Horseflies (*tábanos*) frequent the lake shores and lower areas in summer; lemon juice is best for keeping them away, but can cause skin irritation. For horse trekking trips contact Carol Jones, Casilla 1436 (or through Hans Schulz—see above under **Tourist Agencies**), US$35 half day, US$60 day trips, spectacular, highly rec. Also *Cumbres Patagonia*, Villegas 222, US$40 for 3 hrs, suitable for all levels of experience, enjoyable. Or ask at Club Andino for Valerie, friendly, rec.

Mountain Climbing In the area there is something for every kind of mountaineer. National Park mountain guides are available but can be expensive. Book: *Excursiones, Andinismo y Refugios de Montaña en Bariloche*, by Tonek Arko, available in local shops, US$2, or from the author at Güemes 691. In treks to *refugios* remember to add costs of ski lifts, buses, food at *refugio* and lodging (in Club Andino *refugios*: US$5 per night, plus US$3 for cooking, or US$5 for breakfast, US$8 for dinner). Take a sleeping bag. Best information from Club Andino Bariloche, 20 de Febrero 30, open 0900-1200 and 1500-2000 Mon-Fri and Sat 0900-1200. The Club arranges guides; ask for Sr Ricardo, the secretary, who organizes easy weekend climbs and walks with friendly visitors. Its booklet "*Guía de Sendas y Picadas*" gives details of climbs and it provides maps (1:150,000) and details of all campsites, hotels and mountain lodges. The climbing may mean a ride on horseback or a skilled ascent of the slopes of Cerro Tronador which looms over the area. The Government has built convenient rest lodges at from 1,000 to 2,000m on the mountains. Firing, light and food are provided at these points. Note that at higher levels, winter snow storms can begin as early as Apr, making climbing dangerous.

Swimming in the larger lakes such as Nahuel Huapi and Huechulafquen is not rec, for the water is cold. But swimming in smaller lakes such as Lolog, Lacar, Curruhué Chico, Hermoso, Meliquina, Espejo, Hess and Fonck is very pleasant and the water—especially where the bottom shelves to a shingly beach—can be positively warm.

Skiing There is good skiing during the winter season (July to early Oct), supervised by the Club Andino Bariloche. It is best organized with a tour company, through whom you can secure discounts as part of an inclusive deal. (Skiing is cheaper, however, at smaller resorts, such as Esquel, though more expensive at San Martín de los Andes.) The favourite skiing slopes are on Cerro Catedral (several hotels), and a new ski-lift is to be built higher up, to permit a longer skiing season. (Regular bus service with seasonal timetable from Mercedes bus company at Mitre 161, US$5 return.) There is a cable car (US$10 single, 13 return) and a chair lift (US$120 full week, US$30 full day, 17.50 afternoon only, discount for students but only if you persevere) from the foot of Cerro Catedral to points high on the ridge. Red and yellow markers painted on the rock mark a trail from the top, which leads to Refugio Frey (well equipped, blankets, meals, US$5-8, bed US$5 pp) on the edge of a small mountain lake (allow 6 hours; one can return through the forest to the ski complex the next day and take a bus back to Bariloche). The seasonal cable car, with a chair lift from its upper terminus, takes one higher than the main (2-stage) chair lift. Check at tourist info if cable car is running, as everything closes in Mar. Bus tours from Bariloche to the foot of Cerro Catedral give time for less than 2 hours on top of the mountain. Entrance to the Cerro Catedral ski slopes, below the snowline, is US$ 0.50. The only disadvantage at Bariloche is that the snow is unreliable except at the top. There are other skiing slopes 5 km out of Bariloche, on Cerro Otto (cable car, US$20 pp; open 0900-1900 Jan, Feb, Jul, Aug, and 1400-1800 rest of year; station at foot reached by bus No 50 "Teleférico", 15 mins, US$1, entry to revolving restaurant at top, US$3.50, nice *confitería* belonging to Club Andino on Cerro Otto, 20 mins walk from main *confitería* on summit). Cerro Otto can be reached in 2-3 hours' walk from the town,rec; take the paved Av de los Pioneros, then switch to the signed dirt track 1 km out of Bariloche (splendid views), or in a minibus which goes every ½ hour from a car park near the National Park headquarters (closed public holidays), between 1400 and 1600, US$7 round trip (local bus US$2.10 return). Also at Piedras Blancas (bus US$7 return); on López (try a car trip, rough road, US$14 for a tour, 1400-1830), Dormilón and La Ventana. Ski hire US$5-9 a day, depending on quality, dearer at Cerro Catedral than in town. Ski clothes can also be rented by the day, at US$1-2 per item, from Kiwanis sport stores, Mitre 210, or El Iglú, Galería Arrayanes II, Rolando 244.

Excursions There are numerous excursions: most travel agencies charge the same price. It is best to buy tours on the spot rather than in advance, although they get very booked up in season. Whole-day trip to Lagos Gutiérrez, Mascardi, Hess, the Cascada Los Alerces and Cerro Tronador (950m) leaves at 0800, US$29, and involves 1 hr walk to the Black Glacier, interesting but too much time spent on the bus. Catedral and Turisur have a 9-hour excursion, leaving at 0900 (afternoon dep also Dec-Mar), to Puerto Pañuelo, sailing down to Puerto Blest and continuing by bus to Puerto Alegre and again by launch to Puerto Frías (US$19.50). A visit to the Cascada de los Cántaros is made (stay off the boat at the Cascada and walk around to Puerto Blest through beautiful forest, 1 hr, rec). Several 12-hour excursions to San Martín de los Andes, US$34, rec, through 2 national parks, passing 7 lakes, returning via Paso de Córdoba and the Valle Encantado. This route is covered by public bus (to Osorno as far as La Angostura before turning W) rec.

The area around the resort of Llao Llao offers beautiful scenery for walking: you can choose between the 15 km Circuito Chico and the 17 km "motor tour" route back to Bariloche. A tour of the Circuito Chico costs US$13. At Km 17.7 on the road to Llao Llao there is a chairlift to Cerro Campanario (0900-1200, 1400-1800 daily, US$5), from the top of which there are fine views of Isla Victoria and Puerto Pañuelo. At Km 18.3 a turning to the left leads to Colonia Suiza and Punto Panorámico, and then along Lago Perito Moreno to Puerto Pañuelo (16 km). A trip that can be done independently is to catch a local bus to Llao Llao, US$1, getting off by the chairlift in front of the mountain (closes at 1900). Chairlift costs US$3 each way; it is possible to walk down on a steep slippery trail, in ½ hr. A recommended one-day walk can be done to the Parque Municipal de Llao-Llao, with a lake, Lago Escondido. Take the Llao Llao bus from Bariloche, and get off at Puerto Pañuelo. From here take the road towards Puerto Llao Llao (signposted) until you reach the park on the left-hand side of the road. A trail leads into the park for 3.5 km to Lago Escondido. Beyond this the trail joins up with the road again. Follow the road to the right and continue until you reach a turning on the left, signposted Cerro Llao Llao. It is a walk of 1-1½ hrs along an unpaved road and then a track up to the summit. The track uphill is not clear – there are many forks but all of them seem to lead to the top – and you should be rewarded with beautiful views. To return to Puerto Pañuelo retrace your steps back to the road, and follow this to the left back to the village, to catch return buses to Bariloche. There are a couple of hotels in the vicinity: *Hotel Llao Llao*, and *La Caleta* (see p 176).

A two-day walk can be made from **Pampa Linda** over Paso de los Nubes to Laguna Frías and Puerto Frías on the Chilean frontier. To reach Pampa Linda take the Mercedes bus to Villa Mascardi and then hitch the remaining 50 km. Note that the road to Pampa Linda has a one-way system: up only before 1400, down only after 1600. Register at the Ranger station at Pampa Linda and ask their advice about conditions (campsite at Ranger Station). The route is not always well marked, and should only be attempted if there is no snow on the pass (normally passable only between Dec and Feb). Allow at least 6 hrs to reach Puerto Frías from the pass. From Puerto Frías (campsite opposite the customs post) a 30 km road leads to Peulla (see Chile, section 5). From Pampa Linda 2 other paths lead up Cerro Tronador: one leads to Refugio Otto Meiling, 2,000m, on the edge of the E glacier; the other leads to a refugio on the S side of the mountain.

Club Andino provides an inexpensive but sedate rafting trip up the Río Limay (for novices only). There is better rafting in the Chilean lakes district. A half-day excursion is possible taking a bus to Virgen de las Nieves, walking 2 km to arrive at beautiful Lago Gutiérrez; walk along lake shore to the road from El Bolsón and walk back to Bariloche (about 4 hrs).

A recommended one-day trip by car is Bariloche-Llao Llao-Bahía-Colonia Suiza-Cerro Catedral-Bariloche; the reverse direction misses the sunsets and afternoon views from the higher roads, which are negotiable in winter (even snow-covered). If one is staying only 1-2 days in the area the best excursions are to Cerro Tronador the 1st day, and on the 2nd to Cerro Catedral in the morning and Isla Victoria in the afternoon (possible only Dec-Mar when there are afternoon departures for the latter). The round trip to Cerro Tronador and Cascada Los Alerces is 230 km, takes a full day starting at 0800, goes up to 950m, costs US$22 in a van for 8 people, and is highly rec. Camping facilities are good. Good walks to the *refugio* Italia at Laguna Negra (16 km trail) and to Cerro López (3 hrs, and a *refugio* after 2); in both cases take Colonia Suiza bus (from Moreno or Rolando) and for the former alight at SAC, for the latter at Picada. For *refugio* Italia allow 6 hrs up (first 4 quite gentle, last 2 steep, beside 2 waterfalls), 4 hrs return. The *refugio* is open all year, supposedly manned during season, but take food and sleeping bags. You can continue from this *refugio* to others for a 3-5 day hike; details from Club Andino.

A half-day excursion (1300-1830) may be taken from Bariloche to Puerto Pañuelo, then by boat to Isla Victoria. The full-day excursion (0900-1830, or 1300 till 2000 in season) at US$28 includes the Arrayanes forest on the Quetrihue peninsula further N, and 3 hours on Isla Victoria, picnic lunch advised. It is best to book this trip through an agency, as the boat fare alone is US$21. Some boats going to Arrayanes call first at Isla Victoria, early enough to avoid boat-loads of tourists. These boats carry the names of Paraná river provinces—Corrientes, Misiones, Santa Fe—and they have no open deck. (Turisur have 4 catamarans with a bar and cafeteria.) All boats are very crowded in season, but operators have to provide seating for all passengers. The Arrayanes forest can also be visited by walking 12 km from Villa La Angostura (see next page).

Roads There are 500 km of highways (mostly unpaved) running through the park. The old road to El Bolsón and Esquel is paved for the first 30 km, then narrow, steep and with many S bends between Villa Mascardi and El Bolsón, but goes past the beautiful lakes of Gutiérrez, Mascardi and Guillermo. (A new, faster, but less interesting road is being built between Bariloche and Esquel)

Routes to Chile from Bariloche The preferred route is over Puyehue pass (a third of the cost of the lakes route), on a good broad highway which is paved on the Chilean side up to Termas de Puyehue, and almost entirely paved on the Argentine side (approximately 50 km of gravel road which is difficult in rainy season). Road from Bariloche goes around the E end of Lago Nahuel Huapi, then follows the N side of the lake through the resort town of Villa La Angostura to junction with "Ruta de Los Siete Lagos" for San Martín at Km 94, Argentine customs at Km 109 and pass at Km 125 at an elevation of about 1,280m. (About 22 km from the Argentine customs is Camping Correntoso; 4 km further is Camping El Cruce, ACA, and another 2 km brings you to Camping Osa Mayor, ACA.) Chilean customs at Km 146 in middle of a forest. The frontier is closed at night. *Hotel Termas de Puyehue* is at Km 168. Possible to camp nearby, but take own food as restaurant is expensive. Very pleasant *Motel Ñilque* on Lake Puyehue (Chile) is at Km 174. A six-hour drive, but liable to be closed after snow-falls. Chilean currency can be bought at customs at a reasonable rate.

The alternative is to go via the lakes. The route is Bariloche to Llao-Llao by road, Llao-Llao to Puerto Blest by boat (2½ hrs), Puerto Blest Lago Frías by bus, cross the lake to Puerto Frías by boat (20 mins), then 1½ hrs by road to Peulla. Leave for Petrohué in the afternoon by boat (2½ hrs), cross Lago Todos Los Santos, passing the Osorno volcano, then by bus to Puerto Montt. This route is not recommended in wet or foggy weather.

Several bus companies run services from Bariloche to Puerto Montt, Osorno and Valdivia, via the Puyehue pass: there is at least one bus every day from Argentine side. The majority go via Osorno (6 hrs) and fares range from US$20-25 (US$35 for a 1-day excursion including city tour and Termas de Puyehue); it is no cheaper to go to Osorno and buy a separate ticket from there to Puerto Montt. Companies include Bus del Norte, San Martín 283, Mercedes, B Mitre 161, and Tas Choapa (at Turismo Algarrobal, San Martín 459, T 22774). Sit on left side for best views. You can buy a ticket to the Chilean border, then another to Puerto Montt, or pay in stages in Chile, but there is little advantage in doing this.

Turismo Catedral sells 1 and 2-day crossings to Puerto Montt via roads and lakes (route as stated above). The one-day crossing costs US$90 + cost of lunch at Peulla (US$10.80), credit cards accepted; this excursion does not permit return to Bariloche next day. (1 Sep-31 Mar, take own food, buy ticket day in advance, departs 0700). For a two-day crossing (operates all year round), there is an overnight stop in Peulla. Accommodation at *Hotel Peulla* is in our A2 range. You can make reservations independently (*Hotel Peulla*, PO Box 487, Puerto Montt, Chile). More details about accommodation under Peulla, in **Chile, section 5**. Several tour companies sell this tour, incl transport, board and lodging. Book in advance during the high season. The other agencies sell excursions to Puerto Frías using a Mercedes bus to Puerto Pañuelo, a Turisur boat to Puerto Blest and share a bus and boat to Puerto Frías with excursion groups going on to Chile. Request information at Turismo Catedral which owns the exclusive rights to the excursion via the lakes, using their own boats and bus from Puerto Pañuelo to Puerto Frías (Andina del Sud operates with them on the Chilean side). The most satisfactory way of doing the trip full-circle is by car from Bariloche, going first via Puyehue to Puerto Montt, returning via Tromen Pass (see the Villarrica volcano, good road), then Junín and San Martín de los Andes. No cars taken on ferry on Lago Todos Los Santos.

NB You are strongly advised to get rid of all your Argentine pesos before leaving Argentina; it may be useful to have some Chilean pesos before you cross into Chile from Bariloche. The Argentine and Chilean border posts are open every day; the launches (and hence the connecting buses) on the lakes servicing the direct route via Puerto Blest to Puerto Montt generally do not operate at weekends; check. There is an absolute ban in Chile on importing any fresh food—meat, cheese, fruit—from Argentina. Bariloche Tourist Office may not be up to date on lake crossings to Puerto Montt, check details at travel agencies, particularly if travelling to meet connections.

Further information on border crossings in the Lake District will be found in **Chile, section 5**. Parts of road on the Argentine side of the Puyehue route are being rebuilt, and the lake route is long and tiring.

NB Obtain maps and information about the district in Buenos Aires at the National Park Tourist Office at Santa Fe 690, or at the provincial offices (addresses given on p 77); it is hard to obtain these in the provinces themselves. Park wardens are also useful sources of information.

Villa La Angostura is a picturesque town (pop 3,000) 90 km NW of Bariloche on Lago Nahuel Huapi. It can be reached by excursion bus (day trip, 8 hrs) or local bus (at 1900 daily, returning 0800, Transporte Mercedes, US$7) which requires staying overnight; hotels a little dearer than Bariloche. The port, 3 km from town, is spectacular in summer. 12 km S of the port at the S end of the Quetrihue Peninsula is **The Arrayanes Forest**, containing 300 year old specimens of the rare Arrayan tree. It is best to return to Bariloche if going on to Osorno (Chile): otherwise you have to pay twice the fare to Osorno from Bariloche and arrange for the bus company to pick you up at La Angostura. Daily bus at 1700 to San Martin de los Andes.

Hotels L2 *Hostería Las Balsas*, small, exclusive, high standard, good location; **A3** *Correntoso*, T 94168, has a chalet next door, C for 2 bedrooms, shared use of kitchen and sitting room, luxurious. *Hotel La Angostura*, T 94151. Cheaper are *La Cabañita* and *Don Pedro* in El Cruce, dirty, both **D**. Ask in the tourist office, opposite ACA, for lodgings in private houses, cheaper than hotels. *Hotel Ruca Malen*, 24 km N on lake shore; *Hotel Pichi Trafal*, 53 km N.

Camping *El Cruce*, 500m from centre, US$2 pp, dirty toilets; *ACA Osa Mayor* (2 km along Bariloche road, pleasant, open late Dec to mid-May), *Autocamping San Martin*, *Municipal Lago Correntoso*.

Travel Agent *Turismo Cerro Bayo*, Av Arrayanes s/n, of 5, T (0944) 94401/94412, 10% discount for ISIC and youth card holders on ski packages, trekking, rafting, lake and adventure tours.

Río Villegas, about 80 km S of Bariloche on the road to El Bolsón, is very beautiful. (**E** *Hostería Río Villegas*, pleasant, friendly, restaurant, just outside the gates of the National Park, by the river.)

El Bolsón is 130 km S of Bariloche on the old road to Esquel (unpaved and very rough). It is an attractive small town (pop 8,000) in beautiful country, with many mountain walks and waterfalls (dry in summer) nearby. As it lies in a hollow at about 200m, it can be very hot in summer. It has good fishing and is fully developed as a tourist resort. Within half an hour's drive are Lagos Puelo (see below) and Epuyén (shops and petrol available). The farms and the orchards sell their produce at Bariloche. Famous local fruit preserves can be bought at the factories in town. Handicraft market Thur and Sat. The Balneario Municipal is 300m from the town centre, pleasant river swimming.

Accommodation Very difficult to find in the high season. **B** *Hotel Cordillera*, San Martín 3210, T 92235, clean, warm; *Motel La Posta*, T 92297, smart and new (Route 258). **D** *Hostería Steiner*, San Martín 300, T 92224, clean and pleasant, wood fire, lovely garden; **D** *Henríquez*, Rivadavia 2950; **D** *Familia Sarakoumsky*, San Martín 3003, good. **D** *Hotel Salinas*, Rocas 641, friendly, clean, rec. **E** *Hospedaje Los Amigos*, Las Malvinas y Balcarce, 2 cabins or camping, hot water, shared bath, cooking facilities, breakfast incl, rec (also have cabins and camping 6 km away on Río Azul, good hiking and swimming in river, owners will provide transport); **E** *Campamento Ecológico*, Pagano y Costa del Río, T 92-954, bunks, US$4 camping, hot water, cooking facilities, friendly. Up to 2 days' stay possible at the Franciscan school, but get recommendation from tourist agent.

20 km N of El Bolsón, at Rinconada del Mallín Ahogado (daily bus from El Bolsón) is **B** *Hostería María y Pancho Kramer*, warmly rec, wholefood meals, hot shower, sauna, swimming pool, chess, volleyball, horseback and trekking excursions to lakes and mountains. At Lago Epuyén, 40 km S of El Bolsón, **E** pp *Refugio del Lago*, with breakfast, also full and half pension; meals with fresh food, tours, trekking, riding, French owned, Sophie and Jacques Dupont, Correo Epuyén, 9211 Chubut, or leave a message, T 0944-92753.

Camping *Del Sol*, ½ km from town, F pp, pleasant, friendly, cheap food; many other sites in surrounding area. Several *residencias* and camping sites nearby; the *Aldea Suiza* camping site, 4 km N on Route 258, rec, tennis courts, hot showers, good restaurant. *Nokan Cani*, 4 km S on road towards Lago Puelo, pleasant site near stream, picnic tables, toilets, hot showers, electricity, owner is an acupuncturist, rec. The paying campsite (US$5) at Lago Puelo has beautiful views across the lake to Tres Picos, but the walking is limited, expensive shop and café; free campsite also at Lago Puelo. Frequent public transport from El Bolsón.

Restaurants *Don Diego*, San Martín 3217, good; *Ricar-Dos*, Roca y Moreno, good coffee (food less good). *Parrilla Achachay*, San Martín y Belgrano, basic, but reasonable value. *El Viejo Maitén*, Roca 359, good. *Confitería Suiza*, Antártida Argentina 569, good homemade food; *Amacuy*, San Mateo 3217, good; *Lustra*, Sarmiento 3212, good value; *Parrilla Las Brasas*, Sarmiento y P Hube, clean, good.

Exchange *Hotel Cordillera*, tourist agency ½ block from plaza, or Inmobiliaria Turneo shop, all cash only. It can take a long time to change TCs on Mon as locals queue for money.

Travel Agent *Turismo Translago*, Perito Moreno 360, T (0944) 92523, 10% discount for ISIC and youth card holders on lake excursions to Chilean border and to Valle del Turbio, trekking to Lago Puelo and Cerro Plataforma.

Tourist Office Office on main plaza, open 0900-200. Ask for sketch maps of the beautiful walks in the neighbourhood incl up Cerro Piltriquitrón, rec (6-7 hrs round trip, great views, food and shelter at *refugio*).

Transport Full-day tours from Bariloche are run by Don Otto and Mercedes, 11 hrs, very crowded and difficult to get on in high season. Also local bus by Mercedes from Bariloche, US$10, 3¼ hrs; Empresa Charter offers 10% to ISIC and youth card holders between Bariloche and El Bolsón.

Horse riding Horacio Fernández, Loma del Medio, Apartado Postal 33, El Bolsón, CP 8430; trips of one or more days into the mountains, US$20 per day, plus US$15 for Horacio and his horse, highly rec for all standards. Cross bridge over Río Azul, follow road to right, at power station turn left, follow path straight ahead and on hill is "Cabalgatas" sign on left.

Excursion To *Lago Puelo*, about 20 km S in the Parque Nacional Lago Puelo. Regular buses from El Bolsón go to the lake via Villa Lago Puelo (*Hostería Enebros*, T 99054; *Hostería Lago Puelo*, T 99059; also *cabañas*) where there is a bank, shops and fuel. From here a path runs 12 km W to Chile. Inside the park is the *Albergue El Turbio*, T (0944) 92523, horse and kayak hire, 10% discount for ISIC and youth card holders (information from Turismo Translago in El Bolsón). Good information on the park is available from the wardens at the entrance. Turismo Translago excursions from the paying campsite, or from office in town: ½-day trip across the lake to Valle Río Turbio below Cerro Tres Picos, US$15; also to the Chilean border and Lago Inferior. Canoes can be rented for US$3/hr to appreciate the beauty of the lake. Use "Fletes" truck transport to get to more remote treks and campsites.

About 80 km S of Esquel is **Cholila**, with superb views of Lago Cholila, crowned by the Matterhorn-like mountains of Cerros Dos and Tres Picos. A recommended journey for motorists is to spend the night at El Bolsón, enter the Los Alerces park via Cholila and drive right through it to Esquel, travelling the whole length of Lagos Rivadavia and Futalaufquen. Mercedes bus between Bariloche and Esquel passes daily.

Hotel C *El Trébol*, with bath and breakfast, basic evening meal US$5, comfortable rooms with stoves, bus stops in village 4 km away. **Restaurant** *Hue Telén*, 8 km from El Trébol, irregular opening times, 1 km from ACA (which is reported as poor).

Excursion Good walk around Lago Mosquito: continue down the road from El Trébol past the lake then take a path to the left, following the river. Cross the river on the farm bridge and continue to the base of the hills where a second bridge exists. Follow the path to the lake and walk between the lake and the hills, crossing the exit river via a suspension bridge just past El Trébol—6 hrs (Nick Saunders and Sarah Jaggs, London W1).

At Lago Cholila, 8 km W of Cholila, accommodation is available at the **D** pp *Hostería Estancia Lago Cholila*, views over Cerros Dos and Tres Picos, camping sites. For transport from El Bolsón or Esquel contact Pedro Torres (speaks English) 0944-99039.

Esquel, about 260 km S of Bariloche, was originally an offshoot of the Welsh colony at Chubut, nearly 650 km to the E. It is now a modern town with reasonable amenities (population 18,800). Major skiing location at La Hoya, 7 ski-lifts, 15 km N of Esquel (skiing cheaper than at Bariloche). For skiing information ask at Club Andino Esquel; bus to La Hoya from Esquel, 3 a day, US$7 return, ski pass US$22, gear hire US$7 a day. Esquel is known for its tulips, chocolate, jellies and jams (also for the mazard berry liquor made by the Braese family, interesting, but expensive).

Hotels A2 *Tehuelche*, 9 de Julio 825, T 2421, with shower, heating and breakfast, excellent restaurant, some staff speak English; **B** *Angelina*, Av Alvear 758, T 2763, very friendly and clean good food, warm, run by Italian teacher, highly rec; **C** *Hostería Los Tulipanes*, Fontana 365, T 2748, good rooms and service; **C** *Residencial Esquel*, San Martín 1040, T 2534, clean, friendly, heating, rec; **D** *Hostal La Hoya*, Ameghino 2296, T 2473, on road to airport, 1 km. Also **D** *Hostería La Hoya* at the Centro Deportivo de Ski at La Hoya itself. **D** *Vascongada*, Mitre y 9 de Julio, T 2361, with shower, friendly, good cheap food. **D** *Huentru Niyeu* (no sign), Chacabuco 606, T 2576, clean, quiet, friendly, modern, garage. **D** *Lago Verde*, Volta 1081,

T 2251, doubles only, breakfast incl, modern, comfortable, highly rec; **D** *Zacarias*, Roca 634, T 2270. **D** *Residencial Huemul*, Alvear y 25 de Mayo, T 2149, clean, not very secure, good *confitería*; **D** *Residencial Argentino*, 25 de Mayo 862, T 2237, no singles, basic, clean, heating, camping in season; **D** *Residencial Gingins*, Rivadavia 1243, T 2452, friendly, grubby; **D/E** Sra Helga Hammond, Antártida Argentina 522, friendly, clean, German spoken; **E** Mrs Megan Rowlands' guesthouse at Rivadavia 330, T 2578, Welsh spoken, rec; **E** Sra Olga Daher, Sarmiento 269, friendly, quiet. Ask at tourist office for lodgings in private houses. Hotels are often full in Feb.

Camping Municipal site 5 km from centre on Trevelin road, near gravel-crushing plant, hot showers, rec. In the Parque Nacional there are numerous paying and free campsites beside the lakes, but a permit may be needed from Intendencia at Villa Futalaufquen and campsites are closed in winter. Free campsite at Laguna Z, 5 km along Calle Fontana. Camping at *Cabañas Tejas Negras* (C), good facilities for US$3.50, by *Pucón Pai Motel*, which has its own campsite. Also at La Colina, on hill overlooking town, Darwin 1400, US$3 pp, hot showers, kitchen facilities, lounge with log fire, highly rec. Those with sleeping bags can go to the Salesian school and sleep in the school classrooms, Dec to Mar; get recommendation from tourist office.

Restaurants *Jockey Club*, Alvear 949, reasonably priced; *Ahla Wasahla*, Sarmiento y San Martín, good cheap, friendly, closed Sun; *Red Fox*, Sarmiento 795 y Alvear, a British-style pub with light, but expensive meals, open from 2200, closed Tues. *Parrilla La Estancia*, 25 de Mayo 541, quite good; *El Mesón*, Rivadavia 1034, reasonable, but slow service; *Pizzería Don Pipo*, Rivadavia 924, good pizzas and *empanadas*. *Atelier*, 25 de Mayo y San Martín, good coffee, cheap, open 24 hrs. *Casa Suiza*, good confitería. Rugby fans will enjoy the *Confitería Las Tejas*, 25 de Mayo 745, which shows videos of the game. Home made chocolate and the famous local mazard berry liquor is sold at the *Braese Store*, 9 de Julio 1540.

Bank and Post Office Banco de la Nación Güemes y San Martín, accepts cheques, no commission on Mastercard, open 0730-1300; Viajes Sol del Sur, 9 de Julio 1086, accept cheques; open Mon-Fri, 1000-1300. Viasur, 9 de Julio 1027, Amex cheques only accepted. Post and telecommunications office opposite the bus terminal on Fontana and Alvear (open 0800-2000).

Laundry *Laverap*, B Mitre 543, open Mon-Sat, 0900-2100.

Tourist Agencies *Esquel Tours*, Fontana 754, T 2704, and at airport, good for local tours, to Lagos Menéndez and Cisnes. *Fairway Sports and Adventures*, San Martín 1-43, T 3380, varied programme of tours, highly rec.

Tourist Office Alvear y Sarmiento, very friendly, can arrange lodgings in private homes. Closed Sat and Sun off-season.

Car Hire Fiocaci, 9 de Julio 740, T 2299/2704. **Mechanic** Claudio Peinados, Brown 660, T 0945-3462, highly rec.

Airport 20 km E of Esquel, by paved road, US$14 by taxi. US$2.50 by bus; US$4 by Esquel Tours bus 1 hr before each LADE flight. To Buenos Aires: 4 a week with Austral (T 3413/3614), via San Martín de los Andes. LADE (Alvear 1085, T 2124) flights to Bariloche, Comodoro Rivadavia, and other towns in the Lake District and Patagonia.

Rail From Buenos Aires, Constitución, train leaves Sun and Wed as for Bariloche (above), arriving in *Ingeniero Jacobacci* (E of Bariloche, pop 6,000), after 31 hrs. (Infrequent buses from Bariloche to Ing Jacobacci.) Hotel in Jacobacci: **C** Gran Hotel Argentino, nearly opp station, with shower and heating, very good, may be closed when late trains arrive, restaurant nearby. Enquire at station for bookings. Sleepers from Jacobacci to BsAs are usually fully booked from Bariloche; only a small quota of first class tickets is available in Esquel for connections to BsAs. The Jacobacci-Esquel branch line, on which runs the steam-operated, narrow gauge train described by Paul Theroux in The Old Patagonian Express, was under threat of closure in late 1993. The train (which dates from 1922) is called "El Trencito" and leaves Ingeniero Jacobacci 0430 Fri, arr Esquel 1830. It leaves Esquel Sat 1030, arr El Maitén 1630 (US$7) and Ing Jacobacci 2030 (US$18). If you want to see railway engines, there are only two at Esquel, so go to *El Maitén*, where there is a steam engine cemetery, rec. From El Maitén it is possible to hitch to Bariloche or take the Esquel-Bariloche bus (4 times a week at 1100, US$17, 6 hrs). 2 hotels in El Maitén, same shower, both overpriced, one is *Accomazzo* with good restaurant, the other is **B** La Vasconia, nr station, basic, hot showers.

Buses None direct from Buenos Aires to Esquel so travel via Bariloche. To Comodoro Rivadavia (paved), Don Otto, 4 times a week, US$25 (but usually arrives from Bariloche full in season) or Angel Giobbi, Tues, and Fri 0600, US$25, via Río Mayo. Don Otto to Bariloche, US$30, direct. Empresa Mercedes goes daily (9 hrs) to Bariloche at 0800, best bus for views (and at 2200), US$28.50. To **El Bolsón**, 5 hrs, US$10, rough road, goes alternate days via El Maitén (for train buffs) and via Cholila (for views). To **Trelew**, US$32, 9 hrs, leaves 0900 Tues, Thur, Sat, and 2200 Mon, Wed, Fri; other bus companies on Av Fontana and Alvear (bus terminal) are Empresa Don Otto, Chubut, Denis. Bus terminal T 2233, also for taxis.

Los Alerces National Park Sixty km W of Esquel, also reached by road from Rawson, is the Los Alerces National Park, with centuries-old larch trees. An interesting part of the park can be reached from a separate entrance through Trevelin (see below) following the Río Futaleufú, but one can go only 22 km W because of the new Futaleufú hydroelectric dam. Behind it is Lago Amutui Quimei, which has swallowed Lago Situación and 3 others stretching almost to the frontier. (Futaleufú supplies power to the alumina plant at Puerto Madryn, 500 km to the E.) Entrance by car to see Futaleufú dam is only allowed at 1500, under police supervision; photography not permitted, except on top of the dam itself. There is no public transport to the dam, but buses pass the E side of the lake.

The E side of Los Alerces has much the same natural attractions as the Nahuel Huapi and Lanín parks, but is much less developed for tourism. *Lago Futalaufquen* has some of the best fishing in this huge area, season begins Nov 15. Bus (Mercedes) to Lago Verde passing along the E side of Lago Futalaufquen at 0700, 1300 and 1700 daily in season (it passes 3 hotels and drives into 2 camp sites). Buses also from El Bolsón. Off season transport is difficult but the Esquel—Bariloche bus, twice weekly, passes the lake. At the S tip of the lake is the park administration building (or Intendencia); it has a small museum about the park and a slide show of Argentina's National Parks. Petrol station, 2 expensive supermarkets in Villa Futalaufquen and a lady sells bread and vegetables from her house (buy bread early, or order the day before; meat can be hard to get).

Hotels On the E side of Lago Futalaufquen: *Quime Quipán*, T 22272, rec for fishing, closed in winter; **A2** *Hostería Los Tepúes*, simple, rustic, open all year, family bungalow for rent; **A2** *Pucón Pai*, T 3799, good restaurant, rec for fishermen (holds a fishing festival to open the season); open out of season for large groups only; *Cume Hué*, T 2858, also rec for fishing. Camping at Villa Futalaufquen and at Los Maitenes (closed May-Sep), hot water, store.

On the W side, which is untouched by tourism (by law), is **L2** *Hotel Futalaufquen* just N of Puerto Limonao, T 2648, rec, especially rooms 2/3 and 4/5 which have balconies overlooking the lake, open all year (no heating in rooms); good walking around the hotel, eg to Cinco Saltos, and El Dedal. The latter is a 6-hr hike and back, with great views of the lakes and the cordillera from the top. A good information leaflet describing the flora and fauna encountered along the trail up to Cerro Dedal is available at the park headquarters. Regular full day launch trip from Puerto Limonao (reached by early morning minibus) on Lago Futalaufquen (a sheer delight) through Río Arrayanes to windless Lago Verde (2 campsites, one US$1 pp, one free, very crowded in summer, the free campsite is nicely situated and has a small shop; *Camping Agreste Lago Verde* offers 10% discount to ISIC and youth card holders). From there one can walk out to Lagos Rivadavia and Cholila (see above)—2 days minimum, and to the end of Lago Menéndez, famous for its giant larch trees (US$52 incl launch trip on Lago Menéndez, with Tehuelche Viajes y Turismo, Av Fontana 574, from Esquel); the boat leaves at 1400 but book the day before in Esquel, preferably, as it will not leave if there are not enough passengers; arrive early to claim your space, crossing 90 mins. The dock can be reached by a 30-minute walk across the bridge between lakes Futalaufquen and Verde. There are local guides with outboard motor boats for fishing. Lovely view of Lago Cisne (Swan Lake) to the NW end of Lago Menéndez. One then walks a 3 km nature trail looking across the Andes to Chile before returning. Tours arranged at Esquel (eg Elentur's Lacustre excursion visiting lakes Futalaufquen, Verde, Menéndez and a guided tour around the 2 km walk to Lago Cisne, on which you will see a 2,600-year old alerce, leaves from Puerto Limonao, take food and drink). Other excursion tours offered are less interesting because they only involve short stops in front of points of interest. A road connects all the lakes. The tourist office in Esquel has a pamphlet on all the walks in the Park. **NB** *Refugio Lago Krügger* in the Park offers 10% discount to ISIC and youth card holders, camping and fishing also available.

From Esquel one can also drive to Perito Moreno (**see p 200**) via Teckia (95 km paved), Gobernador Costa (90 km unpaved), La Laurita (61 km paved, ACA service station, breakdown truck and snack bar), 65 paved km to join route 22 (60 km) which is being paved, and on to Río Mayo, with 121 km unpaved road to Perito Moreno.

Crossing into Chile Colectivos leave Esquel for the frontier at La Balsa, 70 km SW via Trevelin, 2 hrs, US$3. Campsite (Camping Río Grande) on Argentine side of river. Cross the frontier river by bridge after passing Argentine customs; Chilean customs is 1 km on the other side of river (1 hr for all formalities). Colectivo from Argentine customs to Futaleufú (10 km) is US$3. Very little traffic for hitching. (For transport from Futaleufú to Chaitén (Chile) see Chile chapter.)

NB At the Futaleufú and Palena border crossings, Argentine border officials only give transit visas: legalize your stay within 10 days either by leaving the country or by renewing your entry stamp at an immigration office.

Trevelin (pop 5,000), 23 km SW of Esquel (local bus, US$0.85, every ½ hour, 0700-1900), is an offshoot of the Welsh Chubut colony (**see p 188**). There is a modern Anglican church beside the Catholic church. It has a Welsh historical museum (entrance US$2) in the old mill.

Accommodation and Food *Hostería Estefanía*, Perito Moreno s/n, T 8148; *Hospedaje Trevelin*, San Martín 327, T 8102. Grills at *Che Ferrada*, good mixed *parrillada* at *El Quincho*, and several tea rooms offering *té galés* and *torta negra* (eg *El Adobe* on Av Patagonia; *Nain Maggie*, rec). *La Cabaña*, 7 km out on the road from Trevelin to Lake Futalaufquen, serves Welsh teas. There is a custom of giving a newly-married couple a "black cake" on their wedding day, to be eaten on their first anniversary. Municipal campsite near centre. On the road to Esquel 3 km from Trevelin, signposted on the righthand side, is *La Granja Trevelin*, owned by Domingo Giacci, macrobiotic meals and good Italian cooking, sells milk, cheese and onions; camping US$1, hot water and wc, bungalows US$15 a day; excellent horses for hire.

Tourist Office Good office in central plaza.

Excursion 17 km on road to frontier are Nant-y-fall Falls, entrance US$0.50 pp incl guide to all 7 falls (1½ hr walk).

PATAGONIA (10)

The vast, windy, treeless plateau south of the Río Colorado: the Atlantic coast is rich in marine life, most easily seen around Puerto Madryn. In the south of the region is the Parque Nacional de los Glaciares, with journeys on lakes full of ice floes and to the Moreno glacier. In the N of the region is Argentina's Welsh community.

Patagonia is sub-divided into the provinces of Neuquén, Río Negro, Chubut, Santa Cruz and Tierra del Fuego. The area covers 780,000 sq km: 28% of the national territory, but has a population of only 600,000, little over 2.7% of the total population; and 57% of it is urban. Wide areas have less than one person to the sq km, and there are virtually no trees except in the N and the Andean foothills.

Over the whole land there blows a boisterous, cloud-laden strong wind which raises a haze of dust in summer, but in winter the dust can turn into thick mud. Temperatures are moderated by the proximity of the sea and are singularly mild, neither rising high during the summer nor falling low during the winter. Even in Tierra del Fuego, where the warmest summer months average 10½°C, the winter days' average can reach a high of about 2°C. Make sure you have plenty of warm clothing, and anti-freeze in your car, available locally. Rain falls mostly in the winter, but not more than 200-250mm a year. The whole E part of the area suffers from a lack of rainfall and the land is more or less desert. Deep crevices or canyons intersect the land from E to W. Few of them contain permanent water, but ground water is easily pumped to the surface. The great sheep *estancias* are along these canyons, sheltered from the wind, and in the depression running N from the Strait of Magellan to Lagos Argentino and Buenos Aires and beyond. During a brief period in spring, after the melting of the snows, there is grass on the plateau. Most of the land is devoted to sheep raising. The wool, which is shipped N to Buenos Aires, is mostly the fine and finecrossbred wool used by the Argentine mills, and is often heavy with sand. Over-grazing leads to much erosion. Wild dogs and the red fox are the sole enemies of the sheep. Because of the high winds and insufficient rainfall there is little agriculture except in the N, in the valleys of the Colorado and Negro rivers. Some cattle are raised in both valleys where irrigation permits the growing of alfalfa.

Patagonia is rich in extractive resources: the oil of Comodoro Rivadavia and

Tierra del Fuego, the little exploited iron ore of Sierra Grande, the coal of Río Turbio, the hydro-electric capacity of El Chocón, plentiful deposits of minerals (particularly bauxite) and marine resources, but their exploitation has been slow. Tourism is opening up too. The wildlife is attractive. Guanacos and rheas are a common sight: there are also *maras*, Patagonian hares. On and off parts of the coast, particularly the Valdés peninsula, seals, sea-elephants, right whales and other aquatic mammals may be seen, as well as penguins, especially between Oct and Apr. Further S, particularly in Tierra del Fuego, the antarctic wild goose (*quequén*) is the most commonly seen of the 152 species of birds (rec reading, *Aves de Argentina y Uruguay*, available, in English, from *Librería ABC* in Buenos Aires).

NB In summer hotel prices are grossly inflated (by as much as 100% in Ushuaia, 75% in Calafate); also in some places there may not be enough hotel beds to meet the demand. Camping is increasingly popular, and *estancias* seem hospitable to travellers who are stuck for a bed. During Argentine summer holidays (Jan, Feb, Mar) getting a hotel room in Ushuaia, Río Grande, Río Gallegos and Calafate is practically impossible. In this connection, remember that ACA establishments, which charge the same prices all over Argentina, are a bargain in Patagonia and Tierra del Fuego, where all other accommodation is expensive. As very few hotels and restaurants have a/c or even fans, it can get uncomfortably hot in Jan. TCs are hard to change throughout Patagonia.

Colonization The coast of Patagonia was first visited by a European late in 1519, when the Portuguese Fernão Magalhães (Magellan), then in the service of Spain, was on his voyage round the world. Early in 1520 he turned W into the strait which now bears his name and there struggled with fierce headwinds until he reached that Sea of Peace he named the Pacific. Later European expeditions that attempted to land on the coast were repulsed by the dour and obdurate local Indians, but these were almost entirely wiped out in the wars of 1879-1883, generally known as the "Campaign of the Desert". Before this there had been a long established colony at Carmen de Patagones; it shipped salt to Buenos Aires during the colonial period. There had also been a settlement of Welsh people in the Chubut Valley since 1865 (see below). After the Indian wars colonization was rapid, the Welsh, Scots and English taking a great part. Chilean sheep farmers from Punta Arenas moved N along the depression at the foot of the Andes, eastwards into Tierra del Fuego, and N to Santa Cruz.

The first European to traverse Patagonia S to N was the English sailor, Carder, who saved his life in a 1578 shipwreck in the Strait of Magellan. He crossed the Strait, walked to the Río de la Plata and arrived in London 9 years later.

The Welsh settlement On 28 July 1865, 150 Welsh immigrants landed at Puerto Madryn, then a deserted beach deep in Indian country. After three weeks they pushed, on foot, across the parched pampa and into the Chubut river valley, where there is flat cultivable land along the riverside for a distance of 80 km upstream. Here, maintained in part by the Argentine Government, they settled, but it was three years before they realized the land was barren unless watered. They drew water from the river, which is higher than the surrounding flats, and later built a fine system of irrigation canals. The colony, reinforced later by immigrants from Wales and from the United States, prospered, but in 1899 a great flood drowned the valley and some of the immigrants left for Canada. The last Welsh contingent arrived in 1911. The object of the colony had been to create a "Little Wales beyond Wales", and for four generations they kept the Welsh language alive. The language is, however, dying out in the fifth generation. There is an offshoot of the colony of Chubut at Trevelin, at the foot of the Andes nearly 650 km to the W, settled in 1888 (see p 187). It is interesting that this distant land gave to the Welsh language one of its most endearing classics: *Dringo'r Andes* (Climbing the Andes), written by one of the early women settlers.

Gary Luton, of the Welsh Patagonia Expedition 1980, writes: "To me Chubut will always foster memories of horses on an open wind-swept plain, or tethered, with brown sheepskin saddles, outside a *pueblo* inn. It is shuttered houses with poplar windbreaks. Chubut is relative prosperity surrounded by shanties of mud brick and tin; it is Coca-Cola and tea houses, sea lions and right whales sounding a short distance from shore; and *asados* washed down with red wine and *mate*. Chubut is a moonscape of neutral colours where sheep lose themselves in the grey-green saltpans of thornscrub, and dust and wind blow across scattered pockets of civilization. And it is the Eisteddfod at Gaiman, a Welsh festival of the arts in a chapel nestled among the poplars, on a cloudless night, where boys in white shirts recite poetry and choirs sing as a culture fights a subsiding battle to maintain itself."

Recommended Reading *In Patagonia* by Bruce Chatwin, a good introduction to the area and its people. *Patagonia*, by Metzeltin and Buscaini (Dall' Oglio, Milan). *At Home with the*

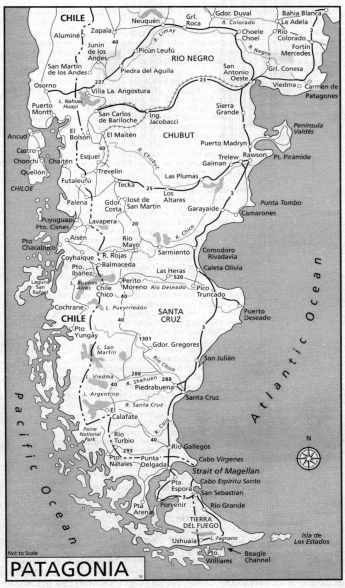

PATAGONIA

Not to Scale

Patagonians, by George Musters (history of 19th century life of Patagonian Indians), ed John Murray, London 1871/1973.

In all Patagonia there is only one town—Comodoro Rivadavia—with a population over 100,000. Most of the towns are small ports, which used only to work during the wool-shipping season but have livened up since the local economy began to diversify. The high tidal range makes it impossible in most of them for ships to tie up at the docks (except at Madryn and Punta Arenas, Chile).

Air Services Aerolíneas Argentinas and Austral from Buenos Aires either direct to Río Gallegos or calling at Bahía Blanca and Trelew or Comodoro Rivadavia on the way. Check if either airline is offering discounts on particular flights, which can result in considerable savings. Beware delays for bad weather. A new company, Almafuerte, flies direct to Puerto Madryn and Calafate.

Many air force LADE flights in the region S of Bariloche must be booked in advance from departure point of flight. The planes are small and fly low; passengers miss little of what there is to be seen, highly recommended for those who enjoy flying. The baggage allowance is 15 kg. Travellers are warned that the flights are often heavily booked ahead, but always check again on the day of the flight if you are told beforehand that it is sold out. Sometimes, through LADE, individual passengers are allowed to fly on air force carriers if planes are full or inopportune. LADE tickets are much cheaper for a long flight with stops than buying separate segments. LADE's computer reservation system is linked to Aerolíneas Argentinas, so flight connections are possible between these airlines. Also LADE's flights synchronize with both AR and Austral flights.

Roads The main road, Route 3, which runs near the coast, is now paved from Buenos Aires via Fitz Roy and down to Río Gallegos. S of this town to Ushuaia is all-weather in a bad state of repair as it is awaiting asphalt. Sometimes passengers going South have to pay for baggage by weight. Many buses do not operate between early Apr and late Oct.

The principal roads in Patagonia roughly form an inverted triangle. Route 3 has regular traffic and adequate services. At the S end, this route enters Chile and crosses the Magellan Straits to Tierra del Fuego by the car ferry at Primera Angostura. The W route (Route 40) zigzags across the moors, is lonely and is good in parts, poor in others (more details given below); there is hardly any traffic except in Dec, Jan and Feb, the tourist season. However, it is by far the more interesting road, with fine views of the Andes and plenty of wild life as well as the Alerces and Glaciares National Parks. Camping is no problem, and there are good hotels at Esquel, Perito Moreno, Calafate and (in Chile) Coyhaique and Puerto Natales. Third class accommodation also at Gobernador Gregores, Río Mayo and Esperanza. The N part of the triangle is formed by the paved highway running from Bariloche through Neuquén to San Antonio Oeste.

Many of the roads in Southern Argentina are gravelled. The price of a good windscreen protector varies according to make of car, but can be US$50 in Buenos Aires. For a VW Kombi they are hard to find at a reasonable price. More primitive versions can be bought for much less—eg US$5 in San Julián, and probably elsewhere—or made from wire mesh, wood and string. The best types to buy are the grid-type, or inflatable plastic ones which are made for some standard-type vehicles, the only disadvantage being some loss of visibility. Drivers should also look out for cattle grids (*guardaganados*), even on main highways. They are signed; cross them very slowly. Always carry plenty of fuel, as service stations may be as much as 300 km apart. Fuel prices are very low in Chubut and Santa Cruz provinces (except Bariloche), US$0.35 per litre, which is about half the price of the rest of the country.

Hitchhiking is generally difficult except on Route 3 in spring and summer; camping equipment is useful as long delays can be expected even in the tourist season.

The upper course of the Río Colorado is the N limit of Patagonia. 160 km S of where it reaches the sea (250 km S of Bahía Blanca), about 27 km from the mouth of the Río Negro, is **Carmen de Patagones** (16,000 people), standing on high ground on the N bank, with **Viedma** (26,000 people) the capital of Río Negro Province, across the river, which is spanned by a connecting rail and road bridge, pleasant setting. There is also a frequent ferry service for pedestrians. On a hill behind Patagones a monument commemorates an attack on the twin towns by a Brazilian squadron in 1827. (Beware of pleasant-looking campsites near this monument; there is an artillery range nearby.) There are three museums, open 1000-1200 only. The swimming is recommended on the Viedma side of the river, where there is a nice shady shore. A law was passed in 1986 nominating Viedma as the site of the new federal capital, but the project is unlikely ever to come to fruition.

Hotels At Viedma: **A1** *Helsingflors Hostería*, San Martín 516, T/F 20719 (BsAs T 824-3634); **C** *Austral*, Villarino 292, T 22019, rec, modern. **D** *Peumayen*, Buenos Aires 334, T 25243; **E** *Hotel Nueva Roma*, basic, fleas. *Restaurant Munich*, Buenos Aires 150, open late.

Camping Good municipal site 500m after crossing the river on the new road bridge on the right, US$14 per tent plus US$4 pp, all facilities incl hot showers, but can be noisy at weekends.

Exchange Travel agency at Namuncurá 78, Viedma, exchanges Amex cheques.

Tourist Office Belgrano 544, 9th floor, Viedma.

Transport Air From Buenos Aires with Austral daily except Sat (the city is also served by LADE). **Buses** Bus terminal at Calle A Zatti y Lavalle about 6 blocks from main plaza. To/from Buenos Aires US$45, La Estrella/Cóndor. To San Antonio Oeste, US$7.50.

Excursion Beautiful beach, El Cóndor, 30 km S of Viedma, 3 buses a day from Viedma in summer, hotel open Jan-Feb, restaurants and shops, free camping on beach 2 km S. 30 km from El Cóndor is a sealion colony (*lobería*); daily bus in summer from Viedma; hitching easy in summer.

Camping Further camping sites on the Río Negro where the main route into Patagonia meets the river (some 170 km from Viedma due NW) with all facilities incl a small shop. Additional shops at General Conesa, 2 km away. Mosquito repellent needed.

Almost due W and 180 km along the coast, on the Gulf of San Matías, is **San Antonio Oeste** (10,000 people). 17 km S is a popular seaside resort, *Las Grutas*, developed in the 1960s with good safe beach (the caves themselves are not really worth visiting); bus from San Antonio hourly US$1.30, ACA has a *Unidad Turística*, with 6-bed rooms, no restaurant. **D** *Tour du Golfe*, friendly, 3-bed rooms, cooking facilities. There are also many good camping sites (eg *La Entrada*, US$5 per tent, on edge of town above beach). Seafood restaurants. The whole of Las Grutas closes down in mid-Mar and retires to Buenos Aires. Between San Antonio and Puerto Madryn is Sierra Grande (ACA garage and café, camping at rear, no facilities but free hot showers at YPF garage in town), where iron-ore deposits are extracted and piped in solution to an ocean terminal 32 km E.

Hotels at San Antonio C *Kandava*, Sarmiento 240, T 21430, with bath, hot water, clean, good. **D** *Golfo Azul*, simple, clean; **D** *Iberia*, Sarmiento 241, with bath, but without breakfast, small rooms, but rec.

Railway via Viedma to **Bahía Blanca** and **Buenos Aires** and W to **Bariloche**. Timetable from Buenos Aires as for Bariloche; train passes through San Antonio Oeste at 1953 en route to Bariloche, 1002 to Bahía Blanca.

Buses From San Antonio N to **Bahía Blanca** and S to **Río Gallegos** and **Punta Arenas** by Transportes Patagónicos. To **Viedma** 0700 daily, US$7.50. To **Puerto Madryn** and **Trelew**, Don Otto, 0200 and 1530, 4 hrs, US$20. To **Buenos Aires**, US$46 via Bahía Blanca, frequent.

Route to Neuquén and Bariloche: paved. From San Antonio Oeste a road runs N 91 km through bush country providing fodder for a few cattle, with a view to the W of the salt flats called

Salina del Gualicho, before joining Route 250 which meets the Zapala-Bahía Blanca highway (Route 22) at Choele Choel, 178 km N of San Antonio Oeste (**see p 170, and Roads** p 171).

About 250 km S, along Route 3 (paved) in Chubut province is **Puerto Madryn**, a port on the Golfo Nuevo. It was founded by the Welsh colonist, Parry Madryn, in 1865. Population, 42,000. Ask at tourist office about visits to the alumina plant. The town is becoming a popular tourist centre, with a casino, skin-diving and nature reserves, both near the town and on the nearby Valdés peninsula. Museo de Ciencias Naturales y Oceanográfico on Domecq García and J Menéndez, informative and worth a visit (open 1600-2000, closed Mon), entry US$2, ask to see video. No Youth Hostel.

Hotels (Often full in summer, make bookings early.) **A1** *Península Valdés*, JA Roca 155, T 71292 4-star, sea view, suites available, comfortable, rec; **A2** *Playa*, Roca 181, T 50732, overpriced but safe, clean, only Spanish spoken; **A3** *Yanco*, Av Roca 626, T 71581, on beach, nightly entertainment programme, free, has rooms for up to 6; **A3** *Gran Madryn I*, L Lugones 40, T 72205, 2-star, friendly, clean, good; **A3** *Hostal del Rey*, Blvd. Brown 681, T 71156, on beach, rec, 2-star, clean, breakfast US$4; **B** *Muelle Viejo*, Yrigoyen 38, T 71284, opposite pier, good restaurant, expensive breakfast, good, clean, quiet; **B** *Hostería Hipocampo*, Bvd Marítimo 33, clean, helpful, but overpriced; **B** *Tolosa*, R Sáenz Peña 250, T 71850, 3-star, friendly, no English spoken, no evening meal, noisy; **C** *Apart-Motel Palma*, Av Roca 7, T 74044, heated, showers, clean, warm, kitchen facilities; **C** *Atalaya*, Domecq García 149, T 73006, with bath, noisy; **C** *Backpackers*, 25 de Mayo 1136, T 74426, clean, friendly, kitchen facilities; **C** *El Dorado*, San Martín 546, T 71026, clean, shower, patio, a bit run down, landlady not keen on backpackers; **C** *Español*, 28 de Julio y San Martín, clean, basic, hot water, restaurant, parking; **C** *Gran Palace*, Av 28 de Julio 390, T 71009, clean; **C** *Motel ACA*, Marcos A Zar e Irigoyen, T 71452; **C** *Residencial Petit*, Alvear 845, T 51460, with bath, clean, quiet, good. **D** *Anciamar*, 25 de Mayo 875, T 51509 clean, quiet, rec; **D** *Antiguo*, 28 de Julio 170, T 71742, good, clean, friendly; **D** *Hospedaje* at 25 de Mayo 763, central, quiet; **D** *Residencial La Posta*, Av Roca 33, T 72422, good, huge rooms, cooking facilities; **D** *Residencial Jo's*, Bolívar 75, T 71433, pleasant; **D** *Vaskonia*, 25 de Mayo 43, T 72581, hot water, friendly, good value.

Camping All closed out of season. At Punta Cuevas, 3.5 km S of town, is ACA site with evening hot showers, good facilities and shady trees (ACA members only, US$8 per tent for 2) but many people camp on beach. There is a swimming pool in the rocks near the ACA camp site, which gets its water at high tide, very pleasant, and free. Two municipal sites: one at Ribera Sur, 1 km before ACA site on same road along beach (gives student discount). All facilities, very crowded, US$3 pp and US$2 per tent for first day. Also rm with bunkbeds, F pp. Bus from town stops 100m before entrance. The other is N of town at Barrio Brown. Camping out can be interesting as one can watch foxes, armadillos, skunks and rheas roaming around in the evening.

Restaurants *Las Aguilas*, MA Zar and RS Peña, rec, good for seafood; *Cantina El Náutico*, Julio Roca and Lugones, good food, especially fish; *París*, RS Peña by Muelle Piedrabuena, good and reasonably priced; *Pizzería Roselli*, Peña y JA Roca, cheap, good, with vegetarian selections; *Parrilla Mayoral*, RS Peña 12; *Parrilla Estela*, RS Peña 27, reasonable prices; *Quijote*, Belgrano 138, reasonable prices, very good; *Barbarians*, 25 de Mayo y 28 de Julio, good coffee. For excellent Welsh afternoon teas, *La Goleta*, Roca 87, 1700-1900 (poor sign, but good tea, US$7).

Banks and Exchange Banco de la Nación, 25 de Mayo y 9 de Julio, go early to avoid long queues, high commission. **Banco del Sud**, Calle Sáenz Peña, advances cash on Visa, 4% commission. **Banco Provincia Chubut**, 25 de Mayo, has Mastercard and Diners ATM (will give dollars). There are no *cambios* as such, apart from Turismo Pu-Ma, 28 de Julio 46 (2% commission for TCs), but fair rates from travel agents (eg Safari Submarino, address below; go in the morning). **La Moneda**, Roca y 28 de Julio, will exchange large sums, not very good rates. Some shops will change US$ cash. High commission on changing cheques, incl at **Banco de la Nación** (but not always, it seems).

Laundromat *Laverap*, 25 de Mayo 529, highly rec.

Post Office Belgrano y A Maiz. **Telephone Office** 28 de Julio, also fax.

Sport Puerto Madryn is being promoted as a diving centre. Tours for those who have never dived before are organized by *Safari Submarino*, Mitre 80; *Pimino* in the harbour, all about US$60 per excursion. A few others along the harbour, ask for Fernando Alonso, rec; all show nature videos at about 1930. Swim in the so-called *parque submarino* amid sunken cars and

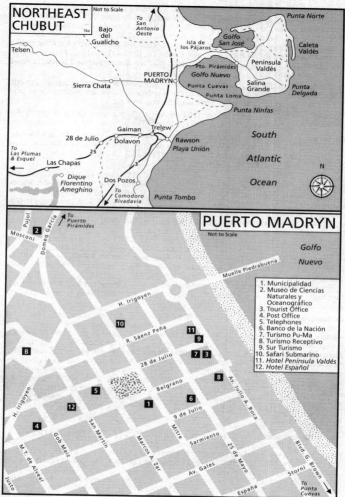

NORTHEAST CHUBUT

To San Antonio Oeste

Bajo del Gualicho

Telsen

Isla de los Pájaros

Golfo San José

Punta Norte

Caleta Valdés

Sierra Chata

PUERTO MADRYN

Pto. Pirámides

Golfo Nuevo

Península Valdés

Punta Cuevas

Salina Grande

Punta Delgada

28 de Julio

Gaiman

Trelew

Punta Loma

Punta Ninfas

Las Chapas

Dolavon

Rawson

Playa Unión

South

To Las Plumas & Esquel

Dique Florentino Ameghino

Dos Pozos

To Comodoro Rivadavia

Punta Tombo

Atlantic

Ocean

N

PUERTO MADRYN

Not to Scale

To Puerto Pirámides

Golfo

Nuevo

Muelle Piedrabuena

1. Municipalidad
2. Museo de Ciencias Naturales y Oceanográfico
3. Tourist Office
4. Post Office
5. Telephones
6. Banco de la Nación
7. Turismo Pu-Ma
8. Turismo Receptivo
9. Sur Turismo
10. Safari Submarino
11. *Hotel Península Valdés*
12. *Hotel Español*

a few fish! Trained divers seriously interested in marine life who have at least a week's stay should contact the Centro Nacional Patagónico at Av Roca. Windsurfing lessons and equipment hire at Brown 871.

Tourist Agencies Several agencies do tours to the Valdés Peninsula, all are for 12 hours, see below. Prices are fixed by law, but itineraries may differ. Tour rates increase by 75% on 15 Nov and again on 15 Dec by the same amount. By far the largest agency is *Sur Turismo*, JA Roca 175, T 73585, whose tours may have over-large groups and give insufficient time (this applies to other agencies too), reports of reservations not honoured and poor organization, check all details with care. Other agencies incl: *Tur-Mar*, T 74104, 25 de Mayo 167, reportedly sensitive approach to conservation; *Pu-Ma*, 28 de Julio 48, T 71482, mixed reports; *Mar y Valle*, Roca 37, T 72872, rec. *Receptivo*, Roca 303 y Belgrano, T 51048, Amex agent, weekend and off-season tours, their guide Luis speaks excellent English and is an expert on marine biology and ornithology, rec; *Prima Tur*, 28 de Julio; *Coyun Co*, Roca 171, T 51845. *Franca del Sur*, Reconquista 378, T 50710, small groups, Spanish only, rec. **Recommended guide**: Dr Pedro Fuentes Gallardo.

Tourist Office, at Julio Roca 223, T 73029, open until 2400 in the tourist season, but only 0700-1800 Mon-Fri in winter; helpful, has notice board for messages, list of current hotel rates and interesting video on the region, but inaccurate bus information.

Car Hire Very expensive (US$150/day, 1994). *Fiorasi*, on Sarmiento; Localiza, Belgrano 196, T 71660; Cuyun-Co, Roca 171. Filling station in Puerto Pirámides are not rec, untrustworthy.

Air Services Daily from Buenos Aires at 1230 via Trelew with Austral; Mon and Sat from Ushuaia with Kaiken; from Comodoro Rivadavia on Mon with LADE. Airport is 7 km from town, no buses, taxi or *remise* only, US$7-8. LADE office at Roca 117, T 51256; Aerolíneas Argentinas, 25 de Mayo 146, T 50110; Almafuerte, Roca 303, T 51108.

Buses Terminal in old railway station: to **Buenos Aires**, US$79; daily at 1415 and 2030, with El Cóndor, and with Costera Criolla at 2115, via San Antonio Oeste, change at Bahía Blanca, 22-24 hrs. To **Río Gallegos**, about 20 hrs, daily at 1730, US$71 (20% student discount). To **Bahía Blanca** 0800 and 1000 daily, 12 hrs, US$32; 10½ hrs, US25, with La Puntual to **Mar del Plata**, changing at Bahía Blanca. Patagónicos to **San Antonio Oeste** at 0800 and 2230, US$20, 4 hrs. To **Trelew** with 28 de Julio company, every 90 minutes, more frequent in summer, 60 mins at 15 mins past hour, US$3.50; driver will stop at entrance to Trelew airport if asked; direct to Trelew airport hourly at half past the hour, US$3.50, 45 mins journey, or Puma (28 de Julio), US$5, leaves 1½ hrs before flight and takes arriving passengers back to Puerto Madryn (taxi to airport US$45). Don Otto to **Comodoro Rivadavia**, Wed, Thur, Fri, Sun 0915 and daily at 1600, US$26. No direct bus to **Bariloche**, change at Trelew and Esquel (7 hr wait), US$60. Taxi rank on the plaza.

For hitching N, try on the industrial estate road, or take a Trelew bus to the main highway then walk 3 km to the service station/truck stop. With luck it is possible to get to Bahía Blanca in one day.

Excursions There are nature reserves at Punta Loma on Golfo Nuevo (sea-lions), only 15 km S of Puerto Madryn area itself, sea-lions even invading the harbour); and also on the Valdés Peninsula at Punta Pirámides (sea-lions) and Isla de los Pájaros (sea birds), Golfo San José and Punta Norte (right whales), see below. (Check opening times of reserves in Puerto Madryn; they vary.) The natural history of the region is most interesting, with other seal and penguin colonies, breeding ground at Golfo Nuevo for right whales, fossils in the cliffs, and guanacos, rheas and armadillos in the countryside. Most animals (except the whale) can be seen in the warm seasons, from Oct to Apr. See whales from perhaps as early as Jun to, at the very latest, end-Dec. Oct-Nov is said to be the time to see the greatest variety of wildlife. There is less wildlife after Dec, a point not made by tour agencies. Past the lighthouse and Naval Zone at Punta Delgada on the other side of the Valdés Peninsula is Salina Grande, 35m below sea level. Naturatur, 9 de Julio 280, have information on local flora and fauna.

The **Punta Loma** sealion reserve is open 0900-1200, 1430-1730, Sep, and Oct, are the best months. Information and video. Entry US$2. Taxis US$25; Tur-Mar does 12-hour US$40 pp trip to Punta Loma and the Florentino Ameghino dam, 110 km inland on the Río Chubut. The dam covers 7,000 ha with water and irrigates 28,000 ha in the lower Chubut valley, as well as producing electric power.

Peninsula Valdes The centre for visits to the Peninsula is **Puerto Pirámides** (pop 100), 90 km E of Puerto Madryn. Entrance fee US$5. About 79 km E of Puerto Madryn, near the entrance to the peninsula, is Isla de los Pájaros. No one is now allowed to visit the island without special permission (only granted to recognized ornithologists). At Punta Norte (176 km) at the N end of the Valdés Peninsula, there are elephant seals (breeding time in first fortnight in Aug, best seen at low tide), late spring and summer (Nov-Mar), reasonably priced restaurant for meals and snacks. At Caleta Valdés, 45 km S of Punta Norte you can see penguins and elephant seals at close quarters, but not at any specific point. Camping at hangar nearby, but take fresh water with you as supplies are unreliable. At Punta Delgada (at the S of the peninsula) most wildlife can be seen except the penguins, which have moved away (*Hotel Faro*, A+, comfortable, excellent food, rec, reservations at *Hotel Peninsula Valdes* in Puerto Madryn). The peninsula is private property. One third belongs to one man, who grazes 40,000 sheep. In theory, the beach on the entire coast is out of bounds, although this is not strictly enforced. A Conservation Officer is permanently stationed at the entrance to the Peninsula (he is very helpful).

Puerto Pirámides Services A2 *ACA Motel*, T 72057, poor restaurant; **B** *Residencial El Libanés*, T 95007; **D** *España*, basic but clean, friendly; *Posada del Mar*, friendly, restaurant; **E** pp *Paradise Pub*, cheapest, good value food and beer, good atmosphere; municipal campsite by the black sand beach (whales may be visible in season) US$5 pp (free out of season), hot showers in evening only, dirty, busy, get there early to secure a place. In summer there are several well-stocked shops, but if staying take sun and wind protection and drinking water. There is a shop that sells original Patagonian Indian work. There is also a small tourist office on the edge of town, useful information for hikes and driving tours. Service station open on Sun. Hydro Sports rents scuba equipment and boats, has a small restaurant, and organizes land and sea wildlife tours (ask for Mariano), boat trips US$20 for 1 hour. Bus (Empresa 28 de Julio) from Puerto Madryn, Thur, Sun at 1000 returns 1800, US$6.50 each way.

Excursions are organized by tourist agencies in Puerto Madryn (addresses above). The usual tour takes in Puerto Pirámides, Caleta Valdés (or Punta Norte) and Isla de los Pájaros (seen through fixed telescopes from a distance of 400m). Shop around, but most agencies charge the same: about US$25-30 pp plus the US$5 entry to the National Park; boat trip to see whales US$20 extra; there are two companies running boat trips from Puerto Pirámides into Golfo Nuevo to see whales, the one on the right as you face the water (Tito Botazzi, T 95016) is better. Trips last about 9 hrs, starting at 0800. On all excursions take drink with you, food too if you don't want to eat in the expensive restaurants (swimsuit, towel and binoculars are also a good idea). Most tour companies stay 50-60 minutes on location, not considered sufficient by some (Siempre Tur are reported to stay longer). Off season tours run regularly only on Thur and Sun, departing at 0955 and returning at 1730. The peninsula is easily reached if one has one's own car, in fact the best way to see the wildlife is by car. Hiring a vehicle is very expensive (US$150 per day), but taking a taxi is worth considering if you can get a group together (taxi US$30 pp for the day). Hitching is very difficult, even at weekends in season. Peninsular roads are variable: from Puerto Madryn to Puerto Pirámides is a good dirt road; from Puerto Pirámides to Punta Norte is degenerating and the road between Punta Norte and Punta Delgada is gravel (tours will not run after heavy rain in the low season).

There are also tours from Puerto Madryn to Punta Tombo **(see p 198)**, US$25 plus US$5 entrance fee with Receptivo, but these usually incl "sight-seeing" in Rawson, Trelew and Gaiman and a lot of time is spent travelling, with only about 1 hr at the Reserve. It is cheaper to visit from Trelew.

NB If possible check all excursion dates in advance; it is very disappointing to arrive in Puerto Madryn only to find that one cannot reach the wildlife reserves. From Mar to Sep (when there is less wildlife to be seen) it may be necessary to take a taxi, but we are informed that the tours run all year, depending on numbers. Tours are cheaper from Madryn than from Trelew, probably because Trelew has the airport.

Along the Río Chubut are several towns. *Rawson* (pop 15,000), the capital of Chubut Province, 7 km from the sea, has law courts, a museum in the Colegio Don Bosco, a fishing port, and a riverside Tourist Office, 9 de Julio 64, T 213. Puerto Rawson is about 5 km down river; you can camp on the beach, and *Cantina El Marinero* serves good seafood (regular buses from Rawson).

Hotels B *Provincial*, Mitre 551, T 81300, clean but dilapidated, good restaurant; *Residencial Papaiani*, A Maiz 377; *Residencial San Pedro*, Belgrano 744.

Some 20 km up the Río Chubut is **Trelew** (pop 61,000), a prosperous town which has lost its Welsh look. There is a pretty red-brick chapel in the centre (rec Sun mornings for Welsh speakers), and a small, interesting museum in the old railway station, open 0700-1300, 1400-2000 Mon-Fri, 1500-1900 Sat, US$3. On the road to Rawson, 500m before the bridge is Chapel Moriah, a beautiful 1880 Welsh chapel, with the graves of many original settlers. The Museo Paleontológico Egidio Feruglio, 9 de Julio 655, open 1600-2300 daily (US$3, Spanish only), has a collection of Patagonian fossils, including some of prehistoric reptiles, and is located in the Parque Paleontológico Bryn-Gwyn. A paved road runs from Rawson through Trelew, Gaiman **(see p 197)** and Dolavon, all on the river, to Las Plumas (mind the bridge if driving) and the upper Chubut Valley, all the way to Esquel **(see p 184)** and Trevelin.

Local Holidays 28 Jul (Founding of Chubut); 13 Dec (Petroleum Day).

Hotels L3 *Rayentray*, San Martín y Belgrano, T 34702, best in town, well run, comfortable; **A2** *Centenario*, San Martín 150, T 30041, expensive restaurant; **A3** *Libertador*, Rivadavia 254, T 35132, without breakfast, 4 blocks from Plaza, good rooms, poor restaurant, quiet, friendly, good value; **B** *Galicia*, 9 de Julio y Rivadavia, T 33803, very warm, without bath, clean; **B** *Parque*, Irigoyen y Cangallo, T 30098, good; **B** *Touring Club*, Av Fontana 240, T 33998, excellent, with bath, a bit dark, book in advance in high season, the social hub of Trelew but run down, chess is played here, colour TV, breakfast rec, coffee the best in town; **C** *Argentino*, Abraham Matthews 186, T 36134, without bath, clean, quiet, breakfast available, good, near bus station; **C** *Provincia*, Yrigoyen 625, T 31544, poor and noisy; **C** *Residencial San Carlos*, Sarmiento 758, T 31538, rec; **C** *Rivadavia*, Rivadavia 55, T 34472, with bath, clean, rec; **D** *Plaza*, with breakfast, on main square, clean, very good rooms; **D** *Residencial Patterson*, Moreno 280, T 31636; **D** *Hostal Avenida*, Lewis Jones 49, T 34172, close to bus station, lots of character, rooms basic but clean, friendly, quiet. Raul G Lerma, Don Bosco 109, offers camping space in garden and local information, speaks English.

Camping By the river, S of the town on the road to Rawson, on right about 200m beyond the bridge over River Chubut, US$12, dirty, run-down, beware of mosquitoes; take Rawson bus, No 7 or 25. The site belongs to the Sports Club and has a public swimming pool.

Restaurants *Don Facundo*, Fontana 213, good, cheap, rec; *Eulogia Fuentes*, Don Bosco 23, good pasta; *El Quijote*, 25 de Mayo 90, good food and service; *Sugar*, 25 de Mayo 247, good fast food; *El Mesón*, Rivadavia 588, seafood; *El Marfil*, Italia 42, good, cheap; *Rotisería La Primera*, San Martín y A P Bell, pasta, pizza, empanadas, good, take-away service; *Cabildo Star*, Roca 88, excellent and cheap pizzas; *Capítulo II*, Roca 393, *tenedor libre*, good and cheap; *La Casa de Juan*, Moreno 360, cosy, good pizzas; *Café Vittorio*, Belgrano 341, good service.

Exchange Lloyds Bank (BLSA), Av 9 de Julio y Belgrano, does not change TCs, unhelpful, cash advance on Visa but high charge for call to verify card; **Banco Provincia del Chubut**, Rivadavia y 25 de Mayo. Local banks. Open 0800-1200. None changes TCs. **Banco del Sud**, 9 de Julio 320, only accepts dollar bills in mint condition; cash advance on Visa, high commission. Difficult to change cheques.

Post Office 25 de Mayo and Mitre. **Telephones** Julio A Roca 1-100 block, open till 2400.

Tourist Agencies *Sur Turismo*, Belgrano 326-330, organize good excursions to Punta Tombo (US$25 pp), Península Valdés (US$58 pp) and Florentino Ameghino dam, T 34550; *Estrella del Sur Turismo*, San Martin 129, T 31282, tours to Valdés Peninsula and Punta Tombo, rec; *Punta Tombo Turismo*, San Martín 150, T 20358; and others. Tours to Valdés Peninsula are more expensive than from Puerto Madryn and take longer, about 12-13 hrs. Best to go in a small tour bus which can get closer to main wildlife viewing sites.

Tourist Office, room 20 on 1st floor of Terminal Terrestre, additionally opens briefly at 0515 for travellers arriving from Esquel, also at airport and at Italia y Rioja, friendly but not always accurate. Free maps and self-guided city tour.

Car Hire Expensive (cheaper to take a tour to Punta Tombo and Península Valdés). 3 companies at the airport; desks are manned only at flight arrival times and cars are snapped up quickly. Localiza, Urquiza 310, T 35344, also at airport.

Air Airport 5 km from centre; taxis cost about US$8. Buses from Puerto Madryn stop at the turning to the airport (10 mins walk; bus from turning to Puerto Madryn, US$3; also hourly buses from terminal to Puerto Madryn, US$3.50, and Puna airport bus, US$5). LADE (Av Fontana 227, T 35925, poor service) flies, **Trelew-Bariloche**, twice a week and to Comodoro Rivadavia twice a week. Aerolíneas Argentinas (25 de Mayo 33, T 34244) flies BsAs-Trelew-Río Gallegos-Ushuaia daily. Austral (same address as AR) also flies to/from BsAs daily. Austral flights from Buenos Aires have a direct bus connection to **Puerto Madryn**. TAN (T 34550) to Neuquén twice a week. LAPA flies BsAs-Trelew-Comodoro Rivadavia-Río Gallegos twice a week and BsAs-Trelew-Comodoro Rivadavia once a week. The Aero Club sells sightseeing flights.

Buses from **Buenos Aires** to Trelew, 4 daily, 21½ hrs (return 0700 and 2130 daily, 1705 Tues, Thur, Fri and Sat, US$83). Bus to **Bahía Blanca**, 734 km, US$32 daily with Don Otto (T 32434), 0600, few a week with La Puntual, 0600; to **Mar del Plata**, changing at Bahía Blanca, US$35 with La Puntual; to **Esquel**, US$32, 2130, 11 hrs with Empresa Chubut (good road, lots of wildlife, spectacular scenery, rec); bus to **Bariloche** daily. Buses to **Rawson** every 15 min; new 1½ hours to **Gaiman** (pop 4,400), US$1.15; every 60 minutes to **Puerto Madryn**, US$3.50 with 28 de Julio; to **Comodoro Rivadavia** daily at 2000, and Sun, Wed, Thur and Fri at 1035, US$26, 4 hrs; to **Río Gallegos**, daily at 1900, US$70. If **hitching** south from Trelew, take the

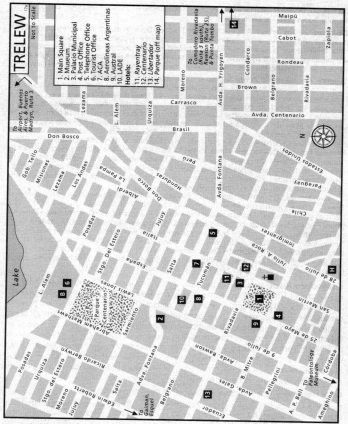

TRELEW
Not to scale

1. Main Square
2. Museum
3. Palacio Municipal
4. Post Office
5. Telephone Office
6. Tourist Office
7. ACA
8. Aerolíneas Argentinas
9. Austral
10. LADE

Hotels:
11. Rayentray
12. Centenario
13. Libertador
14. Parque (off map)

Rawson bus to the flyover 5 km out of town; there is a junction N of town for Puerto Madryn traffic.

Gaiman (pop 4,400), 18 km W of Trelew, a pretty place with well-built brick houses but quite touristy, is now the most Welsh of the Chubut valley towns. It has a museum of the colony, US$0.50, in the old railway station (open in summer, Tues-Sat 1600-2000, in winter, Tues-Sat 1500-1800, curator Mrs Roberts is "full of stories"). The only restaurant seems often to be closed, but tea rooms such as *Casa de Té Gaiman*, Yrigoyen 738, excellent, and those opposite the square, *Plas y Coed*, Miguel D Jones 123 (oldest, excellent tea "and enough food for a week", US$10, Marta Rees speaks English and is very knowledgeable about the area, highly rec) and *Ty Gwyn*, 9 de Julio 111, *Ty Nain* Yrigoyen 283 (excellent, US$12, frequented by tour buses), and *Elma*, Tello 571, serve enormous Welsh teas from 1500 for US$8-10. Small municipal campground by river (poor, no facilities). Interesting local agriculture. Welsh-speakers will be interested in the cemetery above town. The Eisteddfod, Welsh festival of arts, is held in early Oct each year. Interesting walking tours led by volunteer guides (Spanish-speaking—meet in main plaza) incl a private, hand-made (out of beer bottles and string!) theme park (El Desafío—US$5, tickets valid 2 months), a seaweed factory and the *Ty*

Naín tearoom which has a nice display of historical items. All facilities are closed out of season. Regular buses from Trelew in season.

Dolavon, 20 km further W is easily reached by bus from Trelew. It still retains some Welsh character and provides an interesting view of the irrigation system built by the settlers. The old flour mill/museum is superb, but not easy to find: it is completely intact and demonstrations will be given. Key kept by owner of nearby tea-room. There is a campsite: turn right by the service station on the way into town, good facilities, free (Wendy Chilcott and Steve Newman).

Wildlife may be seen at **Punta Tombo** and Camarones. Punta Tombo is 117 km S of Trelew, on a dirt road which branches off the road to Rawson, 5 km SE of Trelew: driving time 1¾ hours (this is incorrectly shown on ACA maps). Park entrance US$5. There the wildlife is very varied: penguins, guanacos, etc. Season for penguins, Sep-Mar (Dec-Jan is the time when the young are taking to the water); the Reserve closes after Mar. Check with the Tourist Office that it is all right to visit the penguins as from late Mar they are "off limits" as they prepare to migrate. When visits are permitted it is a fantastic experience. You can share a taxi from Trelew (US$30 pp). Sur Turismo and others run ½ day tours, spending ½ hour at the site for US$25 (standard fee, not incl park entry). About mid-way between Rawson and Punta Tombo, a road leads off Ruta 1 to Isla Escondida (9 km, signed), no facilities, but lovely rock and sand beach with bird and wildlife (badly littered unfortunately); secluded camping. Good place to camp if you are visiting the wildlife at Punta Tombo early am (the best time). When leaving the park, ask the guard for the shortest route back to Ruta 3. There is an E/W road not shown on most maps.

Camarones, 275 km S of Trelew and 300 km N of Comodoro Rivadavia, is less crowded. There is a large **penguin colony** 35 km away at Cabo Dos Bahías along a dirt road (US$5, open all year); free camping is possible there and in the town itself (**C** *Hotel Kau-i-Keuken*, clean, friendly, good food, rec, owner runs trips to penguin colony; 2 others, **D**, the one by the power station is not rec). Local buses very scarce; two a week, US$10, on Mon and Fri from Trelew (Don Otto), book at Uruguay 590, Trelew; bus leaves 0800 from San Martín and Belgrano, arrives 1130, returns to Trelew same day 1600. In Camarones ask the Guardia Fauna on Mon or Fri for a lift, hitchhiking is difficult, but possible at weekends and taxis are unavailable (a private car will charge US$50-60, ask at Busca Vida).

Comodoro Rivadavia, the largest city in the province of Chubut (pop 158,000), is 387 km S of Trelew. Petroleum was discovered here in 1907 and about 30% of all Argentina's oil production comes from wells to the S and W. A 1,770-km pipeline carries the natural gas to Buenos Aires, and there is a petrochemical plant. Renewed interest in the local oil industry is making the town boom. There is an Oil Museum, with exhibits on exploration and production, 3 km N in Gral Mosconi (bus No 6 from San Martín y Abasolo). From here southward, prices begin to rise very rapidly, so stock up before reaching Río Gallegos (although bear in mind you are not allowed to take food into Chile). Good beach at Rada Tilly, 12 km S (buses every ½ hr) walk along beach at low tide to see sealions.

Local Holidays 28 Jul (Founding of Chubut); 13 Dec (Petroleum Day).

Hotels A3 *Austral*, Rivadavia 190, T 32200, noise from traffic but otherwise comfortable, reasonable restaurant; **A3** *Comodoro*, 9 de Julio 770, T 32300, overpriced, restaurant, night clubs, car rental; **B** *Residencial Azul*, Sarmiento 724, T 24874, comfortable, spotless, rec; **D** *Colón*, San Martín 341, T 22283, run down, but quiet, safe and cheap; **D** *Comercio*, Rivadavia 341, T 22341, friendly, old fashioned, dirty, near bus station, hot showers, good meals; *Pensión Boedo*, Rivadavia 453, cheap restaurant, mediocre food; **D** *Hospedaje Belgrano*, Belgrano 546, T 24313, with bath, clean, hot water; **D** *Diana*, on Belgrano, clean, friendly; **D** *Hospedaje Praga*, España y Sarmiento, shower, clean; **D** *Rada Tilly*, Av Piedrabuena, in Rada Tilly 5 km S, T 51032, modern, clean. *Motel Astra*, access (S) of Route 3, T 25394.

Camping Municipal and ACA, 12 km S at Rada Tilly, may be reached by Expreso Rada Tilly bus from town. Excellent facilities, hot and cold water. There is another, free, campsite at N end of beach, cold water only (watch out for clayslides when it rains).

Restaurants *La Rastra*, Rivadavia 384, very good for churrasco, but not much else; *Cocorico* (better) and *El Náutico*, Playa Costanera. *Pizzería El Nazareño*, San Martín y España, good. *Bom-Bife*, España 832, good food, inexpensive. Several *rotiserías*, much cheaper, on 400 block of Rivadavia, in municipal market.

Banks and Exchange Lloyds Bank (BLSA), Av Rivadavia 276. Oct-Mar 0700-1300; Apr-Sep 1200-1800; no exchange transactions after 1000 in summer, 6% commission on TCs, will pay dollars cash on cheques but minimum US$300; the **Banco de la Nación**, San Martín 108, has the best rates on US$ but does not change TCs. Amex agent is **Orbe Turismo Show**, San Martín 488, T 29699, 5% commission for US$ or peso cheques. *Hotel Comodoro* changes US$ at poor rate. Several travel agencies also change money incl **Roqueta Travel**, Rivadavia y Pellegrini, **Ceferino**, 9 de Julio 852, and **CRD Travel**, Moreno 844 (TCs).

Consulates Belgian Vice-Consul, Rivadavia 283; **Chilean Consul**, Sarmiento 936; **Italian Vice-Consul**, Belgrano 1053.

Post Office San Martín y Moreno.

Travel agencies *Puelche EVT*, Rivadavia 527; *Richard Pentreath*, Mitre 952; *San Gabriel* and *Atlas* at San Martín 488 and 263, respectively; *Monitur*, 9 de Julio 948.

Tourist Office On Rivadavia.

VW dealer, Comercial Automotor, Rivadavia 380, rec. VW concession in Barrio Industrial, Av Irigoyen, also rec.

Air Services Airport, 9 km. Bus to airport from downtown terminal or opp Aerolíneas Argentinas in main street (T 24781), hourly (45 mins), US$0.40; take bus No 6. Once a day to **Buenos Aires** with Aerolíneas (direct) or Austral, stopping at Bahía Blanca daily, except Sun; Austral at 9 de Julio 870, T 22191; Austral daily, except Sun, to **Río Gallegos** and **Río Grande**; LAPA 3 a week to BsAs and Trelew, 2 a week to Río Gallegos; LADE (Rivadavia 360, T 36181) flies once a week (Wed) Comodoro Rivadavia-Perito Moreno-Gobernador Gregores Calafate/Lago Argentino-Río Gallegos-Río Grande-Ushuaia, and on Mon to Puerto Deseado-San Julián-Gob Gregores-Calafate-Río Turbio-Río Gallegos-Santa Cruz; once a week to Bariloche via Trelew and Viedma, or Trelew and Esquel, or via Esquel, El Maitén and El Bolsón; other services to Neuquén via the Lake District (also TAN 6 a week) and to Trelew (also TAN). TAN also flies to Bariloche, Río Gallegos and Puerto Deseado. Kaiken fly to Ushuaia via Río Grande, Río Gallegos and Lago Argentino Tues and Sat. Taxi to airport, US$7.

Buses Bus station conveniently located in city centre; has luggage store, good *confitería* upstairs, lousy toilets, *remise* taxi booth, some kiosks. Bus service to **Buenos Aires** daily at 1200 and 2115, 32 hrs, US$108 (same fare on Costera Criolla; also daily with La Estrella/Cóndor at 1335). Angel Giobbi buses to **Coyhaique** (Chile), US$28.50, 12 hrs, twice a week (Tues and Fri), 0100, Jun-Sep and 3 a week (Mon, Wed, Fri), 0100, Oct-May (weather permitting). Three buses a week to **Bariloche**, US$55 (Don Otto at 2150, Sun, Tues, Thur, stops at Sarmiento midnight, Esquel at 0600 and for ½ hr at El Bolsón at 0900, arrives 0600 at Bariloche). To **Esquel** (paved road) direct, Fri 1230, 10 hrs, via Río Mayo, Mon, Thur, 0100, 15½ hrs, to Río Mayo Tues, Thur, Sun, 1700 and 1900, 5½ hrs. In summer buses heading S usually arrive full. To **Río Gallegos**, Don Otto 2345 daily, and Transportes Patagónica 2200 daily, US$40, reserve or standby. To **Puerto Madryn** and **Trelew**, US$26, at 1200. La Unión colectivo to **Caleta Olivia**, hourly, US$3.50. To **Sarmiento**, US$7, 2½ hrs at 0700, 1300, 1900. To **Mendoza**, daily at 0130, 20 hrs; to **Córdoba**, Tues, Fri, Sun, 1200, 33 hrs.

Hitchhiking There is a truck stop outside Comodoro Rivadavia on Route 3, the road to Bahía Blanca, where you can contact drivers whether heading N or S. Hitch out of the centre on Ruta 3 to "Astra Km 20", or take any bus going N. Expensive truckdrivers' restaurants along the road; buy food in supermarkets.

The road to Chile runs inland from Comodoro Rivadavia, amid oil wells, to (156 km) Colonia Sarmiento (commonly known just as **Sarmiento**), population: 7,000 (archaeological museum with tourist office next to cathedral, check opening times, may be closed at weekends), on Lago Musters, near the large Lago Colhué Huapi. 32 km by dirt road S of Sarmiento there is a large petrified forest, the Bosque Petrificado José Ormachea (**see p 201**), well worth a visit but difficult to reach (contact Sr Valero, the park ranger, for guided tours, ask at *Hotel Colón*).

Hotels and Restaurants *Lago Musters*, P Moreno y Coronel, T 93097; **C** *Hostería Los Lagos*, Roca y Alberdi, T 93046, good, friendly, heating, restaurant; **E** *Colón*, P Moreno 645, restaurant, cheap, friendly; *San Martín*, San Martín y P Moreno, cheap, good restaurant. Food at *El Gaucho*, Route 20, access Sarmiento. *Ismar*, Patagonia 248; *Oroz*, 200 block of Uruguay. In Dec-Mar you may be permitted to sleep in the Agricultural School (take sleeping bag) on the road to petrified forest, opp the ACA petrol station.

Camping Municipal site 2 km N of centre on Route 24, basic, no shower, US$3 for tent, US$1 pp, beside river.

Travel Agency Julio Lew, Roca and Alberdi.

Bus Overnight buses to **Esquel** on Sun, Tues and Thur, stop at Rio Mayo, 0630, take food for journey as cafés on route tend to overcharge. 3 buses a day to **Comodoro Rivadavia**, 0700, 1300, 1900 and Giobbi buses to **Chile** leave at 0200.

From Sarmiento you can reach Esquel (448 km N along Route 40), at the S edge of the Lake District (see p 184). The first 210 km from Sarmiento are paved, then it is mostly a dirt or all-weather road, though short stretches have been paved. Hitching along this road is very difficult, even in summer.

From Sarmiento the road continues W via *Río Mayo* (pop 2,260, 4 hotels, **D** *Covadonga*, very good; **D** *Hotel Pingüino*; **D** *A'Ayones*, T 20044, clean, modern, heating; **F** pp *San Martín*), and the Chilean frontier at Coyhaique Alto to Coyhaique and Puerto Aisén in Chile. The Giobbi buses from Comodoro Rivadavia to Coyhaique, Chile, pass Río Mayo at 0600 on Mon, Wed and Fri, US$14, 6 hrs, but seats are scarce. Mon and Thur at the same hour Giobbi takes Route 40 N direct to Esquel. From Río Mayo Route 40 runs 130 km S to Perito Moreno; 31 km S of Perito Moreno a turning leads W to Lago Blanco, where there is a small *estancia* community, 30 km from the border with Chile (about 150 km from Río Mayo). No hotel, but police are friendly and may permit camping at the police post; wild but beautiful place. No public transport to Chile. From here the road continues to Chile via Paso Huemules and Balmaceda.

Perito Moreno (pop 1,700), at 400m, is close to Lago Buenos Aires, which extends into Chile as Lago General Carrera. Do not confuse the town with the famous glacier of the same name on Lago Argentino near El Calafate, nor with nearby **Parque Nacional Perito Moreno**, see p 210.

Hotels **C** *Americano*, good restaurant; **C** *Argentino*, Buenos Aires 1236, dirty, no showers; **C** *Belgrano*, San Martín 1001, T 2019, with shower, clean, friendly, no heating, with restaurant, rec; **D** *Santa Cruz*, on Belgrano, heating, shared bath and hot water. 25 km S on ruta 40, **C** pp *Telken*, sheep station of the Nauta family offers accommodation Oct-Apr, discounts for families with 2 children, breakfast incl, other meals extra, English and Dutch spoken. Food is very expensive in Perito Moreno. **Restaurant** *Pipach III*, good pizzas and *empanadas*.

Camping Parque Laguna in town, opposite Laguna Cisnes, well shielded, but dirty, US$0.50 pp, US$1 extra for showers, also cabins (slide shows at the tourist office there, information given).

Exchange US$ cash can be exchanged at **Banco de la Provincia de Santa Cruz**. Better rates from Plácido Treffinger, Av San Martín opposite the town hall. Difficult to exchange TCs, though the *Hotel Belgrano* may do so.

Transport Airport is a long way from town, try to hitch as there is only one taxi; LADE flies from Perito Moreno to **Río Gallegos** on Wed, check in well in advance. Hitch-hikers to the S are warned that, outside the tourist season (Jan-mid-Feb), it is usually quicker to head for the coast at Caleta Olivia and go S from there than to take Route 40 via Gobernador Gregores and Piedrabuena.

Excursions South of Perito Moreno are the famous *Cuevas de las Manos*. The series of galleries with 10,000-years-old paintings of human hands and of animals in red, orange, black, white and green, are interesting even for those interested in rock art. The canyon in which the caves are situated is very beautiful, especially in the evening light (entrance US$1). 118 km S of Perito Moreno on Route 40, a marked road goes directly to the caves (44 km). A ranger lives at the site; he looks after the caves and is helpful with information. Camping is permitted but very windy. If it is not busy the ranger may let you sleep inside the park building. No buses, but the tourist office at Perito Moreno can supply names of drivers who can take you there, prices between US$80-100, to be split among a party of visitors. On leaving Perito Moreno on the way to the caves you will pass Cerro de El Volcán, its crater is accessible; after passing the Gendarmería on your right, take the first left (dirt road) at the 3-road junction with Route 40. It is 12 km to the path to the crater—ask permission at the Estancia to know more.

Crossing to Chile From Perito Moreno Route 43 runs south of Lago Buenos Aires to **Los Antiguos**, 67 km W, 2 km from the Chilean frontier (**C** *Hotel Argentino*, comfortable, restaurant; outstanding municipal campsite; service station; salmon fishing; annual cherry festival in early Jan). There is a bus connection (Empresa Co-Mi) from Caleta Olivia (see below) through to Los Antiguos every Mon, Thur, and Sat, at 1030 (from Perito Moreno, leaves from

Hotel Argentino) and back to Caleta Olivia every Tues, Fri and Sun at 0830 (1030 from Perito Moreno), daily in Feb (at least), US$10.

At Km 29 **A3** *Hostería La Serena* offers accommodation in *cabinas*, 10% reduction to *South American Handbook* readers, good restaurant and organizes trips in both the Chilean and Argentine Lake Districts, open Oct-June; further details from Geraldine des Cressonières, Estancia La Serena, Casilla 87, 9040 Perito Moreno, Santa Cruz. Nearby is Los Chilcas where Indian remains can be found (trout fishing). From Los Antiguos Transportes VH buses cross the border by new bridge to Chile Chico, 8 km W, US$2.50, ¾ hr (for routes from Chile Chico to Coyhaique and Puerto Aisén see **Chile section 7**). Another route to Chile is to follow the roads which go around the N side of Lago Buenos Aires to Puerto Ibáñez, but there are no sign posts and it is easy to get lost among the *estancias*.

In Aug 1991, the eruption of Volcán Hudson in Chile buried the area around Lago Buenos Aires in volcanic ash and necessitated its evacuation. The lake itself rose two meters. The effects of the ash were felt as far as the Atlantic coast between Puerto Deseado and San Julián (see below). Much grassland and millions of sheep were killed.

South of Comodoro Rivadavia, Route 3 continues to **Caleta Olivia** (Km 66), pop 13,000. A good start-point for hitching S, Caleta Olivia is the urban centre for important oilfields, and is near Pico Truncado, the gas field which feeds the pipeline to Buenos Aires. On the central roundabout in front of the bus station is a huge granite monument of an oil driller with the tools of his trade.

Hotels **C** pp *Robert*, San Martín 2151, T 61452; **B** *Grand*, Mosconi y Chubut, T 61393; **C** *Capri*, Hernández 1145, T 61132. Camping at Yacht Club.

Buses El Pingüino runs to **Rio Gallegos**, US$34, dep 2100. Many buses to **Comodoro Rivadavia**, 1 hr, US$2.10. To **Perito Moreno** and **Los Antiguos**, Mon, Wed, Fri, 4 hrs, US$18. To **Calafate**, dep 1400, 5 hrs.

73 km further S is **Fitz Roy**, named after the captain of Darwin's ship, *Beagle* (**C** *Hotel Fitzroy*, good, clean, cheap food, camping sometimes possible; petrol station).

This is the area of the **petrified forests,** 70,000,000 years old, of fallen araucaria trees, nearly 3m round and 15-20m long: a remarkable sight. Taxi, Sarmiento to forests, US$39 (3 passengers), incl 1 hr wait, for each extra hour US$9. Hitching is difficult, even in summer, but the Park Warden at Uruguay 43 may give lifts; check return times. There are two sites you can visit: the **Bosque Petrificado José Ormachea**, due W of Comodoro Rivadavia, about 140 km by road (116 km paved—the unpaved part is practically impassable in the wet season), 32 km S of Sarmiento on good gravel road, entry US$5, jeep trip to larger trees US$25 for up to six persons but can be walked in 20 mins; the Víctor Szlapelis park, some 40 km further SW along the same road (follow signposts, road from Sarmiento in good condition). The **Monumento Natural Bosques Petrificados**, W of Puerto Deseado, surrounding the Laguna Grande on a road SW from Fitz Roy, 113 km away, can also be reached from Jaramillo (14 km S of Fitz Roy). This site has the largest examples of petrified trees. A new road has been built from Route 3 about 65 km S of Fitz Roy to the Bosques Petrificados, which reduces the journey by several km.

10 km S of Fitzroy Route 281 branches off Route 3 and runs 123 km SE to **Puerto Deseado**, with a population of 4,100 (airport), at the mouth of the river Deseado which drains Lago Buenos Aires, far to the W. The town was founded on 15 July 1884; its harbour takes large ships. A local tourist attraction is the Cañadón de las Bandurrias, sometimes known as the Grotto of Lourdes, 40m high. Nearby are islands with penguins and other birds, including the unique grey cormorant; local launches available. Lago Buenos Aires is reached by road in 7 hours; 280 km to Las Heras, on to Perito Moreno, near the lake, 177 km, and a further 67 km to the Chilean border at Los Antiguos (see above).

It was at Puerto Deseado that a Welshman in Cavendish's expedition of 1586 gave the name of *pengwyn* (white head) to a certain strange-looking bird. It is only fair to mention the opposing theory that the name is derived from a Spanish word, *pingüe*, meaning fat.

Local holidays 31 Jan (San Juan Bosco); 9 Oct (Coat of Arms day).

Hotels A3 *Los Acantilados*, Pueyrredón y España, T 70167; **B** *Colón*, Almte Brown 450, T 70304, dormitory-style; accommodation may also be available in the sports centre—ask at the

Municipalidad. **Restaurant** *El Quincho*, Av Costanera Marcelo Lotufu, T 0967 70977, rec.

From Fitz Roy Route 3 runs S 268 km to **San Julián** (founded 1901, pop 4,480), the best place for breaking the 834 km run from Comodoro Rivadavia to Río Gallegos. There is much wildlife in the area: red and grey foxes, guanacos, wildcats in the mountains, rheas, etc. The main activities are sheep raising for export, fish canning, and production of kaolin and clay. Clay grinding can be seen at Molienda Santa Cruz and ceramics made at the Escuela de Cerámica; good handicraft centre at Moreno y San Martín. There is a regional museum at the end of San Martín on the waterfront. The ruins of Florida Blanca, a colony 10 km W of town, founded in 1870 by Antonio Viedma, can be visited. The cascade of San Julián is formed by two different tides. Punta Caldera is a popular summer beach. The first mass in Argentina was held here after Magellan had executed a member of his crew. Francis Drake also put in here to behead Thomas Doughty, after amiably dining with him. Near San Julián (15 km) is Cabo Curioso beach, with an attractive cave.

Hotels B *Municipal*, 25 de Mayo 917, T 2300/1, very nice, well-run, good value, but no restaurant. B *Residencial Sada*, San Martín 1112, T 2013, nice, clean, hot water, own bathroom, but sited on busy main road. Also older C *Colón*, Av San Martín 301 and D *Aguila*, San Martín 500 block, sleazy, cheapest in town. Good municipal campsite on the waterfront, US$2 pp, repeatedly rec, all facilities, Av Costanera betweeen Rivadavia and Roca.

Restaurants *Sportsman*, Mitre y 25 de Mayo, excellent value; *Rural*, Ameghino y Vieytes, good, but not before 2100; a number of others. Also bars and tearooms.

Post Office At Belgrano and Av San Martín; telephone exchange also.

Banks Banco de la Nación, Mitre y Belgrano, and Banco de la Provincia de Santa Cruz, San Martín y Moreno.

Pharmacy *Del Pueblo* on San Martín 570. **Hospital**, Av Costanera entre Roca y Magallanes.

Tourist Office In centre of San Martín.

Air Weekly services (Mon) with LADE to Santa Cruz, Río Gallegos, Puerto Deseado, Gob Gregores, Comodoro Rivadavia, Calafate/Lago Argentino and Río Turbio.

Bus Transportadora Patagónica comes from Río Gallegos en route to **Buenos Aires** (also Pingüino, 6 hrs, US$14 to/from Río Gallegos); Transportes Staller goes weekly to **Lago Posadas** stopping in Gobernador Gregores, Hotel Riera, Las Horquetas, Bajo Caracoles and Río Blanco. Transportes El Cordillerano cover the previous route but also stop at **Caleta Olivia**. For hitching, walk 5 km to petrol station on Ruta 3.

An unpaved road (Route 521) runs NW from San Julián to Route 40 along the foothills of the Andes. About halfway is **Gobernador Gregores** (*Hotel San Francisco*, under repair 1994; municipal campsite; good mechanic in town and all grades of fuel available).

Santa Cruz, 153 km S of San Julián, one of the best of the coastal harbours (airport) is near the mouth of the Santa Cruz river which drains Lago Argentino. Founded on 1 December, 1878 and capital of Santa Cruz province until 1904. A deep-water port is being built 22 km outside Santa Cruz at **Punta Quilla**, pop 3,000 (**Hotels** B *Hostal de la Ría*, 25 de Mayo 645, T 8038; *Hostería Turística*; *Anel Aike*, both C). Isla Monte León, 66 km away (Route 1601, then Route 3 and dirt track) has penguins, beaches, fishing and camping facilities (reported closed to visitors).

At **Piedrabuena** (pop 2,600), 35 km W of Santa Cruz (paved road) are B *ACA Motel*, T 7145, simple, functional but good, warm and nice food; B *Hostería El Alamo*, Lavalle 08, T 7249, shower, clean, quiet, breakfast extra, rec; *Andalucia*, Belgrano Oeste 170, hotel and restaurant (good pasta); D *Residencial Internacional*, Ibáñez 99, T 7197, rec; D pp *Hotel Vani*; also campsites N of town on Route 3. ACA breakdown station at Km 247 on Route 3. The *Select* restaurant is very dear for what it offers, but there are several others. Provincial Route 9 (1603 on some maps, unpaved, no petrol) from 43 km S of Piedrabuena to Calafate runs along the edge of a plateau with occasional panoramic views across the valley of the Río Santa Cruz below. Then at about 170 km it drops down into the valley itself to follow the river into the hills and to Lake Argentino. A pleasant run, without being spectacular. Route 288 runs direct to Calafate from Piedrabuena via Tres Lagos. Most traffic to El Calafate goes via Río Gallegos.

Río Gallegos, at the mouth of the Río Gallegos, the capital of Santa Cruz Province, is 265 km S of Santa Cruz; it has a deep-water port with a dry-dock and a large military base. The tidal range here during spring tides is 9.1m. Further N, at Puerto Santa Cruz, maximum tidal range reaches 14.6m. There is a large trade in wool and sheepskins. Population: 75,000. Foundation Day: 9 Dec 1885. The town, although somewhat drab, has a good shopping centre on Roca. "Once beyond Roca and Zapiola, the streets turn to dust, stones and squabbling packs of dogs" (Kevin Healey). The small Plaza San Martín, 1 block from the post office is well tended, with flower beds and statues; outside the post office is the remarkable sight of a balcony (preserved from a demolished house) commemorating the meeting of Presidents Errázuriz and Roca to end Chile and Argentina's 1883 Magellan Strait dispute. The Museo Provincial Mario Echevarría Baleta, Moreno 45 entre Zapiola y Roca, has collections of local history, flora, fauna, rock samples (open 0800-1900, weekends 1500-2000). Museo de los Pioneros, Alberdi y Elcano in the house of a German pioneer family, free, open 1500-2000, rec. Cheap sheepskins (tanned) and very warm leather coats (*gamulanes*) at Puerto Aymond factory of Mr Szasack (half the Buenos Aires price). Argentina's longest road, Route 40, ends at Río Gallegos, or, more precisely, Punta Loyola; it runs from Bolivia for over 4,667 km. **NB** Do not confuse Calle Comodoro Rivadavia with (nearby) Calle Rivadavia. Local holiday 31 Jan.

Hotels **L3** *Aparthotel Niza*, Alcorta 190, T 20958, quiet, good breakfast incl, clean, rec; **A1** *Costa Río*, San Martín 673, new, comfortable, discounts for ACA members; **A3** *Alonso*, Corrientes 33, T 22414, simple, very clean, rm very hot; **A3** *Comercio*, Roca 1302, T 20209, clean, poorly lit, noisy, very busy; **A3** *Santa Cruz*, Roca 701, T 20601, with shower and heating, discount for cash, receptionist speaks English, good coffee bar, breakfast; **B** *Covadonga*, Roca 1214, T 20190, clean, with shower, comfortable, warm, rec; **B** *Nevada*, Zapiola 480, T 25990 (opp bus station for Punta Arenas), with bath, English spoken, good; **B** *Paris*, Roca 1040, T 20111, without bath, grubby, friendly; **B** *Piscis*, Avellaneda y Magallanes, T 25064, pleasant rooms, friendly; **C** *Cabo Virgen*, Comodoro Rivadavia 252, with bath, rec; **C** *Colonial*, Urquiza y Rivadavia, T 22329, shower, cheaper without, hot water, heating, friendly, clean, can be noisy; **D** *Laguna Azul*, rundown but clean and good value; **D** *Central*, Av Roca 1127, central, quiet, cold shower, no heating; close by is **D** *Entre Ríos*, Entre Ríos, good; **D** *Pensión Belgrano*, Calle Belgrano 123, dirty, basic but friendly, has good restaurant; **D** *Residencial Internacional*, Sphur 78, with heating, friendly, but insecure; **D** *Río Turbio*, Zapiola 486, T 22155, good value; **D** *Viejo La Fuente*, Vélez Sarsfield 64-70, T 20304, basic, friendly, rooms near bar are noisy, hot water, restaurant; **E** *Puerto Santa Cruz*, Zapiola 238, T 20099, with bath, passable. Private house: Barrio Codepro II, Casa 71, T 23789, E pp, rec.

NB Accommodation is hard to find in Río Gallegos because of the number of transient workers in town. Apparently no **camping** is allowed around Río Gallegos because it is a military zone apart from the authorized municipal site on Italia y Costa Rica, turn off Route 3 at edge of town heading south (small, basic). There is another site 1 block S of bus terminal (Ruta 3 Norte), US$3 pp + US$1 for tent. Ask at tourist office for new site, being developed alongside a children's playground, cheap, free, hot showers. One is not allowed to take photographs either, for the same reason.

Restaurants Plenty and good, some specializing in seafood, but expensive. *Restaurant Díaz*, Roca 1143, good but dirty, cheap; *La Casa de Miguel*, Roca 1284, good food; *Bifería La Vasca*, Roca 1084, good value, young crowd, rock music, open till 0300; *Jardín*, Roca 1315, good, cheap, popular; *Club Británico*, Roca 935, excellent, reasonably priced; *Montecarlo*, Zapiola 558, good seafood, not the cheapest; opp is good *heladería*. *El Palenque*, Corrientes 73, rec. *Café Carrera*, Fagnano y Roca, good but expensive breakfast; *Le Croissant*, Zapiola y Estrada, good bakery.

Banks and Exchange **Lloyds Bank** (BLSA), Sarmiento 47. Open 1000-1600. Cash advance on Visa and Mastercard. Many banks on Av Roca incl **Banco de Santa Cruz**, 900 block, fair rates, Mastercard. Best rates for TCs, no commission, change cheques here if going to Calafate, where it is even more difficult; fair rates at **Cambio El Pingüino**, Zapiola 469; may also change European and South American currencies. **Cambio Sur**, Av San Martín y Roca, often has good rates. **Banco del Sud**, Calle Alberdi, changes TCs without commission. **Banco de Crédito Argentino**, quick cash advance on Visa upstairs.

Chilean Consulate Mariano Moreno 136, Mon-Fri, 0900-1300; tourist cards issued at border.

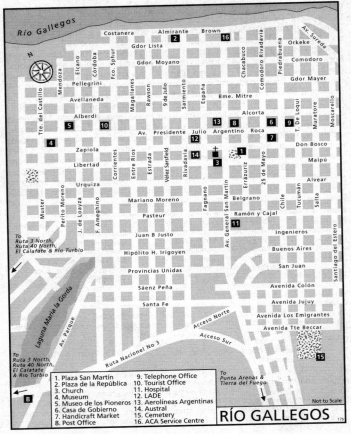

1. Plaza San Martín	9. Telephone Office
2. Plaza de la República	10. Tourist Office
3. Church	11. Hospital
4. Museum	12. LADE
5. Museo de los Pioneros	13. Aerolíneas Argentinas
6. Casa de Gobierno	14. Austral
7. Handicraft Market	15. Cemetery
8. Post Office	16. ACA Service Centre

RÍO GALLEGOS

Laundry Alberdi y Rawson. *Laverap* at Corrientes 277.

Post Office Roca 893. Another branch at the airport. **Telephones**, Roca 613.

Shopping *Artesanías Koekén*, San Martín 336, leatherwork, woollen goods, local produce; *Artesanías Santacruceñas*, Roca 658; *Prepop*, an artisan centre, is worth a visit; *Tía* department store, Roca 700 block, good supermarket section; Supermarket *La Anónima*, Roca y España. Most places take a 2-3 hr lunch break.

Tourist Office Roca y Córdoba, Mon-Fri, 0800-1400, friendly, helpful, English spoken. (Also Alberdi 154, and at airport.) They will phone round hotels for you.

Taxis Hiring a taxi for excursions may be no more expensive than taking a tour bus. Try Sr Miguel Caliguiri, Tres Lagos 445; he charges US$200 to Calafate and Moreno glacier. *A1*, Entre Ríos 350, T 22453, for taxis and car rental, not cheap. **Car Rental** *Localiza*, Sarmiento 237, T 24417, and at airport.

Car parts and repairs at Repuestos Sarmiento, on Sarmiento, owner very friendly and helpful.

Motorcycle Mechanic Juan Carlos Topcic, Costa Rica 25, friendly and helpful.

Air Travel In summer, it is best to make your bookings in advance. AR (San Martín 545, T 22342, airport 20163) flies daily to **Buenos Aires** (Austral flies daily except Sun, via Bahía Blanca, LAPA twice a week, via Comodora Rivadavia and Trelew). AR's Buenos Aires-Auckland-Sydney flight (twice a week) stops at Río Gallegos, but the return journey does not. Several flights to **Ushuaia** (Tierra del Fuego), direct (AR, always booked), but standby seats available with AR, US$59). To **Río Grande**, 40 mins, 6 a week with Austral (Roca 917, T 22038). LADE (Fagnano 53, T 20316) to **Río Turbio** (Wed). To **Comodoro Rivadavia** with LADE twice a week, once via Calafate/Lago Argentino Gob Gregores and **Perito Moreno**, once a week, via Calafate, Gob Gregores, San Julián and Puerto Deseado. Pingüino Río Gallegos-Calafate US$46 (office at airport), 1 hr. TAN to Neuquén, Río Grande Trelew and Comodora Rivadavia. Naval flights (Comando de la Marina, T 22600) up and down the coast every Fri, eg to Buenos Aires, but full of navy personnel. Book seats in Buenos Aires to avoid difficulties with departures.

Airport 4 km from town centre and 3 km from bus terminal. Taxi (*remise*) to/from town, eg opp *Hotel Colonial* US$8 (beware overcharging); Interlagos and Pingüino buses stop at airport, leave 1400 for Calafate direct, US$25 (return US$40, 10% ISIC discount on one way only), 4 hrs; hitching from car park is easy. It is permitted to spend the night at the airport prior to early am flights. **NB** Flights may leave early, sometimes up to 40 mins. LADE flights should be booked as far in advance as possible.

Bus company offices Main companies incl Expreso Pingüino and Interlagos have offices at airport; Pingüino, Zapiola 455, T 22338/25840, open 0800-1300, 1500-2100, Mon-Sat, 0900-1300, 1700-2100, Sun; Transportadora Patagónica, Gobernador Lista 330, T 2330; Mansilla, San Martín 565; Vera, office at bus terminal.

Road Travel New bus terminal at corner of Route 3 and Av Parque, 3 km from centre (no left luggage, small bank, *confitería*, few toilets, kiosks); taxi to centre US$3, bus US$1 (Nos 1 and 12 from posted stops on Roca). To **Calafate**, 4-5 hrs, US$25 (US$40 return), very crowded; turn up with ticket 30 mins before departure: 2 companies—Interlagos and Pingüino—run daily services at 1345 and 1600 between Sep and May, which wait at the airport for incoming flights. In winter both companies operate 3 times a week (El Pingüino has reclining seats, video, toilet, etc, US$50 return, mixed reports). Pingüino offers 2-night excursion to Calafate, sold at airport only, US$93 in single room, credit cards accepted. Route 40, which goes to Calafate (312 km) is paved except the last 40 km; it makes a detour via Río Turbio.

To **Río Turbio**: Expreso Pingüino goes at 1300 daily exc Sat (Sat 1230), 5½-6½ hrs, US$20 (hitching practically impossible); also Mansilla, Sat 1330, and Vera, Mon-Fri 1200; to **Puerto Natales**, Bus Sur and Pingüino twice a week each, 7½ hrs, US$22. Bus to **Punta Arenas**, 260 km, US$23.50 daily at 1300, by Pingüino, also Ghisoni at 1730, except 1415 Tues and Thur, none on Sat, 6½ hrs incl border-crossing process, which is very easy. Make sure your car papers are in order if driving to Chile (go first to Tourist Office for necessary documents, then to the customs office at the port, at the end of San Martín, very uncomplicated). The road to Chile is unpaved but acceptable to the Punta Arenas-Puerto Natales intersection (*hosteria* here, D, with restaurant); there is an 11-km paved strip, single lane, southbound from Punta Delgada (just a restaurant) to the turn-off for the Punta Delgada ferry for Tierra del Fuego. Paving is in progress for 10-12 km E of the Punta Arenas intersection. The 55 km S to Punta Arenas on the main road is paved, 2-lane and good.

Pingüino daily at 2100 to **Caleta Olivia**, US$34, 11 hrs. To **Trelew** and **Puerto Madryn** daily (18 hrs), US$71. To **Comodoro Rivadavia**, 834 km, Patagónica at 2100, stops at Fitz Roy daily at dawn, arr 1000 next day, US$40. For **Bariloche**, take this bus to Comodoro Rivadavia, then the 2150 Don Otto bus to Bariloche (fare to Bariloche US$88). A bus (Andesmar) now goes all the way to **Mendoza**, leaves Fri 1300, arrives 0900 Sun, via Comodoro Rivadavia, Puerto Madryn and Neuquén.

To **Buenos Aires**, 2,575 km, 36 hrs, Pingüino, Mon, Wed, Fri, 2200, daily, 2115, with Costera Criolla, US$107. **Hitchhiking** to Buenos Aires is possible in about 5-7 days; appearance important; hitching to Tierra del Fuego possible from service station on Ruta 3 at edge of town, trucks stop here for customs check, be there before 0700. To Calafate, from police control outside town.

Fishing The S fishing zone incl the Ríos Gallegos, Grande, Fuego, Ewan, San Pablo and Lago Fagnano, nr Ushuaia. It is famous for runs of sea trout. See **Fishing** in **Information for Visitors**, p 229.

Excursion 134 km S, there is a penguin colony at *Cabo Vírgenes* (US$3, run by local authority which puts money directly into conservation). Follow Route 3 then branch off on Route 1 for 3½ hrs (unpaved). "Due to recent oil rush this area is now heavily exploited. Many oil workers take the road to the lighthouse, where they stay, and it's quite easy to hitch to the cape. Take transport (taxi) to junction between Route 3 and the gravel road to the cape. Be there around 0700. Take drinking water. It is possible to arrange return with day trippers from Río Gallegos, or ask at lighthouse or naval station" (Rudiger Schultz, Switzerland). (On the way is El Cóndor ranch, where the manager, Mr Blake, is reported to welcome visitors.) The Navy allows visitors to climb up Cabo Vírgenes lighthouse for a superb view.

From Río Gallegos a railway, the southern-most regular line in the world (no longer in operation), runs 260 km to **Río Turbio** (6,000 people), where Argentina's largest coalfield is located; reserves are estimated at 450m tons and the state coal company YCF is building a deep-water port at Punta Loyola to service it. There is a director of tourism, Prof César Cetta, in the municipality on San Martín. Hotels, always almost full: **B** *Hostería Capipe*, Dufour (9 km from town, T 91240); **B** *Gato Negro*, T 91226; *Albergue Municipal*, by ski-run in hills, 6 km from town, US$10 pp. Visitors can see Mina 1, where the first mine was opened in the hills; area good for trekking and horseback riding. The present mining and industrial area, with the school museum, can also be visited. Río Turbio is 39 km by road from Puerto Natales (Chile). This road is open Oct-Mar only. Alternatively, 55 km N of Río Turbio is Cancha Carrera, from where there is a border crossing, also only open during the summer, into Torres del Paine National Park. The Argentine customs are fast and friendly. 8 km beyond is the Chilean border post, open 0830-1200, 1400-2000, Chilean time. You also have to register at the *carabineros'* office. Buses to Puerto Natales, 2 companies, US$3, regular. To Calafate 4 times a week with Pingüino, 7 hrs, US$27. Expreso Pingüino runs daily at 0600 (plus 1300 Tues, Thur, Sat, 6 hrs) in summer or 1300 Wed, Thur, Sat in winter to Río Gallegos, but LADE flights are cheaper and avoid the numerous passport checks. Pingüino also have flights to Calafate, twice weekly (airport 15 km from town, taxi US$15). *Restaurant El Ringo*, near bus station, will shelter you from the wind.

Calafate (properly El Calafate), on Lago Argentino, 312 km NW of Río Gallegos, pop 3,000, is a developing tourist centre. There is a chapel dedicated to Santa Teresa in the centre; behind it Calle Perito Moreno gently climbs the large hill S of the town, from which one can see the silhouette of the southern end of the Andes, the Laguna Redonda and Isla Solitaria on Lago Argentino. It is the southern gateway to the **Parque Nacional de los Glaciares**, which is 50 km away (the northern end is at Lake Viedma). On the alluvial plain by the lake there are many interesting birds, and in the other direction there is scope for good hill-walking. The Lago Argentino area is very popular, booking all transport in advance is a *must*; accommodation can be difficult to find in Jan-Feb. Obtain maps of the area in advance as none is available in Calafate or in the Park. The tourist office has a list of taxis but undertakes no arrangements; it is helpful but some information may be incorrect, so check. Credit cards are not popular, apart from hotels, and high commissions are charged; most places quote in US dollars.

Festivals People flock to the rural show on 15 Feb (Lago Argentino Day) and camp out with much revelry; dances and *asados* (barbecued sides of sheep). There are also barbecues and rodeo etc on Día de la Tradición, 10 Nov.

Hotels Many hotels are open only from Oct to Apr/May. **L2** *Los Alamos*, Moyano y Bustillo, T 91144, F 91186, comfortable, good food and service, rec; **L3** *Hostería Kau-Yatún*, with bath, many facilities, 25 de Mayo (10 blocks from town centre), T 91059, F 91260, old *estancia* house, comfortable, restaurant and barbecues, horse-riding tours with guides; **L3** *El Mirador del Lago*, Libertador 2047, T/F 91176, good accommodation, acceptable restaurant (wines not rec), better not to take half-board; **L3** *Los Notros*, T/F 91438, 40 km from Calafate on road to glacier, half-board, spacious, rm with glacier views, rec; **A2** *Michelangelo*, Espora 1020, T 91045, F 91058, modern, clean, excellent, reasonable, good restaurant, will accept TCs in payment (at a poor rate, though); **A3** *ACA Hostería El Calafate*, Av San Martín, T 91004, F 91027, modern, good view, 16 rooms, open all year; **A3** *Amado*, Av del Libertador 1072, T 91023, good; **A3** *Upsala*, Espora 139, T 91075, incl breakfast, warm, friendly, rec; **B** *Cabañas Del Sol*, Av del Libertador 1956, T 91439 (D in low season), friendly, clean, good meals, highly rec; **B** *Hospedaje del Norte*, Los Gauchos 813, T 91117, open all year, kitchen facilities, clean, comfortable, owner organizes tours, highly rec, a similar place across the street; **A3** *Hostería Schilling*, Roca 895, T 91453, with bath, lovely rooms, manager speaks good English, safe parking for motorcycles; **C** *Hostería Kapenke*, Av del Libertador 1190, opp *Pizzería Onelli*, T 91093, with bath, breakfast incl, good, rec. Rec bed and breakfast at Espora 60, **E** pp. **C** *La Loma*, B Roca y 15 de Febrero (100 m from bus station), T 91016 (can be booked in Buenos Aires at Av Callao 433, 8a "P", T 371-9123), with bath, breakfast incl, excellent view, modern, highly rec, multilingual, restaurant, tea room: the hotel is cheaper in low season, free

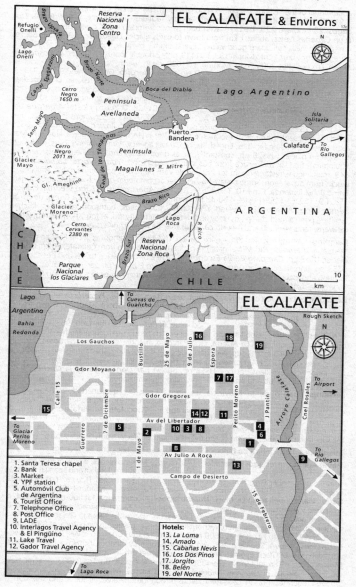

EL CALAFATE & Environs

Reserva Nacional Zona Centro

Refugio Onelli

Lago Onelli

Canal Spegazzini

Brazo Upsala

Brazo Norte

Boca del Diablo

Lago Argentino

Isla Solitaria

Cerro Negro 1650 m

Península Avellaneda

Puerto Bandera

Calafate

To Río Gallegos

Seno Mayo

Cerro Negro 2011 m

Península Magallanes

R. Mitre

Glacier Mayo

Gl. Ameghino

Canal de los Témpanos

Brazo Rico

A R G E N T I N A

Glacier Moreno

Cerro Cervantes 2380 m

Lago Roca

R Rico

CHILE

Brazo Sur

Reserva Nacional Zona Roca

Parque Nacional los Glaciares

C H I L E

0   10
km

EL CALAFATE

Rough Sketch

Lago Argentino

To Cuevas de Gualichu

Bahía Redonda

Los Gauchos

Bustillo

25 de Mayo

9 de Julio

Espora

16

18

19

Gdor Moyano

Calle 15

Guerrero

7 de Diciembre

1 de Mayo

Gdor Gregores

7 17

To Airport

15

Av del Libertador

14 12

10 3 8

Perito Moreno

11

J Pantin

Arroyo Calafate

Chel Rosales

5

2

4
6

1

To Glaciar Perito Moreno

B

Av Julio A Roca

9

To Río Gallegos

13

Campo de Desierto

15 de Febrero

To Lago Roca

1. Santa Teresa chapel
2. Bank
3. Market
4. YPF station
5. Automóvil Club de Argentina
6. Tourist Office
7. Telephone Office
8. Post Office
9. LADE
10. Interlagos Travel Agency & El Pingüino
11. Lake Travel
12. Gador Travel Agency

Hotels:
13. *La Loma*
14. *Amado*
15. *Cabañas Nevis*
16. *Los Dos Pinos*
17. *Jorgito*
18. *Belén*
19. *del Norte*

audio-visual of the last breaking of Moreno Glacier in 1988; **C** *Las Cabañitas*, V Feilberg 218, T 91118, cabins, hot water, kitchen and laundry facilities, helpful, rec; **C** *Residencia Dos Lagos*, 25 de Mayo 220, T 91170, with bath, very comfortable and clean, good value, rec; **D pp** *Cabañas Nevis*, about 1 km from town towards glacier, Libertador 1696, T 91180, for 4 or 8, lake view, full board good value. Several fully cheaper hotels but none less than E pp, eg **D** *Lago Azul*, Perito Moreno 83, T 91419, only 2 double rooms, highly rec; **D** *Hospedaje Belén*, Los Gauchos 300 y Perito Moreno, T 91028, clean, warm, hot water, cooking facilities, very friendly, family welcome, highly rec; **D** *Hospedaje Jorgito*, Gob Moyano 943, T 91323, clean, basic, hot water, cooking facilities, heating, breakfast extra, often full, rec; **D** *Hospedaje Los Dos Pinos*, 9 de Julio 358, T 91271, hot water, cooking and laundry facilities, clean, also cabins (D), dormitory accommodation (F pp), and camping (G pp), arranges tours to glacier, popular; **E pp** *Hospedaje Alejandra*, Espora 60, T 91328. **D** *Youth Hostel Albergue del Glaciar*, Calle Los Pioneros, 200m off Av Libertador, T/F 91243 (reservations in Buenos Aires T 541-447 2338 or 54-321 69416), price per person, camping allowed in the grounds (US$5 pp, dirty, exposed), with use of facilities, E for ISIC or IYHA members, open 1 Nov—31 Mar, rec, hot water, kitchen facilities, English spoken, travel agency, Perito Moreno Tours, runs tours to Moreno glacier (US$28 pp, constantly rec as good value) and elsewhere, rents camping equipment, free shuttle service from bus station and airport. *Youth Hostel La Loma*, Roca 849, multilingual, restaurant, rm for 2-3 people with bath, or **E** pp sharing, IYHA affiliated, 2 blocks from bus station. Some private houses offer accommodation such as Enrique Barragán, Barrio Bahía Redonda, Casa 10, T 91325, E, rec. **F pp** *Apartamentos Lago Viedma*, Paralelo 158, T 91159, F 91158, hostel, 4 bunks to a room, cooking facilities. **F pp** *La Cueva de Jorge Lemos*, Gob Moyano 839, behind YPF station, bunk beds, bathroom, showers, kitchen facilities, popular and cheap but noisy and dirty. If in difficulty, ask at tourist office from which caravans, tents (sleep 4) and 4-berth *cabañas* may be hired, showers extra.

Camping Campsite behind YPF service station, US$4 pp. 3 campsites in the Park en route to the glacier: *Camping Río Mitre*, near the park entrance, 52 km from Calafate, 26 km E of the glacier, US$3 pp; *Camping Bahía Escondida*, 7 km E of the glacier, toilets and hot showers, US$3 pp; unmarked site at Arroyo Correntoso, 10 km E of the glacier, no facilities but nice location and lots of firewood. Take food to all three. Another campsite is *Camping Río Bote*, 35 km, on road to Río Gallegos.

Restaurants Prices rise during Nov and high season lasts until May. *Pizzería Onelli*, Libertador 1197, reasonable, stays open out of season; *Michelangelo*, Espora 1020, very expensive but absolutely magnificent steaks, rec; *Paso Verlika*, Av Libertador 1108, small, 2 courses with wine US$16, credit cards 10% extra, good value; *El Refugio*, Av Libertador 963, Alpine style; *El Rancho*, 9 de Julio y Gob Moyano, large, cheap and good pizzas, popular, free video shows of the glacier, highly rec; *La Rueda*, Gob Paradelo, friendly, cheap, rec; *La Loma*, friendly, home food, picnic lunches supplied, good cakes and chocolates, beautiful view, reasonable prices, discounts for IYHA; *Comedor Family House*, Av del Libertador. Tea rooms: *Maktub*, Libertador 905, excellent pastries, US$8 pp, pricey; *Bar Don Diego de la Noche*, Av del Libertador 1603, lamb and seafood, live music, good atmosphere.

Exchange Banco de la Provincia de Santa Cruz (Av del Libertador) changes cash (commission 1%) and TCs. Advances on Visa and Mastercard (no commission). Travel agencies such as Interlagos also change notes. YPF garage and **Chocolate El Calafate** and some other shops give good rates for cash; also El Pingüino bus company for good rates (but watch the commission); the **Scorpio** snack bar in the main street is reported to give best rates; try also the supermarket in the main street and the *Albergue del Glaciar*. High commission on cheques.

Telephones Public office on Espora, 0700-0100, also has telex and fax facilities.

Travel Agents *Interlagos*, Libertador 1175, tours to Moreno glacier, plenty of time allowed, provide cheapest transport to Fitz Roy (but double check return!), English and Spanish speaking guide, highly rec; *El Pingüino*, Libertador 1025, T 91273, changes TCs, rec; *Los Glaciares*, Libertador 1303, T 91159, rec, prices often cheaper; *Tur Aike*, Libertador 1080, T 91436, and *Gador Viajes*, Libertador 900 block. *Upland Goose*, Av Libertador (1st floor), T 0902-91424, rec. *Hielo y Aventura*, 25 de Mayo, T 91514, organizes 2-hr trek on glacier with champagne, rec. Most agencies charge the same rates for excursions: to the Moreno Glacier US$25 for a trip leaving 0830, returning 1800, without lunch, 3 hrs at glacier; to Lago Roca, at 0930 return 1700, US$25; Cerro Fitz Roy, at 0600 return 1900, US$50, Gualichó caves, 2 hrs, US$8 (see **Excursions**, below). Several hotels also organize tours by minibus incl *Hospedaje del Norte* and *Albergue del Glaciar*, sometimes cheaper and better quality. Jorge Lemos, *Aventrek*, Gob Moyano 839, AP Postal Esp No 7 (9405) El Calafate, Telex Cab pública 86905, runs rec treks with small groups in Glaciares National Park and Fitzroy. *Martín Drake*, Av Roca 2034, T 91364, operates tours in 12-seater minibus throughout the area, as does Dario Serantoni, T

91346. Mountain bikes can be hired from Sr Daniel Alvarez, also rec as source of information, at the Mercado Artesanal on Av del Libertador.

Tourist Information Tourist office on new building by bridge over Río Calafate, friendly. Tour to Moreno glacier information available here. Hotel prices detailed on large chart at tourist office. Sr Jorge Antolín Solache owner of *Hotel La Loma*, Casilla de Correo 36, 9405 Calafate (T 0902-91016, Dec-May), rest of the year Callao 433-8a "P", 1022 Buenos Aires (T 371-9123), has kindly offered to provide any information to travellers in the region. He speaks English, French, Italian and Portuguese. Many shops on main street have maps.

Transport There is a new airport, called Lago Argentino, with an all-weather runway (though flights may be suspended in severe weather). By air from Río Gallegos (LADE twice a week). To Río Gallegos with Pingüino, 1 hr, US$43, daily; to Río Turbio, 3 a week in summer to connect with buses to Puerto Natales and Torres del Paine. Direct flights from Río Gallegos and Ushuaia 3 times a week.

The bus station is on Calle Roca, 1 block from Av del Libertador. Bus Calafate to **Ushuaia** requires four changes, and ferry; total cost of journey US$43. Interlagos Turismo bus runs daily at 0800 (summer) or 0915 Tues, Thur, Sat (winter) to **Río Gallegos** and its airport; in addition El Pingüino runs daily at 0600 and 1630 (Wed, Fri, Sat, in winter) 4½ hrs, US$25, passengers on this bus wishing to go to Chile get off at Güer Aike to catch Pingüino's Gallegos-Río Turbio bus 50 mins later, arriving at 1700. To Río Turbio with Pingüino 4 times a week, 7 hrs, US$27. Taxi to Río Gallegos, 4 hrs, US$200 irrespective of number of passengers, up to 5 people. The Río Gallegos-Calafate road (323 km, all paved) is worth while for the number of animals and birds one sees; however, it is flat and subject to strong winds.

Direct services to Chile: Bus Zaajz Tours, book with Pingüino, Av Libertador (very helpful), Bus Sur and Luis Díaz to **Puerto Natales** via Río Turbio, several times a week, US$25, 7 hrs (rec to book in advance). Travel agencies run regular services in summer, on demand in winter, up to US$50 pp, 5 hrs.

The road trip from Calafate to Punta Arenas is very interesting for wildlife enthusiasts, who will see guanacos and condors at frequent intervals. About 40 km before reaching the border there are small lagoons and salt flats with flamingos. From Calafate take the almost completely paved combination of provincial Route 11, national Route 40 and provincial route 5 to La Esperanza (165 km), where there is a petrol pump and a large but expensive *confitería*. (90 km SE of Calafate Route 40 takes a rough, unpaved and sometimes difficult to follow shortcut which avoids the circuitous La Esperanza route, but even high-clearance vehicles may be unable to cross the unbridged Río Pelque and Chorrillo de Barrancas Blancas after any significant rain. Work has started to improve this section.) East of La Esperanza, gravelled Route 7 joins an improved Route 40 at the Río Coyle. At nearby Fuentes del Coyle, there is a small but acceptable bar/confitería with 2-3 rooms for travellers and a Hotel, D pp, cold, dirty. Road continues to Cancha Carrera (border post Dec-Apr, no town), then 14 km to Chilean border post, Cerro Castillo (2 *hosterías* with rooms, expensive, ask to camp in garden—closed Dec-Apr), then unpaved but good road (63 km) to Puerto Natales and 254 km to Punta Arenas, all paved. There is no direct route from Calafate to Torres del Paine National Park, unless you are prepared to hitch, with some patience, from Cerro Castillo. To take the bus coming from Puerto Natales to the Park, you have to board it in Puerto Natales itself. It is not possible to change Argentine pesos once inside the Park.

Road routes to Calafate By a rough but interesting road from Santa Cruz, Provincial Route 9 (Route 288 is 100 km longer with two bridges replacing old ferry crossings), 5 or 6 hrs by car, but not always possible after rain. South of Esquel, Route 40 is paved south through the towns of Tecka and *Gobernador Costa* (*Hotel Jair, Hotel Vega*, both D; free municipal campsite with all services) in Chubut province; to the W, on the Chilean border, is Lago General Vintter, plus smaller lakes with good trout fishing. 34 km S of Gobernador Costa, gravelled Route 40 forks SW through the town of Alto Río Senguer, while provincial Route 20 heads almost directly south for 81 km (ACA petrol station at isolated La Laurita), before turning E toward Sarmiento and Comodoro Rivadavia. At La Puerta del Diablo, in the valley of the lower Río Senguer, Route 20 intersects provincial Route 22, which joins with Route 40 at the town of Río Mayo (see p 200). This latter route is completely paved and preferable to Route 40 for long-distance motorists; good informal campsites on the W side of the bridge across the Río Senguer.

South of Río Mayo Route 40 becomes quite rough, with no public transportation and very few vehicles of any kind even in mid-summer; persistent enquiries around town may locate a lorry heading to the town of Perito Moreno (see p 200) 124 km to the S, E of Lago Buenos Aires. While there is an excellent paved road connecting Perito Moreno to Caleta Olivia, on the coast, and Los Antiguos, on Lago Buenos Aires, corrugated Route 40 is dismal until tiny, forlorn *Bajo Caracoles* (D *Hotel Bajo Caracoles*, decent but relatively expensive meals). There is a

SOUTHERN SANTA CRUZ & P.N. LOS GLACIARES

PN Los Glaciares:
1. Ventisquero Moreno
2. ACA Restaurant
3. Canal de los Témpanos
4. Brazo Rico
5. Lago Onelli
6. Upsala Glacier
7. Spegazzini Glacier
8. Punta Gualichó
9. Punta Bandera

good grocery store here. 92 km further S of Bajo Caracoles is the town off W to Lago Belgrano. 7 km E, along Route 521 is *Hotel Las Horquetas* with a café/bar, and 15 km beyond this is the Tamel Aike village (police station, water). "Super" grade fuel is available in most places; carry extra, since the only other available source of fuel before Tres Lagos involves a 72-km detour to Gobernador Gregores (**see p 202**).

Midway between Perito Moreno and Gobernador Gregores, at the end of a 90-km spur, is **Parque Nacional Perito Moreno**, one of the Argentine park system's wildest and most remote units, where guanaco and other wildlife roam among a large, interconnected system of lakes below glaciated peaks. The largest of the lakes is Lago Belgrano. Here the mountains are streaked with a mass of differing colours. This is excellent hiking country (ammonite fossils can be found), and a downhill expedition into Chile is possible for intrepid walkers (take all food). On the way to Cerro León is *Estancia La Oriental*, T 0966 2445/2196, guest house and camping site, D pp, A full board, clean, horses for hire. Good chance of spotting condors here. There are few visitors and no formal facilities, but camping (US$2-4 per night) is among the best in South America. The park is situated S of Cerro San Lorenzo, highest peak of the Patagonian Andes. Entrance fee US$5, park ranger has maps and information. Except after heavy rain, the road is better than Route 40 and negotiable by any ordinary vehicle. For more detail, see William C Leitch's *South America's National Parks* (Seattle: The Mountaineers, 1990).

From the Parque Moreno junction to Tres Lagos (accommodation at *Restaurant Ahoniken*, Av San Martín, E pp), Route 40 improves considerably, but after Tres Lagos (one restaurant and supermarket) it deteriorates rapidly and remains very rugged until after the turnoff to the Fitz Roy sector of Parque Nacional Los Glaciares. 21 km beyond is the bridge over Río La Loma, with a hotel which has a bar/café. The remainder of the highway to Calafate, while slow, holds no major problems.

Route 288 runs E from Tres Lagos to Piedrabuena; fuel is available at Laguna Grande, 100 km from Tres Lagos.

NB It is nearly impossible to hitchhike between Calafate and Perito Moreno. There is no public transport, at any time of year along this road. A weekly bus (Sat) from Puerto San Julián goes through Gobernador Gregores, passes *Hotel Las Horquetas*, and on to the village of Bajo Caracoles. There is no public transport into the park but it may be possible to arrange a lift with *Estancia* workers from *Hotel Las Horquetas*.

Excursions Travel by road to the most interesting spots is limited and may require expensive taxis. Tours can be arranged at travel agencies, or with taxi drivers at the airport who await arrivals. Two recommended walks: (1) From the Centro Cívico in Calafate, visit Capilla Santa Teresita in Plaza San Martín; behind it is Calle Perito Moreno; walk to the top of the hill for a view of Calafate. Then go S to the Río Calafate, then to the new section of the town, where the ACA grill is. (2) From the Intendencia del Parque, follow the new road among cultivated fields and orchards to Laguna de Los Cisnes, a bird reserve, with flamingoes, ducks, and abundant birdlife. Walk down to **Lago Argentino**; 15 km along the lakeside are the painted caves at Punta Gualichó. Unfortunately the paintings have greatly deteriorated, but there are fascinating geological formations caused by erosion, on the edge of Lago Argentino, 12 km from Calafate on the road to Río Gallegos. An excursion can also be made to Lago Roca, 40 km S from Calafate. Trout and salmon fishing, climbing, walking, camping and branding of cattle in summer. Good camping here in wooded area, restaurant.

At the far end of Lago Argentino (80 km from Calafate) the **Ventisquero Moreno**, one of the few glaciers in the world that has been growing larger, descends to the surface of the water over a five-km frontage and a height of about 60m. In a cycle of roughly three years it used to advance across the lake, cutting the Brazo Rico off from the Canal de los Témpanos; then the pressure of water in the Brazo Rico would break up the ice and reopen the channel. Owing to rising temperatures from the thinning of the ozone layer, the glacier is reportedly not growing any more (since 1992) and the three-year cycle has been disrupted (it is estimated at 7 years now). Pieces break off and float away as icebergs. The vivid blue hues of the ice floes and the dull roar as they break away from the snout are spectacular, especially at sunset. When visiting the glacier, do not go down too close to the lake as these icebergs can cause great waves when breaking off, and wash people off rocks. New wooden catwalks prevent you from going to the water's edge; there is a fine of up to US$500 for leaving the catwalks.

From Calafate to the glacier's edge there are daily buses by Receptivo Calafate, Pingüino and Interlagos, Sep-May only (daily Nov-Mar, less frequent at other times), return, US$25 from Av Libertador at 0830 returning 1800, giving 3 hrs at glacier; you can use the return fare at no extra cost if you come back next day (student discount available). Trips run by the Youth Hostel cost US$28, go out via the *estancia* and return past the lake. They also do walking tours on the glacier, book ahead. Fares do not incl the US$5 park entrance fee. Taxis, US$80 for 4 passengers round trip. It may be possible to camp in the guardaparque's backyard, but you must ask first. Out of season, trips to the glacier are difficult to arrange, but one can gather a party and hire a taxi; take warm clothes, and food and drink; try asking at hotels or taxis at cooperative, T 91044 (for 4 people). Ask rangers where you can camp out of season, no facilities except a decrepit toilet block. Boat trips are organized by Hielo y Aventura travel agency, T 91414, large boats for up to 60 passengers, US$20 pp on "Safari Náutico" (1 hr), or a day trip ("Minitrekking") incl boat trip and 2½ hrs walk on the glacier, US$70, rec, but not for the fainthearted, take your own lunch.

A worthwhile trip is by motor-boat from Punta Bandera, 50 km from Calafate, to the **Upsala Glacier** at the NW end of Lago Argentino (in early 1995 access to the glacier face was impossible, check in advance if it is possible to go). The trip also goes to Lago Onelli and glacier (restaurant) and Spegazzini glacier. From the dock on Bahía Onelli to Lago Onelli is an easy 2-km trail done with a guide (in English, German or Spanish) through a lovely southern forest wreathed in bearded moss. Small **Lago Onelli** is quiet and very beautiful, beech trees on one side, and ice-covered mountains on the other. The lake is full of icebergs of every size and sculpted shape.

A tour boat usually operates a daily trip to the glacier, the catamaran *Serac*, US$90. The price includes bus fares and park entry fees — pay in dollars and take food. Bus departs 0730 from

Calafate for Punta Bandera. 1 hour is allowed for a meal at the restaurant near the Lago Onelli track. Return bus to Calafate at 1930; a tiring day, it is often cold and wet, but memorable. Out of season it is extremely difficult to get to the glacier. Many travel agencies, eg in Bariloche, make reservations. On the road from Calafate to Punta Bandera, at the foot of Cerro Comisión, is a rock formation that looks like a herd of elephants facing you.

Another worthwhile excursion is to the N end of the Glaciares National Park (entrance US$3.50) to **Cerro Fitz Roy** (Tehuelche name El Chaltén) and Cerro Torre, 230 km NW of Calafate. The Fitz Roy massif can be seen from the village of **El Chaltén**, which is becoming very popular, and one can walk for 2½ hrs to see Cerro Torre (stupendous views: "anyone within 500 miles would be a fool to miss them"—Julian and Cordelia Thomas). It is possible to hike from Chaltén to Cerro Torre base camp and back in one day, crossing the Río Fitz Roy by the new bridge. There are three main trails in the park from the entrance (all well signposted): "Río Blanco" to Fitz Roy glacier, 5 hrs each way, "Cerro Torre" 3 hrs each way and to the Salto, 1 hr each way. Cerro Fitz Roy base camp is 3 hrs easy walk from *Camping Madsen* (which is a better place to stay). Ask at the *gendarmería* (border-police) in Calafate if you can join their truck which goes once or twice a week. On the way to Cerro Fitz Roy (often bad weather) on Route 40, is the Southern Astronomical Observatory, managed by the Observatory of La Plata. Día de la Tradición (10 Nov) is celebrated with gaucho events, riding and barbecue (US$5).

Daily buses in summer from Calafate are run by Caltur, daily at 0600, returning at 1600 (back in Calafate 2000), and Los Glaciares, leaving at 0600 to El Chaltén, at the base of Cerro Fitz Roy, 5 hrs, returns 1600, allowing 2-3 hrs at site, US$50 return. Best to book return before departure during high season (private drivers go off season and charge more). A new road has been built from Route 40 to Chaltén. **Accommodation A3** *Fitz Roy Inn*, 32 beds, restaurant. Cabins sleep 2 (US$50), 3 (US$60) or 4 (US$70). Opposite is *Albergue Patagonia* (US$8 pp private room, US$5 pp communal room, kitchen and laundry facilities, TV and video, book exchange, accepts TCs); **C** pp *Estancia La Quinta*, 3 km from Chaltén, half-board, no heating, prepares lunch for trekkers, rec; **E** pp *Hotel Lago del Desierto*, good, small, showers, new 6-birth cabins D pp with bath. *Confitería La Senyera*, excellent bread, rec; *Josh Aike*, excellent confitería, homemade food, beautiful building, rec; *The Wall Pub. Camping Madsen* (free) at end of village near the paths to Cerros Fitz Roy and Torre (the bus from Calafate goes to and from this site), no facilities; *Ruca Mahuida*, 400m N on route to treks, Paula Marechal (guide and owner), very helpful, camping US$5, showers, stores gear, rec.

A stove is essential for camping as firewood is scarce. Take plenty of warm clothes and a good sleeping bag. Buy supplies in Calafate (cheaper and more choice). It is possible to rent equipment in El Chaltén, ask at park entrance. Beware of straying from the paths. A map is essential, even on short walks (the information centre at park entrance provides photocopied maps of treks). The best is one published by Zagier and Urruty, 1992, US$10 (Casilla 94, Sucursal 19, 1419 Buenos Aires, F 572-5766) and is now available in several shops in Calafate.

Climbing Fitz Roy (3,375m) is approached from Chaltén to Río Blanco, 2-3 hrs, walk, then to Laguna Torre (base camp for Cerro Torre), 3-4 hrs walk. Ask the guide Sr Guerra in Chaltén about hiring animals to carry equipment. The best time is mid-Feb to end-Mar; Nov-Dec is very windy; Jan is fair; winter is extremely cold. There are no rescue services; necessary gear is double boots, crampons, pickaxe, ropes, winter clothing; the type of terrain is ice and rock. Possible targets nearby incl Cerro Torre, Torre Eger, Cerro Solo, Poincennot, Guilleaulmet, Saint-Exupery, La Bífida, La Indómita, Cardón Adela and Hielo Continental (Continental Ice Shelf). Ask for a permit to climb at the Parques Nacionales office in Chaltén. There is no access at all from Chile.

Organized trips to the Glaciares National Park are too short to appreciate it fully; either go on a tour bus, then camp (good gear essential) or hire a taxi/minibus. The travel agencies charge US$200 for up to 8 people, US$300 to take you and return later to collect you; private drivers (eg Martín Drake, see under Calafate **Travel Agents**) charge US$300 for up to 8 to take you and collect later (also does similar arrangements for the Moreno glacier).

TIERRA DEL FUEGO (11)

The island at the extreme south of South America is divided between

Argentina (E side) and Chile (W). The S has beautiful lakes, woods and mountain scenery, and there is much birdlife to see. Boat trips can be made on the Beagle Channel; there is skiing in winter.

Tierra del Fuego is bounded by the Magellan Strait to the N, the Atlantic Ocean to the E, the Beagle Channel to the south—which separates it from the southern islands—and by the Whiteside, Gabriel, Magdalena and Cockburn Channels etc, which divide it from the islands to the W. The local Ona Indians are now extinct. Throughout Tierra del Fuego the main roads are narrow and gravelled. The exceptions are the road for about 50 km out of Porvenir (Chile), which is being widened, and Río Grande-Ushuaia, which is being improved. Part of the south is a National Parks Reserve: trout and salmon in nearly all the lakes and rivers, and in summer wild geese, ducks, 152 other species of birds, and imported musk rats and beaver. **Note** that accommodation is sparse and the island is becoming popular among Argentines in summer. Hotel beds and seats on aircraft may begin to run short as early as Nov. Fruit and meat may not be taken onto the island.

Books *Tierra del Fuego* (3rd edition), in English, by Rae Natalie Prosser de Goodall, US$7.50 (obtainable in Ushuaia and Buenos Aires), colourful maps by the same author. Also *Tierra del Fuego: The Fatal Lodestone*, by Eric Shipton, and *Uttermost Part of the Earth*, by E Lucas Bridges. Available in USA: *Birds of Isla Grande* (Tierra del Fuego) by Philip S Humphrey, and *A Guide to the Birds of South America*, by Rodolphe Meyer de Schauensee.

Mar-Apr is a good time to visit because of the beautiful autumn colours.

There are two ways of crossing the Strait of Magellan to Tierra del Fuego. Coming S from Río Gallegos, an unpaved road turns left for **Punta Delgada** (1 hotel, 2 hosterías). (On the road Río Gallegos-Punta Delgada is Laguna Azul—3 km off main road in an old crater; an ibis breeding ground, beautiful colours). A 30-minute crossing can be made by fast modern ferry from Punta Delgada to **Punta Espora** (no hotel—if desperate, ask the lighthouse keeper). The boats, which take 4 lorries and about 20 cars, run every hour, with schedule determined by tides. Under normal conditions they run from 0800 to 2100 daily, with tidal breaks lasting 4 hours (autumn and winter timetable). Cost is US$1 pp, US$14 per car, ferry-operators accept US dollars or Argentine or Chilean currencies. If going by car, do not go before 1000, as first crossings are taken by buses, etc. At Punta Delgada office the staff can try to reserve the Porvenir/Punta Arenas ferry. There is no bus service from Punta Espora (or Punta Delgada); buses to and from the island only through Porvenir. From Punta Espora (Bahía Azul is ferry terminal) a road runs through Chilean territory to San Sebastián (Chile) and 14 km further to San Sebastián (Argentina, one restaurant and hotel) (usually 15 min delay in crossing borders), Río Grande (road San Sebastián-Río Grande is now paved) and Ushuaia. There is an Esso service station 38 km from Punta Espora. Accommodation is scarce in the Chilean part (except for Porvenir—see **Chilean Patagonia**), and it is not always possible to cross it in one day because of the irregularity of the ferry. It is sometimes possible, coming and going, to spend the night at the guest house of ENAP at Cerro Sombrero (petrol there for employees only, but if you are running out, they may help), but do not count on it. Try *Hostería Karu-Kinka*.

The road from Río Gallegos goes on to Punta Arenas, from where (dock at Tres Puentes 5 km E of town) there are is a daily crossing to Porvenir (passenger US$5, motor car US$30, 2½-3 hours, T Punta Arenas 227020; there is a passenger saloon with small cafeteria; get on first and you are invited on the bridge, get on last and you stand outside in the cold). Return from Porvenir at 1400 (Sun 1630). If crossing with car, don't allow it to be parked too close to other vehicles; the ferry company will not accept responsibility for damage caused by onboard "crashes". If you want to continue, Senkovic buses to Río Grande leave at 1400 on Sat and Tues. A 225-km road runs from Porvenir E to Río Grande (6 hours) via San Sebastián; or by alternative route through Cerro Sombrero (see previous paragraph). Border police at San Sebastián will sometimes arrange lifts to Ushuaia or Río Grande. Hitching after San Sebastián is easy. Distances are roughly as follows in this area: Border with Chile at Monte Aymont; to Río Gallegos 73 km; road to Río Grande via Kimiri-Aike (114 km from Río Gallegos)—no buses; from here to Punta Delgada 30 km; Punta Delgada-Punta Espora (ferry, free for pedestrians) 20 km; on to Punta Sombrero (60 km) and San Sebastián (60 km) reaching Río Grande 80 km on. The best way to hitch from Río Gallegos to Punta Arenas is to take any lorry as far as the turn-off for Punta Delgada ferry. Then there is plenty of Chilean traffic from Punta Delgada to Punta Arenas. *Hotel San Gregorio* will put you up if you get stuck near the turn-off.

Entering Argentina from Chile, be firm about getting an entry stamp for as long as you require. Going in the other direction, don't stock up with food in Argentina, as Chilean border guards will confiscate all fruit, vegetable, dairy and meat products coming into Chile.

Río Grande (pop 35,000), is a port in windy, dust-laden sheep-grazing and oil-bearing plains. The oil is refined at San Sebastián in the smallest and most southerly refinery in the world (**B** ACA motel; service station open 0700-2300). The *frigorífico* (frozen meat) plant in Río Grande is one of the largest in South America; so is the sheep-shearing shed. Government tax incentives to companies in the 1970s led to a rapid growth in population; the subsequent withdrawal of incentives has produced increasing unemployment and emigration. The town is now full of empty temporary housing. Accommodation is difficult if arriving at night. Food is cheaper here than in Ushuaia (*Tía* supermarket rec, good choice). ACA garage on sea-front has free hot showers for men, as has the gymnasium. Fill up with gasoline here.

Local Festivals *Trout Festival*, 3rd Sunday in Feb; *Snow Festival*, 3rd Sun in July; *Woodsman Festival*, 1st week of Dec.

Hotels A3 *Atlántida*, Av Belgrano 582, T 22592, said to be best, always full; **A3** *Los Yaganes ACA*, Av Belgrano 319, T/F 23897, clean, comfortable, restaurant; **B** *Federico Ibarra*, Rosales 357, T 21071, excellent restaurant; **C** *Hospedaje Noal*, Rafael Obligado 557, lots of bread and coffee for breakfast, clean, cosy, friendly, rec; **C** *Residencial Rawson*, Estrada 750, T 21352/24523, with bath, clean, rec; **C** *Villa*, San Martín 277, T 22312, very warm; **D** *Hospedaje Irmary*, Estrada 743, clean and pleasant, rec; **D** *Miramar*, Mackinlay 595, T 22462, without bath, no breakfast, heated, hot water, kitchen facilities, rec; **E** pp *Pensión Stella*, Moreno 835, good, clean.

Restaurants *Yaganes* (good for *centolla*—King crab) expensive; **Don Rico**, Belgrano y Perito Moreno, in ultra-modern building in centre, interesting, closed Mon; *Pizzería La Colonial*, Rosales 666, home made food, friendly. *Confitería Roca*, Roca 629, open all hours, reasonably priced food and bar; likewise **A Todas Horas** in same street. Good workmen's café, *Mary's*, Moyano 373. *Supermarket Sados* on San Martín, near 25 de Mayo. Smart place for a drink, *París*, Rosales 448.

Banks and Exchange Banco de la Nación Argentina, San Martín 200, high commission on TCs; **Banco del Sur**, San Martín; **Superkiosko**, Piedrabuena y Rosales, cash only. Try *Confitería Roca*, Roca 629. Tends to be difficult: if coming from Chile, buy Argentine pesos there.

Post Office Piedrabuena y Ameghino.

Travel Agency *Yaganes*, friendly and helpful.

Tourist Information at the Municipalidad, Mon-Fri, on Calle Sebastián Elcano.

Car Hire Rent-a-Car, Belgrano y Ameghino, T 22657. Localiza, at airport, T 30482.

Car mechanic and VW dealer Viaval SRL, P Moreno 927.

Airport 4 km W of town. Bus US$0.50. Taxi US$5. Río Grande-Buenos Aires flights with Aerolíneas Argentinas – T 22749, daily, 3 hrs 20 mins direct. Austral daily (except Sun) via Bahía Blanca, Comodoro Rivadavia and Río Gallegos. TAN flies to Neuquén, Trelew, Comodoro Rivadavia and Río Gallegos twice a week. To **Ushuaia**, AR 3 a week, LADE 1 a week, Kaiken, daily. LADE also to **Río Gallegos**, 50 mins (book early in summer, 1 a week, Thur), continuing to **Comodoro Rivadavia** via Calafate, Gob Gregores and Perito Moreno. Telephone LADE office (Lasarre 425) open Mon-Fri, 0900-1200 and 1530-1900, 0700-1200 on Sat, T 22968. Conversely, travel with Aeronaval (if you're lucky), mostly Hercules transports, for half the price – enquire at airport. "Rent-a-plane" at airport. You can now fly to Punta Arenas in Chile, through Kaiken Agency, Perito Moreno 937, T 31513, or Aerovías DAP, 9 de Julio 597, T 30249, dep Tues, Thur, Sat, US$80, dep 1300.

Buses leave at 0630 Tues and Sat US$25 (Senkovic, San Martín 959, T 22345), for **Porvenir**, Chile (about 230 km), no food or drink provided, no toilets, nor stops, for 7 hrs, always heavily booked but especially over Christmas/New Year period, meticulous passport and luggage control at San Sebastián. To Punta Arenas, Pacheco (Bilbao 873), runs buses via Porvenir on Tues, Thur, Sat 0700, US$36, 10 hrs, tickets available on day of departure, also with Los Carlos on Mon, Thur, 0730, same price, but at Christmas and New Year tickets are hard to come by. Best to book bus connection in Ushuaia. Very difficult to hitch to Porvenir. Ferry journey from Porvenir to **Punta Arenas** (2 hrs) can be very rough and cold. Daily bus service with Transportes

Los Carlos, to **Ushuaia**, 234 km on an unpaved road (sit on right for better views), US$25, 4 hours, times vary, stopping at *Hostería El Kaikén*, Lago Fagnano, for a drink (rec for the view). Bus departs from Los Carlos office (Estrada 568); arrive 15 mins early. Summer service also by Tecni Austral, daily (exc Sat) at 0730, 3 hrs, US$22.

Excursion 11 km N lies the Salesian mission and the regional museum housed in the original chapel and first parish church of Río Grande. Although the exhibits are not at all organized or classified, there is a great deal to see. There are Ona Indian materials, Salesian mission works, fossils, handicrafts and flora, fauna and mineral exhibits of the area. Just past the mission, on the right side of the road, is the old cemetery.

With a population of 50,000, *Ushuaia*, 236 km SW of Río Grande, is the most southerly town in Argentina, and among the most expensive. Its steep streets (there are mountains, the Cerro Martial, at the back of the town) overlook the green waters of the Beagle Channel, named after the ship in which Darwin sailed the Channel in 1832, on Captain Fitzroy's second expedition. The old prison, Presidio, at the back of the Naval Base can be visited, interesting (see also **Rail** below): tours start from the Museum daily 1600-2300, US$3 (not incl tip for guide). There are impressive views of the snow-clad peaks, rivers, waterfalls and dense woods. There is a naval station at Isla Redonda. The people are engaged in timber cutting, fishing and, nowadays, in factories. The tourist industry is also expanding rapidly, although hotel prices are higher here than on the mainland. A new road has been built between Río Grande and Ushuaia via Paso Garibaldi. Ushuaia and its environs are worth a 2-3 day visit.

Museum Museo Territorial, Maipú y Rivadavia, T 21863, open Mon-Sat 1600-2000, US$2, small but interesting display of early photos and artefacts of the local Indian tribes; relics from the missionaries and first settlers, etc. Also known as the "museum at the end of the world". Highly rec. Building also contains an excellent library with helpful staff, a good bookshop with books in English, and post office, open afternoons when the main one is closed.

NB Prices double on Dec 12 and accommodation may occasionally be hard to find throughout Dec – the tourist office will help. It is best not to drink tap water in Ushuaia.

Hotels L3 *Canal Beagle*, ACA, Maipú 590, T 21117, restaurant (catering usually for tour groups), overpriced; **A1** *Tolkeyen*, at Estancia Río Pipo 5 km from town, with rec restaurant Tolkeyen, 100 m (see below); **A2** *Albatros*, Maipú 505, T 22504, clean, modern, incl breakfast, but rooms a bit cold; **A2** *Las Lengas*, Goleta Florencia 1722, T 23366, superb setting, heating, good dining room; **A2** *Malvinas*, Deloqui 615, T 22626, with bath, breakfast incl, pleasant, helpful, central heating, rec; **A2** *Antártida*, San Martín 1600, T 21896, friendly, restaurant with fine views, rec; **A2** *Cabo de Hornos*, San Martín y Rosas, T 22187, comfortable, often full, TV, spotless, good value (but surcharge on credit cards), restaurant not open to non-residents; **A2** *César*, San Martín 753, T 21460, with bath, comfortable, often full (book in advance), friendly, clean, incl breakfast, rec; **A3** *Maitén*, 12 de Octubre 140, T 22745, good value, clean, but 2 km from town centre, 10% discount for ISIC and youth card holders; **A3** *Posada Fin del Mundo*, Valdez 281, T 22530, family atmosphere, rec; **B** *Casa de Gapgin*, Gob Paz 1380, clean, comfortable, friendly, heating, good breakfast, no sign, rec; **B** *Hospedaje Turístico*, Deloqui 271, T 21316, with private bath, very clean, friendly, parking, TV, kitchen, English spoken, rec; **B** *Hostal Julio Linares*, Deloqui 1522, nr airport, new, good value; **B** *Monte Cervantes*, San Martín y Sarmiento, T 30600, rec; **B** *Mustapic*, Piedrabuena 230, T 21718, multi-lingual owner (Sr Miro, from Croatia, his daughter runs travel agency next door, T 23557, rec), 10% discount for ISIC card holders, no singles, highly rec, exceptionally clean, can leave luggage, rooftop restaurant for breakfast; **C** *Familia Cárdenas*, 25 de Mayo 345, T 21954, near top of hill, rec; **C** *Fernández*, Onachaga y Fitzroy, T 21192, very friendly, hot water, good but expensive meals, but cheaper in bunk-bed accommodation; **C** Sra Marta Loncharich, Magallanes 229, T 24150, shared bathroom, good food and comfort, clean, but overpriced; **D** pp *Alojamiento Internacional* (Hilda Sánchez and Pedro Sieczkovsky), Deloqui 395, 1st floor, T 23483/23622, spartan, friendly, dormitory, take sleeping bag, cooking and laundry facilities, no security, good meeting place, changes money; **D** *Hospedaje Turístico*, Magallanes 196, new, comfortable; **D** pp *Klewel*, Karukinka 22, T 22548, Sandra Gabriela Sainz, tourist information, laundry, café, cocktails, excursions, rec; **D** pp María Guercio, Kuanip 67, T 22234, also large chalet outside town to let; **D** rooms, at home of Ismael Vargas, Kayen 394 (T 21125) 15 mins from centre, clean, doubles only, Sra Vargas speaks English; **E** *Casa Elvira*, Fuegio Basquet 419, T 23123, 10 mins walk from airport, price per person, use of kitchen; Accommodation in private homes (all **C-D**): Familia Beltrame, Gob Valdez 311,

T 22819, rec; Familia Galeazzi, Gob Valdez 323, T 23213, speak English and French, rec; Familia Velásquez, Fadul 361, T 21719, dormitory accommodation, clean, warm, helpful, not enough showers, skimpy breakfast, can leave luggage when hiking. Zulema R Saltzmann, Roca 392 (esq Campos), **D** pp, clean and friendly; Sr Ueno, 12 de Octubre 432, T 24661, full board US$10 pp, rec. The following gives 10% discount to ISIC card holders: Marta Lebhian, Deloqui 641, T 22669, **D** pp, clean, hot water, cooking facilities. There is no YHA in Ushuaia. Hostel for sporting groups only at Sports Complex. Lodging in Ushuaia has recently become rather a problem esp Jan-Mar, but even in winter hotels are very expensive. Enquire at Tourist Office for accommodation in private homes, and for campsites, some of which are free. Many people go to the airport to offer rooms in private houses, in our **E** pp range (minimum).

Camping None in town. After paying US$3.50 entrance fee to park, there are 4 camping sites to choose from, of which 3 are free, but have few or no facilities. The fourth is Camping Lago Roca, at Lapataia, by forested shore of Lago Roca in Parque Nacional, with facilities for car and tent, US$5, dirty, noisy, caters for travellers without car, Dec-Mar, incl gas (18 km from Ushuaia; weather can be bad). Can be reached by bus Jan-Feb. Hot showers evenings (US$3), toilet (US$1), small shop, cafeteria. One free site is by restaurant, with no facilities, on road to Parque Nacional about 4 km from Ushuaia at Río Pipo, and another, 2 km from the Lago Roca campsite close to a beaver dam. The third free site is at Monte Susana, 10 km W. Hot showers at Sports Centre on Malvinas Argentinas.

Restaurants *Tía Elvira*, Maipú 349, very popular, make advance booking, good seafood; *Moustacchio*, San Martín 298, sea food, warmly rec; *Asturias*, Rosas 45, pleasant, reasonable, open 1200-1500, 2030-2300. *Barcleit 1912*, Fadul 148, cordon bleu cooking at reasonable prices. *Kaupé*, Roca 470, English spoken, excellent food and wine, rec, expensive. Best place to eat lamb is at *Tolkeyen*, Estancia Río Pipo, 5 km from town, meal US$15, taxi US$7. *El Viejo Marino*, Maipú 229, nice ambience, excellent food; *Mi Viejo*, Campos 758, good parrillada and buffet, highly rec; *Cafetería, pizzería Ideal*, San Martín 393, good, cheap, hot buffet US$13, very popular with travellers, 10% discount for ISIC card holders; *Los Amigos*, San Martín 130, quick service, some cheap dishes; *Volver*, Maipú 37, interesting decor, good food and service, not cheap; *El Aborigen*, Antártida Argentina 75, inexpensive; *Quick*, San Martín 130, clean, good service, rec, 10% discount for ISIC card holders; also *Split*, Piedrabuena 238, pizzería, offers same discount, cheap. *Turco*, San Martín between Onas y Patagonia, cheap, popular with locals. *Der Garten*, *confitería*, San Martín 638, in Galería shopping arcade. Excellent homemade chocolate sold at a shop at San Martín 785. *Helados Massera*, San Martín 270-72, good. The coffee bar at the airport is very expensive. Ask around for currently available *centolla* (king crab) and *cholga* (giant mussels). Food and drink (apart from the duty-free items) in Ushuaia are very expensive. A popular spot at night is the disco *Extasis* at 9 de Julio y Maipú; another disco is *Barny's*, Antártida Argentina just off San Martín. *Café Latino*, Deloqui y Rivadavia, bar with live music (Argentine and contemporary), in summer gets going around 0200, great atmosphere, high standard.

Banks and Exchange Banks open 1000-1500 (in summer). Useful to have credit cards here as difficult to change cheques and very high commission (up to 10% reported), but **Banco del Sud**, Maipú 600 block, will change cheques (downstairs), also at Shopping Centre Lapataia, San Martín y 9 de Julio, commission US$8. Cash advance on Mastercard at **Banco de Santa Cruz** and **Banco de Tierra del Fuego**, San Martín 1044. Tourist agencies and the *Hotel Albatros* also give poor rates. *Listus* record shop, San Martín 973, sweet shop next door, or *Caminante*, Deloqui 368 for better rates for cash.

Consulates Chile, Malvinas Argentinas y Jainen, Casilla 21, T 21279. **Finland**, Paz y Deloqui; Germany, Rosas 516; **Italy**, Yaganes 75.

Laundromat Rosas 139, between San Martín and Deloqui, open weekdays 0900-2100, US$8.

Post Office San Martín y Godoy, Mon-Fri 0900-1300 and 1700-2000, Sat 0830-1200. **Telephones** and fax on Roca next to Aerolíneas Argentinas.

Shopping Good boots at **Stella Maris**, San Martín 443. **Bookshop** at San Martín y 9 de Julio (Lapataia Arcade). Film is cheaper in Chile. Supermarkets: Surty Sur (with clean toilets, San Martín y Onas) and Sucoop, Paz 1600. Most things are more expensive than elsewhere but some cheap imported goods, eg electrical equipment and cigarettes.

Sport Sports Centre on Malvinas Argentinas on W side of town (close to seafront). Ice skating rink at Ushuaia gymnasium in winter (when lagoon is frozen). Beachcombing can produce whale bones. Fishing: trout, contact Asociación de Caza y Pesca at Maipú and 9 de Julio, with small museum. Fishermen may be interested in visiting the fish hatchery 7 km E of Ushuaia, visiting hours daily 1400-1700. There are brook, rainbow and brown trout and land-locked salmon. Take No 1 bus E-bound on Maipú to the end of the line and continue 2½ km on foot

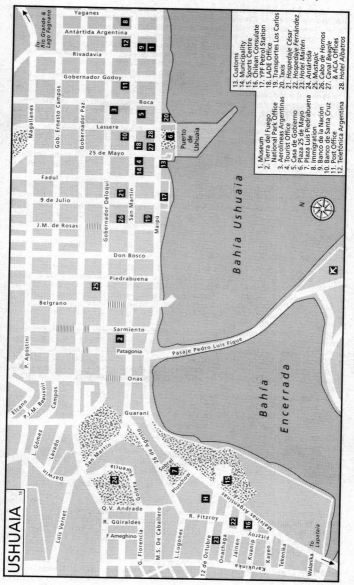

USHUAIA

13. Customs
14. Municipality
15. Sports Centre
16. Chilean Consulate
17. YPF Petrol Station
18. LADE Office
19. Transportes Los Carlos
20. Taxis
21. Hospedaje César
22. Hospedaje Fernández
23. Hotel Maitén
24. Antártida
25. Mustapic
26. Cabo de Hornos
27. Canal Beagle & ACA Offices
28. Hotel Albatros

1. Museum
2. Tierra del Fuego National Park Office
3. Aerolíneas Argentinas
4. Tourist Office
5. Casa de Gobierno
6. Plaza 25 de Mayo
7. Plaza Luis Piedrabuena
8. Immigration
9. Banco de la Nación
10. Banco de Santa Cruz
11. Post Office
12. Telefónica Argentina

to the hatchery. Birdwatchers will also find this ride rewarding. Skiing, hiking, climbing: contact Club Andino, Solís 50, or Caminante. Skiing: A downhill ski run (beginner standard) on Cerro Martial. There is another ski run, Wallner, 3 km from Ushuaia, open Jun-Aug, has lights for night-skiing and is run by Club Andino. The area is excellent for cross country skiing; Caminante organizes excursions "off road". 20 km E of Ushuaia is Valle Tierra Mayoria, a large flat valley with high standard facilities for cross country skiing, snow shoeing and snowmobiling; rentals and a cafeteria; bus am and 1400 from Antartur, San Martín 638.

Travel Agents All agencies charge the same fees for excursions; with 3 or 4 people it is often little more expensive to hire a *remise* taxi. *Rumbo Sur*, San Martín 342, T 21139, runs a range of tours on water and on land and offers a two-day package to Cafayate, US$150 incl transport and hotel, good value. Also organizes bus to ski slope, very helpful. *Antartur*, San Martín 638, T 23240. *All Patagonia*, 25 de Mayo 31, of A, T 24432, F 30707, Amex agent; *Onas Tours*, 25 de Mayo 50, T 23429, just off main street, very friendly. *Aventura Austral*, Maipú 237, catamaran trip to Estancia Harberton, highly rec; *Tiempo Libre*, San Martín 863, T 21017, rec, English spoken. *Caminante*, Don Bosco 319, T 32723, F 31040, organizes walking, climbing tours and horse riding to suit all levels of experience, provides food, tents, equipment, outdoor clothing, detailed map, very friendly and helpful, English and German spoken, highly rec. *Kilak*, Kuanip 67, T 22234, for horse-riding tours. Recommended guide: Domingo Galussio, Intervú 15, Casa 211, 9410 Ushuaia, bilingual, not cheap (US$120), rec.

Tourist Office San Martín 660, T/F (0964) 24550, "best in Argentina", literature in English, German and Dutch, helpful, English spoken. Large chart of hotels and prices and information on travel and staying at Estancia Harberton, off road to Río Grande. Open Mon-Fri 0830-2030, Sat and Sun 0900-2000. National Park Office, on San Martín between Patagonia y Sarmiento, has small map but not much information. The ACA office on Maipú also has maps and information.

Car Hire Tagle, San Martín y Belgrano, T 22744, good, also **Río Grande**, Elcano 799, T 22571, and Localiza, in *Hotel Albatros* and at airport, one T 30663.

Airport Aerolíneas Argentinas, daily to BsAs via Río Gallegos and Trelew, all year round, over 4½ hrs. To **Río Grande**, AR 3 a week, US$26, LADE once a week (irregular, US$24), Kaiken (T 23049/22620), daily, US$27. To **Río Gallegos**, LADE once a week, US$39 incl airport tax, Kaiken, daily, US$49, AR, daily, US$56 (same price as bus). LADE to Comodoro Rivadavia via Río Grande, Río Gallogos, Calafate/Lago Argentino, Gob Gregores and Perito Moreno on Thur. Kaiken to **Punta Arenas** via Río Grande, Mon-Sat, 1100, US$90. Also with Ladeco, Tues and Fri 1540, US$120, continuing to Puerto Montt and Santiago.

Services are more frequent in high season; in winter weather often impedes flights. In the summer tourist season it is sometimes difficult to get a flight out. Since Río Grande airport can take larger planes than Ushuaia (until the new airfield is built), it may be easier to get a flight to Río Grande and travel on from there. At the airport ask around for a pilot willing to take you on a ½ hr flight around Ushuaia, US$38 pp (best to go in pm when wind has dropped). Alternatively ask about flights at the tourist office in town. Taxi to airport, US$3, or 30 mins walk (no bus).

New airport being built, but some say it won't be ready until 2000.

Airline Offices LADE, Av San Martín 564, T 21123, airport T 21700; Austral, Barberis agency, Av San Martín 638, T 23235; Aerolíneas Argentinas, Roca 160, T 21093, airport 21265; Kaiken, San Martín 857, T 23663, or at airport, T 22620/23049.

Rail A Decauville gauge train for tourists runs along the shore of the Beagle Channel between the Fin del Mundo station in Ushuaia to the boundary of the Tierra del Fuego National Park, 2.2 km, US$15; it is planned to continue to Lapataia, 3.8 km. Run by Ferrocarril Austral Fueguino with new locomotives and carriages, it evokes the early "trencito de los presos" (train for prisoners).

Buses run daily between Ushuaia and Río Grande 4 hrs, 0600, 0700, 1900, US$21, Transportes Los Carlos, Rosas 85, T 22337, and Tecni Austral, San Martín 657, T 21945. There are bus services between Río Grande and Porvenir in the Chilean part of the island (242 km, 6-8 hrs) but no air connection. There is a twice-weekly service to Punta Arenas on Mon and Fri, dep 0300 with Transportes Los Carlos, 14 hrs, US$46, a comfortable and interesting ride via Punta Delgada. Trucks leave Ushuaia for the refinery at San Sebastián Mon-Fri, but hitching is very difficult (easier via Bahía Azul and Punta Delgada where there is more traffic). A good place to hitch is from police control on Route 3.

Excursions To the *Parque Nacional Tierra del Fuego*, W of Ushuaia on the Chilean frontier (entrance is 12 km W). At Km 30 from Ushuaia is **Lapataia Bay**. US$3.50 National Park fee (free before 31 Oct). Minibus to National Park from Turismo Pasarela, Fadul 40, T 21735, US$10 return, 4 times a day, first at 1000, last back 2000 from Lago Roca in the Park. In summer Caminante run minibuses to the National Park, departing from Don Bosco 319, 2 or 3 a day, US$15 return. A similar service is operated by two other agencies. Caminante also runs a one day excursion to the Parque Nacional, incl trek, canoeing, *asado* lunch, US$70 inclusive (small groups, book early). Ask at the tourist office about cycling tours in the park, US$65 full day, also "Eco Treks" available and cultural events (ask for Ricardo Araujo, Fundación Antártica). See above for **Camping** possibilities. In winter the temperature drops to as low as -12°C, in summer it goes up to 25°C. Even in the summer the climate can often be cold, damp and unpredictable. It is possible to hitch-hike, as far as Lapataia. Rangers in the park are friendly and will sometimes put people up for a couple of days (as will police) and help with places to visit. A ranger truck leaves Ushuaia every weekday at 1300 and picks up hitch-hikers. Beaver inhabit the Parque Nacional near the Chilean border; one may see beaver dams and with much luck and patience the beavers themselves stand still and down-wind of them: their sense of smell and hearing are good, but not their eyesight. There are many beautiful walks. No maps of the Park are available and hiking can be interrupted by the Chilean border. Good climbing on Cerro Cóndor, rec. Reports that most of the park has been closed off to preserve nature (Feb 1994).

There are excursions to the Cerro Martial and the glacier (itself unspectacular but fine views down the Beagle Channel and to the N) about 7 km behind the town; take road behind *Hotel Antártida*, 2 km to small dam, then 3-4 hour walk along trail to get to chairlift, camping possible. (In winter the Cerro is inaccessible, even on foot; a bus leaves at 1030, 1200, 1400, 1600, 1800, returning 1100, 1230, 1430, 1630, 1830, in summer from in front of Rumba Sur office, US$5 return.) Also to the falls of the Olivia river.

Accommodation At Lago Fagnano: **D Hostería El Kaiken**, T 0964-24427 (ACA) also bungalows, nice site, well-run facilities, cheap drinks, on a promontory 93 km from Ushuaia, has real bath. At Lago Escondido **C El Petrel Inn**, 54 km from Ushuaia after a spectacular climb through Garibaldi Pass, on the road to Río Grande (bus dep 0900, returns 1500, US$17 return, min 4 people), T 24390, trout fishing possible, boat rides, friendly staff. Facilities at *Kaiken* and *Petrel* are open all year round. These inns are rec for peace and quiet.

Los Carlos bus to Lago Fagnano, 2½ hrs, US$10, then from lake to Río Grande 2 hrs, US$11. Tours also arranged to Lagos Fagnano and Escondido, 5-6 hrs, dep 0930, US$25, and aerial excursions over the Beagle Channel (with local flying club, hangar at airport, 3-5 seater planes, 30 mins), Lago Fagnano, Lapataia and Ushuaia Bay. To Lago Escondido/Fagnano US$50; bus to Puerto Almanza (on Beagle Channel), 75 km, 4-5 hrs, US$18.

The Estancia **Harberton**, the oldest on the island, now run by descendents of a British missionary, Mr Bridges. It offers guided walks through protected forest (not Mon) and tea, in Manacatush confitería (T 22742). You can camp. It can be reached by rented car from Ushuaia and by boat (long trip, most of it on the boat and the sea can be very rough, US$65). By car, leave Ushuaia on Route 3, after 40 km fork right on Route J, passing Lago Victoria, then 25 km through forest before the open country around Harberton (85 km in all). Some parts of the road are bad; tiring driving, 5 hrs there and back. Agency tours to the Estancia, by land cost US$30 plus US$6 entrance, but take your own food as the Estancia is expensive. Tours to the Estancia and to the penguin colony by boat and bus, Mon, Tues, Fri, Sun, US$72 plus US$6 entrance, 12 hrs, from all agents, take own food. Some tour agencies in Ushuaia imply that their excursions go to the Estancia though in fact they only go to the bay; others go by inflatable launch from main boat to shore. Check thoroughly in advance.

Sea Trips Rumbo Sur does a whole-day trip by catamaran down the Beagle Channel to see wildlife, with return by bus, highly rec (see above under **Travel Agents**). Similar tours operated by Aventura Travel, US$70. Take food, on board it is overpriced. *Tres Marías* is a fishing boat, tours are 7 hrs, departing 0900, maximum 8 passengers, incl sea lion and sea bird watching, fishing for king crabs, 2 hr trek on Isla de los Lobos (a private island), lunch and a snack incl, US$70 pp (half day US$40 pp), through agencies Antartur, All Patagonia, Caminante, Tiempo Libre. In summer, chartered trips may be taken to see the sealions on Isla de Los Lobos, US$40, 4-5 hrs, or by catamaran, US$25, dep 0930, 1430, 2½ hrs. Ask at Rumbo Sur; the *Ana B* leaves 0930 and 1430 daily, US$30, English and Spanish-speaking guide, expensive food and drinks on board. Interesting boat trips of 3 weeks' duration on the 2,346 ton *Lindblad Explorer* and others cost from US$6,500.

To Puerto Williams, Chile, with Aventura Austral on *Catamaran 14*, 12 hrs, Wed and Sat (end 1993), US$65 pp, take own lunch, post office and postcards available in Puerto Williams, immigration formalities dealt with on board. El Caminante, Don Bosco 319, has also been recommended for trips to Puerto Williams. Luxury cruises around the horn via Puerto Williams are operated by the Chilean company, Tierra Austral, 7/8 days, US$1,260. Ask at the Club Náutico for trips in private launches or catamaran (US$60 pp in Apr 1993), to Puerto Williams.

Isla de los Estados Robert T Cook writes: "This long (75 km) and guarded island lies E of Tierra del Fuego. Except for the caretakers of the lighthouse and an occasional scientist few people ever set foot on this cloud-shrouded reserve of Fuegian flora and fauna that no longer exist on the main island. During the 18th and 19th centuries large numbers of ships were wrecked or lost in the treacherous waters surrounding this island. Much gold, silver and relics await salvage." Information and tours from Rumbo Sur, San Martín 342, Ushuaia.

Argentina apparently has plans for tourist developments in **Antarctica** (accommodation at Marambio and Esperanza stations). Flights can be arranged in Buenos Aires in Jan-Feb through Surexpress, Esmeralda 629, 4th floor, T 325-0252. The plane goes to Ushuaia and you take a boat from there. Also try Andy Macfarlane at Macren Travel, T 322-7988. Complete trips for US$6,000-8,000 for 11 days can be booked at Corrientes 536, 10th floor, T 394-5399. The National Institute of the Antarctic is at Cerrito 1248, T 816-6313/1689, 0900-1500.

INFORMATION FOR VISITORS

Before you go

Entry requirements

● **Documents**

Check visa requirements as they change frequently. Passports are not required by citizens of neighbouring countries who hold identity cards issued by their own Governments. No visa is necessary for US citizens, British citizens and nationals of other Western European countries (except Spain), Canada, Mexico, El Salvador, Nicaragua, Malaysia, Israel, Hungary, Poland, Slovenia and Japan, who may stay for 3 months, a period which can be renewed for another 3 months at the National Directorate of Migration. For all others there are three forms of visa: a business 'temporary' visa (US$28 for UK passport holders, valid 1 year), a tourist visa (US$28), and a transit visa. Australians, New Zealanders and South Africans need visas. (Australians applying for a visa in London must have a letter from Australia House confirming passport ownership.) Tourist visas are usually valid for three months in Argentina and for any number of exits and entrances during that period. If leaving Argentina on a short trip, check on re-entry that the border officials look at the correct expiry date on your visa, otherwise they will give only 30 days. Renewing a visa is difficult and can only be done for 30-day periods. Visitors should carry passports at all times; backpackers are particular targets for thorough searches – just stay calm; it is illegal not to have identification handy. When crossing land frontiers, remember that though the migration and customs officials are generally friendly, helpful and efficient, the police at the control posts a little further into Argentina tend to be extremely bureaucratic in their approach.

At land borders, 90 days permission to stay is usually given without proof of transportation out of Argentina. If you need a 90-day extension for your stay in Argentina, get a new stamp at the first opportunity. Do not be put off by immigration officials in provincial cities who say that the stamp is not necessary, or too complicated to obtain. You can also leave the country, at Iguazú or to Uruguay, and 90 further days will be given on return. Without a valid stamp you will be fined US$40 on leaving.

NB At Argentine/Uruguayan borders one immigration official will stamp passports for both countries. Under Mercosur regulations (1992), borders between Argentina, Uruguay, Paraguay and Brazil are open 24 hrs a day. Argentine immigration and customs officials wear civilian dress. The border patrol, *gendarmeria*, in green combat fatigues, operate some borders.

● **Representation overseas**

Australia, 100 Miller Street, Suite 6, Level 30, North Sydney, New South Wales 2060, T 2922-7272, F 2 923-1798; **Belgium**, 225 Avenue Louise B.3, 1050 Brussels, T 2 647-7812, F 2 467-9319; **Canada**, 90 Sparks Street, Suite 620, Ottawa KIP 5B4, T 613 236-2351, F 613 235-2659; **France**, 6 Rue Cimarosa 75116 Paris, T 1 4553-3300, F 1 4553-44633; **Germany**, Wiesenhuetten-platz 26, 8th Floor, 6000 Frankfurt, T 496 923-1050, F 496 923-6842; **Netherlands**, Herengracht 94 1015 BS, Amsterdam, T 2 023-2723/6242, F 2 062-67344; **New Zealand**, 11 Floor, Harbour View Bldg, 02 Quay Street, PO Box 2320, Auckland, T 9 39-1757, F 9 373-5386; **Spain**, Paseo de la Castellana 53, Madrid 1, Madrid, T 1 442-4500, F 1 442-3559; **UK**, 53 Hans Place, London SW1X 0LA, T 071 584-6494, F 071 589-3106; **USA**, 12 West 56th Street, New York 10019, T 212 603-0400, F 212 397-3523.

● **Tourist information**
Addresses of tourist offices are given in the text.

● **Tourist offices overseas**
Delegations abroad: Bonn, Eduardo Piva, Penthouse 1, Suite F, Bldg AmeriFirst, Adenauerallee 52, 5300 Bonn, T 228-222011; New York, López Lecube, 12 West 56 St, NY10019, T 603-0400; Rome, Luis Ruzzi, Via B Ammamati 6, T 963-60-1485; São Paulo, Ruben Eduardo Ali, Av Paulista 2319, Argentine Embassy, F (5511) 881-4063.

● **Specialist tours**
An increasing number of foreign visitors are birdwatchers. Since at least 980 of the 2,926 species of birds registered in South America exist in Argentina, in places with easy access, enthusiasts head for Península Valdés, Patagonia, the subtropical forests in the NW, or the Chaco savannah in the NE. Tours to observe and photograph the animals are led by expert guides.

● **Maps**
The best road maps are those of the ACA (see above). Topographical maps are issued by the Instituto Geográfico Militar, Cabildo 301, Casilla 1426, Buenos Aires (reached by *Subte* D to Ministro Carranza – or Palermo while Min Carranza is closed for repair – where IGM is one block from station – turn right from station, or take bus 152 from Retiro). 1:500,000 sheets cost US$3 each and are 'years old'; better coverage of 1:100,000 and 1:250,000, but no general physical maps of the whole country or city plans. Helpful staff, sales office accessible from street, no passport required, map series indices on counter, open Mon-Fri, 0800-1300. Pirelli publishes a good series of maps (N, Central and S Argentina), with plenty of tourist information.

Health

Argentina is in general a healthy country to visit, with good sanitary services. In some provinces, like Neuquén and Salta, medical assistance, incl operations, X-ray and medication, is free in provincial hospitals, even for foreigners. Sometimes, though, one must pay for materials. All private clinics, on the other hand, charge. Medicines are more expensive than in Europe (eg US$8.20 for Paracetamol drops for children). Smallpox vaccination no longer required to enter Argentina. If intending to visit the low-lying tropical areas, it is advisable to take precautions against malaria. Chagas' disease (**see Health Information**) is found in NW Argentina. To counter the effects of altitude in the NW, chew coca leaves

or take *te de coca* (use of coca is legal, its trade is not). In the S take plenty of sunscreen to prevent burning owing to the thinning of the ozone layer. Certain shellfish from the Atlantic coast are affected once or twice a year by red algae (*Marea roja*), at which time the public is warned not to eat them. Buy seafood, if self-catering, from fishmongers with fridge or freezer. To be certain, soak fish for 30 mins in water with a little vinegar. Cholera presents no problem except in some remote villages on the Bermejo and Pilcomayo rivers in the tropical lowlands of the Salta and Jujuy provinces, where the Mataco and Toba tribes have been affected by the disease. If travelling through this region, use bottled water and take your own food.

Money

● **Currency**
In Jan 1992 a new currency – the peso – was introduced at par with the dollar. The peso is divided into 100 centavos. Peso notes in circulation: 1, 2, 5, 10, 20, 50 and 100. All old Austral notes were withdrawn from circulation by 31 March 1993. There is an acute shortage of small denomination notes and coins. Coins in circulation: 5, 10, 25 and 50 centavos and 1 peso. It is often difficult to change TCs, particularly in the smaller towns. There is a 3% tax on cheques and commissions can be as high as 10% and in banks is generally 4%. Commission can be avoided if you go to a branch of the issuing bank, especially if changing small amounts. It can take a long time and many forms to transact these cheques. Cheques are often scrutinized very closely: any variation between signatures can lead to their being refused. It is best to take US$ cash (which is widely accepted in larger, more expensive establishments, but take only utterly unblemished notes, dirty or torn notes are usually refused) and American Express TCs, which can be changed at the American Express bank in Buenos Aires. (In N Argentina, while Amex card is widely accepted, Amex TCs are hard to change.) Citibank TCs have been rec; no commission is charged at their own branches around the country. Buy TCs from Citibank itself if possible, as the name is written more clearly. Emergency cash from Amex is available only in Buenos Aires and Bariloche. Because of TCs fraud there are periodic crackdowns on particular types; take more than one type to avoid being stuck without funds. Thomas Cook Mastercard TC refund assistance center, 25 de Mayo 195, 6° piso, Buenos Aires, T 343-8371. It is not advisable to engage in

unsolicited currency transactions on the street as you may be tricked or have problems with the police. Some of the major towns have exchange shops (casas de cambio) and these are given in the text. In Dec 1989, the exchange rate was freed and exchange controls were lifted, so there was no market rate from which travellers could benefit as opposed to the official exchange rate. This régime was in force at the time of going to press, but you are advised to check for changes at the time of your visit. Exchange rates are quoted in major newspapers daily. Money remitted to Argentina from abroad is normally paid out in local currency. It is possible to obtain money from Europe through an express transfer, which takes 2-3 days, and the currency will be subject to tax. For Western Union, T (1) 322-7774. If staying for a long time in Argentina and especially Buenos Aires, you can transfer money from your bank in your home country to a local bank, opening an account in pesos or dollars. Paperwork is not complicated and your money is safe and gaining interest. Check with your bank before leaving.

The provinces of Tucumán, Jujuy and La Rioja have issued bonos (bonds) which circulate at face value alongside the national currency. Two warnings: they are not accepted outside the province of issue and even inside province of issue they are not accepted for some transactions, eg trains, long distance buses. Also, they bear redemption dates, after which they are valueless. Beware!

When crossing a land frontier into Argentina, make sure you have some Argentine currency as there are normally no facilities at the border.

● **Cost of living**
In 1995, Argentina was very expensive for the foreign visitor. Budget travellers should allow US$35-40 a day minimum. High costs can be expected for items such as slide film, and clothing as well as basics, although you can save money by camping and preparing your own food. Imported electronic goods are cheap.

● **Credit cards**
American Express, Diners Club, Visa and Mastercard cards are all accepted. There is a 10% surcharge on credit card transactions in many establishments. Credit cards are readily accepted in all main towns, even in the S, but outside main towns their use is limited. In the S very few service stations accept credit cards (ACA stations only take cards from members) and filling a tank can cost US$40. All shops, hotels and places showing Argencard (head office, H Yrigoyen 878, Buenos Aires, T 331-

2088) signs will accept Eurocard and Access, but you must state that these cards are affiliated to Mastercard. Argencard will not permit cash advances on these cards in outlying regions, and is itself very slow in advancing cash. Lloyds Bank, in many cities, handles Mastercard.

● **Value-added tax**
VAT is not levied on most medicines and some foodstuffs but on all other products and services 18% (raised "temporarily" to 21% 1 April 1995).

Getting there

By Air

● **From Europe**
British Airways (non-stop, 3 times a week) and Aerolíneas Argentinas (AR once, via Paris and Madrid) each fly from London. Aerolíneas also fly to the following European destinations (with other carriers in parentheses): Frankfurt (once a week, Lufthansa, 3 times); Madrid (7 a week, Iberia, daily); Paris (4 a week, Air France, 4 a week); Rome (3 a week, also Alitalia); Zurich (once, Swiss Air, 3 times). KLM flies 3 times a week from Amsterdam. Aeroflot flies from Moscow on Mon with a stopover in Cape Verde Islands.

● **From North America**
Aerolíneas Argentinas fly from the following US destinations (with other carriers in brackets): Los Angeles (6 times weekly, United); Miami (daily, LanChile, American, United); New York (daily, Lan Chile, American, United). Ladeco flies 3 times a week from Baltimore, New York and Miami; American from Dallas daily via Miami; United from Chicago daily. Canadian Air International, fly 3 times a week from Toronto; Aerolíneas fly twice a week from Toronto, once a week from Montreal. **NB** AR is part of Continental's frequent flier programme.

● **From Australasia and South Africa**
Aerolíneas Argentinas fly from Sydney, Australia, via Auckland, New Zealand, on Tues and Fri. On the outward flight from Argentina (Mon), Aerolíneas stop at Río Gallegos, but it is difficult to board there in high season. Malaysia Airlines fly twice a week from Johannesburg and Cape Town.

● **From Latin America**
Aerolíneas Argentinas and Lapsa daily from Asunción; AR (4) and Avianca (4) from Bogotá; Viasa from Caracas (5 a week); Saeta from Quito and Guayaquil, AR from the latter only; AR and LAB twice a week from La Paz via Santa Cruz, once a week from Santa Cruz;

from Lima, AR (3), AeroPerú daily; AR 4 a week from Mexico City; from Montevideo (apart from those given in the Buenos Aires section), AR, Pluna, Varig, United and Iberia (operated by AR); frequent flights also to Punta del Este, with many more in holiday season; from Santiago, Chile, daily with AR, Ladeco and LanChile and other Latin American, European and North American carriers on various days; from Panama City, AR once a week.

From Brazil, AR, Varig and Vasp fly daily from Rio de Janeiro and São Paulo (plus European airlines stopping over at both cities); Varig stops over in Porto Alegre, Transbrasil flies daily from São Paulo and Porto Alegre; AR also fly from Porto Alegre, via Montevideo. See under Brazil, or **Introduction and Hints**, for the Mercosur Air Pass.

By Road

For entering Argentina by automobile see **Motoring, Additional Notes** in **Introduction and Hints**. Tourists can bring into Argentina their own cars, vehicles bought or hired in neighbouring countries for up to 8 months under international documentation. No specific papers are usually required to bring a Brazilian registered car into Argentina.

Customs

No duties are charged on clothing, personal effects, toilet necessities, etc. Cameras, typewriters, binoculars, radios and other things which a tourist normally carries are duty-free if they have been used and only one of each article is carried. This is also true of scientific and professional instruments for the personal use of the traveller. Travellers may only bring in new personal goods up to a value of US$200 (US$100 from neighbouring countries); the amount of duty and tax payable amounts to 50% of the item's cost. There are red and green divisions at airport customs. Baggage claim tags are inspected at the exit from the customs inspection area. All incoming baggage is normally inspected. Keep US$20 notes separate from main money supply; they may be asked for as 'payment'.

2 litres of alcoholic drinks, 400 cigarettes, 40 cigars and 4 kg of foodstuffs are also allowed in duty-free; for tourists originating from neighbouring countries the respective quantities allowed are 1 litre, 200, 20 and 2 kg. You can buy duty-free goods *on arrival* at Ezeiza airport.

If having packages sent to Argentina, do not use the green customs label unless the contents are of real value and you expect to pay duty. For such things as books or samples use the white label if available.

When you arrive

● **Airport information**

Do not send unaccompanied luggage to Argentina; it can take up to 3 days of form-filling to retrieve it from the airport. Paying overweight, though expensive, saves time.

● **Clothing**

Shorts are worn in Buenos Aires and residential suburbs in spring, summer and autumn, but their use is not common outside the capital. Bermuda-type shorts are very fashionable, as are jogging suits. In general, dress tends to be formal (unless casual wear is specified on an invitation) in Buenos Aires and for evening outings to shows, etc. The general standard of dress among Argentines is very high: collar and tie, with jacket, are very much the standard for men, and women 'should always err on the side of elegance' – David Mackintosh. Men wearing earrings can expect comments, even hostility, in the provinces.

● **Hours of business**

Banks, government offices, insurance offices and business houses are not open on Sat. *Government Offices*: 1230-1930 in the winter and 0730-1300 in summer. *Banks*: generally 1000-1500 but time varies according to the city, and sometimes according to the season. (See under names of cities in text.) *Post Offices*: 0800 to midnight for telegrams. Stamps on sale during working days 0800-2000 but 0800-1400 on Sat. *Shops* are open from about 0900 to 1900, though many close at midday on Sat. Outside the main cities many close for the daily afternoon siesta, reopening at about 1700. 24-hr opening is allowed except on Mon; this applies mainly to restaurants, foodshops, barbers, newspaper shops, art, book and record stores.

Dance halls open at 2300 but don't fill up till after midnight; night clubs open after midnight. In city centre, cafés and restaurants are busy till after midnight and many evening events, such as lectures, may not start before 2200.

● **Official Time**

3 hrs behind GMT.

● **Safety**

Argentina is one of the safest countries in South America but in Buenos Aires and other major cities beware of the increasingly common trick of spraying mustard (or ketchup) on you and then getting an accomplice to clean you off (and remove your wallet). If you are sprayed, walk straight on.

NB Never carry weapons, or drugs without prescriptions.

● **Shopping**

Local leather goods in Buenos Aires, eg coats (leather or suede), handbags and shoes. *Ciudad del Cuero*, Florida 940, has clothing, footwear and luggage from 40 manufacturers. NB Leather from the *carpincho* is from the capybara and should not be purchased. A gourd for drinking *yerba mate* and the silver *bombilla* which goes with it, perhaps a pair of *gaucho* trousers, the *bombachas*. Ponchos (red and black for men, all colours for women). *El Guasquero* in Calle Anasagasti specializes in old *gaucho* objects, saddlery, *bolas*, horn items, all genuine and reconditioned by Sr Flores, the owner. The shop is N of Av Santa Fe, near Calle Bulnes, Buenos Aires (postcode 2028). Articles of onyx, specially in Salta. Silver handicrafts. In Buenos Aires, there is a good, reasonable and helpful souvenir shop on Av de Mayo near Chacabuco. Knitted woollens, especially in Bariloche and Mar del Plata. If you like honey, the Casa de la Miel has different honeys from every province. Try Mendoza or Tucumán varieties.

● **Voltage**

220 volts (and 110 too in some hotels), 50 cycles, AC, European Continental-type plugs in old buildings, Australian 3-pin flat-type in the new. Adaptors can be purchased locally for either type (ie from new 3-pin to old 2-pin and vice-versa).

● **Weights and measures**

The metric system is used.

On departure

● **Airport tax**

US$15 for all international flights, except to Montevideo, which is subject to US$3 tax; US$3-6, payable only in pesos also for internal flights (US$1.75 in Ushuaia). When in transit from one international flight to another, you may be obliged to pass through immigration and customs, have your passport stamped and be made to pay an airport tax on departure. There is a 5% tax on the purchase of air tickets.

Where to stay

● **Camping and youth hostels**

Camping is very popular in Argentina (except in Buenos Aires) and there are sites with services, both municipal, free, and paying private campsites in most tourist centres. Most are very noisy and many are closed off-season. Camping is allowed at the side of major highways and in all national parks (except at Iguazú Falls). Wild camping in deserted areas is possible, but note that in Patagonia strong winds make camping very difficult. Many ACA service stations have a site where one can camp, and in general service station owners are very friendly to campers, but ask first. Service stations usually have hot showers. A list of camping sites is available from ACA (labelled for members, but should be easily available and from the main tourist office in Av Santa Fe, BsAs); see Autoclub magazine. References to sites will be found in the text. ACA campsites offer discounts to members, and to holders of the International Driving Licence; European automobile clubs' members are allowed to use ACA sites. The Danmark Organization, Junín 1616, 3rd Flr, Buenos Aires, T (54-1) 803-3700, has a network of clean, cheap youth hostels throughout Argentina (no age limit, but card needed): in Bariloche, El Bolsón, Pinamar, Calafate and the Tigre Delta. There are few other youth hostels (many open only Feb to Mar), but some towns offer free accommodation to young travellers in the holiday season, on floors of schools or church halls; some fire stations will let you sleep on the floor for free (sometimes men only). Many garages have showers that you can use. Good lightweight tents are now available, eg Cacique. Regular (blue bottle) Camping Gaz International is available in Buenos Aires, at an electrical goods store on Av 9 de Julio, near Teatro Colón, and Suntime, Lima 225, Guatemala 5908 (Palermo), Juramento 2452 (Belgrano) and América Pesca, Alfredo Pollini Alvear 1461. Camping Center, Acoyte 1622, Buenos Aires, T 855-0619, rents camping, fishing and backpacking equipment, 5% discount for ISIC holders.

Food and drink

Food

National dishes are based in the main upon plentiful supplies of beef. Many dishes are distinctive and excellent; the *asado*, a roast cooked on an open fire or grill; *puchero*, a stew, very good indeed; *bife a caballo*, steak topped with a fried egg; the *carbonada* (onions, tomatoes, minced beef), particularly good in Buenos Aires; *churrasco*, a thick grilled steak; *parrillada*, a mixed grill, mainly roast meat, offal, and sausages, *chorizos* (incl *morcilla*, black pudding to the British, or blood sausage), though do not confuse this with *bife de chorizo*, which is a rump steak (*bife de lomo* is fillet steak). A *choripán* is a roll with a *chorizo* inside. *Arroz con pollo* is a delicious combination of rice, chicken, eggs, vegetables and strong sauce. *Puchero de gallina* is chicken, sausage, maize, potatoes and squash cooked together. *Empanada* is a tasty meat pie; *empanadas de humita* are filled with a thick paste of cooked corn/maize, onions, cheese and flour. *Milanesa de pollo* (breaded, boneless chicken) is usually good value. *Ñoquis* (gnocchi), potato dumplings normally served with meat and tomato sauce, are tasty and often the cheapest item on the menu; they are also a good vegetarian option when served with either *al tuco* or Argentine roquefort (note that most places only serve them on the 29th of the month, when you should put a coin under your plate for luck). *Locro* is a thick stew made of maize, white beans, beef, sausages, pumpkin and herbs. Pizzas come in all sorts of exotic flavours, both savoury and sweet. **NB** Extras such as chips, *puré* (mashed potato), etc are ordered and served separately, and are not cheap. Almost uniquely in Latin America, salads are quite safe. A popular sweet is *dulce de leche* (especially from Chascomús), milk and sugar evaporated to a pale, soft fudge. Other popular desserts are *almendrado* (ice-cream rolled in crushed almonds), *dulce de patata* (sweet potato preserve), *dulce de membrillo* (quince preserve), *dulce de zapallo* (pumpkin in syrup); these *dulces* are often eaten with cheese. *Postre Balcarce*, a cream and meringue cake and *alfajores*, maize-flour biscuits filled with *dulce de leche* or apricot jam, are also very popular. Sweets: the Havana brands have been particularly rec. Excellent Italian-style ice-cream with exotic flavours. For local recipes (in Spanish) *Las Comidas de Mi Pueblo*, by Margarita Palacios, is rec.

Offices close for 2 to 2½ hours for lunch between 1200 and 1500. Around 1700, many people go to a *confitería* for tea, sandwiches and cakes. Dinner often begins at 2200 or 2230; it is, in the main, a repetition of lunch. Budget travellers should note that especially in Buenos Aires a number of cheaper restaurants are advertised as *tenedor libre* – eat all you want for a fixed price. Those wishing to prepare their own food will find supermarkets fairly cheap for basics.

Drink

Argentine wines (incl champagnes, both charmat and champenoise) are sound throughout the price range. The ordinary *vinos de la casa*, or *comunes* are wholesome and relatively cheap; reds better than the whites. Among the wines highly praised by correspondents, are Etchart Cabernet Sauvignon and Torrontés (white), Michel Torino Torrontés, Weinert, Flickemann, and Santa Ana Cabernet Sauvignon. The local beers, mainly lager-type, are quite acceptable. In restaurants wines have become more expensive (up to US$20/bottle for a good quality wine). Hard liquor is relatively cheap, except for imported whisky. *Clericó* is a white-wine *sangría* drink in summer. It is best not to drink the tap water; in the main cities it is often heavily chlorinated. It is usual to drink soda or mineral water at restaurants, and many Argentines mix it with their cheaper wine, with ice, as a refreshing drink in summer. *Yerba mate*, a very popular home-grown tea, is widely drunk, especially in the interior, continuing the old *gaucho* custom. The tea is called *mate*; the gourd from which it is drunk is called *un mate*.

Getting around

Air transport

Internal air services are run by Aerolíneas Argentinas (AR), Austral, Lapa (reliable turboprop and Boeing 737 services from Buenos Aires to Córdoba, Tucumán, Salta, Mendoza, Iguazú, Bariloche, Villa Gesell, Mar del Plata, Necochea, cheaper than main airlines), TAN (Transporte Aéreo Neuquén) in the S (book tickets through Austral), LAER (Entre Ríos, Mesopotamia), Aeroposta in the S and the army airline LADE (in Patagonia), which provides a good extended schedule with new Fokker F-28 jets. **NB** LADE will not accept IATA MCOs. Inter Austral is a subsidiary of Austral. Deregulation and privatization has permitted the introduction of discounts by the major carriers. Ask at a travel agency. (Even though sometimes offices in various towns may tell you the flights are full, it is usually worth a try out at the airport.) The naval air passenger service, Aeronaval, carries paying civilian passengers, one third cheaper than LADE. No firm schedule though; 2 flights a week between Ushuaia, Río Grande and Río Gallegos; once a week between Ushuaia and Buenos Aires. Some airlines, like Air Kaiken operate during the high season, or are air taxis on a semi-regular schedule. Check with both main airlines about discounts on certain flights. All airlines operate standby systems, at half regular price, buy ticket 2-3 hrs before flight. It is only worth doing this off season. *Plan familiar* tickets allow couples to travel with a 25%

discount for the spouse. Children under 3 travel free. LADE also operates discount spouse (65%) and children (35%) tickets. If travelling by AR or Austral a long linear distance, eg Río Gallegos-Buenos Aires, but wishing to stop en route, it is cheaper to buy the long flight and pay extra (about US$2) for stopovers. **NB** All local flights are fully booked way in advance for travel in Dec. Don't lose your baggage ticket; you won't be able to collect your bags without it. Some travellers have rec checking in 2 hrs before flight to avoid being 'bumped off' from overbooking.

Visit Argentina fare Aerolíneas Argentinas sells a Visit Argentina ticket: 4 flight coupons costing US$450, with US$120 for each extra coupon up to a maximum of 8. It is valid for 30 days and must be purchased outside Argentina and in conjunction with an international flight ticket. Austral sell similar tickets (known as Jetpaq) and they are interchangeable (but cannot be used on Inter Austral). Routing must be booked when the coupons are issued: one change of date and destination is free (but subsequent changes cost US$50). One stop only is permitted per town; this incl making a connection (as many flights radiate from Buenos Aires, journeys to and from the capital count as legs on the airpass, so a 4-coupon pass might not get you very far). If you start your journey outside Buenos Aires on a Sun, when Aerolíneas Argentinas offices are closed, you may have difficulty getting vouchers issued at the airport. If you wish to visit Tierra del Fuego and Lago Argentino it is better fly on the Visit Argentina pass to Río Grande or Ushuaia and travel around by bus or LADE from there than to stop off in Río Gallegos, fly to Ushuaia and thence back to Buenos Aires, which will use 3 coupons. Children travel at a 50% discount, infants 10%. Domestic timetables are given in *Guía Argentina de Tráfico Aéreo* and *Guía Internacional de Tráfico*. It is unwise to set up too tight a schedule because of delays which may be caused by bad weather. Flights between Buenos Aires and Río Gallegos are often fully booked 2 to 3 weeks ahead, and there may be similar difficulties on the routes to Bariloche and Iguazú. If you are 'waitlisted' they cannot ensure a seat. Reconfirmation at least 24 hrs ahead of a flight is important and it is essential to make it at the point of departure. Extra charges are made for reconfirming LADE flights (useful in Santa Cruz and Tierra del Fuego) but they are not high.

Land transport

● Train
See under Buenos Aires, **Railways**: the future of rail services in Argentina is most uncertain.

● Bus
Fares are charged at about US$4.50 per 100 km. Sleeper services from the capital to Mendoza, Córdoba and Bariloche cost US$7/100 km. There are also 'ómnibus truchos' (fake buses), which do not start or end services at bus stations and which have less reliable equipment or time-keeping; they charge less than US$4/100 km (ask at travel agents or hotels). Most bus companies give a 20% student discount if you show an international student card; a YHA card is also useful. The same discount may also be given to foreign, as well as Argentine, teachers and university professors but you must carry documentary proof of your employment. It can be difficult to get reductions between Dec and Mar. Express buses between cities are dearer than the *comunes*, but well worth the extra money for the fewer stops. When buying tickets at a bus office, don't assume you've been automatically allotted a seat. make sure you have one. Buses have strong a/c, even more so in summer; take a sweater for night journeys.

● Motoring
All motorists are required to carry two warning triangles, a fire-extinguisher, a rigid tow bar, a first aid kit, full car documentation together with international driving licence (for non-residents, but see **Car Hire** below), and the handbrake must be fully operative. Safety belts must be worn if fitted. Although few checks are made in most of the country, with the notable exceptions of roads into Rosario and Buenos Aires, checks have been reported on cars entering the country. **NB** Police checks around Buenos Aires can be very officious, even to the point of charges being invented and huge 'fines' demanded. You may not export fuel from Argentina, so use up fuel in spare jerry cans while you are in the country. Always fill up when you can in less developed areas like Chaco and Formosa and especially in Patagonia as filling stations are infrequent. Diesel fuel 'gas-oil' prices are US$0.27 per litre. Octane rating for gasoline ('*nafta*') is as follows: regular gasoline 83 (US$0.65/litre); super 93(US$0.78/litre). Unleaded fuel is not widely available but its use is increasing (it is called Ultra SP and costs a little more than super). ACA sells petrol vouchers (*vales de nafta*) for use in ACA stations. Shell and Esso stations are slightly more expensive.

To obtain documents for a resident (holder of resident visa, staying at least 6 months in the country) to take a car out of Argentina, you can go to ACA in Buenos Aires, which may take up to 4 working days, or you can ask for a list of other ACA offices that can undertake the work; take forms with you from Buenos Aires, and papers may be ready in 24 hrs. You will need at least one passport-size photo, which you can have taken at ACA at a fair cost. If the car is not your own (or is hired), you require a special form signed by the owner and witnessed by a notary public. **NB** Non-residents may buy a car in Argentina but are in no circumstances allowed to take it out of the country; it must be resold in Argentina, preferably in the province where it was purchased. If buying a used car, the procedures are complicated and expensive, and must be handled correctly to ensure that the possessor of the vehicle is actually the owner. The vehicle must be checked by a trustworthy mechanic to see that the motor and chassis numbers agree with those in the ownership documents; the purchaser and owner must go to the local Registro de Automotores to review the documents and then to the Municipalidad to check that tax (*patente*) has been paid. Employ a *gestoria* to undertake all the paperwork, which will cost about US$150 in all, and take you to *gendarmería* to check the vehicle's identification numbers (US$8) and then to the Registro de Automotores to obtain certificate of ownership (*cédula verde*), with your name and local address on it. The new owner has to pay tax at the municipality where it was paid last; if you pay up to the end of the year you will receive a 'libre de deuda' (US$10). At control posts drivers have to show the *cédula verde*, proof of payment of tax, sometimes a driver's licence, the items required mentioned above, and all lights and tyres may be checked. If you move to another province, your new address has to be registered on all the vehicle documents with a 'cambio de radicación'. Third party insurance is obligatory; best obtained from the ACA, for members only.

Most main roads are paved, if rather narrow (road maps are a good indication of quality), and roadside services are good. Road surface conditions vary once one leaves main towns: high speeds are quite possible on the dirt and gravel roads, as long as you have the essential guard for the windscreen. Most main roads now have private tolls, ranging from US$2 to US$10; tolls are spaced about every 100 km. Secondary roads (which have not been privatized) are generally in poor condition. Sometimes one may not be allowed to reach a border if one does not intend to cross it, stopping eg 20 km from the border.

Automóvil Club Argentino (ACA), Av Libertador General San Martín 1850, 1st flr, touring department on 3rd flr, 1425 Buenos Aires, T 802-6061/9, open 1000-1800 (take colectivo 130 from LN Alem and Corrientes down Alem, Libertador and F Alcorta, alight opp ACA and walk 1 block through park; to return take the 130 from corner of Libertador on left as you leave building), office on Florida above Harrod's, 2nd flr, has a travel document service, complete car service facilities, insurance facilities, road information, road charts (*hojas de ruta*-about US$2.35 each to members, if available) and maps (dated with the code letters in the bottom corner – road map of whole country, with service stations and *hosterías* shown, US$4 to members, US$9.50 to non-members, and of each province), a hotel list, camping information, and a tourist guide book sold at a discount to its members and members of other recognized, foreign automobile clubs upon presentation of a membership card. (YPF, the state oil agency, also produces good maps for sale.) **NB** Members of other recognized automobile clubs are advised to check if their club has reciprocity with ACA, thus allowing use of ACA facilities and benefit from lower prices for their rooms and meals at ACA *hosterías*. The Club has service stations, some with parking garages, all over the country. If you are not a member of ACA you will not get any help when in trouble. ACA membership permits you to pay with Eurocard (Argencard) for fuel at their Service stations, gives 20% discount on hotel rooms and maps, and discounts at associated hotels, and 10% discount on meals.

ACA accommodation comes in 4 basic types: *Motel*, *Hostería*, *Hotel*, and *Unidades Turísticas*, and they also organize campsites (see below). A *motel* may have as few as 3 rooms, and only 1 night's stay is permitted. *Hosterías* have very attractive buildings and are very friendly. *Hotels* are smarter and more impersonal. All have meal facilities of some kind. Anyone can get in touch with the organization to find out about accommodation or road conditions.

Hitch-hikers, as well as motorists, are rec to contact the ACA for its wealth of information.

Touring Club Argentino, Esmeralda 605 and Tucumán 781 3rd flr, T 392-6742 has similar travel services but no service stations.

● **Motorcycle**
Repairs at Eduardo Olivera, Mecánica Ruben SA, Lavoiser 1187-1674, Sáenz Peña, Buenos

Aires, T 757-4285, excellent BMW mechanic with good selection of spares. Juan Carlos Topcic, Costa Rica 25, casa 48, 9400 Río Gallegos, T 0966-23572, all makes.

● **Motorhomes**

Casa Import Trailer, Av Juan de Garay 331, T 361-5674, sells articles for motorhomes. Casa Car, Humberto Primo 236, T 30-0051, rents motorhomes. Rancho Móvil, Luis Viale 2821, T 59-9470, is club for motorhome owners; all in Buenos Aires. Porta-Potti toilets are widely sold in Argentina, sometimes under a different name.

● **Car hire**

To rent a small car (for four plus luggage) costs from US$40 to US$110 a day, not incl mileage, fuel, insurance and tax (20%); highest prices are in Patagonia. Discounts are available for several days', or weekly rental. Minimum age for renting is 25 (private arrangements may be possible). A credit card is useful. You must ensure that the renting agency gives you ownership papers of the vehicle, which have to be shown at police and military checks. At tourist centres such as Salta, Posadas, Bariloche or Mendoza it may be more economical to hire a taxi with driver, which includes the guide, the fuel, the insurance and the mechanic. Avis offers a good and efficient service with the possibility of complete insurance and unlimited mileage for rentals of 7 days or more, but you should prebook from abroad. No one-way fee if returned to another Avis office, but the car may not be taken out of the country. Localiza, a Brazilian company, accepts drivers aged at least 21 (according to Brazilian rules, but higher insurance). They also offer 4WD vehicles, though only from Buenos Aires. Taking a rented car out of Argentina is difficult with any company. Other companies are given in the text.

If you do not have an international driver's licence, you can get a 3-month licence from Dirección de Transportes de la Municipalidad, Av Roca 5225, Buenos Aires, T 602-6925, Mon-Fri 0800-1300; bring documentation from home.

● **Hitchhiking**

Argentina seems to be getting increasingly difficult for this. Ask at petrol stations. Traffic can be sparse, especially at distances from the main towns, and in Patagonia. It may be useful to carry a letter from your Consulate. Though they tend to be more reserved in manner than most Latin Americans, Argentines are generally friendly and helpful, especially to foreigners (display your flag, but not the Union Jack).

Communications

● **Language**

Spanish, with variant words and pronunciation. English comes second; French and Italian (especially in Patagonia) may be useful.

The chief variant pronunciations are the replacement of the "ll" and "y" sounds by a soft "j" sound, as in "azure" (though note that this is not done in Mendoza), the omission of the "d" sound in words ending in "-ado" (generally considered uncultured), the omission of final "s" sounds, the pronunciation of "s" before a consonant as a Scottish or German "ch", and the substitution in the N and W of the normal rolled "r" sound by a hybrid "rj". In grammar the Spanish "tú" is replaced by "vos" and the second person singular conjugation of verbs has the accent on the last syllable eg *vos tenés, podés,* etc. In the N and NW, though, the Spanish is more akin to that spoken in the rest of Latin America.

● **Newspapers**

Buenos Aires dailies: *La Nación, La Prensa.* Tabloids: *Clarín, La Razón.* Evening papers: *Crónica.* English language daily: *Buenos Aires Herald.* Magazines: *Noticias, Gente, Redacción, Mercado, El Gráfico* (sports). The daily, *Página Doce,* is very popular among students and intellectuals. English language magazines: *The Review of the River Plate* (commercial, agricultural, political and economic comment), and *The Southern Cross* (Irish community). German-language weekly, *Argentinisches Tageblatt,* available everywhere, very informative. There is a weekly international edition of *La Nación,* priced in Europe at US$1.30. Write for further information to: La Nación, Edición Internacional, Bouchard 557, 1106 Buenos Aires.

● **Postal services**

Letters from Argentina take up to a month to get to the UK and the USA (but service is improving). Rates for letters up to 20 grams: US$0.75 Mercosur, US$1 rest of Latin America, US$1.25 rest of world (add US$2 for *certificado*); up to 150 grams, US$1.50, US$2.25, US$3 respectively.

Small parcels only of 1 kg at post offices; larger parcels from Encomiendas Internacionales, Centro Postal Internacional, Av Antártida Argentina, near Retiro Station, Buenos Aires, and in main provincial cities, about US$40 for 5 kg. Larger parcels must first be examined, before final packing, by Customs, then wrapped (up to 2 kg, brown paper; over 2 kg must be sewn in linen cloth), then sealed by Customs, then taken to Encomiendas Internacionales for posting. Cheap packing service available. Open 1100-1700 on weekdays. Used clothes have to be fumigated before they will be accepted. Having parcels sent to Argentina incurs a customs tax of about US$3/package. *Poste restante* is available in every town's main post office, fee US$1.

● **Radio**
English language radio broadcasts can be heard daily on short wave: 0100-0130 on 6060 KHz 49m, 0230-0300 on 11710 KHz 25m, 0430-0500 and 2230-2300 on 15345 KHz 19m; Radiodifusión Argentina al Exterior, Casilla de Correo 555, 1000, Buenos Aires. This is a government station and broadcasts also in Japanese, Arabic, German, French, Italian and Portuguese. Broadcasts by foreign radio stations (incl the BBC) are receivable on short wave.

● **Telephone services**
Two private companies operate telephone services, Telecom in the N and Telefónica Argentina in the S. Buenos Aires Federal District and the country as a whole are split roughly in two halves. For the user there is no difference and the two companies' phone cards are interchangeable. For domestic calls public phones operate on *cospeles* (tokens) which can be purchased at news stands. On weekdays, 2200-0800, and from Sat 1300 to 0800 Mon inland and local calls cost one third (Telefónica Argentina) and international calls are reduced by 20%; other offices have different reduced rate hours. Rates per minute for international calls, full rate (Mar 1995): USA US$3.52; Paraguay, Chile US$3.55; Spain, Italy US$4.22; Canada, UK, France US$5.10; Japan, Hong Kong US$6.37. All charges are payable only in pesos. In main cities there are also privately-run 'Centros de Llamadas', offering a good telephone and fax service. International public phones display the DDI sign (Discado Directo Internacional); DDN (Discado Directo Nacional) is for phone calls within Argentina. Provide yourself with enough tokens or phone cards in Buenos Aires because, in the regions, phone booths exist, but the tokens and cards are not on sale. Most telephone company offices in principal cities have a phone for USA Direct; if they do not, they can direct you to one. There is frequently a high mark-up on calls made from hotels; beware of erroneous charges for international calls on hotel bills. No reverse-charge calls to South Africa. It is now easy to call reverse charge to Australia. Operator speaks English. Fax: American Express in Buenos Aires allows card holders to receive Faxes at US$1 per sheet and to send them at

US$8/sheet (to Europe). Telefónica and Telecom send faxes abroad for US$1.23/page, plus cost of the call, and US$1.82/page to receive.

NB Owing to modernization, many 2- and 3-digit prefixes are being changed (**see p 75**).

Sport

Fishing The three main areas for fishing are the Northern Zone, around Junín de los Andes, extending S to Bariloche; the Central Zone around Esquel; the Southern Zone around Río Gallegos and Río Grande. To fish anywhere in Argentina you need a permit, which costs US$10/day, US$30/week, US$100/year. In the Northern Zone forestry commission inspectors are very diligent. For tours arranged from the UK, contact Sport Elite (JA Valdes-Scott), Woodwalls House, Corscombe, Dorchester, Dorset, DT2 0NT.

Walking and skiing Details on outdoor activities in Argentina can be found in *Weekend* (Spanish), good photos and excellent maps. Information on trails in NW Argentina, the Lake District, and Tierra del Fuego is given in *Backpacking in Chile and Argentina*, 3rd edition 1994 (Bradt Publications, 41 Nortoft Road, Chalfont St Peter, Bucks, SL9 0LA, UK). Note that Bradt Publications' *South America Ski Guide* (1992) gives details of Argentine ski resorts.

The skiing season is May to end-Oct; best sites are Las Leñas (Mendoza, which has many other small sites), Chapelco, San Martín de los Andes, Bariloche and La Hoya (nr Esquel, cheapest, but shorter runs).

Holidays and festivals

The main holiday period, generally to be avoided by business visitors, is Jan-Mar, though some areas, such as Tierra del Fuego, begin to fill up in Nov/Dec. Winter school holidays, in which travelling and hotels may be difficult, are the middle two weeks of Jul. No work may be done on the national holidays (1 May, 25 May, 20 June, 9 July, 17 Aug, 12 Oct and 25 Dec) except where specifically established by law. There are no bus services on 25 and 31 Dec. On 1 Jan, Holy Thursday and Good Friday, and 8 Dec employers are left free to decide whether their employees should work, or banks and public offices are closed. Banks are also closed on 31 Dec. There are gaucho parades throughout Argentina, with traditional music, on the days leading up to the Día de la Tradición, 10 Nov. On 30 Dec (not 31 because so many offices in centre are closed) there is a ticker-tape tradition in downtown Buenos Aires: it snows paper and the crowds stuff passing cars and buses with long streamers.

Further reading

Federico B Kirbus has written the highly informative *Guía de Aventuras y Turismo de la Argentina* (with comprehensive English index – 1989), obtainable at El Ateneo, or from the author at Casilla de Correo 5210, 1000, Buenos Aires. Kirbus has also written the *Guía Ilustrada de las Regiones Turísticas Argentinas*, 4 volumes, NW, NE, Centre, S, with about 300 black and white photos, colour pictures and colour plates on flora and fauna (published by El Ateneo); also *La Argentina, país de Maravillas*, Manrique Zago ediciones (1993), a beautiful book of photographs with text in Spanish and English. *Nuestros Paisanos Los Indios* by Carlos Martínez Sarasola is an excellent compendium on the history and present of Argentine Indian communities, rec. The Fundación Vida Silvestre (conservation organization and bookshop), Defensa 245/251, has information and books on Argentine flora and fauna. Field guide to Argentine birds: *Guía para la identificación de las aves de Argentina y Uruguay* by T Narosky and D Yzurieta, with drawings and colour illustrations. Among a number of guide books to the country, recent rec additions are *Travel Companion: Argentina* by Gerry Leitner, the *Pirelli Guide* by Diego Bigongiari, US$18, incl maps, rec for cultural, historical and nature information, and the *Insight Guide* to Argentina.

British business travellers are strongly advised to read '*Hints to Exporters: Argentina*', obtainable from DTI Export Publications, PO Box 55, Stratford-upon-Avon, Warwickshire, CV37 9GE. Similar information is provided for US citizens by the US Department of Commerce.

Acknowledgements

We wish to offer our profound thanks to Alan Murphy for doing the updating. For their generous assistance we wish to thank Federico Kirbus, Herbert S. Levi and Brad Krupsaw (all from Buenos Aires), and Carola Burton (Bariloche). Thanks are also due to the following residents and travellers: Anika Absolan (Vienna, Austria), Daniel Aeberhard (Slough, UK) an excellent contribution, Louise Bach (Vestbjerg) and Tine Tang Kleif (Aarhus, Denmark), David Barton (Willenhall, UK), Niki Beattie (Cobham, Surrey), Janie Bergeron and François Vitez (Longueuil, Canada), Phil and Jenny Blackman (Bath, UK), Stephen Bone (Lingfield, UK), Ruth Brandt (Israel), Anke Brednich (Frieburg, Germany), Terrie Catlow (Buenos Aires, Argentina), Ludovic Challeat (Lamastre, France), Diego Puls (Amsterdam, The Netherlands), Carmelita Chávez (Vista, USA), Etienne Claes (Brugge, Belgium), Bernard Cloutier (Montreal, Canada), Judith Stanton and Mark Collins (London, UK) a helpful up-date, Mary Crow (Ft Collins, USA), Kathrin and Henning Dictus (Neuwied, Germany), Karl Dokter (Munich, Germany), Jae and Gerry Duffy (Elizabeth, USA), Olivier Dumoulin (Buenos Aires, Argentina), Jayne Dyer and Nicholas Hird (Bexhill-on-Sea, UK), Eddie Edmundson (British Council, Recife, Brazil), Urs Eggli (Zurich, Switzerland), Jakob Engström and Richard Björlin (Brussels, Belgium), Gonzalo I Fernández (Viña del Mar, Chile), Stefanie Floegel (Vilsbiburg, Germany), Valerie Fraser and Tim Butler (Lima, Peru) many long and informative letters, Gisa Gericke (Wetzlar), Nicole Hofmann (Weisbaden), and Tanja Wirth (Flörsheim, Germany), Mariecke van der Gias (Utrecht, The Netherlands), Michael Gonin (Canberra, Australia), Nicole Gotze (Bariloche, Argentina), Loukas Grafakos (Papagou, Greece), Herbert Gramm (Cambridge, USA), Matt Griffin (Seattle, USA), Sylvia Grisez (Warren, USA), Erez Guilatt (Jerusalem, Israel), John W Guinee (Reston, USA), Jay Hassani (Baltimore, USA), Sibylle Hössler (Munich, Germany), Carlos and Seba Orellana (Buenos Aires), A Jachnow and A Kuhn (Berlin, Germany), Marten H Jacobsen and Brit R Lauritsen (Denmark), Guy Jarvi (Bondi, Australia), Kate Jenikes (Eugene, USA), Patrick J Paludan (Valby) and Erik Hassenkamm (Valby and Skanderberg, Denmark), Sonja Jovanovic and Andrew Thompson (London, UK) a helpful letter S and Othmer KamerGüntert (Uetikon, Switzerland), Mark Kent (Asunción, Paraguay), May-Britt Koopman (Triesen, Switzerland), Kato and Mark Kostrzewa (Mountain View, USA), M Leufgens and M Jollands (Alsdorf, Germany), Riika Levoranta (Vammala) and Vesa Lampiner (Möjärvi, Finland), Thomas Lüscher (Rümikon, Switzerland), Claire Marin and Jean-Claude Praz (Baar/Nendaz, Switzerland), Egon Otto Mayer (Mendoza, Argentina), Peter McFadden (Conwy, UK), Oliver Meiser (Pfullingen, Germany) a very detailed contribution Mr Max Mizejewski (Kerby, USA), Rachel Morán (Ruxton, USA), Christiane Moser (Frieburg, Germany), Christina Müller (Hanau, Germany), Martijn Mugge (Enschede, The Netherlands), Mark Muhlbacher (Lucerne, Switzerland) for many letters Hans-Peter Neusch (Stuttgart, Germany), Holly O'Callagnan (Durazno, Uruguay), Paul Olai-

Olssen (Oslo, Norway), T P O'Sullivan (Loughborough, UK), Serge Ouddane (Paysandú, Uruguay), Luzia Portmann and Rolf Studer (Lucerne, Switzerland), Margorie Powell (Cambridge, UK) extensive contribution, Cindy Raider (Concepción del Louguay, Argentina), Lawrence Railton and Susan Boyd (London, UK), Guillermo Ramires (Kings Cross, Australia), Urs Riegger (Zurich, Switzerland), Thomas and Petra Sbampato (Wallisetten, Switzerland), Burkhard Schack and Michael Zickgraf (Seelbach, Germany), Doris Schmittat (Weisbaden, Germany), Herbert K Schmitz (Potomac, USA), Therese Schöb (Zurich) and Urs Steinmann (Gruningen, Switzerland), Rüdiger Schultz (St Gallen, Switzerland), Ken Simons (London, UK), Jorge Antolín Solache (Calafate, Argentina), Marianne and Jürg Weber, Claudia Hess Steiner and Thomas Steiner (Lyss, Switzerland), Patrick Sterckx (Grez-Doiceau, Belgium), J R Stourton (Cirencester, UK), Alexandra Strickner and Peter Buda (Vienna, Austria), Urs and Verena Stuber (Schindellogi, Switzerland), Astrid Studer and Andreas Hediger (Reinach, Switzerland), Pim and Irma Sybesma (Leiden, The Netherlands), Ilay Tamari (Ramat-Hasharon, Israel), Rainer Teck (Solingen, Germany), Ron and Dorothy Thyer (Blackburn, Australia), A.ndrios Tieleman and Ditty Bakker (Haarlem, The Netherlands), Peter Titz (Oberwil, Switzerland), Jean Tremlett (Carshalton, UK), Arnaud Troost and Fenna den Hartog (Rotterdam, The Netherlands), Samuel Urech (Niederhasli, Switzerland), Eric and Ingrid Van den Broeck (Leuven, Belgium), Ruben Vázquez (Santa Cruz, Argentina), Margot Verhagen and Carel van der Velden (Holland), Infanger Vinzenz (Erstfeld, Switzerland) an extensive contribution Dre Visscher (Tilburg, The Netherlands), Ron Wain (Teddington) and Steve 'Ribs' Harrop (Cardiff, UK), Noemi Wallingre and Al Bianco (Buenos Aires, Argentina), Dr Volker Weinmann (Blumenau, Brazil), Jane Westlake (London, UK), Jacqui White (Salta, Argentina), Marc Williamson (Melbourne, Australia) an extensive contribution, Natalie and Derek Windsor (Durham, UK), Christian Leonards and Sandra Winterhalter (Insel Reichenau, Germany) and P Lamartine Yates (Cuvat, France).

BOLIVIA

INTRODUCTION

BOLIVIA, straddling the Andes, is a land of gaunt mountains, cold desolate plateaux and fertile, semi tropical lowlands. In area it is about twice the size of Spain. It is land-locked, with Chile and Peru to the W, Brazil to N and E, and Argentina and Paraguay to the S.

The Andean range is at its widest, some 650 km, in Bolivia. The Western Cordillera, which separates Bolivia from Chile, has high peaks of between 5,800 and 6,500m and a number of active volcanoes along its crest. The passes across it are above 4,000m. To the E of this range lies the bleak, treeless, windswept Altiplano, much of it 4,000m above sea-level. It has an average width of 140 km, is 840 km long, and covers an area (in Bolivia) of 102,300 sq km, or nearly 10% of the country. Its surface is by no means flat, for the Western Cordillera sends spurs into it which tend to divide it into basins. The more fertile northern part is the more inhabited; the S part is parched desert and almost unoccupied, save for a mining town here and there. Nearly 70% of the population lives on it, for it contains most of the major cities; almost half of the people are urban dwellers.

Lake Titicaca, at the northern end of the Altiplano, is an inland sea of 8,965 sq km at 3,810m: the highest navigable water in the world. Its maximum length and breadth are 171 and 64 km, and the greatest known depth is 280m. There are large annual variations between high and low water levels; 95% of the water flowing into it is lost by evaporation, making it more salty than most freshwater lakes. The immense depth of the water keeps the lake at an even all-the-year-around temperature of 10°C. This modifies the extremes of winter and

1 La Paz, Titicaca & the Peruvian Frontier
2 The Yungas
3 Oruro & Routes to Chile and Argentina
4 Potosi, Sucre and the Southern Highlands
5 The Cochabamba Basin
6 The Northern Lowlands
7 Eastern Bolivia

BOLIVIA

Not to Scale

night temperatures on the surrounding land, which supports a large Aymara indian population, tilling the fields and the hill terraces and tending their sheep and llamas.

The Altiplano is a harsh, strange land, a dreary grey solitude except for the bursts of green after rain. The air is unbelievably clear—the whole plateau is a bowl of luminous light. A cold wind blows frequently in the afternoons, causing dust storms. During the winter temperatures fall below freezing point; there is frost every night in July and August, but during the day the tropical sun raises temperatures over 20°C.

The animals of the Altiplano are fascinating. Llamas serve as pack animals. They carry up to 22 kg loads up to 20 km a day and yield about 2½ kg of wool when sheared at intervals of from two to five years. The alpaca, bred not for work but for wool, belongs to the same group; the two may be distinguished by differences in the texture of their coats and shape of their tails. The vicuña, chinchilla and red fox are the main wild animals. The vicuña, an untamed smaller member of the family to which the llama and the alpaca belong, is found, though in diminishing numbers, on the bleak pampas. It may not be hunted, but its fine silky, tawny coloured wool may be sold.

Agriculture in the Altiplano is also interesting: the potato and the *oca* (another tuber), eaten in the dehydrated form of *chuño* and *tunta*, are the main crops. *Quinoa*, a kind of millet, and *cañava*, a smaller and darker grain, are the main cereals; both are extremely nutritious. *Chicha*, the national intoxicant, is brewed from maize (corn). Edible fish (small *boga*, large white-fleshed *pejerrey* and the rainbow and salmon trout with which Lake Titicaca has been stocked) are widely sold in the towns of the Altiplano.

Since the colonial period mining has been far more important to the economy of the Altiplano than agriculture. In 1545 the Spanish discovered Indian mine workings and vast reserves of silver, tin, bismuth and tungsten in a mountain which they called Cerro Rico (the "rich hill"). Interested only in silver, they built Potosí at its base, 4,070m above sea level. Today a much more important mining centre is Oruro, 210 km S of La Paz at the base of the Eastern Cordillera, where a low belt of hills supplies tin, copper, silver and tungsten. Nearby are the mines of Huanani, formerly owned by the tin magnate Simón Patiño, and Colquiri. Since the collapse of the world tin market in 1986, most of the other mines in the area have been closed or are now worked as small-scale cooperatives, including the ex-Patiño mines at Catavi, which used to produce nearly half the tin of Bolivia. Lack of investment and the high cost of producing Bolivian tin was a major contributor to the industry's decline. Silver is still mined or extracted from the tailings left by past generations, and variable amounts of lead, bismuth, antimony, tungsten and zinc from pockets in the Cordillera are exported. Large deposits of silver have been found S of the Altiplano, near Lípez, and mines are being reopened, and their tailings reprocessed, two centuries after the Spaniards abandoned them.

Recommended reading: *We Eat the Mines and the Mines Eat* Us by June Nash, New York, 1979, and *The Potosí Mita* 1573-1700 by Jeffery Cole, Stanford University Press, 1985.

From the Altiplano rises, to the E, the sharp façade of the Eastern Cordillera. As luck would have it there is a gently graded passageway along the plateau at the foot of the Eastern Cordillera from Lake Titicaca, in the N, to the Argentine frontier, in the S. From Viacha, near La Paz, a railway line runs S along this passageway to Villazón on the Argentine border with connections to Chile (from Uyuni). The giant masses of the northern parts of the Eastern Cordillera rise to very great heights in the Cordillera Real to the E of Lake Titicaca: four peaks soar to above 6,000m. This magnificent sight can be seen on a clear day from the top of a ridge on the more S Titicaca-La Paz road, which goes past Tiahuanaco. The far sides of the Cordillera Real fall away to the NE, very sharply, towards the Amazon basin.

These heavily forested north E slopes are deeply indented by the fertile valleys of the Nor Yungas and Sud Yungas, drained by the Río Beni and its tributaries, where cacao, coffee, sugar, coca and tropical fruits are grown. The problem of transport from here to the consuming centre of La Paz is formidable: the connecting all-weather road, hair-raising in places, climbs 3,430m in 80 km to surmount La Cumbre pass, at 4,725m within 24 km of La Paz.

Further S, from a point just N of Cochabamba the Eastern Cordillera is tilted, not to the NE, but to the E. This part of the Eastern Cordillera rises abruptly in sharp escarpments from the Altiplano, and then flattens out to an easy slope E to the plains: an area known as the Puna. The streams which flow across the Puna are tributaries of the Río Grande flowing NE to the basin of the Amazon, and of the Pilcomayo flowing SE through the Chaco to the Río de la Plata system. They cut increasingly deep incisions as they gather volume until, to the E, the Puna is eroded to little more than a high remnant between the river valleys. These valleys are densely inhabited; a variety of grain crops and fruits is grown. All these semi-tropical mountain valleys are known as Yungas: the generic name is not confined to the valleys of the Provinces of Nor and Sud Yungas to the E of La Paz. Rainfall in the Yungas is from 700 to 800 mm a year, as opposed to the 400 to 700 mm of the northern Altiplano and much less further S. The heaviest rain is during December, January and February. The mean average temperature is between 16° and 18°C, with high humidity.

The very fertile basins in which Cochabamba, Sucre, and Tarija lie send food and cattle to the towns of the Altiplano, but the other valleys have, until recently, lacked the communications to do so.

The lowland tropics, stretching from the foothills of the Eastern Cordillera to the frontiers with Brazil to the NE and E and with Paraguay and Argentina to the SE and S, take up 70% of the total area of Bolivia, but contain only about 20% of its population. Rainfall is high but seasonal, and large areas suffer from alternate flooding and drought. The climate is hot, ranging from 23° to 25°C in the S and to 27°C in the N. Occasional cold dust-laden winds from the S, the *surazos*, lower the temperature considerably. In the N and E the Oriente has dense tropical forest. Open plains covered with rough pasture, swamp and scrub occupy the centre. Towards the end of the 18th century this was a populous land of plenty; for 150 years Jesuit missionaries had controlled the area and guided it into a prosperous security. A symbol of their great effort is the cathedral at San José de Chiquitos: a gem of elegance and dignity. But the Jesuits were expelled in 1767; years of maladministration, spoliation and corruption reduced the area to lethargy.

This once rich land, drained by the Madre de Dios, Beni and Mamoré rivers into the Madeira, a tributary of the Amazon, has been isolated from the rest of the country. It is as difficult to get at from the E as from the W, for there are rapids and falls in the Madeira which limit navigation. In its heart lie the seasonally inundated tropical Llanos de Mojos, ringed in by rain forest or semi-deciduous tropical forest: 230,000 sq km with only 120,000 people. Roads and river connections are being improved; roads link Trinidad with La Paz and Santa Cruz, Guayaramerín and Riberalta with La Paz and Todos Santos and Puerto Villarroel with Cochabamba. Meat is now shipped from Trinidad, capital of Beni Department, and from airstrips in the area, to the urban centres of La Paz, Oruro, and Cochabamba.

The forests and plains beyond the Eastern Cordillera sweep S towards the Río Pilcomayo, getting progressively less rain and merging into a comparatively dry S land of scrub forest and arid savanna. The main city of this area is Santa Cruz de la Sierra, founded in the 16th century, now the second city of Bolivia and a large agricultural centre. Here conditions favour the growing of sugar-cane, rice, oil plants and citrus fruit. The plains to the E are mainly used as grazing lands with small areas under cultivation, but in this area are extensive oil, gas, and iron-ore deposits, possibly Bolivia's greatest asset when developed.

Climate There are four distinct climatic zones: (1) The tropical departments of Santa Cruz and Beni, drained by the Amazon; altitude between 150 and 750m; average temperature, 29°C. (2) The Yungas north of La Paz and Cochabamba, among the spurs of the Cordillera; altitude, 750-1,500m; average temperature, 24°C. (3) The Valles, or high valleys and basins gouged out by the rivers of the Puna; average temperature, 19°C. (4) The Puna and Altiplano; average temperature, 10°C, but above 4,000m may get down to -25°C at night in June-August. The period from December to April is considered the rainy season throughout Bolivia. Little rain falls upon the western plateaux between May and November, but the rest of the year can be wet. There is rain in all seasons in the E part of the country, heaviest from November to March.

History At Tiwanaku (Tiahuanaco), near Lake Titicaca, stand the impressive remains of a pre-Inca civilization. The Aymara speaking Indians in this area emerged around 1000 BC into a civilization characterized by massive stone buildings and monuments, exquisite textiles, pottery and metalwork. This phase seems to have been ended abruptly by some unexplained calamity around AD 900 (possibly the failure of the agricultural system). When the Quechua-speaking Incas of Cuzco conquered the area around AD 1200, they found the Aymaras at Tiahuanaco living among ruins they could no longer explain. The Aymaras resisted obstinately and were not finally conquered until the latter part of the 15th century in the reign of Inca Túpac Yupangi (1471-93). Even so, they kept their traditional social structures and language, and fought for the Incas under their own leaders. Only religion was formally imposed by the Incas. Kollasuyo, Inca Bolivia, was only a small part of the Inca empire and lasted only about 80 years.

Francisco Pizarro landed in Peru in 1532. Six years later Spain conquered Bolivia, and the next year La Plata, now Sucre (still the official capital), was founded. The excellent Inca communications system and economic organization fell into ruin. In 1559 La Plata became capital of the *audiencia* of Charcas, in the Viceroyalty of Peru. As a result of the discovery of silver at Potosí in 1545, Charcas became one of the most important centres of the Spanish colonial economy, sending a constant supply of silver to Spain. By 1610 Potosí, with a population of over 160,000 was the largest city in the Americas, but, as the richest deposits were exhausted and new mines opened in Mexico, Alto Peru, as present day Bolivia was known, went into decline.

Revolutionary movements against Spanish colonial rule began early; there were revolts at La Paz in 1661, at Cochabamba in 1730 and at Sucre, Cochabamba, Oruro and La Paz from 1776 to 1780. In 1809 the University of San Francisco Xavier, at Sucre, called for the independence of all Spain's American colonies. Finally, on 9 December 1824, Simón Bolívar's general, Gen Antonio José de Sucre, won the decisive battle of Ayacucho in Peru and invaded Alto Peru, defeating the Spaniards finally at the battle of Tumusla on 2 April 1825. On 9 February 1825, when he first entered La Paz, Sucre had already promulgated the decree of independence, but his second in command, Santa Cruz, was for retaining links with Peru; Bolívar was in two minds. Sucre had his way and Bolivia was declared independent.

For most of the period since independence, three main features have dominated Bolivian history: the importance of mining; the loss of territory through disputes and wars with neighbouring countries; and chronic political instability. Although silver had been so important in the colonial period, the Bolivian economy has depended for much of this century on exports of tin. The construction of railways and the demand for tin in Europe and the USA (particularly in wartime) led to a mining boom after 1900. By the 1920s the industry was dominated by three entrepreneurs, Simón Patiño, Mauricio Hochschild and the Aramayo family, who exercised great influence over national politics. The importance of mining and the harsh conditions in the isolated mining camps of the Altiplano led to the rise of a militant miners movement.

Bolivian politics have been even more turbulent than elsewhere in Latin America. Although in the nineteenth century the army was very small, officers were key figures in power-struggles, often backing different factions of the landowning elite. Between 1840 and 1849 there were 65 attempted coups d'etat. The longest lasting government of the nineteenth century was that of Andrés Santa Cruz (1829-1839), but when he tried to unite Bolivia with Peru in 1836, Chile and Argentina intervened to overthrow him. After the War of the Pacific (1879-1883) there was greater stability, but opposition to the political dominance of the city of Sucre culminated in a revolt in 1899 led by business groups from La Paz and the tin-mining areas, as a result of which La Paz became the centre of government.

Since independence Bolivia has suffered continual losses of territory, partly because of communications difficulties and the central government's inability to control distant provinces. The dispute between Chile and Peru over the nitrate-rich Atacama desert in 1879 soon dragged in Bolivia, which had signed a secret alliance with Peru in 1873. Following its rapid defeat in the War of the Pacific Bolivia lost her coastal provinces. As compensation Chile later agreed to build the railway between Arica and La Paz. Railways traded for valuable territory has been Bolivia's fate. A railway to Yacuiba was Argentina's return for annexing some of the Chaco. When Brazil annexed the rich Acre Territory in 1903, Bolivia was compensated by yet another railway, but this Madeira-Mamoré line never reached its destination,

Riberalta, and proved of little use; it was closed in 1972.

There was not even an unbuilt railway to compensate Bolivia for its next loss. A long-running dispute with Paraguay over the Chaco erupted into war in 1932. Defeat in the so-called Chaco War (1932-1935) resulted in the loss of three quarters of the Chaco (**see Paraguay chapter, p 1065**).

The Chaco War was a turning point in Bolivian history, increasing the political influence of the army which in 1936 seized power for the first time since the War of the Pacific. Defeat bred nationalist resentment among junior army officers who had served in the Chaco and also led to the creation of a nationalist party, the Movimiento Nacional Revolucionario (MNR) led by Víctor Paz Estenssoro. Their anger was directed against the mine owners and the leaders who had controlled Bolivian politics. Between 1936 and 1946 a series of unstable military governments followed. This decade witnessed the apparent suicide in 1939 of one president (Germán Busch) and the public lynching in 1946 of another (Gualberto Villarroel). After a period of civilian government, the 1951 elections were won by the MNR but a coup prevented the party from taking office.

In April 1952 the military government was overthrown by a popular revolution in which armed miners and peasants played a major role. Paz Estenssoro became president and his MNR government nationalized the mines, introduced universal suffrage and began the break-up and redistribution of large estates. The economy, however, deteriorated, partly because of the hostility of the US government. Paz's successor, Hernán Siles Zuazo (president 1956-1964), a hero of the 1952 revolution, was forced to take unpopular measures to stabilize the economy. Paz was re-elected president in 1960 and 1964, but shortly afterwards in November 1964 he was overthrown by his vice president, Gen René Barrientos, who relied on the support of the army and the peasants to defeat the miners.

The death of Barrientos in an air crash in 1969 was followed by three brief military governments. The third, led by Gen Torres, pursued left-wing policies which alarmed many army officers and business leaders. In August 1971 Torres was overthrown by Hugo Banzer, a right-wing general who outlawed political parties and trade unions. Banzer's government, though repressive, was mild by comparison with contemporary regimes in Argentina and Chile. After Banzer was forced to call elections in 1978, there was another period of short-lived military governments, which overruled elections in 1978 and 1979 giving victories to Siles Zuazo. One of these, led by Gen García Meza (1980-1981) was notable for its brutal treatment of opponents and its links to the cocaine trade which led to its isolation by the international community. In August 1982 the military returned to barracks and Dr Siles Zuazo assumed the Presidency in a leftist coalition government with support from the communists and trade unions. Under this regime inflation spiralled out of control. The elections of 14 July 1985 were won again by Víctor Paz Estenssoro, who imposed a rigorous programme to stabilize the economy. In the elections of 7 May 1989, Gonzalo Sánchez de Lozada of the Movimiento Nacionalista Revolucionario, MNR (chief architect of the stabilization programme) won most votes but the result was so close that Congress had to choose a president from the three leading contenders. Jaime Paz Zamora of the Movimiento de la Izquierda Revolucionaria (MIR) who came third in the elections, was inaugurated as President on 6 August 1989 after having made an unlikely alliance with the former military dictator, Gen (retired) Hugo Banzer (Acción Democrática Nacionalista), in return for certain cabinet posts.

At the end of Paz Zamora's term, the former military dictator General Luis García Meza was sentenced to 30 years in prison at a much-publicized trial. Although several of his accomplices were imprisoned at the same time on human rights charges, García Meza himself managed to escape during the trial. He was captured in Brazil in early 1994 and held there by the military until February 1995, when he was extradited to Bolivia. He is now held in solitary confinement in a prison outside

La Paz.

The presidential election of 6 June 1993 was fought between Acuerdo Patriótico, led by Hugo Banzer, a coalition of MIR, Banzer's own ADN and two other parties, Gonzalo Sánchez de Lozada of the MNR, Unidad Cívica Solidaridad (UCS), led by the brewery owner Max Fernández, and the populist Conciencia de Patria (Condepa) of Carlos Palenque. Gonzalo Sánchez de Lozada won the greater number of votes but failed to gain the required 51% majority to win the presidency outright. Shortly afterwards, however, the other candidates recognized Sánchez de Lozada's victory and withdrew from the contest.

The People Of the total population some two thirds are Indians, the remainder being *mestizos*, Europeans and others. The racial composition varies from place to place: Indian around Lake Titicaca; more than half Indian in La Paz; three-quarters *mestizo* or European in the Yungas, Cochabamba, Santa Cruz and Tarija, the most European of all. Since the 1980s, regional tensions between the "collas" (*altiplano* dwellers) and the "cambas" (lowlanders) have become more marked. Under 40% of children of school age attend school even though it is theoretically compulsory between 7 and 14.

About two-thirds of the population lives in adobe huts, and medical services are sketchy outside the towns and mining camps. Epidemics are comparatively rare on the Altiplano, but malaria and yellow fever are still problems in the Oriente and Santa Cruz, and hepatitis and Chagas disease (**see Health Hints in Introduction**) are endemic in the warmer parts of the country.

The most obdurate of Bolivian problems has always been that the main mass of population is, from a strictly economic viewpoint, in the wrong place, the poor Altiplano and not the potentially rich Oriente; and that the Indians live largely outside the monetary system on a self-sufficient basis. Since the land reform of 1952 isolated communities continue the old life but in the agricultural area around Lake Titicaca, the valleys of Cochabamba, the Yungas and the irrigated areas of the S, most peasants now own their land, however small the plot may be. Migration to the warmer and more fertile lands of the E region has been encouraged by the Government.

The highland Indians are composed of two groups: those in the N of the Altiplano who speak the guttural Aymara (an estimated 1 million), and those elsewhere, who speak Quechua, the Inca tongue (3 million). Outside the big cities many of them speak no Spanish, but knowledge of Spanish is increasing. In the lowlands are some 150,000 people in 30 groups, including the Ayoreo, Chiquitano, Chiriguano, Garavo, Chimane and Mojo. The lowland Indians are, in the main, Guaraní. About 70% of Bolivians are Aymara, Quecha or Tupi-Guaraní speakers. The first two are regarded as national languages, but were not, until very recently, taught in schools, a source of some resentment. There are also about 17,000 blacks, descendents of slaves brought from Peru and Buenos Aires in 16th century, who now live in the Yungas.

The Indian women retain their traditional costume, with bright petticoats, and in the highlands around La Paz wear, apparently from birth, a flattish brown or grey bowler (locally called a *bombín*). In Cochabamba they wear a white top hat of ripinoled straw. In Potosí, the women's hat is like a "stove-pipe". According to Peter McFarren (*An Insider's Guide to Bolivia*) there are over 100 styles of hat. The angle at which it is worn is significant, the variety is evidence of the strength of traditional costume, but the hat is also practical (protection against the sun and wind). Indians traditionally chew the coca leaf, which deadens hunger pains and gives a measure of oblivion. Efforts to control the cultivation of coca is one of many sources of friction between the indigenous population and the authorities; others include landlessness, and exploitation of labour. On feast days they drink with considerable application, wear the most sensational masks and dance till they drop.

NB Remember to refer to rural Indians not as "indios" (an insult) but as "campesinos" (peasants).

The Economy Bolivia is the poorest country on the South American mainland. Its poverty is partly attributable to its rugged terrain, which makes communications between the various parts of the country extremely difficult, and to its landlocked position.

The agricultural sector employs over one third of the working population and contributes 17% to gdp. Employment in agriculture has fallen since the mid-1960s because of increasing urbanization. Production of crops for food takes place primarily in the Altiplano, mainly by subsistence farmers, while crops for industrial use (cotton, sugar and soya) are concentrated around Santa Cruz. Most commercial agriculture is in the E, where there are a number of food-processing plants: vegetable oils, a maize mill and sugar refineries. The controversial area in agriculture is the cultivation of the coca leaf, used for chewing by the Indians and to make the drug cocaine. In the 1980s the extreme economic depression and rising unemployment drove increasing numbers in search of the lucrative cocaine trade. Coca is easy to grow, up to four crops a year can be harvested, and Bolivia's production is believed to be worth about US$2bn a year, although less than a third of that actually returns to the country.

In contrast to agriculture, mining, including oil, contributes 7.7% of gdp, yet about half of export earnings. Bolivia is a major producer of tin, antimony, wolfram and bismuth. Silver, lead and zinc are also produced and there are large unexploited reserves of lithium and potassium. Tin used to be the major mineral export, but because of the collapse of the world tin market, it has lost its dominant position in overall exports to natural gas and zinc.

Estimated reserves of natural gas are 111bn cu m, sufficient to meet domestic demand and export commitments for 30 years, but oil reserves, at 108 million barrels in 1994, were being exploited faster than the rate of discovery. Production of around 19,175 b/d was just sufficient to meet domestic demand, but would be insufficient were there to be a general economic recovery.

The recession which afflicted most Latin American countries from 1980 hit Bolivia with six consecutive years of contraction of gdp, accompanied by accelerating inflation, massive and frequent devaluations of the currency and social unrest. Government spending to support key export sectors was hampered by widespread inefficiency, corruption and strikes in state enterprises, which led to massive public sector deficits and external indebtedness. Economic problems were compounded in 1983 by a severe drought in the Altiplano and floods in the E lowlands, which devasted farming. The resulting food shortages exacerbated existing inflationary pressures and led to hyperinflation with annual rates reaching over 20,000%.

In the mid-1980s the government of President Paz Estenssoro introduced severe austerity measures to stabilize the economy, in which price controls were lifted, subsidies removed, public sector wages frozen and the currency linked to the US dollar in a controlled float. Tax reform was passed, a new currency, the boliviano, was created, worth 1 million pesos, the IMF agreed to disburse a standby credit, bilateral and multilateral lending began to flow again and steps were taken to buy back the external commercial bank debt. Inflation came down to 10-20% a year, although unemployment continued to rise and living standards to fall. Nevertheless, by the 1990s there were encouraging signs that growth and employment were recovering and structural adjustment had put Bolivia on a firmer footing (gdp grew by 4.2% in 1993 with inflation at 9.3%, 7.5% in 1994). Growth was insufficient, however, to relieve Bolivia's profound poverty and this, combined with widespread corruption, continues to fuel discontent. In 1994 President Sánchez de Lozada initiated a plan to privatize six state companies: private investors would take up to half the equity in each company without payment, but would agree to substantial, long-term investment. The remaining shares would be divided among the adult population, to be held in pension funds. The aim of the scheme, due to start in 1995, is to generate investment, jobs and economic growth.

Government The Constitution of 1967 vests executive power in the President, elected by popular vote for a term of 4 years; he cannot be immediately re-elected. Congress consists of two chambers: the Senate, with 27 seats, and the Chamber of Deputies, with 130 seats. There are nine departments; each is controlled by a Delegate appointed by the President.

Bolivia has, in effect, two capitals. Although Sucre is the legal capital, La Paz is in almost all respects the actual capital, being the seat of the Government and of Congress. The Supreme Court, however, still holds its sessions in Sucre.

Communications After centuries of isolation new roads are now integrating the food-producing eastern zones with the bulk of the population living in the towns of the Altiplano or the W-facing slopes of the Eastern Cordillera. Under Spanish rule there were four great trails in use within the country: three of them led through passes in the western Cordillera to the Pacific; the fourth led from La Paz S into Argentina. At the turn of the century, railways replaced the llamas and mules. By far the shortest line is the one from La Paz to Arica (Chile), completed in 1913. Arica ships a large part of the exports together with Antofagasta (Chile) and Matarani (Peru).

Bolivia has 3,774 km of railway. There are two private railways: Machacamarca-Uncia, owned by the Corporación Minera de Bolivia (108 km) and Uyuni-Pulacayo (52 km) owned by the Empresa Minera Pulacayo. A railway to link Cochabamba and Santa Cruz, as part of a Pacific-Atlantic rail network, has been under study with Inter-American Development Bank assistance since 1989. Bolivia has over 14,000 km of navigable rivers, which connect most of the country

Bolivia : fact file

Geographic

Land area	1,098,581 sq km
forested	51.2%
pastures	24.5%
cultivated	2.2%

Demographic

Population (1994)	7,888,000
annual growth rate (1989-94)	2.4%
urban	57.7%
rural	42.3%
density	7.2 per sq km
Religious affiliation	
Roman Catholic	92.5%
Birth rate per 1,000 (1993)	32.8
	(world av 26.0)

Education and Health

Life expectancy at birth,	
male	60.3 years
female	65.3 years
Infant mortality rate	
per 1,000 live births (1990-95)	75.1
Physicians (1991)	1 per 2,561 persons
Hospital beds (1990)	
	1 per 1,183 persons
Calorie intake as %	
of FAO requirement	84%
Population age 25 and over	
with no formal schooling	23.3%
Literate males (over 15)	84.7%
Literate females (over 15)	70.7%

Economic

GNP (1992 market prices)	US$5,084mn
GNP per capita	US$680
Public external debt (1992)	
	US$3,694mn
Tourism receipts (1991)	US$90mn
Inflation (annual av 1988-93)	14.8%
Radio	1 per 1.9 persons
Television	1 per 12 persons
Telephone	1 per 38 persons

Employment

Population economically active (1992)	
	2,530,409
Unemployment rate	19.0%
% of labour force in	
agriculture	38.9
mining	2.1
manufacturing	8.8
construction	5.1
Military forces	33,500

Source *Encyclopaedia Britannica.*

with the Amazon basin. The national highway system at the end of 1988 totalled 41,642 km, of which only 4% were paved and under 25% gravel-surfaced.

Music and Dance   The heart of Bolivia is the 2-mile (3¼ km) high Altiplano and it is the music of the Quechua- and Aymara-speaking Indians of this area that provides the most distinctive Bolivian musical sound. Although there is much that is of Spanish colonial origin in the Indians' dances, the music itself has more Amerindian style and content than that of any other country in South America. It is rare to find an Indian who cannot play an instrument and it is these instruments, both wind and percussion, that are quintessentially Bolivian. The clear sounds of the *quena* and *pinkullo*, the deeper, breathier notes of the *tarka*, *tarka*, *pututo* and *sicuri* accompanied by *huankaré*, *pululu* and *caja* drums can be heard all over the Altiplano, the *charango* being virtually the only instrument of European origin. The Indian dances are mainly collective and take place at religious fiestas. The dancers wear colourful costumes with elaborate, plumed headdresses and some of them still parody their ex-Spanish colonial masters. Such are the Auqui Auquis and Pakhochos dances. The Khachua dance on the other hand dates from the time of Inca Túpac Yupangi. Other notable dances are the Wititis, Wila Khawani, Jucumaris, Takiri de Kharmisa and Sikuris de Ayata.

The principal popular dances that can be regarded as "national" in their countrywide appeal are the Cueca and Huayño. The Bolivian Cueca is a close relative of the Chilean national dance of the same name and they share a mutual origin in the Zamacueca, itself derived from the Spanish Fandango. The Huayño is of Indian origin and involves numerous couples, who whirl around or advance down the street, arm-in-arm, in a "Pandilla". Other similar, but more regional dances are the Bailecito Chuquisaqueño, Khaluyo Cochabambino, Rueda Tarijeña from the SE and Carnavalito Cruceño and Taquirari Beniano from the tropical lowlands. Justly celebrated is the great carnival Diablada of Oruro, with its hordes of grotesquely masked devils, a spectacle comparable to those of Rio in Brazil and Barranquilla in Colombia.

The region of Tarija near the Argentine border has a distinctive musical tradition of its own, based on religious processions that culminate with that of San Roque on the first Sunday in September. The influence is Spanish, the dance is the Chapaqueada and the musical instruments are the *caña*, *erke* and *violin chapaco*. The first named is an immensely long bamboo tube with a horn at the end, aimed at the sky, on which different "Toques" are played.

There are many professional folk groups on record, the best known being Grupo Aymara, Los Runas, Los Laris, Los Masis, Kolla Marka and Bolivia Manta, some of which have now established themselves in Europe and North America.

Recommended reading: Herbert S Klein, *Bolivia: The Evolution of a Multi-Ethnic Society* (Oxford University Press). Latin American Bureau's *Bolivia in Focus*, on history, culture, politics and economics.

LA PAZ (1)

La Paz, Lake Titicaca and Mount Illimani are probably the three most familiar sights of Bolivia, set amid high Andean Altiplano and the Cordillera Real. The region around La Paz is known as Little Bolivia, containing snow-peaks, desert and sub-tropical jungle in Coroico, just one day's breathtaking bus-ride away.

La Paz, the highest capital in the world, lies in a steep canyon; Plaza Murillo in the centre, at 3,636m, is about 370m below the level of the Altiplano and the new city of El Alto. Mount Illimani, with its snow-covered peaks (6,402m), towers over the city. One of the best ways to appreciate the setting is from the air. East-west flights pass by Illimani with beautiful views of the summit; the rim of the Altiplano, with El Alto built up to the edge, the old city descending the canyon, is very dramatic. The Spaniards chose this odd place for a city on 20 October 1548, to avoid the chill winds of the plateau, and because they had found gold in the Río Choqueyapu, which runs through the canyon. Beware of *soroche* (altitude sickness), especially if arriving from much lower altitudes by air. The mean average temperature is 10°C, but it varies greatly during each day, and the nights are cold. It rains almost every day from December to February, but the sun usually shines for several hours. The rest of the year is mostly clear and sunny. Snow is rare.

In 1993, the population of La Paz was estimated at 1.2 million, over half of it Indian. Orientation is relatively simple; a major avenue, changing its name from Av Mariscal Santa Cruz to Av 16 de Julio (this section is generally known as Prado) runs SE from Plaza San Francisco down to the Plaza del Estudiante. The business quarter, government offices, university and many of the main hotels and restaurants are situated in this area. On the hills above Plaza Mendoza are the poorer parts of the city. From the Plaza del Estudiante, Av Villazón and its extensions lead further SE towards the wealthier residential districts, which run from Sopocachi to the bed of the valley at Obrajes, 5 km from the centre and 500m lower than Plaza Murillo. Sopocachi, through which runs Av 6 de Agosto, has many restaurants, discos, bars, etc; the Mercado Sopocachi, on F Guachalla, is good but not cheap (a bimonthly *Sopocachi* magazine of cultural events, with map, is sold at newsstands). Beyond Obrajes are the upper-class districts of Calacoto and La Florida. The main sports and social clubs are in these districts.

El Alto is now a city in its own right. Apart from the district known as Ciudad Satelite, it is almost 100% indigenous; almost everyone is an emigrant from the countryside. It is growing at 10% per year, compared with 4% growth in the wealthier districts of La Paz. Costs are much lower than in La Paz, but construction, etc is much more basic. There is a market on Thursday and Sunday in Avenida Alfonso Ugarte, more interesting for its size than the items for sale. El Alto is connected to La Paz by motorway (toll US$0.50, cycles free). Buses from Plaza Aguino and Pérez Velasco leave regularly for Plaza 16 de Julio, El Alto.

There are few colonial buildings left in La Paz; probably the best examples are in the Calle Jaén. Late 19th/early 20th century architecture, often displaying heavy European influence, can be found in the streets around Plaza Murillo, but much of La Paz is modern. Emilio Villanueva added local features to European styles, eg the Tiwanaku-style decorations on the University building, but much 20th-century architecture was influenced by Frank Lloyd Wright, eg the new Correo. The Plaza del Estudiante (Plaza Franz Tamayo), or a bit above it, marks a contrast between old and new styles, between the traditional commercial and the more elegant. The Prado itself is lined with high-rise blocks dating from the 1960s and 1970s. Plaza

---

La Paz: Key to map

1. Plaza Murillo; 2. Congreso Nacional; 3. Museo Nacional de Arte; 4. Cathedral; 5. Palacio Quemado; 6. General Post Office; 7. Iglesia La Merced; 8. Museo de Costumbres; 9. Museo y Casa de Murillo; 10. Iglesia Santo Domingo; 11. Museo Nacional de Etnografía y Folklore; 12. Entel; 13. Casa de la Cultura; 14. Basílica de San Francisco; 15. Mercado de Hechicería; 16. Parque Prehistórico Tiahuanaco (Museo Semisubterráneo); 17. Alcaldía; 18. US Embassy and Citibank; 19. Banco Central; 20. Tourist Office; 21. TAM; 22. Museo Arqueológico de Tiahuanaco; 23. Lloyd Aéreo Boliviano; 24. Biblioteca Municipal. Hotels: 25. *Presidente*; 26. *Sucre Palace*; 27. *Gloria*; 28. *Libertador*; 29. *Plaza*; 30. *El Dorado*; 31. *Panamericano*; 32. *Res Rosario*; 33. *Milton*; 34. *La Paz*. 35. *Plaza*; 36. *Sagárnaga* and *Alem*; 37. *Hostal República*; 38. *Continental*; 39. Restaurant/Peña *Los Escudos*; 40. *Casa del Corregidor*, Markets; 41. Rodríguez; 42. Camacho; 43. Lanza; 44. Main Indian Market; 45. Negro. Parks and Squares; 46. Plaza del Estudiante; 47. Plaza Venezuela; 48. Plaza Scure; 49. Garita de Lima; 50. Plaza Mendoza; 51. Plaza Velasco; 52. Plaza Riosinio; 53. Plaza Antofagasta; 54. Plaza Vicenta Eguino; 55. Estadio Hernando Siles; 56. Universidad Mayor San Andrés; 57. Immigration Office.

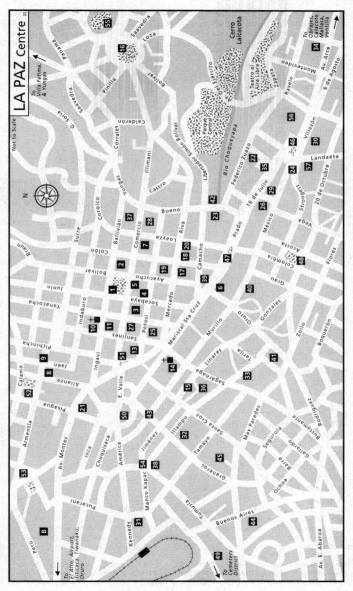

LA PAZ Centre

Not to Scale

Murillo, 3 blocks N of the Prado, is the traditional centre. Facing its formal gardens are the huge Cathedral (modern but very graceful); the Palacio Presidencial in Italian renaissance style, usually known as the Palacio Quemado (burnt palace) twice gutted by fire in its stormy 130-year history; and on the E side the Congreso Nacional. In front of the Palacio Quemado is a statue of former President Gualberto Villarroel who was dragged into the plaza by an angry mob and hanged in 1946. Across from the Cathedral on Calle Socabaya is the Palacio de los Condes de Arana, dating from 1775, now the Museo Nacional del Arte. Calle Comercio, running E-W across the Plaza, has most of the stores and shops. On Av Libertador Simón Bolívar (to which Mount Illimani provides a backdrop), is the Central Market (called "Mercado Camacho"), a picturesque medley of Indian victuals and vendors presiding raucously over stalls, their black braids topped by hard-brimmed bowler hats. Further E is the residential district of Miraflores. Another good view of Illimani can be had from the top of the rise on Calle Illimani.

At the upper end of Av Mariscal Santa Cruz is the Plaza San Francisco with the church and monastery of San Francisco, dating from 1549, well worth seeing: the church is richly decorated on native religious themes (the mestizo baroque façade clearly displays how the traditional baroque vine motif is transformed into an array of animals, birds, fruits and plants), the interior contains huge, square columns and gilt altars on which stand many saints; Indian weddings can be seen on Sats 1000-1200. Behind the San Francisco church a network of narrow cobbled streets rise steeply. Much of this area is a permanent street market. Handicraft shops line the lower part of Calle Sagárnaga; further up, from Illampu to Rodríguez and in neighbouring streets, is the local Rodríguez market. Turning right on Max Paredes, heading W, is Avenida Buenos Aires, one of the liveliest streets in the Indian quarter, where small workshops turn out the costumes and masks for the Gran Poder festival. Continuing W along Max Paredes towards the cemetery district, the streets are crammed with stalls selling every imaginable item, household goods, clothing, hats, food, festive goods. Transport converges on the cemetery district (for more information see **Buses** below. Do not expect to go anywhere in a hurry in this part of the city; there are good views of Illimani from these heights.

Other churches of more than passing interest are Santo Domingo (originally the cathedral) on the corner of Calles Ingavi and Yanacocha, with its decorative 18th-century façade (next door is the University Pacensis Divi-Andreae, 1826, and the Colegio Nacional San Simón de Ayacucho, a pink building); La Merced, on a plazuela at Calles Colón and Comercio; San Juan de Dios, on Loayza between Merced and Camacho, with a carved portico, circular paintings of the life of Christ and, above the altar, figures holding lighted (electric) candles around a statue of the Virgin; and San Sebastián, the first church to be built in La Paz, in Plaza Alonso de Mendoza (named after the church's builder). On Plaza Sucre (with trees, benches and photographers) is San Pedro church, Av 20 de Octubre y Colombia, built 1720; large paintings of the life of Christ along the nave, a huge chandelier below the dome and a gilt altar.

A worthwhile walk is to Mirador Laicacota on Avenida del Ejército: one of the delights of La Paz is the change from day to night, when all the lights begin to twinkle on the surrounding hillsides.

Museums

Museo Nacional de Arte, across from the Cathedral at Calle Socabaya 432, housed in the 18th century baroque palace of the Condes de Arana, with beautiful exterior and patio. It has a fine collection of colonial paintings including many works by Melchor Pérez Holguín, considered one of the masters of Andean colonial art, and also exhibits the works of contemporary local artists. Open Tues-Fri 0930-1230, 1500-1900, US$0.25, Sat 0930-1330, entry US$0.50, students US$0.25.

Museo Tiahuanaco (Tiwanaku), or Museo Nacional de Arqueología, easily reached by going down the flight of stairs by María Auxili church on the Prado. This modern building, simulating the Tiwanaku style, contains good collections of the arts and crafts of ancient Tiwanaku and items from the E jungles. It also has a 2-room exhibition of gold statuettes and objects found in Lake Titicaca. Tues-Fri 0930-1230, 1500-1900, Sat 1000-1230, 1500-1800, Sun 1000-1400. Entry US$1.20.

Museo Semisubterráneo, or Templete del Estadio, in front of National Stadium, with restored statues and other artefacts from Tiahuanaco. It's in a sunken garden and much can be seen from street level. No explanations are given and the statues are being badly eroded by pollution.

Museo Nacional de Etnografía y Folklore, on Calle Ingavi 916, is housed in the palace of the Marqueses de Villaverde, worth seeing (exhibits on the Chipaya and Ayoreo Indians), quite good library adjoining. Mon-Fri 0830-1300, 1430-1800.

The following four museums, all on Calle Jaén, are included on a single ticket, which costs US$0.75 (free on Sat), from Museo Costumbrista. All are open Tues-Fri 1000-1200, 1430-1830, Sat and Sun 1000-1230, and all are delightful, with well-displayed items in colonial buildings. Calle Jaén, a picturesque colonial street with many craft shops, is well worth seeing for itself.

Museo Costumbrista, Plaza Riosinio, at top of Jaén. Miniature displays depict incidents in the history of La Paz and well-known Paceños. Also has miniature replicas of reed rafts used by Norwegian, Thor Heyerdahl and Spaniard, Kitin Muñoz, to prove their theories of ancient migrations, T 378478.

Museo Casa Murillo, on Jaén, T 375273 was originally the home of Pedro Domingo Murillo, one of the martyrs of the abortive La Paz independence movement of 16 July 1809. This colonial house has been carefully restored and has a good collection of paintings, furniture and national costumes of the period; there is also a special room dedicated to herbal medicine and magic (Kallawaya) along with two rooms of paintings. Warmly rec.

Museo de Metales Preciosos, Jaén 777, well set out with Inca gold artefacts in basement vaults, also ceramics and archaeological exhibits, warmly rec, T 371470.

Museo de Litoral, Jaén 789, with artefacts of the War of the Pacific, and interesting selection of old maps.

Mineral Museum, Banco Minero, 6 de Agosto 2382, esq Belisario Salinas. Open Mon-Fri 0900-1300, 1430-1630. Good gold and silver exhibits; free.

Núñez del Prado, Ecuador 2034, Mon-Fri, 0900-1200, 1400-1800, excellent sculpture.

Museo Tambo Quirquincho, Calle Evaristo Valle, nr Plaza Mendoza (Tues-Fri, 0930-1200, 1500-1900, Sat-Sun, 1000-1230, US$0.50, Sat free), in a restored colonial building, displaying modern painting and sculpture, carnival masks, silver, early 20th century photography and city plans, highly recommended.

Museo de Historia Natural, Calle 26, Cota Cota, ½ hr from centre by micro-bus marked Cota Cota from Plaza San Francisco, small but quite well-presented. Check for opening times.

Festivals Particularly impressive is the Alacitas Fair held from last week of Jan to first week of Feb, on the upper part of Plaza Villarroel, mostly on Calle Tejada Zorzano (take *micro* B, K, H, 131 or X). "It is dedicated to Ekeko, an Indian household god. You can buy plaster images of him at many of the booths. He is a red-nosed cheerfully-grinning little personage laden with an assortment of miniature cooking utensils, coins, balls of wool, tiny sacks of sugar, coffee, salt, rice and flour; a kind of Bolivian Santa Claus. Ekeko is said to bring prosperity and to grant wishes. If you buy a toy house, or a cow, or a sheep at the Alacitas, you will get a real one before the year is out. There are also model motor-cars and planes, for the extreme optimists." (Christopher Isherwood, "The Condor and the Cows.") Beginning of May, Corpus Christi. End May/early June, Festividad del Señor de Gran Poder, the most important festival of the year, with a huge procession of costumed and masked dancers. Fiestas de Julio, a month of concerts and performances at the Teatro Municipal, offers a wide variety of music, including the University Folkloric Festival 8 December, festival around Plaza España, not very large, but colourful and noisy. On New Year's Eve fireworks are let off and make a spectacular sight, and a din, view from higher up. **See also p 333** for festivals outside La Paz.

Hotels Try to arrive in La Paz early in the day as accommodation, especially at the cheaper end of the market, can be hard to find. Prices include tax and service charge (20% in all).

Expensive Hotels: **L3** *Radisson Plaza*, formerly *Hotel La Paz* (still referred to as *Sheraton*), Av Arce 2177, T 316163, F 343391, good 5-star hotel with all facilities; **L3** *Plaza*, Av 16 de Julio 1789, T 378317, F 343391, excellent, restaurant is good value and open to the public, fine view (check bill); peña show on Fridays; **L3** *Presidente*, Potosí 920 y Sanjines, T 368601, F 354013, including breakfast, "the highest 5-star in the world", pool, gymnasium and sauna all open to non-residents, bar, disco, excellent service, comfortable, good food, rec; **A1** *El Rey Palace*, Av 20 de Octubre 1947, T 393016, F 367759, inc breakfast, large suites, excellent restaurant, stylish, modern; **B** *Sucre Palace*, Av 16 de Julio 1636, T 363453, F 392052, hot water a problem, overpriced, *Karin* snack bar on ground floor, excellent, expensive, disappointing restaurant on 1st floor; **A2** *Camino Real*, Ravelo 2123, T 314542, F 365575, self-catering apartments, incl breakfast, TV, parking, new; **A3** *Gloria*, Potosí 909, T 370010/18,

F 391489, central, 2 restaurants, one on top floor with good view, one vegetarian, excellent food and service, rec; **B** *Eldorado*, Av Villazón, T 363355, F 391438, with breakfast, may be able to bargain for longer stays, safe luggage deposit, secure parking nearby; **B** *Libertador*, Obispo Cárdenas 1421, T 351792, F 391225, very good value, colour TV, good cheap restaurant, helpful (baggage stored), highly rec; **B** *Max Inn*, Plaza Sucre 1494, T 374391, F 341720, all rooms with bath, heating, TV, smart, very clean, poor service; **C** *Hostería Blanquita*, Santa Cruz 242, T 352933, "baroque", incl breakfast, hot showers, comfortable; **C** *Hostal Embajador*, Juan de la Riva 1438, T 392079, with bath, TV, heating, breakfast included, German spoken, helpful; **C** *Hotel Copacabana*, Av 16 de Julio 1802, T 352244, with bath, central, restaurant and grill room (lunch only at latter), good service, safe deposit, rooms a bit small and fusty, rec; **C** *Residencial Rosario*, Illampu 704, T 326531, F 375532, Turisbus travel agency downstairs (see under Travel Agents), with bath (electric shower—safe design), D without, very popular with foreigners, avoid noisier rooms near foyer, sauna, laundry, good restaurant, "superb", stores luggage, most highly rec; **C** *Sagárnaga*, Sagárnaga 326, T 350252, F 360831, with bath, E without, basic breakfast included, good location, laundry, English spoken, rec.

For people staying several weeks, often looking for permanent residences, boarding houses (*pensiones*) are popular, eg Illimeier, Sopocachi, Calle Resequin 1978, D with breakfast, English and German spoken.

Medium-priced hotels: **D** *Continental*, Illampu 626, T 378226, with bath, hot water, clean; **D** *España*, Av 6 de Agosto 2074, T 354643, hot water, TV, quiet, friendly, rec; **D** *Hostería Claudia*, Av Villazón 1965, T 372917, with bath, E without, breakfast extra, clean, secure, friendly, rec; **D** *La Joya*, Max Paredes 541, T 324346, F 350959, with bath and TV, phone, E without bath or TV, breakfast incl, clean, modern and comfy, helpful, restaurant, bar, in the heart of market district, highly rec; **D** *Latino*, Perú 171, T 358341, near bus terminal, with bath; **D** *Milton*, Illampu y Calderón No 1124, T 368003/353511, F 365849 (PO Box 5118), with bath, hot water, popular with travellers, will store luggage, excellent views from roof, good restaurant, rec, local market outside, so no taxis to the hotel at weekends; **D** *Neumann*, Loayza 442, T 325445, with bath (E without), bargaining possible for students; **D** *Residencial Copacabana*, Illampu 734, T 367896/375378, hot water, clean but basic and run down, changes TCs; **D** *Residencial La Estancia*, Mexico 1559, T 324308, with bath and breakfast,

helpful, good restaurant; **D** *Hostal República*, Comercio 1455 (T 357966), with bath, E without, breakfast, beautiful old house of former president, very clean, hot water, luggage stored, helpful, laundry service, rec, also a separate house is available, sleeps 6, all facilities, US$25 a night; **D** *Tambo de Oro*, Armentia 367, T 322763, near bus station, hot showers, clean, friendly, helpful and safe for luggage; **D** *Viena*, Loayza 420, T 323572, with bath, E without, beautiful old building with elegant entrance and patio, gloomy rooms, friendly staff, clean, rec, arrive early, often full, tours with Vicuña Tours, good.

E *Alem*, Sagámaga 334, T 367400, hot water, cheaper without bath, clean, helpful, rec; **E** *Andes*, Av Manco Kapac 364, T 323461, clean, good beds, hot water 24 hrs a day, good value (one of the few that offers single rooms at F), discount for IYHA card holders, rec; **E** *Austria*, Yanacocha 531, T 351140, without bath, clean, hot water, but insufficient showers, safe deposit, very cosy, good for longer stays, use of kitchen, laundry, TV, friendly and helpful staff, very popular, arrive early, highly rec; opposite is **E** *Hostal Yanacocha*, large clean rooms, dirty bathrooms, hot water, secure; **E** *Bolivia*, Manco Kapac 287, T 375030, opp railway station, clean, shared tepid showers, good views from back, upper rooms; **E** *Italia*, Av Manco Kapac 303, T 325101, with bath, try upper floor for quieter rooms, clean but showers usually cold; **E** *Alojamiento Illimani*, Av Illimani 1817, T 325948, hot water, friendly, clean and safe, uncomfortable beds, laundry facilities, often full; **E** *Ingavi*, Ingavi 727, nice rm, poor service, good value; **E** *Hostal Latino*, Junín nr Sucre, clean, hot water, motorcycle parking, luggage stored, helpful; **E** *Panamericano*, Manco Kapac 454, T 340810/378370, with hot showers, near railway station and main bus terminal, helpful, good restaurant, rec; **E** *Res Plaza*, Plaza Pérez Velasco 785, T 322157, a bit run-down, but clean and hot water, F without bath, washing and luggage storage facilities; **E** *Res Sucre*, Colombia 340, opp Plaza San Pablo, T 328414, cheaper without bath, warm water, big rooms, clean; **E** *Torino*, Socabaya 457, T 341487, central, hot water on request (electric showers) with bath (F without), formerly the gringo hotel but run down, poor beds, dirty, noisy, from disco especially at weekends till 0300, 2400 curfew, has noticeboard, stores luggage, book exchange, bar; **E** *Max Paredes*, Max Paredes 660, T 362726, with bath (cheaper without), modern, clean; **F** *Hostal Chiquiago*, Plaza San Francisco, simple, friendly, secure, luggage stored; **F** *Alojamiento Illampu*, Illampu 635, T 342274, hot water, laundry facilities, very small rooms with poor soundproofing, check prices carefully; *Alojamiento París*, Sucre 949, T 356836, hot showers, friendly but not very clean, and noisy; **F** *Alojamiento Universo*, Inca 175, dormitories, basic, motorcycle parking. Cheapest possibly is **F** *Posada El Carretero*, Catacora 1056, y Pichincha y Sanjinés, T 322233, 5 beds to a room, helpful, pleasant, hot shower extra, can use kitchen for breakfast.

Youth Hostel association, **Asociacón Boliviana de Albergues Juveniles**, ABAJ, Edif Alborada piso 1, of 105, Calle Juan de la Riva 1406 y Loayza, T 361076/321597, has hostels at *Hostal Duendes*, Av Uruguay 470, T 351125, Casilla 8765, and *Hotel Andes*, Manco Kapac 364, US$3.50 and 2.80 respectively, pp, without breakfast; other hostels around the country are given in the text. To use hostels you must have a Bolivian YHA card, US$2, two photos needed, available from ABAJ, which also sells international cards, US$20.

Camping No organized site, but Mallasa (Municipal Park, unmarked, turn left at Aldeas Infantiles SOS), Valencia and Palca below the suburb of La Florida have been recommended. Club Andino Boliviano (T 794016) rents equipment. *Caza y Pesca*, Edif Handal Center, Av Mcal Santa Cruz y Socabaya, *Sajama*, Sagárnaga 177, 2° piso, or *Epcot*, Av 6 de Agosto 2190, local 9, T 342424, for camping equipment and camping gas. Kerosene for pressure stoves is available from a pump in Plaza Alexander. Public showers at Duchas La Paz, 20 de Octubre 1677.

HOTEL MILTON ✦✦

LA PAZ, BOLIVIA

- Offers 50 comfortable and ample rooms (Singles, doubles and triples) all of them with TV, private bath, heat, hot water 24 hrs a day (steam boiler system), telephone, music and family ambiance.
- Elevator, laundry, safety boxes, luggage storage, coffee shop.
- Located in the commercial Handicraft and Tourist Centre of the City, 3 blocks from the main Avenue. On weekends, an interesting and traditional fair.
- Low rates and special rates for groups and for Hostess with long stay.

Illampu Esq. Calderon No. 1124
Tel: 353511/368003 Fax: 591 2 365849/368003
PO Box 5118 La Paz Bolivia

Restaurants in La Paz can be roughly divided into two categories: either they serve international cuisine and are expensive or they serve local dishes and are fairly cheap. The restaurants with international cuisine are to be found mainly on three streets, Av 16 de Julio (the Prado), Av 6 de Agosto and Av 20 de Octubre. Service charges and tax of up to 23% are usually included on the bill but it is customary to leave a tip of 10% anyway. Always check prices before ordering, and then your bill and change.

Av 16 de Julio: (street numbers given in brackets). There are many snack bars, including *Confitería Elis* (1497), with good plate lunches, excellent soups, breakfasts (waffles, pancakes, French toast, pay extra for coffee refills) and pastries, not cheap, also *Eli's Pizza Express* in same block (very good), English spoken, highly rec; *Denny's*, No 1605, US-style, one of a chain; *La Mía Pasta* (1665 and Av Salinas at Plaza Abaroa) good pasta, salad buffet; *Patito Pekín* (1687), good Chinese, reasonably priced; *California Donuts II* (1695), American-style food, expensive, US$2-10, opens 1230 (*No I* is at Av Camacho 1248, *No III* is on Av Arce); *Utama*, in *Plaza* hotel (1789) excellent salad bar, highly rec; *Tokio* (1832), good, also has tea room and patisserie and rec for *salteñas*, but look out for high prices not written on menus, expensive; *Super 10* (1991 y Villazón), very good, *almuerzo* US$4, open Sun evenings. On Plaza Estudiante, *Pizza I'Passo II*, good but expensive; *Il Fiore*, snacks, ice cream, pizza; *Café Ciudad*, 24 hr coffee shop, full menu, good, pricey. *Mary's Tee*, near Plaza Estudiante, for excellent pies and cakes.

S of Plaza del Estudiante and Av Arce: *El Batau*, Landaeta 402, T 342518, German owner, Bolivian and international cuisine, rec; *Don Francisco*, Av Arce 2312, good steaks, especially à la Pepe; *Pizzeria Morello*, Av Arce 2132, very good but very expensive, also *La Suisse*, Av Arce 2164, good steaks and raclette, fair fondue, closed Sat and Sun, gourmet restaurant on first floor, expensive; *Viva La Pizza*, J José Pérez 322, rec, expensive; *Kranky*, Av Villazón 1987, good, cheap sandwiches, burgers, ice cream, rec; *Chifa Emy*, Cordero 257, best Chinese, very good service, takes credit cards, US$12.50 pp with drinks; *Rigo's*, Plaza Organo, near Museo Semisubterráneo, pleasant and good set lunch; *Vienna*, Federico Zuazo 1905, T 391660, German, Austrian and local food, excellent, at moderate prices, very fashionable with Bolivians and popular with foreigners too.

In the Sopocachi district: up-market Italian cuisine at *Pronto*, Jauregui 2248, T 355869, Mon-Sat 1830-2230 (below Imprenta Quipus behind 6 de Agosto between Guachalla and Rosendo Gutiérrez), beautiful decor, about US$7 pp, serves three different types of pasta: regular, integral and "pasta de quinoa", "must be unique in South America", popular, good service, poor coffee; *Montesano*, Sánchez Lima 2279, nr Plaza Abaroa, excellent Italian US$35

VIENNA

RESTAURANT • BAR

European style restaurant offering traditional cuisine and dining amid antiques, old prints and wood.

English and German spoken.

Our kitchen is open
Monday-Friday
12:00-14:00 18:30-22:00
Sundays
12:00-14:30

Federico Zuazo 1905 • Casilla 56
• Tel: 391660 •
La Paz – Bolivia

for 2, also fish and steaks. Several restaurants on Belisario Salinas, eg *El Honguito* (steak sandwiches), *Bar Pub*, and others. Among those **on Av 6 de Agosto:** *El Arriero* (No 2535, Casa Argentina), best barbecue with large portions, but quite expensive; *Mocambo*, 6 de Agosto y L Gutiérrez 319, good food and service, Spanish, US$15 pp; *Oriental*, good, cheap, Chinese; while **on Av 20 de Octubre** there is *Mamma Mia*, art gallery by day, good Italian restaurant at night, expensive but good pizzas; *La Quebecoise*, near Plaza Abaroa, French Canadian, good value, pleasant atmosphere; *El Gaucho*, No 2041, steakhouse, good, about US$20 pp. Close to 20 de Octubre: Brazilian *feijoada* on Sat and Sun, at *Ipanema*, Av Ecuador 2139, between Aspiazu and F Guachalla, T 372306, rec, closed Mon. *Gringo Limón*, Plaza Abaroa, good but expensive steaks; *Filippo*, just off Plaza Abaroa, for good *salteñas*. *La Caldera Mágica*, JJ Pérez 322 y 20 de Octubre, nice atmosphere, good lunches, bar. Rec Mexican place: *Tacos Teru K*, Ignacio Cordero 1294, San Miguel (behind Loreto College) T 794513.

On the continuation of the **Prado** going west, in Av Mariscal Santa Cruz, is *Los Escudos* (Edif Club de La Paz, T 322028/350586), Munich-type bierkeller with fixed 4-course lunch, food and shows, Fri and Sat nights

(2000-2400). On the corner of Colón with Santa Cruz is *Restaurant Verona* for good economical *plato del día*, very popular in the evenings; *La Fiesta*, Santa Cruz 1066, excellent, good lunches, rec. On Plaza Velasco is *Kory Punku*, which serves excellent *parrilladas*, cheap and popular, live music some evenings.

On Calle México, running parallel S of the Prado: *La Estancia*, No 1553, good *almuerzo*, rec; *Capullito*, No 1490, pleasant café and *confitería*. México continues W as Murillo: at No 1040 is *Casa del Corregidor*, T 353633, centrally heated, behind Correo, Spanish colonial restaurant with Bolivian and European dishes, food not cheap, bar *El Horno*, open Mon-Sat, lunches from US$2.50 including vegetarian, *peña* at nights (see **Entertainments** below); *Crístal*, No 726, outdoor, quite cheap, good.

On Sagárnaga: *Naira*, next to *Peña Naira* (No 161 downstairs), which serves good food (see **Entertainments** below), and above the Peña, is *Resolana*, often confused with the *Naira* restaurant, very good pizzas and puddings but not cheap, live jazz most evenings, rec. Next to *Naira*, at street level, is *Panadería San Jorge*. *El Montañés* (No 323), opposite *Hotel Sagárnaga*, good, clean, family-run, homemade dishes. *Imperial*, Sagárnaga y Murillo, good and inexpensive local food, clean, balcony tables, cheap *almuerzo*, vegetarian dishes, frequently rec. In same area, *El Lobo*, Santa Cruz 441, good, clean, rec (Israeli dishes, good meeting place, noticeboard, limited menu, very popular); good cheap meals at Illampu 773, closed Sun evening. *Snack América*, Av América 192, good hamburgers; also *Los Laureles*, Av América 67, rec. On Calle Evaristo Valle there are several inexpensive typical restaurants. Excellent set lunch at *Clávida*, opp train station, including potatoes and cheese in peanut curry sauce.

In the shopping and business district N of the Prado: there are numerous snack bars and cheap restaurants. *Club de la Prensa*, Calle Campero, set in a pleasant garden, the limited menu is typical Bolivian—meat only, in copious quantities—and the company is lively; *Confitería Club de la Paz*, Camacho 1202, on the corner where Ayacucho joins Av Mcal Santa Cruz, good tea room, traditional, serious atmosphere, meeting place for businessmen and politicians, great coffee, expensive; *Torino*, at the hotel in Socabaya, is rec for excellent set lunch, US$1.50; next to *Torino*, *Chifa Jardín*, Socabaya 48, good, cheap Chinese; nearby, also in Socabaya is *Salteñería Super Salteña*; *Confitería California*, Potosí 1008, Centro Comercial Cristal, does good set lunches for US$2, also on Potosí, *Repostería Alemana* (*Nollo*)

for breakfasts, *La Kantuta*, in *Hotel Presidente*, No 920, excellent food, good service, *Subterráneo* (No 1120), cheap and OK, *Chez Pierre* (1320) good lunches, US$1.25, *Rincón Tarijeño La Choza*, good food at reasonable prices, and *Hogar Austriaco*, good lunches, pleasant. On Yanacocha, *La Fregata* (No 525), good value, and *La Tertulia*, near Ingavi, small, simple, charming, hot drinks and pastries. *Dumbo*, Camacho y Loayza, large portions, clean, very good; *Confitería Arabesque*, Mercado y Loayza, excellent *café con crema*; *Snack Conny*, Loayza opp San Juan de Dios, confitería, lunches, etc; *Casa Chang*, Juan de la Riva y Bueno, good set course Chinese meals, highly rec; *Los Pinochos*, Sanjines 553, excellent cheese empanadas and steaks, good food in large portions, popular café; *La Casa de los Paceños*, Sucre 856, very good, especially its *fritanga*. There are many other snack bars and Chinese restaurants on Calles Comercio (eg *Café Comercio*, next to *Hostal República*, *La Fuente de Soda*, No 801, good burgers, and *Salteñería Comercio*, No 1439, excellent *salteñas* and Bolivian food, outdoor seating) and Colón. *Taiwan*, opp Mercado Camacho, large portions, excellent. *Confitería Rivoli*, Colón 415, small and pleasant snack bar, good and cheap food. At Av Ayacucho 206 is the *Internacional*, a lunch-time favourite of local businessmen and has good shows Friday and Saturday nights.

Cheap vegetarian restaurants to recommend are the *Hotel Gloria Naranjos*, Potosí 909, buffet lunch, US$2, very popular, be there by 1200 for a table, closed Sun; *Andromeda*, Arce 2116, French, pricey but good, live music; *La Huerta*, Plaza Isabel La Católica, Av Arce, 1st floor, excellent salads, lunchtime and early evening, rec; *Natur Center*, Cañada Strongest 1852, lunches only, closed Sun; *Viscachani*, México 1290, lunches only, closed Sun. Vegetarian dishes served at *Palacio del Buen Gusto*, 18 de Julio 1698, closed weekends, not cheap.

Burgers: A good chain is *Clap's*, Centro Comercial El Patio, Av Arce, Calle Ayacucho, Calle Belisario Salinas, another chain is *Denny's*. Stalls in the Indian quarter sell hamburgers for US$0.75 each including chips, egg and tomato, have 2 for a filling meal, but don't have aji, mayonnaise or mustard if worried about hygiene and watch your burger being cooked.

Comedor Popular, often referred to as *Comedor Familiar*, for strictly limited budgets, cheap but filling local meals around US$0.80-1.50, available at Camacho and Lanza markets. The foodstalls at the top of Jiménez sell good T-bone steak cheaply. Bread from street vendors and Cochabamba wholemeal bread (*pan integral*) sold at the main markets, is rec. Fresh dairy produce at *Pil* on Bueno y Cárdenas. *Kremrik* is a chain of ice-cream parlours, with outlets in Plaza Murillo 542, and on Av Villazón, just off Plaza del Estudiante, good ice-cream. Good coffee at *Solo Café*, Potosí 1108, esq Socobaya and *Café Pierrot*, in *Hotel Gloria*. Patisseries: a good one at Bueno y Camacho, with apple pie and cakes; *Kuchen Stube*, Rosendo Gutiérrez, Ed Guadelquivir (closed Mon), and Edificio Mcal Ballivián, Mercado 1328 (hard to find), Mon-Fri 0930-1230, 1500-1900, very good cakes, coffee and German specialities.

The *Calacoto* district situated in The Valley 15 mins S of the city, "La Zona Sur" (US$0.40 by *trufi* or minibus), is home of the resident community. Calacoto has recently developed into an important area in its own right: international shopping centres, supermarkets stocked with imported items and some of the best restaurants and bars in La Paz. The area begins after the bridge at La Florida where there is an attractive park, Plaza Humbolt – exhibitions of local art work on Sun and a collection of kiosks selling cheap snacks. The main road, Av Ballivián begins here at Calle 8 and continues up the hill to the shopping district of San Miguel on Calle 21 (about a 20 min walk). On the main avenue, corner of Calle 8 is *El Viejo Tonel*, Brazilian rodizio restaurant, bar and disco (young crowd). Next, on the right side of the avenue, between Calle 9 y 10 is *Rumors*, an American/Mexican bar, restaurant, excellent music, popular late night place. *Puerto del Sol*, good Chinese on the left on the corner of Calle 11. Opposite, still on the main road, is an excellent arts and handicrafts shop, weavings, ceramics, silver etc. Continuing up the hill on Av Ballivián between Calle 15 y 16 on the left is *The Britannia*, Bolivia's only authentic English pub, open Tues-Sun from 1700, cosy, popular with regular ex-pat crowd. Batemans XXXB best English bitter, bar snacks, darts etc. English owner, Tom Clough, moved this well-known local from its former location on the shores of Lake Titikaka in Dec 1994. Highly rec. Next door to The Britannia on the avenue is *Abracadabra*, open 7 days for lunch and dinner, great ribs, best hamburgers and pizza in La Paz, American owner, rec. Five minutes walk further up the hill on the right is Calle 21 – the church of San Miguel on the corner of the avenue is an easy landmark – which has a huge variety of shops, fast-food cafés, banks and a post office. Back on the main avenue and continuing up the hill between Calle 24 y 25 is *The Suisse Chalet*, excellent fondue, steaks, expensive but rec, and almost next door *The Galeon* for some of the city's best seafood.

Airline Offices Lloyd Aéreo Boliviano (LAB), Camacho 1460, T 367701/7/367718/371020; Aero Sur, 16 de Julio 1607, T 371834, F 390457; British Airways at Martín Travel, Av 20 de Octubre 2164, T 340831/355541, F 391641; KLM, Av Arce 2355; American Airlines, Av 16 de Julio 1440, Edificio Herman, T 372009. In Edif Avenida, 16 de Julio 1490 are AeroPerú, 2nd floor, T 370002-4, and Viasa, planta baja, T 327223. Aerolíneas Argentinas, Edificio Banco de la Nación Argentina, Av 16 de Julio 1486, T 351711/351624; Qantas, Av 16 de Julio, Ed Cosmos, planta baja, T 322903. Varig, Av Mcal Santa Cruz 1392, Edif Cámara de Comercio, T 314040, F 391131.

Banks Money is changed in hotels or *casas de cambio* rather than in banks. **Citibank**, on the Prado (cashes its own TCs, very high commission and will receive money sent from any US bank), but will not advance cash to holders of Citibank Mastercard. **Banco Industrial**, Av Gral Camacho 1333, open 0830-1700, Sat 1000-1300, good service, changes cash and TCs. Cash advance (in bolivianos) on Visa and Mastercard at **Banco de La Paz** on Prado (limit US$300 per day, no commission), **Banco Santa Cruz de la Sierra**, **Banco Mercantil**, ground floor, **Banco Popular**, **Banco Nacional** and **Banco Boliviano Americano**, among others; Banco Santa Cruz branch in Shopping Norte is open Sat pm. **Visa** has an office on Av Camacho 1448, 11th and 12th floors, T 369975/357014, F 354066, for cancelling cost or stolen credit cards. Automatic cash dispensers for Visa and Mastercard can be found at several sites in the city including Av Camacho 1223, the airport and Shopping Norte shopping centre (look for the sign Enlace – Visa at branches of ATC). **Amex**, Av 16 de Julio 1490, piso 5, T 323954/341201.

Exchange Houses **Sudamer**, Colón 256, good rates also for currencies other than US$ (1% commission on TCs into dollars, frequently rec); **Unitours**, Mercado 1300, 1% commission on TCs. **Casa de Cambio Silver**, Mercado 979, charges 1% commission to change TCs into dollars; similarly **D'Argent**, Mercado 1328, free coffee and drinking water, US$ only (will change TCs into dollars at 1% commission).**Kantuta**, Av Mcal Santa Cruz 1326. Some *cambios* verify passports. Some deal in Argentine and Chilean pesos. Street changers can be found at corners around Camacho, Colón and Prado. It is not worth dealing on the black market since there is virtually no difference between black and official rates. NB if arriving on Friday night, bring bolivianos or US dollars cash as it is difficult to change TCs at the weekend (try *El Lobo* restaurant, which usually changes TCs at any time, good rates, or *Hotel Gloria* which gives good rates for most western currencies). If you leave Bolivia with bolivianos you may not be able to change them in neighbouring countries. Watch out for forged currency, especially dollars and Chilean pesos.

Embassies and Consulates **Argentine Consulate**, Sánchez Lima 497, T 353089/343516; **Brazilian Consulate**, Av 20 de Octubre, 20-38 Edificio Fonconain, Embajasy piso 11, visa office, piso 9, T 352108, 0900-1300, Mon-Fri (visas take 2 days). **Chilean Consulate**, H Siles 5843, corner of Calle 13, Obrajes district, T 785269, open Mon-Fri 0830-1130 (visa same day if requested in the morning, take microbus N, A or L from Av 16 de Julio). **Ecuador** 16 de Julio 1440, piso 14, T 321208. **Paraguayan Consulate**, 7th floor Edificio Venus, Av Arce 2105, just below Calle Montevideo (very good visa service), T 322018; **Peruvian Consulate and Embassy**, 6 de Agosto 2190 y Calle F Guachalla, Edif Alianza, T 353550, 0930-1300 (a visa costs US$10 in US$ bills, issued same day if you go early); **Venezuelan Embassy and Consulate**, Av Arce 2678, Ed Illimani, 4th floor, T 375023 (consulate open Mon, Wed, Fri 0900-1200 – visas are only given to Bolivian residents, if you need one, get it in your home country).

United States Embassy and Consulate, Av Arce 2780, opp Edif Illimani, T 350120/430251, F 359875, Casilla 425. **Canadian Consulate**, Av 20 de Octubre 2475, Plaza Avaroa, T 375224, Mon-Fri. 0900-1200. **Japanese Embassy**, Rosendo Gutiérrez 497, esq Sánchez Lima, PO Box 2725, T 373151.

Austrian Consulate, Edif Petrolero, 7th floor, Oficina 1, Av 16 de Julio 1616, T 326601, 1600-1800; **British Embassy and Consulate**, Av Arce 2732-2754, T 357424, F 391063, Casilla 694, Mon-Thur 0900-1200, 1400-1600, Fri 0900-1300, has a list of travel hints for Bolivia, doctors, etc; **Danish Consulate**, Federico Zuazo 1598, Edif Park Inn, Piso 11, Casilla 662, T 360655/1, F 376380; **Finnish Consulate**, Mercado 1004, c/o Sibo SA, T 350900/367227; **French Consulate**, Av Hernando Siles 5390, esq Calle 08, Obrajes, T 786114 (take bus No 11 or microbus N, A or L down Av 16 de Julio); **Belgian Embassy** is 1 block from French at No 5290, T 784925; **German Embassy**, Av Arce 2395, T 390850, slow service, Mon-Fri 0900-1200; **Italian Embassy**, 6 de Agosto 2575, PO Box 626, T 323597, F 391075; **Netherlands Consulate**, Av Arce 2031, Edif Victorio, 2nd floor, T 355701; **Norwegian Consulate**, Calle Presbítero Medina 2516, T 322528; **Spanish Consulate**, Av Arce y Calle Cordero, T 343518; **Swedish Consulate**, Av Arce 2856, Casilla de Correo 852, T 327535, open 0900-1200; **Swiss Embassy**, Av 16 de Julio 1616, 6th floor, T 353091, F 391462, Casilla 9356, open 0900-1200, 1400-1500; **Israeli Embassy**, Av Mcal Santa Cruz, Edificio Esperanza, 10th floor, T 358676/371287, Casilla 1309/1320.

Entertainment Best entertainment for visitors are the folk shows (*peñas*). Outstanding folk show at *Peña Naira* (US$5, includes first drink), Sagárnaga 161, T 325736, every night about

2215. Various restaurants have shows worth seeing. At these, visitors will be able to listen to the wide variety of local musical instruments, the different types of flutes, including the *quena*, and the *charango*, a small guitar with five strings, the body of which was originally made from the shell of an armadillo. Enquire at the *Rumillajta* shop (in the *galería* close to San Francisco church) about future performances by the famous folk group of that name. Good *peña* at *Casa del Corregidor*, Calle Murillo 1040 (T 363633), dinner show Mon-Thur, no cover charge, Fri and Sat *peña* US$4, colonial atmosphere, traditional music and dance (see also under **Restaurants**); nearby is *La Luna*, Oruro y Murillo, great live bands, contemporary music. See also under restaurants for *Los Escudos*. Another *peña* is *Marko Tambo* on Calle Jaén, US$7 (all incl) repeatedly rec (also sells woven goods). Indian dance halls, for example on Max Paredes, should only be visited in the company of Bolivians. If you wish to learn a local indstrument, contact *Academia "Walisuma"*, Av Apumalla 512 (old Cemetery District between José M Asin and José M Aliaga): Pedro Mar teaches bi-lingual courses, English/Spanish, for *quena*, *zampoña* and *charango*.

Good salsa at *El Loro en su Salsa*, on Rosendo Gutiérrez on corner of Av 6 de Agosto, open Thur, Fri and Sat pm. *Bar Socavón*, Aspiazu y 20 de Octubre 2172, Sopocachi, T 353998, has live music Thur-Sat, music videos Wed, very popular. On Calle Belisario Salinas in Sopocachi Bajo, is *Piano Bar*, cosy, with a fireplace, live piano music, good drinks and snacks. On the same street in *Panyco*, live music, rec; and *Caras y Caretas*, live music, food, good atmosphere. *Café Montmarte*, Fernando Guachalla, off Av 6 de Agosto, next to Alliance Française, set lunch US$4, bar with live music Thur, Fri, Sat. Excellent jazz at *Marius Club*, Presbitero Medina y Salazar (near Plaza Avaroa). Local radio station, *Radio Fides*, Calle Sanjines y Sucre, Andean music on Thur, when it is open to public (2000, US$0.75), not all year round, check in advance, T 359191.

La Paz has a resident ballet and symphony orchestra, but no theatre company. There are some good **cinemas**, films being mainly in English. For film buffs there is the excellent Cinemateca Boliviana, Pichincha y Indaburo, La Paz's art film centre with festivals, courses, etc (entry US$0.75 for students). **Casa Municipal de la Cultura "Franz Tamayo"**, almost opp Plaza San Francisco, hosts a variety of exhibitions, paintings, sculpture, photography, videos, etc, most of which are free. The **Palacio Chico** (Ayacucho y Potosí, in old Correo), operated by the Secretaría Nacional de Cultura, also has exhibitions (good for modern art), concerts and ballet. The SNC is also in charge of many regional museums. Listings available in Palacio Chico.

There are clown and mime shows in Parque del Ejército on Sunday, colourful and popular; the Parque Central has a children's amusement park, US$0.20.

Hospitals *Clínica del Accidentado*, Plaza Uyuni 1351, T 328632/321888 offers first aid. Efficient and well run nursing homes such as **Clínica Americana** (Av 14 de Septiembre 78, T 783509), **Clínica Alemana** (6 de Agosto 2821, T 323023/327521/373676, good), *Clínica Rengel* (T 390792/8), *Clínica Santa María*, Av 6 de Agosto 2487, efficient and not too expensive, *Clínica del Sur*, Av Hernando Siles y Calle Siete, Obrajes. **Red Cross** opposite Mercado Camacho will give inoculations if required, T 323642. **The Methodist Hospital** (12th block of Obrajes, T 783809, take "A" *micro* from the Prado) runs clinic at US$5, telephone for appointment.

Health and Hygiene If suffering from *soroche*, ask in chemists/pharmacies for suitable medication. Malaria pills and yellow fever vaccination, US$15.50 including certificate are available at *Centro Piloto de Salva*, Av Montes y Basces, T 369141 about 10 mins walk from Plaza San Francisco, N of the main bus station, rec as helpful and friendly. *Laboratorio Inti*, Socabaya 266, has been recommended, also for vaccines (human immunoglobulin, cholera, rabies vaccine - but make sure you know precisely how it should be administered). Tampons may be bought at most *farmacias* and supermarkets; others say they are impossible to find, especially outside La Paz. The daily paper, *Presencia*, lists chemists/pharmacies on duty (*de turno*). For contact lenses, *Optaluis*, Comercio 1089, a stock of 5,000 lenses, including "semiduros".

Doctors Check that any medical equipment used is sterilised. Dr Ricardo Udler, Edificio Mcal de Ayacucho, Calle Loayza, T 360393/327046, speaks very good German, rec. Dr César H Moreno, Pinilla 274, Edif Pinilla, T 433805/792665 (home), rec. Dr Eduardo Fernández, Edif Avenida, Av 16 de Julio, 9th floor of 3, T 370385 (surgery)/795164 (home), speaks English, rec. **Dentists** Dr and Dra Osorio at *Hostal Austria*, Yanacocha 531. Dr Horacio M Rosso, Av 20 de Octubre, Edificio Guadalquivir, T 35475, his wife speaks German, rec. Also rec: Dr Benjamín Calvo Paz, Edificio Illimani, Av Arce esq Campos, T 343706, and Dra Esperanza Eid, Edificio Libertad, Potosí, Piso 9, No 909, both speak English. Tourist Office has a list of doctors and dentists who speak foreign languages.

Language Schools Centro Boliviano Americano (address under **Libraries** below) US$140 for

2 months, 1½ hrs tuition each afternoon. *Alliance Française* (see also below). *Fastalk*, T 812341, offers Spanish and Portuguese courses, 1 week or 1 month, 3 hrs a day; *Instituto de La Lengua Española*, Calle 14 Final Derecha Esq Aviador No 80, Achumani, T 796074. For English language teaching try *Pan American English Centre*, Av Villazón y Pasaje Bernardo Trigo 429, T 379654, Casilla 5244, native speakers only, minimum stay 3 months.

Laundromats Wash and dry, 6-hour service, at *Gelmi-Lava-Sec*, 20 de Octubre 2019, suite 9, T 352930, helpful service, US$1.40 for 1 kg; *Lavandería Cinco Estrellas*, 20 de Octubre 1714, US$3 for 3 kg. *Limpieza Rosario*, Av Manco Kapac, nr Hotel Andes; *Lavandería Bandel*, Av Mcal Santa Cruz 1032, local 10, T 353563; *Lavandería Select*, Av Arce, down from *Hotel La Paz*; 3-hour service, rec; *Limpieza Finesse*, Illampu 865. Usual charge US$1 per kg. Normally leave laundry early morning and collect same evening. Laundry service at *Oficina Gregoria Apazá*, Colombia y Almirante Grau, T 369607, phone first. Sra Elena Aranda offers laundry and repairs service, meets people on ground floor of Post Office. Dry cleaning, Calle Murillo 1366, US$.15 per kg, *La Esmeralda*, Colón 558.

Libraries *Centro Boliviano Americano* (CBA), Parque Zenón Iturralde 121, T 351627/342582 (10 mins walk from Plaza Estudiante down Av Arce), has public library and recent US papers (Mon-Fri 0900-1230, 1500-1930). *USIS* has lending library and 2nd-hand paperbacks. *Alliance Française*, F Guachalla 399 y 20 de Octubre, T 324075 (open Mon-Fri 1600-2000), has an old library. *Goethe-Institut*, Av 6 de Agosto 2118, T 374453 (Mon-Thurs, 1600-2000), good library, recent papers in German, videos in German and Spanish.

Post Office Correo Central, Av Mariscal Santa Cruz y Oruro (Mon-Sat 0800-2200, Sun 0900-1200 only). Stamps are sold only at the post office. Good philately section on first floor. There are a number of shops selling good postcards, etc. Poste Restante keeps letters for 3 months, good service, no charge. Procedure for sending parcels: all is arranged downstairs (open office hours only, Mon-Fri 0800-1200, 1430-1830); you must buy official packaging, US$1 for each parcel. Find out the price of postage before mailing parcels as the service is very expensive. Don't forget moth balls (difficult to buy – try Calle Sagárnaga) for textile items. To collect parcels costs at least US$0.50. Express postal service is on the top floor, expensive.

DHL, Av Mcal Santa Cruz 1297.

Telecommunications Entel (T 367474) office for telephone calls is at Ayacucho 267 (the only one open on Sun), and in Edif Libertad, Calle Potosí. Pay for overseas calls in advance. Long wait for incoming calls. Fax also from Ayacucho 267.

Places of Worship Protestant Community Church (inter-denominational), in English, American Co-operative School, Calle 10 Calacoto (T 795639 or 792052). Sunday service at 1100, but there are "lots of activities during the week". Anglican-Episcopalian services are held at the Community Church on the third Sunday of each month. **Synagogues** Calle Landaeta 330 (Sat am services only); Colegio Boliviano Israëlito, Cañada Strongest 1846 for Friday service—it looks like a private house.

Shopping Look around and bargain first. There are good jewellery stores throughout the city (eg *Joyería Cosmos*, Handal Center, Loc 13, Socabaya y Camacho, Inca and Bolivian designs in gold and silver, colonial objects) but visit the gold factories for lower prices and special orders. There is inexpensive silver and jewellery in the little cabinets outside Lanza market on Av Santa Cruz. Up Sagárnaga, by the side of San Francisco church (behind which are many handicraft stalls in the Mercado Artesanal), are booths and small stores with interesting local items of all sorts, best value on Sunday am when prices are reduced. The lower end of Sagárnaga is best for antiques. At Sagárnaga 177 is an entire gallery of handicraft shops: *Artesanía Nacional Tiwanaku*, for paintings, silver jewellery and woven goods, and, although there have been complaints about quality and price, a visit is a must. Upstairs is *Artesanía Sajama*, rec for woollens. *Millma*, Sagárnaga 225, and in *Hotel Radisson*, for alpaca sweaters (made in their own factory) and antique and rare textiles. *Wari* on Sagárnaga will make to measure very quickly, English spoken, prices reasonable; also *Toshy* on Sagárnaga for top quality knitwear. *Artesanía Sorata*, Linares 862, and Sagárnaga 311, 0900-1930, Mon-Sat, specializes in dolls, sweaters and weavings made by a women's cooperative and handmade textiles. Along Murillo and between Sagárnaga and Santa Cruz are various little shops selling old ponchos and rugs. For musical instruments: *Rumillajta*, one of the Galería shops adjacent to the San Francisco church entrance; many shops in Linares, eg *Sumaj Supay*, No 851, also sell woollen goods, also *Coral* at No 852 (very good waistcoats, rugs, etc.). Other music shops (LPs, CDs, cassettes) on Evaristo Valle. Alpaca goods are about 50% dearer than in Puno; sweaters are much more expensive than Peru (beware of moths in woollen goods). The maximum you can bargain prices down is 20%. Handmade clothing for children is good value. Most shops close Saturday afternoon and Sunday. Very cheap rubber stamps are made on Sagárnaga, to your own, or local designs. See also the "witchcraft market" on Calles Melchor Jiménez, and Linares, which cross Calle Santa Cruz above San Francisco, fascinating items for sale.

Artículos Regionales in Plaza de los Estudiantes is rec. *Suma Ampara*, Av Villazón 1958, wide variety of woven goods, but prices not as low as in street markets. The rec *Casa Fisher* (see Cochabamba **Shopping**) has an outlet in Handal Center, Store No 2, Calles Mcal Santa Cruz y Socabaya, T/F 392948. Antique stores at El Prado 1615, Javier Núñez de Arco downstairs, his father upstairs, nice items, very expensive, also old photographs.

The Indian market is a good place for ponchos and local handicrafts. Many Indian objects are sold near Av Buenos Aires, and Indian musical instruments on Calle Granier, near the General Cemetery. On Calle Los Andes, above Buenos Aires, there are several embroidery shops. At Gallardo 1080, 1 block above Buenos Aires, there is the small workshop of the late master mask maker, Antonio Viscarra, now run by his daughter and son-in-law. Costume, mask and trinket shops for Gran Poder abound above Buenos Aires. Food market is the Mercado Camacho (Camacho y Bolívar). The Tourist Office has a full list of all markets.

Shopping Norte, Potosí y Socabaya, is a new, modern mall with restaurants and expensive merchandise.

Bookshops Large stock of English, French and German books, and US magazines, at *Los Amigos del Libro*, Mercado 1315, also Edificio Alameda, Av 16 de Julio (1 block from *Plaza Hotel*) and El Alto airport, rec; they also sell a few tourist maps of the region from Puno to the Yungas, and walking-tour guides. Amigos del Libro will ship books. *Gisbert*, Comercio 1270, books, maps, stationery, will ship overseas, rec. *Multi-Libro*, Loayza 233, T 391996, small, good for maps, politics, religion, psychology etc (ask if you don't see what you want), open till 2100 Mon-Fri, and am Sat and Sun. *El Umbral*, Potosí 1375, T 361282, and *Hisbol*, Zapata 178, for academic subjects. *Librería La Paz*, Colón y Ballivián (wide selection of maps). Historian Antonio Paredes-Candia has a kiosk selling rare historical works on Villazón, opp San Andrés University. *Librería Martínez Acchini*, Arce 2132, good for technical books. There are 2nd-hand stalls on Av Ismael Montes; there are occasional book fairs on the Prado. German books available at Goethe Institut (see below).

Films For Kodak, Casa Kavlin, Calle Potosí 1130; Laboratorio Fuji Color, Potosí 1316; Foto Linares, Mercado y Loayza, will develop both Ansco and Agfa colour film, 1-day service on black-and-white, rec. *Foto 88*, Ayacucho 224, quick for slide developing (24 hrs), prints in 2 hrs, colour not so good. *Full Color* is the cheapest chain for developing but quality is variable; *Fotoplan* on Calle Graneros highly rec. Fuji transparency film available at half shop price in

market, and Agfa transparency film for about US$5. Cheap Fuji, Kodak and Konika film from stalls nr San Francisco. In all cases check dates on film. **Repairs** at Av Sánchez Lima 2178 by Rolando Calla C, just ring bell (1400-1700), there is no sign; also at Potosí 1316, between 1000-1200, T 373621, very helpful, professional, fair prices.

Sport There are two golf clubs (Mallasilla, the world's highest, and Pinos). Non-members can play at Mallasilla on weekdays: club hire is possible, green free, clubs, balls, and caddie US$37, the course is empty on weekdays, no need to book; it is in good condition and beautiful. After your round have a drink in the small outside bar. There are two tennis clubs (La Paz Tennis and Sucre Tennis); and two riding clubs. Football is popular and played on Wed and Sun at the Siles Stadium in Miraflores, two clubs (Micro A); there are reserved seats. Basketball is played in Plaza del Estudiante on Mon, Wed and Fri in season. YMCA sportsground and gymnasium, opposite the University of San Andrés, Av Villazón, and clubhouse open to the public, Av 20 de Octubre 1839 (table tennis, billiards, etc); regular meetings Tues and Thurs 1930 of a mountaineering group which runs weekend excursions. **Snooker/Pool** *San Luis*, Edificio México, 2do Sótano, Calle México 1411, *Picco's*, Edificio 16 de Julio, Av 16 de Julio 1566, both places rec for good tables and friendly atmosphere. See also under **Skiing** and **Mountaineering** under **Excursions** below.

Cycle Spares Try the shop at the Velódromo in Alto Irpavi, about 10 km out of town; the cheap cycle chains made in India and sold in shops in the centre of La Paz are not rec.

Tour Companies and Travel Agents *Crillon Tours*, Av Camacho 1223, Casilla 4785 (T 374566, F 391039), with 24-hr ATM for cash on credit cards; in USA, 1450 South Bayshore Dr, suite 815, Miami, FL 33131, T (305) 358-5853, F (305) 372-0054. *Transturin*, Camacho 1321 (T 328560/363654, F 391162, Telex 2301 TRTURIN BV): these two agencies offer full travel services, with tours ranging from La Paz to the whole country; full details of their Lake Titicaca services will be found on **p 274**. *Turismo Balsa*, Capitán Ravelo 2077 (T 357817, F 391310) and Av 16 de Julio 1650 (T 354049), PO Box 5889, city and local tours (rec), **see also under Lake Titicaca, p 274**; *Turisbus* (Illampu 702, Casilla 442, T 325348/369542, F 375532), helpful, trekking equipment rented, agent for Peruvian railways, ENAFER, tickets (to Puno and Cuzco—US$12 and US$31, also local and Bolivian tours), rec. *Exprinter*, Edificio Herrman, Plaza Venezuela (also operates exchange facilities) to Cuzco via Copacabana, US$30.

MAIN OFFICE:
Calle Hermanos Manchego No. 2469
(behind Plaza Isabel La Católica)
Phones: 34-1018, 35-3558, 34-2759,
Fax: (591 2) 32-9625
BRANCH OFFICE: Camino Real
Aparthotel
Calle Capitán Ravelo No. 2123
(At the back of Radisson Plaza hotel)
Phone/Fax: 0811-2707
P.O. Box 106 La Paz - Bolivia

Paititi
classic-adventure travel

SINCE 1985, THE AGENCY WITH THE
MOST COMPETITIVE PRICES, BEST PERSONALIZED SERVICES, MOST VARIED ALTERNATIVES

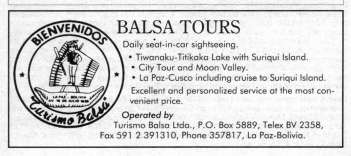

BALSA TOURS

Daily seat-in-car sightseeing.

- Tiwanaku-Titikaka Lake with Suriqui Island.
- City Tour and Moon Valley.
- La Paz-Cusco including cruise to Suriqui Island.

Excellent and personalized service at the most convenient price.

Operated by
Turismo Balsa Ltda., P.O. Box 5889, Telex BV 2358,
Fax 591 2 391310, Phone 357817, La Paz-Bolivia.

BIENVENIDOS

LA PAZ - BOLIVIA
AV. 16 DE JULIO 1650
Turismo Balsa

Magri Turismo, Av 16 de Julio 1490, 5th floor, T 323954/341201, F 366309, Amex representative: gives TCs against American Express card, but cannot give cash or exchange TCs; offers all other Amex emergency services and clients' mail, recommended for tours in Bolivia, travel services. *Pachamama Tours*, Av Mcal Santa Cruz y Colón, Galería Ed Litoral, subsuelo, of 17, T 322311, recommended for tours of La Paz, Tiwanaku, Titicaca, etc, also arranges tours throughout Bolivia; *Diana Tours*, Sagárnaga 328, T 340356/375374/350252, F 360831, some English spoken, good tour to Coroico but Tiwanaku expensive; *Titikaka Tours*, Loayza between Riva and Camacho, good for flights; *Tawa Tours*, Sagárnaga 161 and Rosenda Gutiérrez 701, T 325796, run jungle tours to their own camp as well as the Salt Lake areas, friendly, good guides (also charter flights to Europe and USA). *Shima Tours*, Potosí 1310, very helpful, good for flight tickets; *Cóndor Tours*, Sagárnaga, cheap; *Combi Tours*, Illampu 734, T 367896; *Seul Travel*, Plaza San Francisco, arranges tours to the Yungas for more than one day, helpful; *Transamazonas*, Edificio Cosmos, Piso 10, Oficina 3, Av 16 de Julio 1800, T 350411, tours to Salt Lakes and the Beni (also at the *Restaurant El Lobo*). *Fremen*, Plaza Abaroa, T 327073/376336, F 367329, range of tours incl to the Beni. *Paititi SRL*, Calle Pedro Salazar 848, T 353558/341018/342759, F 329625, organizes adventure tours, rec, Javier Prudencio is helpful and speaks several languages. *Peru Bolivian Tours*, Loayza, Ed Mcal de Ayacucho PB - Of 8, T 363720, F 365845. *Expediciones Guarachi*, Plaza Alonso de Mendoza, Edif Santa Ana, of 314, T 320901/310655, F 392344, treks and mountaineering to many lesser-known and remote destinations, highly rec for their expertise and efficiency. Also *Carmoar Tours*, Calle Bueno 159, which is headed by Günther Ruttger (T/F 340633), has information and maps for the Inca Trail to Coroico, rents trekking gear. For information on and arrangement of climbing and adventure tours, *Colibrí*, Sagárnaga 309, see under **Mountaineering** below. *Reinaldo Pou Munt*, Capitán Ravelo 2401, T 327226, Casilla 13632, expensive, offers excellent tours of the city and environs, speaks English and German. *Nuevo Continente*, Manco Kapac 366, T 373423/812479, rec for trip to Zongo, Clemente is a good driver, cheap service to airport, very friendly and helpful. Roberto Méndez, speaks English, rec for private tours, contact through Marta in the Mercado de Hechicería, Calle JM Linares, near Sagárnaga, opp No 896. Many agencies arrange excursions or travel to Peru (Puno, Cusco, Arequipa), as well as local tours. A one-day tour to Coroico is popular, US$22. See also names and addresses under "Exchange Houses", p 253.

NB Unless indicated in the list above, services offered by travel agents are expensive, some being criticised as overpriced. We have also been told that many services to Peru and beyond deteriorate markedly once Bolivia has been left (commitments unfulfilled, buses changed, extra passengers taken on—but see also Peru to Bolivia—Peru, Section 5). Note also that flight tickets can be bought more reliably from airlines than through agencies.

Tourist Office Secretaría de Turismo, Mercado 1328, between Loayza and Colón, Edif Mcal Ballivián, 18th floor, T 358213, F 374630, open Mon-Fri 0830-1200, 1430-1830. Information office at the bottom end of Av 16 de Julio (Prado) on Plaza del Estudiante on corner with C México, free leaflets, map of La Paz US$2.25. Telephone directories in La Paz have economic and tourist information in English on all the provinces.

Maps Instituto Geográfico Militar, Av 16 de Julio 1471, T 364416, open Mon-Fri 0900-1200, 1500-1900. The IGM head office is at Estado Mayor General, Av Saavedra Final, Miraflores. You must show your passport to enter the head office, but any map can be delivered to the Prado office, which has copies of all those available, within 24 hours. Topographic maps cost US$5.25 per sheet, US$4 for a photocopy (scale 1:50,000) and US$8, US$7 photocopy (scale 1:250,000). A 3-sheet map of La Paz costs US$5.25 per sheet; a 3-sheet map of La Paz Department, including Lake Titicaca, costs US$9.20; 1-sheet national communications map, US$6; 4-sheet country map, political 1988, 1:1,500,000 US$10.50; 9-sheet hydrographical map, 1990 1:1,000,000, US$17. Departmental road maps are meant to be available in the tourist offices in the capitals of each department but often they are out of stock. Senac (the national road service) publishes a Red Vial 1989 map, which is probably the best, but is still inaccurate, about US$4.50 from the office on 8th floor of Ministerio de Transporte y Communicaciones, Av Mcal Santa Cruz, tall building behind Correo, open till 1800, have to show passport. Also reported as inaccurate are the maps of the Automóvil Club Boliviano. Maps are generally hard to find. Maps are sold at Ichthus bookshop on the Prado, No 1800; also at Librería La Paz and Amigos del Libro (See p 256). Tourist map of La Paz, US$2.25.

Useful Addresses Instituto Nacional de Arqueología de Bolivia, Calle Tiwanaku 93. **Immigration**, to renew a visa go to Migración Bolivia, Av Camacho 1433 (opp Banco de Santa Cruz), T 359665, Mon-Fri 0900-1200, 1600-1800. **Tourist Police**, Mercado 1328, Edif Ballivián 18° piso, for insurance claims after theft, English spoken, helpful. **YMCA**, 20 de Octubre 1839, Casilla 963. **Asociación Boliviana de Agencias de Viajes y Turismo**, Edif Litoral, Mariscal Santa Cruz 1351, Casilla 3967.

Local Buses   There are three types of city bus: large Fiat buses run by the city corporation, on fairly limited routes; *micros* (Bluebird-type buses), which charge US$0.30; and minivans, marginally more expensive, but quicker than *micros*.

Taxis   US$1-1.25, for short trips within city limits. *Trufis* are fixed route collective taxis which charge US$0.35 within city limits. Fares out of town are given under **Excursions** below. Taxi drivers are not tipped. Don't let the driver turn the lights out at night. Radio taxis, many companies, eg Alfa T 322427, La Rápida 392323 (standard fare in centre US$1.10, to suburbs US$2.20).

Car Hire   Cars may be hired direct from **Imbex**, Av Montes 520, T 379884, F 322947, well maintained Suzuki jeeps (US$45/day, highly rec); **National**, F Zuazo 1935, T/F 376581, rec; **Avis** at Martin Travel, Plaza del Estudiante 1920; **Rent-a-Car International**, F Suazo 1942, T 357061; **Kolla Motors**, Rosendo Gutiérrez 502, T 341660/351701 who have well-maintained four-wheel drive Toyota jeeps (which seat 6), insurance and gasoline extra. **Petita Rent-a-car**, Cañada Strongest 1857-A, T 379182, F 322596, Swiss owners Ernesto Hug and Aldo Rezzonico, rec for well-maintained VW "beetles" and 4WD jeeps, etc, also offer adventure tours, **Jeeping Bolivia**, German, French, English spoken, rec. One can also hire experienced drivers for US$25 a day plus accommodation and meals. Eduardo Figueroa, T 786281, taxi driver and travel agent, recommended. Adolfo Monje Palacios, in front of *Hotel El Dorado* or T 354384 highly rec for short or long trips. Oscar Vera, Simón Aguirre 2158, Villa Copacabana, La Paz, T 230453, specializes in trips to the Salar de Uyuni and the Western Cordillera, speaks English, rec.
   Motorcycle rental: Moto Rent, Av Busch 1255, Miraflores Norte, T 357289, 650 Kawasaki endurance type, US$50/day unlimited mileage, US$250/week.

Garage   for VW and other makes: Ernesto Hug, Av Jaime Freyre 2326, T 342279 (see also **Car Hire** above) highly rec. *Car Park* on corner of Ingavi and Sanjines, US$1.75 for 24 hrs, safe and central.

Airport   El Alto, above La Paz, the highest commercial airport in the world (4,018m) connected to the city by motorway, T 810122. A taxi between the centre and airport takes about 30 mins, US$8 but may be negotiated down; current prices, including luggage, should be on display at the airport exit (enquire at the tourist office in town, or at the airport). Cotranstur minibuses, white with "Cotranstur" and "Aeropuerto" written on the side and back, go from anywhere on the Prado and Av Mcal Santa Cruz to the airport between 0800-0830 to 1900-2000, US$1.50, best to have little luggage, departures from the airport every 5 mins or so; colectivos from opposite *Hotel Crillón* (Plaza Isabel La Católica) charge US$2.65 pp, carrying 4 passengers. Micros marked "El Alto", "Río Seco", "Alto Lima", "Ceja", 30 mins to summit, then ½-hr walk to airport. There is a duty-free shop but it can sometimes forget to open. Bank in international departures hall will change cash. The international departures hall is the main concourse, with all check-in desks and is the hall for all domestic arrivals and departures. Small tourist office at the Airport, some maps available, English spoken, helpful (when staffed). The coffee shop inexpensive and serves good breakfasts.

Air Taxis   Contact Major Pericón of Taxi Aéreo Urkupiña, T 350580, 812099. Aero Inca, T 361018. Alas Doradas T 354070.

Air Services   LAB, Aero Sur (T 371833), TAM and Kantuta (T 390290) fly to the main cities and towns. Fares are comparatively low for internal flights. (For details, see under destinations.)

Bus Services   (for information, T 367275/367274); buses to: **Oruro**, **Potosí**, **Sucre**, **Cochabamba**, **Santa Cruz**, **Tarija** and **Villazón**, leave from the main terminal at Plaza Antofagasta (micros 2, M, CH or 130), see under each destination for details. Beware of taxi rip-offs, false police and theft from buses as they pull in at the bus station. The terminal (open 0700-2300) has a post office, ENTEL, restaurant, luggage store and agencies, such as Turisbus, Diana, Vicuña (cheaper than their offices in town).
   Buses to **Sorata**, **Copacabana** and **Tiahuanaco** do not leave from the bus station but from the Cemetery district. Companies located here include Flota Copacabana, Manco Kapac, 2 de Febrero, Ingavi, Morales. To get to the Cemetery district, take any bus or kombi marked "Cementerio" going up Calle Santa Cruz; the route is Santa Cruz, Max Paredes, Garita de Lima, Mariano Bautista, Plaza Félix Reyes Ortiz/Tomás Katari (look out for the cemetery arch on your left). On Plaza Reyes Ortiz are Manco Kapac (T 350033) and 2 de Febrero (T 377181) for Copacabana and Tiquina. From the Plaza go up Av Kollasuyo and at the 2nd street on the right (Manuel Bustillos) is the terminal for kombis to Huatajata and Huarina, and buses for Sorata (Trans Tur Sorata and, nearby, Larecaja). Several micros (20, J, 10) and kombis (223, 252, 270, 7) go up Kollasuyo; look for "Kollasuyo" on the windscreen in most, but not all, cases.
   Buses to **Coroico and the Yungas** leave from Villa Fátima (25 mins by micros B,V,X,K, 131,

135, or 136, or *trufis* 2 or 9, which pass Pérez Velasco coming down from Plaza Mendoza, and get off at the service station, Calle Yanacachi 1434).

International Buses To **Buenos Aires**, daily at 1800, Expreso Panamericano, 3 days, US$135 incl meals, 10% student discount, but you have to insist. Service advertised as direct, but you have to change at Villazón and walk across the border. (Cheaper to book to Villazón and rebook in Argentina). To **Arica** via the frontier at Tambo Quemado and Chungará the only reliable service is at 0500 Tues and Fri, US$20, with Litoral, T 358603 (office No 19 bus terminal), 18-19 hrs; there is also Tues and Fri at 2030, US$21, Expreso Panamericano. To Arica via the frontier at Charaña and Visviri in stages (no direct service), Senobus (Calle Hujutri, 400 m from train station in direction of Cementerio), Tues, Fri, Sat evenings (US$8.50) or (cheaper) El Cariñoso. In Charaña take taxi to Visviri (US$0.50), then colectivo taxi to Arica US$10. It is a beautiful, exhausting trip, but doing it in stages, rather than straight through, involves extra waiting at the border, all companies involve several changes of bus ("an 18-hr passage, swallowing dust all the time, but worth it at half the cost of the *ferrobus*"). Military checks can be expected both sides of the frontier. To **Iquique** and Arica, Tues, Thurs and Sat at 1830, US$32, Geminis (T 378585, when office in bus station is closed, Diana Tours at office No 5 also sell tickets), Iquique 20 hrs, Arica 24 hrs. To **Tacna**, also with Litoral, Thurs or Sun 0700, US$17.50, 13-16 hours; a very bad road, but an alternative if all other routes to Arica are fully booked (there are no Bolivian customs or immigration at the border for exit stamp, Peruvian entry is given in Tacna). Colectivos and agencies to **Puno** daily with different companies (eg Colectur) most easily booked through travel agencies, US$10-12, 10 hrs. **NB** Of the various La Paz-Puno services, only Transturin does not make you change to a Peruvian bus once over the border. For luxury and other services to Peru see under **Lake Titicaca** below.

Trains It is imperative to check times before travelling as changes are frequent and timetables contradictory. For this reason, schedules given in the text (under destinations) should be treated with caution. For information T 353510/352510/373069. Towns served are Oruro, Potosí, Sucre, Cochabamba, Villazón and intermediate stops. In early 1994, many services, including *ferrobuses*, had been withdrawn. Micros which go to the station are A, M, N, P, 130, 131, C. The ticket office, at the rear of the building at the N end of main station, opens 0700, but get there at least 2 hrs beforehand.

To **Villazón** (minimum 20 hrs) for Argentina, dep Fri at 1300. Trains also leave Oruro Mon and Thur at 1900; no sleepers; restaurant car. Book ahead at central station; queue at 0600 on previous day (queuing numbers are given out), take passport. If all train tickets are sold out, go to station 2 hrs before departure for returned tickets, try Exprinter travel agency, try and board train anyway and pay the guard, or fly to Tarija and then go by road to Villazón.

Railways to/from the Coast (1) By the Southern Railway of Peru from Arequipa to Puno, on Lake Titicaca then by road to La Paz, incorporating if desired one of the lake crossings described below under **Lake Titicaca** and **Crossing the Peruvian Frontier**.

(2) **La Paz-Arica International Railway**, 447 km: In the Bolivian section the line climbs to El Alto and then runs SW to Viacha (Km 32) the junction of lines to Antofagasta, Guaqui (freight only) and Villazón. It coninues to Corocoro, the copper mining town, crosses the Río Desaguadero at Calacoto (Km 98) and then runs SW to the border at Charaña (Km 208 – see below) a very cold place to change trains or wait for a bus. The mountain peaks visible include Illimani, Sorata, Huayna-Potosí, Mururata, and many others. For description of the Chilean part, **see Chile, The Desert North, Section 1. NB** Chilean pesos can be bought in La Paz at a better rate of exchange than in Arica.

There is a Bolivian *ferrobus* service straight through to Arica, on Mon and Fri at 0700, arrives 1900, US$52, US$95 return, incl breakfast and lunch, meals and refreshments after this charged extra ("bill in bolivianos, paid for in US dollars, change given in Chilean pesos"), max 20 kg baggage is free, extra charge for excess, worth it for the views, change money on train (poor rates), book ticket one-two weeks in advance, especially in high season (when extra trains are added). Alternatively take a train to Charaña every other Thur from Viacha at 0300 (no chance of seeing the spectacular scenery), then change to a colectivo to Arica (US$10), or, on 2nd and 4th Wed of each month a train leaves Charaña at 0930, arriving Arica at 1800 (every Wed Jan-Mar). The return from Charaña to Viacha is in daylight. Fares: Viacha-Charaña: US$3.05 pullman. Bus Charaña-La Paz US$7.50.

(3) **La Paz-Antofagasta**, by Antofagasta and Bolivia Railway, 1,173 km, now definitely a trip for the adventurous who are impervious to cold at night, or blazing sunshine at tedious daytime border changes. The train is full of contrabandistas, impromptu folk music, but the ride is very rough and subject to long delays. The train starts at Oruro (but check in La Paz in advance), to where you must go by bus, then train as far as Calama in Chile, then by bus (240 km) to Antofagasta. This, the most S of the three railway routes connecting La Paz with the Pacific

coast, passes through magnificent scenery. The train leaves Oruro at 1930 on Sun only (schedules often change), reaching Uyuni sometime after 0300 on Mon (US$4.10 Oruro-Uyuni), then there is a wait of up to 11 hrs, then another 4 hrs to Avaroa, the border (US$5 Uyuni-border, US$6.65 Oruro-border); 1 hr to change trains, then 40 minutes to Ollagüe, where Chilean customs take 4-12 hrs. As Cathy and Alan Hook of Bromley say, there is a ridiculous line-up in Chile, with officious checks (including a blood-pressure test for cholera), then "battle to get searched, all for the prize of waiting on the windswept railway line for the train to reappear." After that it is 6 uncomfortable hours to Calama (US$16 Oruro-Calama, US$5 border-Calama). In Bolivia, seats can be reserved as far as the border; tickets are sold in Oruro 0730-1100 on day of departure, in Uyuni 30 minutes before train arrives, or at 1800 the day before. Restaurant car and waiter service. If taking your own food, eat fresh things first as the Chileans do not allow dairy produce, teabags (of any description), fruit or vegetables to be brought in. There are no exchange facilities at the border. It is advisable to buy Chilean currency and sell bolivianos before journey, or on the train. All passports are collected and stamped in the rear carriage, they should be ready for collection after 1-2 hours; queue for your passport, no names are called out (beware, as the train goes down to Chile, carriages are added; the reverse happens in the other direction).

(4) La Paz-Buenos Aires: No trains now run to Argentina as this service was suspended in March 1993.

By Road from La Paz to the Pacific Coast
There are 2 routes: the shortest and most widely used is the road from La Paz to Arica via border towns of Tambo Quemado (Bolivia) and Chungará (Chile). The majority of Bolivia's imports, including foreign cars, jeeps and large vehicles from Chile's Pacific sea-ports, Arica and Iquique, are brought to La Paz by truck via this route. From La Paz take the main highway S towards Oruro to **Patacamaya** (104 km – about 1½ hrs from central La Paz on good paved road – 130 km N of Orwo); Sun market, no tourist items; **G** *Los Angeles*, basic, no electricity, candles provided, other cheap accommodation and restaurants. At Patacamaya (ask for directions – no road signs) turn right (W towards the cordillera) towards Tambo Quemado. From Patacamaya, the "road" which climbs to altitudes of around 5,000m and which is, at times, unmarked except for the tracks of heavy lorries, becomes dirt, sand, stones, mud and water. Allow 6-8 hours to cover the next 220 km to Tambo Quemado. Four-wheel drive obligatory. Take extra petrol (none available after Chilean border until Arica) food and water. Watch out for river crossings and seek advice before travelling during or just after rainy season (Dec-April).

"In the right vehicle, the journey is, in itself, a worthwhile adventure; the views, particularly to the W, of the volcanoes in distant Lauca National Park, Chile (see Chile - **The Desert North** (1) are breathtaking" (Tom Clough, La Paz). There are plans to pave this section: when completed the journey time between La Paz and Arica is expected to be about 7 hrs.

Mid-way between Patacamaya and Tambo Quemado is the town of Curahuara de Carangas. Watch for speed restrictions upon entering town past military school. Police control point in main plaza. Possible overnight stop in Sajama Village (4,200m) 22 km E of Tambo Quemado at the foot of Mt Sajama (see **South from La Paz (2) - Excursions from Oruro**). Lagunas, 12 km further on is a popular "truck-stop". Petrol available. Restaurant/bar *Lagunas* offers cheap set menu, helpful, friendly. Owner can usually find accommodation somewhere in the village, US$1, take your own sleeping bag, extra blankets, warm clothing. Facilities are at best very basic; you may well be sleeping on a straw mattress on a dirt floor. No water or electricity, gas lamps or candles are usual. Nights can be bitterly cold and very windy but the array of stars in crystal clear skies makes it worthwhile. In the daytime there are spectacular views of nearby snowcapped Mt Sajama.

The Bolivian border control at Tambo Quemado consists of customs, "tránsito" (highway police), immigration, and international police. Approx US$3.50 per "particular" ("private non-commercial) vehicle. Check with Automóvil Club Boliviano, La Paz for any special documents which may be required, depending on the registration of your vehicle. Bolivian vehicles require a Temporary Export Certificate in order to leave Bolivia (to be obtained in La Paz prior to travel), and Temporary Import Certificate approx US$2.50 from customs at Chungará on entering Chile. Best to change a small amount of currency into Chilean pesos in La Paz. Temporary Import/Export Certificates are normally valid 90 days. It is worth double checking all documents including visa requirements with the Consulate of Chile in La Paz before travelling. From Tambo Quemado there is a stretch of about 16 km of "no-man's land" (the road is more appalling than ever) before you reach the Chilean frontier at Chungará. Here the border crossing, which is set against the most spectacular scenic backdrop of Lake Chungará and Volcán Parinacota is strictly controlled. Open: 0800-1200; 1430-1800. Expect a long wait behind lines of lorries; avoid Sundays; best to travel midweek. Drivers must fill in "Relaciones de Pasajeros", US$0.25 from kiosk at border, giving details of driver, vehicle and passengers.

Border control consists of Ministry of Agriculture and Livestock (SAG - control of animals entering Chile is rigidly enforced; do not take any fruit, vegetables, or dairy products, into Chile). Immigration, Customs and Police.

From Chungará, the road is paved; the first 50 km section to Putre goes through spectacular Lauca National Park. Look out for some treacherous bends as the road descends dramatically to sea-level where it meets the Pan Amerian Highway (Route 5) 12 km North of Arica.

An alternative, on which there are no trucks, is to go by good road from La Paz via Viacha to Santiago de Machaco (130 km, petrol); then 120 km to the border at **Charaña** (*Galojamiento Aranda*); immigration is behind the railway station, only 30-day permit given on entry), very bad road. In Visviri (Chile) there is no fuel, accommodation, bath or electricity, ask for restaurant and bargain price. From Visviri a regular road runs to Putre, then as above.

A variation from Viacha is take the roads which more-or-less follow the railway to Charaña (4WD essential). On this scenic route, with interesting rock formations, you pass Comanche (puya raimondii flowers grow near here) and General Campero in the Ciudad de Piedra (near the football field in Gen Campero is a house which lets a room and has water). From Gen Campero roads go to Gen Pérez, Abarao and Charaña. From this route treks can be made S to the mountains towards Sajama and, from Charaña, to Sajana itself.

Excursions from La Paz There is trout fishing in the many glacial lakes and streams near La Paz.

The best near-by excursion is to Río Abajo and Mallasilla golf course: through suburbs of Calacoto and La Florida follow the river road past lovely picnic spots and through some weird rock formations, known as the **Valle de la Luna**, "Moon Valley". Kombi A, Nos 231 and 273 pass the Valle de la Luna en route to the Mallasa recreation area, a large weekend excursion area near Mallasa village. (No 231 can be caught at Plaza Belzu; if you do not want to walk in the valley, stay on the bus to the end of the line and take a return bus, 2 hrs in all.) About 3 km from the bridge at Calacoto the road forks; sharp right leads to the Caza y Pesca Club and Mallasilla golf course. Get out of the minibus at the turning and walk a few minutes E to the Valle entrance, or get out at the football field which is by the entrance. Take good shoes and water. Alternatively take Micro 11 ("Aranjuez"-large, not small bus) from Calle Sagárnaga, near Plaza San Francisco, US$0.50, and ask driver where to get off. Just before the Valle are the Aranjuez Forest, the Aniceto Arce cactus gardens (badly eroded) and the *Playa de Aranjuez*, a bathing spot popular for lunch at weekends. Most of the local travel agents organize tours to the Valle de la Luna (which are very brief, 5 minutes stop for photos in a US$12 tour of La Paz and surroundings); taxis are not dear (US$12), especially if shared; make sure the price is per car and not per person. Just past the Valle de la Luna and the Mallasilla Golf Course is Mallasa where several small roadside restaurants and cafés have opened; also *Oberland*, T 796818, a Swiss-owned, chalet-style restaurant (good meat) and resort, popular at weekends, especially with the expat community: cabañas, sauna, swimming pool, racket ball, tennis. It has been recommended for superb fondue, raclette, pasta and salads. Book in advance. Also *Los Lobos*, highly rec for *churrasuir* steaks, US$4.50.

Zoo, on road to Río Abajo, entrance just past Mallasa, well-housed animals in beautiful, wide open park-like setting. The climate in this valley is always much warmer than in the city, where the zoo previously was. Open daily 0900-1200, 1430-1800, US$0.60 adults, US$0.40 children.

To Achumani (past Valle de la Luna) for good views of the valley and houses of the wealthy. Walk back along the valley and catch frequent buses into town. Further beyond Ashumani is the new residential zone of Chasquipampa on the Palca road, near which is the Valle de las Animas. Here the eroded landscape is similar to, but much larger than, the Valle de Luna; good for walking and picnics. Take Kombi 239 from University to Chasquipampa. On the way back there are good views of the S districts and the city above.

To La Muela del Diablo, a gigantic, tooth-shaped rock which can be seen from the Valle de la Luna road, take Micro "Ñ" from Murillo y Sagárnaga or from the University (last stop Cota Cota) minibus 213 to Rosales, or *trufi* 288 from Cementerio, Plaza Isabel La Católica to

Urbanización Pedregal (ask driver where to get off). Cross the river and climb through the village to the cemetery; from there it is 1½ hrs easy climb to the rock, "more impressive especially if the wind is blowing than Moon Valley". The road continues to Ventilla, the start of the Inca trail.

To the Zongo Valley: a steep but scenic ride down past several of La Paz's electric power plants. Either take taxi for US$4/hr, allow at least 5 hrs, or take Micro 52, EMTA or 101 to Plaza 16 de Julio, El Alto (US$0.50) from where you can hire a taxi for US$2.25-4.50 pp or take Trans 16 de Julio (Plaza Ballivián) on Tues, Thurs and Sat, 0600. It is quite safe to drive yourself (in suitable vehicle) and hike. The road passes a series of lakes and a water course (on left); at each junction en route turn left. 20 minutes past a miners' cemetery (also on left) and a large deserted mining camp, you come to the last hydroelectric dam and on the right, a white guard house (4,750 m). Alight here. Walk up and over the small hill on the righthand side of the road until you meet the water channel again. Follow the water course for 45 minutes; this needs special care as it is cut into the side of a sheer cliff in places. You eventually come to an aqueduct which you can either cross, straddling the water, or walk beneath to the other side. At the end of the bridge, turn right up hill to a marker of rocks piled one on top of the other. Continue over the hill, cross a stream and go straight up the next hill at a similar rock marker. From the top of the hill, it is only a few minutes down to the site of the former ice cave (about 1¼ hour's walk in all). Global warming has completely destroyed the ice cave, which used to be the main attraction of the valley.

For the acclimatized only: A climb to **Corazón de Jesús**, the statue at the top of the hill reached via the steps at the N end of Calle Washington, then left and right and follow the stations of the cross. Worth the climb for the views over the city and the Altiplano, but watch out where you put your feet. Do not go alone, there is a risk of robbery; beware of dogs. Take a bus to Ceja El Alto (eg No 20 or 22) to save yourself some of the walk.

To see Puya Raimondii flowers, go to the village of Comanche, 2½ hrs from La Paz (micros from railway station to Viacha—1 hr—then truck to Comanche—rough, dusty and cold, or by train, Tues 2200, back on Wed only at 1500, US$1.50 each way); some travel agencies arrange tours.

Hikes near La Paz For the *Takesi* (Inca) road hike, take a Sector Bolsa Negra bus at 1000, US$1.25, daily from between Calles Riobamba and Burgoa, 2 blocks N of Plaza Líbano (another location may be Boquerón y Rodríguez, by the Mercado Rodríguez) to Ventilla on Palca road, arrive 1 hr early for seat, 3 hrs, return 0930 (alternatively take a Cota Cota bus Ñ to the end of the line or a taxi to Ovejura vehicle checkpoint above Cota Cota, US$6.35, then truck to Ventilla). Take the track to the left, parallel to the Río Palca for 10 km track to San Francisco mine. At Choquecota, before San Francisco, there are shops. If you leave Ventilla before 1300, you should reach Takesi village before nightfall (it's worth seeing the village). The "camino de Takesi" goes over the pass (4,650m), passes the Laguito Loro Keri and then follows the valley which ends at Chojlla (colectivo to La Paz US$2, 0730 and 1200 daily) and on 5 km to Yanacachi (one hotel, one *alojamiento*), meals available in private homes (only colectivo to La Paz at 0700 US$2.85, daily except Sat—or Sun, check, buy ticket day before), 4 hrs (if you miss that, it's a 45-min walk down to Santa Rosa, which is on the main La Paz-Chulumani road). One powerful river can be crossed by asking at houses on the bank, where they will rig up a pulley for you for US$1-2. *Backpacking in Peru and Bolivia* (Bradt Publications), and the La Paz tourist office leaflet with sketch map both describe this 3-5 day walk, which shows exceptionally fine Inca paving in the first part. Several reports say that it is much tougher than descriptions suggest (especially for the the less-than-fit), and is very unpleasant in the wet season. Please take care not to add to the litter already on the route. The highest point is 4,650m and the lowest 2,100. The scenery changes dramatically from the bitterly cold pass down to the humid Yungas. At Chojlla one can sleep at the school house for US$0.80, or the *Sheraton Inn*, basic, US$1 or less. At the village of Kakapi (3 hrs beyond Takesi, 2½ hrs before Chojlla) Don Pepe provides campsite or you may also be able to stay in the schoolhouse. Ask for Señor Genaro Mamani, a very helpful local expert and guide. The trail can also be used as a starting point for reaching Chulumani or Coroico.

Another trail is the **Choro** hike from La Cumbre pass to Coroico, descending from the snow-covered heights to tropical vegetation. Take any early bus to the Yungas from Villa Fátima (see p 246 for transport details) to the statue of Christ at La Cumbre, US$1, where the trail starts (a pick-up is unlikely to take you). Look out for condors at the start of the trail. The speedy can do the hike in under 3 days; lesser mortals will need around 4 days. The start of the trail is signposted. It is 4-5 hrs from La Cumbre to Chucura (campsite, reports of theft and begging); 5-6 hrs further to the village of Choro (campsite; on this stretch is Challapampa where Doña Juana lets rooms, G, also campsite); 8-9 hrs further along a very overgrown path and across a major river without a bridge (cross in a group; do not attempt in the wet season) to **Sandillani** (camping possible at 3 places beyond Choro, after 1 hr, 1 hr 20 mins next to water, and 1½ hrs near big empty house. In Sandillani a Japanese man welcomes visitors and will let you camp in his orchard, an excellently situated campsite, clean water, fire pit, and small shelter for packs and drying laundry. He likes postcards, stamps, old magazines or money from your home country, he keeps a log-book for any hikers to sign. Another family sell food and drinks. Thereafter it is 3 hours/7 km to Chairo. Be sure to cross the river as you enter Choro (the path resumes clearly on the other side after 200 m); the trail rises high above here to Chairo. Water is available all the way, but take water purification pills. A tent is essential. (The tourist office has a map of the trail, but it is unreliable.) From Chairo (accommodation—US$2.50,or sleep under eaves of the school, and food with Familia Paredes de la Tienda, very friendly, swimming pool), there is a daily truck to Coroico at 0500. It is a stiff, 3-hr climb up to the main road below Coroico (occasional jeeps). From this junction hitch to Yolosa (1½ hrs walk), or take a truck to Coroico. From Yolosa there are minibuses to Chuñavi and trucks from there to Chulumani (see below and p 276).

Take all supplies with you. See the warning in **Hiking**, p 332.

For both hikes, Carmoar Tours in La Paz (address above) has been recommended for equipment rental (tents US$4.10/night) and maps. Also the Club Andino Boliviano, México 1638.

A third hike is **Yunga Cruz**, from Chuñavi to Chulumani in the Sud Yungas (sketch map available from La Paz tourist office, though not very accurate or helpful). 5-7 days walking and spectacularly beautiful, many birds to be seen en route, from condors to hummingbirds. H-W Neumann and Gabi Zahn from Frankfurt, Germany, reported that it "needs a minimum of 5-6 days hard walking, mostly uphill. Great views but little water after passing the highest point". Simone Fecht from Stockach, Germany, adds that "it takes nearly a day to get to **Chuñavi** from La Paz. A bus leaves at 0800-0830 from Plaza Líbano on the corner of Calle Venancio Burgoa, go early as it is often full and no reservations possible. Accommodation in Chuñavi at the school or in the garden, ask for permission. There are two campsites near Chuñavi, one 35 mins walk and another 45 mins walk away. After these there are no more camping sites for another 6-8 hours walking, until you reach a small plain after the first river crossing".

Mountaineering Increasing numbers are visiting the Cordillera Real, to the E of La Paz. The range has the marked advantages over many half massifs of settled weather from end April-Sept, easy access via numerous mine tracks, and favourable starting altitudes (4,200-4,700 m). The Cordillera Real is 150 km long with six peaks over 6,000 m (20,000 ft)—Illampu 6,380 m (see under Sorata, below), Ancohuma 6,420 m, Chearoco 6,100 m, Chachacomani 6,100 m, Huayna Potosí 6,090 m, Illimani 6,460 m. All can be reached relatively easily from La Paz, the latter two within a few hours' driving. There are also a large number of impressive 5,000m-plus peaks.

The route to **Illimani** is via Calacoto and Huancapampa. Trucks leave Calle Zoilo Flores (behind *Hotel Milton*) 0600, 4½ hrs to Estancia Uno. From here you can hire mules, US$6 (Antonio Limachi rec), 4 hrs to base camp (4,400m), then climb to Nido de Cóndores (5,750 m) and set out for summit at 0300. The route to **Huayna Potosí**, an attractive peak (2 days) starts from Zongo Lake. (Minibus from Plaza Ballivián in El Alto Mon, Wed, Fri 0800-0900, US$4 one way, taxi US$35; trucks from Plaza Ballivián each morning. On Sundays a truck belonging to Corpac, the state electricity company, goes from Av Montes, near the bus station, to its plant by the lake.) Huayna Potosí requires mountaineering experience for ice and crevasses on the way to the top; however, bad weather, apart from mist, is rare. (*Refugio Huayna Potosí*, at base camp, 60 km, 2 hrs, from La Paz, has bedrooms, kitchen, electric light, water and food, accommodation for 20, contact Hugo Berrios, Calle Illampu 626, *Hotel Continental*, T 795936/323584, Casilla 731; transport and guiding service available.) Climbing on this mountain is now well-organized and, with a guide (recommended) it is good for gaining experience in mountain climbing. Before setting out you must register at *Refugio Huayna Potosí*.

Condoriri or Pequeño Alpamayo are reached in one or two days from Tuni at Km 21 on the La Paz-Tiquina road. Base camp is at 4,700m. From here recommended walks are to summit of Apacheta (5,300m) and Paso Jallayco (5,100m). If climbing in the Condoriri area, make sure return transport is arranged in advance; there is no traffic apart from the odd tour. People at Tuni are very friendly, but expect payment for guarding base camp. Theft from tents has been reported.

Quimza Cruz, "the future of Bolivian mountaineering", rock climbing, some ice-climbing, the highest point is 5,300 m, starting at 3,000 m. Any excursion there requires 4 days minimum, plus one day there and one back. In the N part, the Araca group, there are good rock climbs on solid granite. Snow and ice-climbing can be found in the central part. There is no direct road from La Paz; either drive to Mocoya, 280 km, 8 hrs by car, or take a bus from La Paz to

Veloco, 5 km before Mocoya, a tin mine at 4,100 m. The route, also made by truck, is to take the autopista towards Oruro. At Pan Duro take an unpaved road, direction Inquisivi, to Caxata. From Caxata it is 4 hrs to Veloco. In this region there is nowhere to buy food.

For the Western Cordillera with the peaks of Sajama, Parinacota and Pomerape, **see under Sajama, p 284, below**. The Cordillera Apolobamba, the N extension of the Cordillera Real, with many 5,000m-plus peaks, can be reached by public transport from La Paz, the main starting out points being **Charazani**, **see p 275** (trucks from La Cancha del Tejar on Calle Reyes Coronados, 10 hrs in dry weather) and Pelechuco (buses and trucks from La Paz).

Normal alpine experience and equipment will enable most peaks to be ascended, and many new routes remain to be explored. Several peaks can be climbed in a day, but the 6,000 m mountains usually require 2-4 days. There are no huts (except Chacaltaya ski-lodge and the *refugio* at Huayna Potosí). Do not underestimate altitude problems: at least 1-2 weeks' acclimatization is usually necessary before exceeding 5,500 m. (A visit to Chacaltaya and its ski-slopes is an easy way of judging one's reaction to altitude). Also, rescue services are virtually non-existent; prudence, proper gear and experience (incl crevasse rescue abilities) are indispensable. Note that mountaineering gear and high altitude camping equipment cannot normally be bought in Bolivia, though you may be able to buy it from climbers leaving the country. Club Andino Boliviano will be very pleased to accept, or buy, good "surplus" gear after climbing is finished.

A good guidebook is *The Southern Cordillera Real*, R Pecher & W Schmiemann, Plata Publishing Ltd (1977), possibly obtainable in La Paz; distributor: Los Amigos del Libro (W Guttentag), Casilla 450, Cochabamba. Also numerous expedition reports. Maps covering most of the range are the photo-surveyed 1:50,000 IGM Series, US$5 each. The Royal Geographic Society in London has an excellent map of the Cordillera Apolobamba, copies of which are available for US$6. Colonial Travel, Mexico 1733, provide information and advice on routes, organizes transport.

Guides *Alfredo Martínez* at the *Club Andino Boliviano*, Calle México 1638, T 365065, Casilla 5879, is the country's foremost guide, or contact **Hugo Berrios**, the Club secretary, T 795938, F 326724, who is also a guide. Also rec is: *Bernardo Guarachi*, Plaza Alonso de Mendoza, Edif Santa Anita, oficina 314, T 320901, Casilla 20886, La Paz (he has equipment for hire). *Colibrí SRL*, Sagárnaga 309, T 371936, F 355043 att Colibrí, *Oscar Sainz* and *Juan Villarroel*, specialize in climbing, with up-to-date information, trips arranged for all levels of experience and adventure tourism in all parts of Bolivia, very helpful, rec, full range of equipment hire. *Andes Expediciones*, Plaza Alonso de Mendoza, Edif Santa Anita, 3° piso, of 314, experienced guides, rec. *Sajama*, Calle Sagárnaga, La Paz, rec for equipment. *Iván Blanco Alba, Asociación de Guías de Montaña y Trekking*, Calle Chaco 1063, Casilla 1579, La Paz, T 350334, has been recommended (the association has about 10 guides in all and arranges climbing and hiking expeditions). Also recommended, *José Camarlinghi* (licensed by the German Alpine Club), Casilla 3772, Pedro Kramer 924, La Paz (T 352266) and *Ricardo Albert* at Inca Travel, Av Arce 2116, Edificio Santa Teresa. *Dr Juan Pablo Ando*, Casillo 6210, T 783495, trained in Chamonix, for mountaineering, rock climbing, trekking and ecological tours. In Europe the following have been recommended for group tours: *Adventura Ultimos*, Arzgruben weg 1, 8102 Mittenwald, Germany, and *Dr Erich Galt*, A-6020 Innsbruck, Amraser Str 110a, Austria. For guiding, *Norbert Kloiber*, Herrenstrasse 16, 8940 Memmingen, West Germany (T 08331-5258). *Trek Bolivia*, Sagárnaga 392, T/F 317106. The experienced Alex Munroy organizes expeditions in the Cordillera as well as trips to Peru.

The **Club de Excursionismo, Andinismo y Camping**, CEAC, helps people find the

cheapest way to go climbing, trekking, etc; foreigners may join local groups, T 783795, Casilla 8365, La Paz, or ask at the University or for Catherina Ibáñez at Plaza Tours, Av 16 de Julio 1789, T 378322, F 343301 (she has an information service for CEAC). Each week there is a meeting and slide show.

Skiing Ninety minutes by car from La Paz (36 km) is *Chacaltaya*, the highest ski run in the world. Season: November to March, sometimes longer. Skiing equipment may be hired, and a rope-tow reaches a maximum altitude of 5,221m. The facilities are sub-standard, emergency services non-existent and the rope tow should be used with extreme caution (it is of a design no longer permitted in Europe). Midweek skiing is often not possible owing to the absence of staff. Taxi or minibus US$30 (whole car) for a half-day trip, or similar to the top by rented car costs about US$60, and really only at weekends; no visitor should miss the experience and the views. However the trip can be hair-raising, buses carry no chains. Often the buses and tours only go half way. The Club Andino Boliviano, México 1638 y Otero de la Vega, runs its own Saturday and Sunday buses (mixed reports, Marco is a good guide); the day trip, beginning at 0730 and returning at 1600, comes to about US$30 for bus ticket, ski pass and equipment for the day; your bus ticket (US$13) gives free access to the ski station restaurant, otherwise US$2 entrance, hot drinks only. Equipment for hire is available (US$13 skis and boots from the Ski School—in the same building as the Ski Club, very limited, poor equipment for hire, queue at once), but better take your own. A good tip is to share equipment since, at that altitude, you will need a long break between activities. The lift pass costs US$1.50—out of season the lift only goes if there are 5 or more people. Reports suggest that Club Andino's Chacaltaya programme is not totally reliable; people have been stranded at the run, resulting in a 5-hr walk back to La Paz in the dark. (NB Club Andino's oxygen bottle at the Chacaltaya station may not always be full.) Many agencies do day trips, US$12.50, often combined with Valle de la Luna. Club Andino also occasionally arranges trips to Mount Illimani. One can walk to the summit of Chacaltaya for views of Titicaca on one side, La Paz on the other, and Huayna Potosí. Tiring, as it is over 5,000m, but one has most of the day to do the climb. Laguna de Milluni, near Chacaltaya, is a beautiful lake to visit, but do not drink its water; it is dangerously contaminated by acid residues from mining. For the really hardy, accommodation costs US$3 at the Chacaltaya ski station, but take very warm clothes and sleeping bag, food and water, as there is no heating, or bedding and the caretakers are unhelpful. (Chacaltaya skiing is described in Bradt's *South America Ski Guide*.)

Take plenty of mineral water when going to the mountains as it's thirsty work in the rarefied air. To avoid *soroche* after skiing drink *mate de coca*.

Urmiri Take road S towards Oruro, turn left at Urmiri sign at Km 75. To get this far take Flota Bolívar or Flota Copacabana bus; lifts from the crossroads are few and far between. A steep scenic descent leads to pool filled by mineral springs and a pleasant primitive inn. Worth visiting, it's a 2½ hour trip one way. The La Paz Prefectura runs buses to Urmiri, where they have a hotel (D), price includes food.

Tiahuanaco (*Tiwanaku*) The ruins of Tiwanaku, not far from the village of Tiahuanaco, are 72 km W of La Paz, near the S end of Lake Titicaca. The road from El Alto is graded and dusty. It passes through the village of *Laja* (Laxa), the first site of La Paz, at the junction of the roads between Potosí and Lima and Potosí and Arica. Because there was no water, La Paz was moved to its present site on the Río Choquepayu. Laja's church was the first cathedral of the region. On its mestizo baroque façade, note the fruits and plants, the monkey (an Indian symbol of reconstruction), the double-headed Habsburg eagle (the Spanish king, Charles I, was also Habsburg Emperor), and the faces of King Ferdinand and Queen Isabella as Indians on the left bell tower (the right bell tower was built in 1903). The church has a solid silver altar, but is closed to visitors. Simple meals at US$0.80 available in village. At the highest point on the road between Laja and Tiwanaku are wide views of the Cordillera and a site where offerings to Pachamama are made.

Many archaeologists believe that Tiwanaku existed as early as 1600 BC, while the complex visible today is estimated to have been built between the 8th and 10th centuries AD. Recent research suggests that the site was a ceremonial complex at the centre of an empire which covered almost half Bolivia, S Peru, N Chile and NW Argentina. It was also a hub of trans-Andean trade. The reason for the demise of the Tiwanaku civilization is not entirely clear, although studies by Alan Kolata of the University of Illinois indicate that the area had an extensive system of raised fields, capable of sustaining a population of 20,000, which may have been flooded by rising water levels in Lake Titicaca. This could have precipitated the empire's fall. The Pumapunka section, 1 km S of the main complex may have been a port, as the waters of the lake used to be much higher than they are today. The raised field system is being reutilized in the Titicaca area.

The main structures are: Kalasasaya, meaning "standing stones", referring to the statues found in that part. Two of them, the Ponce monolith (centre of inner patio) and the Fraile monolith (SW corner), have been re-erected. In the NW corner is the Puerta del Sol, originally at Pumapunku: the split in the top probably occurred in the move. Its carvings, interrupted by being out of context, are thought to be either a depiction of the creator God, or a calendar. The motifs are exactly the same as those around the Ponce monolith. This figure displays many of the typical Tiwanaku features: puma faces looking downwards, condor faces, two left hands, the snake with a human face on his left arm, the crying god. The Templo Semisubterráneo is a sunken temple whose walls are lined with faces, all different, according to some theories depicting states of health, the temple being a house of healing. The Akapana, originally a pyramid, was the largest structure, but is now no more than a hill. At Pumapunku, some of whose blocks weigh up to 100 tonnes, the widespread confusion of fallen stones suggests a natural disaster putting a sudden end to the construction before it was finished.

The entrance ticket to Tiwanaku costs US$2.50 for foreigners, including entry to museum; the site opens at 0900. There is a small museum at the ticket office; it has a toilet. An older museum, the other side of the railway from the main site, on the way to Pumapunku, is due for relocation. Most of the best statues are in the Museo Tiahuanaco or the Museo Semisubterráneo in La Paz. Indians trade arrowheads and bronze figures (almost all fakes); the llamas paraded at the site for photo opportunities spit and attack people. Allow 4 hours to see the ruins and village.

Tiahuanaco, the present-day village, has arches at the four corners of its square, dating from the time of independence. The church, built 1580-1612, used precolumbian masonry. In fact, Tiwanaku for a long while was the "quarry" for the altiplano. There is a very basic *alojamiento* on Calle Bolívar, cheap, good views. There is little chance of buying a meal, except food on market day. Across the Pan-American Highway from the ruins, a café sells refrescos, sandwiches, etc.

Fiestas At Tiwanaku, 21 June, before sunrise, colourful dances, llama sacrifices, etc. In Tiahuanaco village, on the eighth day of carnival (Sunday), local carnival, colourful, souvenirs for sale, bargain hard, do not take photographs. Market day in Tiahuanaco is Sunday; do not take photos then either.

Guidebook in English *Tiwanaku*, by Mariano Baptista, Plata Publishing Ltd, Chur, Switzerland, or *Discovering Tiwanaku* by Hugo Boero Rojo. They are obtainable from Los Amigos del Libro (or 2nd-hand from stalls in Av Ismael Montes). *Guía Especial de Arqueología Tiwanaku*, by Edgar Hernández Leonardini, a guide on the site, recommended. Written guide material is difficult to come by; hiring a good guide costs US$10.

Transport Transportes Ingavi, José María Azú y Eyzaguirre (take any Micro marked 'Cementerio') US$1.20, 2 hrs, 4 daily (frequency may change according to demand—the earlier you go the better). They are usually full. Tickets can be bought in advance. Taxi for 2 costs about US$20 (can be shared), return, with unlimited time at site. (US$30-40 inc El Valle de la Luna). Some buses go on from Tiahuanaco to Desaguadero; virtually all Desaguadero buses stop at Tiahuanaco, US$0.50. Return buses (last one back 1730-1800) can be caught at the crossroads in the village at the "Tránsito" sign. They are always very crowded and cannot be booked in advance, but there are usually plenty available.

Tours from La Paz cost US$15 return; they stop at Laja and the highest point on the road before Tiwanaku. Some tours include El Valle de la Luna.

If driving between Tiwanaku and La Paz, especially if en route from Desaguadero, note that the police checkpoint at Tambillo is not above bribery for trumped-up charges.

Lake Titicaca

Lake Titicaca is two lakes joined by the Straits of Tiquina: the larger, N lake (Lago Mayor, or Chucuito) contains the Islas del Sol and de la Luna at its S end; the smaller lake (Lago Menor, or Huiñamarca) has several small islands. The waters are a beautiful blue, reflecting the hills and the distant cordillera in the shallows of Huiñamarca, mirroring the sky in the rarified air and changing colour when it is cloudy or raining. Periodically the water level rises, inundating low-lying land, but its size is much reduced from prehispanic times. There are various legends concerning the origin of the name, some surrounding the *titi*, a wild cat of the lake shore, whose pelt is much prized by witch doctors. The trout fished in the lake and served in many restaurants is not native. There is some trout farming but stocks are low enough for trout to have become too expensive for many locals, who catch *pejerrey* and *karachi*. Also beginning to be farmed are the Lake's giant frogs, whose legs are served, fried, with chips, in several places. The totora-reed boats are still made, more as museum pieces than for practical purposes. Wood and fibreglass vessels last much longer. Totora reed, harvested on the shore, as well as for boatbuilding, can be used for thatching, straw, animal feed, and the young shoots can be eaten as a salad vegetable. A trip on the lake is a must if in the area; boat services are given below.

Tristan Jones, who crossed South America in his sailing cutter *Sea Dart*, spent over eight months cruising Lake Titicaca (see his book *The Incredible Voyage*, Futura Publications). He says "the Titicaca Indians' most interesting music, and quite rare, is at masses held for the dead". *An Insider's Guide to Bolivia*, by Peter McFarren, gives a good historical background, including an interesting article about archaeological discoveries in Lake Titicaca, by Johann Reinhard (available in many bookshops and large hotels in La Paz). Reinhard also contributed a chapter on "Underwater Archaeological Research in Lake Titicaca" to *Ancient America, Contributions to New World Archaeology*, edited by Nicholas J Saunders (Oxford: Oxbow Monograph 24, 1992).

Copacabana, 158 km from La Paz, is an attractive little town on Lake Titicaca. It has a heavily restored, Moorish-style cathedral containing a famous 16th century miracle- working Dark Virgin of the Lake, also known as the Virgin of Candelaria, the patron saint of Bolivia. Candlelight procession on Good Friday. The cathedral itself is notable for its spacious atrium with four small chapels; the main chapel has one of the finest gilt altars in Bolivia. The basilica is clean, white, with coloured tiles decorating the exterior arches, cupolas and chapels. Vehicles are blessed in front of the church daily, especially on Sunday. An *hospicio* (serving now as an almshouse) with its two arcaded patios is worth a visit; ask permission before entering. There are 17th and 18th century paintings and statues in the sanctuary and monastery. Good food and drink at the hotels and in the market.

There are good walks beside the lake, or on the hills around the town. On the headland which overlooks the town and port, Cerro Calvario, are the Stations of the Cross. On the hill behind the town (Cerro Sancollani) overlooking the lake, roughly SE of the Basilica, is the Horca del Inca, two pillars of rock with another laid across them (probably a sun clock rather than a gallows, now covered in graffiti). With the church entrance behind you turn right up PD Murillo towards the green house at the street end. At the green house turn right and immediately left up a rocky hill. There is a path marked by white stones. Boys will offer to guide you: fix price in advance if you want their help. Above the Horca, on the other side of the ridge, is the Flecha del Inca, an arrow-shaped hole in a rock. Back down at the green house, turn left instead of right to the cemetery at the Asientos (Seats) del Inca, close to town. Further from town is El Baño del Inca, about 2 km (an hotel and museum are under construction here). Ask for directions on reaching the woods. Copacabana's water supply can be intermittent. Beware of sunburn especially on the lake, even when it does not feel hot. **NB** The local police have been known to accuse travellers of "photographing secret buildings" and "fine" them US$10-20, or confiscate "false" US$ bills or travellers cheques. New arrivals may also be pressurized into paying for 'entry' to the town; the fee is in fact for the sanctuary.

Fiestas 2-5 May, very colourful; 5-8 August, when the town gets very full, hotel prices quadruple and theft is common in broad daylight.

Hotels C *Playa Azul*, 6 de Agosto, full board (rooms fair, but chilly, half-board a possibility),

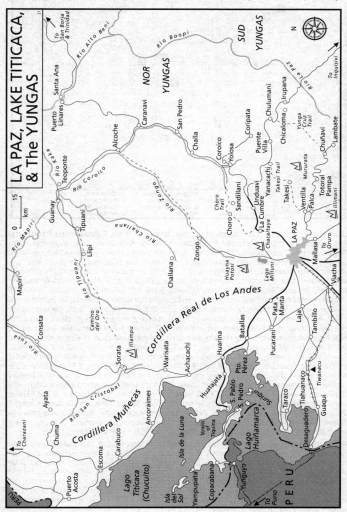

LA PAZ, LAKE TITICACA, & The YUNGAS

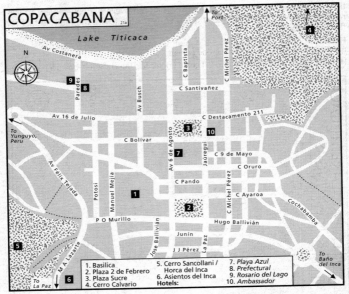

COPACABANA

Lake Titicaca

1. Basilica	5. Cerro Sancollani / Horca del Inca	7. Playa Azul
2. Plaza 2 de Febrero	6. Asientos del Inca	8. Prefectural
3. Plaza Sucre	**Hotels:**	9. Rosario del Lago
4. Cerro Calvario		10. Ambassador

tepid electric showers, water supply poor, good food, T 320068; **C** *Residencial Rosario del Lago*, Rigoberto Paredes between Av Costanera and Av 16 de Julio, same ownership as *Res Rosario*, La Paz, inc breakfast, colonial style, hot water (solar power), Turisbus office, due open Jan 1995; **D** *Prefectural*, with good meals, some rooms have lake view, very mixed reports; **F** *Alojamiento Aransaya*, Av 6 de Agosto 121, T 229, basic but clean and friendly, hot shower, with good restaurant (specializes in trout), about US$2 a dish; **F** *Alojamiento Aroma*, Av Jauregui, towards beach, clean, hot showers, very helpful and informative owner; **F** *Alojamiento Imperio*, Calle Visconde de Lemos, some hot water (shower US$0.50 extra), will change money; **F** *Residencial Sucre*, Murillo 228, T 2080, hot water, bath, parking, quiet, clean; **F** *Ambassador*, Bolívar y Jauregui, T 216, balcony, request heater, clean, with bath, cheaper without, good restaurant, reduction with YHA card; **F** *Kota Kahuaña*, Av Busch 15, blue house, hot showers (water not available all day), cheap, clean, some rooms with lake view, rec. **F** *Residencial Copacabana*, Oruro 555, T 220, warm water, reasonable; **F** *El Turista*, Pando 378, rec, friendly, cheap and clean, inadequate shower facilities; **F** *Residencial Porteña*, by market on Jauregui, clean, safe, rec; **F** *Solar*, Jauregui, new, clean; **F** *Emperador*, Calle Murillo, behind the Cathedral, clean, popular with travellers, laundry service and laundry facilities, communal baths, hot showers all day (electric), breakfast served in your room, very highly rec; many others on Murillo, eg **G** *Illimani*, basic, clean, Cochabamba; **G** *Las Playas*, overlooking beach, hot showers, dirty, laundry facilities; **G** *San José*, next to *Ambassador*, T 215, 1 block from lake, clean, basic, hot water, some rooms with lake view; *Alojamiento Bolívar*, Jauregui 158, bright blue, good views, hot shower, pleasant, simple, clean, rec. Many other residenciales in F and G categories. Prices increase at Easter and during fiestas.

Restaurants On Plaza 2 de Febrero (main square) are *Napolés*, clean, reasonable prices, "cold rice and tough meat on plastic plates", changes money; *La Patria*, very good *pique* dish, not too expensive; *Colonial*, decent lunch, good trout. Several on 6 de Agosto inc *Snack 6 de Agosto*, good trout, salad and chips, big portions, serves breakfast, closed in evenings, *Tourist Palace*, cheap, reasonable, *Puerta del Sol*, good, and *Pensión Flores*, lunch only. Watch out for gringo pricing of food and in restaurants. *Peña Clima* has music on Saturdays, behind the market. Many other restaurants offer acceptable US$2 meals; trout rec; good breakfasts and other meals, especially fish, in the market.

Services ENTEL, behind the church on road from La Paz. Motorcycles and bicycles can be hired; ask boys at the beach, but bargain. (If planning to cycle far hire mountain bikes.) Bank only opens Wednesday-Sunday (does not change TCs or sell soles); a few restaurants and shops give poor rates for US$, but not for soles, so, if coming from Peru, buy bolivianos in Yunguyo (beware, much counterfeit money here, poor rates) before crossing frontier. Difficult to change TCs (try David Suxo's *artesania* shop on the plaza, or *Bidesa*, 6 de Agosto, poor rates). Post Office on Plaza 2 de Febrero. Open Wed to Sun 0900-1200, 1400-1700. Many shops are closed on Mon and Tues, as they are open on Sundays.

Transport By car from La Paz to Copacabana (direct), 4 hrs, take exit to "Río Seco" in El Alto; the road is paved as far as Tiquina. Bus from La Paz: either take an agency bus for US$12-15 approximately (pick up at your hotel; eg Turisbus, Diana Tours); or public bus: 2 de Febrero, T 377181, 6 a day; Manko Kapac, T 350033, 3 a day, 4½ hrs, US$3, last bus 1700, book day before; both companies' offices in La Paz are in Plaza Reyes Ortíz, opposite entrance to cemetery. Note that buses for La Paz are very full on Sunday afternoons. One day trips from La Paz are not recommended as they allow only 1½-2 hrs in Copacabana. To reach Copacabana you cross the lovely straits of Tiquina (for details of the ferry crossing see below). Bus Copacabana-Yunguyo (Peru), hourly when full, US$0.40, from Plaza Sucre below *Hotel Playa Azul*. Agency buses between La Paz and Puno can be picked up (slightly cheaper to pay La Paz-Copacabana and Copacabana-Puno separately). No public bus services to Puno: you have to go to Yunguyo and catch a bus from there. Bus to Huarina (difficult connection for Sorata), US$2.50. **NB** It is impossible to travel from Copacabana to Guaqui direct, because of border crossings.

Isla del Sol. The site of the Inca creation legend is a short distance by boat from Copacabana. A sacred rock at its NW end is worshipped as the birthplace of Manco Kapac and Mama Huaca, the first Incas. On the E shore near the jetty for Crillon Tours' hydrofoils and other craft is the Fuente del Inca, a pure spring, and Inca steps leading up from the water. A 2-km walk from the landing stage takes one to the main ruins of Pilko Caima (the Sun Gate from the ruins is now kept in the main plaza in Copacabana), a two-storey building with false domes and superb views, entry US$1.20. Southeast of the Isla del Sol is the Isla de la Luna (or Coati), which also may be visited—the best ruins are an Inca temple and nunnery, but they have been sadly neglected. It is worthwhile staying overnight on the Isla del Sol for the many beautiful walks through villages and Inca terraces, some still in use. It is not possible to see all the sites on the Isla del Sol (a 4-hour round trip on foot) and return to Copacabana in one day. Take camping equipment, all food and water (or water sterilizers), or ask Don Juan, next to the school on the beach at Challas (NW coast) for lodging in one of his rooms (US$0.80). He serves thirsty walkers with beer or refrescos. Also enquire near the Inca steps for lodging. **G** *Casa Blanca* in the main village above the landing area, rec as clean and comfy, owners will cook meals to order. Also *Albergue Inca Sama*, next to Pilko Caima, restaurant serving fish dishes, excellent views, basic accommodation (G pp) at Yumani, 30 mins walk from Pilko Caima, campsite (contact via *Hotel Playa Azul*, Copacabana, or La Paz T 356566/357817). The owner, Sr Pusari, offers boat service from Copacabana, US$33 one way, US$50 return, or the 15-min crossing Yampupata-Pilko Caima.

Boats can be hired in Copacabana, at the beach or through many *residenciales* (including *Emperador*), to go to Islas del Sol and de la Luna. Few boats are available in the low season. You can go either to the S end of Isla del Sol, or to the N, or both, and on to La Luna. Whatever you choose to do it is imperative to agree with the boatman what is included in the price, how long you will stay ashore and, if staying overnight, when you will be collected (preferably in writing). Fares vary according to type of boat (motor or sail), its capacity, length of trip, etc; by sail to the S end costs US$15, by motor US$30, by motor boat to N and S US$40, similar to include Isla de la Luna. Between Islas del Sol and de la Luna, US$10 return. All prices for 5-7 passengers. Note that sailing boats may suffer from lack of wind and that motor boats generally hold more passengers. Warning: Several reports have been received of boat excursions giving less than value for money, and often giving free rides to the owner's friends and relatives encountered en route. Many boat owners are also reluctant to do more than a morning trip (0730-1300). Don't always take the cheapest possible offer, ask around and check what is included for your money. Cheaper boats can be found by walking 15 km N along the lakeside from Copacabana to Yampupata where fishermen cross the narrows in rowing boats to Isla del Sol in ½ hour, US$3, return. This is a lovely walk in itself (allow 3½ hrs), through unspoilt countryside, but it is too rough for cycling. At the village of Sequañe ask for Señor Hilario Paye Quispe who will row you across and bring you back another day if you plan to stay on the Isa del Sol.

Tour boats to Isla del Sol often stop only briefly at the jetty by the Fuente del Inca. All the time visitors are ashore they are pestered by people with llamas and children for photographs to be taken, after which payment is demanded.

To hire a rowing boat in Copacabana costs US$4.50 per hour.

From Copacabana to La Paz: the unpaved road from the Peruvian border and Copacabana goes to San Pedro, the W side of the Straits of Tiquina, the main base of the Bolivian navy. On the E side is San Pablo. Vehicles are transported across on barges, US$3. Passengers cross separately, US$0.20 (not included in bus fares) and passports are checked. Expect delays during rough weather, when it can get very cold. In San Pablo there is a clean blue restaurant with excellent toilets. After the crossing, the route is through **Chúa**, where there is fishing, sailing and Transturin's catamaran dock (see below). The public telephone, Cotel, office is on the plaza just off the main road. No restaurants or accommodation. About 2 km further along the main road is a turning to the right (signed) to *La Posada del Inca* restaurant, open Sat, Sun and holidays for lunch only, in a beautiful colonial *hacienda* setting (good trout, average prices). After another 4 km the road passes through **Huatajata**, with restaurants, *Yacht Club Boliviano* (restaurant open to non-members, open Sat, Sun lunch only, sailing for members only) and Crillon Tours International Hydroharbour and *Inca Utama Hotel* (see also below). At Huarina, 42 km E of Tiquina, is the turn off for Achacachi, Sorata and the road along the E shore of Titicaca to Puerto Acosta (see below). Between Huatajata and Huarina (at Km 65 from La Paz) is the **B Hotel Titicaca**, T La Paz 374877, F 391225, beautiful views, friendly, sauna, pool, good restaurant, very quiet during the week (address in La Paz, Potosí y Ayacucho 1220, 2° piso). The main road to the capital continues through Batallas (see below). Bus La Paz—Huatajata/Tiquina, US$0.80, Transportes Titikaka, Av Kollasuyo 16, daily from 0400, returning between 0700 and 1800.

In Huatajata, next to Crillón's *Inca Utama*, is *Restaurant Huatajata Utama*, highly rec, then *Inti Raymi*, with boat trips, *El Lago*, *Panamericano*, *La Playa* and *Hostal Restaurante Lago Azul* (cramped rooms, basic, overpriced). The restaurants are of varying standard, most offering trout and *chairo* (*chuño* soup with meat or quinoa or barley). Most seem to come to life at weekends and in the high season. Beside *Lago Azul* is Máximo Catari's *Inti Karka* restaurant on the road (full menu, open 7 days, average prices, good fish but small portions), and hotel, a 3-storey building on the waterfront (F pp, breakfast extra, basic, shower, water unreliable, some rooms with lake view, ask for extra blankets, T 813212). Catari arranges boats to the islands in Lago Huiñamarca, Pariti, Kalahuta and Suriqui: prices, to Suriqui US$22 for 4-5 people, to all 3 islands US$40, 1-hr boat trip US$7.50, sailing boat for 3 US$16 for a day (Catari's prices, boat trips rec). Paulino Esteban (see below) is also rec, contact through Servitur, PO Box 8045, La Paz, T 340060, F 391373. On **Suriqui** (1½ hrs from Huatajata) you can visit the museum/craft shops of the Limachi brothers (now living at the *Inca Utama* cultural complex) and Paulino Esteban, who helped in the construction, out of totora reeds, of Thor Heyerdahl's *Ra II*, which sailed from Morocco to Barbados in 1970. Heyerdahl's *Tigris* reed boat, and the balloon gondola for the Nazca (Peru) flight experiment (**see Peru chapter, Section 4**), were also constructed by the craftsmen of Suriqui. Reed boats are still made on Suriqui, probably the last place where the art survives. On **Kalahuta** there are *chullpas* (burial towers), old buildings and the town of Kewaya (no one lives there). On **Pariti** there is Inca terracing, the weaving on the island is very good. Boats can also be hired in Tiquina for trips to Suriqui, US$3 pp in a group. No food is available on Suriqui.

Three major La Paz travel agents base their Titicaca operations on the shores of Lago Huiñamarca: 1) Crillon Tours (address under La Paz **Travel Agents**), run a hydrofoil service on Lake Titicaca with a bilingual guide – "excellent and willing to resolve any problem". Among Crillon's vessels is the *Glasnost Arrow*, a gift from Leonid Brezhnev to Richard Nixon. All Crillon's tours stop at the cultural complex at *Inca Utama*: in the daytime visitors see the archaeological and ecological museum (recorded commentary, quite brief, but interesting), in the evening the

Kallawaya (Native Medicine) museum, including a meeting with a Kallawaya fortune teller. The *Inca Utama* hotel has a health spa based on natural remedies; the rooms are comfortable, with heating, good service, bar, good food in restaurant (5-star accommodation, **A**, reservations through Crillon Tours, T La Paz 374566/350363). Also at *Inca Utama* are an observatory (*Alajpacha*) with retractable thatched roof for viewing the night sky, a new panoramic restaurant, a bar on the lake, a new colonial-style building with 12 de-luxe suites and 2 conference rooms. Health, esoteric, mystic and ecological programmes are offered. Leaving La Paz at 0600, you get to Huatajata for breakfast and a visit to the "admirable" museum 0800. The hydrofoil sets off at 0830, moves past reed fishing boats, and stops in the Straits of Tiquina for a few minutes to watch the wooden ferry boats crossing. Only the Isla del Sol is visited to see the ruins (30 mins). You arrive at Copacabana for sightseeing and a trout lunch. The short tour returns to La Paz from Copacabana via *Inca Utama*; the longer one continues to Puno (Peru) to connect with the Puno-Cuzco rail service (customs and immigration handled by Crillon). Trips can be arranged to/from Cuzco and Machu Picchu, hydrofoil and train one way, flight the other; other combinations of hydrofoil and land-based excursions can be arranged (also jungle and adventure tours). Charge: US$156 from La Paz to Puno, US$119 for day excursion from La Paz (US$114 for day trip to Tiwanaku and Huatajata). Expensive but fascinating, not least for the magnificent views of the Cordillera on a clear day. All facilities and modes of transport connected by radio.

2) Transturin (see also La Paz **Travel Agents**) run catamarans on Lake Titicaca, either for sightseeing or on the La Paz-Puno route (US$127 La Paz-Puno; day trips US$70-90; overnight at *Hotel Titicaca* and tour US$130). From their dock at Chúa, 3-hour trips go to Copacabana, with bar, video, sun deck and music on board. One-night tours to Copacabana are also available. The catamarans are slower than the hydrofoils of Crillon so there is more room and time for on-board entertainment. Transturin runs through services to Puno without a change of bus, and without many of the usual formalities at the border. Transturin has offices in Puno, Av Girón Tacna 149-147, T 352771, and Cuzco, Av Portal de Panes 109, of 1, T 222332.

3) **Hotel Las Balsas**, owned and operated by Turismo Balsa (see La Paz **Travel Agents**), T La Paz 357817, F 391310, in a beautiful lakeside setting at Puerto Pérez, with views of the cordillera; all rooms have balcony over the lake. Large new salon caters for groups, seminars. Hotel is advertised as 5-star; **A3**, but willing to negotiate to reduce price out of season; fitness facilities incl massage. jacuzzi, sauna, racket ball; T/F (2) 813226; restaurant expensive, but fixed price lunch or dinner good value at US$12. Turismo Balsa operate boat trips to Suriqui and Kalahuta, and services to Puno and Cuzco.

Note: these three travel agencies also offer a full range of packages and travel services; contact their La Paz offices.

Puerto Pérez is the closest point to La Paz on Lake Titicaca (72 km, less than 1 hr by car). The road to the port turns off the main road at *Batallas*, a typical Altiplano market town so named because of the final battles between Almagro and Pizarro. The views of the lake and mountains from Puerto Pérez are superb; the sunsets are spectacular, too. The port was the original harbour for La Paz, founded in the 19th century by British navigators as a harbour for the first steam boat on the Lake (the vessel was assembled piece-by-piece in Puno). Colourful fiestas are held on New Year's Day, Carnival (Mon and Tues before Ash Wednesday), 3 May and 16 July. For transport to Puerto Pérez there is a regular minibus service from La Paz Cementerio district: across from the cemetery, above the flower market, ask for buses to Batallas, price US$0.75.

Crossing the Peruvian Frontier

There are 3 routes from La Paz to Puno: 1) Along the W side of Lake Titicaca. The road and railway (no passengers) go from La Paz 91 km W to **Guaqui**, formerly the port for the Titicaca passenger boats. Guaqui was flooded by a 3-metre rise in the lake's water level in 1985. The line was repaired in 1990. **G** *Residencial Guaqui*, good value, basic, friendly; tiny restaurant on the Plaza de Armas has been rec. On the last weekend of July, Guaqui celebrates the festival for the Apóstol Santiago. Arrive early morning to join in the end of all-night carousing (what little accommodation there is, is all fully occupied). The road crosses the border at *Desaguadero* 22 km further W (*Hotel Bolivia*, near Bolivian customs, reasonable 4-course meals) and runs along the shore of the lake to Puno. A side road which branches off to the N leads to Yunguyo and back across the border to Copacabana. The route La Paz-Guaqui-Puno is being paved so that, eventually La Paz to the Peruvian ports of Matarani/Mollendo will be paved throughout.

Transport Buses from La Paz to Guaqui and Desaguadero depart from Ignavi office (José María Asu y Eyzaguirre) 0830 and 1000, US$1.50, 3½ hrs, avoid putting luggage on roof. From Desaguadero to La Paz 1430. To Puno US$6.50, 3 hrs. To Puno from La Paz US$15, 8 hrs.

2) Via Copacabana (see under Copacabana for description of the route to Copacabana). From Copacabana an unmetalled road leads S to the frontier near Yunguyo. For La Paz tourist agency services on this route **see under International Buses (p 260)** and under Lake Titicaca above.

This is now a very straightforward border crossing, with customs and immigration posts at either side of the border; the buses/colectivos stop at each one (or you can walk, 400m, and a small hill, between the two posts; transport does not start till Yunguyo, a further 600m). Taxis and tricycles run between the border and Yunguyo. Make sure, if arranging a through ticket La Paz-Puno, that you get all the necessary stamps en route, and ascertain whether your journey involves a change of bus. Note the common complaint that through services La Paz-Puno (or vice versa) deteriorate once the border has been crossed, eg smaller buses are used, extra passengers taken on, passengers left stranded if the onward bus is already full, drivers won't drop you where the company says they will.

At Yunguyo, do not photograph the border area. Beware of "out of hours" charges on the Peruvian side; if returning immediately to Bolivia, with a new visa, a US$5 bribe is asked for by Peruvian officials to avoid the statutory 72 hours outside Bolivia. There are many money changers on the Peruvian side. When leaving Peru, take as few soles as possible since they are very difficult to change. Arrive at the Peruvian border in the morning to ensure transport into Bolivia.

If crossing into Bolivia with a motorcycle, do not be fooled into paying any unnecessary charges to police or immigration.

3) Along the E side of Lake Titicaca. The Peruvian authorities do not officially recognize the road as being a border crossing. (Officially, you must get your entry stamp in the Department of Puno, but as this is next to impossible on this route, you will run into difficulties later on.) The road passes through Achacachi (**see p 280**), Ancoraimes (small Sun market), Carabuco (with colonial church), **Escoma**, which has a large Aymara market every Sunday (it finishes before 1300, watch out for drunks in the afternoon) and **Puerto Acosta**. The area around Puerto Acosta is good walking country and the locals are friendly. From La Paz to Puerto Acosta the road is fine during the dry season (approximately May to Oct). North of Puerto Acosta towards Peru the road deteriorates rapidly and should not be attempted except in the dry season.

There is an immigration office, beware extortionate demands by guards, but it is advisable to get an exit stamp in La Paz first. **G** *Alojamiento Espinosa*, basic, friendly, but no restaurants. Bus La Paz (Cementerio district)-Puerto Acosta, US$2.50, Fri 1130, Sat/Sun 0630. Many trucks travel La Paz-Puerto Acosta on Tues and Fri afternoons. The only transport beyond Acosta is early on Wed and Sat mornings when a couple of trucks go to the markets, some 25 km from Puerto Acosta on the border (no formalities); the Peruvian and Bolivian markets are completely different.

At Escoma a road branches N, roughly parallel with the border, going to Chuma, and to **Charazani** (Juan José Pérez; Ulla-Ulla *fiesta*, 16 July, witch doctor; **G** pp *Hotel Charazani*, good, clean, friendly; 2 restaurants; one bus a week from La Paz, otherwise trucks; by car 2 days from La Paz). The road ends at Apolo.

The road from Escoma to Charazani is very scenic, climbing to 4,500m. At the highest point is a sign to the **Reserva Ulla Ulla**, where llamas, alpacas, vicuñas, vizcachas and many birds can be seen, with the backdrop of the Cordillera de Apolobamba. Camping is possible (but cold), ask for the thermal springs, or for permission at farms (payment welcome). Sendero Luminoso activity was reported in the area in late 1994. Ulla Ulla-Charazani by car 3-4 hrs. Charazani is in the Yungas, with thermal springs. 2-3 hrs away is Curva, one of the bases of the Kalawaya (native medicine doctors), now reported to be unwilling to practice for visitors (too many of the latter). Also in the area is **Iskanwaya**, a major archaeological site on the eastern Andean slopes. A road from the Escoma-Charazani road crosses a 5,000m pass before descending to Aucapata; continue down a very poor jeep track then hike 1 hr down a cactus-filled canyon to the ruin (at about 1,500m). The city stands on two built-up platforms, with delicate walls, plazas, narrow streets, storerooms, niches, pot shards, etc. Admission to the museum in Aucapata is by donation. Great care is needed not to damage this site. (With thanks for information to Gregory W Frux, New York, and Dr J Kleinwächter, AM Wetzelsberg, Germany.)

THE YUNGAS (2)

Lush forested slopes behind the mountains to the N of La Paz; this is the main production area of citrus, bananas, coffee and coca leaves for the capital. It is also a favourite retreat for those escaping the Andean chill.

NB The Yungas are a coca-growing region, so it is advisable not to wander too far off the beaten track.

The Yungas can be approached either via La Cumbre, NE of La Paz, or by turning off the road which skirts the E shore of Lake Titicaca and crossing the Cordillera to Sorata. Both routes join at Caranavi, so a circular route can be made (**see map, p 269**).

The route NE out of La Paz circles cloudwards over La Cumbre pass at 4,725m; the highest point is reached in an hour; all around stand titanic snowcapped peaks and snowfields glinting in the sun. Then at Unduavi the paving ends; the road becomes "all-weather" and drops over 3,400m to the luxuriant green rain forest in 80 km. The roads to Coroico and Chulumani divide just after Unduavi, where there is a *garita* (check point), the only petrol station, but no good place to eat. Police may ask drivers of private vehicles for a voluntary contribution at the checkpoint near Unduavi. Note, if travelling by truck from La Paz to the Yungas via La Cumbre, the best views can be seen in May and June, when there is least chance of fog and rain on the heights. If you want to alight at La Cumbre, ensure you tell the driver beforehand for it is easy to miss in fog or cloud. It is very cold at La Cumbre and, further down, there are waterfalls at San Juan that baptise open vehicles—be prepared. For details of the La Cumbre-Coroico hike (Choro), **see p 263**.

Chulumani, the capital of Sud Yungas, is the main regional centre. Citrus fruits are the main products from this area as well as some coffee.

Hotels B *Motel San Bartolomé* (T 358386), pleasant, some family rooms and cabins cheaper, superb jungle setting with fabulous views of mountains, swimming pool, can be booked through the *Hotel Plaza*, La Paz, T 378311, Ext 1221 (or Plaza Tours in La Paz); C *Motel San Antonio*, pleasant cabins and swimming pools (both Motels are out of town, a taxi ride or long walk away). D *Prefectural*, on outskirts, full board, swimming pool (not always full, open to non-residents for US$0.50). D *Residencial El Milagro*, good views, at entrance to town by *tránsito*, very clean, very attentive landlady, garden; D *La Hostería*, Junín, T (0811) 6108, with bathroom, breakfast included, clean and friendly, restaurant; E *Panorama*, with pool, basic rm, poor service, restaurant; F pp *García*, on main square, with toilet, cheaper without, basic, clean and cheap, rec, but noisy at weekends from disco; *Hotel Bolívar*, cheap, clean and friendly.

C *Hotel Tamapaya*, 95 km from La Paz, just outside Puente Villa (the lowest point on the road), is in a beautiful setting, with shower, good rooms, swimming pool, rec.

Restaurants *Don Miguel* on main street, doesn't look much, but very good. Cheap food at *García* and at *Pensión Viviana*, Calle Lanza, for freshly-squeezed orange juice.

Bus From La Paz, Flota Yungueña, Av Las Américas 354, Villa Fátima, 120 km, Sat 0830, 6 hours, US$3.30. Minibus from Villa Fátima, La Paz, 0830/1430 daily, and returns early afternoons daily, US$3.50, 3-4 hrs, more comfortable than the bus.

Excursion From Chulumani you can continue to *Irupana* (fiesta 5 August, hotel F, clean with pool); the road passes through fruit, coffee and coca plantations. Bus from Chulumani less than US$1, or take any passing truck. In Irupana you can hire transport for *Chicaloma*, the centre of Bolivia's black population (½ hr, US$13 with waiting; 2 hrs walk). The village is in a tremendous location.

The other branch from Unduavi leading to Yolosa, the junction 7 km from Coroico, has been described as "life-endangering". True, it is steep, twisting, clinging to the side of sheer cliffs, and it is very slippery in the wet, but the danger lies in not knowing the rules of the road, especially at weekends. Uphill vehicles always have right of way; downhill must wait or reverse to a passing place. Uphill drives on the cliff side, be it left or right, downhill on the outside. Speed and ignorance on the narrow road leads to drivers plunging over the edge.

The little town of **Coroico** is perched on a hill at 1,525m; the scenery is beautiful. The hillside is covered with orange and banana groves; there are delightful walks through paths down to the river where warm pools are ideal for bathing (and if you're not up to 2-3 hrs walk each way, lifts are usually available in Coroico). The trail to the river starts at the left corner of the football pitch, looking downhill; it forks often, keep right. Another pleasant short walk starts at El Calvario (follow the Stations of the Cross by the cemetery, off Calle Julio Zuazo Cuenca which leads uphill from the main square). Facing the chapel at El Calvario, with your back to the view of the town and its setting, look for a path on the left, which soon becomes well-defined. It leads in 1 hour to the Cascada y Toma de Agua de Coroico (the source of the town's water supply); the path runs quite level along the hill's edge.

Festivals There is a colourful four-day festival on 19-22 October, when accommodation is hard to find. It is great fun, but wait a day or two before returning to La Paz (hung-over drivers). On 2 November, All Souls' Day, the local cemetery is festooned with black ribbons.

Hotels *San Carlo*, 1 km outside town, 3-star, T 813266 (La Paz T 372380), with restaurant, pool and sports facilities, modern, rec. Also out of town is *El Viejo Molino*, 4-star, with pool, T 0811 6004 (or represented in La Paz by Valmar Tours, T 361076, F 352279). **D** *Don Quijote*, 800 m down Coripata road (up from square, then left, then right), new, pool, restaurant. **D** *Prefectural*, down the steps from the square, past the convent and beyond the football pitch, building a bit dated, but clean and pleasant, nice garden, good views, swimming pool (may not have water), full board (E without food), food quite good, has bus service to La Paz. **E** *Lluvia de Oro*, on street off square by Entel, good value (but confirm price), food rec, cheap, swimming pool, top floor rooms are best, opp is **G** pp *Res Coroico*, dormitory accommodation. **E** *Sol y Luna*, uphill past cemetery, and Umopar (narcotics police) station, ¹/₂-hr walk from town (ask for La Alemana, La Gringa, Victoria or Sigrid Fronius—all the same person!), dormitory accommodation **G** pp, meals available (Indonesian food), cooking facilities, also 2 *cabañas* for rent D, camping US$1 pp, swimming pool, garden, laundry service, highly rec (also, Sigrid offers Shiatsu massage for US$7), in La Paz reserve through Chuquiago Turismo, Planta Baja, Edif La Primera, Av Santa Cruz 1364, Casilla 4443, T 362099/359227. On road to *Sol y Luna* is **E** pp *Esmeralda*, T 811-6017, with bath (**F** pp without), German owner, good views, hot showers, TV, restaurant, changes money, rec. **E** *Hostal Kori*, at top of steps leading down from square, swimming pool (open to all, US$1), with bath, cheaper without (weekly rates available), very popular, not very clean, top floors most highly rec, restaurant. **E** *La Casa*, just down the hill from *Hostal Kori*, small, swimming pool, clean, with restaurant (below), rec; **G** pp *Residencial de la Torre*, next to Veloz del Norte office, showers, nice garden. *Res 20 de Octubre* is ABAJ youth hostel affiliate, US$2.50 pp. Camp site by the small church on the hill overlooking the town—a stiff climb though. Hotels can be difficult at holiday weekends and as the area is a popular retreat for the rich from La Paz, prices are higher.

Restaurants *La Casa* is German-run, good food and setting but not cheap, excellent salads, vegetarian dishes, fondue and raclett for dinner (reserve in advance), wonderful views, rec. The convent opposite *La Casa* has been rec for its biscuits, peanut butter and coffee liqueurs, and interesting cheap white wine. *Don Pasante*, J S Cuenca, up the hill to *Hotel Esmeralda*, local and international food, breakfasts, rec. Also try second to last stall on right in Mercado Municipal, highly rec. *Daedalus Bar*, main plaza, for cocktails. Honey is sold in various places.

Horse Riding Patricio and Dany (French), who live at *Rancho Beni* by the new hospital in Comunidad de Aparto, have 6 horses for hire, US$5/hr, US$9 for 2 hrs inc guide, US$30 for all-day trek, with breakfast, lunch and swim at Río Vagante, also trekking in the mountains or just a few hours' riding; very friendly, rec. Dany makes excellent, home-grown coffee. Reservations in La Paz: Shuriya, Plaza Abaroa, Av 20 de Octubre 2463, T 322041, 1100-1300, 1530-1930.

Services Entel, main plaza, for international and local calls; Cotel next to church, phones, public TV. No banks; nowhere to change TCs. Pío Rolando Gutiérrez Linares rec as knowledgeable about local plantlife (Spanish only).

Transport Buses, minibuses, trucks and pick-ups from La Paz all leave from Villa Fátima, where transport companies have their offices: Flota Yungueña, Av Las Américas 354; Trans Tours Hotel Prefectural, Yanacachi 1434; Veloz del Norte, Virgen del Carmen 1329, T 311640; Don Juan, Av Las Américas y Ocobaya. Three buses a day, 2 companies, US$3, 3-5 hrs; several companies eg Trans Tours Hotel Prefectural, Don Juan, Turibus Totaí, Turismo Nuevo Continente, run 14 seater minibuses, US$4, 3-4 hrs and perhaps slightly less hair-raising, worth booking in advance; trucks (best for views) US$2. Also pick-ups, usually from company offices. Sit on right in the mountains, on left hand side on the descent to Yungas. In Corcoico: Flota Yungueña in

Comedor Municipal, on road to Caranavi; Trans Tours Hotel Prefectural at *Restaurant Las Peñas/Res 20 de Octubre*; Veloz del Norte, next to *Restaurant Disco Safari* uphill from square; Don Juan, on square next to Artesanías Arco Iris. Extra services run on Sundays. It can be difficult to book journeys to La Paz on holidays and on Sun evenings/Mon mornings (though these are good times for hitching). Buses and pick-ups may drop you at Yolosa, 7 km from Coroico; there is usually transport Yolosa-Coroico, US$0.50, or you can walk, uphill all the way, 2 hrs. In Coroico trucks leave from the market. Buses and pick-ups run from Yolosa to **Caranavi**, 3-4 hrs, US$2.50, **Guanay**, 7 hrs, US$4 and **Rurrenabaque**. Also trucks.

On the road from Puente Villa to **Coripata** (F *Hotel Florida*), which is also reached by road from Coroico, you enter the main coca growing area of N Bolivia. The countryside is quite different from that near Coroico, where coffee, as well as coca and fruits, is the main crop.

From the road junction at Yolosa the lower fork follows the river NE to **Caranavi**, a very ugly town 164 km from La Paz, 75 km from Yolosa, at times along a picturesque gorge, towards the settled area of the Alto Beni . Market day is Saturday; lots of transport in late afternoon.

Hotels Mainly along Av Mcal Santa Cruz, the main street: E *Landivar*, most expensive, pool; F *Caranavi*, clean and friendly, rec; F *Residencial Avenida*, friendly, basic and cheap; F *Alojamiento Capitol*, basic; F *México*, basic.

Restaurants *Paradiso*, cheap; *Tropical*, good set menu and cheap.

Bus From Villa Fátima in La Paz, Veloz del Norte and Yungueña buses, US$4, daily, 6-7 hrs; also Turibus Totai, 4 a day, US$4.50 and trucks, 12½ hrs. Trans Tours Hotel Prefectural Coroico (address above) 0900 and 1400 to Caranavi, 0900 continues to Guanay, US$2.50; to Rurrenabaque, 2000, 12 hrs, US$9. Direct bus Coroico-Caranavi on Sundays, or you can take a truck, US$1.65. If you want to continue into the Beni Lowlands without going into Caranavi, wait at the checkpoint before the town where all transport has to stop and ask for a ride there. Rurrenabaque and Trinidad can be reached by road.

Some 70 km NW of Caranavi lies the gold mining town of **Guanay**, an interesting, friendly place at the junction of the Tipuani and Mapiri rivers. Other gold mining sites are Tipuani and Mapiri (see below). Buses direct from La Paz, Yungueña and Estrella Azul, about US$8, also trucks, which have frequent stops and diversions. The bridge just before Guanay was washed away in 1994: travellers change buses and cross by a temporary footbridge. (Transport from Caranavi is very erratic: buses run if there are enough passengers, if not take a pick-up.)

Hotels, Restaurants, Services E *Panamericana*, helpful, popular with tour groups; F pp *Perla Andina*, clean, friendly, cold water, rooms on street less hot than those on courtyard, fans in rooms but electricity 1800-2400 only; F *Hotel Ritzy*, on main plaza, very clean, with mosquito nets; G pp *Alojamiento Los Pinos*, opp football pitch, cold water, basic, clean, may arrange exchange of TCs (with commission — cash can be changed with shopkeepers or gold dealers); G pp *Estrella Azul*, basic, friendly; G pp *Pahuichi*, clean, nice restaurant. Camping is possible next to the football field. *Restaurant La Bamba*, opp *Panamericana*, good value, English spoken. Many other eating places on main street have fixed-price meals; one, with courtyard, monkey and parrot, serves excellent value breakfast of steak, eggs and tomato for US$0.75. Electricity is rationed—every 10 mins or so – and water is available before 1200 only.

Boats go down the Río Beni from Guanay to Rurrenabaque (see p 314), 8-12 hrs, US$11-18 depending on how successfully you negotiate and availability of vessels. Cargo is now carried by road so you have to wait till the boat is full, which can take several days. Latest reports suggest that boatmen are unwilling to go with fewer than ten passengers. "Expreso" boats can also be hired from Flota Fluvial, opposite *Perla Andina*, at a price (US$150-300 depending on size and your ability to bargain). The journey goes through gold mining settlements, then narrow, fertile river banks sown with peanuts.

From Guanay boats leave from the dock 3 blocks from the square for **Mapiri**, a mining town on the river of the same name (Accommodation **F**). Boats leave daily at 0700, or later if not full, US$10, 5-7 hrs; cargo boats may run at other times, but do not rely on it. Mines can be seen along the way, in among the tropical vegetation.

From Mapiri, an adventurous route goes up into the mountains via Sorata Limitada (a mining town, not to be confused with Sorata) and Santa Rosa to Sorata, thence, completing the Yungas circuit, back to La Paz. *Camionetas* run to Santa Rosa (**G** *Hotel Las Cinco Estrellas*, small rooms, tiny beds, cleanish, pool), US$2. At Sorata Limitada there are 2 basic *alojamientos*, both G, the one beside the football pitch is quieter than the one beside the bar. *Camionetas* leave for Sorata from Sorata Limitada, US$10, 14 hrs and from Santa Rosa, US$8, 10 hrs. The scenery is superb, but the road is narrow, slippery, dangerous and dirty, especially in the rainy season. Try to get yourself as comfortable a seat as possible; the driver usually carries carpet to protect passengers against rain, but there is also a lot of dust. Have warm clothing handy for the road crosses the pass at 4,700m before dropping to Sorata.

Rather than going straight through to La Paz, it is worth breaking the journey at **Sorata**, a beautiful place at 2,695m. There is also good transport from La Paz (see below). All around Sorata are lovely views and ideal country for hiking and climbing since it is in a valley at the foot of Illampu. The town square, with its trees and, on a clear day, the snow-capped summit of Illampu as a backdrop, is delightful. The market area is beside the square; market day is Sunday. Fiesta 14 September.

Hotels D *Prefectural*, at entrance to town, C full board, bath, hot water, good but dear food, bar, pool (US$0.80 for non-residents), nice building and garden, rec; **E** *Paraíso*, Villavicencio 117, with bath, breakfast extra, hot water, smart, restaurant; **F** pp *Copacabana*, down the hill from the centre (look for the signs), shared hot showers, meals (including vegetarian and German breakfast – called "Americano" – but not cheap), clean, simple rooms; **F** pp *San Cristóbal*, Muñecas 350, near market, basic, shared bath, meals available, friendly; **G** *Alojamiento Central*, main square No 127, basic, no showers, but nice rooms. **G** pp *Residencial Sorata*, just off main square, mansion (formerly major export/import house) in process of renovation, shared bathrooms, hot water unreliable, clean, large reading room and table-tennis, good restaurant, laundry facilities, friendly staff incl Louis from Quebec, highly rec.

Restaurants *Casa de Papaco*, follow signs from main square, pizzas, homemade pasta, meat and vegetarian dishes, Bolivian dishes, good food, nice building, friendly, not cheap but worth it. *La Terraza*, good, friendly, cheap, good breakfast; *Santa Rosa*, main square, cheap meals; *El Tigre*, main square, cheap lunches. Good and cheap set meals at *Pensión Larecaja*, just off the main square.

Services Two Entel offices for telephones. Money exchange in the hotels, or good rates for cash at the Oficina Parroquial, next door to the church. For handicrafts, *Artesanía Sorata* on the main square.

Transport Buses from La Paz with Transtur Sorata (Bustillos 670, Cemetery district; in Sorata, just off square at No 101) and Larecaja (Bustillos y Angel Bobia, Cemetery district; in Sorata, 14 de Septiembre 206, just off square on road into/out of town), both have departures at 0700-0715, return from Sorata 1130-1300, US$2, 4 hrs "directo", 6 hrs stopping (Larecaja). On Mon there is a 0530 bus to La Paz. Plenty of trucks in am from Cemetery district, La Paz, to Sorata. Sit on left from La Paz.

Hiking and Climbing The climbing season is end-April to beginning-September. Sorata is the starting point for climbing *Illampu* (experience and full equipment necessary).

Hotel Copacabana rents equipment and can arrange treks, guides and mules – at a price. Much cheaper to make arrangements yourself.

When trekking in this area do not trust any water, it may be infected by vizcacha urine or with micah from the snow melt; it is best to filter it.

There are lots of walking possibilities. The most popular is to San Pedro cave, most easily reached by road, a 12 km walk (2 hrs) each way. The cave is beyond the village of San Pedro (where the road splits, take the lower road and look for the white building above). You can swim in the underground lake, which is 20.6°C. Entry US$1.25; do not go alone, do not swim alone. Latest reports say the cave is filthy and vandalized (1994). It is also possible to walk to the cave along the Río San Cristóbal; on leaving Sorata on the San Pedro road, look for the round sign to the Seminario. Go down that road and join the river. Initially you may have to walk on the river bed, or through fields (only for a short way), then the path becomes clearer, following the gorge. After 2 hrs, you come to a small plain with white boulders. After 3 hrs, you reach a bigger plain with scrub, above which is a large, whitish rock. In about the middle of the plain is a small gorge, on the far side of which, by a tree, a path leads right through the scrub up to the white rock. Just follow this path steeply up until you reach the road. The last part is difficult to follow. It is imperative to take water, at least 1 litre per person (or else take sterilizing tablets and fill up at the tap in San Pedro). Ask for the house selling refrescos by the litre in San Pedro.

A highly recommended hike is to Laguna Chillata and Inca Marka, a strenuous full-day walk, climbing from Sorata to 4,207m (either take plenty of water, or a water filter). Go with a guide because this is a sensitive area; the lake is sacred and Inca Marka is a burial place, dating back to the precolumbian Mollu culture. Camping is forbidden; do not touch anything, not even bits of paper, bottles, etc, which may be offerings.

Werner Bischoff from Steffisburg in Switzerland recommends the "Circuito Illampu", a 7-day high-altitude trek (5 passes over 4500 m) around Mt Illampu. "It can get very cold and it is a hard walk, though very beautiful with nice campsites on the way. Food can be bought in Cocoyo on the third day. A very good trek for getting acclimatized if you intend to climb a high peak".

Sorata is the starting point for two treks into the Yungas. The **"Camino de Oro"** or "Gold Digger's Trail", a 7-8 day hike to Guanay (see above), rises to 4,800m before going to Ancoma (1½ days from Sorata), then Wainapata, Chusi, 18 hrs from Ancoma (shop), Llipi, 8 hrs from Chusi and Unutulumi (2-3 hrs from Llipi, from here a *camioneta* runs daily to Guanay, US$5, 0930, winding through the many gold-digging towns in the Tipuani valley). After Ancoma it is very hot. The Ancoma-Llipi section is the most interesting, following the Tipuani river, climbing Inca staircases, crossing rivers on precarious plank bridges and going through an Inca tunnel. Very strenuous, not much flat ground for camping. See the warning in **Hiking**, p 332.

The **Mapiri Trail** opens up a road; claimed by some to be prehispanic and paved since Mollu times and used by Colonel Faucett, but certainly used by quinine and rubber traders, gold miners as well as the Bolivian army on the way to defeat by Brazil in 1903. It is 150 km, 7-8 days, and tough; a guide is essential. Travel light, take water purification and capacity for at least 3 litres pp. From Mapiri, you continue to Guanay by boat.

Anne Girardet (Nyon, Switzerland) writes: "It starts in the freezing cold town of Ancoma at 4,200m, follows for much of its length a ridge allowing beautiful views and ends in tropical Mapiri at 800m" adding "It is not a luxury to hire mules to carry the heavy load for the first three days." Matthew Parris (London E14) adds: "Your camps must be waterproof and insect-excluding. If you don't like flies, wasps, bees and ants, don't go. Much of your time will be spent crawling along rock-bottomed trenches and under logs. You will be rewarded with parrots, butterflies, flowers, tree-ferns, millions of tons of moss and with unbelievable views over thousands of square miles of near-vertical cloud forest, utterly unpenetrated by man."

It is also possible to hike from Sorata to Lake Titicaca. It is much cheaper to go to Sorata and ask about trekking there than to book up a trek with an agency in La Paz.

Sorata to La Paz The road to the capital leaves Sorata, descends to the river, crosses a bridge and climbs up the side of the valley. It continues climbing, in a landscape of huge valleys and ridges, to a pass in fields with stone walls and boulders before reaching the openness of the altiplano. Between Warisata and Achacachi is a tremendous marsh, with sheets of water, dykes, farms, cattle, people working the fields and many birds; in the distance snow-capped peaks can be seen. At **Achacachi**, there are 3 *alojamientos: Huancayuno*, opposite school, bathroom, water, *San Pedro*, no bathroom, *Tu Residencial*, all G, none too clean and all reported hostile, better stay somewhere else; 2 restaurants to the left of *Huancayuno*; market behind the main plaza (which looks as if it was once prosperous). Interesting Sun market. Fiesta 14 September. There are good views of Lake Titicaca from the church up the hill from the left side of the plaza. It is also possible to walk to the lake in 1½ hrs. Plenty of buses to La Paz in the morning, US$1; from La Paz to Achacachi every 15 mins from Cemetery district (opposite side of Av Kollasuyo from Sorata buses). Achacachi is a good place for connections if coming from Peru to Sorata: from Copacabana take a bus to Huarina, change there for a bus to Achacachi, then take a truck to Sorata. Sorata to Peru: take a La Paz bus and get out at Huarina; from there take a bus to Copacabana (best done in the morning).

ORURO AND ROUTES TO CHILE AND ARGENTINA (3)

Flamingoes shimmering in the glare of salt-flats, geysers and volcanoes on the Chilean border and, around Oruro, the poverty of the mines belies former wealth.

Oruro, 230 km SE of La Paz, is built on the slopes of a hill at an altitude of 3,704m. The population, mostly Indian, is 195,000. Although Oruro is famous as a mining town, there are no longer any working mines. It is, however, an important railway junction and the commercial centre for the mining communities of the altiplano. Several fine buildings in the centre hint at the city's former importance, notably the baroque concert hall (now a cinema) on the main square (Plaza 10 de Febrero) and the Casa de la Cultura (**see below under Museums**) built as a mansion by the tin "baron" Simón Patiño. There is a good view of the city from the Cerro Corazón de Jesus, near the church of the Virgen del Socavón, 5 blocks W of Plaza 10 de Febrero at the end of Calle Mier. Excellent daily market, near railway station. The zoo is not really worth a special visit. Along Calle La Paz, the continuation N of Soriano Galvaro, are many of the workshops in which costumes and masks for the Diablada are made. The disused San José mine, worked for over 450 years for silver, tin and other minerals, lies 3 km W of the city and can be visited with a permit (permit and guide arranged through the tourist office). A 20,000 tons-a-year tin smelter has been built nearby at Vinto; open to visitors, but a permit has to be applied for, 24 hours in advance, in Oruro.

La Diablada At carnival on the Saturday before Ash Wednesday, Oruro stages the Diablada ceremony in gratitude to Pachamama, the Earth Mother. Two figures, a bear and a condor, clear the way for a procession of masked dancers, led by two luxuriously costumed masqueraders representing Satan and Lucifer. Alternating with them in the lead are St Michael the Archangel and China Supay, the Devil's wife, who plays the role of carnal temptress. Behind them come hundreds of dancers in ferocious diabolical costumes, leaping, shouting, and pirouetting. The parade ends in the crowded football stadium, where the masqueraders perform various mass and solo dances. These are followed by two masques: the first is a tragic re-enactment of the Conquest, in the second the golden-haired Archangel conquers the forces of evil in battle.

In the contest between good and evil, the result in favour of the good is pronounced by the Virgen del Socavón, the patroness of miners, and after the performance the dancers all enter her chapel, chant a hymn in Quechua and pray for pardon. The Diablada was traditionally performed by Indian miners, but three other guilds have taken up the custom.

The costume always features the heavy, gruesome mask modelled in plaster, with a toad or snake on top; huge glass eyes; triangular glass teeth; a horsehair wig; and pointed, vibrating ears. Tied around the neck is a large silk shawl embroidered with dragons or other figures, and the dancer also has a jewelled, fringed breastplate. Over his white shirt and tights he wears a sash trimmed with coins, and from it hang the four flaps of the native skirt, embroidered in gold and silver thread and loaded with precious stones. Special boots equipped with spurs complete the elaborate outfit. Satan and Lucifer wear scarlet cloaks, and carry a serpent twisted around one arm and a trident. The working-class Oruro district known as La Ranchería is particularly famous for the excellence of the costumes and masks made there. One of the most famous folklore groups is the stately Morenada. The opening procession begins at around 0800 on Saturday and dancing continues until 0300 the following day. Carnival lasts 8 days with displays of dancing by day and night often superior to those given on the opening Saturday. There are two options for seating: municipal seats around the main plaza and on Av Cívica, which cost US$5 a day, booked in advance; Av Cívica is a good spot because the street is wide and the dancers are unrestricted. The alternative is seating outside shops (US$4 a day, also booked beforehand) where the streets are narrower so you are closer to the dancers, and to the water-bombers. To wander among the dancers you are officially supposed to purchase a professional photographer's ticket for US$15, but little checking seems to be done (amateurs need pay only US$1.50, show your small camera and insist). Seats can be booked at the town hall.

Tony Baker writes, "Do not wear a raincoat as protection against water bombs; you will merely become a prime target, or rather more of a prime target since gringos get soaked as a matter of course. The best thing to do is buy a water-cannon and arm yourself to the teeth, try to buy seats near a water supply, wear few clothes as possible, and, though you will get soaked, at least you will get some revenge... Fortunately hostilities cease as it gets dark, so you can get changed into something warm and dry and really enjoy the nights' entertainment. *Leche de tigre* is drunk against the cold: hot milk with a heavy shot of singani."

Latest reports suggest that the processions on the opening Saturday are fine, but degenerate thereafter as all the participants are drunk; also participants now have to be wealthy to afford to take part, so *campesinos* have been forced to the periphery (selling food, etc). The Friday before carnival, traditional "challa" ceremonies are held at mines, including the slaughter of a white llama. It is essential to go with a guide and get permission to visit (eg Pepé-Elmer Chávez at the Tourist Office). The weekend before carnival the groups practise, which is almost

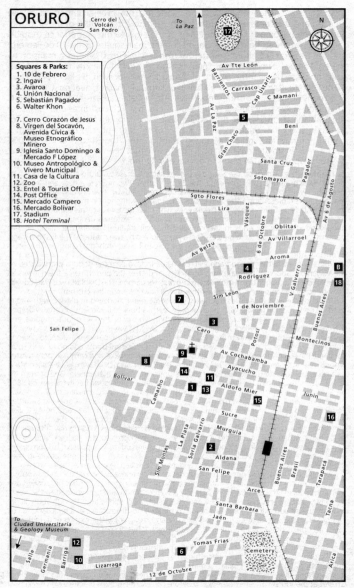

ORURO

Cerro del
Volcán
San Pedro

Squares & Parks:
1. 10 de Febrero
2. Ingavi
3. Avaroa
4. Unión Nacional
5. Sebastián Pagador
6. Walter Khon

7. Cerro Corazón de Jesus
8. Virgen del Socavón,
   Avenida Cívica &
   Museo Etnográfico
   Minero
9. Iglesia Santo Domingo &
   Mercado F López
10. Museo Antropológico &
    Vivero Municipal
11. Casa de la Cultura
12. Zoo
13. Entel & Tourist Office
14. Post Office
15. Mercado Campero
16. Mercado Bolívar
17. Stadium
18. *Hotel Terminal*

To
La Paz

Av Tte León

Barrientos
Carrasco
Cap Ustaniz
C Mamani

Av La Paz

Gran Chaco

Beni

Santa Cruz

Pagador

Sotomayor

Av 6 de Agosto

Sgto Flores

Lira

Vásquez

6 de Octubre

Oblitas

Av Villarroel

Av Belzu

Aroma

Rodriguez

V Galvarro

Sim León

1 de Noviembre

Buenos Aires

San Felipe

Caro

Potosi

Montecinos

Av Cochabamba

Ayacucho

Bolivar

Camacho

Aldofo Mier

Junín

Sucre

La Plata

Soria Galvarro

Murguia

Sim Montes

Aldana

San Felipe

Buenos Aires

Brasil

Tarapacá

Arce

Tacna

Santa Barbara

Jaén

To
Ciudad Universitaria
& Geology Museum

Salle

Germania

Barriga

Lizarraga

Tomas Frias

Cemetery

12 de Octubre

Arica

as good as the main event. On the Saturday after Carnival all the groups perform in the football stadium, less atmosphere, less crowded, but good for photos. *Beware of sharp practices during the period of carnival.* Accommodation, increases in the prices of which are officially controlled, must be booked in advance for carnival; the Senatur office in the Edificio Prefectural will find accommodation with families, US$5 pp; book a few days in advance. Transport prices from La Paz triple. Organized tours from La Paz cost US$50, including transport, food and a seat in the main plaza, but it is probably more interesting to go independently.

Museums Museo Etnográfico Minero, under the Church of the Virgen del Socavón, W end of Calle Mier, containing mining equipment and other artefacts from the beginning of the century as well as a "tío", entry via the church 0900-1200, 1430-1800, US$0.50; **Casa de la Cultura**, Galvarro 5755, formerly one of the Patiño residences, now run by the Universidad Técnica de Oruro, contains European furniture and a coach imported from France, also houses temporary exhibitions, open Mon-Fri 0900-1200, 1430-1800, US$1; **Museo Antropológico**, S of centre on Av España (take micro A heading S or any trufi going S) has a unique collection of stone llama heads as well as impressive carnival masks, open Tues-Sun 1000-1200, US$0.75, no guide, all in Spanish; **Museo Mineralógico**, part of the University (take micro A South to the Ciudad Universitaria), with over 3,000 mineral specimens, claimed as one of the best in South America, open Mon-Fri 0800-1200, 1430-1700.

Guide *Carnival de Oruro.* Dance costumes and masks, Calle La Paz, 400 block.

Hotels In the centre: **C** *Nikkei Plaza*, Plaza 10 de Febrero, T 54799, with bath and breakfast, modern, comfortable; **D** *Repostero*, Sucre 370 y Pagador, T 50505, with bath, hot water, clean, pleasant, comedor; **D** *Gran Sucre*, Sucre 510, T 53838, run-down but pleasant, has new wing; **D** *América*, Bolívar y Pagador, T 60707, with bath, E without, clean, restaurant; **E** *Ideal*, Bolívar 386, T 52863, with bath, F without, basic but clean, poor beds; **E** *Gloria*, 15 de Octubre, with bath, F without, basic, clean, hot water. **Near the bus terminal**: **C** *Terminal*, above bus terminal, T 53797, modern, heating, good views, expensive restaurant, higher rates charged for foreigners, noisy; **E** *Bolivia*, Rodríguez 131 y 6 de Agosto, T 41047, with bath, F without, hot water, clean restaurant; **E** *Lipton*, Av 6 de Agosto 225, T 41538, with bath, F pp without, clean, secure, parking extra; **E** *Residencial Verano*, 200 m from bus terminal, T 41742, without bath, modern, clean; **F** pp *Residencial El Turista*, 6 de Agosto 466, T 41888, without bath, unhelpful, safe parking. **Near the railway station**: all on Galvarro, all **G** pp and very basic, no hot water: *Hispano-Americano* (No 6392, T 61117); *Alojamiento Copacabana* (No 6352, T 54184); *Ferroviario* (No 6278, T 60079); 5 blocks N is **F** *F85MIAlojamiento 15 de Octubre*, 6 de Agosto 890, T 40012, without bath, hot shower US$2 extra, clean, good value.

Restaurants *La Casona*, Pres Montes 5970, opp Post Office, good *pizzería*; *La Tarantella*, Bolívar y 6 de Octubre, pizzas and Chinese dishes; *La Gaviota*, Junín 676, reasonable; *Nayjama*, typical Oruro cuisine; *Club Social Arabe*, Junín 729 y Pres Montes, good value lunches; *Los Escudos*, Montecinos y 6 de Agosto, good value; good *salteñas* at *Super Salteñas*, Bolívar 490. *Bamin*, Potosí 1640, excellent and not expensive, friendly; *Libertador*, Bolívar 347, excellent set lunch for US$1; *Cafetería París*, just off main square, excellent cakes. Vegetarian: *El Huerto*, Bolívar 359, cheap. Cheap meals in the Mercado Fermín López.

Banks and Exchange Cash advances on credit cards at **Banco de La Paz**, US$3.75 authorisation charge. TCs can be changed at **Banco Boliviano Americano**, 5% commission and at **Banco de Santa Cruz**, Bolívar 670 (also office at Pagador y Caro, open Sat 0900-1200). It is quite easy to change dollars (cash) on the street: good rates on Av V Galvarro, opposite train station, or at Ferretería Findel, Calle Pagador 1491, near the market (large hardware store), or try Don Ernest at Av V Galvarro 5998, T 60520.

German Consulate at Adolfo Mier y Galvarro.

Laundry Alemania, Aldana 280.

Post Office Presidente Montes 1456. **Telecommunications** Entel, Bolívar, 1 block E of plaza.

Sauna Ayacucho y Galvarro, wet or dry, showers US$0.75. Duchas Oruro, 500 block of Av 6 de Agosto (near bus terminal); Santa Bárbara, Pagador 6801.

Shopping *Infol*, Ayacucho 426 for alpaca, high quality but not cheap nor a large selection and *Reguerín* on the junction with Mier; also sell devil masks. An un-named shop at Av La Paz 4999 is recommended for all kinds of masks, good quality and prices. The municipal market has an interesting witchcraft section, said to be far better than the one in La Paz. A good handicraft shop is on Av Cochabamba, opposite the market, although handicrafts are generally cheaper in Cochabamba.

Travel Agent Jumbo Travel, 6 de Octubre 6080, T 55005/55203, friendly and efficient. A recommended driver and guide is Freddy Barron, Casilla 23, Oruro, T (052) 41776, who offers a programme of excursions and aventure tours. Juan Carlos Vargas, T 40333, also rec as tour guide, contact via tourist office.

Tourist Office The kiosk at Bolívar y Galvarro, 1 block E of Plaza 10 de Febrero, T 50144, open Mon-Fri 0900-1200, 1400-1800, Sat/Sun 0900-1000, supplies a map of the city.

Trains Check in advance which services are running, T 60605. 4 hrs 20 mins from/to **La Paz** Wed only. To **Cochabamba**, Wed and Fri at 0800. To **Potosí**, Wed at 2100, US$4.25 *especial*, US$5.75 *pullman*. To **Villazón**, Mon and Thur, 1900, 16-19 hours (US$6.80 *especial*, US$9 *pullman*), exhausting but exhilarating to the hardy traveller. Ticket office opens at 0700, best to be there early. **Calama**, for Antofagasta (Chile), 30-36 hrs, very prone to delay. Sun 1930, US$16, be at ticket office at 0700. For details see above under La Paz, **Railways to/from the Coast** (3).

Buses Terminal 10 blocks N of centre at Buenos Aires y Aroma, T 53689. To/from **La Paz**, 3 hours, seven bus lines work the route, hourly in the day, US$2.50, also at US$3.10; to **Potosí**, 8-10 cold and rough hours, US$3.15-3.75; to **Cochabamba**, 4½-6 hrs, US$4, Cometa frequent, several other companies. To **Sucre**, best to go via Cochabamba if wet as the road to Potosí is so bad. Roads to **Río Mulato** and **Uyuni** are very bad, Panasur and 11 de Julio, 2 days a week each, US$6.30 and US$4.20, some trucks work the route; train (4½-8 hours) recommended. Trucks to Potosí and Sucre leave from Av Cochabamba near the Mercado Bolívar. Note: if coming to Oruro and travelling on a tight budget, do not take a bus which arrives late at night as cheap accommodation will be shut; only the expensive *Hotel Terminal* will be open.

Excursions To the hot springs at **Obrajes**, 23 km N, where there is the choice of private baths or swimming pool, both hot (not very clean, but excellent for the dirty traveller), entry US$1.20. Also to springs at Capachos, less good. Free facilities for clothes washing in the natural hot water. Wait at the bus stop at Calle Caro for the (intermittent) bus to both places, US$0.50 to Capachos. Go early as return transport difficult after 1600. Taxis sometimes make the run. Take picnic lunch. Avoid Sun when it is very crowded.

To **Lago Poopó**, about 80 km S, and the **Santuario de Aves Lago Poopó**, an excellent bird reserve. Moreno Ortelli from Como, Italy, writes "If you do not have your own transportation, stay in Challapata (120 km S of Oruro), accessible by bus or train from either Potosí or Oruro. There is a basic *alojamiento* where you can rent a bike or motorbike to ride the approx 10 km to the lake-shore. Some Uro indians live in the region, belonging to the Muratos sub-group."

To **Llallagua**, 3,881m, 95 km SE, a mining town at which visitors are not always made welcome (**F** *Hotel Bustillo*; *Santa María*; **G** *Hotel Llallagua*, small beds, no bath, seldom has water, perhaps the best, but not really rec; few restaurants). *Fiesta*: Asunción. Nearby is the famous Siglo Veinte, once the largest tin mine (ex-Patiño) in the country (now closed), but being worked by small cooperatives. There is an acute water shortage. Llallagua can be reached by bus from Oruro (Bustillo, 7 a day, Enta 0900, 1700 daily, 3 hrs, US$2), continuing twice a week to Sucre (Bustillo), buses also to Potosí, beautiful but uncomfortable. Also buses 1900 from La Paz. Nearby at **Uncía** (Km 102; small *alojamiento* near the prison, **G**, clean, safe, basic; poor restaurants, eat at the market) there are more former Patiño mines and good hot springs (reached by *trufi*).

Travellers with a 4WD vehicle might explore the country SW of Oruro towards the Chilean frontier. It's a day's drive to the western mountains following tracks rather than roads. There are no hotels in any of the towns, but lodging can often be found by asking a local school-teacher or mayor. At Toledo, 38 km SW, there is a colonial church. **Escara**, further SE, is a lovely village with a beautiful square; it is a friendly place, has bike rental. From Escara it is only 25 km S to **Chipaya**, 190 km from Oruro, which is less welcoming, the main settlement of the most interesting Indians of the Altiplano. They speak a language closely related to the almost extinct Uru; their distinctive dress and unique conical houses are beginning to disappear as the community changes. This is a very difficult trip without your own transport; there is transport once a week in either direction from Huachacalla on the Oruro-Sabaya road. In Chipaya, the town council charges visitors US$50 for free access and hospitality. For a smaller, or no, contribution you will be much less welcome. There is very little for the visitor to do and it is very cold.

A one-day drive to the W is the **Parque Nacional Sajama**, established in 1945 and covering 60,000 hectares. The park contains the world's highest forest, consisting mainly of the rare Kenua tree (Polylepis Tarapana) which grows up to 5,200m. The scenery is wonderful and includes views of three volcanoes (**Sajama** – Bolivia's highest peak at 6,530m – Parinacota, Pomerape). The road is very bad. Take the Litoral La Paz-Arica bus (La Paz 0500 Tues and Fri;

from Arica same days 0900), ask for Sajama. and pay the full fare. A cheaper way is to take a La Paz-Oruro bus as far as Patacamaya (1½ hrs from La Paz), then take a truck to Estación Tomarapi (dusty, but very interesting, US$2). There are restaurants in the park but no fresh food, so take plenty from La Paz (water no problem, but take purifying tablets). If continuing into Chile (same buses) remember that no meat, dairy products, fruit or vegetables may be taken across the border. Crampons, ice axe and rope are needed for climbing the three volcanoes which are not technically difficult; the routes to base camp and beyond are fairly obvious. In Sajama village (altitude 4,200 m, population 500), Peter Brunnhart (Señor Pedro) and Telmo Nina have a book with descriptions of the various routes to the summit (Telmo Nina keeps the visitors book, Park entry fee US$1); basic accommodation available. It can be very windy and cold at night (good sleeping bag essential). Mules can be hired, US$6/day. Good bathing in hot springs 5 km N of village, interesting geothermic area 6 km W of village. The Sajama area is a major centre of alpaca wool production and llama meat is still the main food. This area will become more accessible when the new La Paz-Arica highway is completed.

A road and railway line run S from Oruro, through Río Mulato, the junction for trains to Potosí, to Uyuni (323 km). The road is sandy, and after rain very bad, especially S of Río Mulato.

Uyuni, population about 10,000, lies bitterly cold and unprotected at 3,665m near the eastern edge of the Salar de Uyuni, claimed to be the largest salt lake in the world. Still a commercial and communication centre, Uyuni was, for much of this century, important as a major railway junction. A giant statue of an armed railway worker, erected after the 1952 Revolution, dominates Av Ferroviaria. Most services are near the station. Uyuni's main point of interest is as a centre for excursions to the Salar de Uyuni, Laguna Colorada and Laguna Verde (see below). Note that water is frequently cut off and may only be available between 0600 and midday. Market Sun. **Fiesta** San Miguel.

Hotels and Services D *Avenida*, Av Ferroviaria, opp station, T 878, in renovated wing, rooms with bath, hot water, F without bath in old wing, clean, hot showers (timed) US$1 extra, bar, breakfast, unfriendly, has a book for comments on trips to the Salar and Lagunas. **F** *Residencia Sucre*, new, clean, padlocks on doors, glass in windows. Three *Residenciales* all on Av Arce, all **G** pp: *Copacabana*, no hot water, basic, clean rm, dirty bathrooms; *Urkupiña*, basic and quite clean, hot water; *Uyuni*, small rooms, basic, dirty, hot showers extra. *Restaurant 16 de Julio*, Av Arce, best in town, good cheap meals, friendly. *Salteñas* go on sale about 0900 daily. The stalls around the municipal market are well-stocked with regional contraband. Banco del Estado will not change money, best rates at *Restaurant 16 de Julio*, or try the pharmacy on Av Arce, or shops. Nowhere to change TCs but tour agencies and some shops accept payment in TCs. The Immigration Office is on Calle Potosí; only issues 30-day stamps, for 90 days go to Potosí. The tourist office opposite is helpful.

Transport The train service to Calama, Chile, is described under **Railways To/From the Coast**, (3), **p 260**. Uyuni is also a stop on the La Paz-Oruro-Villazón line: Oruro-Villazón (Mon, Thur at 1900) and Oruro-Tupiza (1 *ferrobus*) all stop here. Uyuni-La Paz (Expreso del Sur, Sat 1430, US$11.55; to Oruro, *ferrobus*, Tues, Wed 1330, local train Mon, Thur 1430. Fares: Oruro-Uyuni US$3.15 *especial*, US$4.25 *pullman*, 8 hrs. Daily freight train to Ollagüe, US$4.50, 6 hrs.

Bus to **La Paz** and **Oruro**, Panasur, Wed, Sun 1800, US$8, 15 hrs, terrible road as far as Huari (US$6.30 to Oruro), 11 de Julio also to Oruro, Mon and Fri 1800, US$4.20; to **Tupiza**, Wed 1530, US$4, 7½ hrs; to **Potosí**, American, daily 1030, other companies, 6 hrs, US$5, spectacular journey on unpaved roads. Trucks to Potosí are unpredictable, umpteen different versions of what's going on, but a great 8-9 hr trip when you get it, US$4.

By Road to Chile Motorists must be warned against the direct route from Uyuni into Chile by way of Ollagüe. There is the danger of getting lost on the many tracks leading over the deserted salt lakes, no gasoline between Uyuni and Calama (Chile), and little hope of help with a breakdown on the Bolivian side unless you don't mind waiting for perhaps a week. After rain the route is impassable and even experienced guides get lost. Maps give widely differing versions of the route. "Where the road has been built up, *never* forsake it for the appealing soft salt beside it. The salt takes a man's weight but a vehicle breaks through the crust into unfathomable depths of plasticine mud below."—Andrew Parkin.

To hitch to Chile via Ollagüe, trucks first go N, then across the Salar de Ollagüe. The scenery on this route is amazing and, once in Chile, you will see lakes similar to Lagunas Colorada and Verde. There is nowhere to stay in Ollagüe, but police and border officials will help find lodging and transport for hitchers.

Excursions To *Llica*, the capital of Daniel Campos Province, 5 hrs W of Uyuni across the Salar de Uyuni by truck, daily, 1100, bus daily, 1200. There is a new, basic **F** *Alojamiento Municipal* in town. Also Angel Quispe in the plaza has 3 beds. Meals are available in private houses. There are no shops and no electricity. There is a teachers' training college but not much special to see. Two fiestas: July 26 and August 15. Good for llama and other wool handicrafts. To *Pulcayo*, 20 km E on the road to Potosí, a largely abandoned mining town with a railway cemetery and alpaca wool factory (**G** *Hotel Rancho No 1*, without bath, large old rooms, hot water, good meals).

The standard excursions are NW to the *Salar de Uyuni* and S to *Laguna Colorada* and *Laguna Verde*. "When it still has water in it (up to 4 or possibly 6 inches), being in the middle of the Salar de Uyuni is like being an ant on a gigantic mirror. The blue sky merges into the blue water, the islands are perfectly reflected and since there is no horizon they appear suspended in space. Some areas may be dry, in which case the salt crust is as blinding-white and featureless as the most perfect snowfield (sunglasses essential)."—Stephen Saker.

Dan Buck and Anne Meadows write (with additional details from other travellers): *Laguna Colorada*, about 350-400 km SW of Uyuni, 12 hours' straight driving over unmarked, rugged truck tracks, is featured in Tony Morrison's two books, *Land Above the Clouds* and *The Andes*. It is one of Bolivia's most spectacular and most isolated marvels. The rare James flamingoes, along with the more common Chilean and Andean flamingoes, breed and live in its red algae-coloured waters. The shores and shallows of the lake are crusted with gypsum and salt, a bizarre arctic-white counterpoint to the flaming red waters. From afar, with their loping, John Cleese walks and pinkish feathers, the flamingoes look alike. The leg and bill colorations are the easiest way to distinguish the three breeds. Chilean: brownish-blue legs with red knee-joints; almost white bill with brown-black tip. Andean: bright yellow legs; black front half on yellow bill. James: dark, brick-red legs; small black tip on bright yellow bill. See: *The Birds of Chile*, AW Johnson, or *Land Above the Clouds*, Tony Morrison.

The standard outing (see below for operators) lasts four days and takes visitors from Uyuni N to the Salar de Uyuni, S on to Lagunas Colorado and Verde, and then back to Uyuni. Day one: Uyuni to Colchani, thence to the Salar, including a salt-mine visit, lunch on the cactus-studded Isla Pescado, and overnight at a village, eg, San Juan, S of the Salar (simple lodging, ask around, electricity 1900-2100, running water). Between Colchani and Isla Pescado is **D** *Hotel Playa Blanca* run by Teodoro Colque, new in 1994, warm, well-designed. Day two: To Laguna Colorada (4,775m), passing active Volcán Ollagüe and a chain of small, flamingo-specked lagoons. Overnight at Laguna Colorada (Eustaquio Berna runs the *campamento* and still appreciates small gifts – cigarettes, oranges, etc, US$1 to stay, dirty, windy. Permission to lodge at the nearby, modern ENDE, electricity company, facilities must be obtained in writing from Cochabamba headquarters.) Day three: Drive past belching geysers at Sol de Mañana (do not walk near the geysers) and through the Pampa de Challviri (4,800m, via a pass at 5,000m) where telluric outcroppings sprout from sand dunes surrounded by wind-scoured mountains, to the wind-lashed, frothy jade waters of the **Laguna Verde** (4,600m) at the foot of Volcán Licancábur, and back to Laguna Colorada. *Refugio* at Laguna Verde, US$2, small, mattresses, running water, view of lake. Day four: Return to Uyuni. A three-day version eliminates the Salar de Uyuni.

The excursion price from Uyuni depends on the size of the vehicle, the number of days and the demand. Expect to pay up to US$100 per day, divided by the number of passengers. (Whether you return to Uyuni or proceed into Chile, you pay for a round-trip.) For example, the four-day trip is US$300 in a double-cab Datsun pickup (one to four passengers) with Uyuni Tours or US$400 in a Toyota Land Cruiser (one to seven passengers) with Transamazonas. Although some haggling is allowed, don't get your hopes up. Price includes gas but excludes lodging, which costs about US$1 pp per night, and food. Tents are not required, but a warm sleeping bag is essential. Packing your vehicle with the maximum number of passengers will lower the per-head tariff, but bouncing cheek-by-jowl for several days over dusty, corrugated roads is tedious.

Tour Agencies Tours can be organized in Uyuni, or in Potosí or La Paz (some of the Uyuni companies are connected with Potosí and La Paz travel agencies). In Uyuni most agencies are on Av Ferroviaria, including: Transamazonas; Uyuni Tours, T 878, owners Ciprián and Antonia Nina, rec; Brisa Tours, frequently rec; Transandino Tours (Wilma Ignacio Apala) has been recommended (Casilla 18, T 0693-2132, or La Paz 820353); Tunupa Tours (Elias Cruz Romero, warmly rec), good value; Koala Tours (see under Potosí for head office). Prices are reported to be much higher in La Paz. Reports disagree on the ease of arranging a tour by turning up in Uyuni and hunting for others to form a group (this can take several days). Do not try to form a group at Carnival; everyone is at Oruro.

Temperatures at Laguna Colorada can easily drop below -20°C even out of the persistent strong winds. It is imperative that trips carry sufficient food, water and fuel and that the vehicle is equipped with spares and is up to the task. Take warm bedding, candles, hat, swimming costume and high factor sun tan lotion. **NB** Reports vary on the quality of tours. Obtain a written contract and be firm. Try to check the vehicle before agreeing terms. Insist on taking spares and try to ensure the vehicle is filled with fuel the evening before (in case of power cuts). It is worth taking two drivers and choosing an agency with experienced drivers and radio contact. Drivers are reported habitually to try to cut a day off a 4-day tour. Tour agencies will, if requested, leave travellers at Hito Cajones on the border with Chile (see below for the problems of travelling between Hito Cajones and San Pedro de Atacama). They can also arrange for a Chilean company to meet you at San Pedro de Atacama (eg *Nativa*: see San Pedro de Atacama **Tourist Agencies**, p 639, and **To Bolivia**). Check whether the cost of this service is per person or per vehicle. Tours do not run at Christmas/New Year.

If you plan to enter Chile via one of the unattended border crossings in the SW region, you must get an exit stamp at the Bolivian immigration office on Calle Potosí (Mon-Fri only). There are (reportedly) no immigration offices SW of Uyuni. The stamp is valid for three days, ie, you have 72 hrs to get out of Bolivia, but reports suggest that more than 72 hrs is permitted if you state the exact date you intend to leave Bolivia. Before issuing the exit stamp, Bolivian immigration requires that you present proof of travel, ie, your excursion contract. Your tour company can run your passports over to immigration, which opens at 0900, the morning you are leaving.

To San Pedro de Atacama (Chile) From Laguna Verde it is 7 km to Hito Cajones, the frontier post with Chile and a further 8 km to La Cruz, the junction with the E-W road used by trucks carrying borax and sulphur from the mines to San Pedro. There are reports of a daily bus Hito Cajones-San Pedro, but the frequency of other traffic and the ease of finding transport is uncertain. Tour guides may be very over-optimistic: if you are unlucky you will have to walk a long way in difficult conditions. Adequate, food, water and clothing essential. **Do not underestimate the dangers of getting stuck without transport or lodging at this altitude**.

South of Uyuni, 200 km, is *Tupiza* (2,990m, 20,000 people), a centre of the silver, tin, lead, and bismuth mining industries. The statue in the main square of Tupiza is to Victor Carlos Aramayo, the founding member of the Aramayo mining dynasty, pre-eminent in the late 19th, early 20th centuries, together with the Patiños and the Hoschilds. Chajra Huasi, a palazzo-style, abandoned home of the Aramayo family across the Río Tupiza, may be visited. It was expropriated by the government after the 1952 revolution. An archaeology museum, part of the University of Tupiza, has been opened just off plaza (US$1.75). IGM office, for maps, is in the Municipal building.

Hotels and Services F *Hotel Mitru*, run down, private shower and bath, water unreliable, poor plumbing, downstairs rooms might be better, laundry can take 3 days, but still the best, restaurant has good *almuerzo*, but no dinner, annex has snack shop and restaurant, both open for dinner; next to it is **F** *Residencial Crillón*, very run down, with good motorcycle parking; much better for motorcyclists is **F** *Res Valle Hermoso*, Av Pedro Arraya, T 589, hot showers, good, will let you park bikes in restaurant; **G** pp *El Rancho*, Av Arrayo 200 block, without bath; also **G** pp *Residencial Monterrey*, opposite railway station, clean, hot water, and 2 blocks from the station, **F** *Hotel Centro*, clean, friendly and quiet; *Restaurant Gallo de Oro*, Calle Chorolque, cheap *parrillada*; *Restaurant Chicheño*, near market, typical food; *Picantería Las Brisas*, on opposite side of river, open Sat and Sun only, large helpings.

   TCs can be changed at Empresa Bernall Hmnos, but only in the presence of the owner, good rates, many shops will also change dollars at better rates than in Villazón. Good food market on Sat and Sun. Hospital Ferroviário (nr *Hotel Mitru*), Dr Rolando Llano Navarro and staff, very helpful.

Transport Trains to Villazon, 3 a week, 3 hrs. Trains to Uyuni, *expreso* US$9. Bad road from Potosí which goes on S to Villazón; often closed in rainy season because road fords the Río Suipacha. Bus to Villazón 3 hrs, US$2, 1000 and 1500; to Potosí, US$5.25, Expreso Tupiza and Flota Chicheño, both daily. To Uyuni, US$4, 7½ hrs. No direct bus to La Paz, only via Potosí. A new road is being built from Uyuni to Atocha.

Wendy Chilcott and Steve Newman (Sussex) write: "Follow the road to the left of the cathedral out of town between the cemetery and a barracks. Continue as road curves right until you reach a dry river bed. Follow this to the left towards the hills. After 200 m take the right fork in the river bed. Here are some superb rock formations... huge pinnacles of rock and soil, only 4 inches thick—seem to defy gravity! The valley narrows rapidly but the path follows a stream bed for several hundred metres to a picturesque waterfall. Any further progress requires difficult scrambling but will eventually lead to the altiplano. " The whole walk takes 2 hrs, worth it for the rock formations alone, take water and food. Beautiful sunsets over the fertile Tupiza can be seen from the foot of a Christ statue on a hill behind the plaza.

Tupiza is the centre of Butch Cassidy and the Sundance Kid country. On 4 November 1908, they held up an Aramayo company payroll N of Salo. (Aramayo *hacienda* in Salo, one hour N of Tupiza, still stands. Roadside kiosks serve excellent roast goat, *choclo, papas*, soup.) Two days later they encountered and were killed by a four-man military-police patrol in **San Vicente** (pop 400, 4,500 m), 103 km, 4 to 6 hours on a good dirt road, NW of Tupiza. Supposedly truck transport from Tupiza on Thur early am from near football stadium. Alternatively hire a vehicle: Fermín Ortega at Taller Nardini, Barrio Lourdes, rec; Don Manuel at *Hotel Mitru* can suggest others, US$30 to US$80 one-way. (Also accessible and a bit closer from Atocha, but fewer vehicles for hire.) Travel up spectacular canyon with red and white, wind-carved rock formations. Basic *alojamiento* on main street marked "Hotel;" restaurant "El Rancho" next-door; several *tiendas* sell beer, soda, canned goods, etc. Shootout site off main street—ask locals. Cassidy and Sundance are buried in an unmarked grave in the cemetery, but the grave has yet to be found. An investigation of the supposed grave, by the Nova project in 1991, proved negative, but see *Digging Up Butch and Sundance*, by Anne Meadows (New York: St Martin's Press, 1994). Whether Butch and Sundance did die here or not, San Vicente has been described by one correspondent as "a very sad place to die".

Dr Félix Chalar Miranda, President of the local historical society offers jeep tours to the hold-up site near Salo, the escape route and San Vicente. He can also arrange excursions to Laguna Colorada and Laguna Verde, T 467 (office), 509 (home) or contact via *Inquietud* newspaper office at Av Cul Arraya 205.

The Argentine border is at **Villazón**, population 13,000, altitude 3,443 m, 81 km S of Tupiza. From Villazón there is an improved road to Tarija. The road linking Potosí with Villazón via Camargo is in poor condition and about 100 km longer than the better road via Tupiza. For information on border crossing with Argentina **see Argentina Section 3**; remember Jujuy province, Argentina is 1 hour ahead. Little to see in Villazón (has two cinemas) and not at all welcoming; border area must not be photographed. Entering Bolivia, guards will let you pass through after hours to sleep in Villazón, but you must get your passport stamped next day. There is an entry/exit tax of US$4.

Hotels at Villazón E *Residencial El Cortijo*, clean, good value, intermittent hot water, restaurant; F pp *Grand Palace*, behind bus station, safe, sheets taken at 0700 for washing; F *Hotel Bolivia*, one block from border, clean small rooms, good value breakfast, hot showers extra; F *Panamericano*, clean, laundry facilities, rec. F *Residencial Martínez*, ½ block from bus station, well signed, hot water when town's supply is on, basic but clean and well-maintained; F *Residencial 10 de Febrero*, next door, very basic. Restaurants opposite bus station and on first floor of covered market, for example *Repostería*, about US$1 a head. The Mercado Municipal de Vivanderos is near the frontier, parallel with main street, across the railway.

Banks and Exchange Money-changing at Cambio Porvenir or other *cambios* on main street, rates said to be good (some take TCs), also at Cambio Trébol, shop by border that sells train tickets (see below) but with 6% commission on TCs; Banco del Estado does not change TCs. Out of hours try the Ciné Rex. No exchange facilities in La Quiaca. **Warning** Do not show passport or money to men claiming to be plainclothes police.

Argentine Consulate in main plaza, open 1400-1700, Mon-Fri; not very helpful.

Buses To Potosí several between 0830 and 1830, 10-15 hrs, US$4.20-5.25 (unsurfaced road—terrible in the wet, can take 24 hrs); to **Tupiza**, 0700 and 1500, US$2; to **Tarija**, beautiful journey but most buses overnight only, daily at 1900/2000, US$5, 6 hrs, very cold on arrival but passengers can sleep on bus until daybreak; trucks for Tarija from beside bus station. From **La Paz**, several companies: journey takes 25 hrs, costs US$13.25, eg Panamericana and Chicheña, even though buses called "direct", you may have to change in Potosí, perhaps to another company, eg Villa Imperial. 1830 depart La Paz, 0700 arrive Potosí, 0830 leave Potosí, 1930 arrive Villazón. The same procedure applies from Villazón to La Paz. Bus station is near the main square, behind Ciné Teatro Libertador Bolívar; it is 5 blocks from the border. Taxi to border, US$0.20 or hire porter, US$1, and walk across.

Trains Station about 1 km N of frontier on main road, taxi US$1.80. To **Oruro** for La Paz (very dusty and cold journey), twice a week (US$9 Pullman, US$6.80 special). Train stops at Tupiza, Atocha, Uyuni and Oruro. The express from La Paz/Oruro connects with a bus to **Tarija** (in theory), tickets from railway station. Ticket office opens 0800, long queues, or tickets to La Paz can be bought (US$1 commission per ticket) at the first shop on the right next to the border.

POTOSI, SUCRE AND THE SOUTHERN HIGHLANDS (4)

The World Cultural Heritage Sites of Potosí, with its rich mining past and its current mining misery, and Sucre, the white city. In the S of this region, Tarija is known for its fruit and wines and its traditions which set it apart from the rest of the country.

Potosí (pop 110,000), 551 km SE of La Paz, stands at 4,070m, the highest city of its size in the world. The climate is often bitterly cold and fireplaces are few; warm clothes essential. It was founded by the Spaniards on 10 April 1545, after they had discovered Indian mine workings at Cerro Rico, the hill at whose foot it stands.

Immense amounts of silver were once extracted from this hill. In Spain "éste es un Potosí" (it's a Potosí) is still used for anything superlatively rich. By the early 17th century Potosí was the largest city in the Americas, but over the next two centuries, as its lodes began to deteriorate and silver was found elsewhere, Potosí became little more than a ghost town. It was the demand for tin—a metal the Spaniards ignored—that lifted the city to comparative prosperity again. Silver, copper and lead are also mined.

Large parts of Potosí are colonial, with twisting, narrow streets and an occasional great mansion with its coat of arms over the doorway. UNESCO has declared the city to be "Patrimonio de la Humanidad." Some of the best buildings are grouped round the Plaza 10 de Noviembre, the main square. The old Cabildo and the Royal Treasury—Las Cajas Reales—are both here, converted to other uses. The Cathedral (open Mon-Fri 0930-1000, 1300-1500, Sat 0930-1000, guided tour only, US$1) faces the square, and near-by is the Mint—the Casa Real de Moneda (founded 1572, rebuilt 1759-1773)—one of the chief monuments of civil building in Hispanic America (Calle Ayacucho, T 22777). The Moneda (entrance US$2, US$3 to take photos), has a museum in many sections occupying 30 of its 160 rooms. The main art gallery is in a splendid salon on the first floor. One section is dedicated to the works of the 17th-18th century religious painter Melchor Pérez de Holguín, one of Bolivia's most acclaimed artists (and dubbed "the El Greco of America"). Elsewhere are coin dies and huge wooden presses which made the silver strip from which coins were cut (there are plans to resume minting in Potosí – on a different site). The smelting houses have carved altar pieces from Potosí's ruined churches. There are also sections on armaments and on minerology. You cannot fail to miss the huge, grinning mask over an archway between two principal courtyards; its significance is uncertain, perhaps to hide a coat of arms at the time of Independence. You are advised to wear warm clothes, as it is cold inside; a guided tour (obligatory) starts at 0900 and 1400 approximately, and lasts for 2 hours, Spanish only (if you want an English guide, get a group together, or turn up at opening time and hope that others arrive). The rooms are only opened for the tours. Open Mon-Sat 0900-1200 and 1400-1700. The Convento y Museo de Santa Teresa at Chicas y Ayacucho, T 23847 (entry US$1.50, Mon-Fri 0900-1200, 1300-1800, Sat 0900-1200, but check at Tourist Office) has an interesting collection of colonial and religious art, obligatory guide. Among Potosí's baroque churches, typical of the Andean or "mestizo" architecture of the 18th century, are the Compañía (Jesuit) church, on Ayacucho, with an impressive bell-gable (1700, closed for restoration in 1992), San Francisco (Tarija y Nogales) with a fine organ

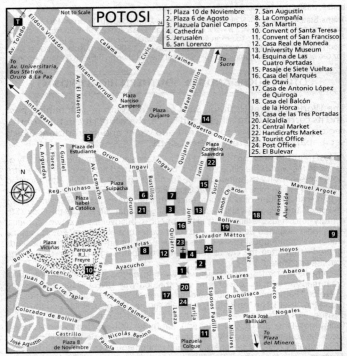

POTOSI

Not to Scale

1. Plaza 10 de Noviembre
2. Plaza 6 de Agosto
3. Plazuela Daniel Campos
4. Cathedral
5. Jerusalén
6. San Lorenzo
7. San Augustín
8. La Compañía
9. San Martín
10. Convent of Santa Teresa
11. Convent of San Francisco
12. Casa Real de Moneda
13. University Museum
14. Esquina de Las Cuatro Portadas
15. Pasaje de Siete Vueltas
16. Casa del Marqués de Otavi
17. Casa de Antonio López de Quiroga
18. Casa del Balcón de la Horca
19. Casa de las Tres Portadas
20. Alcaldía
21. Central Market
22. Handicrafts Market
23. Tourist Office
24. Post Office
25. El Bulevar

(can be visited in morning and evening, worthwhile for the views from the tower and roof, museum of ecclesiastical art, underground tunnel system, open 1400-1600, Mon-Fri, entry US$1), and San Lorenzo, with a rich portal (1728-1744, Calle Héroes del Chaco); fine views from the tower. San Martín on Calle Hoyos, with an uninviting exterior, is beautiful inside, but is normally closed for fear of theft. Ask the German Redemptorist Fathers to show you around; their office is just to the left of their church. Other churches to visit include Jerusalén, close to the *Hotel Centenario*, and San Agustín (only by prior arrangement with tourist office) on Bolívar y Quijarro, with crypts and catacombs (the whole city was interconnected by tunnels in colonial times). Tour starts at 1700, US$0.10 admission. From San Cristóbal, at Pacheco y Cañete, one gets a fine view over the whole city. Teatro Omiste on Plaza 6 de Agosto is under restoration; it has a fine façade. The University has a museum with some good modern Bolivian painting (Mon-Fri, 1000-1200, 1500-1700, entrance US$1, Calle Bolívar, T 22248).

In Potosí, 2,000 colonial buildings have been catalogued. The city is being repainted in traditional colours of teracotta, cream and blue. A suggested tour round the town is to start at San Agustín at the corner of Bolívar and Quijarro and walk down Quijarro which, in colonial times, was Calle Ollería - potmakers - and Calle de los Sombreros. The whole block behind San Agustín belonged to the monastery; there are many wooden balconies, many houses retain colonial interiors with balconies, patio, rings for tying horses, etc, but much restoration is needed. At Quijarro and Omiste is the Esquina de las Cuatro Portadas (four houses with double doors), or Balcón de Llamacancha. Quijarro is one of Potosí's best preserved streets, with many emblems over doorways. Go right up Omiste for one block then turn right again into Junín, at Plaza Cornelio Saavedra (Mercado de Artesanías). See the Pasaje de Siete Vueltas (the passage of the seven turns) on your left. There is a fine stone doorway (house of the Marqués de Otavi) in Junín between Matos and Bolívar. Cross Plaza 10 de Noviembre diagonally to Lanza to see at No 8 (now a school) the house of José de Quiroz and of Antonio López de Quiroga. Turn up Chuquisaca and after 3 blocks right into Millares: here on the left is a sculpted stone doorway and on the right a doorway with two rampant lions in low relief on the lintel. Turning left up Nogales you come to an old mansion in a little square. Turn left along La Paz and one block along there is another stone doorway with suns in relief. At the corner with Bolívar is the Casa del Balcón de la Horca. Turn left and you reach the Casa de las Tres Portadas, then it's 2½ blocks back to San Agustín.

Festivals San Bartolomé, or the Fiesta de Chutillos, is held from the middle of August, with the main event being processions of dancers on the last weekend, Saturday featuring Potosino, and Sunday national, groups. Costumes can be hired in artesanía market on Calle Sucre. In May there is a market on Calle Gumiel every Sunday, with lotteries and lots of fun things for sale. On three consecutive Saturdays at the end of May, beginning of June llama sacrifices are made at the cooperative mines in honour of Pachamama; the same occurs on 1 August, the Ritual del Espíritu. Other mining festivals are the Carnaval Minero and the Fiesta de los Compadres in February, for decorating El Tío (the Dios Minero) and one's work place. Potosí is sometimes called the "Ciudad de las Costumbres", especially at Corpus Cristi, Todos Santos and Carnaval, when special cakes are baked, families go visiting friends, etc. In October, Festival Internacional de la Cultura, in Potosí and Sucre.

Hotels Unless otherwise stated hotels have no heating in rooms. **C** *Claudia*, Av Maestro 322, 3-star, T 22242, helpful, modern, highly rec; **C** *Hostal Colonial*, Hoyos 8, a pretty colonial house (T 24809) near the main plaza, rec, with heating, has names and T numbers of guides, even if you're not staying there very helpful, very expensive for long-distance phone calls; **C** *Hostal Libertador*, Millares 58, T 27877/24629, Casilla 324, heaters in rooms, with bath, hot water, clean, quiet, comfortable, viewpoint, parking, highly rec (owner is Sr Wilson Mendieta Pacheco, director of Casa Real de la Moneda); **D** *Hostal Felimar*, Junín 14, T 24357, 2-star, hot water, breakfast, 2 roof-top suites, solar-powered, 1st floor rm have no exterior windows but warm, quiet; **D** *Santa María*, Av Serrudo 244, T 23255, clean, hot water; **D** *Jerusalem*, Oruro 143, T 22600, recently modernized, pleasant, helpful, *comedor*, with bath, F without, parking, laundry, highly rec; **D** *El Turista*, Lanza 19 (T 22492), also LAB office, helpful, hot showers all day, breakfast (US$1) highly rec; **D** *Hotel IV Centenario*, Plaza del Estudiante, T 22751, hot water all day, large cold rooms, central, very run down, poor service, apparently cheaper for Israelis and Danes; **E** *Central*, Bustillos 1230 y Linares, T 22207, hot shower, breakfast, basic, very mixed reports; **E** *Hotel Carlos V*, Linares 42 on Plaza 6 de Agosto, T 25151, friendly, breakfast, without bath, occasional hot water, clean, luggage store, rec; **E** *Residencial Sumaj*, Gumiel 10, T 23336, small rm, double rm on top floor good, with windows and views, hot water, shared bathrooms only, good value, clean and friendly, highly rec; **F** *Alojamiento La Paz*, Oruro 262, T 22632, central, basic, clean; **E** *Residencial Copacabana*, Av Serrudo 319, T 22712, individual or shared rooms, restaurant, clean, hot showers, will change $ cash, safe car park (owner, Dr Hugo Linares Fuentes will give medical assistance), rec; **E** *Res Felcar*, Serrudo 345 y Bustillos, T 24966, 1-star, clean, hot water, friendly, rec; **G** *Alojamiento Ferrocarril*, Av E Villazón 159, T 24294, basic, clean (hot showers US$0.55), friendly, close to the railway station; **G** *Alojamiento San Lorenzo*, Bustillos 967, T 24842, close to market, very basic, no shower or hot water; **G** pp *Casa de María Victoria*, Chuquisaca 148, T 22132, clean, stores luggage, popular, friendly, kitchen and laundry facilities, unpredictable plumbing, rec. In times of drought there may be rationing of water for showers etc. **Youth hostels** **D-E** *Res San Antonio*, Oruro 136, T 23566, US$2 pp without breakfast, dirty and **F** *Alojamiento El Barquito*, Oruro 7, T 22600 (not obviously spotted, good, rustic, rec).

5 km from Potosí in the village of San Antonio is *Hotel El Tambo*, Km 5 Carretera a Oruro, T 25597, F 22985, 3-star, colonial/rustic architecture, 3 restaurants, Bodega Bar, all details from Hidalgo Tours (see below).

Restaurants *Sumaj Orcko*, Quijarro 46, excellent food including fried vizcacha, large portions, cheap set lunch, reasonably priced Chilean wine, very popular with foreigners and locals, heating, slow service; *Plaza*, next door, serves a cheap set lunch, good and friendly; *Confitería Royal*, just off main plaza, small selection of good snacks and cakes; *El Aldabón*, Linares 35, good set meal, US$1; *El Mesón*, corner of Plaza 10 de Noviembre near Tarija, irregular opening, European-style, very pricey (prices not written on menus, beware of overcharging), variously reported as excellent, poor, or pretentious; *Pizzería Argentina*, Linares 20, rec, cheap, tasty *salteñas* and pizzas, good service; *Las Vegas*, Padilla y Linares, 1st floor, cheap *almuerzos*, dinner more expensive, good; *La Tranquita*, Bolívar 957, good; *Anexo El Criollo*, Bolívar 581, good, excellent steaks; *Don Lucho*, Bolívar 765, large and tasty servings, but not cheap, meat good, *peñas* on Fri, check entrance fee for show before eating. *The Sky Room* at Bolívar 701 has interesting views of the town and the Cerro, pricey. On Sucre, *Confitería Capricornio*, good sandwiches, light meals, cheap, clean, rec. *La Carreta*, Gumiel, excellent, pleasant service, mid-price range; *Quillahuasi*, Junín 56, good. *Snack bar Bamby*, just off top of main square, good cheap lunches. Breakfast can be a difficult meal to find, but it is available in the Mercado Central, Calle Bolívar from 0700 (also other meals – not always hygienic): worthwhile to see if the hotel serves it as most restaurants seem to be closed at this time. *Coffee Shop*, Plaza Alonso Ibáñez, good coffee and cakes and *Confitería Cherys*, Padilla 12 y Linares, friendly, good cakes, coffee, burgers, very popular, attractive, breakfast. Other *confiterías*: *Kivo's*, Quijarro 12, *Santa Clara*, Plaza Principal (nice and clean), and *Chaplin*, Bustillos 979.

Banks and Exchange Banco Nacional, Sucre near Plaza, exchange for US$ cash. Many shops and restaurants around main plaza on Padilla and on Bolívar between Sucre and Junín (most display "compro dólares" signs). Amex cheques may only be changed at Morales, Bertram y Schuett, Matos 19; TCs may also be changed at Distribuidora Cultural Sud, same address. **Casa de Cambio Fernández**, Sucre 10. **Banco La Paz** on Plaza 10 de Noviembre, for cash withdrawals on Visa and Mastercard, with US$1.25 authorization charge Mon-Wed only. Banco Popular, Bolívar y Junín, cash withdrawals on Visa, friendly.

Clinic Clínica Británica, on Oruro near *Alojamiento La Paz*, clinics am and pm English spoken.

Sauna Bath and showers in Calle Nogales. Sauna Florida, Plaza Chuquimina, near bus station, open Thurs and Fri, US$1.50 (also has racquetball).

Laundry *Limpieza la Veloz*, Calle Quijarro, corner of Mattos, Edificio Cademin, and at Camacho 258, US$1.3 per kilo.

Post Office Lanza 3, open Sat till 1900, Sun 0900-1200; unreliable for overseas mail. **Telephone** Entel, Calle Camacho, T 43496; also at Av Universitaria near bus terminal.

Shopping Silver (sometimes containing nickel) and native cloth. Silver coins, jewellery and coca leaves in market between Av Camacho and Héroes del Chaco. Coca leaves (for *soroche*) also available in streets near the market. There is an interesting gift shop in the post office. Silver is sold in the main market near the Calle Oruro entrance. There is an informal swap market every Friday night at the Plazuela, at Bolívar and Quijarro. There is a small handicraft market at the junction of Calle Sucre and Plaza Saavedra (rec) but very expensive. Some Fridays the merchants organize music, food and drink (*ponche*), not to be missed. Almost opposite is *Andina*, Sucre 94, for handicrafts and antiques. The Triángulo Productivo, in front of San Lorenzo, has handicrafts for sale. For musical instruments, Arnaud Gerard (Belgian), Los Alamos 18, workshop *Killay* behind Mercado Artesanal, makes beautifully made and tuned pieces, designed to be played, will make to order. Art gallery of Carlos Cornejo L, Simón Chacón 19, open every afternoon and some evenings, very good (also does trips to, and gives information on, Tarapaya, see **Excursions**). The best bookshop is at the University, open Mon-Fri, 1000-1200, 1500-1700.

Tourist Agents *Hidalgo Tours*, Junín y Bolívar, T 28293, F 22985, Casilla 310, *ferrobus* tickets for La Paz/Sucre, specialized services within the city and to Salar de Uyuni (with all meals, accommodation at Albergue San Juan, aperitifs, wine, radio-controlled), highly rec for mine visits (see below); *Potosí Tours*, corner of Padilla, on the Plaza, good tours of the city and mine (see below); *Transamazonas*, Bolívar 982, Edif Cámara de Minería, T 27175, F 24796; *Cerro Rico Travel*, Plaza Alonso Ibáñez 21, T 25552; *Koala Tours*, Ayacucho 5, frente a la Casa de Moneda, PO Box 33, T 24708, F 22092 mine tours (see below) and has a branch in Uyuni for Salar trips; *Turismo Balsa*, Plaza Alonzo de Ibáñez, T 26272, English spoken, daily city and mine tours (see also La Paz **Travel Agents**).

Some agencies offer trips to the Salar de Uyuni, Laguna Colorada and Laguna Verde (**see above p 286**) but reports suggest that this is more expensive and more time-consuming than excursions to these places from Uyuni. Tours from Potosí cost US$160-180 pp and last 5-6 days. It is essential to get a written contract (a tourist police requirement) and make sure that the guide is approved by the police. The trip needs a suitable vehicle, sufficient fuel, food and water (if not included in the price, take your own or tell the guide precisely what you need), first aid, and proper organization.

Tourist Office On 2nd Floor, Cámara de Minería, Calle Quijarro (T 25288), ½ block from main plaza, and booth on main plaza (both closed Sat and Sun and unreliable opening times during the week); sells town maps (US$0.25), information booklet (US$2.50), helpful. Instituto Geográfico Militar, Calle La Paz, possible to buy maps, 0900-1200, 1400-1800.

Useful Addresses Police station On Plaza 10 de Noviembre. **Migración** La Paz 1001, can renew tourist permit here for 1 month, 10 bolivianos.

Local Transport Taxi within city limits US$0.60; approx US$1/km for longer journeys. Buses US$0.10.

Airport Aerosur (Bolívar y Junín, T 22087) to La Paz daily except Sun at 1005 (US$130 return), with connections to Cobija, Cochabamba, Guayaramerín, Santa Cruz, Tarija and Trinidad. LAB fly to La Paz (US$120 return), also Santa Cruz (US$100 return), Sucre and Cochabamba. Book flights well in advance. Airport is 5 km out of town on the Sucre road.

Trains Potosí is on the La Paz, Oruro, Potosí, Sucre line; latest report is of a *ferrobus* twice a week to Potosí from Oruro/La Paz, Tues and Sat at 1820 (US$11), continues to Sucre (US$14.50). Full information from Enfe at the station, T 23101 (ask at Hidalgo Tours, who sell Enfe tickets, about Hidalgo Express, special service).

Buses Bus terminal out of town, on Av Universitaria, below railway station, 30 min walk, steeply uphill to main plaza (or *micros* C, I or L); through buses from La Paz call here at the toll gate, as they are not allowed to enter city limits. There is an information office at the terminal, T 26075, an express mail service, and a terminal tax, 50 centavos. To **Tarija**, Andesbus Mon, Thur, Sat 1400, US$10.50, rec, or San Jorge (T 26214), San Lorenzo or *Emperador* (T 25580), all daily, US$10.50 at 1600 or 1630 from bus terminal; Tarija is reached by car or lorry leaving Plaza Minero (Bus "A"), full range of scenery. To **Villazón**, several companies daily, usually departing 1800-1900, 12 hrs (but O'Globo 0800), US$4.20-5.25 (Trans Tupiza, T 24264, rec). To **Cochabamba**, US$5.25-7.35, 12 hrs, several companies inc Copacabana, T 24041, 1900. Many buses to **La Paz** (mostly overnight in either direction, 10-14 hrs, US$5.25-8.50, you get what you pay for), Trans Copacabana luxury service with heat and video, US$12.60, 10 hrs, spacious, rec. Avoid Flota Copacabana. To **Oruro** US$3.15-3.75, Bustillos, T 25672, Universo and Imperial, 8 hrs, leaving between 1900 and 1930. To **Uyuni**, at least 4 companies: Diana Tours, American (T 27162), 11 de Julio (T 28126, rec), Expreso Parco, all have offices around Av Toledo y Av Antofagasta, at least 1 a day 1100-1215, 6-8 hrs, unpaved road, OK in dry season, US$4, book in advance, especially on the day when the bus connects with the Oruro-Calama train. To **Sucre**: two types of service, the more luxurious being Andesbus, Bustillos 1094, T 25050, 3½ hrs, US$5, rec, similar service with Transtin, Cochabamba 104, T 22056, Alave, Bustillos 1066, T 27655, and Emperador, Camacho 281, all at 0700 and 1700. Less comfortable are companies such as 10 de Noviembre (not rec, not safe), all US$3.15. The road to Sucre is being paved, so a lot of dust, or mud, depending on the weather; all but 30 km have been paved. To **Santa Cruz**, Trans Copacabana, 1900, and Flota Copacabana, 1930, both US$12.55. Trucks for **Tarabuco** leave from Plaza San Francisco. Heavy overbooking reported on buses, also, timetables change frequently; the trucks from the plaza are an alternative.

Excursions to the mines: The state mines in Cerro Rico were closed in the 1980s and are now worked as cooperatives by small groups of miners. A 4½ hr morning tour to the cooperative mines and ore-processing plant involves meeting miners and seeing them at work in conditions described as "like stepping back into the nineteenth century". Visitors need to be reasonably fit as parts are very hard going, not recommended for claustrophobics or asthmatics. Guided tours are offered by former miners. By law all guides have to work with a travel agency. Guides recommended include: Eduardo Garnica Fajardo, Hernández 1035, Casilla 33, T 24708/22092 (Koala Tours), he speaks English, French and some Hebrew (frequently rec, and sometimes impersonated by unprofessionals). Also highly rec as an English-speaking guide for small groups is Julio César Morales of Koala Tours. Koala Tours offer breakfast at 0600, "plato típico" with llama meat; they also donate part of their fee to buy medicines (donations can be sent to Eduardo Garnica). Raul Braulio, Millares 147 (Transamazonas Tours), T 25304, experienced guide, speaks some English; David Almendras, Colombia 631, T 25552 (Cerro Rico Travel), highly rec; Santos and Marco Mamami, Pacheco 60, T 27299 (Cerro Rico Travel); Roberto Méndez E, Campamento Pailaviri 4, T 26900 (Turismo Balsa), speaks English, very knowledgeable, rec; Salustio Gallardo, Calle Betanzos 231, near Plaza Minero; Juan Carlos González, Av Japón 10, T 26349 (Turismo Balsa), rec, Spanish spoken only. Efraín Huanca (Hidalgo Tours) warmly rec as friendly and very informative. Guides provide essential equipment – helmet, lamp and usually protective clothing (but check when booking). Wear old clothes and take torch and a handkerchief to filter the dusty air. The price of tours is regulated (US$5 pp) and includes transport. A contribution to the miners' cooperative is appreciated as are medicines for the new health centre (*Posta Sanitaria*) on Cerro Rico. New projects (a radio, drinking water) have been, or will shortly be realized. You will also be asked to contribute towards buying presents for the miners – dynamite, coca leaves, cigarettes. The size of tour groups varies – some agencies, eg Koala, limit groups to 8, some groups are as large as 20 people, which is excessive. The Pailaviri State mine is closed temporarily as of April 1995.

Thermal Baths at *Tarapaya*, on the road to Oruro. Trucks go straight to Tarapaya where there are public baths, US$0.30, and private, US$0.60; the private baths, higher up, may be cleaner. If you get out of the truck or bus at the bridge at Km 25, cross the bridge and take any trail up, you reach the 50 metre-diameter crater lake on the other side of the river from Tarapaya. The temperature of the lake is 30°C, a beautiful spot; take sun protection. Below the crater lake are boiling ponds. Bus from market nr train station, Av Antofagasta, US$0.50. Taxi US$6 for a group, hitch back; do not go in late afternoon, there is no transport back to Potosí (no problem at weekends). A good place to spend a lazy day resting, or to freshen up after visiting the mines (mine guides often offer transport after a mine tour). On the way to Tarapaya is the village of El Molino (15 km), in a green valley; no accommodation or shop, but nice landscape. Take a colectivo from Plaza Chuquimia. Also baths at Chaqui (by truck or bus from Plaza Uyuni, 1 hr, clean, pleasant baths, closed Wed), Tora and San Diego (on the main road to Sucre, it also has a restaurant).

The following walk, originally proposed by Hallam Murray, has proved popular. It takes 8-9 hrs at a gentle pace and covers about 24 km (map Hoja 6435, serie H631, from Instituto Geográfico Militar, and a compass are useful). Take Av Hoyos E out of Plaza 10 de Noviembre and continue beyond the Iglesia San Martín. Aim initially for Laguna San Ildefonso SE of the city. Ask directions: after a brickworks on the paved road to the ore-processing plant by Cerro Rico, a footpath heads E over a gentle hill planted with young trees. Follow this path until the second junction with a dirt road, then turn left/N and continue to the W shore of the lake. It was built in 1767 to provide water for the city and is in a wonderful position. It has duck, and fish deep down in the clear water. Beyond, to the E, are lumpy hills and mountains. Go round the W shore, cross a small river at the lake's N end and at the next intersection turn left. Follow up the valley, passing herds of llama and old mine openings. This valley is full of fascinating plants, animals, and rock formations.

  Continue along the left side of the valley beyond a second unnamed, and possibly dried-up lake (visible only when close to it) and turn S to climb steeply to the adjoining valley (very tough for the unacclimatized), just beyond the peak of Cerro Masoni (4,920m). The time from the Plaza to the highest point between the two valleys is 5-6 hrs. The views from this point are spectacular, with mountain peaks to the S towards Argentina. Closer at hand is moon-like scenery. This is an excellent spot for a picnic. Continue down and back to Potosí via the small lake which can be seen from the high point. Probably best to keep high to the left (S) of Lagunas San Sebastián and to approach Cerro Rico on its E flank. The walk back into Potosí is depressing and bleak, passing miners' houses, close to a heavily polluted stream and with the most extensively worked face of Cerro Rico to your left, but this is a side of Bolivia which should also be seen.

A recommended Sunday trip is to Manquiri, a sanctuary in the mountains. Wait from 0730 at Garita de San Roque or at Plaza Uyuni for a truck. At **Betanzos** (1 hr on the Sucre road; **G** nameless *alojamiento*, basic), the Feria de Papas is held within the first two weeks of May: folk dances, music and costumes (buses from Plaza Uyuni, Potosí).

Another trip is to **Caiza** on a road which forks off the Tarija road at Ingenio Cucho; there is one small hotel, near main square, *San Martín de Porres*, clean, with restaurant. Two buses a day from Potosí, from Plaza del Minero at 1330 but they are sometimes late. Caiza is where cooperatives produce handicrafts in tin and some silver. Silverware is being encouraged. On 4 August, the entry of the Virgen de Copacabana is celebrated with dancing and traditional costumes. For information go to the tourist office in Potosí, or Programa de Autodesarrollo Campesino, Av Argentina y Gareca, Ciudad Satélite, Potosí, T 32013/32028. Caiza is about 2 hrs from Potosí, at a much lower altitude, so it is hotter and can provide relief from *soroche*.

Sucre (pop 112,000), the official capital of Bolivia, is 164 km NE of Potosí. A branch road runs to it from Epizana on the old Cochabamba-Santa Cruz highway. The altitude is 2,790m, and the climate is mild (mean temperature 12°C, but sometimes

24°C in November-December and 7°C in June).

Founded in 1538 as the city of La Plata, it became capital of the audiencia of Charcas in 1559. Its name was later changed to Chuquisaca. The present name was adopted in 1825 in honour of the first president of the new republic. In 1992 UNESCO declared the city a "Patrimonio Histórico y Cultural de la Humanidad". The city is an important administrative and educational centre: there are 2 universities, the oldest dating from 1624. Long isolation has helped it to preserve its courtly charm; by tradition all buildings in the centre are painted in their original colonial white. It is sometimes referred to as La Ciudad Blanca. Throughout the city, the public buildings are impressive. The main square is Plaza 25 de Mayo, which is large, spacious, full of trees and surrounded by elegant buildings. Among these are the Casa de la Libertad, formerly the Assembly Hall of the Jesuit University (open Mon-Fri 0900-1130 and 1430-1830, Sat, 0930-1130, US$0.30, US$0.65 to take photographs, US$2.65 to use video), where the country's Declaration of Independence was signed (it contains a famous portrait of Simón Bolívar by the Peruvian artist Gil de Castro "... hecho en Lima, con la más grande exactitud y semejanza" - the greatest likeness); also on the Plaza is the beautiful 17th century Cathedral, entrance through the museum in Calle Ortiz (open Mon-Fri 1000-1200, 1500-1700, Sat 1000-1200, entry US$1, if door is locked wait for the guide). Worth seeing are the famous jewel-encrusted Virgin of Guadalupe, 1601, works by Viti, the first great painter of the New World, who studied under Raphael, and the monstrance and other church treasures including giant lanterns of pure silver weighing 46 kilos. Four blocks NW of Plaza 25 de Mayo is the modern Corte Suprema de Justicia, the seat of Bolivia's judiciary (entry free but must leave passport with guard, no photographs allowed). The nearby Parque Bolívar contains an obelisk, a small triumphal arch and a miniature of the Eiffel tower which can be climbed (the park used to be a lovers' meeting place but improved lighting has turned it into a favourite place for students to revise at night). The obelisk opposite the Teatro Gran Mariscal, in Plaza Libertad, was erected with money raised by fining bakers who cheated on the size and weight of their bread. Also on this plaza is the Hospital Santa Bárbara. Sucre University was founded in 1624. Early 17th century wooden ceilings (alfarjes) are found in San Miguel (see below) and San Francisco (0700-0930 and 1600-1930).

SE of the city, at the top of Calle Dalence, lies the Franciscan monastery of La Recoleta (see below under **Museums**) with good views over the city. Behind the monastery a road flanked by Stations of the Cross ascends an attractive hill, Cerro Churuquella, with large eucalyptus trees on its flank, to a statue of Christ at the top. The cemetery is worth a visit, to see mausoleums of presidents and other famous people, boys give guided tours; take Calle Junín S to its end, 7-8 blocks from main plaza.

Churches Church opening times seem to change frequently, or are simply not observed. **San Miguel**, completed in 1628, has been restored and is very beautiful with Moorish-style carved and painted ceilings, pure-white walls and gold and silver altar. In the Sacristy some early sculpture can be seen. It was from San Miguel that Jesuit missionaries went S to convert Argentina, Uruguay and Paraguay (open 1130-1200, no shorts, short skirts or short sleeves). **San Felipe Neri**, church and monastery, neoclassical, attractive courtyard with cloisters (note above the crucifix an inscription in Hebrew letters saying, from right to left, TALE - lamb, one of the signs for Christ in the zodiac, on each side of the cross are two replicas of the Israeli *menora*, the lamp from the Temple). The monastery is used as a school. The church, sadly is closed. Access to the roof (note the penitents' benches), which offers fine views over the city, is only open for an hour between 1600 and 1800 (times change) US$0.50 entrance with a free guide from Universidad de Turismo office, opposite the convent, at N Ortiz 182. **Santa Mónica** (Arenales y Junín) is perhaps one of the finest gems of Spanish architecture in the Americas, note the main altar and pulpit in filigree (it is no longer a church but may be visited when functions are being held inside or daily 1500-1800). **San Francisco** in Calle Ravelo has altars coated in gold leaf; the bell is the one that summoned the people of Sucre to struggle for independence (open 1800 most days). **Capilla de la Rotonda** (Av L Cabrera, near the railway

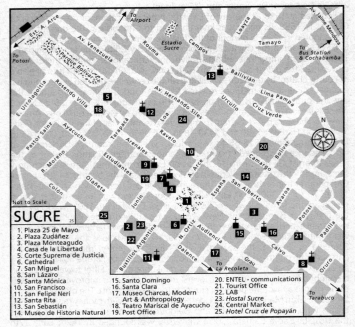

SUCRE

1. Plaza 25 de Mayo
2. Plaza Zudáñez
3. Plaza Monteagudo
4. Casa de la Libertad
5. Corte Suprema de Justicia
6. Cathedral
7. San Miguel
8. San Lázaro
9. Santa Mónica
10. San Francisco
11. San Felipe Neri
12. Santa Rita
13. San Sebastián
14. Museo de Historia Natural

15. Santo Domingo
16. Santa Clara
17. Museo Charcas, Modern Art & Anthropology
18. Teatro Mariscal de Ayacucho
19. Post Office
20. ENTEL - communications
21. Tourist Office
22. LAB
23. *Hostal Sucre*
24. Central Market
25. *Hotel Cruz de Popayán*

station), **Santa Rita**, **San Sebastián** (reconstructed in 1990). **Santo Domingo**, corner of Calvo and Bolívar (1545), open only Frid and Sun night. Next door at Calvo 212 is the **Santa Clara museum** (see below). **San Lázaro**, Calvo y Padilla, built in 1538, is regarded as the first cathedral of La Plata (Sucre). On the nave walls are six paintings attributed to Zurbarán; it has fine silverwork and alabaster in the Baptistery, open daily for mass 0700-0745. **La Merced** (Azurduy and Pérez) has gilded altar pieces.

Museums These include the University's anthropological, archaeological, folkloric, and colonial collections at the **Museo Universitario Charcas** (Bolívar 698), and its presidential and modern-art galleries (open Mon-Fri 0830-1200, 1500-1800, Sat 0830-1200, US$1, photos US$1.50). The **Museo de Santa Clara** (Calle Calvo 212), displays paintings, books, vestments, some silver and musical instruments (including a 1664 organ); there is a window to view the church; small items made by the nuns on sale, entry US$1, open Mon-Sat 1000-1130, 1430-1700. The **Museo de la Recoleta** (Calle Pedro de Anzúrez, open Mon-Fri 0900-1130, 1500-1630, US$0.55 for entrance to all collections, guided tours only) is at the Recoleta monastery, on a hill above the town, notable for the beauty of its cloisters and gardens; the carved wooden choirstalls above the nave of the church are especially fine (see the martyrs transfixed by lances); in the grounds is the Cedro Milenario, a thousand-year old cedar. **Museo de Historia Natural**, Calle San Alberto 156 (open Mon-Fri 0830-1200/1400-1800), US$0.50. **Caserón de la Capellanía**, San Alberto 413, houses the textile museum run by Antropológicas del Surandino. Rec for explanations of Indian groups and their distinctive textiles, open Mon-Fri 0830-1200, 1500-1800, Sat 0900-1200, free.

Warning Police all wear uniform and carry ID cards with photographs. Note: you do not have to show your passport to anyone on the street, be they in or out of uniform. On arrival at a hotel your passport number is registered and then given to the tourist police; each hotel's list is handed to the tourist office. If in doubt call 110 radio patrol or the tourist office (see below). Insist on going to the police station, if possible with a witness, before showing passport or money to anyone without credentials. Common targets are lone tourists who don't speak

Spanish; places where scams frequently occur are the plaza, Cerro Churuquella, Recoleta and Santa Clara. Cons can be very elaborate, involving an initial approach from a fellow "tourist from Peru" who is in league with the false "policeman" who later approaches, demanding inspection of passport, luggage, etc, and with the "taxi driver" enlisted to take you all to the police station.

Festival   Independence celebrations, 24-26 May, most services, museums and restaurants closed. Oct: Festival Internacional de la Cultura, 10 days, shared with Potosí.

Hotels A3 *Real Audiencia*, Potosí 142, T 32809, F 30823, excellent restaurant, modern, rec; **C** *Hostal Cruz de Popayán*, Loa 881, T 25156/31706, rec, a beautiful colonial house with interior courtyard, no heating, colour TV, excellent breakfast served in rm or in patio; **C** *Colonial*, Plaza 25 de Mayo 3, T 24709/25487, F 21912, expensive but rec all round and for good breakfast; **C** *Hostal Libertad*, Arce y San Alberto, 1st floor, T 23101/2, clean, spacious and comfortable rooms, friendly and efficient with excellent restaurant, highly rec; **D** *Hostal España*, España 138, T 25765, inc breakfast, TV, clean, pleasant; **D** *Hostal Sucre*, Bustillos 113, T 21411/31928, good, clean, dining room, patio, friendly staff, rec; **C** *Municipal*, Av Venezuela 1052 (T 21216), rec, restaurant; **D** *Hostal los Pinos*, Colón 502, T 24403, clean, comfortable, hot showers, TV in room, garden, quiet, peaceful, good breakfast; **D** *Londres*, Av H Siles 949, T 24792, 3 blocks uphill from station, with shower, restaurant, good; **D** *Hostal San Francisco*, Av Arce 191 y Camargo, T 22117, bath or shower, with bath, E without, pleasant, meals available, clean, quiet, comfortable, safe motorcycle parking, rec; **E** *Alojamiento Austria*, Av Ostria Gutiérrez 518, T 24202, hot showers, good value, restaurant, near bus station as well as **E** *Alojamiento Central*, Ostria Gutiérrez 456, T 23935, hot showers charged extra, and **F** *Alojamiento Chuiguisaca*, Ostria Gutiérrez 33, T 24459, shared bathrooms, clean, friendly, safe car parking (US$0.50 per day). **E** *Residencial Avenida*, Av H Siles 942, T 21245, clean, hot showers, breakfast extra, laundry, friendly and helpful, rec; **E** *Residencial Bolivia*, near plaza, San Alberto 42, T 24346, with electric showers, cheaper without bath, spacious rooms, hot water, breakfast included (clothes washing not allowed); **E** *Residencial Bustillo*, Calle Ravelo 158, T 21560, without bath (D with bath), tiny rooms, clean, hot water, will store luggage at a price; **E** *Residencial Charcas*, Ravelo 62, T 23972, with bath, F without, good value breakfast, hot showers, some rooms small, quiet except for first floor (best rooms nos 15-19), clean, helpful, opp market, laundry facilities, rec; **E** *Residencial Oriental*, Calle San Alberto 43, T 21644, with bath, F without, clean, friendly but basic, tiny rooms, unlockable interior windows, hot water, motorcycle parking; **F** *Alojamiento Abaroa*, Loa 419, hot showers, uncomfortable beds, friendly, basic; **F** *Alojamiento El Turista*, Ravelo 118, T 23172, clean, hot showers 0700-1200 only, safe, basic, laundry facilities, cheap meals, terrace, doors closed at 2300; **F** *Alojamiento La Plata*, Ravelo 26, T 22102, without bath, limited shower facilities, clean, central, opp market, noisy, very friendly; **F** pp *Grand*, Arce 61, T 22104, large rm, with bath, restaurant, laundry service. Many cheap and basic places opp central market. **Youth hostel**, *Hotel Londres*, Av Hernando Siles 949.

Restaurants   *Piso Cero*, Venezuela 241, good but expensive; *Las Vegas* on SE side of Plaza, Nos 31 and 37, main restaurant and annex (less grand), mixed reports but generally good (icecream, no breakfast, at lunchtime no drink without food, evening meals); *Pizzería Napoletana*, on Plaza, 25 de Mayo 30, excellent pizzas (evenings and some lunchtimes) and good home-made ice cream, not cheap; *Plaza*, also on main square, with balconies, good food and pisco sours, good live music on Friday nights, very popular with locals. *Kactus*, on Calle España, just off the main square, nice bar and restaurant, pizzas, not expensive, highly rec. *Pecos Bill Pizza*, Argentina 27, between plaza and *Hostal Sucre*, serves *almuerzo*, mixed reports. *La Taverne* of the *Alliance Française*, Aniceto Arce 35, 1/2 block from main square, closed Sun, good value, soft music—also regular films and cultural events, good meeting place; *Picolíssimo*, San Alberto entre Avaroa y Bolívar, rec, good value lunch, otherwise expensive, popular; *Alcázar*, Av Arce 105, opp San Francisco, attractive, popular, a bit more expensive than others. On Ortiz, near Plaza 25 de Mayo, are *Snack Paulista* (No 14), no food but excellent fruit juices and milk shakes; *Bibliocafé Sureña* (No 30) good pasta and light meals, music, opens 1800, closed Mon; and *Arco Iris* (No 42), good service, pricey but good, *peña* on Sat, excellent *roesti*, Swiss potato dish, live music some nights; *Kultur-Café Berlín*, Avaroa 326, opens 1530, good food but limited selection and small portions, German newspapers, *peña* every other Friday, closed Sunday (in same building as Instituto Cultural Boliviano Alemán—ICBA), popular meeting place. *Rainbow Room Café*, Calvo y Potosí, cheap meals, live music, English language magazines (next to Centro Boliviano Americano). *El Germen*, Av Arce near San Francisco church, good lunches, cosy. *Don Sancho*, Ostria Gutiérrez 130, good, clean, rec. *Confitería Palet*, Plaza 25 de Mayo 6, good coffee. *Le Repizza*, Calvo 70, very good value lunches, small but good pizzas in evening, rec; *Café Cupido Corazón*, Olañeta 77, nice coffee shop, snacks available. *Los Bajos*, Loa 759, serves special sausages (*chorizo* chuquisaqueño), good, daytime only. *Doña Máxima*, Junín 411, usually only cold food; *El Solar*, Bolívar 800, good but expensive and no prices written on menus (Sun closed); *Snack Miryam*, España 67, good *salteñas*; also on España, No 140 is *Snack Lucy*, recommended for snacks; *Tucanito* on Estudiantes, wide choice of sandwiches, hot and cold drinks, pleasant, popular with local students; *Amanecer*, Pasaje Junín 810-B, German *pastelería*, run by social project supporting disabled children, excellent. *New Hong Kong II*, 25 de Mayo 29, good Chinese; a good Chinese restaurant is *Canton*, San Alberto 242, clean, large portions and tea, reasonable prices. *El Tropezón*, Junín, ½ block from Post Office, good set meal for US$1. *Bunkers*, Ravelo next to *Res Charcas*, good breakfasts; *Chop Clock Café*, Audiencia Grau, 1 block from plaza, good breakfasts; *Café Hacheh*, Pastor Sainz 241, coffee bar and art gallery near university, interesting to visit, tasty sandwiches and fresh fruit juices, highly rec. *La Carreta*, Estudiantes 34, good fruit juices, cakes, coffee. Good chicken and chips cafés on Camargo between Arce and Loa; many others on Calles Loa and H Siles. Typical of many Bolivian cities, not many restaurants open for breakfast, but there are many fruit juice and snack stalls in the market (No 24 on map); stall No 11, Rosa, is rec for her *vitamínico*; stalls also sell cheap lunches until 1400. The local brewery produces an interesting sweetish porter or stout. The local sausages (eg at *Chorizería*, Loa between Estudiantes y Olañeta, not cheap but good) and the local chocolate, Taboada and Para Tí, are recommended.

Banks and Exchange Banco Nacional, Calle España, cash given on Visa card, good rates. TCs changed, 1% commission. Banco de la Paz, Plaza 25 de Mayo, for cash on Visa and Mastercard. Travel agencies' rates are good and at casa de cambio on corner of Calvo y Plaza Monteagudo. Ambar, *casa de cambio*, San Alberto 7, T 31339, good rates, TCs cashed for US$ cash at 1.5% commission. Most shops and hotels will change money. Street changers on Hernando Siles/Camargo between España and Junín, and in market.

Cultural Institutes The Instituto Cultural Boliviano - Alemán (Delegación de Enseñanza del Goethe Institute), Avaroa 326, Casilla 304, T 22091, shows films, has German newspapers and books to lend (0930-1230 and 1530-2000), runs Spanish, German, Portuguese and Quechua courses and it has the *Kulturcafé Berlín* (see above). Spanish lessons cost from US$3.50 for 45 mins for one person, with reductions the more students there are in the class. The ICBA also runs a folk music *peña* on Fridays. Alianza Francesa, Aniceto Arce 35, T 23599, noticeboard on Plaza 25 de Mayo (Casa de Libertad side) announces events. Centro Boliviano Americano, Calvo y Potosí, in the Colegio Simón Rodríguez. The *Café Hacheh* (see above), is run by Felix Arciénega, Bolivian artist of national fame. He organizes folk and jazz concerts, conferences and discussions, and is the editor of an art and poetry journal "Hacheh". The cafe also puts on exhibitions by other local artists, has an extensive library and a large collection of native, jazz and classical records.

Folklore Centro Cultural Masis aims to promote the traditional Yampara culture: textiles, ceramics, figurines and music. It offers instruction in Quechua, traditional Bolivian music (3 hrs a week for US$12 a month, rec) and handicrafts; once or twice a week there are musical events and the snack bar holds exhibitions of textiles and photographs. Items are for sale, including musical instruments to the highest professional standard. Open 1530-2130. The director, Roberto Sahonero, who will give further details, is to be found at Bolívar 561 DS (T 23403, Casilla 463); he is usually at the centre Mon, Wed and Fri, 1900.

Consulates West German, Arenales 215 (T 21862). Spain, Pasaje Argandoña (T 21435); Italy, Vice Consul, Dalence 33.

Hospital Recommended, staffed by Japanese and locals. **Doctor** Dr Gaston Delgadillo Lora, Colón 33, T 21692, speaks English, French, German, highly rec. **Dentist** Dr Carlos Sánchez C, San Alberto 75.

Laundry Laverap, Bolívar 617, between Audiencia and Dalence, quick, US$2.50 wash and dry. Lavandería Paola, Bolívar 543, T 32477, rec.

Motorcycle Mechanic Sr Jaime Medina, Motorservi Honda, Calle René Calvo Arana, T 25484. Will service all makes of machine. **Car Mechanic** at Camargo 450, rec for Toyotas.

Post Office Junín y Ayacucho/Estudiantes, open till 2000. **Poste Restante** is organized separately for men and women. **Telephone and Fax** Entel, España 271, open till 2245.

Saunas Acuario, San Alberto 680; El Tropical, Calle Guillermo Andrade.

Shopping Permanent market is bounded by Ravelo, Loa, Camargo and Junín, for food and household goods. A bus from the central market will take you to the *campesino* market. *Artesanías Calcha*, Arce 109, in same arcade as *Hostal Libertad* (San Alberto 13 other entrance), rec, very knowledgeable proprietor. *ASUR*, Antropológicos del Surandino, have a museum and project shop at San Alberto 413, Caserón de la Capellanía, T 23841, weavings